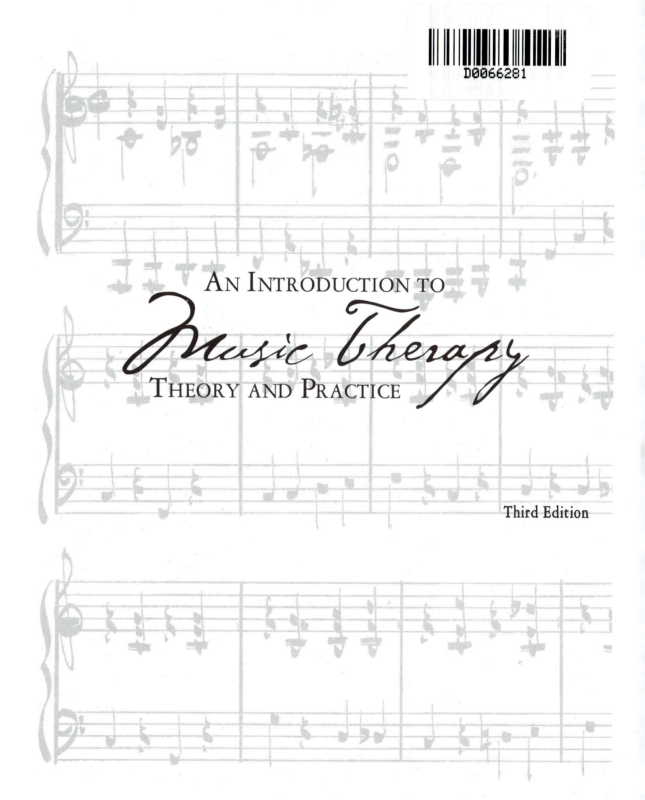

An Introduction to

Music Therapy

Theory and Practice

Third Edition

William B. Davis, Ph.D., RMT
Colorado State University

Kate E. Gfeller, Ph.D., RMT
The University of Iowa

Michael H. Thaut, Ph.D., RMT
Colorado State University

An Introduction to

Music Therapy

Theory and Practice

Third Edition

Published by The American Music Therapy Association, Inc.
Silver Spring, Maryland

ISBN: 978-1-884914-20-1

Editors: **William B. Davis, Ph.D., RMT**
                         Colorado State University
                         Kate E. Gfeller, Ph.D., RMT
                         University of Iowa
                         Michael H. Thaut, Ph.D., RMT
                         Colorado State University

Technical Assistance: **Wordsetters**
                         Kalamazoo, Michigan

Cover Design: **Tawna Grasty, GrassT Designs**

Typesetting: **Angie K Elkins, MT-BC**

Printed in the United States of America

Dedications

For my wife, Carol, my sons, Philip and Andrew, my mother, Myra McGregor,
and the music therapy students at Colorado State University.

WBD

I dedicate this to the memory of my father, Norman Gfeller. I am grateful to my mother,
Stella Gfeller, my husband, Kyran Cook, and my colleagues, students, and friends,
whose generosity of wisdom, kindness, and spirit has made this effort possible.

KEG

I dedicate this book, in gratitude to the unceasing love of my family, to the lives of the
patients we care for and the students we teach to care for them.

MHT

Music exalts each joy, allays each grief,
Expels diseases, softens every pain,
Subdues the rage of poison and of plague.
—*John Armstrong, 1744*

Acknowledgments

Revising a textbook is a shared process requiring collective efforts from numerous people. The editors would first like to acknowledge the individuals who authored or co-authored many of the chapters that you are about to read—thanks to you for your expertise and for graciously adhering to strict deadlines and writing style. Gratitude goes to Dr. Michele Forinash and Dr. Cathy McKinney for their careful review and input on information found in Chapter 15. We would also like to thank Dr. Andrea Farbman, Executive Director of the American Music Therapy Association, who made this project possible; without her support and assistance this book would not have become a reality. We would also like to express appreciation to Hope Smith, who patiently edited the book, reconciling diverse writing styles into a coherent whole. Our gratitude also goes to Angie Elkins for her professional production expertise in preparing this text for publication, and to Tawna Grasty, who created the cover. Indexing a book is a tedious task; the editors extend their appreciation to Nicole Wilshusen for her precise work on the index. Brian Kinnaird also deserves thanks for his hard work assembling the selected readings, glossary of terms, and definitions. Finally, we would like to acknowledge the assistance received from Virginia Driscoll, Meganne Masko, Rachel Strauss, Kristin Webster, and Kathryn Polutnik in proofreading, formatting references, and locating resources.

Preface to the Third Edition

The organization and content of the three editions of *An Introduction to Music Therapy: Theory and Practice* reflect the evolution of the field of music therapy over the past 15 years. An important goal of the first edition, published in 1992, was to provide a comprehensive overview of the music therapy profession for undergraduate students enrolled in entry level courses. The second edition, published in 1999, continued in that vein, offering updated information, including the most recent theoretical and empirical research in the field.

Similar to the first and second editions of this text, the third edition reviews the concepts and knowledge that have accrued since the turn of the 21st century. However, this new edition represents a substantial reconceptualization and organization that aims to reflect the explosive growth in music therapy research and practice. First and foremost is the use of additional authors. This new format may bring to mind the classic text *Music in Therapy*, published in 1968 and edited by pioneering music therapist E. Thayer Gaston. In that book, multiple authors contributed chapters in their respective areas of practice and research. Similarly, the new contributors in the third edition of this textbook are leading practitioners and researchers in the field, whose chapters reflect many years of experience as well as familiarity with the most current research findings and clinical techniques. The addition of new contributors provides greater breadth of perspective as well as considerable depth of expertise regarding subspecialties within music therapy.

A second change in the third edition is a chapter on music therapy in hospice care. The use of music therapy with persons who are terminally ill has seen remarkable growth since the publication of the second edition, and so deserves the thorough discussion found in this new edition. A third change in the newest edition is an expanded chapter on clinical practice, which includes a basic overview of some prominent theories or methodological approaches used in contemporary music therapy.

Although written primarily as an introductory text on music therapy, the book is also relevant in other undergraduate music therapy courses, including those covering clinical populations and techniques, clinical practice, and research methods. In addition, this book can serve as a reference for music therapy clinicians who wish to learn about unfamiliar clinical populations, update their knowledge about the current state of music therapy, or prepare for the Board Certification exam.

In recent years, the special needs of children and adults with disabilities have become the shared responsibility of educators and health professionals. This interrelationship has increased the need to become familiar with the educational and therapeutic strategies of other disciplines. The text introduces music therapy to a broad range of health and human services students and professionals, such as those in special education, medicine, nursing, occupational therapy, physical therapy, psychology, recreational therapy, counseling, gerontology, psychology, social work, and human development.

Specifically, our goals for the third edition of this text are as follows:

- To introduce the field of music therapy to the reader in a clear, straightforward manner, including the definition of music therapy, education and training of music therapists, clinical populations served by music therapists and employment options.
- To provide a historical perspective on the development of the music therapy profession.
- To provide an understanding of human response to music.
- To describe characteristics and needs of those populations most commonly served by music therapists, and to introduce music therapy interventions.
- To introduce the basic concepts of referral, assessment, treatment planning, intervention, and evaluation.
- To introduce the role of research and several prominent research methods used in music therapy.
- To introduce key legislative and accreditation issues that impact health care delivery, especially those that relate to music therapy practice.
- To provide a bibliography of research, books, and materials used by music therapists.

ORGANIZATION

The book is organized into three major sections:

PART ONE — AN OVERVIEW OF MUSIC THERAPY

PART TWO — POPULATIONS SERVED BY MUSIC THERAPISTS

PART THREE — PROFESSIONAL ISSUES IN MUSIC THERAPY

Part One, An Overview of Music Therapy, is comprised of three chapters that introduce the reader to the basic concepts of music therapy. The first chapter defines music therapy, provides an overview of the clinical settings and populations served by music therapists, and describes the education and training of a music therapist. Chapter 2 discusses the historical development of the use of music in therapy, focusing on developments in the United States during the 19th and 20th centuries. Chapter 3 describes human response (physiological, psychological, and social) to musical stimuli across the lifespan. This overview of music as a human phenomenon provides a foundation for therapeutic uses of music described in other chapters.

Part Two, Populations Served by Music Therapists, makes up the majority of the text, with 11 chapters devoted to this topic. In this section, we introduce the clinical populations most frequently served by music therapists. Special efforts were made to present concepts in a manner that may be easily understood by readers with little prior familiarity with music therapy. Each chapter is similarly structured, beginning with a definition and general information about the disability, followed by a discussion of the use of music therapy with that condition.

Chapters 4, 5, 6, 7, and 8 provide a thorough description of four population groups that are served most frequently by music therapists: people who have developmental disabilities (intellectual disabilities, autism spectrum disorders), physical disabilities, behavioral-emotional disorders, and age-related disabilities. Chapters 9 through 14 describe other important clinical groups that music therapists work with, including people with learning disorders, sensory impairments, medical conditions, and stroke or traumatic brain injury, as well as those in hospice and in prison.

Part Three, Professional Issues in Music Therapy, provides the reader with information about the music therapy treatment process and research. Chapter 15, divided into two sections, is devoted to the clinical treatment process and professional accountability, including the responsibilities of assessment, the planning of therapeutic music activities based on goals and objectives, and the evaluation of treatment progress. The second part of Chapter 15 discusses prominent theories and methodological approaches commonly used in music therapy. Chapter 16, the final chapter, describes the importance of research in music therapy. Four major research methods—descriptive, experimental, historical and qualitative—are presented. In addition, we have included information about how to effectively read a research journal article.

In its whole, this book presents a comprehensive overview of the music therapy profession. It looks at where we have been, where we are today, and where we might be in the future. Efforts to enhance the lives of persons with disabilities demand the attention of many skilled professionals, the music therapist included. Technical knowledge is but one component of helping people with disabilities to recognize their full potential. Music therapy professionals must also believe in themselves and in their ability to make a contribution. This book was written especially for the dedicated students and professionals who believe they can make a difference in the lives of these people who have special needs.

SPECIAL FEATURES

An Introduction to Music Therapy: Theory and Practice includes a number of learning aids that will help the student study successfully.

Chapter Outlines

Each chapter begins with an outline, which allows the reader to quickly surmise how the chapter is organized and what major topics are included.

Tables and Illustrations

Throughout the book, the reader will find tables and illustrations to help clarify ideas and assist in reviewing material.

Chapter Summaries

At the end of each chapter, a concise summary helps the reader grasp the major concepts. In addition, the reader may want to preview a chapter by reading the concluding statements.

Study Questions

Study questions at the end of each chapter allow the student to test his or her understanding of the information that was presented. The format of these questions is short answer/essay.

Selected Readings

For those readers who would like additional information about a specific topic or are in search of references for a research paper, we have included a list of books that will be helpful in beginning the research project.

Glossary

We have used bold font to highlight important terms used in each chapter. These key words and phrases will be defined and listed alphabetically at the end of the book, providing a convenient study aid for students who wish to review definitions f important terms.

Index

An index of the important topics and names is included at the end of the book. By consulting this reference tool, the reader can quickly and easily locate the page or ages containing a particular topic or name.

Table of Contents

Acknowledgments v

Preface vi

PART ONE: AN OVERVIEW OF MUSIC THERAPY 1

Chapter 1. Clinical Practice in Music Therapy 3

What Is Music Therapy? 5
With Whom Does a Music Therapist Work? 8
Where Do Music Therapists Work? 10
What Are the Personal Qualifications of a Music Therapist? 12
What is the Educational Preparation of a Music Therapist? 13
What Is the Overall Profile of the Music Therapy Profession? 14

Chapter 2. Music Therapy: Historical Perspective 17

Music Therapy in Preliterate Cultures 18
Music and Healing in Early Civilizations 19
Uses of Music in Antiquity: Healing Rituals 19
Music and Healing in the Middle Ages and Renaissance 20
Music Therapy in the United States 22
    18th-Century Writings on Music Therapy 22
    Literature from the 19th Century 23
    Music Therapy in 19th-Century Educational Institutions 24
    Early 20th-Century Music Therapy 27
The Development of the Music Therapy Profession 32

Chapter 3. Music: A Human Phenomenon and Therapeutic Tool 41

Humans as Musical Beings 42
Music as a Life Span Activity 43
    Musical Development of Children 44
    The Musical Adolescent 49
    The Musical Adult 49
Music Is a Varied and Flexible Art Form 51
    Style, Structural Features, and Engagement 51
Functions of Music 53

Functional Domains..54
    Physical Systems 54
    Music and Cognition...57
    Music as Communication 60
    Music and Emotions...61
    Music, Culture, and Society 67

PART TWO: POPULATIONS SERVED BY MUSIC THERAPISTS 77

Chapter 4. Music Therapy with Children and Adults with Intellectual Disabling Conditions..79

A Brief Historical Perspective 80
Conception and Definition of Intellectual Disabilities..81
An Important Link to the Current Definition of Intellectual Disabilities: Five Assumptions 84
Extent and Classification of Intellectual Disabilities...85
    Mild Intellectual Disability 86
    Moderate Intellectual Disability..86
    Severe and Profound Intellectual Disabilities 86
    Severity Unspecified 87
Causes of Intellectual Disabilities..87
Prevention of Intellectual Disabilities 89
    Primary Prevention..89
    Secondary Prevention...90
    Tertiary Prevention 90
Developmental Profiles of Persons with Intellectual Disabilities 91
    Cognitive Development...91
    Language Acquisition..92
    Physical and Motor Development 93
    Social and Emotional Characteristics..94
Educational Placement of Persons with Intellectual Disabilities.......................................95
Educational Strategies Used with Persons Who Have Intellectual Disabilities....................96
Music Therapy for Persons With Intellectual Disabilities..96
Music Therapy Treatment Goals for Persons Who Have Intellectual Disabilities 98
    Music Therapy for Development of Social and Emotional Behaviors........................98
    Music Therapy for Development of Motor Skills..101
    Music Therapy for Development of Communication Skills 103
    Music Therapy for Development of Pre-Academic Skills 105
    Music Therapy for Development of Academic Skills...108
    Music Therapy for Development of Leisure Skills 109

Chapter 5. Individuals with Autism and Autism Spectrum Disorders (ASD) 117
   Definition and Diagnosis...118
   Etiology 120
   Characteristics 121
      Communication 121
      Social Interactions 123
      Sensory Processing 124
      Behavioral Issues...125
   Music Therapy Goals and Interventions 127
      Music Therapy to Improve Communication Skills 128
      Music Therapy to Improve Social and Emotional Skills................131
      Music Therapy to Improve Behavior 132
      Music Therapy to Improve Academic, Physical/Motor, and Leisure Skills 135

Chapter 6. Music Therapy for Children and Adults with Physical Disabilities 143
   Physically Disabling Conditions 145
      Cerebral Palsy..145
      Muscular Dystrophies 146
      Spina Bifida 147
      Clubfoot..148
      Congenital Dislocation of the Hip 148
      Arthrogryposis 148
      Juvenile Rheumatoid Arthritis...148
      Dwarfism 149
      Osteogenesis Imperfecta 149
      Thermal Injuries 149
      Spinal Cord Injuries 150
      Acquired Amputations..150
      Poliomyelitis 151
   Music Therapy with the Physically Disabled: An Outline 151
      Settings 151
      Background Knowledge 151
      The Interdisciplinary Team Member 152
      Goals..152
   Music Therapy in the Treatment of Physical Disorders 153
      Motor Skills 154
      Communication Skills 160
      Cognitive Skills 167
      Social Skills...172
      Emotional Skills...173
      Musical Skills...175

Chapter 7. Music Therapy and Elderly Populations 181

An Introduction to Aging 181
Gerontology: The Study of Aging 183
The Graying of America: Demographics of Older Adults 183
Definitions of Age 184
    Biological Age 185
    Psychological Age 185
    Psychosocial Age 185
Age-Related Disorders 186
    Age-Related Psychological Disorders 187
    Age-Related Physical Disorders 188
Aging and the Changing Workforce 192
Community Integration and the Older Adult 192
The Functional Approach to Treatment 193
Clinical Practice in Music Therapy 194
    Assessment Using Music 195
    An Approach to Music Therapy Treatment Design 196
    Music Application for Therapeutic Outcomes 197
    Music Therapy Activities 198
    Music Therapy and Evidence-Based Practice 199
    The Therapeutic Relationship in Music Therapy Practice 201

Chapter 8. Music Therapy in the Treatment of Behavioral-Emotional Disorders 209

Behavioral-Emotional Disorders: An Introduction 210
Some Common Categories of Behavioral-Emotional Disorders 211
    Schizophrenia 212
    Mood Disorders 215
    Anxiety Disorders 217
    Personality Disorders 219
    Substance-Related Disorders 221
    Other Psychiatric Disorders 222
Philosophical Orientations to Psychiatric Treatment 223
    Treatments That Focus on Affect 224
    Treatments That Focus on Behavior 225
    Treatments That Focus on Cognition 227
    Treatments That Focus on Physical Factors: Biomedical Model 229
    Eclectic Orientation 232
Clinical Uses of Music Therapy in the Psychiatric Setting 233
    Considering Individual Differences in Age and Culture 233
    Categories of Music Activities Used in Therapy 234

Levels of Group Therapy Based on the Client's Functional Level 237
    Supportive, Activity-Oriented Music Therapy *238*
    Reeducative, Insight-and-Process-Oriented Music Therapy *239*
    Reconstructive, Analytically and Catharsis-Oriented Music Therapy *240*
Changes in Health Care Delivery: Short-Term Care 241

Chapter 9. Group Music Psychotherapy in Correctional Psychiatry 247

Music Therapy in Correctional Psychiatry: Rationales and Goals 248
Professional Considerations for the Correctional Music Therapist 249
Three Types of Group Music Psychotherapy 251
    Guided Music Listening and Counseling *251*
    Therapeutic Music Improvisation *251*
    Music and Relaxation *252*
A "Musical Semantics" Model of Therapeutic Musical Improvisation 252
Clinical Considerations 256

Chapter 10. Music Therapy in Neurologic Rehabilitation 261

Rehabilitation Techniques in Neurologic Rehabilitation 262
    Principles of Neurologic Rehabilitation *262*
    Cognitive Deficits *264*
    Communication Deficits *264*
    Physical Deficits *265*
    Socioemotional Deficits *266*
Neurologic Music Therapy 266
    Neurologic Music Therapy with Cognitive Deficits *267*
    Neurologic Music Therapy with Speech and Language Deficits *268*
    Neurologic Music Therapy with Sensorimotor Deficits *269*
Stroke 271
    Prevalence *271*
    Definition *271*
    Etiology and Diagnosis *271*
    Assessment *273*
Traumatic Brain Injury 277
    Prevalence *277*
    Definition *277*
    Etiology and Diagnosis *277*
    Assessment *278*
    Treatment for Stroke and Traumatic Brain Injury *281*
Neurologic Music Therapy for Patients with Stroke and Traumatic Brain Injury 281
    Neurologic Music Therapy with Cognitive Deficits *282*
    Neurologic Music Therapy with Communication Deficits *284*
    Neurologic Music Therapy with Physical Deficits *286*
    Music Therapy with Socioemotional Deficits *289*

Parkinson's and Huntington's Disease 290
    Prevalence 290
    Definition 290
    Etiology and Diagnosis 291
    Assessment 291
    Treatment for Patients with Parkinson's or Huntington's Disease 292
Neurologic Music Therapy for Patients with Parkinson's or Huntington's Disease 293
    Neurologic Music Therapy with Cognitive Deficits 293
    Neurologic Music Therapy with Communication Deficits 293
    Neurologic Music Therapy with Physical Deficits 294
Multiple Sclerosis 295
    Prevalence 295
    Definition 295
    Etiology and Diagnosis 295
    Assessment 296
    Treatment for Patients with Multiple Sclerosis 297
Neurologic Music Therapy for Patients with Multiple Sclerosis 298

Chapter 11. Music Therapy, Medicine, and Well-Being **305**
A Biopsychosocial Perspective of Health and Illness 308
Music in the Promotion of Health and Well-Being 310
Medical Applications of Music Therapy 311
    Biological Needs 312
    Psychological and Social Needs 325
Assessment Procedures 331
    Self-Report Measures 331
    Observation of Behavioral Responses 332
    Clinical Measures 332

Chapter 12. Music Therapy in Hospice and Palliative Care **343**
Hospice and Palliative Care: What Are They? 344
Who Benefits from Hospice or Palliative Care? 344
Music Therapist as Part of the Hospice Team 344
Issues at End-of-Life, Typically Addressed by Music Therapists 345
    Physical Issues 345
    Psychosocial Issues 348
Music Therapy Goals and Interventions Commonly Used in Hospice and Palliative Care 350
    Music Therapy to Alleviate Physical Symptoms 352
    Music Therapy for Psychosocial Support 356

Chapter 13. Music Therapy in the Treatment of Sensory Disorders 365

Part I: Hearing 366
  Sound and the Auditory System 368
    Sound Energy 368
    The Hearing Mechanism 369
  Profiles of Hearing Loss 369
    Types of Hearing Loss 369
    Degree of Hearing Losses 370
    Configuration of Hearing Loss 371
    Onset of Hearing Loss 371
    Hearing Aids and Cochlear Implants 372
  The Relationship Between Hearing Loss and Mode of Communication 373
  Other Terms and Sociocultural Issues Related to Hearing Loss 376
    Deaf Culture 377
    Music in Deaf Culture 377
  Problems Associated with Hearing Loss 378
    Problems Resulting from a Hearing Loss in Early Childhood 378
    Problems Resulting from a Hearing Loss Acquired in Adulthood 379
  Music Therapy with Persons Who Have Hearing Losses 380
    Music Perception and Enjoyment 380
    Accommodations in Music Therapy and Music Education 383
  Treatment Goals for Persons with Hearing Losses 384
    Music Therapy to Promote Auditory Training 385
    Music Therapy for Speech Development 386
    Music Therapy for Language Development 387
    Music Therapy for Social Skills Development 388
Part II: Vision 390
  Visual Impairments: Definitions and Etiology 391
    Definitions of Vision Loss 391
  Characteristics of Persons with Visual Impairments 393
    Cognition 393
    Language 393
    Academic Achievement 394
    Social Development 394
    Motor Development 394
  Music Therapy Objectives 395
    Listening Skills 395
    Orientation and Mobility Skills 395
    Daily Living Skills 396
    Social and Interpersonal Communication Skills 396
    Emotional Expression and Development 397
    Academic Skills 397
    Reducing Sensory Stimulation Behaviors That May Accompany Blindness 397

Chapter 14.   Music Therapy in Special Education 405
Important Events in the History of Special Education 406
Individuals with Disabilities Education Act (IDEA) 407
Disability Categories under IDEA 408
Mainstreaming and Inclusion 410
Principles of Inclusion 411
Models of Educational Services 411
Changing Roles of Music Therapists in Schools 413
Music Therapy as a Related Service 413
Music Therapy in a District-wide Setting 414
Adaptive Strategies for Including Students with Disabilities in Music 415
The Importance and Role of Collaboration in Schools 416
Managing the Therapeutic Classroom 419
The Use of Music as a Strategy to Manage Behavior 421
Conclusions 423

PART THREE: PROFESSIONAL ISSUES IN MUSIC THERAPY 427

Chapter 15.   The Music Therapy Treatment Process 429
Part I: The Clinical Process 430
Referral 431
Assessment 432
Why Is Assessment Important? 433
Assessment Tools 436
Treatment Plan 437
Therapeutic Goals and Objectives 438
Documentation of Progress 442
Evaluation and Termination of Treatment 443
Professional Ethics and Personal Qualifications 444
Professional Ethics 444
Cultural Competence 446
Personal Qualifications 448
Part II: Music Therapy Approaches 451
Definitions 453
Historical Trends That Have Influenced Music Therapy Approaches 454
Recent Trends That Have Influenced the Development of Music Therapy Approaches 455
Advances in Scientific Knowledge Regarding Health and Illness 455
Societal Changes 456
Research and Clinical Initiatives in the Music Therapy Field 456

Factors That Influence Clinical Choices...457
    Differences in Clientele Served 457
    Policies or Attitudes at the Work Place...459
    The Clinical and Educational Background of the Therapist 460
    The Personal Strengths, Limitations, and Beliefs of the Individual Therapist.......................460
Prominent Approaches to Music Therapy 460
    Approaches Developed within Music Education and Pedagogy 461
    Approaches Developed within the Field of Music Therapy.....................465
    Music Therapy Approaches Reflecting or Based upon Psychological
        Philosophies, Theories, or Models...468
    Music Therapy Approaches Reflecting Biomedical Models......................473
    Eclectic or Integrative Approach 477
Conclusions 479

Chapter 16. The Role of Research in Music Therapy **487**
Introduction to Research in Music Therapy 487
The Value of Research..488
Definition of Research...488
How Research Can Influence Music Therapy Practice 489
Types of Research 491
    Descriptive Research...491
    Experimental Research...506
    Historical Research...516
    Qualitative Research...525
Current Status of Research in the Profession...534

ADDITIONAL RESOURCES **539**

Glossary of Terms...541

Index 555

PART **One**

An Overview of Music Therapy

CLINICAL PRACTICE IN MUSIC THERAPY

Kate E. Gfeller
William B. Davis

CHAPTER OUTLINE

WHAT IS MUSIC THERAPY?
WITH WHOM DOES A MUSIC THERAPIST WORK?
WHERE DO MUSIC THERAPISTS WORK?
WHAT ARE THE PERSONAL QUALIFICATIONS OF A MUSIC THERAPIST?
WHAT IS THE EDUCATIONAL PREPARATION OF A MUSIC THERAPIST?
WHAT IS THE OVERALL PROFILE OF THE MUSIC THERAPY PROFESSION?

Music therapy—what's that? This question is often asked by people with no musical background as well as by those with substantial training as musicians. Most people have a general idea of what professionals such as doctors, teachers, accountants, or construction workers do, since they have encountered numerous examples in everyday life. In contrast, the music therapy profession is relatively young and the total number of music therapists is smaller than one finds in older professions. Therefore, many people have little personal experience with this unique career and have questions concerning its scope and methods. We will begin this chapter with some brief examples of how music therapy is used in different settings and with different clientele.

John is a music therapist at New Horizons Rehabilitation Center. His clients come to the center because they have difficulty, as the result of accidents or neuromuscular conditions, with basic physical movements such as walking, eating, writing, and other important tasks. This afternoon, John is working with his gait training group, that is, a small group of adults who once walked naturally and with ease, but who now have an irregular gait (walking motion) due to neurological damage. Research has shown that a steady rhythmic beat can function as a timing cue that helps reestablish a more regular gait. Therefore, John and the center's physical therapists have their clients practice gait training to music that has a strong steady beat and is at a suitable tempo. The clients also seem to be more motivated

3

and less frustrated when they practice their gait training to music that they really enjoy. Therefore, John takes into account the favorite musical styles of each client as well as the tempo and beat when selecting music for gait training. In summary, John uses music to provide a timing cue and to sustain the motivation level of adults in physical rehabilitation.

Across town, Lisa works as a music therapist in a preschool program for children who have language delays. Lisa and the children are singing together a favorite childhood song, "The Wheels on the Bus." As they come to the verse, "The wheels on the bus go round and round," they all draw circles in the air with their fingers. Next, they bob up and down as they sing, "The people on the bus go up and down." This session looks much like any preschool group because musical songs and games are such a natural part of young childhood. However, Lisa has selected therapeutic music interventions and song lyrics that illustrate or reinforce specific language concepts being emphasized in speech therapy, and that are consistent with their therapy goals. Because Lisa has done such a skillful job of selecting musical materials that are developmentally appropriate and engaging, these youngsters don't even realize that they are working hard on important language skills. If you ask them, music is just for fun!

Holly is a music therapist at Greenbrier Retirement Village, where her clients are all senior citizens. Some of the seniors are quite frail and need a lot of nursing care. However, this afternoon, Holly is working with a group of older adults who live in their own apartments, but who come to the social center at Greenbrier to participate in their weekly bell choir rehearsal. Each person is responsible for playing one or more of the bells. All together, they can create a complete song. They just finished giving a concert at the local civic center and will start preparing for their next concert today. Violet, who has been with the group for several years now, has recently had a slight stroke. Consequently, she has difficulty using her left hand. Therefore, Holly has given Violet a part that requires her to use only one hand. In the coming months, Holly will check with Violet's physical therapist to determine if a specially adapted handbell might provide Violet with some motivation to practice regaining use of her left hand. Melvin has trouble with his eyesight, so Holly has given him a bell part that is rung less frequently, and she notates his part in extra large print. Harriet is a very active and alert senior who is looking for a challenge, so Holly assigns to Harriet four different bells. Harriet also helps with the choir's newsletter and concert schedule. The bell choir provides an enjoyable and musically satisfying context in which these seniors can maintain their physical dexterity (e.g., handling the bells), stay mentally alert (e.g., following their part and playing only at the correct time), and keep involved socially.

Paul is a music therapist at the community mental health center. This afternoon, he is meeting with a group of adults who suffer from chronic depression. One of the first things you might notice about this group is that no one is talking! Rather, each member of the group is actively improvising on musical instruments, an interesting observation given the fact that none of the clients are trained musicians. As a music therapist, Paul has been trained to help people of all kinds of backgrounds and abilities to participate in musical activities in meaningful and therapeutic ways. In this session, musical improvisation serves as a medium for self-expression, and the members of the group are using this nonverbal mode of communication to share how they are feeling today with other members of the group.

Kellie is a music therapist at the local general hospital, and in that capacity, she works with many different kinds of patients who have different health problems. Today, she is consulting with a Lamaze group, in which expectant mothers learn techniques to help them cope with the pain that occurs in natural childbirth. Kellie is explaining how music can be used to assist with physical relaxation and as a focal point to help them during painful portions of labor. In cooperation with the Lamaze teacher and each mother-to-be, Kellie will prepare a personalized tape of music that each mother can use during labor. In addition, Kellie and the Lamaze teacher are instructing the women on how to use music to cue a relaxation response. Kellie is using well-researched principles of relaxation, cognitive pain management, and her knowledge of human response to music to help these women prepare for this important moment in their lives.

From these few examples, it should be clear that music can be used in a variety of ways with a variety of people and in different kinds of facilities. Consequently, the question "What is music therapy?" does not easily lend itself to a short, concise answer. Using these examples as a point of departure, let's address some commonly asked questions about music therapy:

- What is music therapy?
- With whom does a music therapist work?
- Where do music therapists work?
- What are the personal qualifications of a music therapist?
- What is the educational preparation of a music therapist?
- What is the overall profile of the music therapy profession?

WHAT IS MUSIC THERAPY?

In music therapy, the word *music* is used to describe the particular medium used. Music is used as a therapeutic tool, but its optimal benefit in therapy depends on the appropriate use by the therapist. It is not a cure-all. For example, what would happen if we were to give musical recordings or concert tickets to people who have cerebral palsy or depression? Those individuals may enjoy the music or may even feel a temporary shift in mood as a result of enjoying the concert. However, it is unlikely that they would experience significant or lasting improvements in physical or emotional functioning as a result of those brief musical experiences. That sort of informal usage of music, which people can provide for themselves each day, does not take into account the underlying cause of the health problem. Nor is the music utilized in a manner consistent with well-tested theories of treatment. The effectiveness of music as a therapeutic tool applied for particular use depends on the skill and knowledge of the therapist.

In the examples at the opening of this chapter, different kinds of music were used in different ways. For example, in his work at the rehabilitation center, John uses recordings of highly rhythmic music to serve as a timing cue and to enhance motivation. Lisa and the children in the preschool group are singing commonly known children's songs, but the choice of songs is, in part, due to the particular language concepts embedded in those particular songs. Paul's clients at the mental health center are actually creating their own music on the spot and using their improvisation as nonverbal communication. Just as physicians use a variety of procedures and equipment (i.e., performing surgery, prescribing medicine, listening to people's problems, etc.) depending on the medical condition, so do music therapists tailor their uses of music to the individual needs of their clients.

Because music is a universal phenomenon, people of all ages and all cultures listen, perform, create, and enjoy it. Some music is highly complex and challenging to understand. Other music is very simple and easy to follow. Some people like to compose or perform music, while others derive considerable pleasure simply by listening. The variety of musical styles and the manifold ways in which people can be involved make music a highly flexible therapeutic medium. (Chapter 3 describes different structural features of music and its functions in society that contribute to music's effectiveness as a therapeutic tool.)

Now, let's consider the word *therapy*. This is a commonly used word that is often used to mean assisting or helping a person. Often, it is used in the context of physical or mental problems. As we know from everyday life, therapy can occur in a variety of forms. For example, psychologists primarily listen and talk to their clients, dieticians educate people on which foods are most nutritious and suitable for their individual needs, and physical therapists assign various physical exercises or develop special splints or mobility devices. Surgeons use special tools like scalpels and clamps to repair damaged body parts. Music therapists use music and musical activities to facilitate therapeutic processes.

Given the various ways in which music is used as a therapeutic tool, it is difficult to articulate a brief yet comprehensive definition of *music therapy*. Certainly, a number of different definitions have been proposed over the years as the profession has evolved. In the first decade of professional development, a brochure entitled "Music Therapy as a Career" (National Association for Music Therapy [NAMT], 1960) defined music therapy as "the scientific application of the art of music to accomplish therapeutic aims. It is the use of music and of the therapist's self to influence changes in behavior."

In the early days of the profession (see Chapter 2 for additional information on the history of the profession), music therapists were fewer in number and were trained in one of a handful of university programs. Further, the variety of clientele served and procedures used in those early years were much narrower than in the present day. Thus, this rather brief and narrow definition of music therapy probably seemed appropriate at the time.

Two decades later, that same professional organization had grown considerably in membership. By this time, new techniques and standards of practice had been developed to meet an ever more diverse client base. Thus, it is no surprise that a new definition was in order. NAMT's 1980 brochure, "A Career in Music Therapy," described the profession in the following way:

> Music therapy is the use of music in the accomplishment of therapeutic aims: the restoration, maintenance, and improvement of mental and physical health. It is the systematic application of music, as directed by the music therapist in a therapeutic environment, to bring about desirable changes in behavior. Such changes enable the individual undergoing therapy to experience a greater understanding of himself and the world about him, thereby achieving a more appropriate adjustment to society. As a member of the therapeutic team, the professional music therapist participates in the analysis of individual problems and in the projection of general treatment aims before planning and carrying out specific music activities. Periodic evaluations determine the effectiveness of the procedures employed.

Since 1980, the music therapy profession has continued to evolve as new knowledge and new health care practices have emerged. In 1997, the American Music Therapy Association published the following definition of music therapy in their brochure regarding professional opportunities:

> Music Therapy is an established allied health profession using music and music activities to address physical, psychological, cognitive, and social needs of individuals with disabilities. The profession was established in 1950 because of work done using music with patients in Veterans' Hospitals

following World War II. Today, over 5,000 music therapists are employed throughout the United States in settings such as hospitals, clinics, day care facilities, schools, community mental health centers, substance abuse facilities, nursing homes, hospices, rehabilitation centers, correctional facilities, and private practices. Nearly half a century of research in music therapy supports the effectiveness of music therapy in many areas such as facilitating movement and overall physical rehabilitation; motivating people to cope with treatment; providing emotional support for clients and families; providing an outlet for expression of feelings and providing process oriented psychotherapy.

More recently, the website for the American Music Therapy Association (www. musictherapy.org) offered the following definition:

> Music Therapy is an established healthcare profession that uses music to address physical, emotional, cognitive, and social needs of individuals of all ages. Music therapy improves the quality of life for persons who are well and meets the needs of children and adults with disabilities or illnesses. Music therapy interventions can be designed to: promote wellness, manage stress, alleviate pain, express feelings, enhance memory, improve communication, and promote physical rehabilitation. Research in music therapy supports its effectiveness in a wide variety of healthcare and educational settings. (Retrieved June 1, 2008)

This definition of music therapy emphasizes various types of health problems assisted through music therapy but offers little information about other aspects of the profession (e.g., how music functions as a therapeutic tool). Music therapy means different things to different people and is shaped by the individual therapist's values, philosophy, training, clinical setting, and cultural background. It is likely that each music therapist might modify this particular definition a little or a lot, depending on his or her own professional experiences. As you read further on in this book, you will find information about the various structural features and societal functions of music that contribute to its effectiveness as a therapeutic medium. You will also read about the many different ways in which music functions as a therapeutic tool with different clienteles. Once you have finished reading this book, you should have in mind a much more comprehensive idea of this profession.

WITH WHOM DOES A MUSIC THERAPIST WORK?

As the opening vignettes imply, a wide variety of people can benefit from music therapy. For example, John works with people who have physical disabilities.

Paul works with adults who have emotional disorders. Lisa works with little children who have delays in language development. These are only a few of the many clienteles served by music therapists today.

In the past, music therapists have most frequently worked with those who have behavioral and emotional disorders or have intellectual disabilities. With increased emphasis on providing preventive health care, integrating disabled children into the public schools, and increasing services to the elderly population, music therapists are expanding into new clinical areas. Music therapy is now used in pain control, stress management, infant stimulation, adult day care, nursing homes, wellness programs, childbirth, prisons, and medical care.

As is the case in other health care professions (e.g., nursing, physical therapy, occupational therapy, speech language pathology, etc.), music therapy methods and techniques vary greatly among these clinical settings. For example, Holly uses methods and materials that are suitable for well and fragile older adults. Kellie's use of music with expectant mothers is based on principles of pain management and requires sensitivity to the physical needs during pregnancy. Lisa has to take into account normal patterns of child development, especially as related to language development, in planning her session. The therapeutic goals selected and the interventions used are influenced by the individual client's needs, facility policies and programs, and input from other therapists. Therefore, music therapists need to learn not only basic music therapy methods, but also specialized techniques applicable for particular clienteles.

Below is a breakdown of the major populations served by music therapists based on a 2007 survey conducted by the American Music Therapy Association (AMTA, 2007):

- behavioral and emotional disorders (19%)
- developmentally disabled (12%)
- elderly and Alzheimer's (9%)
- medical/surgical (9%)
- neurological disorders (5%)
- all others (46%)

Approximately 40% of all music therapists work with clients who have behavioral and emotional disorders or developmental disabilities, or with older adults. Historically, mental illness and intellectual disabilities have been the disabilities most prevalently served by music therapists, but recently, music therapists are serving a more diverse population of clienteles. In the past two decades, increasing numbers of music therapists are working with older adults. This is consistent with the overall growth of the elderly population and its need for increased medical and social services, including music therapy.

The types of clients served by music therapists continue to change over time. For example, only a few decades ago, many premature babies died shortly after delivery. Now, many of these at-risk babies survive but may have special education and health care needs that could be addressed by a music therapist. Other trends, such as the AIDS epidemic and the growth of hospice and palliative care, have also changed the type of clientele that music therapists serve. Therefore, this profile of clients served by music therapists will continue to change over time. These changes bring about changes in professional training and job opportunities.

In order to learn more about the sorts of people served by music therapists, students can seek experience, such as in volunteer or paid positions. By working with children, adolescents, or adults with special needs, the aspiring therapist learns about one or more clinical populations and can make a more informed career choice (Knoll, et al, 1999).

WHERE DO MUSIC THERAPISTS WORK?

As the profiles of the music therapists at the beginning of this chapter suggest, music therapists work in a variety of settings. For example, the community mental health center where Paul works is a renovated Victorian home, which has been remodeled to include offices of counselors and larger rooms for group therapy. The clients do not live at the center, but rather arrive when they have individual or group therapy. Kellie, on the other hand, works in a general hospital. Her office, where she does her planning, is in the activity therapy area; often, she provides music therapy right in the patients' rooms or therapy areas on the different wards. Lisa's preschool classroom is at the end of one wing of a public school. The parents bring their children to preschool on weekday mornings. As you can see, music therapists do not necessarily work in hospitals. The type of treatment facility will vary greatly depending on the nature of the individual's health problem. However, these various options for provision of treatment have not always existed.

The places in which people receive treatment have changed dramatically over the centuries. In ancient times, we know that people who had mental or physical impairments were sometimes killed, abandoned, or left to fend for themselves as street beggars (Rudenberg, 1981). In the 1800s, the public attempted to care for those with disabilities by establishing special institutions for the blind, the "feebleminded," the deaf, and the insane (Trent, 1994). It was usual for very young children with severely disabling conditions to be sent to a residential institution where they would be raised and educated and perhaps spend their entire lives.

The quality of institutions varied greatly. Some were, unfortunately, little more than walls and beds, providing essentially custodial care. Other institutions run by administrators that were more enlightened included rehabilitation or recreational programs. Some institutions included music programs for the residents, including orchestra, band, chorus, or other groups. Often, exceptionally talented residents were identified and became "lifelong" members of the performance groups of the facility. These institutional music programs were sometimes organized by musically talented personnel or philanthropically minded music teachers. In other instances, music therapists were hired by the institution to develop a music program (Graham & Beer, 1980).

The initial purpose of these music programs was to develop performance groups. As time went on, educators and health care specialists began to notice additional benefits of music programs for the disabled. For example, in programs for persons with intellectual disabilities, music was seen as an opportunity for developing speech and social skills. Early reports from schools for the deaf indicated that rhythmic activities were perceived as beneficial for training the residual, or usable, hearing of the residents (Darrow & Heller, 1985; Graham & Beer, 1980).

In the 20th century, significant changes in educational and rehabilitative practices have occurred. People began to raise concerns about those institutions that provided poor care and further questioned whether people with disabilities should be isolated from their families and communities. Gradually, the general public became more concerned with the rights of individuals with physical and mental limitations (Graham & Beer, 1980; Shore, 1986; U.S. Department of Education, 1988). In response to pressure by parents and advocacy groups who felt that the educational and social opportunities within the institutions were of lesser quality than programs found in the public schools (Biklen, Lehr, Searl, & Taylor, 1987; Shore, 1986), regulatory changes in the educational practices for disabled students occurred.

In 1975, the U.S. federal government passed a landmark bill, Public Law 94-142, entitled the **Education for All Handicapped Children Act** of 1975 (Shore, 1986; U.S. Department of Education, 1988). This bill called for sweeping changes in the education of children with disabilities, including appropriate placement within the public school setting (called mainstreaming); the development of **Individualized Education Programs (IEPs)** was implemented in schools across the nation in 1978. So, rather than educating students with disabilities in remote residential institutions, children from the ages of 3 through 21 with wide-ranging disabilities were enrolled in local public schools (Graham & Beer, 1980).

Today, music therapists are employed in a variety of health care and educational settings, including medical hospitals, clinics, group homes, centers for persons with developmental disabilities, prisons, schools, and mental health facilities. Some music therapists engage in private practice or serve as consultants. Others teach, supervise music therapy interns, or become administrators.

The most prevalent work settings served by music therapists (AMTA, 2007) include children's facilities or schools (18%), geriatric facilities (15%), mental health settings (13%), self-employment/private practice (13%), and medical settings (10%). Job opportunities vary depending on geographic location, availability of funding, and other factors, such as regional and institutional practices.

According to the 2007 membership directory of AMTA, major growth areas for employment include school-related facilities, geriatric facilities, private practice, and hospice/bereavement services. Employment opportunities can be expected to change with future developments in educational and health care trends. Music therapists' salaries are comparable to those of other professionals in allied health professions, such as special education teachers and social workers.

WHAT ARE THE PERSONAL QUALIFICATIONS OF A MUSIC THERAPIST?

A music therapist must be both a good musician and a good therapist. What does this mean? Musically, the individual must have excellent functional musical skills (e.g., playing social instruments such as guitar, piano, etc.), must have a broad knowledge of different styles of music (e.g., popular music, classical, jazz, religious, etc.), and should be able to use music flexibly, creatively, and in an aesthetically satisfying manner. Being a talented musician, however, is not enough. Some excellent musicians lack the interpersonal qualities so essential to a good therapist.

Because a therapist's work can be both physically and mentally demanding, certain personal characteristics are requisite to being a successful care giver. Good physical health is important for stamina. Emotional stability is essential since a music therapist must relate effectively with many different types of people of all ages and should serve as a good role model. A sincere interest in helping others, patience, tact, understanding, and a good sense of humor are important. Because the music therapist works with particularly vulnerable individuals, it is especially important that the therapist be reliable, genuine, and ethical. For example, becoming a therapist primarily to have a steady job to "fall back on," as opposed to having genuine interest and good therapeutic skills to offer others, suggests that the therapist is using the client for his or her own financial security. This sort of "use" of the client is unethical.

The music therapist must accept that many of the rewards in a helping profession are intangible. He or she must be able to cope with frustration and must be able to look at situations with clinical objectivity. In short, the successful music therapist is a good musician as well as being creative and imaginative; demonstrates excellent interpersonal skills with clients, supervisors, and peers; and is reliable, genuine, and ethical.

WHAT IS THE EDUCATIONAL PREPARATION OF A MUSIC THERAPIST?

As you will learn later in this chapter, the education and training of a music therapist is multidisciplinary, encompassing other subject areas in addition to music. The music therapy student can expect to learn about physiology, anatomy, biology, psychology, counseling, anthropology, and movement/dance. As you can see, music therapy is a diverse field that is influenced by many factors. The training received by music therapists is unique among college programs, because it requires not only a thorough knowledge of music, but also in-depth education in the biological sciences, sociology, anthropology, psychology, and oral and written communication.

Music therapy programs are approved by the **American Music Therapy Association** (AMTA). Although there is some variation in the particular course titles and number of semester hours in each area from one program to the next, programs typically require course work in the following general areas: music therapy, music, behavioral/health/natural sciences, general education, and general electives. The content to be covered in these courses is summarized in the AMTA's list of professional competencies, knowledge and skills that should be included in the undergraduate program. Study in the area of music therapy includes courses in music therapy principles, the psychology of music, and practical clinical experiences (including an internship that follows completion of course work). Typically, classes cover theories, observation, assessment and measurement techniques, research literature, methods and materials, and ethics. Students can expect to learn about the application of these topics to a variety of disability groups. The course work in music therapy is normally completed in four years if you are a full-time student and is followed by an internship at a clinical facility.

Music courses include theory, history, performance on primary and secondary instruments, functional knowledge of orchestral and band instruments, and music leadership skills. Students in music therapy should expect to master a primary instrument (clarinet, piano, violin, voice, etc.) as well as gain functional skills on guitar, piano, voice, autoharp, and other instruments. The part of the program devoted to the behavioral/health/natural sciences includes course work in psychology, sociology, human development, and research methods. It is recommended that studies in physiology, kinesiology, neurology, and biology also be included. General education consists of those courses required by the individual institution. A school's general curriculum often includes math, English, philosophy, physical education, and basic computer skills. Additional course work in the humanities, such as art, dance, theater, and movement, is suggested.

A small portion of the curriculum may be devoted to general electives: studies chosen by the student. These courses may be in the areas of music, behavioral/health/natural sciences, or additional work in music therapy. After completing course work, the student enters into a clinical internship at an AMTA or university-approved site. During the internship, the student refines his or her clinical skills under the supervision of a Board Certified music therapist. This experience simulates a full-time job in music therapy and provides the student with practical experience in all aspects of music therapy practice. Once this phase of training is completed, the student is eligible to take the Certification Board exam. This exam is administered by the Certification Board for Music Therapists (CBMT), an independent accrediting organization. The test measures the candidate's knowledge about music therapy foundations and principles, clinical theories and techniques, general knowledge about music, and professional roles and responsibilities. Once the exam has been passed, the candidate becomes Board Certified and can apply for professional certification.

WHAT IS THE OVERALL PROFILE OF THE MUSIC THERAPY PROFESSION?

The *2007 AMTA Member Sourcebook* indicated that there are about 2,400 professional music therapists in AMTA. Of the individuals responding to the 2007 survey, approximately 86% of the members are women and 14% are men. The membership profile by age is as follows: ages 20–29=22%; ages 30–39=18%; ages 40–49=24%; ages 50–59=22%, and ages 60 or older=10%. Twenty-six percent of the membership holds masters or doctoral degrees. Approximately 87% of the AMTA membership is Caucasian, 6% Asian and Asian American, 2% African-American, and 2% Hispanic. Thus, at this point in time, young women with undergraduate degrees make up the largest proportion of the profession. Increased diversity by gender and by ethnicity are important goals for the association, especially given the diverse population served and the fact that musical preferences and responses are related to cultural background.

SUMMARY

A career in music therapy offers challenge, opportunity, and reward to those interested in working with children and adults who require special services because of behavioral, learning, or physical disorders. We defined music therapy as a behavioral science concerned with changing unhealthy behaviors and replacing them with more adaptive ones through the use of musical stimuli. The person considering a career in music therapy should be a competent musician who is physically and mentally healthy with good interpersonal skills.

Music therapists work with a variety of clinical populations including, most frequently, people with behavioral-emotional disorders, people with intellectual disabilities, and older adults. Facilities that employ music therapists are equally diverse. Currently, many music therapists are employed in schools and in settings that serve older adults.

The American Music Therapy Association requires a rigorous educational and training program. Course work in music therapy, music, the health/behavioral/ natural sciences, clinical techniques, and general courses comprise a typical program in which the aspiring music therapist will engage.

The following chapters of this book will elaborate on this basic information and, in addition, will discuss historical bases for the uses of music therapy and how music affects the emotional, psychological, and physical health of disabled populations. We will also consider the music therapy treatment process, the role of research in music therapy, and future trends in this unique field.

STUDY QUESTIONS

1. How is a music therapist different from a music educator?

2. Before deciding on a career in music therapy, why is it important to gain experience working with disabled populations?

3. What are the three clinical populations most frequently served by music therapists?

4. Describe the music programs found in early institutions. How did they differ from the music therapy programs offered today?

5. List at least three health care settings that employ music therapists.

6. What are three qualifications that a person should have to become a successful music therapist?

7. What is the purpose of the internship required by the American Music Therapy Association?

8. What is the function of the Board Certification exam? When is a music therapist eligible to take the exam?

REFERENCES

American Music Therapy Association. (1997). *Music Therapy Makes a Difference* [Brochure]. Silver Spring, MD.

American Music Therapy Association. (2007). *2007 AMTA member sourcebook*. Silver Spring, MD: Author.

Biklen, D., Lehr, S., Searl, S., & Taylor, S. (1987). *Purposeful integration . . . inherently equal.* Syracuse, NY: The Center on Human Policy, Syracuse University.

Darrow, A. A., & Heller, G. N. (1985). Early advocates of music education for the hearing impaired: William Wolcott Turner and David Ely Bartlett. *Journal of Research in Music Education, 33*, 269–279.

Graham, R. M., & Beer, A. (1980). *Teaching music to the exceptional child.* Englewood Cliffs, NJ: Prentice-Hall.

Knoll, C. D., Henry, D. J., & Reuer, B. L. (1999). *Music works: A professional notebook for music therapists* (3rd ed.). Stephenville, TX: Music Works.

National Association for Music Therapy. (1960). *Music therapy as a career* [Brochure]. Lawrence, KS: Author.

National Association for Music Therapy. (1980). *A career in music therapy* [Brochure]. Washington, DC: Author.

Rudenberg, M. T. (1981). *Music therapy for handicapped children: Orthopedically handicapped.* Washington, DC: National Association for Music Therapy.

Shore, K. (1986). *The special education handbook.* New York: Teachers College Press.

Trent, J. (1994). *Inventing the feeble mind: A history of mental retardation in the United States.* Berkeley, CA: University of California Press.

U.S. Department of Education. (1988). *Summary of existing legislation affecting persons with disabilities.* Washington, DC: Government Printing Office.

CHAPTER 2

MUSIC THERAPY: HISTORICAL PERSPECTIVE

William B. Davis
Kate E. Gfeller

CHAPTER OUTLINE

MUSIC THERAPY IN PRELITERATE CULTURES
MUSIC AND HEALING IN EARLY CIVILIZATIONS
USES OF MUSIC IN ANTIQUITY: HEALING RITUALS
MUSIC AND HEALING IN THE MIDDLE AGES AND RENAISSANCE
MUSIC THERAPY IN THE UNITED STATES
 18th-Century Writings on Music Therapy
 Literature from the 19th Century
 Music Therapy in 19th-Century Educational Institutions
 Early 20th-Century Music Therapy
THE DEVELOPMENT OF THE MUSIC THERAPY PROFESSION

Scholars from diverse disciplines, including anthropology, psychology, musicology, and physiology, have long questioned why music has been in our behavioral repertoire for thousands of years (Hodges, 1996; Winner, 1982). Music has no apparent survival value, yet it has been an important part of all cultures, past and present. Music has been called "the universal language" and "the greatest good that mortals know." Throughout recorded time, it has been credited with the power to "solace the sick and weary" and to express unspoken emotions (Stevenson, 1967). It is remarkable that music has claimed such a valued role throughout history. This chapter will discuss the role of music in preliterate cultures, the relationship between music and healing during the advent of civilization, the early practice of music therapy in the United States, and the development of the music therapy profession.

MUSIC THERAPY IN PRELITERATE CULTURES

Preliterate societies are those which possess no system of written communication. Early nomadic people banded together in small groups for survival and eked out a living as hunters and food gatherers. They had no agriculture, political structure, or permanent housing. These small groups developed distinct customs and rituals that set them apart from other similar groups. We can only speculate about the musical component of prehistoric life, but we can gain some clues by studying how music is used in preliterate cultures that exist today. This knowledge helps us to understand human response to music and provides some background about the close relationship between music and healing (Nettl, 1956).

Members of preliterate cultures generally believe they are controlled by magical forces and surrounded by an evil, unpredictable environment. To remain healthy, they feel compelled to obey a complex set of regulations that protect them from the hostile forces of nature and their fellow human beings. They perceive magic as an integral part of a healthy and peaceful life (Sigerist, 1970).

Members of preliterate cultures believe in the power of music to affect mental and physical well-being. Music is often connected with supernatural forces. For example, among certain preliterate societies, the songs used in important rituals are thought to have come from superhuman or unearthly sources (Merriam, 1964; Sachs, 1965). These songs, with their unexplainable powers, are used for entreating the gods and in all activities requiring extraordinary assistance, such as in religious or healing rites.

In some preliterate societies, an ill person is viewed as a victim of an enemy's spell. He or she is blameless and thus enjoys special treatment from the group. In other societies, however, it is believed that a person suffers illness to atone for sins committed against a tribal god. As long as the afflicted member continues to contribute to the well-being of the family and community, status does not change. If the person becomes too ill to uphold social responsibilities, he or she is considered an outcast and ostracized. In these cultures, the cause and treatment of disease is primarily determined by the "medicine man," who often applies elements of magic and religion in order to exorcise the malevolent spirit or demon from the patient's body. The type of music used is determined by the nature of the spirit invading the body.

Because of slightly different concepts of disease among preliterate societies, the role of the musician/healer and style of music vary. In most instances, the tribal musician/healer holds a place of importance within society. It is this person's duty not only to determine the cause of the disease, but also to apply the appropriate treatment to drive the spirit or demon from the patient's body. Sometimes, music functions as a prelude to the actual healing ceremony. Drums, rattles, chants, and songs may be used during the preliminary ritual and also throughout the actual ceremony (Sigerist, 1970). It is important to note that the musician/healer usually does not act alone. Preliterate societies recognize the power of the group and include family and society members in the ritual. Healing séances or choruses provide spiritual and emotional support in order to facilitate a quick recovery (Boxberger, 1962). As noted earlier, we must speculate about the customs of preliterate societies from ancient times. If, as many scholars believe, that current practices among contemporary preliterate societies offer a "window" into the past, then is likely that music was an important part of healing ceremonies very early in human history.

MUSIC AND HEALING IN EARLY CIVILIZATIONS

The hunters and food collectors of preliterate cultures predominated for about 500,000 years. The advent of agriculture 8,000–10,000 years ago led to a more stable existence, the growth of larger populations, and the rise of civilization. Civilization is characterized by the evolution of written communication, the growth of cities, and technological achievement in areas that include science and medicine. It is a way of life for a large group of people living in a more or less permanent alliance with a particular set of customs and view of nature. The first civilizations appeared between 5000 and 6000 B.C. in an area that is now Iraq and became firmly established by 3500 B.C. Music played an important part in "rational medicine" during this time as well as in magical and religious healing ceremonies.

USES OF MUSIC IN ANTIQUITY: HEALING RITUALS

With the advent of civilization, the magical, religious, and rational components of medicine began to develop along separate lines. In ancient Egypt (c. 5000 B.C.), these elements existed side by side, but healers generally based a treatment philosophy on only one. Egyptian music healers enjoyed a privileged existence, due to their close relationship with priests and other important government leaders. Egyptian priest-physicians referred to music as medicine for the soul and often included chant therapies as part of medical practice (Feder & Feder, 1981).

During the height of the Babylonian culture (c. 1850 B.C.), disease was viewed within a religious framework. The sick person suffered as penance for sins committed against a god and was viewed by society as an outcast. Treatment, if offered, consisted of religious ceremonies to placate the offended deity (Sigerist, 1970). Healing rites often included music.

Music was regarded as a special force over thought, emotion, and physical health in ancient Greece. In 600 B.C., Thales was credited with curing a plague in Sparta through musical powers (Merriam, 1964). Healing shrines and temples included hymn specialists, and music was prescribed for emotionally disturbed individuals (Feder & Feder, 1981). The use of music for curing mental disorders reflected the belief that it could directly influence emotion and develop character. Among the notables of Greece who subscribed to the power of music were Aristotle, who valued it as an emotional catharsis; Plato, who described music as the medicine of the soul; and Caelius Aurelianus, who warned against indiscriminate use of music against madness (Feder & Feder, 1981).

By the 6th century B.C., rational medicine had almost completely replaced magical and religious rites in Greece. Although a minority still attributed illness to supernatural powers, the majority supported rational investigation into the causes of disease. For the first time in history, the study of health and disease was based on empirical evidence (Sigerist, 1970).

The predominant explanation of health and disease became the theory of the four cardinal humors. This theory was described by Polybus, son-in-law of Hippocrates, in his treatise, "On the Nature of Man," circa 380 B.C. The four humors were blood, phlegm, yellow bile, and black bile, and each element contained a unique quality. Good health was the result of maintaining a balance among the four humors, whereas an imbalance of two or more elements led to illness. Sick individuals were considered to be inferior. With only slight modification, this theory influenced medicine for the next 2,000 years, becoming most important during the Middle Ages.

MUSIC AND HEALING IN THE MIDDLE AGES AND RENAISSANCE

Although much of the splendor of classical Greece was lost during the Middle Ages, this time period (c. 476–1450 A.D.) represents an important connection between antiquity and the present. After the fall of the Roman Empire, Christianity became a major force in Western civilization. The influence of Christianity prompted a change in attitudes toward disease. Contrary to earlier thinking, a sick person was neither inferior nor being punished by gods. As Christianity spread throughout Europe, societies began to care for and treat their sick members. Hospitals were established to provide humanitarian care to people with physical ailments. Sufferers of mental illness, however, were not as fortunate. Mentally ill people were believed to be possessed by demons and were often incarcerated and abused (Boxberger, 1962).

Although Christian beliefs heavily influenced attitudes toward disease during the Middle Ages, the practice of medicine was still based on the theory of the four humors developed during Greek civilization. This framework also provided the basis for the role of music in treating illness. Numerous statesmen and philosophers believed in the curative powers of music, including Boethius, who claimed that music either improved or degraded human morals. Cassiodorus, like Aristotle, viewed music as a potent type of catharsis, whereas St. Basil advocated it as a positive vehicle for sacred emotion. Many believed hymns to be effective against certain unspecified respiratory diseases (Strunk, 1965).

During the Renaissance, advances in anatomy, physiology, and clinical medicine marked the beginning of the scientific approach to medicine. Despite developments in the laboratory, however, treatment of disease was still based on the teachings of Hippocrates and Galen and a sophisticated interpretation of the four humors. During this period, there was some integration of music, medicine, and art. For example, it was not unusual to find writings, such as those of Zarlino (a musician) and Vesalius (a physician), that touched on the relationship between music and medicine (Boxberger, 1962).

Music during the Renaissance was not only used as a remedy for melancholy, despair, and madness, but also prescribed by physicians as preventive medicine. Properly dispensed music was recognized then, as it is today, as a powerful tool to enhance emotional health. For those who could afford the luxury of attending live performances, music helped to maintain a positive outlook on life. Optimism was particularly important during this time, because Europe was being ravaged by epidemics that sometimes decimated entire villages (Boxberger, 1962).

During the Baroque period (1580–1750), music continued to be linked with the medical practice of the day, based as before on the theory of the four humors. In addition, the theory of temperaments and affections by Kircher (1602–1680) provided a fresh viewpoint on the use of music in the treatment of disease. Kircher believed that personality characteristics were coupled with a certain style of music. For example, depressed individuals responded to melancholy music. Cheerful people were most affected by dance music, because it stimulated the blood (Carapetyan, 1948). Thus, it became necessary for the healer to choose the correct style of music for treatment. Supporting the use of music to treat depression, Burton, in his *Anatomy of Melancholy*, stated that "besides that excellent power it hath to expel many other diseases, it is a sovereign remedy against Despair and Melancholy, and will drive away the Devil himself" (Burton, 1651). Other writers, such as Shakespeare and Armstrong, also included numerous examples of music as therapy in their plays and poems (Davis, 1985).

By the late 18th century, music was still advocated by European physicians in the treatment of disease, but a definite change in philosophy was underway. With increased emphasis on scientific medicine, physicians and scientists began to investigate scientifically supported explanations for illness, rather than religious or superstitious explanations. Consequently, the use of music to "soothe" the gods would no longer be consistent with contemporary views on illness and healing. While many aspects of medicine from that time period would be viewed through contemporary eyes as naive or simply wrong, there was important progress regarding scientifically based medical treatment. During this time period, music was relegated to special cases and applied by only a few physicians who viewed treatment from a holistic (multitherapeutic) framework. The belief that music influenced mood was one way in which music was considered relevant to medical practice at this time. This shift in medical practice and the role of music within healing practices were evident during the growth and development of music therapy in the United States.

MUSIC THERAPY IN THE UNITED STATES

The practice of music therapy in the United States has a long, storied history. Although music therapy as a profession became organized only in the 20th century, music has been used in this country to treat physical and mental ailments since the late 18th century.

18th-Century Writings on Music Therapy

The earliest known reference to music therapy in the United States was an unsigned article in *Columbian Magazine* in 1789. The article, entitled "Music Physically Considered," presented basic principles of music therapy that are still in use today and provided evidence of music therapy practice in Europe. Mainly using the ideas of Descartes (a French philosopher), the anonymous author developed a case for using music to influence and regulate emotional conditions. An interesting conclusion drawn by the author was that a person's mental state may affect physical health. The author also asserted that music, because of its effect on emotions, was a proven therapeutic agent. One other important point in this article was the author's advice that the skilled use of music in the treatment of disease required a properly trained practitioner. This advice is as pertinent now as it was in 1789 (Heller, 1987).

Another article published during this period was entitled "Remarkable Cure of a Fever by Music: An Attested Fact." This article was published in 1796 in the *New York Weekly Magazine*. The anonymous author described the case of an unnamed French music teacher who suffered from a severe fever. After nearly two weeks of constant distress, a concert was performed at the patient's request. His symptoms reportedly disappeared during the performance but returned upon its conclusion. The music was repeated throughout the man's waking hours, resulting in the suspension of his illness. In two weeks' time, the music teacher recovered completely.

Both authors based their conclusions of the music's effectiveness on anecdotal rather than scientific evidence. Such claims lack credibility by today's standards, but these articles suggest that some practitioners during the 18th century were interested in using music in medical treatment. At that time, medical care was crude and often dangerous, so a gentle treatment like music therapy was likely welcomed by the public, who often suffered at the hands of the unregulated medical profession (Heller, 1987).

Literature from the 19th Century

During the 19th century, several authors wrote about the use of music to treat physical and mental illness. Articles appeared in music journals, medical journals, psychiatric periodicals, and medical dissertations. Although these reports varied in length as well as quality, they supported the use of therapeutic music as an alternative or a supplement to traditional medical treatment.

The earliest documents produced during this period were dissertations written by two medical students, Edwin Atlee and Samuel Mathews, who attended the University of Pennsylvania. Atlee's work, entitled *"An Inaugural Essay on the Influence of Music in the Cure of Diseases,"* was completed in 1804. He cited literary, medical, and scholarly sources, including material from theorist Jean-Jacques Rousseau, physician and psychiatrist Benjamin Rush, poet John Armstrong, and British musicologist Charles Burney, as well as personal experiences.

The purpose of Atlee's brief dissertation was "to treat the effects produced on the mind by the impression of that certain modification of sound called music, which I hope to prove has a powerful influence upon the mind, and consequently on the body." After defining important terms used in his text, he suggested that music has the ability to arouse and affect a variety of emotions, including joy and grief. The final part of Atlee's dissertation discussed the beneficial effects of music on a variety of mental and physical illnesses and described three cases in which he successfully treated patients with music. In one of his examples, he encouraged a client to resume playing the flute.

Samuel Mathews wrote *"On the Effects of Music in Curing and Palliating Diseases"* in 1806. His dissertation was in some respects similar to Atlee's, but more sophisticated in its use of sources and in the amount of information presented to the reader. Mathews outlined the benefits of music in the treatment of diseases of the mind and body. For example, in order to alleviate depression, he recommended using music that matched the mood of the patient (today this is known as the **iso principle**), because "with the precaution, we may gradually raise the tunes from those we judge proper in the commencement [of a depressed state] to those of a more lively nature." In addition to other citations, Mathews used the Bible to support his assertions, recounting the story of the therapeutic effects of David's harp playing on Saul's psychological difficulties (Gilbert & Heller, 1983).

The dissertations of Atlee and Mathews were strikingly similar in form, content, and physical appearance. Of the many sources they cited, no one person was relied on more heavily than physician/psychiatrist Benjamin Rush, who was a professor at the University of Pennsylvania and a strong advocate for the use of music to treat mental disease. Rush played a major role in creating interest in music therapy during the beginning of the 19th century and likely encouraged Atlee and Mathews to write on the topic (Carlson, Wollock, & Noel, 1981). Their dissertations made a unique contribution to music therapy during the early years of the 19th century.

Music Therapy in 19th-Century Educational Institutions

The use of music therapy in educational institutions for persons with disabilities began in the 19th century. In 1832, the Perkins School for the Blind was founded in Boston by Dr. Samuel Gridley Howe (Heller, 1987). Perhaps due to the urging of his wife, Julia Ward Howe (who composed the lyrics to "Battle Hymn of the Republic"), Dr. Howe, the school's administrator, included music in the curriculum from the beginning. Dr. Howe was instrumental in engaging prominent Boston musicians to help establish ongoing music programs at the school. One of the first of these musicians was Lowell Mason, who taught at the school from 1832–1836. He was responsible for teaching vocal music and piano lessons as well as other music activities. By the time Mason left the school, he had established a strong curriculum in music instruction, which is still in effect today (Darrow & Heller, 1985).

There are other examples of music therapy in institutional settings during the mid-1800s. George Root, a music pupil and friend of Mason, taught at the New York School for the Blind from 1845 to 1850 (Carder, 1972). During the 1840s, William Wolcott Turner and David Ely Bartlett developed a successful music program at the American Asylum for the Deaf, located in Hartford, Connecticut. One student, identified only as Miss Avery, successfully completed a difficult course of piano study. Turner and Bartlett reported her accomplishment in an article entitled "Music Among the Deaf and Dumb," which appeared in the October 1848 issue of the *American Annals of the Deaf and Dumb* (Darrow & Heller, 1985). Music programs were also developed for students with physical disabilities during the early to mid-1800s.

During this period when music therapy was being developed in educational settings, there was also renewed interest in its use as treatment for disease. Three unsigned articles (all entitled "Medical Powers of Music") appeared in *Musical Magazine* within a span of two months in 1840–1841. These reports focused on the linkage of therapeutic music with history, philosophy, and religion, but added little in the way of new information. Much of the material in the articles came from British music historian Charles Burney, whose book *A General History of Music* was published in 1789. One prominent example was the story of King Philip V of Spain, who suffered from depression. During the late 1730s, the famous Italian baroque castrato, Farinelli, who had retired to Spain, was summoned to Madrid to perform for King Philip. It was reported that the king was so moved by the singing of Farinelli that all signs of his chronic depression disappeared, thus assuring the singer lifelong gratitude from the Spanish monarch. The final article in the series cited stories from composers, writers, historians, and performers who had firsthand experience with the therapeutic effects of music (Heller, 1987). Despite their questionable credibility, these articles indicated ongoing interest in music therapy during the first third of the 19th century.

The next substantial support for music therapy was not published until 1874. The article penned by physician James Whittaker entitled "Music as a Medicine," cited an impressive number of American and European sources to support his theory that musical response was linked to physiological, psychological, and sociocultural attributes. Numerous examples were provided to support his belief in the power of music to influence mind and body. Whittaker concluded that the greatest effects from the use of music were on mild forms of mental illness, whereas the treatment of physical ailments and severe mental distress with music was temporary at best.

A second article during that decade was published in the *Virginia Medical Monthly* in 1878. "Music as Mind Medicine" was an edited version of a piece that originally appeared in *The World,* a New York newspaper, dated March 6, 1878. The journal article, edited by Landon B. Edwards, described a series of experiments that took place at Blackwell's Island (now Roosevelt Island), an infamous facility for the care of New York City's indigent, insane citizens. These sessions were held to test "lunatics'" reactions to live music provided by instrumental and vocal soloists. The report began with introductory information about the purpose of the experiment and the people who participated. The principals included the distinguished American pianist John Nelson Pattison, who was credited with initiating the project. Also taking part were New York City Charities Commissioner William Brennan, several physicians, and a number of New York City government officials. A large entourage of musicians also accompanied Pattison and the others to the hospital. The group included 40 members of D. L. Downing's Ninth Regiment Band and several vocalists from the New York Musicians Guild.

The musicians provided music for a large group of patients following a series of nine individual sessions. Pattison directed the individual sessions from a piano, while the doctors assisted by taking physiological data and recording each patient's reaction to the music. The government officials apparently were onlookers, although this was not specifically stated. The article reported that similar sessions had taken place on four previous occasions, about which no information has been located.

The music experiments on Blackwell's Island marked an unprecedented attempt to alleviate the suffering of a large group of persons with mental illness. Authorities who were in a position to implement and maintain such programs, an occurrence not seen previously in the United States, supported the concerts and individual sessions.

During the final decade of the 19th century, two important papers appeared that provided strong support for music therapy in institutional settings and in private practice. In January 1892, George Alder Blumer's treatise titled "Music in Its Relation to the Mind" appeared in the *American Journal of Insanity*. Although the author recognized the therapeutic value of music, he did not support the extravagant claims made by others. Blumer believed that music was a part of moral treatment. The combination of art, reading, music, and physical education provided a well-rounded therapy program for persons with mental illness. Blumer held music in such high regard that he hired immigrant musicians to perform for the patients at Utica State Hospital in New York, where he served as Chief Executive Officer. In fact, Blumer may have been the first person to establish an ongoing music program in an American hospital and should be considered a pioneer in the music therapy movement in the United States.

James Leonard Corning, a prominent neurologist, made another innovative contribution to the advancement of music therapy practice in the late 19th century. His article, titled "The Use of Musical Vibrations Before and During Sleep— Supplementary Employment of Chromatoscopic Figures—A Contribution to the Therapeutics of the Emotions," was published in the *Medical Record* in 1899. Corning's work represented the first controlled attempt to treat mental illness with music. He kept up to date with trends in psychology and neurology and used the information from both professions to fashion his unusual treatment procedures, which he called vibrative medicine.

Using an interesting array of equipment, Corning maintained a consistent environment for testing his patients' reactions to music. He presented music and visual images to his patients as they passed from presleep to sleep. Corning believed that during sleep a person's thought processes became dormant, allowing the penetration of "musical vibrations" into the subconscious mind. Appropriate musical selections (classical music only) helped to transfer those pleasant images and emotions into the waking hours, which suppressed and eventually eliminated the morbid thoughts that plagued his patients. Corning's theories about the relationship between sleep, emotions, and health were based on assumptions that have not been validated by modern research. His work, however, was important, because it represented the first documented attempt to systematically record the effects of music on mental illness.

Throughout the 19th century, music therapy was championed by musicians, physicians, psychiatrists, and other individuals interested in promoting this unique form of therapy. However, these advocates worked independently of each other, so there was little overall growth in its use. During the final decade, articles about music therapy began to appear more frequently in popular and professional journals, and the public began to gain an awareness of the therapeutic possibilities (Davis, 1987). This growth continued into the early years of the 20th century.

Early 20th Century Music Therapy

At the turn of the 20th century, medical care and treatment in the United States was very different than from today. For example, mortality rates were high, many "cures" were still unpleasant, antibiotics had not been developed, and mental illness and intellectual disabilities were largely misunderstood. Hospitals were frequently little more than warehouses designed to isolate but not treat people with disabilities or illness; stays were often long (in 1923 the average hospital stay was almost 13 days compared to today's average of about 4 days). If you were diagnosed with an intellectual or mental disability, hospitalization could last a lifetime. (Starr, 1984; Trent, 1994).

The use of music in hospitals as a soothing, healing, or normalizing agent can be better understood as one considers the extended length of hospitalization and the difficulty of providing care for difficult or "hopeless cases" that did not respond to medical practices of the day. For persons who faced weeks, months, or years of confinement in a hospital or asylum, music was something that could comfort or brighten the mood of patients whose medical needs could be addressed only marginally by typical medical care.

Given the limited understanding of illness and its cause at that time period, it is no surprise that during the first years of the 20th century music therapy gained support only sporadically and its use was often based upon informal observations by physicians or nurses who believed in the potential benefit of music. From time to time, physicians, musicians, psychiatrists, and the general public presented their cases for music therapy in scientific publications, newspapers, and the popular press. Clinical and experimental research provided data to support therapists' contentions that music could be effective in a variety of settings. In addition, a number of short-lived organizations promoted music therapy programs in hospitals, especially for returning World War I and II veterans (Taylor, 1981).

One of the most influential figures to advance the cause of music therapy during the first two decades of the 20th century was Eva Vescelius. She promoted music therapy through numerous publications and the National Therapeutic Society of New York, which she founded in 1903. In *Music and Health*, a publication completed shortly before her death in 1918, she provided a fascinating view of music therapy based on both age-old and contemporary concepts of health and disease. Vescelius felt that the object of music therapy was to return the sick person's discordant vibrations to harmonious ones. She gave precise instructions for the treatment of fevers, insomnia, and other ailments with music.

Perhaps her most unique contribution was the publication of the short-lived journal *Music and Health*. Published in 1913, only three issues appeared in print. Each contained poems and articles by Vescelius and others on the therapeutic applications of music. Additionally, there were advertisements for a course in "musicotherapy" offered by Vescelius. After her death, her sister Louise carried on her work for a short period of time (Davis, 1993).

The first course work in music therapy offered through a university was organized and taught by Margaret Anderton, an English-born pianist who had provided music therapy services to Canadian soldiers suffering from physical and mental disabilities during World War I. During 1919, she taught classes at New York City's Columbia University that prepared musicians for working in hospitals as therapists. She believed that "it is the object of the course to cover the psychophysiological action of music and to provide practical training for therapeutic treatment under medical control" ("Columbia University to Heal Wounded by Music," 1919, p. 59). Like Vescelius, she strongly felt that musicians should be thoroughly trained as therapists before working with patients.

Anderton advocated two principal ways to administer music therapy. For soldiers suffering from psychological conditions, the therapist should provide the music. For those afflicted with physical conditions, the patient should be responsible for producing the music, because it would help to strengthen an injured arm or leg. She also favored the use of woodwind instruments (especially for psychological conditions), because, according to her research, the timbre produced healing effects (Taylor, 1981).

Isa Maud Ilsen, a musician, nurse, and hospital executive, founded the National Association for Music in Hospitals in 1926. Previously, she had served as a teacher of musicotherapy at Columbia University with Margaret Anderton in 1919. She had also been Director of Hospital Music in World War I reconstruction hospitals for the American Red Cross. Ilsen viewed music as a way to alleviate pain for surgical patients and those with physical ailments. Her 20 years as a hospital musician helped to refine her theories concerning music therapy, and, like Eva Vescelius, she viewed a healthy person as one who is in harmony (Ilsen, 1926). Ilsen believed rhythm to be the vital therapeutic component in the music, although she believed that certain styles of music, such as jazz, were inappropriate for treatment.

Like other musicians and physicians during the first half of the 20th century, Ilsen prescribed a specific treatment regimen, using primarily classical music for the relief of a variety of disorders. For severe insomnia, for example, she prescribed a "dose" of Schubert's "Ave Maria." For terminal illness, she believed that Brahms waltzes or

Sousa marches were appropriate. She sometimes used ethnic songs and instrumental music in making her selections, which would suggest some consideration of the patient's music preferences ("Music Prescriptions," 1919, p. 26). Like many other early music therapists, she wanted hospitals to use qualified individuals to administer music therapy programs. Isa Maud Ilsen should be considered an important pioneer in the movement to promote music therapy in American hospitals (Boxberger, 1962).

Like Ilsen and Anderton, Harriet Ayer Seymour worked with World War I veterans as a music therapist, gaining experience and insight into the therapeutic value of music. Inspired by the writings of Eva Vescelius, she published her own guide for the aspiring music therapist in 1920, titled *"What Music Can Do For You."* Over the next 25 years, she actively promoted music therapy through her writings and practical demonstrations. During the Depression of the 1930s, she became involved in the Federal Music Project of the Works Progress Administration, which was an employment program implemented by the Roosevelt administration. Under her guidance, music programs were presented at numerous New York City hospitals and prisons. She conducted experiments to determine the effectiveness of certain types of music on physical and mental disorders (Davis, 1997). Seymour founded the National Foundation for Music Therapy in 1941. As president, she presented lectures and taught classes, emphasizing music therapy techniques used with returning World War II veterans. Her career culminated with the 1944 publication of the first text outlining a course of study in music therapy (Boxberger, 1962; Seymour & Garrett, 1944).

An Instruction Course in the Use of Practice of Musical Therapy presented Seymour's ideas about the appropriate applications of music with a variety of clinical populations. Only brief consideration was given to specific techniques. Essentially, her therapeutic strategy was the same for all clients, consisting of a variety of light classical music selections and folk songs performed by a small group of musicians under the guidance of a lead therapist. According to Seymour, a successful therapeutic experience was achieved through a combination of the music and positive thought, or musical meditation. Because the book was crude in its appearance, organized in a confusing manner, and printed with errors in typesetting and spelling, it is unlikely that the book received wide distribution or use. Despite those shortcomings, Seymour may have used the text to help train some of the 500 music therapy students that she claimed to have worked with between 1941 and 1944 (Davis, 1996).

Although the number of reports of music therapy activity in institutional settings increased dramatically during the first half of the 20th century, music therapy was not widely accepted as a profession by the medical community. The attempts of Vescelius, Ilsen, and Seymour to establish permanent jobs in hospitals, prisons, and schools met with only partial success, probably because of limited support from physicians and hospital administrators (Davis, 1993).

Some doctors, however, actively promoted music therapy. In 1914, Dr. Evan O'Neill Kane, in a letter to the *Journal of the American Medical Association*, enthusiastically endorsed the use of the phonograph in the operating arena for the purposes of distracting and calming patients undergoing surgical procedures. The music was particularly important during the administration of anesthesia, because "the phonograph talks, sings, or plays on, no matter how anxious, busy or abstracted the surgeon, anesthetist and assistants may be, and fills the ears of the perturbed patient with agreeable sounds and his mind with other thoughts than that of his present danger" (Kane, 1914, p. 1829).

In 1915, Dr. W. P. Burdick, who often worked with Kane in the operating room, reported in *The American Yearbook of Anesthesia and Analgesia* that the phonograph was being used not only in operating rooms, but also in wards as a diversion from discomfort and an aid to sleep. Burdick indicated that even the most serious cases improved while the music was playing and that 95% of his patients expressed interest in having the music as part of the healing process (Burdick, 1915).

In 1920, Esther Gatewood further emphasized the use of music in the operating arena, especially during the administration of anesthesia. Like Kane and Burdick, Gatewood advocated patient-preferred music during surgical procedures but believed that it was important to initially match the music to the mood of the client, then to change the temperament of the patient by degree. Gatewood was describing the technique that would later be named the *iso principle*. This principle became more fully developed in the 1940s by Ira Altshuler (Taylor, 1981).

As more reports appeared, the use of music spread from the operating room to other treatment areas. In 1929, Duke University included music for patients not only in operating and recovery areas, but also in both children's and adult wards. Every patient had access to radio reception through earphones or speakers located throughout the hospital. This development represented the first extensive commitment to music therapy by a major American hospital (Taylor, 1981).

In 1930, J. A. McGlinn published an article that reviewed the side effects of anesthesia used in obstetric and gynecological procedures. McGlinn reported that music could effectively reduce patient anxiety during the administration of anesthesia without disrupting operating room routine. Specifically, he recognized four benefits of music, which was chosen to fit the mood of the patient: (1) it effectively masked the sounds in the operating room; (2) it engaged the attention of the patient under local or spinal anesthesia; (3) it relaxed operating room personnel, including nurses, doctors, and other assistants during the surgical procedure; and (4) it provided a source of entertainment for the custodial crews cleaning up after the operation. McGlinn also indicated a bias against jazz and "sentimental" music, believing that it had no place in the hospital (McGlinn, 1930).

Dr. A. F. Erdman continued to champion the cause of music during surgical procedures in the 1930s. Like McGlinn, Erdman believed that music was effective in diverting the patient's attention from the impending operation. Instead of providing music for the entire staff, however, Erdman experimented with a Western Electric music reproducer and earphones, which allowed the patient to hear both the music and instructions from the surgeon. Preferences of the patient were considered when selecting the music prior to the surgical procedure (Erdman, 1934).

Besides its use during surgical procedures, music therapy was also employed in hospital orthopedic and pediatric wards. Harriet Ayer Seymour, founder of the National Foundation for Music Therapy, prescribed specific styles of music for children suffering from ailments such as tuberculosis and physical disabilities. Later, music was successfully used by physicians, including K. L. Pickerall and others, in all phases of a patient's hospital stay, from admission to discharge. In addition to the reduction in anxiety provided by the music, Pickerall noted that medication levels were often reduced and that recovery time was shorter than with clients not receiving music (Taylor, 1981).

Willem Van de Wall was another music therapy innovator noted chiefly for his contributions to the development of music therapy programs in mental hospitals and prisons between World War I and World War II. The Russell Sage Foundation, a philanthropic organization devoted to improving the human condition, provided financial support for his work. Grants led to the publication of a number of important books on music therapy, including a comprehensive work titled *Music in Institutions*, published in 1936.

Van de Wall, like Anderton and Ilsen, lectured on music and health at Columbia University from 1925 to 1932. He also served on the State of Pennsylvania's Bureau of Mental Health, where he was a field representative in charge of music and other therapeutic programs. This position was developed to improve conditions in Pennsylvania mental hospitals (Boxberger, 1963). The first hospital music program developed by Van de Wall in the Commonwealth of Pennsylvania was at Allentown State Hospital for Mental Diseases during the late 1920s.

In 1944, Van de Wall was appointed Chairman of the Committee for the Use of Music in Hospitals, whose purpose was to oversee the progress of music therapy programs in psychiatric hospitals. Boxberger (1963) considered Willem Van de Wall one of the most important 20th-century figures in the development of music therapy in hospitals and institutions.

Ira Altshuler, a contemporary of Van de Wall, was another important individual active in promoting music therapy during the mid 20th century. In 1938, Altshuler initiated one of the first large-scale music therapy programs for persons with mental illness at Detroit's Eloise Hospital. His innovative programs combined psychoanalytic techniques and music therapy methods specifically designed for use with large groups of clients. He later trained some of the first music therapy interns in the United States, working closely with students and faculty from Michigan State University. Dr. Altshuler tirelessly promoted music therapy through numerous publications and presentations and was a founding member of the National Association for Music Therapy in 1950 (Davis, 2003).

Although substantial music therapy activity was recorded during the first four decades of the 20th century, there was no trend toward its regular use. Despite support from such people as Van de Wall, Vescelius, Ilsen, Altshuler, and Seymour, music therapy had still not developed as an organized clinical profession (Boxberger, 1962).

THE DEVELOPMENT OF THE MUSIC THERAPY PROFESSION

In the 1940s, the use of music in the treatment of psychiatric disorders became more widespread, partly due to a gradual change in treatment philosophy. Many therapists, including the eminent psychiatrist Karl Menninger, began to advocate a holistic treatment approach (one that incorporates a variety of treatment modalities). With this shift in philosophy and increased knowledge about its effective applications, music therapy finally became an accepted treatment modality in many hospitals. In addition, the belief that music was somehow "magic" was starting to be dispelled as hospitals and clinics began to sponsor scientific research in music therapy. Much of this effort can be attributed to Frances Paperte, founder of the Music Research Foundation in 1944, and later Director of Applied Music at Walter Reed General Hospital located in Washington, D.C. (Rorke, 1996).

During World War II, numerous organizations, including the Musicians Emergency Fund, the Hospitalized Veterans Music Service, Sigma Alpha Iota, Mu Phi Epsilon, the American Red Cross, and Delta Omicron, provided musicians to Veterans Administration hospitals and later to state institutions. These volunteers assisted hospital staff in organizing ongoing music programs for patients.

By the conclusion of World War II, many United States medical facilities, recognizing the value of music as therapy, employed music programs to assist in the physical and mental rehabilitation of returning soldiers. Although not explicitly referred to as music therapy, the goals were unmistakable: activities implemented by volunteer musicians and music performances by men and women's military bands and choirs were designed as an important element of a wounded soldier's "reconditioning." (Robb, 1999; Sullivan, 2007).

Before the formation of the **National Association for Music Therapy** in 1950, most "music therapists" were unpaid, part-time staff members who worked under the supervision of hospital personnel and who lacked professional status. Many people began to recognize that future growth of the profession would be predicated on effective leadership of trained music therapists. During the 1940s, institutions such as Michigan State University, the University of Kansas, Chicago Musical College, College of the Pacific, and Alverno College started programs to train music therapists at both the undergraduate and graduate levels (Boxberger, 1962). Graduates of these programs comprised the first group of professionally trained music therapists, most of whom worked with persons who were mentally ill.

While music therapy training programs were being developed at a few colleges and universities, movement toward the formation of a national organization was also taking place. The Committee on Music in Therapy of the Music Teachers National Association (MTNA) presented programs during the late 1940s to educate musicians, physicians, psychiatrists, and others in the ways that therapeutic music could be used in schools and hospitals. Ray Green chaired an organizational committee to form a national music therapy association (Boxberger, 1962). The first meeting of the new organization took place in June 1950. Attendees adopted a constitution, set goals, developed membership categories, and appointed a standing committee for research. The National Association for Music Therapy, Inc. (NAMT) was born. The first annual conference was held in conjunction with MTNA in Washington, D.C., during December 1950.

The years following the founding of NAMT focused on improving education and clinical training as well as establishing standards and procedures for the certification of music therapists. Professional publications also enhanced the credibility of the young organization. Monthly newsletters, annual publications, and quarterly periodicals preceded the establishment of the *Journal of Music Therapy (JMT)* in 1964. This journal, edited by William Sears, was (and still is) devoted to research efforts of music therapists.

Probably the most important leader in the field of music therapy during the formative years of NAMT was E. Thayer Gaston (1901–1971). As chairman of the Music Education Department at the University of Kansas, he championed the cause of music therapy during the decades of the 1940s, 50s, and 60s. In collaboration with the renowned Menninger Clinic, a facility in Topeka, Kansas that specialized in the treatment of mental disorders, he established the first internship training site in the United States. In addition, Gaston started the first graduate music therapy program in the United States at the University of Kansas. His "insatiable thirst for knowledge, dedication to scholarship, and unquestioned integrity led to his preeminent position in this field, and many of his associates referred to him as the 'father of music therapy'"(Johnson, 1981, p. 279).

Perhaps the most important action taken by NAMT during its early years was the establishment of the Registered Music Therapist (RMT) credential. This designation was established in 1956 in conjunction with the National Association for Schools of Music (NASM), who served as the accrediting agency. The RMT credential provided assurance to employers that the therapist had met educational and clinical standards set by NAMT and NASM.

As the number of RMTs increased, so did the types of populations served. During the early years of NAMT, music therapists worked primarily with psychiatric patients in large, state-supported institutions. By the mid 1960s, music therapists were also working with adults and children with intellectual disabilities, people with physical disabilities, individuals with sensory impairments. By 1990, music therapy clients included elderly people in nursing homes, patients with medical conditions, and prisoners. During the early years of the 21st century, music therapists continue to work with increasingly diverse clinical populations. In addition to the conditions listed above, significant numbers of music therapists are improving the lives of persons with Rhett's syndrome, AIDS, substance abuse, and terminal illness.

A second organization, the **American Association for Music Therapy**, was established in 1971. Initially called the Urban Federation for Music Therapists (UFMT), the American Association for Music Therapy (AAMT) developed policies and procedures on education, training, and certification that differed from those of NAMT (see Chapter 1). In January of 1998, the National Association for Music Therapy and American Association for Music Therapy merged to create a single organization, the American Music Therapy Association (AMTA).

Since the inception of NAMT in 1950, AAMT in 1971, and AMTA in 1998, the profession of music therapy has continued to grow, with both organizations emphasizing high standards for education, clinical training, and clinical practice. In addition, publications have added to the development of the profession. *Music Therapy*, published annually by AAMT, began in 1980, while a second NAMT periodical, *Music Therapy Perspectives*, began publication in 1984. This semiannual journal provides information on music therapy techniques with specific populations. Since 1998, the *Journal of Music Therapy* and *Music Therapy Perspectives* have served as the two official journals of AMTA. In 1985, a **Board Certification exam** sponsored by both NAMT and AAMT was implemented to strengthen the credibility of the profession. By 2007, more than 2,000 music therapists in the United States worked in diverse settings with a variety of disability groups. The music therapy profession is strong and viable and anticipates continued growth into the 21st century.

SUMMARY

The earliest references to the relationship between music and medicine are found in ancient preliterate cultures. In some of those societies, which exist in parts of the world today, an ill person was seen as a victim of an evil spell, and in others, as a sinner against a tribal god. Music was used extensively in healing rituals by "medicine men," either to appease the gods who had caused the illness or to drive away evil spirits from the patient's body.

Throughout the development of civilization, the relationship between music and healing has complemented the theory of disease prevalent at the time. This evolutionary process has included periods of magic, magico-religious, and rational interpretations of disease. By the 6th century B.C., rational medicine had almost completely replaced magical and religious treatment in Greece. For the first time in history, the study of health and disease was based on empirical evidence. The predominant theory at the time was that of the four cardinal humors developed during the time of Hippocrates.

During the Middle Ages, Christianity influenced attitudes toward sick people, who were viewed as neither inferior nor being punished for their sins. Hospitals were established to provide humanitarian care to persons with physical ailments, although the mentally ill population was still mistreated. The theory of the four cardinal humors was still predominant and provided the basis for the use of music in the treatment of disease.

Advances in anatomy, physiology, and clinical medicine during the Renaissance marked the beginning of the scientific approach to medicine. However, treatment of disease was still based upon the theories of the Greek physicians Galen and Hippocrates. Music was often used in combination with medicine and art to treat medical conditions and also as a preventive measure against mental and physical disorders.

During the Baroque era, the theory of the four cardinal humors continued to dominate but was joined by Kircher's theory of temperaments and affections. Music continued to be closely linked with medical practice. Music was used to treat physical ailments as before but also played an increasing role in the amelioration of mental disorders, such as depression.

Music in the treatment of disease was still popular during the last few decades of the 18th century, but a shift was underway to a more scientific approach to medicine. This change was evident in Europe as well as in the United States. Accounts of music therapy in the United States first appeared during the late 18th century, as various physicians, musicians, and psychiatrists supported its use in the treatment of mental and physical disorders.

During the 19th and the first half of the 20th centuries, music therapy was used regularly in hospitals and other institutions but almost always in conjunction with other therapies. The reports that appeared in books, periodicals, and newspapers persuaded early 20th-century pioneers, such as Vescelius, Anderton, Ilsen, Van de Wall, and Seymour, to promote music therapy through personal crusades and organizations, which were, unfortunately, short-lived. Researchers such as Gatewood, Seymour, and Altshuler attempted to study the reasons why music was effective in the treatment of certain physical and mental disorders; however, their efforts were overshadowed by the lack of trained music therapists and unsubstantiated claims of effectiveness that stunted the growth of the profession until collective research efforts and the establishment of undergraduate and graduate curricula began during the mid 1940s.

During World War II, music therapy was used primarily to boost the morale of returning veterans, but it was also used in the rehabilitation of leisure skills, socialization, and physical and emotional function. Most music therapists during this time served as volunteers under the supervision of doctors and other hospital staff.

With the formation of NAMT in 1950 and AAMT in 1971, professional recognition to the women and men working as music therapists was finally forthcoming. The development of a standardized curriculum, regular publications, an efficient administrative organization, and the merger of NAMT and AAMT to form the American Music Therapy Association in 1998 have all contributed to the growth of the profession. Today, music therapy is recognized as a strong, viable profession.

STUDY QUESTIONS

1. What is the concept of cause and treatment of disease in preliterate cultures?

2. Define and discuss the importance of the four cardinal humors in relationship to the ancient Greek concept of health and illness.

3. What part did music play in the treatment of disease during the Renaissance?

4. What was the importance of the unsigned article printed in *Columbia Magazine* in 1789?

5. Some of the prominent people in the mid 19th century who established music therapy programs in institutional settings include _____.

6. Why were the music therapy experiments conducted on Blackwell's Island in 1878 considered important?

7. Describe the contributions of James L. Corning to music therapy.

8. Eva Vescelius was a music therapy pioneer in the early 20th century who edited and published the first music therapy periodical in the United States. This journal was called _____.

9. Who taught the first U.S. university courses in music therapy and where?

10. How was music used in the operating arena during the early part of the 20th century?

11. What was the status of the music therapy profession during World War II?

12. Two periodicals published by the American Music Therapy Association include _____ and _____.

13. What were the events of the late 1940s that led to the formation of NAMT?

14. In what year were the following organizations established: NAMT? AAMT? AMTA?

15. Discuss the importance of the Board Certification (BC) in the music therapy profession.

REFERENCES

Atlee, E. A. (1804). *An inaugural essay on the influence of music in the cure of disease.* Philadelphia: B. Graves.

Blumer, G. A. (1892). Music in its relation to the mind. *American Journal of Insanity, 5,* 350–364.

Boxberger, R. (1962). Historical bases for the use of music in therapy. In E. H. Schneider (Ed.), *Music Therapy 1961,* 125–166. Lawrence, KS: National Association for Music Therapy.

Boxberger, R. (1963). A historical study of the National Association for Music Therapy, Inc. In E. H. Schneider (Ed.), *Music Therapy 1962,* 133–197. Lawrence, KS: National Association for Music Therapy.

Burdick, W. P. (1915). The use of music during anesthesia and analgesia. In F. H. McMechan (Ed.), *The American yearbook of anesthesia and analgesia,* 164–167. New York: Surgery.

Burney, C. (1957). *A general history of music from the earliest ages to the present period* (Reprint ed.). New York: Dover. (Original work published 1789)

Burton, R. (1651). *The anatomy of melancholy.* Oxford, England: Henry Cripps.

Carapetyan, A. (1948). Music and medicine in the Renaissance and in the 17th and 18th centuries. In D. M. Schullian & M. Schoen (Eds.), *Music and medicine,* 117–152. New York: H. Wolff.

Carder, M. P. H. (1972). *George Frederick Root, pioneer music educator: His contributions to mass instruction in music.* Unpublished doctoral dissertation, University of Maryland, College Park.

Carlson, E. T., Wollock, J. L., & Noel, P. S. (Eds.). (1981). *Benjamin Rush's lectures on the mind.* Philadelphia: Philadelphia Philosophical Society.

Columbia University to heal wounded by music. (1919, March 1). *Literary Digest, 60,* 59–62.

Corning, J. L. (1899). The use of musical vibrations before and during sleep—A contribution to the therapeutics of the emotions. *Medical Record, 14*, 79–86.

Darrow, A. A., & Heller, G. N. (1985). Early advocates of music education for the hearing impaired: William Wolcott Turner and David Ely Bartlett. *Journal of Research in Music Education, 33*, 269–279.

Davis, W. B. (1985). *An analysis of selected nineteenth-century music therapy literature.* Unpublished doctoral dissertation, University of Kansas, Lawrence.

Davis, W. B. (1987). Music therapy in nineteenth-century America. *Journal of Music Therapy, 24*, 76–87.

Davis, W. B. (1993). Keeping the dream alive: Profiles of three early twentieth century music therapists. *Journal of Music Therapy, 30*, 34–45.

Davis, W. B. (1996). An instruction course in the use and practice of musical therapy: The first handbook of music therapy clinical practice. *Journal of Music Therapy, 33*, 34–46.

Davis, W. B. (1997). Music therapy practice in New York City: A report from a panel of experts, March 17, 1937. *Journal of Music Therapy, 34*, 68–80.

Davis, W. B. (2003). Ira Maximilian Altshuler: Psychiatrist and pioneer music therapist. *Journal of Music Therapy, 40*, 247–263.

Edwards, L. B. (1878). Music as mind medicine. *Virginia Medical Monthly, 4*, 920–923.

Erdman, A. F. (1934). The silent gramophone in local anesthesia and therapy. *Scientific American, 149*, 84.

Feder, E., & Feder, B. (1981). *The expressive arts therapies.* Englewood Cliffs, NJ: Prentice-Hall.

Gilbert, J. P., & Heller, G. N. (1983). *Mathews' "On the effects of curing and palliating diseases" (1806): First imprint in music therapy.* Unpublished manuscript, University of Kansas.

Heller, G. N. (1987). Ideas, initiatives, and implementations: Music therapy in America, 1789–1848. *Journal of Music Therapy, 24*, 35–46.

Hodges, D. A. (Ed.). (1996). *Handbook of music psychology* (2nd ed.). San Antonio, TX: IMR Press.

Ilsen, I. M. (1926). How music is used in hospitals. *Musician, 31*, 15, 30.

Johnson, R. E. (1981). E. Thayer Gaston: Leader in scientific thought on music in therapy and education. *Journal of Research in Music Education, 29*, 279–285.

Kane, E. O. (1914). The phonograph in the operating room. *Journal of the American Medical Association, 57*, 1829.

Mathews, S. J. (1806). *On the effects of music in curing and palliating diseases.* Philadelphia: P. K. Wagner.

McGlinn, J. A. (1930). Music in the operating room. *American Journal of Obstetrics and Gynecology, 20*, 678–683.

Medical powers of music. (1840). *The Musical Magazine; or, Repository of Musical Science, Literature and Intelligence, 52*, 423.

Medical powers of music. (1841a). *The Musical Magazine; or, Repository of Musical Science, Literature and Intelligence, 54*, 31.

Medical powers of music. (1841b). *The Musical Magazine; or, Repository of Musical Science, Literature and Intelligence, 55*, 45–47.

Merriam, A. P. (1964). *The anthropology of music.* Evanston, IL: Northwestern University.

Music physically considered. (1789). *Columbian Magazine, 111*, 90–93.

Musical prescriptions. (1919, August 23). *Literary Digest, 60*, 26.

Nettl, B. (1956). Aspects of primitive and folk music relevant to music therapy. In E. T. Gaston (Ed.), *Music therapy 1955* (pp. 36–39). Lawrence, KS: Allen Press.

Remarkable cure of a fever by music: An attested fact. (1796). *New York Weekly Magazine, 11*, 44.

Robb, S. L. (1999). Marian Erdman: Contributions of an American Red Cross hospital recreation worker. *Journal of Music Therapy, 36*, 314–329.

Rorke, M. A. (1996). Music and the wounded of World War II. *Journal of Music Therapy, 33*, 189–207.

Sachs, C. (1965). *The wellsprings of music.* New York: McGraw-Hill.

Seymour, H. A. (1920). *What music can do for you.* New York: Harper and Brothers.

Seymour, H. A., & Garrett, E. E. (1944). *An instruction course in the use and practice of musical therapy.* New York: National Foundation of Musical Therapy.

Sigerist, H. E. (1970). *Civilization and disease* (3rd ed.). Chicago: University of Chicago Press.

Starr, P. (1984). *The social transformation of American medicine.* New York: Basic Books.

Stevenson, B. (Ed.). (1967). *The home book of quotations: Classic and modern* (10th ed.). New York: Dodd, Mead.

Strunk, D. (1965). *Source readings in music history.* New York: W. W. Norton.

Sullivan, J. M. (2007). Music for the injured soldier: A contribution of American women's military bands during World War II. *Journal of Music Therapy 44,* 282–305.

Taylor, D. B. (1981). Music in general hospital treatment from 1900 to 1950. *Journal of Music Therapy, 18,* 62–73.

Trent, J. W. (1994). *Inventing the feeble mind: A history of mental retardation in the United States.* Los Angeles: California Press, Ltd.

Turner, W. W., & Bartlett, D. E. (1848). Music among the deaf and dumb. *American Annals of the Deaf and Dumb, 2,* 1–6.

Van de Wall, W. (1936). *Music in institutions.* New York: Russell Sage Foundation.

Vescelius, E. A. (1913). Music in its relation to life. *Music and Health, 1,* 5–10.

Vescelius, E. A. (1918). Music and health. *Musical Quarterly, 4,* 365.

Whittaker, J. T. (1874). Music as medicine. *The Clinic, 6,* 289–294.

Winner, E. (1982). *Invented worlds.* Cambridge, MA: Harvard University Press.

CHAPTER 3

MUSIC: A HUMAN PHENOMENON AND THERAPEUTIC TOOL

Kate E. Gfeller

CHAPTER OUTLINE

HUMANS AS MUSICAL BEINGS
MUSIC AS A LIFE SPAN ACTIVITY
  Musical Development of Children
  The Musical Adolescent
  The Musical Adult
MUSIC IS A VARIED AND FLEXIBLE ART FORM
  Style, Structural Features, and Engagement
FUNCTIONS OF MUSIC
FUNCTIONAL DOMAINS
  Physical Systems
  Music and Cognition
  Music as Communication
  Music and Emotions
  Music, Culture, and Society

Abbey just completed her degree in music therapy, and now she's on the job market. She heard that a local hospital is interested in starting a music therapy program as part of their physical rehabilitation unit, so she submitted her resume to the Human Resources office. She was thrilled when they called to schedule an interview. The Human Resources director from the hospital has asked Abbey to prepare a 30-minute presentation about music therapy for the board of directors, doctors, and physical and occupational therapists on the staff. They would like her to describe some typical interventions for their clients as well as some basic scientific background on how music works as a therapeutic tool.

Abbey's smart. She realizes that some people attending her talk may not have the intuitive and deep understanding of the power of music that she has—after all, she has been involved in music since she was just 4 years old. Her audience will be primarily medical personnel who are accustomed to discussing treatment in relation to scientific theories. Therefore, Abbey needs to explain, in a manner that these medical personnel will understand, how humans respond to music and how it functions as a therapeutic tool.

This chapter focuses on various characteristics of music that contribute to its influence on human behavior. First, it will cover how humans respond to music throughout the lifespan. Second, it will address the many styles, structures, and forms of engagement that make music accessible to most all humans. Third, it will describe common functional uses of music found in cultures around the world. Finally, it will outline the many ways in which music is related to our physical, cognitive, communicative, emotional, and sociocultural functioning. Knowledge of human response to music provides an important foundation for therapeutic uses of music that will be presented in other chapters of this book.

HUMANS AS MUSICAL BEINGS

Humans and higher vertebrates of the animal kingdom are alike in many ways. Like humans, animals seek food and shelter, mate and form families, nurture their young, fight for territory, and even communicate through special vocalizations and body movements. One of the ways in which humans differ from animals, however, is through the creation of and purposeful involvement in music. This special form of communication is not necessary for survival, yet it is deeply embedded in the culture and history of humankind. It is a prevalent part of everyday life and can be found in every known culture (Clair, 1996; Huron, 2004; Nettl 1956; Radocy & Boyle, 1979). Throughout recorded time, music has soothed fretful infants, elicited joyful dancing and play, expressed social conscience and religious faith, and expressed grief as we bid loved ones goodbye.

Music has always spoken for people and to people when words are inadequate (Gaston, 1968). "From the lullaby to the dirge"—these words suggest an important feature of music: the fact that music can be a valued art form from the first days of life through old age. This fact contributes to music's versatility and usefulness as an art form and a therapeutic medium.

MUSIC AS A LIFE SPAN ACTIVITY

Sheila and Robert Williams are hosting the Thanksgiving dinner for their extended family this year. Robert's parents, Yvonne and Joe, who are in their mid 70s, are thrilled to be meeting their new great-grandchild for the first time. Sheila and Robert's daughter, Keisha, and her husband, Jonathan, have made the trip home to introduce their adorable 3-month-old baby girl, Jada, to the whole family. Sheila and Robert's son, Jahleel, who is in high school, is looking forward to meeting his new niece, but he is even more excited about showing his grandma and grandpa his medal from music contest, at which he got a 1 rating on his trumpet solo. After all, Grandpa Joe used to be a pretty mean trumpet player himself.

*None of the Williams family members are professional musicians, but a peek into their Thanksgiving weekend reveals that music is important to every family member, young and old. Sheila and Jonathan are in the kitchen making final preparations for the big Thanksgiving feast. Sheila is pretty tired from getting the house ready for guests, on top of her usual responsibilities. She keeps the energy high by tuning in to her favorite radio station, which plays classic tunes from the years she was in high school and college. Not only does the music put her in an energetic and happy mood, but some of those songs bring back memories of when she and Robert were first dating. She stops her slicing and dicing and says to Jonathan—"I just **love** Lou Rawls. You know, this tune was playing the night that Robert proposed to me. I still get goose bumps all over whenever I hear it."*

Robert, who is trying to keep that middle-age spread under control, is getting in a last-minute workout before the big meal. As he leaves the house for a jog around the neighborhood, he grabs Jahleel's iPod onto which he has added his favorite workout music to Jahleel's collection of hip hop. The musical beat helps him run at a steady pace, and the energetic tunes keep him motivated. While Robert is going for high energy, Keisha wants a quiet, calm environment. Keisha and baby Jada are bonding in the guest bedroom. As Keisha cuddles and rocks her precious baby, she sings the lullaby that her mom sang to her 25 years ago. Keisha just loves to see baby Jada coo and smile in response to this magical song.

Down in the family room, Jahleel was planning to surprise Grandpa Joe with the 1st place contest medal, but Grandpa Joe has a surprise of his own. After Joe retired, he felt he needed something new to add a little zip to his life. Instead, he ended up going to something old—the old trumpet he found up in the attic. About two months ago, Joe started playing his trumpet with some other jazz hounds from way back when. Grandpa Joe has brought along some charts of "Caravan" and "Solitude" to play with Jahleel. Although this musical moment belongs to Jahleel and Joe, Sunday morning the whole family will pile into the van to hear Grandma Yvonne sing a solo in the choir at church. As the Williams family illustrates, music can be a satisfying and influential part of life for people of all ages.

One reason that music is such a flexible and powerful therapeutic tool is because people are responsive to music across the lifespan. While some activities such as reading, riding a bike, drawing pictures, playing baseball, or conversing with friends require adequate mental or physical development for participation, human beings can engage in music from cradle to grave. Newborns all around the world respond to the gentle lullabies or rhythmic nursery rhymes of care givers, and the oldest of our older adults are known to appreciate music. However, the manner in which we respond to or create music varies as we grow older. The following sections will describe musical development across the lifespan, emphasizing physical, mental, social, and emotional aspects of musical participation and enjoyment.

Musical Development of Children

Musical skills, like nonmusical skills (i.e., walking or talking), emerge at somewhat different times from child to child; nevertheless, under normal circumstances, developmental milestones occur in a relatively predictable sequence. Although a number of existing theories describe the process of child development, one prominent developmental theory is that of Jean Piaget, a Swiss psychologist, who outlined four primary stages of child development: (1) **sensorimotor**, (2) **preoperational**, (3) **concrete operations**, and (4) **formal operations**. During each of these stages, children demonstrate a readiness for a particular level of mental, social, and motor ability. In other words, at the outset of each of these stages, the normally developing child has matured (e.g., neurological and muscular development) to the point that he or she can perform the tasks characteristic of that stage.

Development is a process through which physical (including neurological) maturation interacts with environmental conditions; an environment rich with age-appropriate forms of stimulation promotes physical development. For example, in order to take his first steps, a toddler must have adequate neuromuscular maturation to control his legs and trunk in purposeful movement. Think about the halting wobbly first steps of a toddler, often supported by the strong supportive arms of a care giver. With repeated practice, those tiny muscles become stronger, and the child's steps become more sure and precise. If a child is confined for an unnaturally extended time in a crib or bed, the natural sequence of development will be slower or impaired.

While Piaget did not address musical development specifically in his writings, we know that musical response and involvement require a host of mental, motor, and social skills that have been documented by developmental psychologists. Researchers have studied musical milestones for each stage of child development, and participation in musical activity contributes to continued mental, social, and motor development.

Sensorimotor development (ages newborn–2). This stage of development is aptly named. During this stage, children learn about the environment through their senses and through motor activity. A newborn infant "gets to know" his mother through the sound of her voice, the smell of her body and milk, and her touch. Healthy babies respond to their environment with sucking, mouthing objects, grasping, kicking, cooing, and crying. As their motor skills develop, they will begin to explore an increasingly larger universe through creeping, crawling, and other exploratory activities. For the child in this stage of development, music offers manifold opportunities for sensory stimulation and motor activity.

In the first days of existence, the infant will receive both sensory and motor stimulation as the parent rocks the baby and sings lullabies. Newborns are active listeners (Bayless & Ramsey, 1982). Even though hearing is not fully developed at birth, young infants can discriminate one sound from another and seek out the source of the sound (De L'Etoile, 2006: McDonald & Simons, 1989; Standley & Madsen, 1990; Trehub, 2004). Infants are particularly attracted to the voice of their mother, **infant-directed speech** (speech that is typically slower, higher pitched, and has greater inflection), and lullabies or songs that contain characteristics associated with infant-directed speech (De L'Etoile, 2006; Hanson-Abromeit, 2003; Standley & Madsen, 1990)

Infants as young as two days old will respond to fluctuations in a rhythmic beat (Spiegler, 1967); babies of 2 months will fix attention on a singer or musical instrument. As the baby matures, he or she will respond with an expanding range of responses to musical sounds and objects. Musical bells or chimes can elicit smiles or wiggles from a 3-month-old. During the first 6 months of life, children respond to music with generalized movements, and they begin to match the vocalizations of their care givers (Campbell & Scott-Kassner, 1995). Babies seek out sensory stimulation and attend selectively to musical sound sources such as lullabies, chants and rhymes, music boxes, rattles, and the musical inflection of the care giver's voice (Standley & Madsen, 1990). Bright-eyed babies coo with delight as they discover the silvery sound created as they kick the ankle bells on their booties.

Over the first year and a half, the child's listening skills evolve. Initially, he or she will be able to discriminate musical dynamics (loud vs. soft) and differences in timbre (i.e., environmental sounds and different types of musical instruments). Eventually, the ability to discriminate pitch patterns, phrase endings, intervals, and rhythm will evolve (Campbell & Scott-Kassner, 1995; Greenberg, 1979; Moog, 1976; Zimmerman, 1971).

By the age of 6 months, gross physical response to music becomes more apparent. The infant of 6 months responds to music with generalized body movements. As physical maturation occurs, these movements eventually become purposeful arm and leg movements that occasionally synchronize briefly with an external beat (Campbell & Scott-Kassner, 1995; McDonald & Simons, 1989). During this stage, the baby advances from reflexive to deliberate movements such as rolling over, sitting up, crawling, and eventually walking. Concurrently, the baby will learn to manipulate objects, including shaking rattles and kicking ankle bells. The toddler banging on his mother's pots and pans is learning about sounds, shapes, and sizes (Campbell & Scott-Kassner, 1995).

Increasing variety in motor activity occurs not only in the limbs and trunk, but in the vocal mechanism as well. Vocal play and babbling (making repetitive sounds such as "buh, buh, buh" or "dadadadada") emerge between the ages of 12 to 18 months. These first babblings are important steps in developing motor control of the tongue, teeth, and lips. By 19 months, some melodic and rhythmic patterns appear in vocalization, followed by increasing use of spontaneous songs made up of short melodic phrases and flexible, irregular rhythmic patterns (Campell & Scott-Kassner, 1995; Davidson, McKernon, & Gardner, 1981). As children play in their cribs and sandboxes, the observant listener can hear brief melodic phrases that are paving the way for more sophisticated speech and songs.

Truly, the sensorimotor child is a musical child. Music, a sensory stimulation that promotes motor activity, is an ideal medium for learning in these tender years. Music is a natural and enjoyable part of childhood and encompasses a range of responses including sensation, cognition, communication, socialization, and motor activity. Musical activities can be designed with the child's present developmental level in mind. Thus, it is a flexible and useful therapeutic and educational tool through which a child can practice and eventually master a host of important developmental tasks. As you will learn in other chapters, music functions as an excellent therapeutic medium for infants and toddlers (i.e., high-risk infants, hospitalized babies and toddlers, etc.) (Hanson-Abromeit, 2003; Standley, 2001), as well as for severely disabled persons who, despite an older chronological age, are functioning at a mental age equivalent to the sensorimotor level of development (Farnan, 2007).

Preoperational stage (ages 2–7). The preoperational stage of development is characterized by rapid language and conceptual growth. In this stage, the child can use words as symbols to represent objects and events in the environment rather than functioning solely through perceptual acts. For example, the child in the sensorimotor stage experiences the concepts of *"fast"* and *"slow"* by direct observation of, or participation in, events that exemplify these contrasting tempi (such as playing quickly and slowly on a drum). During the preoperational stage, the child begins to label these concepts with the words *fast* and *slow* and is no longer completely dependent upon physical involvement with the object or event for understanding. In music activities, the rapid development of language is apparent as the child learns to label musical objects and events, such as "big drums" and "little drums" or "loud music" and "soft music."

Burgeoning verbal communication is paralleled by increasing vocalization during music activities. In the earliest years of this developmental stage, the child may improvise short, melodic patterns, or join in on a few words of a song. For example, as the adult sings "Old MacDonald Had a Farm," the 2- or 3-year-old may join in on "E-I-E-I-O." More accurate imitation of pitch patterns and greater vocal involvement will occur as the child reaches ages 4 or 5. Make-believe, action and story songs, and imitations are not only favorite singing experiences but also excellent opportunities for playful practicing communication and learning vocabulary (Barrickman, 1989; Bayless & Ramsey, 1982; Campbell & Scott-Kassner, 1995; Humpal, 1998; McDonald & Simons, 1989; Ringgenberg, 2003).

In addition to language growth, the preoperational stage of development is a time of increasing social awareness. In the first few years of this stage, children are very egocentric. In other words, they are unaware of others' points of view or needs. Children may play next to one another, engaged in similar activities, but cooperation or interaction is rare. This type of playtime interaction is called **parallel play**. Around ages 4 or 5, youngsters show increasing willingness to share and cooperate with their peers. Although still egocentric, children from ages 4 through 6 can be expected to follow directions, take turns, cooperate with others, and engage in the other social amenities required for musical activities. Musical games such as "Farmer in the Dell" or "London Bridge" or playing rhythm instruments together provides opportunities to practice and develop social skills.

Gradual motor development facilitates increasing coordination and a larger repertoire of movements (Campbell & Scott-Kassner, 1995; McDonald & Simons, 1989). From ages 2 to 4, toddlers may show brief moments of beat synchrony to rhythmic music. **Beat competency** (being able to maintain a steady beat), however, requires greater physical maturation, the rate of which varies from child to child. By age 3 or 4, walking, galloping, and jumping can all be incorporated in musical games.

Motor development is accompanied by increasing sophistication in spatial concepts, such as over, under, up, and down. Musical games such as the "Hokey Pokey," which require directed motor movement, encourage practice of these emerging spatial and motor skills. In the later years of the preoperational stage, normally developing children will master skipping, basic eye-hand coordination, and clapping to a beat (Campbell & Scott-Kassner, 1995).

Although children in the preoperational stage of development are no longer reliant solely upon sensory or motor experiences for understanding their world, activities with sensory and motor involvement are still valuable aids for learning (Gfeller, 1990, 2002a; McDonald & Simons, 1989) and form an important connection between direct experiences and symbolic representation. Many of the new language concepts, such as labeling of directions or size, are paired with visual aids or motor experiences in the educational setting.

As the individual matures through the preoperational stage of development, music continues to be an effective, enjoyable modality for learning. Music activities that require language, social cooperation, and physical activity promote practice and mastery of the skills that characterize this stage of development in therapeutic settings as well as in everyday life. Because music is such a natural part of childhood, music can bring a feeling of normalcy and fun into the therapeutic regimen.

Concrete operations (ages 7–11). Around age 7, the normally developing child begins to understand his or her world in a new way. Youngsters in this developmental stage can think systematically and solve problems mentally as long as the situation is related to immediate reality (i.e., concrete situations common in their own experience). This ability to think logically helps the young musician to learn musical notation and acquire concepts of rhythm and harmony. At this stage, children can sustain, or conserve, a melody or rhythm in their memory, despite distraction of harmony or competing melodies. For example, children can sustain a musical descant while other children sing another melody line (Campbell & Scott-Kassner, 1995).

The egocentrism of the preoperational child is giving way to a greater sense of community involvement. Social experiences outside the home, such as Girl Scouts, day camp, and soccer, are valued events. Musical activities such as choirs, bands, and complex folk dancing offer special opportunities for cooperation and group involvement. Children at this stage experience a sense of group pride as they prepare for and present concerts.

By age 7, normally developing children have attained and refined their basic motor movements. Activities such as folk dances require sequencing of gross motor skills. Fine motor coordination is required for mastery of symphonic (string, woodwind, brass) and social instruments (guitar, autoharp) (Campbell & Scott-Kassner, 1995).

For music therapy clients who are within the concrete operations stage of development, music acts effectively as a focal point for fostering social interaction and cooperation in groups. Furthermore, musical activities can provide ample opportunity for the development of motor functioning and for personal achievement and mastery of musical skills.

Formal operations (age 11–adulthood). The most notable characteristic that distinguishes this stage of development is the ability to think abstractly. During the stage of concrete operations, children can think systematically and solve mental problems as long as the experience is related to their own world of events. However, in formal operations, people are able to grapple mentally with ideas outside their own realm of existence. For example, the young child of 7 or 8 may learn about world hunger from seeing the faces of starving children, or from missing his or her own lunch. The adolescent, however, can think about world hunger through abstract figures of crop production and population decline. Although the capacity to use abstract thinking is in place by junior high, formal thinking will be refined through a multitude of learning experiences throughout adulthood.

The Musical Adolescent

By adolescence, those children who have achieved formal operations have at their disposal a wide range of musical experiences. Some teenagers may participate in formal musical organizations such as choirs, bands, orchestras, dance companies, or drum and bugle corps. Others may start up their own informal musical groups, such as rock bands or jazz ensembles. However, playing music is not the only avenue of musical involvement. Teenagers spend many hours watching music videos or listening to musical recordings (Christenson & Roberts, 1998; North, Hargreaves, & O'Neill, 2000; Zillman & Gann, 1998). Rock music, hip hop, and rap are among styles important within teen culture, and music is often used as an outlet for feelings of rebellion and confusion that accompany this time of life (Brooks, 1989; Gardstrom, 1999). Because music is such an important part of adolescent culture, it can be an extremely powerful therapeutic tool for use with clients in this age group.

The Musical Adult

A small percentage of people develop musical skills to high levels of sophistication. These individuals become professional performers, music teachers, composers, and music therapists. Although the level of musical involvement and skill level varies greatly from adult to adult, music is a valued art form for many people. Some adults find considerable satisfaction in avocational music activities, such as the church choir, civic band, or social dancing. As is the case with children, adults with no special musical talent or training can obtain considerable enjoyment from listening to music.

Our society spends large sums of money each year attending concerts, buying stereo equipment, and listening to recordings in order to bring music into our lives (Huron, 2004). All of these activities, whether active or passive, can contribute to a sense of community, enjoyment, and personal expression. Consequently, most adults enjoy listening to some type of music and associate particular musical selections with important moments in their lives. This makes music a flexible and powerful therapeutic medium for evoking emotions, memories, and social connections.

Older adults. In our youth-oriented society, aging is often associated with senility, passivity, indifference, and incapacity. However, improved health care and a subsequent increase in lifespan have rendered such perspectives as incorrect and out of date. The larger proportion of older adults is basically healthy and enjoys independent, productive lives (Hoyer & Roodin, 2003). What is more, staying engaged in activities that challenge mental and physical functioning (such as playing musical instruments or dancing) is associated with lower risk of Alzheimer's disease and other forms of dementia (Verghese et al., 2003). Research on the musical preferences, skills, and abilities of the elderly indicates that many older adults (sometimes referred to as healthy elderly) enjoy the intellectual and social benefits of participating in musical activities such as choir, band, or music appreciation (Clair, 1996; Coffman & Adamek, 1999; Coffman, 2002).

It is true that hearing loss often accompanies the process of aging (Hoyer & Roodin, 2003). Furthermore, research suggests that discrimination of small pitch changes or complex rhythm patterns may be more difficult for adults age 65 or older (Gibbons, 1982, 1983). However, musical enjoyment does not necessarily decline during the years of retirement. In particular, older adults often enjoy music that was popular in their early years (Clair, 1996; Gibbons, 1977). What is more, the tapping toes of the elderly as they listen to big band music from their youth dispel the myth that older people like only quiet, sedate music.

Passive listening is not the only avenue for musical involvement during retirement years. Many older adults express interest in singing and playing musical instruments (Clair, 1996; Coffman & Adamek, 1999; Coffman, 2002). In fact, musical hobbies that were initiated during early childhood may re-emerge after the pressures of making a living subside (Larson, 1983). As is the case with other age groups, preference for various styles of music will vary depending on the individual's past musical training and cultural background (Clair, 1996; Coffman, 2002; Gfeller, 2002c; Gilbert & Beal, 1982; Lathom, Peterson, & Havlicek, 1982).

As we will learn in future chapters, music can be used therapeutically with older adults, including well elderly and those with health problems. Music can be used to encourage social involvement and physical activities (i.e., music for social dancing or sing-alongs) (Bright, 1972; Clair, 1996; Palmer, 1977). In addition, music can be used to express tender emotions. For example, some terminally ill adults may choose special songs to express their religious faith as they face their own mortality (Clair, 1996; Munro, 1984).

In summary, music is an art form that is a valued part of our lives from infancy to our final days. The fact that music can be enjoyed by people of all ages contributes to its flexibility as a therapeutic tool. Effective music therapists take into consideration the developmental aspects of musical skills and preferences as they design treatment goals and interventions in order to maximize participation and therapeutic benefit.

MUSIC IS A VARIED AND FLEXIBLE ART FORM

Style, Structural Features, and Engagement

The variety of styles, structural features, and forms of engagement is another characteristic of music that contributes to its therapeutic effectiveness. Think of how many different types of music you have heard throughout your life. Try this brief exercise: Take five minutes and write down as many musical selections as you can. Perhaps you wrote down some pop tunes you heard on the radio today, a sonata that you have been practicing for your lesson, or a salsa hit that you danced to over the weekend. Maybe you wrote down the soundtrack to a movie or a song you sang in kindergarten. You may have listed a folk song, a Gregorian chant, or a jazz tune. Your memory may have retrieved a vocal solo, a string quartet, a jazz combo, a marching band, or a symphony. Perhaps the simple ring tone on your cell phone came to mind, or a complicated Mahler symphony. The list seems endless! This banquet of musical sounds makes it an engaging and flexible therapeutic medium (Clair, 1996; Gfeller, 2002a).

Musical diversity. As noted above, one way in which music is diverse is with regard to style and cultural heritage. The word *music* represents a gigantic universe of sounds that range from the austere chants of monks, to the exuberant rhythms of salsa, and everything in between. Most every well-established culture has a history of musical sounds that are characteristic; however, as a result of globalization, there are many musical fusions that have evolved. For example, American jazz has been strongly influenced by the rhythms of Latin culture and the unique musical scales of the Middle East. Rock music has been influenced by jazz, hip hop, rhythm and blues, and a host of other musical styles. The musical styles from around the globe offer a rich buffet of rhythms, melodies, harmonies, and timbres that can tap into a wide range of emotions and can suit a range of social and aesthetic circumstances. Most people can identify at least one style of music that they find musically satisfying or that connects them with their culture.

Structural components of music. Musical sounds also vary greatly in their structural components. Music is made up of combinations of pitch (which are organized in sequential patterns to form melodies, and simultaneous combinations to form harmony), rhythm, timbre, and dynamics. Some music, such as children's songs, may consist of short, repetitive melodic patterns with relatively simple rhythms (Gfeller & Hanson, 1995). In contrast, a Bruckner symphony will have as many as 100 musicians playing many different pitches, rhythms, timbres, and dynamics all at once. A music therapist can select or compose musical materials that are an ideal match for the functional level and therapeutic needs of clients, taking into account their individual developmental level; cognitive, communicative, and physical abilities; and personal preferences (Gfeller & Hanson, 1995).

Forms of musical engagement. There are many different ways and situations in which music can be enjoyed. People can enjoy listening to music in the solitude of their own room or join hundreds of other in the excitement of a rock concert. You can relax as soothing music in the background washes over you, or you can use it to pump up your energy level. You can be swept up in its emotional message, or pay rapt attention as you analyze each structural element. You can sing, play a musical instrument, or dance. You perform the works of others, compose music, or improvise musical sounds. Consequently, music is accessible to people of all functional levels and in various functional states (Gfeller, 2002a; Gfeller & Hanson, 1995).

Because musical engagement takes on so many forms that range from passive to active, music therapists can select music and music activities that are appropriate for persons in a coma or for those who are hyperactive. Clients can engage in music listening, music making, or moving to music. Activities can be designed for individuals, small groups, or large groups, depending upon the therapeutic objectives at hand. In short, **the diversity of musical styles, structures, and types of engagement provide the music therapist with a rich menu of musical materials from which to choose. The challenge is to select music that is culturally meaningful, stylistically preferred, appropriate in complexity, within the abilities and interests of individual clients or groups, and appropriate for a given therapeutic objective** (Clair, 1996; Gfeller & Hanson, 1995).

Another characteristic of music that contributes to its therapeutic potential is that it serves a wide variety of functions within most societies. Consequently, music can be easily integrated into a wide range of therapeutic protocols and can be used to enhance functionality and quality of life in many ways. The next section describes some of the primary functions of music observed in nearly all cultures.

FUNCTIONS OF MUSIC

Scholars who study the lives of people around the world tell us that music is present in all known cultures. "There is probably no other human cultural activity which is so all pervasive [as music] which reaches into, shapes, and often controls so much of human behavior" (Merriam, 1964, p. 218). Music has a certain universality in that it is present within every culture known to us (Nettl, 1956).

If we think about the many ways in which music is used in our everyday lives, the list is almost endless. Music is heard on TV and radio, in places of business, at church, in schools, at sporting events, at concerts and dances, and at home, to name just a few. People spend millions of dollars annually on compact disc players, iPods, tickets to concerts, and musical instruments (Huron, 2004). Music is enjoyed by young and old, rich and poor, male and female, and people from all walks of life. This prevalence means that music is relevant for most people, which in turn contributes to its effectiveness as a therapeutic tool (Clair, 1996).

While the varied uses of music in society are too numerous to list, many years ago, ethnomusicologist Alan Merriam (1964) developed a useful classification of broad categories of music's uses in society. Merriam was interested in the influence of music on social, physical, and verbal behaviors, as well as the importance of cultural and social factors in music making. He studied music in a variety of cultures around the world and noted similar uses of music across cultures. Eventually, he set up categories of 10 **functions** (broad purposes or reasons for) of music that existed in most cultures: (1) music as an influence on physical response, (2) music as a form of communication, (3) music as a form of emotional expression, (4) music as **symbolic representation**, (5) music to enforce conformity to social norms, (6) music to validate social institutions and religious rituals, (7) music to contribute to the continuity and stability of culture, (8) music to contribute to the integration of society, (9) music for **aesthetic** enjoyment, and (10) music for **entertainment**. In short, music fulfills many functions or broad purposes within cultures worldwide.

As we consider the influence of music on humans, especially within the context of music therapy, these functions of music are related to key domains of human functioning: the body's physical systems, cognition, communication, emotions, and social/cultural affiliation. The following portion of this chapter describes the influence or role of music relative to each functional domain of human behavior. Implications for music therapy practice are presented.

FUNCTIONAL DOMAINS

Physical Systems

> It's around 4:30, and Waving Grass, Iowa, is a town on the move. Over at the high school, the marching band is striding down the field to the strains of Sousa's "Stars and Stripes Forever." In the adjacent athletic field, April, Becky, and Marly are working on endurance for their long-distance marathons with a little help from their favorite music downloaded on their iPods. Over at the Fowler Dance Academy, Adriana's dance class is leaping and turning to the strains of Tchaikovsky's "Swan Lake." Over at the local McDonalds, the action is of another sort altogether: Kyle and Brian are bolting down some burgers and fries as the MUZAK plays upbeat tunes over the loud speakers.

> Ms. Kwoun, the 6th grade teacher, murmurs to herself, "I've had enough action for one day." She just arrived home after taking her class on an all-day field trip at a local nature trail. She's decided a little deep breathing and yoga to music would be a great way to relax and rejuvenate.

These are a few of the many examples of physical response to music. Our body (sometimes referred to as our physical system) responds to music in a variety of ways, including large muscle movements that are easy to see, as well as some responses that are less obvious, such as the intake of sound waves into our auditory system.

Music as a sound energy and sensory stimulation. From a physical standpoint, music is a form of energy perceived by the auditory and tactile senses. Whether the sound source is a violin, music box, or voice in song, each musical source creates sound energy that causes the surrounding air molecules to move in patterns of greater (compression) or lesser (rarefaction) density. These patterns are known as sound waves. One of the biggest differences between music and other environmental noises is the fact that musical sound waves tend to be organized in a somewhat regular fashion over time, which comprises what we perceive as pitch, timbre (tone quality), and loudness.

The sounds waves are funneled into the **ear canal** and toward the **middle ear** structure, beginning with the tympanic membrane (eardrum) and three small bones of the middle ear, known as the **ossicles**. These middle ear structures vibrate in synchrony with the sound energy and transmit this mechanical energy to the inner ear structure known as the **cochlea**. Sensory receptors for hearing found within the cochlea encode the mechanical energy into an electrical signal, which is then sent via the **auditory nerve** to the brain (Wagner, 1994). (Note: Additional detail regarding the hearing mechanism appears in Chapter 13.) While the ear picks up and transmits the sound, it is in the brain where the sound is organized and assigned meaning. For example, are the notes high or low? Does the music sound smooth or discordant? How long does each note last?

Although the sense of hearing usually comes to mind when we think of musical perception, sound waves are also perceived by the **tactile** sense, or sense of touch (sometimes referred to as **vibrotactile** stimulation). For example, in your apartment or dorm room, you may feel the pulse of the rhythm from your neighbor's stereo in your chest cavity, even if you cannot hear the tune. Some sounds tend to be felt in the abdomen and chest, while other frequencies resonate in the cranial bones. Because of this tactile transmission of music, even people with severe hearing loss can perceive musical stimuli.

Therapeutic aspects of musical sounds. At this most basic level, music as auditory and tactile stimulation has the potential to be a therapeutic medium. For example, some individuals who are tactually defensive (difficulty accepting physical touch) because of neuromuscular abnormalities may benefit from tactile desensitization techniques. In this type of intervention, the music therapist plays instruments called tone bars that produce sound waves in the low frequency range. The sound waves play a part in improved sensory processing and integration so that the individual has more normalized acceptance of touch and reduction of motor rigidity (Farnan, 2007). The vibrotactile element of music may foster alerting responses (i.e., blinking, smiling, making eye contact, tears, etc.) in nonverbal individuals with neurological damage. In other words, the auditory and tactile stimulation of music can be a valuable tool in eliciting initial or more adaptive responses from persons who are not responsive at a verbal level (Gfeller, 2002a). The vibrotactile aspect of music also serves as a valuable form of sensory input for persons who are profoundly deaf, who get little input through the sense of hearing.

The effects of music on the central and autonomic nervous system. For many years, scholars have been interested in how internal systems of the body, such as the circulatory or respiratory systems, respond to music (Hodges, 1996; Thaut, 2002). These kinds of internal and automatic functions are called autonomic responses and are controlled by the autonomic nervous system. Scientists have studied the effects of various styles or tempi on body functions such as pulse rate, respiratory rate, blood pressure, and muscular response. The bulk of studies on physical response to music supports the notion that music influences physiological response. However, researchers have discovered a variety of responses to different kinds of music (Dainow, 1977; Hodges, 1996; Thaut, 2002). For example, we cannot say with certainty that all people will show an increase in heart rate if they hear Beethoven's "Fifth Symphony" and a decrease in heart rate with Brahms' "Lullaby."

Human beings, in general, show such a variety of physical responses to any given stimulus. Not all people will react to a happy or fearful situation with exactly the same physical response. People have very individual reactivity patterns to many types of stimuli, including music (Thaut, 2002). In addition, music is a complex stimulus that rapidly changes over time and which is perceived differently from one person to the next. However, a music therapist, through careful assessment of an individual, can often find musical selections that promote steady and regular breathing, evoke positive images or emotions, provide distraction from stressors, and, consequently, assist physical relaxation (Thaut, 2002; Thaut & Davis, 1989). Studies of **Guided Imagery and Music (GIM)**, which will be introduced later in this book, indicate that relaxation and imagery in conjunction with music listening can reduce blood pressure, reduce hormones associated with stress, and help boost immune functioning (McKinney, Antoni, Kumar, Tims, & McCabe, 1997; McKinney, Tims, Kumar, & Kumar, 1997).

Motor response to music. A growing body of research concerning the role of auditory perception in motor learning indicates several basic ways in which a predictable and regularly recurring rhythmic signal (such as the underlying steady beat in music) is believed to facilitate muscular control of movement patterns (Thaut, 2002, 2005). A rhythmic beat can (1) influence the timing and readiness (called potentiation) of the nervous system, which in turn controls physical movement; and (2) assist automatic movement by providing a cue for timing. In addition to motor readiness, music can have an impact on psychophysiological factors affecting motor performance, such as fatigue.

The motor system is sensitive to arousal by the auditory system. According to studies conducted by several scientists (Pal'tsev & El'ner, 1967; Rossignol & Jones, 1976), sound primes the motor system by arousing the motor neurons in the spinal cord and thus sets the motor system in a state of heightened readiness and excitability. When sound is organized in repetitive rhythmic patterns, the priming effect begins to arouse the motor neurons and activates muscle patterns in a predictable time structure, thus creating a physiological auditory-motor entrainment effect. That is, the motor system tends to synchronize movement responses to the time structure of auditory rhythmic stimuli. This synchronization remains very stable, even when the rhythm changes (Thaut, 2005; Thaut & Schauer, 1997).

Research (Thaut & Miller, 1994; Thaut, Miller, & Schauer, 1998) suggests that synchronization occurs in the following manner: after hearing one- or two-beat intervals, the brain very rapidly computes a representation of the duration of the beat interval, then the brain matches the duration of the movement to the beat interval, and after establishing a preferred comfortable timing between the beat and movement response, synchronization is maintained by matching the duration of the movement to the rhythmic beat interval. This has important implications for the use of rhythm to cue movement. Examples from everyday life come to mind: marching to a drum cadence, dancing to rhythmic music, or doing aerobic exercise to music that has a strong beat. In these sorts of situations, the person listening to the rhythmic beat can use the regularly recurring beat to help anticipate the correct speed of movement.

In addition to the effect of rhythm on readiness and timing, music can influence one's affective (emotional) state. Positive arousal, motivation, and attention to a positive auditory stimulus can divert attention from physical discomfort or fatigue that can accompany motor activity and physical rehabilitation (Marteniuk, 1976). This can assist with motor persistence, and is probably one of the reasons that so many people like to listen to music while they jog or work out.

As we will find in Chapters 4, 6, and 10, the affect of music on physical response can be exploited in a variety of ways in order to maintain or improve physical functioning. Music can be used (1) as tactile stimulation (Farnan, 2007; Gfeller, 2002a); (2) to stimulate motor readiness (i.e., in rhythmic gait or aerobic exercise); (3) as a structure for motor movements; and (4) as motivation or distraction to encourage persistence during labored or painful movement (Jeffery & Good, 1995; McIntosh, Brown, Rice, & Thaut, 1997; Miller, Thaut, McIntosh, & Rice, 1996; Prassas, Thaut, McIntosh, & Rice, 1997; Staum, 1983; Thaut, 2005; Thaut, McIntosh, Rice, & Prassas, 1993). Thus, music can be a powerful tool for persons regaining motor control (e.g., recovery from stroke or brain injuries) or to help people requiring an exercise routine (such as cardiac patients or persons with weight problems) to persist toward their therapy goals.

Physical response is only one of many ways in which we are affected by music. The next section will focus on music's function in cognition (mental functioning).

Music and Cognition

There's music in the air over at Lincoln Elementary School, but today it's not coming from the music room. Ms. Mendez, the Spanish teacher, is teaching the 4th grade class how to count in Spanish with a catchy little tune: "Uno, dos, y tres, cuatro, cinco, seis, siete, ocho, nueve, I can count to diez." Over in the 3rd grade classroom, Ms. Stowe is having her students practice their multiplication tables using the "Multiplication Rock." In Mrs. Driscoll's 6th grade class, the students are singing "Fifty, nifty United States from thirteen original colonies; Fifty, nifty stars in the flag that billow so beautifully in the breeze." This little ditty, "Fifty, Nifty United States," helps them memorize the 50 U.S. states in a fun, engaging way.

Perception of music involves many parts of the brain that are connected through complex neural networks (Peretz & Zatorre, 2004). Even a seemingly simple activity such as humming a familiar tune necessitates complex processing mechanisms, attention, memory storage, retrieval, motor programming, and so forth (Zatorre, 2005). Brain imagining and studies of persons with discrete areas of brain damage indicate that different aspects of music (e.g., pitch, interval ratios, differentiation of different timbre, consonance vs. dissonance, etc.) are processed in a variety of locations in the brain (Peretz, 2001; Peretz et al., 1994). This neural processing of music is an incredibly interesting but complex topic.

Neuroanatomical studies (which parts of the brain are involved in what aspects of music listening) are beyond the scope of this class. You can learn more about this topic in numerous journal articles, textbooks, and in advanced courses on the Psychology of Music. At this point, the focus will be on observable examples of music and cognitive (mental) functioning that affect our everyday life: attention, perceptual processing, and memory.

Fei-lin is driving to work. She lives in a large city, so she is among the thousands of commuters on the freeway. Because she is focusing primarily on the flow of traffic, whether she's within the speed limit, and scanning the freeway signs for her exit, she is barely aware of other environmental stimuli around her—such as the readings on the clock and temperature gauge on her dashboard, the billboard advertising a new hotel, or the number of people in the car to her left. Suddenly, her attention is diverted from the flow of traffic to her car radio, as she hears Beethoven's "Emperor Piano Concerto." She has always loved that composition!

Attention is the process of seeking out stimuli that are of interest. The attention system requires the coordination of many aspects of the brain and is a foundation for memory, language, and many other mental functions. Our environment typically has an enormous amount of information available through the senses, stored memories, and other mental processes, but we can attend to only a limited amount at a given time—often information that is particularly important in the current situation (such as the stoplight at an intersection), or information that is novel or engaging. Because good composers excel at creating compositions with beautiful textures and interesting contrasts, music is a powerful medium for attracting our attention (Thaut, 2005).

Once our attention is drawn to music, there is the process of sustaining attention and focusing on particular elements of the music. This is more complex that you might think. Consider, for example, all the distractions at a concert: The person coughing in the back, the cell phone ring two rows ahead of you, or the child whispering to his dad. Even without these distractions, there is the complex act of attending to particular elements of the music, such as a melodic theme or the tone quality of specific instrument. Then there is the task of **sustaining** your attention, as you listening to a long extended melody or theme; this requires sustained attention (concentration). As we listen to a fugue played by a quartet, we may **shift** our attention from the first violin to the cello, as each instrument takes up the theme, or **divide** our attention between listening to the music and searching for a cough drop in our purse or pocket as we feel a tickle in our throat. Sustaining, shifting, and divided attention all requires effort and can be particularly difficult if we are tired, preoccupied, or have some type of neurological problem.

In therapy, the motivational quality of preferred music can help to grab a client's attention. Because music is made up of interesting and ever-changing patterns of repetition and contrast, music can be used in cognitive rehabilitation to practice sustained attention, shifting attention, and divided attention. The therapist can select or compose music of suitable complexity to meet the current functional level of each client (Gfeller, 2002b; Thaut, 2005).

Perception involves the psychological processes through which people recognize, organize, synthesize, and give meaning in the brain to information received through the senses. For many years, psychologists have studied laws of perceptual organization, that is, how we organize small parts into wholes. Human beings organize information into structures that are as simple as possible (good Gestalts). Music is often made up of **good Gestalts**—well-organized rhythmic, melodic, and harmonic patterns, which can enhance the perceptual process, as we filter, select, and organize information for further processing. For example, the Alberti bass commonly heard in a Mozart sonata has a regular and predictable melodic, harmonic, and rhythmic structure that makes it easy to organize, learn, and recall.

Memory is the means by which we draw on past knowledge that has been stored for use in the present (**retrieval**). Music can be an effective **mnemonic device** (memory tool) for several reasons. First, attention to a given stimulus is required in order for the information to be **encoded**. As noted above, interesting or preferred music can assist with the attention process. Then, the information to be learned must be processed adequately (usually through adequate repetition or pairing with already-known information) to promote **storage** into **long-term memory**. The repetitive nature of many musical lyrics (such as lyrics in a chorus) as well as the good Gestalt of many songs can facilitate the rehearsal process. In addition, new information can be paired with an already-known song. For example, some people have paired the order of letters in the alphabet with the familiar tune, "Twinkle, Twinkle, Little Star."

The music can also act as a memory cue when we go to **retrieve** information stored in long-term memory. The example of learning to count in Spanish, or remembering the 50 states of the U.S. illustrates the use of music as a mnemonic (memory) device (Gfeller, 2002a, Thaut, 2005).

In summary, the engaging and structural properties of music with regard to attention, perceptual processing, and memory are several reasons that music can be an effective therapeutic tool to promote learning, including with persons who have learning disabilities, intellectual disabilities, or brain injury (Gfeller, 2002a; Thaut, 2005).

Music as Communication

When we think of communication, we tend to think of words. For example, the letters *c a d,* when put together, bring to mind a sleazy womanizer who charms young naive ladies with flattery and promises. However, when we play the notes C A D on the piano, no specific meaning comes to mind. Musical symbols are abstract in nature and are not readily translatable (Gfeller, 2002b; Kreitler & Kreitler, 1972; Winner, 1982). One musical phrase essentially refers to another musical phrase, not to a specific idea or object. For example, in traditional harmony of music from the Western compositional practice (as you may have studied in music theory), a tonic (I) chord can progress to almost any chord. A dominant chord (V) or leading (VII) tone, however, as a result of stylistic convention, will often time resolve to (progress toward) the tonic chord. To those readers without music theory background, this basically means that there are certain musical combinations that we become accustomed to, to the point that they sound "correct" and we can predict what note should come next. Music, like speech, is considered form of communication, for it is made up of a system of symbols with specific rules of organization through which people can express themselves (Berlyne, 1971; Gfeller, 2002b; Kreitler & Kreitler, 1972).

Perhaps you have observed the musical communication that takes place in a jazz ensemble. A jazz performance is often based upon a familiar tune or musical phrase that will become the "theme" upon which the musicians improvise. One might liken it to the topic of a conversation. The ensemble members take turn playing variations on the theme; the musicians in essence talk to one another through their instruments. The audience hears a back-and-forth banter and expanding of musical ideas, occasional reference to other musical themes, and even musical jokes. Although there are no words, there is obvious communication among the musicians.

Speech and music are both considered forms of communication, and they do share some characteristics. For example, both have rules of syntax specific to a given culture; both have oral and written forms; both are processed by the auditory system. Speech and music are also different in important ways: Spoken language is an efficient way to impart specific information that is considered basic to everyday functioning (such as the letters *b e d*, referring to a particular type of furniture). Music (without lyrics) does not refer to specific thoughts, ideas, or events. Instead, it communicates intrinsic meaning; that is, one musical phrase leads us to expect a related or contrasting musical idea.

Recent neuroanatomical studies indicate some interesting differences in how the brain processes speech and music (Gfeller, 2002b; Gottselig, 2000; Peretz et al., 1994). This difference in processing has implications for the use of music in some types of rehabilitation, such as for persons who have problems with spoken communication. As you will discover in other chapters, the music therapist may be able to recruit (use) those neural networks involved in music processing in order to compensate for or facilitate impaired spoken communication (Hobson, 2006; Thaut, 2005). Music is also a valuable nonverbal communication that offers an alternative form of emotional outlet and meaningful interaction with others (Clair, 1996).

E. Thayer Gaston, an early leader in music therapy, describes music's power in the following way:

> *From a functional viewpoint, music is basically a means of communication. It is far more subtle than words. In fact, it is the wordless meaning of music that gives it potency and value. There would be no music and, perhaps, no need for it if it were possible to communicate verbally that which is easily communicated musically.* (Gaston, 1958, p. 143)

In summary, speech and music are both forms of communication, but they are processed somewhat differently (Hobson, 2006). In addition, they convey different kinds of information. Speech is considered primarily referential (semantic) in nature, while many consider music's most powerful quality its ability to evoke moods and emotions (Gfeller, 2002b). The next section delves further into the relationship between music and emotional expression.

Music and Emotions

Music has long been associated with emotional expression and is frequently called the "language of emotions" (Gfeller, 2002b; Langer, 1942; Winner, 1982). Research indicates that music induces positive or negative moods, and thus, people often use music to regulate their own emotions (Balch, Bowman, & Mohler, 1992; Eich, Macaulay, & Ryan, 1994; Kwoun, 2005). Recent studies in neuroscience indicate that those areas of the brain activated during emotionally rewarding stimuli such as excellent food or sex are also involved when we listen to personally meaningful music (Zatorre, 2005). According to one study, the emotional experience in music is probably the main reason that people choose to listen to music (Sloboda & O'Neill, 2001).

As a purveyor of emotions, music plays an important role in society, since it provides a vehicle for expression of ideas and emotions that are not easily expressed through ordinary discourse (Radocy & Boyle, 1979). In some instances, such as times of sorrow or loss, we may find words inadequate for expressing our deepest feelings. In other instances, such as times of social protest, music is an acceptable way to express ideas that may be considered controversial or unacceptable if spoken. For example, teenagers or members of political groups have often used music as a vehicle for speaking out against the ills of society. Some have called this use of music to "let off steam" regarding social issues a **"safety valve" function** (Merriam, 1964; Radocy & Boyle, 1979).

Within a given culture, music alone conveys emotional content or mood (Gaston, 1968; Merriam, 1964; Radocy & Boyle, 1979). Music, in conjunction with textual or visual information, can also intensify or alter the message found in words or images (Galizio & Hendrick, 1972; Gfeller, 2002b; Gfeller, Asmus, Eckert, & Eckert, 1991; Gfeller & Coffman, 1991; McFarland, 1984; O'Briant & Willbanks, 1978; Thayer & Levenson, 1983; Wintle, 1978). The extent to which music, a nonverbal language, can convey feelings and ideas can be illustrated by the use of music in sound tracks to movies and television programs (Gfeller, 2002b; Kwoun, 2005).

> *Julie and Jenny decided to go to a film festival highlighting classic movies of favorite film makers such as Billy Wilder and Alfred Hitchcock. They laughed until their sides split during the old comedy "Some Like It Hot," but Alfred Hitchcock's movie, "Psycho" was no laughing matter. Even though Julie and Jenny covered their eyes for the infamous murder scene with Janet Leigh in the shower, they remained terrified as they heard the hideous high, shrill sounds of the violin in the movie sound track.*

Why is music so often used as an expression of emotion? Many scholars have attempted to answer this question over the past decades, and a variety of explanations has been proposed. Some have suggested that the emotional meaning conveyed by music is learned as a result of **extramusical associations**—that is, as a result of cultural and life experiences, we begin to associate particular musical sounds with various emotions. Others have suggested that emotional expression is embodied, or found directly, in the structural features of the music itself (Kwoun, 2005). This second perspective is sometimes known as expressionism. We will briefly examine these two points of view.

Extramusical associations and emotions. There are two general types of extramusical association commonly described in studies of music and emotion: (1)

cultural convention, and (2) referentialist theory of music and emotion. Each is described below.

Cultural convention is a term that refers to the unique musical sounds associated with different cultures. Although many people describe music as the universal language, in actuality, no single style of music is meaningful to all people. Although music is a universal phenomenon, it is not a universal language; the traditions and beliefs of each culture influence musical creation and response (Clair, 1996; Nettl, 1956). For example, in Western culture, much of our music has been organized around a series of half and whole tones that make up major and minor scales. We have often associated music based on a major scale with positive happy feelings, while music in a minor key often has connotations of melancholy or sadness. The dark, low timbre of an English horn may represent melancholy, while the bright triadic outline of a trumpet fanfare would be more likely to connote triumph and exultation.

In contrast, traditional music from India is organized around scalar patterns made up of smaller musical intervals, or semitones. For example, between our notes of C and D on the piano, an Indian scale may have several notes, not just one halftone (C#) in between. An American accustomed to listening to classical or pop music from the Western musical tradition will probably find it difficult initially to organize and understand the music of traditional Indian music. According to some theorists, this also impedes one's ability to interpret the emotional sentiments expressed by the music.

In short, the moods expressed in music operate within the context of a particular culture (Merriam, 1964). Within any given culture, musical communication of mood and sentiments become somewhat standardized (Meyer, 1956). These conventional musical patterns connote a shared meaning to people with the same cultural background, and in so doing, act as an efficient purveyor of emotion.

Referentialist theory reflects the belief that the meaning in music arises from connections the listener makes between the music itself and some nonmusical object or event. For example, composers like Beethoven in his "Pastoral (Sixth) Symphony" used high-pitched trills on instruments such as the flute to imitate the sounds of birds. This musical reference brings to mind the pleasant sights, sounds, and smells of a walk through a sylvan glen. In contrast, the roll on a timpani drum might be used to connote the ominous sound of thunder or cannons of war. This imitation of nonmusical events or objects is called **iconicity**. In addition to these more obvious imitations of nature or events, other structural qualities of music have been used to refer to nonmusical events or feelings. For example, depression, a feeling that often results in downcast facial expressions and slow, lethargic movement, might be represented musically through slow tempo or descending musical scales. The use of music to imitate human emotions and movements is sometimes referred to as **isomorphism** (Gfeller, 2002b; Gottselig, 2000; Kreitler & Kreitler, 1972).

Iconicity and isomorphism are not the only mechanisms through which music can refer to nonmusical events. **Association through contiguity** is another way in which music can refer to objects or events in life (Radocy & Boyle, 1979). This phenomenon occurs when a particular musical selection or style of music has been paired with a specific event. The music alone can eventually elicit the same types of feelings that occurred when an event took place.

> *Deanna is listening to her car radio as she drives to the grocery store. The apple blossoms and forsythia are just starting to pop, the sky is blue, and the sun is shining. It's a beautiful day, but tears are streaming down Deanna's face. On the radio, she hears the song, "Wind Beneath My Wings," which is the song that her family chose to be sung at her older brother's funeral three years ago. It's as if she's right back at the service, missing her big brother all over again.*

Most of us can think of special songs or musical styles that bring back memories and feelings of past events. However, we can experience an emotional response to music we have never heard before. Scholars of the expressionistic school of thought would argue that the true meaning in music is not reliant on extra musical references but emerges from the structural qualities of the music itself. In other words, the emotional meaning of music is embodied in the music itself.

Structural features and emotional expression: An expressionistic point of view. From an expressionistic point of view, music's meaning results from the musical sounds themselves and nothing more (Gfeller, 2002b; Radocy & Boyle, 1979). It is the structural characteristics of the music itself, as opposed to extra musical associations, that excite feelings and emotions in the listener. Research indicates the tempo, melodic line, rhythm, harmony, and dynamics are linked to different emotional meanings in music (Juslin & Sloboda, 2001; Kwoun, 2005). Research also indicates a neurological basis for extracting emotional cues from particular structural features of music, such as tempo or mode (Peretz, 2001).

A theory known as "**optimal complexity theory**" (Berlyne, 1971) indicates that we feel pleasurable feelings if the structural features of the music are at an optimal or ideal level of complexity and/or familiarity. Music that is too complex or unfamiliar in style can leave the listener with a sense of confusion, chaos, and discomfort. In contrast, if music is too simple or has been heard again and again so that it lacks freshness, the listener may feel bored and unsatisfied.

Berlyne's theory can be illustrated by considering "top ten" hits on the radio. When new songs are introduced on the radio, their style of music is often similar to many other popular songs, so some familiarity already exists. This familiarity helps people to organize and make sense of what they are hearing. However, some songs attract particular attention because they contain novel and interesting elements, such as a unique beat or unusual lyrics. But these top ten hits will eventually drop from the top of the charts. Why? Because as they gain in popularity, radio disc jockeys tend to play them again and again—so often, in fact, that they lose some of that novelty or newness that attracted the listener in the first place. The rock hit at the top of the charts is, for that week, an example of a song that still contains the ideal balance between being unique and yet familiar. According to Berlyne, this balance arouses pleasant feelings in the listener.

Another prominent theory regarding emotions and structural features of music is known as the **theory of expectations**. According to this theory, which is associated with theorist Leonard Meyer (1956), people have an emotional response to music when the musical sounds they *expect* to hear do not actually occur (are inhibited). When we listen to music written in a familiar style, we often can anticipate subsequent notes or phrases—that is, we have expectations regarding what notes are most likely to follow. For example, imagine that someone plays the following notes on a piano: C, D, E, F, G, A, B, and then stops. Most people from Western cultures would be surprised because they expect to hear the scale completed with another note, C. Some people may respond by actually humming the final note, some people may giggle, and some people may show surprise on their faces. In short, the expectations of the listener are inhibited when the typical musical pattern is not completed; an emotional response of surprise results.

Leonard Meyer's theory of expectations might also be illustrated by portions of Haydn's "Surprise Symphony." In this composition, the music proceeds along in a fairly predictable manner, when suddenly Haydn inserts an uncharacteristically loud chord. When people first hear this symphony, it often brings chortles or startled responses. According to Meyer's theory, these emotional responses are the result of inhibited or arrested expectations. It is the balance of the expected and unexpected within a composition that helps to bring meaning and emotion to music.

Culture, experience, and structure. In recent years, researchers have developed models that indicate the contributions of culture, personal experience, and musical structure in the emotional content of music. In particular circumstances, one explanation may be more viable than another, but it seems that all of these factors contribute to music's ability to convey moods. One such theory that considers culture as well as structure, and one that emerged from cross-cultural research, is known as the **Cue Redundancy model.**

The Cue Redundancy model has emerged from recent cross-cultural studies that have examined the relative contributions of cultural convention and structural features of music to emotional response. Balkwill and Thompson (1999), who studied the responses of persons raised in Western culture to Hindu music, proposed a model of emotional response called Cue Redundancy. According to this theory, listeners from other cultures can pick up some emotional cues from structural features such as tempo, while other elements of music such as mode or tonality are more culture-specific. That is, people from another culture will have more difficulty extracting the emotional content from tonality alone. A person raised in a given culture has multiple cues (thus the term *cue redundancy*) of structural features as well as cultural learning for determining the emotional content within music of his or her own culture. A listener from outside the culture has fewer accessible cues for detecting the emotional gist of the music.

More recent research by Kwoun (2005), focusing on the responses of native Koreans and U.S. listeners from two different age groups (older adults who had spent most of their lives in Korea or the U.S., respectively, versus younger adults from Korea and the U.S. who have had more exposure to music from other cultures through globalization), gave additional support to the accuracy of this model. Kwoun found that expression of music embodies both universal auditory cues (structural features) that communicate emotional meaning across cultures, as well as culture-specific cues resulting from cultural conventions. Furthermore, the age and life experiences of the person can influence the extent to which cultural conventions predominate as a cue.

While many people would agree that music is linked with emotions, how does this relate to music's use in therapeutic settings? As we will discover in later chapters, many of the clients served in music therapy are struggling to express or cope with feelings in a healthy and appropriate way (Cassity & Cassity, 2006; Clair, 1996; Gfeller, 2002b). For example, people with mental illness, or elderly persons facing impending death, may feel overwhelmed by sadness, a sense of isolation, anger, or other uncomfortable emotions. Rather than expressing their feelings directly, they may become withdrawn or may even use aggressive ways such as attempting suicide or striking out at others if unable to express emotions and needs more directly. Modification of emotional states plays an important role in psychotherapy, and the experience and expression of emotions has a curative aspect (Greenberg & Paivio, 1997; Greenberg & Safran, 1991).

Sometimes individuals who have difficulty verbally expressing uncomfortable feelings have found music a less threatening or alternative way to share emotions.

Music evokes memories, which in turn can evoke happiness, sadness, or other powerful feelings. Music can be a useful stimulus for reminiscence and life review in older adults, or for persons facing serious crises. Music as an outlet for expressing emotions has enormous potential as a therapeutic tool for clients who have difficulty coping with or expressing emotions (Clair, 1996). As Gaston (1968) remarked, music can often express deep emotions when words no longer suffice. In addition, music can affect one's arousal level and decrease anxiety during relaxation (Thaut & Davis, 1989).

Music, Culture, and Society

It's a brisk but sunny autumn day in Madison, Wisconsin. Over in Camp Randall Stadium at the University of Wisconsin, the football game is over. Next comes the tradition known to UW fans as the "Fifth Quarter." Enthusiastic Badger fans join Bucky Badger, the school mascot, and the UW marching band members in doing the polka to the "Bud Song." As the song comes to a close, they all shout out and sing, "When you say WISCONSIN you've said it all!" Hard to believe such a huge and potentially disorganized crowd could come together in unison!

A few blocks away, the Rubinstein and Strauss families have gathered for the wedding reception of their daughter, Rachel, and son, Aaron. In response to the music, "Hava Nagila," the wedding party and guests clasp hands in a circle to dance the hora. Rachel's mom, Mrs. Rubinstein, (known to all as an excellent dancer) does a complex grapevine step along with some energetic kicks. Her elderly father, Mr. Froman, is happy simply to keep up with the moving circle. Hearts are full as family and friends celebrate the bride and groom, who have now been lifted on chairs in the middle of the circle as the dancing continues. What a wonderful celebration!

Across town, yet another group is gathering, but for a more somber purpose. Mrs. Murphy, the matriarch of a large and well known Irish family in town, recently passed away, and the downtown congregation at St. Patrick's has gathered to honor her memory and to support her family. The strains of "Ave Maria," Mrs. Murphy's favorite song, waft through the sanctuary and over the congregation.

Music, social values, and social integration. According to Crozier (1998), "The enjoyment of music is essentially a social experience" (p. 67). Music is a part of many ceremonies or rituals that mark significant events in people's lives, such as weddings, funerals, bar mitzvahs, parties, dances, church services, Thanksgiving, state ceremonies, political rallies, and dancing.

Music is not, as one sometimes hears, a "universal language," for the music from one culture may not be understood or even tolerated by those in another culture (Clair, 1996). Music is, however, considered a universal phenomenon, in that there is no culture that does not have music as an art form (Clair, 1996; Nettl, 1956). The meaning of music and musical preferences can vary not only by major cultural groups based on nationality or race, but also by smaller subcultures such as those based upon religion or age (Clair, 1996; Froman, 2006). For example, think of the sharp contrast in musical favorites among adolescents who affiliate with Goth rock music, as opposed to senior citizens from northern Wisconsin who get together to polka every Saturday.

Music provides identification with other like-minded peers (Crozier, 1998). Songs directly or indirectly inform members of society about proper behavior (Merriam, 1964; Radocy & Boyle, 1979), thus enforcing conformity to social norms. For example, during times of war, people have used music to rally support for the troops (e.g., "Over There," "Soldier Boy"), or to express resistance toward war (e.g., "Given Peace a Chance" or "War"). Music is also used to validate social institutions and religious rituals. For example, our national anthem is sung at many major gatherings (i.e., sports events, school meetings, etc.). Universities typically have a fight song that expresses school loyalty. Most religions have a body of music that expresses the major tenets upon which faith is founded (Froman, 2006). These ritualized uses of music emphasize and transmit the most important attitudes and beliefs at the center of an organization or religion. As music enforces conformity to social norms and validates social institutions and religious rituals, cultural values and beliefs are shared among members of the community and transmitted from one generation to the next, thus contributing to the continuity and stability of culture (Merriam, 1964, p. 225).

According to Merriam (1964), music also forms a solidarity point for social congregating, cooperation, and coordination. Consider the many musical events that require the combined efforts of many toward a common goal: church choirs, community choruses, civic musicals, orchestras and bands, duets, trios, quartets, sing-alongs around a camp fire, bell choirs, bluegrass fiddlers at a square dance, jazz and rock groups—the list is almost endless. These musical activities call for a strong measure of cooperation, since the extent to which the entire composition has merit depends on the contributions of each individual. The elements of rhythm, melody, and harmony require a level of order and structure created by the combined efforts of the group.

Sociocultural issues in the therapeutic process. Because music is so commonly found in everyday life, it is easy to take for granted its power as a bearer of cultural values. However, we can no doubt all remember times when we joined our fellow humans in song for a religious or political event. "The Battle Hymn of the Republic," "Amazing Grace," and "We Shall Overcome" have buoyed our spirits and strengthened our resolve. As music therapists work with individuals who are struggling with pain or emotional distress, music as a bearer of culture can help support the individual in his or her quest for meaning and quality of life.

As we consider the power of music as a bearer of culture, it is important to realize, however, that each culture has its own musical heritage. Musical meaning is shaped not only by national citizenship, but by our membership in a variety of subcultures. Religious affiliation is a strong cultural context through which we perceive and interpret music (Froman, 2006). The hymn "Amazing Grace" may have great spiritual and sentimental value to a member of the Methodist church. In contrast, the complex, chromatic incantations of the rabbi will hold greater significance to people of Jewish heritage. Our membership within a socioeconomic group can also affect our cultural perspective (Radocy & Boyle, 1979). Several studies have shown preference for different styles of music based on income and formal education. In short, the value and meaning that we attribute to any given musical selection will be filtered through our own cultural context.

The selection of musical stimuli for any music therapy intervention should take into account the cultural traditions of those clients involved. For example, a therapist may find that clients from a predominantly Latino urban neighborhood along the Texas border are more comfortable with different styles of music than are Caucasian, blue-collar clients from the heart of Nashville, Tennessee. In short, no single style of music will be valued by all people, since music's ability to function depends on a commonality of experience with music in the appropriate functional context (Radocy & Boyle, 1979).

While social integration may seem to be a natural byproduct of everyday life, for many clients served by music therapists, social interaction is difficult or limited. For example, people with emotional disorders may demonstrate withdrawn or aggressive behaviors, which can prevent appropriate socialization. Other people, such as the elderly, may long for companionship and social opportunities but may lack the physical strength or resources to initiate community involvement. Improved social interaction has been identified as an important goal in many music therapy settings. Because music activities often occur in groups, appropriately structured musical events can provide "experience in relating to others" (Sears, 1968, p. 31). In fact, a perusal of research within music therapy journals over the past few decades indicates that improved socialization is a common goal in music therapy practice (Clair, 1996; Gfeller, 1987, 2002b).

In conclusion, music is an important part of our lives and functions in many different ways. Merriam's (1964) functions of music in society point out the breadth of roles that this art form plays in our everyday lives. At its most basic, music is a form of sound energy that can stimulate the auditory or tactile senses. It can prime the nervous system for physical movement such as marching or dancing. Music is also a form of nonverbal communication exquisitely capable of expressing our deepest thoughts and most tender emotions. It is an art form that can bind us together toward a common resolve. Because music is such a flexible medium, it serves as a powerful tool for the professional music therapist in a variety of therapeutic objectives.

SUMMARY

There are many reasons why music can be used as a flexible and therapeutic tool. **One advantage in using music is that some type of musical enjoyment or involvement is possible for people of any age.** From the earliest days of infancy through old age, music can be appreciated by people both with and without formal musical training. Musical involvement will differ, however, depending on the level of development. Young children will experience music as a sensorimotor stimulus and can benefit from direct experiences making and listening to musical sounds. As the child grows older, participation in music as a social activity will become more and more common. In adulthood, music can be enjoyed through listening or direct participation, and as an individual or group member. Musical enjoyment can extend into the retirement years, offering a source of beauty and social involvement.

Another aspect of music that makes it a flexible therapeutic medium is that it is comprised of diverse styles and combinations of sounds from simple to very complex. Music can also be enjoyed through a variety of forms, such as listening, singing, playing instruments, or composing. Because music includes such a wide range of sounds and forms of involvement, the music therapist has ample material from which to choose in meeting specific therapeutic goals and the personal preferences of individual clients.

Another reason music can function so effectively for a variety of therapeutic purposes is the many uses of music in society. Merriam (1964) has outlined 10 functions of music, which relate to five functional domains: physical systems, cognition, communication, emotions, and sociocultural functioning. **Music is a pervasive art form that influences our daily lives in each of these domains.** This influence can be applied to therapeutic needs of persons of all ages.

STUDY QUESTIONS

1. Describe the musical responses of a child in the sensorimotor stage of development.

2. What types of musical activities are engaging to a child in the preoperational stage of development?

3. Describe the musical capabilities of children who have reached the concrete operations stage of development.

4. What is the most notable cognitive characteristic of the formal operations stage of development?

5. How do the musical preferences and abilities of older adults compare to those of adults below the age of 65?

6. List Merriam's 10 functions of music in society.

7. Compare and contrast the referentialist and expressionist view of music and emotions.

8. What does association through contiguity mean in the context of music and emotions?

9. Which psychologist is associated with the optimal complexity theory?

10. What scholar is associated with the theory of expectations?

11. Is music a universal language? Explain your answer.

12. Compare and contrast the use of music for aesthetic purposes and for entertainment.

13. Describe our present research knowledge concerning the influence of music on autonomic responses.

REFERENCES

Balch, W., Bowman, K., & Mohler, L. (1992). Music dependent memory in immediate and delayed word recall. *Memory and Cognition, 20*(1), 21–28.

Balkwill, L., & Thompson, W. F. (1999). A cross-cultural investigation of the perception of emotion in music: Psychophysical and cultural cues. *Music Perception, 17*(1), 43–64.

Barrickman, J. (1989). A developmental music therapy approach for preschool hospitalized children. *Music Therapy Perspectives, 7*, 10–16.

Bayless, K. M., & Ramsey, M. E. (1982). *Music, a way of life for the young child.* St. Louis, MO: C. V. Mosby.

Berlyne, D. E. (1971). *Aesthetics and psychobiology.* New York: Appleton-Century-Crofts.

Bright, R. (1972). *Music in geriatric care.* New York: St. Martin's Press.

Brooks, D. M. (1989). Music therapy enhances treatment with adolescents. *Music Therapy Perspectives, 6*, 37–39.

Campbell, P. S., & Scott-Kassner, C. (1995). *Music in childhood.* New York: Schirmer Books.

Cassity, M., & Cassity, J. (2006). *Multimodal psychiatric music therapy for adults, adolescents, and children* (3rd ed.). Philadelphia: Jessica Kingsley.

Christenson, P. G., & Roberts, D. F. (1998). *It's not only rock & roll: Popular music in the lives of adolescents.* Cresskill, NJ: Hampton Press.

Clair, A. A. (1996). *Therapeutic uses of music with older adults.* Baltimore: Health Professions Press.

Coffman, D., & Adamek, M. (1999). The contributions of wind band participation to quality of life of senior adults. *Music Therapy Perspectives, 17*, 27–31.

Coffman, D. D. (2002). Music and quality of life in older adults. *Psychomusicology, 18*(1–2), 76–88.

Crozier, W. R. (1998). Music and social influence. In D. J. Hargreaves, & A. C. North (Eds.), *The social psychology of music.* (pp. 67–83). New York: Oxford University Press.

Dainow, E. (1977). Physical effects and motor response to music. *Journal of Research in Music Education, 25*, 211–221.

Davidson, L., McKernon, P., & Gardner, H. (1981). The acquisition of song: A developmental approach. *Documentary report of the Ann Arbor symposium: National Symposium on the Applications of Psychology to the Teaching and Learning of Music.* Reston, VA: Music Educators National Conference.

De L'Etoile, S. K. (2006). Infant-directed singing: A theory for clinical intervention. *Music Therapy Perspectives, 24*, 22–29.

Eich, E., Macaulay, D., & Ryan, L. (1994). Mood-dependent memory for events of the personal past. *Journal of Experimental Psychology: General, 123*(2), 201–215.

Farnan, L. A. (2007). Music therapy and developmental disabilities: A glance back and a look forward. *Music Therapy Perspectives, 25*(2), 80–85.

Froman, R. (2006, November). *Music therapy with Jewish clients in the United States of America.* Paper presented at the 8th annual national conference of the American Music Therapy Association, Kansas City, MO.

Galizio, M., & Hendrick, C. (1972). Effect of musical accompaniment on attitude: The guitar as a prop for persuasion. *Journal of Applied Social Psychology, 2*, 350–359.

Gardstrom, S. C. (1999). Music exposure and criminal behavior: Perceptions of juvenile offenders. *Journal of Music Therapy, 36*, 207–221.

Gaston, E. T. (1958). Music in therapy. In J. H. Masserman & J. L. Moreno (Eds.), *Progress in psychotherapy* (pp. 142–148). New York: Grune and Stratton.

Gaston, E. T. (1968). *Music in therapy.* New York: Macmillan.

Gfeller, K. E. (1987). Music therapy theory and practice as reflected in research literature. *Journal of Music Therapy, 24*, 176–194.

Gfeller, K. E. (1990). A cognitive-linguistic approach to language development for the preschool child with hearing impairment: Implications for music therapy practice. *Music Therapy Perspectives, 8*, 47–51.

Gfeller, K. E. (2002a). The function of aesthetic stimuli in the therapeutic process. In R. F. Unkefer & M. H. Thaut (Eds.), *Music therapy in the treatment of adults with mental disorders* (pp. 68–84). St. Louis, MO: MMB.

Gfeller, K. E. (2002b). Music as a therapeutic agent: Historical and sociocultural perspectives. In R. F. Unkefer & M. H. Thaut (Eds.), *Music therapy in the treatment of adults with mental disorders* (pp. 60–67). St. Louis, MO: MMB.

Gfeller, K. E. (2002c). Music as communication. In R. F. Unkefer & M. H. Thaut (Eds.), *Music therapy in the treatment of adults with mental disorders* (pp. 42–59). St. Louis, MO: MMB.

Gfeller, K. E., Asmus, E., Eckert, E., & Eckert, M. (1991). An investigation of emotional response to music and text. *Psychology of Music, 19*(2), 128–141.

Gfeller, K. E., & Coffman, D. (1991). An investigation of emotional response of trained musicians to verbal and musical information. *Psychomusicology, 10*(1), 3–18.

Gfeller, K. E., & Hanson, N. (1995). *Music therapy programming for individuals with Alzheimer's disease and related disorders.* Iowa City, IA: West Music.

Gibbons, A. C. (1977). Popular music preferences of elderly people. *Journal of Music Therapy, 14,* 180–189.

Gibbons, A. C. (1982). Music aptitude profile scores in a non-institutionalized elderly population. *Journal of Research in Music Education, 30,* 23–29.

Gibbons, A. C. (1983). Primary measures of music audiation scores in an institutionalized elderly population. *Journal of Music Therapy, 14,* 21–29.

Gilbert, J. P., & Beal, M. (1982). Preferences of elderly individuals for selected music education experiences. *Journal of Research in Music Education, 30,* 247–253.

Gottselig, J. M. (2000). *Human neuroanatomical systems for perceiving emotion in music.* Unpublished doctoral dissertation, The University of Iowa, Iowa City.

Greenberg, L., & Paivio, S. C. (1997). *Working with emotions in psychotherapy.* New York: Guilford Press.

Greenberg, L., & Safran, J. (1991). *Emotions, psychotherapy and change.* New York: Guilford Press.

Greenberg, M. (1979). *Your children need music.* Englewood Cliffs, NJ: Prentice-Hall.

Hanson-Abromeit, D. (2003). The Newborn Individualized Development Care and Assessment Program (NIDCAP) as a model for clinical music therapy interventions with premature infants. *Music Therapy Perspectives, 24,* 60–68.

Hobson, M. R. (2006). The collaboration of music therapy and speech-language pathology in the treatment of neurogenic communication disorders: Part II–Collaborative strategies and scope of practice. *Music Therapy Perspectives, 24*(2), 66–72.

Hodges, D. A. (Ed.). (1996). *Handbook of music psychology* (2nd ed.). San Antonio, TX: University of Texas at San Antonio IMR Press.

Hoyer, W. J., & Roodin, P. A. (2003). *Adult development and aging* (5th ed.). Dubuque, IA: McGraw Hill.

Humpal, M. E. (1998). Information sharing: Song repertoire of young children. *Music Therapy Perspectives, 16*(1), 37–42.

Huron, D. (2004). Is music and evolutionary adaptation? In I. Peretz & R. Zatorre (Eds.), *The cognitive neuroscience of music* (pp. 57–78). New York: Oxford University Press.

Jeffery, D. R., & Good, D. C. (1995). Rehabilitation of the stroke patient. *Current Opinion in Neurology, 8,* 62–68.

Juslin, P. N., & Sloboda, J. A. (2001). *Music and emotion: Theory and research.* New York: Oxford University Press.

Kreitler, H., & Kreitler, S. (1972). *Psychology of the arts.* Durham, NC: Duke University Press.

Kwoun, S. (2005). *An examination of cue redundancy theory in cross-cultural decoding of emotions in music.* Unpublished doctoral dissertation, The University of Iowa, Iowa City.

Langer, S. (1942). *Philosophy in a new key.* New York: Mentor Books.

Larson, P. S. (1983). An exploratory study of lifelong musical interest and activity: Case studies of twelve retired adults (Doctoral dissertation, Temple University, 1983). *Dissertation Abstracts International, 44,* 100A.

Lathom, W., Peterson, M., & Havlicek, L. (1982). Musical preferences of older people attending nutritional sites. *Educational Gerontology: An International Bimonthly Journal, 8,* 155–165.

Marteniuk, R. G. (1976). *Information processing in motor skills.* New York: Holt, Rinehart and Winston.

McDonald, D. T., & Simons, G. M. (1989). *Musical growth and development.* New York: Schirmer Books.

McFarland, R. A. (1984). Effects of music upon emotional content of TAT stories. *Journal of Psychology, 116*, 227–234.

McIntosh, G. C., Brown, S. H., Rice, R. R., & Thaut, M. H. (1997). Rhythmic auditory-motor facilitation of gait patterns in patients with Parkinson's disease. *Journal of Neurology, Neurosurgery, and Psychiatry, 62*, 22–26.

McKinney, C. H., Antoni, M. H., Kumar, M., Tims, F. C., & McCabe, P. M. (1997). Effects of guided imagery and music (GIM) therapy on mood and cortisol in healthy adults. *Health Psychology, 16*, 1–12.

McKinney, C. H., Tims, F. C., Kumar, A., & Kumar, M. (1997). The effect of selected classical music and spontaneous imagery on plasma beta-endorphin. *Journal of Behavior Medicine, 20*, 85–99.

Merriam, A. P. (1964). *The anthropology of music.* Evanston, IL: Northwestern University Press.

Meyer, L. B. (1956). *Emotion and meaning in music.* Chicago: University of Chicago Press.

Miller, R. A., Thaut, M. H., McIntosh, G. C., & Rice, R. R. (1996). Components of EMG symmetry and variability in Parkinsonian and healthy elderly gait. *Electroencephalography and Clinical Neurophysiology, 101*, 1–7.

Moog, H. (1976). The development of musical experience in children of pre-school age. *Psychology of Music, 4*, 38–47.

Munro, S. (1984). *Music therapy in palliative/hospice care.* St. Louis, MO: Magnamusic-Baton.

Nettl, B. (1956). *Music in primitive cultures.* Cambridge, MA: Harvard University Press.

North, A. C., Hargreaves, D. J., & O'Neill, S. (2000). The importance of music to adolescents. *British Journal of Educational Psychology, 29*(115), 613–621.

O'Briant, M. P., & Willbanks, W. A. (1978). The effect of context on the perception of music. *Bulletin of the Psychonomic Society, 12*, 441–443.

Palmer, M. D. (1977). Music therapy in a comprehensive program of treatment and rehabilitation for the geriatric resident. *Journal of Music Therapy, 14*, 162–168.

Pal'tsev, Y. I., & El'ner, A. M. (1967). Change in the functional state of the segmental apparatus of the spinal chord under the influence of sound stimuli and its role in voluntary movements. *Biophysics, 12*, 1219–1226.

Peretz, I. (2001). Listen to the brain: A biological perspective on musical emotions. In P. N. Juslin & J. A. Sloboda (Eds.), *Music and emotion: Theory and research.* New York: Oxford University Press.

Peretz, I., Kolinsky, R., Tramo, M., Labrecque, R., Hublet, C., Demeurisse, G., et al. (1994). Functional dissociations following bilateral lesions of auditory cortex. *Brain, 117*, 1283–1301.

Peretz, I., & Zatorre, R. (Eds.). (2004). *The cognitive neuroscience of music.* New York: Oxford University Press.

Prassas, S. G., Thaut, M. H., McIntosh, G. C., & Rice, R. R. (1997). Effect of auditory rhythmic cuing on gait kinematic parameters in hemiparetic stroke patients. *Gait and Posture, 6*, 218–223.

Radocy, R. E., & Boyle, J. D. (1979). *Psychological foundations of musical behavior.* Springfield, IL: Charles C. Thomas.

Ringgenberg, S. (2003). Music as a teaching tool: Creating story songs. *Young Children, 58*(5), 76–79.

Rossignol, S., & Jones, G. (1976). Audio-spinal influence in man studied by the H-reflex and its possible role on rhythmic movements synchronized to sound. *Electroencephalography and Clinical Neurophysiology, 41*, 83–92.

Sears, W. (1968). Processes in music therapy. In E. T. Gaston (Ed.), *Music in therapy* (pp. 30–44). New York: Macmillan.

Sloboda, J. A., & O'Neill, S. A. (2001). Emotions in everyday listening to music. In P. N. Juslin & J. A. Sloboda (Eds.), *Music and emotion: Theory and research* (pp. 415–430). Oxford, England: Oxford University Press.

Spiegler, D. (1967). Factors involved in the development of prenatal rhythmic sensitivity. (Doctoral dissertation, West Virginia University, 1967). *Dissertation Abstracts International, 28,* 3886B.

Standley, J. (2001). Music therapy for the neonate. *Newborn and Infant Nursing Reviews, 1*(4), 211–216.

Standley, J. M., & Madsen, C. M. (1990). Comparison of infant preferences and responses to auditory stimuli: Music, mother, and other female voice. *Journal of Music Therapy, 27,* 54–97.

Staum, M. (1983). Music and rhythmic stimuli in the rehabilitation of gait disorders. *Journal of Music Therapy, 20,* 69–87.

Thaut, M. H. (2002). Physiological and motor responses to music stimuli. In R. F. Unkefer & M. H. Thaut (Eds.), *Music therapy in the treatment of adults with mental disorders* (pp. 33–41). St. Louis, MO: MMB.

Thaut, M. H. (2005). *Rhythm, music, and the brain.* New York: Routledge.

Thaut, M. H., & Davis, W. B. (1989). The influence of preferred relaxing music on measures of state anxiety, relaxation, and physiological responses. *Journal of Music Therapy, 26*(4), 168–187.

Thaut, M. H., McIntosh, G. C., Rice, R. R., & Prassas, S. G. (1993). Effect of rhythmic cuing on temporal stride parameters and EMG patterns in hemiparetic gait of stroke patients. *Journal of Neurologic Rehabilitation, 7,* 9–16.

Thaut, M. H., & Miller, R. A. (1994). Multiple synchronization strategies in tracking of rhythmic auditory stimulation. *Proceedings of the Society for Neuroscience, 146,* 11.

Thaut, M. H., Miller, R. A., & Schauer, M. L. (1998). Multiple synchronization strategies in rhythmic sensorimotor tasks: Phase vs. period corrections. *Biological Cybernetics, 79*(3), 241–250.

Thaut, M. H., & Schauer, M. L. (1997). Weakly coupled oscillators in rhythmic motor synchronization. *Proceedings of the Society for Neuroscience, 298,* 20.

Thayer, J. F., & Levenson, R. W. (1983). Effects of music on psychophysiological responses to a stressful film. *Psychomusicology, 3,* 44–52.

Trehub, S. E. (2004). Musical predispositions in infancy: An update. In I. Peretz & R. Zatorre (Eds.), *The cognitive neuroscience of music* (pp. 3–20). New York: Oxford University Press.

Verghese, J., Lipton, R. B., Katz, M. J., Hail, C. B., Derby, C. A., Kulslansky, G., et al. (2003). Leisure activities and the risk of dementia in the elderly. *The New England Journal of Medicine, 248,* 2508–2516.

Wagner, M. J. (1994). *Introductory musical acoustics* (3rd ed.). Raleigh, NC: Contemporary.

Winner, E. (1982). *Invented worlds.* Cambridge, MA: Harvard University Press.

Wintle, R. R. (1978). *Emotional impact of music on television commercials.* Unpublished doctoral dissertation, University of Nebraska, Lincoln.

Zatorre, R. (2005). Music, the food of neuroscience? *Nature, 434,* 312–315.

Zillman, D., & Gan, S. (1998). Musical taste in adolescence. In D. J. Hargreaves, & A. C. North (Eds.), *The social psychology of music* (pp. 161–187). New York: Oxford University Press.

Zimmerman, M. P. (1971). *Musical characteristics of children.* Reston, VA: Music Educators National Conference.

PART **Two**

Populations Served by Music Therapists

MUSIC THERAPY WITH CHILDREN AND ADULTS WITH INTELLECTUAL DISABLING CONDITIONS

William B. Davis
Laurie A. Farnan

CHAPTER OUTLINE

A BRIEF HISTORICAL PERSPECTIVE
CONCEPTION AND DEFINITION OF INTELLECTUAL DISABILITIES
AN IMPORTANT LINK TO THE CURRENT DEFINITION OF INTELLECTUAL
    DISABILITIES: FIVE ASSUMPTIONS
EXTENT AND CLASSIFICATION OF INTELLECTUAL DISABILITIES
    Mild Intellectual Disability
    Moderate Intellectual Disability
    Severe and Profound Intellectual Disabilities
    Severity Unspecified
CAUSES OF INTELLECTUAL DISABILITIES
PREVENTION OF INTELLECTUAL DISABILITIES
    Primary Prevention
    Secondary Prevention
    Tertiary Prevention
DEVELOPMENTAL PROFILES OF PERSONS WITH INTELLECTUAL DISABILITIES
    Cognitive Development
    Language Acquisition
    Physical and Motor Development
    Social and Emotional Characteristics
EDUCATIONAL PLACEMENT OF PERSONS WITH INTELLECTUAL DISABILITIES

EDUCATIONAL STRATEGIES USED WITH PERSONS WHO HAVE INTELLECTUAL
    DISABILITIES
MUSIC THERAPY FOR PERSONS WITH INTELLECTUAL DISABILITIES
MUSIC THERAPY TREATMENT GOALS FOR PERSONS WHO HAVE INTELLECTUAL
    DISABILITIES
    Music Therapy for Development of Social and Emotional Behaviors
    Music Therapy for Development of Motor Skills
    Music Therapy for Development of Communication Skills
    Music Therapy for Development of Pre-Academic Skills
    Music Therapy for Development of Academic Skills
    Music Therapy for Development of Leisure Skills

School mornings are much like those for many families in Colin's house. After awakening, there are dressing and grooming tasks to complete, breakfast to eat, and preparations to make for a full day at school. There are, however, differences in how these tasks are carried out, because Colin has an **intellectual disability**. Although he is 10, he must have assistance with personal activities of daily living including eating, dressing, and hygiene. Colin is educated in a special education classroom at the public school that his brothers and sisters attend. He learns pre-academic skills, such as the identification of basic colors, words, and numbers. He also learns social skills and works on communication and language arts skills. Colin requires help with gross and fine motor planning and skills, so he works on an individual basis with an occupational therapist twice a week. He also attends an adapted physical education program at school. He also works with a speech pathologist, a school psychologist, and a music therapist on a regular basis. Colin, like millions of other children and adults who have intellectual disabilities, exhibits developmental delays in language acquisition, cognitive abilities, motor skills, and social adaptation.

A BRIEF HISTORICAL PERSPECTIVE

A brief overview of past attitudes toward intellectual disabilities enables us to better understand the current climate. With such a historical perspective, we can appreciate the various approaches to caring for a population that has been successful—and not so successful—over time. For many years, progress toward understanding the condition of intellectual disabilities has depended on a few individuals with a compassionate and caring attitude. It is these people that have provided the impetus for changes that have improved the quality of life of persons with intellectual disabilities (Drew & Hardman, 2007; Farnan, 2007).

Not too many decades ago, people with intellectual disabilities (ID) were a hidden segment of American society. Misunderstood, feared, scorned, segregated, persecuted, and punished sometimes to death, these individuals were not given the chance to learn and contribute to society (Scheerenberger, 1989). Times have changed, and today many people with intellectual disabilities lead productive and interesting lives.

Before the 18th century, intellectual disabilities were not considered a serious problem in any society, because people with milder intellectual disabilities usually functioned well in the predominantly agrarian culture of the time. Individuals with significant intellectual disabilities were likely to die from natural causes; those who survived but could not contribute to the productivity of society were often eliminated (Scheerenberger, 1983).

The move to improve care and treatment of people with intellectual disabilities began during the 19th century in France and Switzerland, then spread to the rest of Europe and finally, to the United States. Two Frenchman—Jean Itard, a physician, and Edouard Seguin, an educator, developed programs to teach social, academic, language, and gross and fine motor skills to adults and children with intellectual disabilities (Scheerenberger, 1983). During the late 1800s, Seguin introduced his educational concepts to American institutions. Some of his ideas are still in use today, including a multidisciplinary approach to teaching, small class sizes, and the use of well-trained teachers. Seguin also advocated the use of music to teach listening skills and speech and to develop gross and fine motor skills. Because of his influence, many 19th century schools for students with intellectual disabilities used pianos and rhythm instruments to augment traditional teaching techniques (Kraft, 1963).

Since 1900, the quality of education for individuals with intellectual disabilities has continued to improve, albeit unevenly at times. Educational settings have ranged from large state-supported residential facilities to, more recently, small group homes and public school classrooms.

From the middle of the 19th century, music therapy has played an important role in the treatment of individuals with intellectual disabilities in both institutional and educational settings. In this chapter, we will define intellectual disabilities, learn about their causes, discuss teaching strategies, and learn how music therapy can be used to help acquire skills for personal independence, enhance quality of life, and increase societal inclusion for these individuals.

CONCEPTION AND DEFINITION OF INTELLECTUAL DISABILITIES

The often-used term *mental retardation* has developed into an objectionable description of what we now refer to as an intellectual disability (ID). Intellectual disabilities are not a particular medical diagnosis, such as cancer or influenza, nor are they considered a mental illness. Intellectual disabilities are one of the four areas of developmental disabilities identified by the federal government in 1975. The other developmental disabilities include autism, cerebral palsy, and epilepsy, discussed in later chapters (Farnan, 2007).

Persons with ID have a significant deficit in intellectual ability that may limit development in such areas as communication, abstract reasoning, social behavior, and motor development. Persons with ID vary in ability but, with proper supports, can almost always improve their quality of life (Drew & Hardman, 2007).

In past times, societies have often used a ranking approach to describe persons who were perceived not to be fully "able bodied." In 1601 in England, for example, the Elizabethan Poor Law identified three major categories: the vagrant, the involuntarily unemployed, and the helpless. In 1877, the first definition endorsed by the American Association on Mental Retardation (AAMR; now called the **American Association for Intellectual and Developmental Disabilities—AAIDD**) was developed based solely on level of intellectual function. In 1910, the United States government offered the following tripartite classification of intellectual disability:

1. Idiot: mental development does not exceed that of a normal child of about 2 years old.
2. Imbecile: mental development is higher than that of an idiot but does not exceed that of a normal child of about 7 years.
3. Moron: mental development is above that of an imbecile but does not exceed that of a child of about 12 years. (Scheerenberger, 1983, 1987)

By 1959, the AAMR outlined five levels of intellectual disability: borderline, mild, moderate, severe, and profound as determined by the Stanford-Binet intelligence tests. The definition of intellectual disability was changed again in 1961, 1973, 1983, 1992, 2002, and most recently in 2007. With each definition there was attention directed to changing the IQ ranges, dropping categories, and adding language describing adaptive behaviors (Farnan, 2007).

Today, the most widely used and accepted definition was developed by the American Association on Intellectual and Developmental Disabilities. The AAIDD definition of intellectual disabilities states that "Mental retardation is a disability characterized by significant limitations both in intellectual functioning and in adaptive behavior as expressed in conceptual, social, and practical adaptive skills. This disability originates before the age of 18" (AAIDD, 2002, p. 1). The 2002 definition remains current with the exception of replacing the term *mental retardation* with *intellectual disabilities* (Farnan, 2007).

There are three key components to the AAIDD definition of intellectual disabilities: a measure of intelligence, presence of severe functional limitations in adaptive behavior, and age of onset. Let us now look at the three components in detail.

1. Intellectual disabilities are characterized by significantly subaverage intelligence. Intellectual function is usually determined from an intelligence quotient (IQ) test. On the Stanford-Binet Intelligence Scale, an IQ level below 70–75 signifies a deficit in intellectual performance. This figure will vary slightly depending upon the psychometric scale used. When compared to peers of average or higher intelligence, adults and children with intellectual disabilities are less likely to remember information, use abstract concepts, display logical reasoning, and make good decisions. Based on intelligent test scores only, approximately 3% of the total population is considered to have ID, but this figure is reduced to 1% when appropriate helping strategies are provided to the individual with ID (Drew & Hardman, 2007).

2. Intellectual disabilities exist concurrently with limitations in **adaptive behavior.** Adaptive behavior, comprising conceptual, social, and practical skills, may be defined as skills that people must learn to function effectively in daily life. Note that subaverage intelligence by itself is not sufficient for a diagnosis of intellectual disability; adaptive behavior deficits must also be present. This part of the definition was added following observations that some adults and children functioned well in life despite deficits in intellectual functioning (Drew & Hardman, 2007). Examples of adaptive behavior skills include:

   • Conceptual skills: receptive and expressive language, writing, reading, using money

   • Social skills: interpersonal, responsibility, self-esteem, gullibility, naiveté, following rules, obey laws

   • Practical skills: personal activities of daily living such as eating, dressing, toileting, mobility, personal grooming; instrumental activities of daily living such as preparing meals, taking medication on schedule, using the telephone, managing personal finances, using private or public transportation, maintaining a clean and safe living environment, and occupational skills.

3. Onset of intellectual disabilities occurs before age 18. In most Western societies, 18 marks the age of adulthood. This portion of the definition continues to the criticized because intellectual disabilities sometimes do not manifest until after the age of 18. A number of experts believe that the definition should be expanded to include adults with intellectual disabilities who are in need of services such as vocational training. Public

schools frequently use the age of 18 (and sometimes 22) to terminate public education for students with intellectual disabilities (Drew & Hardman, 2007; Thomas, 1996).

AN IMPORTANT LINK TO THE CURRENT DEFINITION OF INTELLECTUAL DISABILITIES: FIVE ASSUMPTIONS

The 2002 AAIDD definition is supported by five assumptions that center on the functioning of an individual with intellectual disabilities within his or her familiar environments such as home, school, and work. The 2002 definition also recognizes the importance of environmental influences that may impact an individual's performance, such as cultural, economic, and linguistic background (Drew & Hardman, 2007). The five assumptions are as follows:

1. "Valid assessment considers cultural and linguistic diversity as well as differences in communication and behavioral factors." Failure to assess the individual's cultural background, primary language, communication requirements, and behaviors may result in an invalid assessment of a person's strengths and weaknesses. The inclusion of a multidisciplinary treatment team can contribute to a cogent assessment of the person with intellectual disabilities.

2. "The existence of limitations in adaptive skills occurs within the context of community environments typical of the individual's age peers and is indexed to the person's individualized needs for supports." Community environments typical of the individual's age peers may include the home, neighborhood, school, and other places which the person frequents. Age peers are important because consideration must be given to the cultural or linguistic background of the individual. An analysis of supports or services needed is important to help the person function as well as possible in his or her social context.

3. "Specific adaptive limitations often coexist with strengths in other adaptive skills or other personal capabilities." It is important to remember that persons who have intellectual disabilities will, in addition to obvious weaknesses, demonstrate certain strengths. For example, an individual may have strong social skills while having severe deficits with motor skills, or have poor communication skills while possessing functional reading skills.

4. "An important purpose of describing limitations is to develop a profile of needed supports." Supports are developmental and educational approaches provided by parents, educators and therapists designed to assist the person with intellectual disabilities to function at their optimal ability.

5. "With appropriate supports over a sustained period, the life functioning of the person with intellectual disabilities will generally improve." Most every person with intellectual disabilities can improve adaptive skills over time with appropriate services. Some may need supports over a lifetime, while others may need only intermittent assistance to help with integration into the community. In unusual situations, the goal may be to preserve current functioning or slow regression. (AAIDD, 2002, pp. 8–9)

The concept of supports first appeared in the AAMR's 1992 definition and continues as an important strategy in the habilitation of individuals with intellectual disabilities. Supports are the combined efforts of parents, teachers, peers, physicians, and other professionals to identify the level of services needed to assist individuals with ID to meet their best possible level of function. Supports include providing physical, emotional, social cognitive, employment, health, and safety strategies to help the individual with intellectual disabilities to improve personal functioning to the greatest extent possible. Having proper supports can also promote inclusion within the community (Weis, 2008).

EXTENT AND CLASSIFICATION OF INTELLECTUAL DISABILITIES

After a person has been identified as having an intellectual disability, the next step is to ascertain the level of severity. Classification is an attempt to sort individuals with intellectual disabilities into categories on the basis of ability and/or achievement and is often tied to gaining access to funding sources for that person.

Classification systems for intellectual disability have varied over time much as definitions have. Before 1992, most classification systems focused on two important criteria: severity and cause of the disability. Terminology such as that used in the current edition of the *Diagnostic and Statistical Manual-IV-TR* (*DSM-IV-TR*; American Psychiatric Association [APA], 2000) employs descriptors like *mild, moderate, severe, profound retardation,* and *retardation, severity unspecified* that are related to the degree of disability and adaptive behavior. Music therapists and other professionals may find the *DSM-IV-TR* classifications useful to assist in the planning and implementation of an appropriate treatment program. The following are descriptions of functioning level based on the *DSM-IV-TR* categories:

- Mild mental retardation: IQ level from 50–55 to 70
- Moderate mental retardation: IQ level of 35–40 to 50–55
- Severe mental retardation: IQ level 20–25 to 35–40
- Profound mental retardation: IQ levels below 20 or 25
- Severity unspecified: intelligence not testable by available methods

Mild Intellectual Disability

A person with mild intellectual disabilities has the capacity to learn basic math, reading, and writing skills up to about the sixth-grade level. These individuals are capable of living independently in the community but may need assistance and support when confronted with extraordinary social or vocational stress. They can usually become economically independent or semi-independent.

A child with mild intellectual disabilities is often mainstreamed (integrated into regular classrooms) in the public schools (Harris, 2006). Most individuals with intellectual disabilities appear physically normal and may not manifest signs of intellectual disabilities until they enter school and fail to keep pace with their age-mates' academic progress (Weis, 2008). This category comprises approximately 85% of those defined as having intellectual disabilities (*DSM-IV-TR*; APA, 2000).

Moderate Intellectual Disability

People with moderate intellectual disabilities are capable of learning functional academic skills up to about the second-grade level, including basic reading proficiency, simple number concepts, and limited verbal communication skills. These individuals can learn self-help skills to meet their basic needs, such as personal grooming and hygiene, dressing, and eating. They can develop meaningful interpersonal relationships with family members, friends, and acquaintances. The adult with moderately intellectual disabilities may work in a supervised work setting, such as a sheltered workshop (Brantley, 1988; Harris, 2006).

Despite their abilities, however, adults and children with moderate intellectual disabilities may require supervision and economic support throughout their lives. Today, small residential group homes provide this support and supervision while simultaneously allowing residents to gain a measure of social and economic independence.

Children with moderate intellectual disabilities are normally found in segregated classrooms within the public school setting. Along with intellectual deficits, they may exhibit secondary disabilities, such as speech and language disorders, neurological problems (e.g., cerebral palsy), sensory impairments (e.g., deafness and/or blindness), and poor eating and dental practices. This group makes up approximately 10% of the total population with intellectual disabilities (*DSM-IV-TR*; APA, 2000).

Severe and Profound Intellectual Disabilities

In addition to subnormal intelligence, many individuals with severely/profoundly intellectual disabilities experience medical conditions that delay or completely arrest development of adaptive skills. The approximately 4–6% of persons in this category also exhibit the disabilities described above, but with more frequency and severity (*DSM-IV-TR*; APA, 2000). In addition, musculoskeletal impairments (e.g., contractures of hands, arms, or legs) and debilitating emotional and psychiatric problems can accompany severe intellectual disabilities. While many of the individuals in this category are able to attain some level of social competence in a highly structured, supervised setting, all need support and care throughout their lifespan.

Children who are severely/profoundly intellectually disabled are sometimes placed in segregated public school classrooms but are frequently educated within the residential facility setting. Curriculum focuses on self-care skills (e.g., eating, dressing, bathing) and rudimentary verbal and nonverbal communication skills (Drew & Hardman, 2007; Harris, 2006).

A 6-year-old child with mild or moderate intellectual disability has a life expectancy comparable to that of a child without disabilities. For children with severe and profound intellectual disabilities, however, average life expectancy can be significantly less, although some individuals will live to the age of 70 or 80 with appropriate health care. It is likely that this group of people with severe/profound level of intellectual disabilities will live longer in the future due to advances in medical treatment and care. This change will present challenges to both caregivers and policymakers (Drew & Hardman, 2007).

Severity Unspecified

The diagnosis of intellectual disability, severity unspecified is used when there is a strong certainty of intellectual disability but the person cannot be tested by available methods such as standardized intelligence tests (*DSM-IV-TR*; APA, 2000). An example of persons with intellectual disabilities in this category would be those too limited or unaware to be assessed, or an infant who cannot be tested by available psychometric tests such as the Bayley Scales of Infant Development or Cattell Infant Intelligence Scales. As a rule, the younger the age, the more difficult it is to assess intellectual disabilities with the exception of those with profound impairments.

CAUSES OF INTELLECTUAL DISABILITIES

The AAIDD 2002 etiology classification comprises four risk factors (biomedical, social, behavioral, and educational) spread over three time periods: prenatal (before birth), perinatal (during birth), and postnatal (after birth). Biomedical factors refer to biological conditions such as poor nutrition and genetic disorders, while social factors may include lack of environmental stimulation. An example of behavioral factors would include maternal drug or alcohol abuse; educational factors refer to the quality of educational opportunities available and development of adaptive skill (AAIDD, 2002; Jones, 1996).

The time before and shortly after birth is extremely critical to the health and well-being of a child. It is perhaps astonishing that most infants emerge into the world with no serious disabilities. Intellectual disabilities may be caused by a number of conditions that can damage the brain before birth, during birth, or during childhood. Over 300 causes have been identified, but in about 30–40% of cases, the **etiology** cannot be determined (*DSM-IV-TR*; APA, 2000). The three major causes of intellectual disabilities are **Down syndrome, fetal alcohol syndrome,** and **Fragile X syndrome** (Brown & Percy, 2007). As much as we know about ID, it can still be difficult to ascertain the exact cause and it is not unusual to see the cause of ID listed as *multiple congenital anomalies, etiology unknown.*

Etiology can be categorized as follows:

Prenatal causes: Chromosomal abnormalities and genetic errors are genetic disorders that cause intellectual disabilities. Disorders such as Down syndrome or Fragile X syndrome are caused by changes in the number or structure of specific chromosomes. Phenylketonuria (PKU) is a genetic metabolic disorder that causes severe brain damage due to the body's inability to break down a chemical called phenylalanine. A special diet started soon after birth will effectively prevent intellectual disabilities caused by PKU. Rubella and syphilis are examples of infections that can damage the brain and central nervous system of an unborn child. Drugs or toxic substances, such as tobacco, alcohol, or cocaine, ingested by a pregnant woman can lead to mental deficiency in her child. Other disorders in this category include tumors of the brain, the central or peripheral nervous system, or other organ systems. These conditions, many of which are hereditary, manifest in the postnatal period. Intellectual disabilities can also be caused by the failure of the mother to maintain a balanced diet during pregnancy or have adequate access to prenatal health care.

Perinatal causes: Most any unusual stress or birth trauma during birth, such as deprivation of oxygen (anoxia), may injure the infant's brain. Prematurity and low or excessive birth weight are additional examples of conditions that can cause delayed cognitive development at birth. Teenagers, women over the age of 35, undernourished or obese women, and women with diabetes or a history of genetic disorders have a higher risk of bearing a child with a gestational disorder. Prematurity and low birth weight, more than any other condition, are the leading predictors of serious health problems.

Postnatal causes: Common diseases of childhood, including whooping cough, chicken pox, and measles, can, in a small number of cases, lead to

meningitis and **encephalitis**, which can cause intellectual disabilities. Other postnatal factors such as a blow to the head; near drowning; or ingestion of lead, mercury, or other poisonous substances can lead to damage to the brain and nervous system. It has been estimated that most intellectual disabilities with a known cause are due to adverse social, environmental, and economic conditions. Numerous studies have confirmed the connection between poverty and intellectual disabilities. Poor living conditions, malnutrition, inadequate prenatal and postnatal health care, and dysfunctional family situations have all been linked to mental deficiency (Drew & Hardman, 2007; Harris, 2006).

In recent years, great strides have been made in the reduction of the number of cases of intellectual disabilities through improved prenatal care. Almost 98% of babies born after the 32nd week of gestation survive, and it is now possible to estimate the physical maturation of a newborn infant. This is important because care and any needed treatment can be administered early, which has dramatically reduced infant mortality in the United States (Drew & Hardman, 2007).

PREVENTION OF INTELLECTUAL DISABILITIES

Through basic and applied research, advances have been made in the prevention of intellectual disabilities, identification of genetic markers, and metabolic testing. As much progress as there has been, much remains to be discovered. We will briefly examine progress in the three categories of prevention: primary, secondary, and tertiary.

Primary Prevention

Specific prenatal care strategies reduce the risk of giving birth to a child with intellectual disabilities. Proper prenatal care, which begins before pregnancy, is the best method of reducing that risk. The prospective mother should refrain from consuming alcohol, tobacco, drugs, and other toxic substances. Chronic medical conditions, such as diabetes, heart disease, and high blood pressure, also present a potential danger to the fetus. Such conditions should be monitored throughout pregnancy.

Teenage mothers, women over the age of 35, and mothers who have given birth multiple times are also considered at high risk, because they have a higher than normal probability of giving birth to a low-birth-weight infant. Babies weighing less than 1,500 grams have a high mortality rate, and those children who survive are more likely to be intellectually disabled. Proper nutrition plays a major role in reducing the number of premature and underweight infants born to women of all ages. This, in turn, can help to reduce the number of children born with intellectual disabilities and other disabling conditions (Drew, Hardman, & Logan, 1996; World Health Organization, 2007).

Secondary Prevention

Secondary prevention is based on identifying potential parents with a high probability of having a child with intellectual disabilities. Recent advances in prenatal diagnostic techniques, such as amniocentesis and ultrasound, have made it possible to detect **genetic abnormalities, metabolic errors,** and **inherited conditions** that might lead to intellectual disabilities.

Testing for prenatal birth defects is justified under the following circumstances: advanced age of the mother or father (35 and 55, respectively), a family history of an inherited disorder (such as Down syndrome or Fragile X syndrome), a record of miscarriage or infertility, a history of inborn malformations in the parents or a previous child, a chronic medical condition in the mother that requires medication or x-ray treatment, or parents who are close biological relatives.

The sophistication in prenatal diagnosis and treatment techniques continues to grow. In the future, increasingly advanced intrauterine surgical techniques to reduce the problems related to **hydrocephaly** and **spina bifida**, modification in the mother's diet to reduce the baby's probability of metabolic disorders, and drugs that positively influence fetal development will decrease the birthrate of infants with intellectual disabilities (World Health Organization, 2007).

Tertiary Prevention

Tertiary prevention seeks to minimize the long-term effects of intellectual disabilities in children. Research has indicated that infant stimulation programs and early education programs have helped children with intellectual disabilities achieve gains in communication skills, social abilities, and academic competence. Due to the overwhelming evidence in favor of early intervention for intellectual disabilities, federal legislation requires educational services for children with disabilities between the ages of 3 and 5. There are also financial provisions in this legislation to assist families in providing services for their disabled children as young as 1 day old. These and other programs, such as the interdisciplinary programs of the University Affiliated Facilities and Head Start, are crucial in minimizing the effects of intellectual disabilities and maximizing each individual's potential (World Health Organization, 2007).

Although important research into the prevention of intellectual disabilities continues at the primary, secondary, and tertiary levels, progress is slow. There is still much to be learned before we can assure the birth of a healthy child.

DEVELOPMENTAL PROFILES OF PERSONS WITH INTELLECTUAL DISABILITIES

Just as the general population displays individual variations in the developmental timetable, so does the population with intellectual disabilities. However, there are similarities among individuals who are intellectually disabled in the way they develop language skills, adapt socially and emotionally, acquire physical skills, and process information. In this section, we will examine some of these characteristics (Drew & Hardman, 2007).

Cognitive Development

Limited cognitive ability is the most evident characteristic of children with intellectual disabilities. Basically, they learn in the same developmental sequence as their peers without disabilities, except at a slower pace with less retention of information. Rate of information acquisition and retention is related to the severity of intellectual disability. Individuals with severe and profound intellectual disabilities acquire and retain less information than their peers with mild and moderate intellectual disabilities. Other learning characteristics include a short attention span, difficulty in using abstract concepts, and problems generalizing information to other settings (Westling & Fox, 2004).

How do persons with intellectual disabilities think and process information? It is not enough to know what their learning difficulties are. We must also have an awareness of how they think, because it affects the teaching strategies used in the classroom and in therapy sessions. Information processing can be divided into three operations:

Reception: The perception of a visual, aural, or other sensory stimulus.

Central Processing: The categorization of the incoming stimuli using memory, reasoning, and evaluation.

Expression: The ability to select an appropriate response to the incoming stimuli from a variety of choices.

These operations are controlled by **executive function**, which is the process governing the moment-to-moment decisions that a person makes each day. Each decision is based on several factors, including the information received from a stimulus (reception), the ability to classify the stimulus (central processing), and, finally, the choice of response from an assortment of possibilities (expression). Expression leads to feedback for the individual from the initial stimulus. The information provided by the feedback becomes the new stimulus, to which the person then reacts by reapplying the three information processing steps.

The following example will help clarify how the information processing model works. A young girl is walking down the sidewalk. A man approaching from the other direction is the stimulus. She becomes aware of the man's presence (reception). The girl does not recognize the man. She remembers that her parents and teachers have urged her to be cautious around strangers (central processing). The girl's behavioral choices include walking away from the man, walking toward him to speak with him, or ignoring him. She decides to walk away from the man (expression).

This model can be used to identify cognitive problems in adults and children with intellectual disabilities. Cognitive deficits can occur in any or all of the three stages of information processing or in the executive function process. People with intellectual disabilities are often unable to attend to relevant stimuli, organize information, and choose an appropriate response. For example, if a girl with intellectual disabilities were in the situation described above, she might not remember what her teachers and parents have told her about talking to strangers and therefore might not exercise due caution. Thus, her ability to make the best decision might be compromised due to her intellectual disability.

Another cognitive problem experienced by persons with intellectual disabilities is the inability to accurately categorize information. For example, most 10-year-old children have little difficulty classifying eagles, robins, and sparrows as birds, whereas Colin, our 10-year-old boy with intellectual disabilities introduced at the beginning of this chapter, has difficulty making those distinctions.

Individuals with intellectual disabilities often have difficulty retaining information, which interferes with generalization, the ability to take information learned in one setting (such as a classroom) and apply it to a different setting (the home). Teachers, parents, and therapists must work closely together on similar goals and approaches so the client has a chance to practice what he or she has learned in a variety of situations.

Language Acquisition

The ability to use language effectively is vital for success in our complex society. For adults and children with intellectual disabilities, the characteristic delay in language development is perhaps the most incapacitating and often frustrating aspect of the disability (Thomas, 1996).

Most researchers agree that the rate and quality of language acquisition is dependent upon cognitive development. As you have learned, cognitive ability develops slowly in individuals with intellectual disabilities, which, in turn, impedes the development of language (Kirk, Gallagher, Anastasiow, & Coleman, 2005).

In most children, the preverbal forms of communication (babbling, cooing) are replaced by two- or three-word phrases by the 20th month of life. By the beginning of the third year, pronouns are incorporated into the child's speech, and by the age of 4, most children are able to ask questions, manipulate words, and, in general (many parents would agree!), talk incessantly. At age 5, meandering speech patterns have been replaced by more concise language skills (Baroff, 1986).

Children with intellectual disabilities follow the normal sequence of language development but generally exhibit lags in language acquisition based upon the severity of impairment. Individuals with severe and profound intellectual disabilities have much more difficulty developing language skills than do their peers with mild and moderate intellectual disabilities.

People with intellectual disabilities nearly always exhibit some difficulties with language. As mentioned above, language deficits hamper cognitive, social, and emotional growth. Even a child with mild intellectual disabilities exhibits language patterns markedly different from those exhibited by a peer. Quantity is diminished, content is deficient, and language structure is rudimentary. As the severity of disability increases, language development is even more impaired due to the potential of neurological damage to the language areas of the brain. Such impairment makes speech highly unlikely for some individuals. Other conditions can also negatively influence language development. Children with Down syndrome, for example, have a high incidence of mild hearing loss that is difficult to detect but can contribute to delayed language skills (Kirk et al., 2005). Also, because of the shape of their mouth and tongue, articulation, pronunciation, and clarity of words can be daunting.

Physical and Motor Development

Most children with intellectual disabilities exhibit challenges with physical fitness, gross and fine motor control, agility, posture, endurance, and stamina. Conditions that frequently accompany intellectual disabilities, such as cerebral palsy, spina bifida, and epilepsy, can also hinder or even prohibit development of physical and motor skills.

Studies have shown that persons with intellectual disabilities perform at a level lower than that of their peers on physical tasks requiring strength, endurance, coordination, running speed, flexibility, and reaction time (Kirk et al., 2005). Their average rate of achievement is two to four years behind, but some persons with mild and moderate intellectual disabilities perform at a level comparable to their age-mates without disabilities.

It has been suggested that many of the problems in motor performance experienced by children with mild and moderate intellectual disabilities might be due to a lack of problem-solving skills and failure to understand the assignment, both cognitive tasks, rather than inherent deficits in motor planning and execution.

In addition, individuals with severe and profound intellectual disabilities frequently have damage to the motor cortex and spinal column (Drew & Hardman, 2007).

Certain groups of adults and children, such as those with Down syndrome, exhibit unique physical problems. Many are short and obese and often exhibit **hypotonia** or lack of muscle tone. Frequent respiratory infections, heart defects, and a type of misalignment of the upper spinal column called **atlantoaxial instability** are also common among this population. The therapist or teacher must be aware of the presence of these medical conditions and make appropriate adjustments (Brown & Percy, 2007).

Social and Emotional Characteristics

Adults and children with intellectual disabilities often display maladaptive behaviors that interfere with learning and interacting appropriately. Some behaviors, such as short attention span, low frustration tolerance, hyperactivity, aggressive behavior, and **self-injurious behavior**, can result from the person's frustrations at lack of success in the classroom and in other settings rather than from the intellectual disability. Other problems arise from relationships with classroom peers. The development of self-esteem and social patterns occurs during a child's early years through play behavior. A child with intellectual disabilities may be avoided by peers, or because of limited cognitive ability may demonstrate less interest in play. The resulting lack of experience and quality interaction with role models can contribute to poor self-esteem. In addition, a delay in language acquisition significantly interferes with social adaptation (Drew & Hardman, 2007; Jones, 1996).

The environment also influences social skills development. Many adults and children with intellectual disabilities who years ago used to reside in residential facilities may display maladaptive behaviors, perhaps from a combination of inadequate attention, poor training, and stress due to lack of privacy. A trend toward deinstitutionalization of persons with intellectual disabilities began during the late 1960s and continues throughout the world today. Many residents moved out of large state-supported institutions into small group homes, often located in residential areas. Usually housing no more than eight residents per home, these facilities seek to provide a more normalized setting in which to learn the skills necessary to function at school, in a work setting, and in the community. In many cases, especially for residents with mild and moderate intellectual disabilities, these homes have positively influenced self-esteem by reducing failure; providing positive, consistent role models; and creating a more homelike environment (Baroff, 1986; Dunn & Fait, 1989; Kirk et al., 2005). At the same time, larger residential facilities are also changing and becoming more homelike. Extensive physical plant remodeling has transformed what used to be called *wards* into more contemporary, comfortable, private, and homelike atmospheres called *apartments* (Central Wisconsin Center for People with Developmental Disabilities, 2004).

EDUCATIONAL PLACEMENT OF PERSONS WITH INTELLECTUAL DISABILITIES

Until the passage of **PL 94-142** (Education for All Handicapped Children Act) in 1975, children with intellectual disabilities were usually educated in an environment segregated from nondisabled peers, often in institutional settings. The 1975 law was the result of years of litigation dealing with discrimination against children with disabilities. For the first time in United States history, all school-age children were entitled to a free and appropriate education. In 1990, Congress passed PL 101-476, the **Individuals with Disabilities Education Act (IDEA)**, which strengthened the earlier law. Specifically, IDEA requires:

- Nondiscriminatory and **multidisciplinary assessment**
- An **individualized education program** (IEP)
- Parental involvement
- Education in the **least restrictive environment**

The role of the Individualized Education Program (IEP) in a disabled child's rehabilitation program is extremely important. IDEA mandates that an individual program plan be developed for every disabled child (including all children with intellectual disabilities) enrolled in a public school. This written plan includes an assessment of the child's strengths and areas of need, concrete goals and objectives, the names of the people administering the program, and a process for evaluation. The classroom placement of a student with intellectual disabilities depends primarily on his or her level of cognitive and social functioning, sometimes referred to as the functional or behavioral age. For example, our 10-year-old Colin is assessed as functioning at a 5.7-year-old level. Some children with mildly and moderately intellectual disabilities are mainstreamed into regular classrooms with their normal peers, but they may require special services. Frequently, remedial help is provided for reading, math, speech, motor development, and psychological needs. This assistance is usually provided in a special resource room, which is staffed and equipped to help students with intellectual disabilities with their particular difficulties (Thomas, 1996).

More students with severe disabilities also attend public schools but are assigned full-time to a special classroom designed for their more complex needs. A specially trained teacher and assistants usually work with small groups of students on pre-academic skills, personal grooming, safety, and social skills.

Education in a residential facility is reserved for those who need a more highly structured setting, including many children with severe and profound intellectual disabilities as well as students with mild and moderate intellectual disabilities with severe emotional or behavioral disturbances. Students in this setting learn personal care skills, such as eating, dressing, hygiene, safety, and fundamental communication. (For a more complete discussion on legislation directed at the education of all children with disabilities, please refer to Chapter 14.)

EDUCATIONAL STRATEGIES USED WITH PERSONS WHO HAVE INTELLECTUAL DISABILITIES

According to Kirk et al. (2005), one of the most important educational goals for a student with intellectual disabilities is to change or replace behaviors that interfere with the learning process and social skill development. It is not surprising, therefore, that schools stress the acquisition of social skills. Three other areas are important in instructional programs for children with mild and moderate intellectual disabilities: (1) academic skills (reading, writing, and math); (2) communication skills (verbal and, if indicated, nonverbal techniques, such as signing and use of assisted technology); and (3) prevocational and vocational training (cooperation, on-task behavior, promptness, dependability, and specific job skills). Achieving social competence is also the primary functional objective for students with severe and profound intellectual disabilities. Other goals usually focus on communication, safety, and personal grooming skills. Music therapy can play an important role in improving the lives of adults and children with intellectual disabilities. Let us now turn our attention to music therapy used with this population.

MUSIC THERAPY FOR PERSONS WITH INTELLECTUAL DISABILITIES

In the United States, the use of music therapy in the treatment of persons with intellectual disabilities dates back to the middle of the 19th century. During this time, a few private and public schools used pianos, guitars, and rhythm instruments to assist in the development of language, motor skills, and social competence. Public training schools for the "feebleminded" in Massachusetts, Illinois, Pennsylvania, Ohio, and Kentucky included music as an integral element of their curriculum. Private facilities, most of which were located in urban areas on the East Coast, were attended by the few children whose parents could afford specialized training (Kraft, 1963). In the late 1800s in the Midwest, state-run residential facilities focused on a more rural setting and a farm-like atmosphere for the benefits of fresh air and vocational skill development (Northern Wisconsin Center, 2007).

By the turn of the 20th century, some state institutions were becoming overcrowded. Persons with intellectual disabilities lived a less than full life and the

medical model of treatment prevailed. Conditions, awareness, and policy gradually improved over the years, and by the 1950s, the use of music therapy with clients who have intellectual disabilities was regularly reported in the literature (Brewer, 1955; Isern, 1959; Loven, 1957; Peterson, 1952; Wendelin, 1953). Music therapists noted that music elicited affective (emotional) responses and improved memory, communication, and social and motor skills, even in the individuals with the most complex conditions and needs.

The decade of the 1960s brought about significant improvements in the treatment of adults and children with intellectual disabilities. First, a shift in government policy led to increased funding for state residential facilities. New programs were developed to teach residents personal care, and social, motor, and language skills. Music therapy became an integral part of many residential treatment programs during this time. Second, the quantity and quality of music therapy research literature improved, which further strengthened the rationale for its inclusion in treatment programs (Reynolds, 1982). Third, the medical model of intellectual disability, which viewed the condition as a disease without a cure, was gradually replaced with a developmental model emphasizing the acquisition of social, pre-academic and academic, motor, and language skills (Coates, 1987). Music therapy was considered an important service to enhance the developmental process and expand functional life skills.

Until 1975, most children with intellectual disabilities lived in residential facilities, which provided for their educational as well as other needs. However, a few public school classrooms offered music and other special services to other students with disabilities. Unfortunately, these students were segregated from their nondisabled peers and achieved minimal academic progress. Passage of the Education for All Handicapped Children Act (PL 94-142) in 1975 dramatically changed the educational process of children with disabilities between the ages of 3 and 21. Many children previously placed in residential facilities were now placed in foster homes, in small group homes, or back with their biological parents (Coates, 1987). In addition to opening new doors for individuals with intellectual disabilities, the law provided new employment opportunities for music therapists.

For many years, music therapists have observed that adults and children with intellectual disabilities often respond more positively to music than to other educational and therapeutic strategies (Atterbury, 1990; Boxhill, 1985; Farnan, 2007; Howery, 1968; Lathom, 1980). Today, 13% of all music therapists work with persons who have developmental disabilities, including intellectual disabilities, in such settings as residential institutions, intermediate care facilities, public and private schools, and private practice (American Music Therapy Association, 2007).

The term *Active Treatment* is a useful concept from Title XIX, an important piece of federal legislation passed in 1970, and is pertinent to how music therapists practice. The federal standard for Active Treatment states that programs for persons with disabilities must be directed toward "(a) the acquisition of the behaviors necessary for the client to function with as much self-determination and independence as possible; and (b) the prevention or the deceleration of regression or loss of current optimal functional status" (State of Wisconsin Department of Health and Family Services, 1989, p. 43).

Recall our earlier discussion about typical areas of need in adults and children who have ID. Depending on level of severity, the person with intellectual disabilities may need help with communication skills, cognitive development, and motor development, or with improving social skills. As music therapists and members of an interdisciplinary team, we use our therapeutic and musical abilities to help the individual with ID meet the goals outlined by Title XIX.

MUSIC THERAPY TREATMENT GOALS FOR PERSONS WHO HAVE INTELLECTUAL DISABILITIES

Music therapy goals for adults and children with intellectual disabilities can be grouped into six categories: (1) as a strategy for developing social and emotional behavior, (2) as a means of developing motor skills, (3) as a tool for developing communication abilities, (4) as an aid in developing pre-academic skills, (5) as a tool to develop academic skills, and (6) as a strategy to develop leisure skills (Atterbury, 1990; Boxhill, 1985; Carter, 1982; Coates, 1987; DeBout & Worden, 2006; Farnan, 2007; Graham & Beer, 1980; Lathom, 1980; Michel, 1979). Because the needs of persons with intellectual disabilities vary, treatment strategies must be individualized, even though most music therapy occurs in groups.

Music Therapy for Development of Social and Emotional Behaviors

Adults and children with ID often have problems acquiring effective and appropriate social skills. Structured therapeutic music interventions that incorporate movement, songs, and rhythmic activities provide a stimulating environment in which social behaviors can be practiced and learned. Because of the group nature of music therapy sessions, experiences can be structured to promote cooperation, sharing, taking turns, and learning appropriate ways to greet people. For example, a "hello song" teaches names of group members, a proper greeting (e.g., shaking hands), and taking turns. The pleasure of participating in musical activities is a powerful reinforcer and usually captures the client's attention and cooperation.

Interfering behaviors, such as talking out-of-turn, verbal or physical aggression, and out-of-seat behavior, can sometimes be a problem for many persons with intellectual disabilities. Because participating in music therapy is enjoyable for most participants, inappropriate behaviors can often be reduced, replaced, or even completely eliminated. A skilled music therapist combines a pleasurable music activity, such as performing on instruments, listening or moving to music, singing, or creating music, with positive reinforcement to increase cooperative behavior (Lathom, 1980). It is important to keep in mind that most behaviors that might be considered inappropriate are actually an attempt to communicate needs. If a certain behavior is to be reduced, then another behavior must be offered as replacement (Farnan, 2007). The following example illustrates the use of playing instruments as a replacement behavior for self-injurious hand biting.

> Let's explore involvement in active music therapy for Melissa, a 23-year-old young woman. She is classified as having severe to profound intellectual disabilities caused by anoxia (lack of oxygen) during a complicated delivery. Melissa is currently living in a group home and has recently graduated from a high school special education program. Since aging out of educational services at 21, she has become more self-abusive. When she is asked by staff to do something, she screams and bites her right hand, causing self-injury. The staff at the group home has tried various approaches with Melissa, but she seems to be the most content when in her room listening to the Beatles through her headphones. Her father used to listen to recordings with her when she lived at home and they would sing together; this was an enjoyable activity for both father and daughter and is an activity that continues to be pleasurable for Melissa. Melissa's current case manager has asked that she be referred to an inpatient 28-day assessment program at a well respected residential facility. While she is in this short-term program, she will be seen by an interdisciplinary team comprised of a physician; psychologist; pharmacist; psychiatrist; dentist; dietician; and recreation, occupational, physical, speech, and music therapists. While all of these disciplines will meet and work as a team to develop the best person-centered plan for Melissa, our focus will be on what the music therapist would do in the assessment sessions and what recommendations could be made to improve the quality of life for Melissa.

> In reading through the admission summary, the music therapist takes note that Melissa has some limited expressive speech and is reported to be able to sing on pitch. The music therapist will seek to identify what causes Melissa stress and what the behavior of hand-biting and screaming is trying to communicate, and will then make suggestions for replacement behaviors.

Table 1 provides a sample of what an initial assessment session might look like.

Table 1
Music Therapy Session Plan with Melissa

Outline	Procedure
Opening	Sing "Hello, Goodbye" by the Beatles and shake hands with Melissa while welcoming her to music. Encourage her singing.
Open hand drum with tubanos	Therapist will ask Melissa to either look at, touch, or point to which drum she would like. Therapist will start a slow, steady, quiet beat and invite Melissa to join in on her drum.
Drumming as replacement behavior for inappropriate self hand-biting	Therapist will praise Melissa for using her hands in such a good way. If Melissa becomes upset, ask her if she is finished and remove the drum.
Expression of choices	Offer Melissa a choice of two different instruments. After she has communicated her choice, improvise a simple song with positive lyrics about Melissa and good use of her hands.
Movement experiences	Present Melissa with a colorful cord or stretch cloth that will allow her to hold on to part of it and get into a movement exchange with the therapist. Use "Blackbird" or "Good Day Sunshine" by the Beatles as background music and to structure the movements. Praise Melissa for doing such good things with her hands. Encourage singing.
Foreshadow the next transition for Melissa	In the closing song, sing a few phrases reflecting the positive things Melissa has done and then alert her to where she is going next in her day to help her accommodate to the transition without becoming upset.
Closing	Thank Melissa for coming and participating and use a therapist-composed song for her to sing the word "bye" at the end of the phrase.

In this example, the music therapist would not write specific objectives for Melissa (for more information on writing goals and objectives, refer to Chapter 15), but rather offer recommendations to the staff when she returns to her group living setting. Along with a report that details the content and material used in the music therapy session, the following recommendations were suggested to help Melissa:

1. Melissa appears to be able to better self-regulate her anxiety and behavior when the situations focus on her positive abilities. Find the things she does well and praise her for a job well done.

2. She becomes increasingly more anxious and self-injurious behaviors escalate if she is requested to do something new or asked to speed up a response. She seems to do better when given time to complete a task.

3. Involve Melissa in Very Special Arts in her community. [Very Special Arts recently changed their name to VSA arts, which stands for *Vision of an inclusive society*, *Strength of shared resources, and Access to artistic expression that unites us all*.] VSA offers group music sessions that she might enjoy, and instrument play would provide a replacement behavior for self-biting. It would also allow Melissa to meet other people of her own age and abilities, providing a social opportunity that has been lacking since finishing high school.

Music Therapy for Development of Motor Skills

The development of motor skills is highly correlated with learning (Boxhill, 1985; Cratty, 1974). Music, because it is time-ordered (must be continued without interruption to complete an idea), is an ideal stimulus to help coordinate movement. All movements involve the central nervous system, which arouses and controls muscular activity. This highly complex system is immature at birth. In many infants, it matures rapidly, and by the age of 6, most children are capable of complex motor skills, such as hopping, galloping, and skipping. In individuals with intellectual disabilities, however, the central nervous system develops slowly or incompletely. Voluntary control of movement can be difficult or impossible. Movement activities allow participants to explore the environment, and development of motor skills creates a foundation for learning. Music and movement activities, therefore, are a vital part of a music therapy program for persons with intellectual disabilities.

Individuals with intellectual disabilities who have mild or moderate needs can generally learn complex gross and fine motor skills, although at a less sophisticated level than their nondisabled peers. Adults and children with severe and profound needs, on the other hand, usually have difficulty coordinating even basic movements, due to physical and cognitive limitations. Nonetheless, music therapy experiences that promote movement enable these individuals to interact more fully within the environment. Movement therapeutic music experiences can range from very simple tasks, such as nodding the head or tapping a foot to a simple beat, to complex motor tasks, like the steps of an intricate folk dance (Lathom, 1980).

The rhythmic element of music provides structure and motivation for helping clients learn to walk, run, hop, skip, and gallop. In turn, these skills are associated with improvements in body image, balance, locomotion, agility, flexibility, strength, laterality (side-to-side movement), directionality (up/down, right/left, back/forth movement), and general learning. Initially, attempts to move rhythmically are more important than successes. As the participant becomes more comfortable with movement, the therapist encourages him or her to coordinate movements with the music. Gross motor activities, such as folk dancing, strengthen large muscles and help to develop coordination, agility, and balance. Instrumental activities, such as playing the piano, guitar, or autoharp, promote fine motor control, which can contribute to improvements in such activities as writing and drawing (Boxhill, 1985; Farnan, 2007; Lathom, 1980; Moore & Mathenius, 1987).

> *Paul is a 45-year-old man with Down syndrome, described as having mild intellectual disabilities. He has put on weight and his knees are causing him enough pain that he is resisting getting out of his chair and not engaging in activities that he used to enjoy. He now lives at home with his 70-year-old mother. He attends a vocational workshop but now is becoming more reluctant to leave the house to go to work and is in danger of losing his job. He has started to use a walker that seems to help his mobility, and he loves to sing. His mother thinks maybe music therapy could help him become more active again. What could the music therapist do?*

> *After meeting Paul and being granted approval to read his medical records, Michelle, his music therapist, realizes that the extra weight is causing his knee strain. Fortunately, there is nothing structurally wrong with his knees, so Michelle can include recommendations for treatment from the physical therapist. She decides to begin in-home sessions designed to help Paul become more active, burn calories, build endurance, and strengthen leg muscles. The music therapist's goal is to help Paul do the types of activities he used enjoy by improving his mobility and encouraging him to return to a more regular routine and break out of his cycle of isolation. Therapeutic music interventions using a strong rhythmic component are the most powerful tool that Michelle can offer Paul in this situation. The rhythmic element of music provides structure, motivation, and timing and will assist Paul to walk better.*

Table 2 on the following page shows an example of an individual music therapy session plan for Paul.

Table 2
Music Therapy Session Plan with Paul

Outline	Procedure
Opening	Gentle stretching and warm-ups with recorded music Paul likes. Ask Paul to suggest arm and hand movements.
Upper extremity focus	Therapist and Paul reach together with a stretch band while singing on a neutral syllable to build Paul's endurance and deep breathing.
Upper extremity fine motor focus	Paul selects three hand-held instruments. Therapist and Paul reach up to shake and play with the series of instruments.
Lower extremity focus	Warm up ankles and feet with rhythmic music Paul has selected.
Lower extremity strengthening	While seated in a chair, therapist and Paul kick to the beat of a drum.
Active gross motor	Therapist and Paul stand up and sit down to the beat of the music.
Ambulation practice	Paul uses a drum to beat out his steps across the room: rest – return – repeat.
Cool down	Return to deep breaths and stretching with the instrumental music.
Carry over	Paul promises to do this plan on his own with his music. His mother and he will keep a chart on Paul's progress to show the therapist at the next session.

Music Therapy for Development of Communication Skills

Speech and language are all part of a larger communication system that includes facial expressions, gestures, words, and movements to help express our ideas to others. We seek out many methods to get our point across, and individuals with ID are no different. Adults and children with ID employ a combination of modes of communication to express their needs. If a person is nonverbal, there are picture signs, words, phrases, and automated talkers that can give voice to their ideas. If a person is verbal, sometimes clear articulation for understandable speech can be a challenge but should be encouraged.

Speech and language have two distinct aspects, which include receptive language and expressive language. Receptive language abilities are the skills one uses to receive the message, process it, and understand what was said. Expressive language abilities are the skills used to communicate needs, wants, and ideas to others. A person with ID may have great receptive language (understanding) but little expressive language (speaking) or may exhibit problems in both areas. Think of it like an audio system with the in/out signal. One line can be working, while the other line is disconnected or loose.

As we learned earlier, one of the most incapacitating problems for a person with intellectual disabilities is the limited ability to communicate. Whereas an adult or child with moderate or mild needs will likely develop functional speech, persons with severe/profound disabilities must develop nonverbal means of communication, such as basic sign language, a communication board with pictures of important objects in the environment, or assistive technology such as voice output communication aids and synthesized speech (Atterbury, 1990; Carey, Friedman, & Bryen, 2005; DeBout & Worden, 2006; Carey, Friedman & Bryan, 2005). Music is an ideal tool for teaching communication skills, because the therapist can use melody, rhythm, tempo, pitch, dynamics, and lyrics to develop expressive language, receptive language, and the capability to follow directions. In addition, therapeutic music experiences can help improve vocal range, pitch discrimination, articulation, and vocal quality (Boxhill, 1985; Farnan, 2007; Grant, 1989).

Auditory awareness, or the perception of sounds in the environment, is a necessary skill for language comprehension. Individuals with intellectual disabilities often lack the ability to distinguish between meaningful and irrelevant aural stimuli; thus, they are unable to grasp the communicated message. The music therapist can help "fine-tune" the auditory system by devising music attention control exercises for tracking, locating, identifying, and discriminating among sounds (Grant, 1989; Lathom, 1980; Thaut, 2005).

A music therapy session should include many language experiences, by using age-appropriate songs with some repetition of melodies and lyrics (to help our clients remember important material), and by emphasizing the important words in each song. It is important for the therapist to speak clearly, use facial expressions and simple sentences, and allow the person a sufficient length of time to respond (Farnan, 2007; Lathom, 1980). To further enhance learning, the use of visual cues is recommended. For example, songs about Thanksgiving can include pictures of a turkey, Pilgrims, Native Americans, and other appropriate symbols.

> *Eric is an 8-year-old boy who has been classified as having severe intellectual disabilities due to inadequate prenatal care available to his mother during her pregnancy. He lives in an apartment with his single mother and his grandmother, who is his primary caregiver. Eric attends an after-school music therapy group at a nearby clinic with other similar children. Eric has some degree of receptive language as exhibited by looking and smiling when he hears his name and by following simple directions. He demonstrates some degree of expressive communication through his*

facial expressions, gestures, and a few words (yes, no, stay, go, done, etc.). Currently, he speaks in one-word responses and does not sequence words to form a sentence. At the music therapy clinic, his group is working on a choir performance for an upcoming community festival.

Table 3 provides a sample session plan to help improve Eric's communication.

Table 3
Group Music Therapy Session Plan

Outline	Procedure
Opening	Therapist leads group to sing a fill-in-the-blank song saying or waving "Hello" and naming each of the children in the group.
Vocal warm-ups	Therapist leads children to sing triads up and down on a neutral syllable, emphasizing and demonstrating breath support.
Articulation exercise	Therapist leads children to sing triads and articulate consonants using m/t/v/b/s, etc., emphasizing and demonstrating articulation and pronunciation.
Song practice	Therapist has written several different songs for the children using a narrow pitch range, rhythms that match the words, and predicable lyrics that repeat using specific proficiency words: *yes, no, no thank you, go, stay, more, done, stop, happy, sad, mad,* etc.
Closing	Therapist leads song that has a fill-in-the-blank for good-bye.

When using the microphone during the "I want to say Yes!" song, Eric has learned to articulate an audible "yes" at the appropriate time in the song. This is an important step for Eric, because he is beginning to use expressive language for the first time in his life and is ready to take the next step by learning to use two-word phrases.

Music Therapy for Development of Pre-Academic Skills

Certain behaviors must be present before learning can take place, including a sufficient attention span, the ability to follow directions, and eye contact. We will examine how music can be helpful in developing these fundamental skills, often impaired in individuals with intellectual disabilities.

Attention. Many adults and children with intellectual disabilities have difficulty focusing on a simple task, due to the challenges they experience in filtering out irrelevant stimuli and attending to important directions (Harris, 2006). Using aural, visual, tactile, and other sensory cues, the therapist can help improve the attention of these learners by providing structure and motivation. For example, a group therapeutic music experience may require a client to wait for a musical cue, such as the beat of a drum, before playing his or her part. The success of the activity will depend, in part, on the ability to play at the right time. The therapist can increase sustained attention by gradually lengthening the client's waiting time (Atterbury, 1990).

Following directions. Effective learning requires the ability to follow simple requests. Activities to develop this skill focus on sequencing directions into one-, two-, or three-step requests. For example, a client first learns to follow one-step directions, such as, "Stand up." Once proficient, a two-step sequence is introduced, such as, "Stand up, then pick up the tambourine." An example of a three-step direction is, "Stand up, pick up the tambourine, and give it to Raphael." Music activities with directions in the lyrics are effective in helping clients to learn a sequence of directions.

Eye contact. The inability to initiate and maintain eye contact interferes with the development of attention span and the ability to communicate. Many important messages are conveyed nonverbally and are therefore missed if eye contact has not been established (Lathom, 1980). Interesting therapeutic music experiences help the therapist obtain eye contact with the client. The duration of eye contact can then be systematically lengthened using behavior modification and other techniques. It is important to remember that eye contact is perceived in different ways by many cultures of the world. For example, in Tibetan culture, it is considered disrespectful for a student to look directly at a teacher or a person in authority. In Japanese culture, eye contact is avoided or not maintained as long as in Western societies because Japanese people may consider it impolite to sustain eye contact with someone of a higher social status. So becoming aware of and sensitive to the cultural background of the client is very important in designing effective and respectful interventions.

> Carlos is 13 and has a moderate intellectual disability with a diagnosis of Fragile X syndrome, the most common form of inherited intellectual disability. He lives at home with his mother, father, and two older siblings and attends a school full-time in his neighborhood. Carlos, like many children with this type of intellectual disability, has a diagnosis of attention deficit disorder, a common coexisting condition with Fragile X syndrome (Harris, 2006). He struggles in his integrated classroom (an educational setting that includes peers with intellectual disabilities and students who are nondisabled) to understand basic academic concepts such as colors and numbers, concepts that he is capable of learning when he is paying attention to his teacher. His school is fortunate in that it has a strong music therapy program that will assist Carlos to develop the pre-academic skills he will need to learn useful academic concepts. Tricia, the school music therapist, has been assigned to work with Carlos individually to improve attention

span and ability to follow directions. Tricia wisely decides to use Carlos' favorite instruments—hand drums and the Q-Chord (a type of electronic autoharp) in their music therapy sessions held three times per week. There will be two small group sessions and one individual 20-minute session each week.

The small group session example in Table 4 focuses on academic skills, impulse control, sustained attention, and listening skills for Carlos and three of his classmates.

Table 4
Small Group Music Therapy Session Plan with Carlos

Outline	Procedure
Opening	Echo opening song with an opportunity to insert individual names when the drum is passed to each participant.
Rules rap	Using the back beat of the Q-chord, the group chants out the "rules" for the session. *"We will wait, we will listen, we will share with each other!"*
Impulse control	Using the rhythm to help organize motor responses, the therapist starts the beat on the drum. When all the students are playing, she first chants, *"Get ready to listen and **stop**. Get ready to listen and **play**."* This is followed by each student taking a turn at the responsibility of the leadership position.
Play with colors	The therapist has selected groups of instruments the three different colors of the stop lights—red, yellow, and green. The "conductor" will hold up a matching colored card when that color is to play. After the students select their first instrument, the therapist will start a basic beat on the drum to add structure to the experience. The students will also state the color that has been shown. Colors will change as needed.
Counting is fun	Therapist and students sit in a small circle with a bucket filled with colored shaking eggs. As the therapist picks up one egg to pass around, the group sings, *"Here comes our number one egg!"* The egg goes around the circle to the other bucket and the group sings, *"There goes our number one egg."* This process goes on for different amounts of eggs each time.
Closing and self-affirmation	Therapist leads a song titled, *"Tell me one good thing you did today in Music Therapy!"* When it is the students' turn, they state something they did well in the session in the context of the lyrics.

Music Therapy for Development of Academic Skills

Therapeutic music experiences can be used to teach academic concepts, such as identifying colors and shapes (object classification); grouping objects by size, number, or attribute (seriation); learning up/down and in/out (spatial relationships); and recognizing the differences between first, second, and last (temporal relationships). As an illustration, colors can be taught through the use of different-colored instruments, and high/low can be conveyed with musical pitches (Gfeller, 1990).

Individuals with intellectual disabilities often have difficulty with short-term memory, the ability to recall information shortly after it has been presented. Music can help clients remember important academic information. For example, an enjoyable, familiar melody paired with learned information is an effective way to improve retention. Multisensory activities, which involve the presentation of material in two or more sensory modalities, also improve the ability to retain short-term information. For example, pictures of animals could be used with the song "Old MacDonald." In addition, music to enhance information retention needs frequent repetition and a relatively slow tempo.

> *Omar is 17 years old and has a severe intellectual disability due to unknown, unspecified causes. Like Carlos, he is enrolled in a school that provides educational support in an integrated classroom. Omar is working with Randy, the school's music therapist, to learn primary colors using songs written especially for him at his after-school program site. When the therapist sings "Where is the blue drum?" Omar is able to identify and tap the blue drum consistently (while ignoring the red and green drums), indicating that he has learned to recognize the color blue. He has also learned to identify red and green by the same method. Randy is now teaching Omar to recognize spatial relationships through enjoyable music experiences. By developing music and lyrics with specific music cues, he can help Omar learn the concepts of up and down by using high pitched sounds to represent up and lower pitches to designate the concept of down.*

Table 5 on the following page gives a sample music therapy session plan for Omar.

Table 5
Music Therapy Session Plan with Omar

Outline	Procedure
Opening	The therapist greets Omar with a handshake and a drum beat to get started.
Spatial concepts	The therapist and Omar work together on the song, "*Cool Guys Drum.*" The therapist has composed this song to allow Omar enough time to listen, observe, and match the movements of up and down with his arms as they play standing floor drums.
Musical cues for practical skill development	
Phone practice	Omar's aunt has programmed his home phone number into his simple cell phone. She wants him to learn to identify the number 5 to call home. The therapist has written a *"Dial 5 to stay alive"* song where Omar will touch a large number 5 on a touch talker button that will say, "5 will call home." The catchy rhythm of the song helps Omar to touch the switch in the song and associate the number 5 with reaching someone who can help him if he needs it. Later they will work together with the phone to practice this important skill.
Money management skills and learning to identify coins and currency.	The music therapist has found laminated and enlarged photos of quarters, dimes, and pennies and will be placing those photos on drums and tambourines for use with Omar. The therapist will also be composing a song that will allow Omar enough time to recognize pictures and make a response.
Closing	Randy and Omar high five to end the session.

Music Therapy for Development of Leisure Skills

Integrating persons with intellectual disabilities into community life by developing leisure skills has been an important goal since the implementation of deinstitutionalization more than 30 years ago (Harris, 2006). Music therapy can help individuals with intellectual disabilities to achieve this important but often overlooked goal. During the early years of community integration, clients learned to work in vocational settings (sometimes referred to as a sheltered workshop), interact in a socially appropriate manner, and care for their basic needs. However, many of these people had little knowledge about how to use their free time at the end of the workday, during weekends, and on holidays. Many newly deinstitutionalized people engaged in activities such as petty crimes or substance abuse, resulting in disciplinary action and possible placement in a more restrictive living environment (Mahon & Bullock, 1992; Mahon & Goatcher, 1999).

The music therapist can encourage the leisure time use of music in several ways. Clients such as Paul and Melissa, whom we met earlier in this chapter, can learn how to operate an audio system and how to purchase or use the library to borrow prerecorded music. Paul can join community music groups or attend concerts. Learning to play a musical instrument can be another means of leisure gratification (Coates, 1987; Howery, 1968). Additionally, the music therapist should become familiar with resources in the community where the person with intellectual disabilities will be living and make appropriate contacts for him or her. For example, is there a music teacher willing to provide piano or guitar lessons to a person like Paul? What types of concert opportunities are available? Is there a church choir or civic music group for the client to join?

Music as a meaningful leisure activity may help to promote a successful community adjustment for adults and children with intellectual disabilities. Let us now look at how the music therapist is organizing music leisure activities for 30-year-old Jazmine.

Jazmine survived a near drowning event when she was 7 and was without oxygen long enough to cause irreversible brain damage. The case manager for Jazmine recently completed her Essential Life Plan as part of what is now referred to as a person-centered process approach to service delivery and planning. Essential Lifestyle Planning is a detailed person-centered planning method, which focuses on the person's particular likes and dislikes. This approach also recognizes that the client is in a partnership with service providers. Jazmine communicates what she wants to do as an active member of her own team and selects opportunities to engage in social, educational, and recreational activities, including those involving music.

Jazmine is in transition from an intermediate care residential setting to a smaller, four-bedroom group home located in a nice residential neighborhood. Working with her job coach, she has found an excellent employment opportunity bagging groceries at the local supermarket. However, there are concerns about loss of opportunities for leisure activities in her new placement. Kate was Jazmine's music therapist when she lived in the residential setting. As part of the discharge planning for Jazmine, Kate has included recommendations for future community-based experiences for Jazmine, even though Jazmine will not receive active music therapy services after her new placement. Through astute observation of community music and service trends, Kate is knowledgeable about opportunities to engage Jazmine in interesting music experiences. For example, there is a choir comprised of adults with intellectual disabilities and nondisabled peers conducted by a music therapist that Jazmine is looking forward to joining and also classes in visual arts, private music instruction in voice, and dance classes. Along with her new job, Jazmine is excited by her new home and opportunities to interact with her new friends in the community.

The preceding music therapy examples illustrate the effectiveness of music therapy in addressing important functional life skills in persons with intellectual disabilities, including social and emotional behavior, motor development, expressive and receptive communication, pre-academic and academic knowledge, and appropriate leisure activities.

The most important people in this chapter are the uniquely gifted individuals with intellectual disabilities. The focus of the music therapist is on enhancing the overall quality of life for the individual so that person can enjoy the benefits of living in a free and inclusive society. Remember Colin from the beginning of this chapter? He recently won a first-place ribbon in the Special Olympics State Meet for the softball throw. He is still wearing his ribbon to school and continues to enjoy the success of his endeavors, as do his teachers, coaches, therapists, and friends.

SUMMARY

I n this chapter, we learned that intellectual disabilities, characterized by deficits in intelligence and adaptive skills, affect millions of adults and children living in the United States. Intellectual disability is defined by areas of need, including: (1) social/emotional development, (2) physical/motor development, (3) speech and language acquisition, (4) pre-academic skills, (5) academic skills, and 6) leisure skill development.

Educational and community placement depends on the ability to adapt to societal demands that are impacted by political and economic influences.

In this discussion, we identified four classifications of intellectual disability: (1) mild, (2) moderate, (3) severe/profound, and (4) severity unspecified. Intellectual disability can be caused by genetic and metabolic disorders, toxic agents, environmental factors, trauma, infections, or injury, but most cases are of unknown etiology.

For many years, music has been an important component of treatment for adults and children with intellectual disabilities. Music therapists working with this population individualize treatment goals according to six broad categories:

1. As a strategy for improving social and emotional behavior. Musical activities can be structured to promote appropriate behaviors and/or minimize or replace less acceptable behaviors.

2. As a means of improving motor skills. Music and movement activities can help develop motor skills and enhance the ability to learn.

3. As a tool for improving communication skills. Music therapy experiences can promote language development and improve articulation and vocal production.

4. As an aid in teaching pre-academic skills. Well planned therapeutic music experiences can help teach basic skills, such as attending, following directions, maintaining eye contact, and cooperating with others.

5. As tool to assist teaching academic skills. A well trained music therapist can use therapeutic music experiences to help adults and children learn numbers, colors, spatial relationships, letters, money concepts, etc.

6. As a leisure activity. Music therapists can help individuals with intellectual disabilities incorporate meaningful musical activities into their leisure time, by listening or performing, or both.

STUDY QUESTIONS

1. The three components of the AAIDD's definition of intellectual disabilities include _____, _____, and _____.

2. Intellectual disabilities can be divided into four categories according to severity of intellectual disability. List the four categories, and then discuss the differences among them.

3. List at least five causes of intellectual disabilities.

4. Progress is being made in the prevention of intellectual disabilities. Name, then define, three categories of prevention discussed.

5. What types of adaptive skill deficits are you likely to encounter in a person with mild intellectual disabilities?

6. Why is learning social adaptive behaviors so important to an adult or child with intellectual disabilities?

7. Why is music therapy an effective strategy to helping persons with intellectual disabilities to learn?

8. List at least three important music therapy goals developed for persons with intellectual disabilities.

9. What is IDEA and how has this legislation impacted the educational opportunities for children with intellectual disabilities?

10. Discuss speech and language development in persons with intellectual disabilities.

REFERENCES

American Association for Intellectual and Developmental Disabilities. (2002). AAIDD definition of mental retardation. Retrieved May 10, 2008, from http://www.aamr.org/Policies/faq_mental_retardation.shtml

American Music Therapy Association. (2007). *AMTA member sourcebook*. Silver Spring, MD: Author.

American Psychiatric Association. (2000). *Diagnostic and statistical manual of mental disorders* (4th ed., text revision). Washington, DC: Author.

Atterbury, B. W. (1990). *Mainstreaming exceptional learners in music*. Englewood Cliffs, NJ: Prentice-Hall.

Baroff, G. S. (1986). *Mental retardation: Nature, cause, and management* (2nd ed.). Washington, DC: Hemisphere.

Boxhill, E. H. (1985). *Music therapy for the developmentally disabled*. Rockville, MD: Aspen Systems.

Brantley, D. (1988). *Understanding mental retardation*. Springfield, IL: Charles C. Thomas.

Brewer, J. E. (1955). Music therapy for the mentally deficient. In E. T. Gaston (Ed.), *Music therapy 1954* (pp. 113–116). Lawrence, KS: Allen Press.

Brown, I., & Percy, M. (2007). *A comprehensive guide to intellectual and developmental disabilities*. Baltimore: Paul H. Brooks.

Carey, A., Friedman, M., & Bryen, D. N. (2005). Use of electronic technologies by people with intellectual disabilities. *Mental Retardation, 43*(5), 322–333.

Carter, S. A. (1982). *Music therapy for handicapped children: Mentally retarded*. Lawrence, KS: National Association for Music Therapy.

Central Wisconsin Center for People with Developmental Disabilities. (2004). *Wisconsin Forward Award Application* (p. xi). Madison, WI: Author.

Coates, P. (1987). "Is it functional?" A question for music therapists who work with the institutionalized. *Journal of Music Therapy, 24,* 170–175.

Cratty, B. J. (1974). *Motor activity and the education of retardates* (2nd ed.). Philadelphia: Lea and Febiger.

DeBout, J. K., & Worden, M. C. (2006). Motivators for children with severe intellectual disabilities in the self-contained classroom: A movement analysis. *Journal of Music Therapy, 43*(2), 123–135.

Drew, C. J., & Hardman, M. L. (2007). *Intellectual disabilities across the lifespan* (9th ed.). Englewood Cliffs, NJ: Prentice Hall.

Drew, C. J., Hardman, M. L., & Logan, D. R. (1996). *Mental retardation: A life cycle approach* (6th ed.). Englewood Cliffs, NJ: Prentice Hall.

Dunn, J., & Fait, H. (1989). *Special physical education: Adapted, individualized, developmental* (6th ed.). Dubuque, IA: William C. Brown.

Farnan, L. A. (2007). Music therapy and developmental disabilities: A glance back and a look forward. *Music Therapy Perspectives, 25,* 80–85.

Gfeller, K. E. (1990). A cognitive-linguistic approach to language development for the pre-school child with hearing impairment: Implications for music therapy practice. *Music Therapy Perspectives, 8,* 47–51.

Graham, R. M., & Beer, A. S. (1980). *Teaching music to the exceptional child*. Englewood Cliffs, NJ: Prentice-Hall.

Grant, R. E. (1989). Music therapy guidelines for developmentally disabled children. *Music Therapy Perspectives, 6,* 18–22.

Harris, J. C. (2006). *Intellectual disability: Understanding its development, causes, classification, evaluation and treatment*. New York: Oxford University Press.

Howery, B. I. (1968). Music therapy for intellectually disabled children and adults. In E. T. Gaston (Ed.), *Music therapy 1968* (pp. 47–55). New York: Macmillan.

Isern, B. (1959). The influence of music on the memory of intellectually disabled children. In E. H. Schneider (Ed.), *Music therapy 1958* (pp. 162–165). Lawrence, KS: Allen Press.

Jones, C. J. (1996). *An introduction to the nature and needs of students with mild disabilities.* Springfield, IL: Charles C. Thomas.

Kirk, S. A., Gallagher, J. J., Anastasiow, N. J., & Coleman, M. R. (2005). *Educating exceptional children* (11th ed.). Boston: Houghton Mifflin.

Kraft, I. (1963). Music for the feebleminded in nineteenth-century America. *Journal of Research in Music Education, 11*, 119–122.

Lathom, W. (1980). *Role of music therapy in the education of handicapped children and youth.* Lawrence, KS: National Association for Music Therapy.

Loven, M. A. (1957). Value of music therapy for intellectually disabled children. In E. T. Gaston (Ed.), *Music therapy 1956* (pp. 165–174). Lawrence, KS: Allen Press.

Mahon, M., & Bullock, C. (1992). Teaching adolescents with mild mental retardation to make decisions in leisure through the use of self-control techniques. *Therapeutic Recreational Journal, 26*, 9–26.

Mahon, M., & Goatcher, S. (1999). Later-life planning for older adults with mental retardation: A field experiment. *Mental Retardation, 37*, 371–382.

Michel, D. E. (1979). *Music therapy: An introduction to therapy and special education through music* (2nd ed.). Springfield, IL: Charles C. Thomas.

Moore, R., & Mathenius, L. (1987). The effects of modeling, reinforcement, and tempo on imitative rhythmic responses of moderately retarded adolescents. *Journal of Music Therapy 24*, 160–169.

Northern Wisconsin Center. (2007). History web page. Retrieved May 25, 2008, from http://dhfs.wisconsin.gov/dd_nwc/aboutnwc/history.htm

Peterson, E. D. (1952). Music to aid the mentally handicapped. In E. G. Gilliland (Ed.), *Music therapy 1951* (pp. 19–21). Lawrence, KS: Allen Press.

Reynolds, B. J. (1982). Music therapy literature related to intellectual disabilities. In S. A. Carter (Ed.), *Music therapy for handicapped children: Intellectually disabled* (pp. 43–56). Lawrence, KS: National Association for Music Therapy.

Scheerenberger, R. C. (1983). *A history of mental retardation.* Baltimore: Brooks.

Scheerenberger, R. C. (1987). *A history of mental retardation: A quarter century of promise.* Baltimore: Brooks.

Scheerenberger, R. C. (1989). *The fate of persons with mental retardation under Nazi Germany.* Fairfax, VA: National Association of Superintendents of Public Residential Facilities for the Mentally Retarded Monograph Supplement No. 1 to the "Superintendents' Digest."

State of Wisconsin Department of Health and Family Services, Division of Health, Bureau of Quality Compliance. (1989). *Federal regulations document: Interruptive guidelines– Intermediate care facilities for the mentally retarded.* Madison, WI: Author.

Thaut, M. H. (2005). *Rhythm, music, and the brain.* New York: Routledge.

Thomas, G. E. (1996). *Teaching students with mental retardation.* Englewood Cliffs, NJ: Merrill.

Weis, R. (2008). *Introduction to the abnormal child and adolescent psychology.* Los Angeles: Sage.

Wendelin, A. (1953). Instrumental music for the intellectually disabled. In E. G. Gilliland (Ed.), *Music therapy 1952* (pp. 133–138). Lawrence, KS: Allen Press.

Westling, D. L., & Fox, L. (2004). *Teaching students with severe disabilities* (3rd ed.). Englewood Cliffs, NJ: Prentice Hall.

World Health Organization. (2007). *International statistical classification of diseases and related health problems* (10th rev.). New York: Author.

CHAPTER 5

Individuals with Autism and Autism Spectrum Disorders (ASD)

Mary S. Adamek
Michael H. Thaut
Amelia Greenwald Furman

CHAPTER OUTLINE

DEFINITION AND DIAGNOSIS
ETIOLOGY
CHARACTERISTICS
    Communication
    Social Interactions
    Sensory Processing
    Behavioral Issues
MUSIC THERAPY GOALS AND INTERVENTIONS
    Music Therapy to Improve Communication Skills
    Music Therapy to Improve Social and Emotional Skills
    Music Therapy to Improve Behavior
    Music Therapy to Improve Academic, Physical/Motor, and Leisure Skills

Autism is a **pervasive developmental disability** that affects a person's ability to communicate and interact with others. The term *autism spectrum disorder* (ASD) refers to the fact that this condition affects individuals in different ways and to varying degrees (Autism Society of America, 2008). ASD affects approximately 1 in 150 people in the United States (Rice, 2007), which means that approximately 1.5 million Americans today have some form of autism. It is four times more prevalent in boys than in girls, and the rate of children diagnosed with autism is increasing by 10–17% each year. At this rate, the number of people with autism could reach 4 million within the next decade (Autism Society of America, 2008).

Many music therapists work with children and adults with autism in schools, residential settings, and community agencies. According to the U.S. Department of

Education (2007), over 92,000 students ages 6–17 with autism received some form of special services under IDEA during the 2001–2002 school year. (See Chapter 14 for more information about IDEA.) The majority of music therapy services with individuals with autism are provided to children, primarily in school and community settings. Adults with severe autism may receive music therapy services in residential facilities for people with developmental disabilities, or they may receive services in community settings with other adults who have developmental disabilities. This chapter will focus on the characteristics and needs of children with autism and music therapy interventions for children with autism. For more information on music therapy with adults who have developmental disabilities, refer to Chapter 4.

DEFINITION AND DIAGNOSIS

Leo Kanner (1943), a psychiatrist at Johns Hopkins University, was the first person to identify autism as a distinct developmental disorder. He described a group of children who were relatively normal in physical appearance but who exhibited severely disturbed behavior patterns that included the following: extreme social aloofness or aloneness; lack of emotional responsiveness; avoidance of eye contact; failure to respond to auditory or visual stimulation; lack of language development or failure to use language adequately for communication; excessive attachment to objects; and preoccupation with ritualistic, repetitive, and obsessive behaviors. Because the symptoms were presented in early infancy, Kanner coined the term *infantile autism.*

Since those early years, the definition and diagnostic criteria of autism have been changed and refined, mostly in terms of broadening the definition. Autism is described as a spectrum disorder, meaning that there are a variety of possible disorders and characteristics having differing levels of developmental delay ranging from mild to severe. Thus, generalizations are difficult to make since individuals with autism can be very different from one another, and there is a wide range of abilities and deficits.

Autism Spectrum Disorder (ASD) falls under the umbrella category of **Pervasive Developmental Disorders (PDD)**, listed in the *Diagnostic and Statistical Manual of Mental Disorders* (American Psychiatric Association, 2000). This category includes neurological disorders such as autism, **Rett's Syndrome,** and **Asperger's Syndrome**, which are characterized by severe and pervasive impairments in many areas of development (American Psychiatric Association, 2000; Autism Society of America, 2008). Autism and ASD affect children of all social classes, financial levels, educational levels, cultures, and races throughout the world (Autism Society of America, 2008; Scott, Clark, & Brady, 2000).

Persons with autism have serious deficits in communication and social skills, and they may display behaviors that are unusual compared to their typically developing peers. Symptoms of autism begin before the age of 3 and continue throughout a person's life. All of the following diagnostic criteria must be present from early childhood in order to make a diagnosis of autism:

- *Qualitative impairment in reciprocal social interaction,* based on what is typical for developmental level. This may manifest in poor eye gaze, disinterest in personal relationships, and limited use of gestures.

- *Qualitative impairment in verbal and nonverbal communication,* based on what is typical for developmental level. This may manifest in language acquisition delay, limited or lack of speech, lack of spontaneous and varied make-believe play.

- *Restricted repertoire of interests and activities,* based on developmental level. This may manifest in stereotypical or repetitive movements such as rocking, hand flapping, or spinning as well as limited or abnormally intense interest areas. (Frith, 2003)

As a spectrum disorder, the range of abilities and degree of developmental delay result in unique profiles among persons with ASD; however, all children with autism have some sort of difficulty with communication, social skills, and behavior (Frith, 2003; Johnson, 2004; Mastropieri & Scruggs, 2000; Scott et al., 2000). Those who have difficulty with verbal communication and expressing needs may point, use gestures, or use other nonverbal forms of communication such as pictures or icons. Many, but not all, children with ASD also have cognitive impairments; however, children with Asperger's Syndrome have high cognitive abilities combined with severe impairment in reciprocal social interaction and restricted interests. A person with autism may have a combination of the characteristics listed in Table 1 on the following page (Centers for Disease Control and Prevention, 2008), which will be discussed more extensively later in this chapter.

Table 1
Continuum of Abilities and Limitations for Persons with Autism

AREA OF FUNCTIONING	VARIABILITY LEVELS
Measured Intelligence	Severely impaired ----------------Gifted
Social Interaction	Aloof ------Passive -----Active but odd
Communication	Nonverbal ------------------------Verbal
Behaviors	Intense -------------------------------Mild
Sensory	Hyposensitive ----------Hypersensitive
Motor	Uncoordinated -------------Coordinated

Individuals with autism or ASD may display some of the following specific traits or characteristics. It is important to note that not all people with this diagnosis have all of these traits, and the severity of the disorder varies by individual (Autism Society of America, 2008).

- Repeating words or phrases, **echolalic** language
- Unresponsive to verbal cues or directions; may appear to be deaf due to unresponsiveness
- Difficulty interacting with peers; minimal spontaneous socialization
- Oversensitivity or undersensitivity to stimuli or to pain
- Resistance to change; insistence on routine
- Minimal direct eye contact
- Odd or unusual play, particularly sustained play or attachment to objects

Contrary to common beliefs, children with ASD may make eye contact, develop good functional language and communication skills, socialize with peers, and show affection. Their skills in these areas might be different or less sophisticated than typically developing peers, but it is very likely that with appropriate educational and social interventions, children with ASD may develop functional and appropriate skills in all of these areas. Other behavioral or emotional disorders may co-occur with ASD as a secondary diagnosis, including obsessive/compulsive disorder, anxiety disorder, depression, and attention-deficit/hyperactivity disorder. (See Chapter 8 for a review of behavioral-emotional disorders.)

ETIOLOGY

When autism was first recognized as a distinct disorder, psychiatrists attributed it to an early emotional trauma or to faulty parenting. The unusual array of symptoms (i.e., relatively normal physical appearance and isolated skills coupled with the emotional unresponsiveness, social aloofness, and difficulty with language) led many researchers to believe that autism was the result of an emotional trauma in very early childhood. However, because no consistent patterns of social or emotional history emerged in these children, other etiological considerations emerged.

Since the 1960s, accumulated research evidence strongly suggests that autism is a developmental disorder of brain function that is manifested in a variety of perceptual, cognitive, and motor disturbances. To date, there is no single known cause of autism; however, there is general agreement that autism is related to abnormalities in the brain structure and function. Researchers have found differences in brain scans between brains of individuals with autism and individuals with typical development (Frith, 2003). Research is underway to test several theories related to the causes of autism. Some theories link the disorder to genetics and heredity, while others cite environmental risks as causal factors related to the development of autism. Currently, many national organizations are funding and conducting research to determine the causes of autism and best practices for intervention (Autism Society of America, 2008; Autism Speaks, 2008; Centers for Disease Control and Prevention, 2008).

The following sections describe three functional domains in which children with autism often have difficulties. Typical educational approaches to support learning will be described.

CHARACTERISTICS

Communication

As noted previously, a child with autism has qualitative impairment in language and communication skills. Some children may have no ability or interest in communicating verbally or nonverbally with others. Some have **echolalic** language, in which previously heard words or phrases are repeated without any intent to convey meaning. Children with autism have a marked difference in language skills compared to children who are typically developing. Impairments may be characterized by:

- lack of spontaneous social imitation (e.g., waving and saying "goodbye")
- failure to use language correctly (e.g., syntactic problems, not using verbs)
- limited vocabulary and semantic concepts, poor intonation patterns
- pronoun reversal (e.g., saying "you" instead of "I")
- lack of gesture or mime when trying to make needs known
- difficulty understanding spoken language

- failure to develop joint attention skills in preverbal children (e.g., pointing to a toy to share one's pleasure with another person). (Heflin & Alaimo, 2007; Mundy & Stella, 2000)

Children who have severe levels of autism may have little or no receptive or expressive language, while students with mild levels of autism may have developed language skills that allow them to communicate with others. Because communication is a primary deficit for individuals with ASD, the development of communication skills is often a key focus for therapy. This may include the development of verbal communication or effective use of alternative or augmentative communication systems.

There are many **alternative and augmentative communication (AAC) systems** available, which may enhance a child's verbal communication skills or become a child's primary means of communication. These alternative systems help a child express wants and needs, initiate and maintain conversations, and receive and understand information from others. AAC systems can be simple systems of pointing to pictures, words, or letter boards, or more sophisticated methods, such as use of sign language, voice output computers, or visual tracking devices (National Research Council, 2001; Scott et al., 2000). These communication systems can provide a means for students to communicate with others in a meaningful way and can facilitate two-way, interactive communication between the student with autism and others.

The **Picture Exchange Communication System (PECS)** is a good example of an AAC system that is used in many homes and classrooms. PECS is system that teaches children to use pictures and symbols in order to ask for wants and needs, respond to others, and initiate conversations. Using PECS, a child learns the meaning of a set of pictures or symbols by exchanging those symbols for something he or she wants or needs. Using a sentence strip that says "I want _____," the child learns to fill in the blank with a picture (attached to the sentence strip with Velcro) that stands for whatever he or she wants; then the child hands the sentence strip back to the teacher, therapist, or other conversational partner in exchange for the desired object (Bondy & Frost, 1994; Frost & Bondy, 1994; Kravits, Kamps, Kemmerer, & Potucek, 2002). Other AAC systems might be a simple picture/symbol book, board, or wallet used for making requests or responding to questions. Some children may use basic signs to communicate with others. More sophisticated technology such as computers with voice output systems can also provide an effective means of communication. Music therapy implications for the use of ACCs will be discussed later in this chapter.

Social Interactions

Social skills play a major role in child development and support a child's ability to function in integrated classrooms or community settings. Appropriate social skills are necessary for successful interactions with peers without disabilities and for participation in normalized activities. Individuals with ASD have core deficits in social interaction and social perception, which manifest in difficulty initiating interaction, difficulty maintaining social relationships, and difficulty understanding the perceptions of others (Scott et al., 2000). Social deficits can range from mild (such as difficulty making and maintaining eye contact), to severe (such as the inability to share experiences and interests with others). Some individuals with less severe deficits may interact spontaneously with others, while those with severe social deficits may seem oblivious to others and the environment. Even individuals with higher functioning skills may have problems understanding the perspective of others, and understanding that the thoughts, beliefs, and intentions of others may be different from their own. Some children have difficulty with physical touch or in maintaining socially acceptable personal space. For example, some children stiffen and avoid physical contact, while others may be clingy and have inappropriate boundaries (such as always wanting to sit on the therapist's lap or in uncomfortably close proximity to others). Social behaviors can also vary over time.

Because social deficits are a key feature of autism, these children need direct training to improve social skills in a variety of settings. While children with autism can develop more socially appropriate behaviors through social skills training, it is important to note that communication skills provide the foundation for developing and maintaining social relationships; consequently, children with autism need to develop functional communication *along with* social skills in order to enhance interactive skills, make friends, and be included in classroom and social activities.

A variety of techniques can be used to teach social skills to children with these deficits. When choosing social skill interventions, teachers and therapists must keep in mind the age, language skills, developmental level, and interests of the child in order to develop effective approaches. Some current educational approaches used to teach social skills include:

- **Direct instruction**—teaching children directly to interact with peers with the support of prompts, modeling, or physical assistance during the interaction
- **Social communication training**—teaching children to ask questions and seek out information in a social setting
- **Use of social stories**—stories developed to teach social skill concepts and strategies (Gray & Garand, 1993); these stories can also be set to music to create social story songs

- **Leisure-related social skill development**—teaching social interaction and rules of play through leisure skills. (Scott et al., 2000)

Sensory Processing

Children who are typically developing have intact sensory systems that help them perceive the world around them. Their senses of vision, hearing, touch, taste, and smell work in an integrated fashion to help them make sense of their environment. Many children with autism have sensory processing problems. To a child with sensory processing problems, the environment may be confusing, painful, or even frightening. Some children with autism have sensory processing problems that can cause oversensitivity or undersensitivity to certain stimuli. For instance, some children with autism are particularly sensitive to high or loud sounds; when presented with this type of sound, they will shriek, hold their ears, or become aggressive in some way. Because they may process and respond to information in different ways, children with autism may exhibit atypical, inappropriate, unusual, or **stereotypical behaviors.** They may exhibit aggressive or self-injurious behaviors when they are unable to understand or unable to communicate their confusion. Keep in mind, however, that not all children with autism exhibit these types of behaviors.

Because musical sounds are such an integral part of music therapy, the processing of and response to musical sounds by children with autism is of particular interest. A number of research studies with this population document unusual sensitivity and attention to music. In fact, in 1964, a prominent researcher, Bernard Rimland, even listed unusual musical capabilities as a diagnostic criterion for autism (Rimland, 1964). Sherwin (1953), in a case study of boys with autism, noted strong melodic memory; recognition of classical music selections; and strong interest in playing the piano, singing, and listening to music. Observations of 12 children with autism over a two-year time period indicated heightened response and interest in musical sounds as compared with other environmental stimuli (Pronovost, 1961). Studies by Frith (1972), O'Connell (1974), Blackstock (1978), and Thaut (1987) showed improved task performance or attention on tasks involving music compared with those using other modalities.

Studies by Applebaum, Egel, Koegel, and Imhoff (1979) and Thaut (1987) indicated that children with autism could perform similarly to age-matched children with typical development on musical tasks involving imitation or improvisation. Koegel, Rincover, and Egel (1982) described music as an efficient motivator and modality for enabling autistic children to learn nonmusical material and emphasized its use as positive sensory reinforcement in decreasing self-stimulation behaviors.

Recent studies provide evidence that a high level of musical responsiveness can co-exist with low functioning in other cognitive areas in autistic children (e.g., Heaton, 2003; Heaton, Hermelin, & Pring, 1998; Heaton, Pring, & Hermelin, 2001; Hermelin, O'Conner, & Lee, 1997; Mottron, Peretz, & Menard, 2000). In addition, research examining the unique auditory perception of children with autism indicates higher performance in perceptual tasks involving music compared with other acoustic stimuli (e.g., verbal language [Foxton et al., 2003; Heaton, 2003, 2005; Heaton & Wallace, 2004; Mottron, Peretz, Belleville, & Rouleau, 1999; Nieto del Rincon, 2008; Young & Nettelbeck, 1995]). It is important to note, however, that some children with autism may show unusual and negative sensitivity to some musical sounds, or some combinations of music and movement.

It is, as of yet, unclear why many children with autism show heightened interest in and more typical responses to music than to other types of stimuli. However, the fact that music can be engaging and can support optimal functioning in children with autism explains in part why music therapy can be an excellent therapeutic choice for this population.

Behavioral Issues

Some children with autism have behaviors that are difficult to manage in a variety of settings such as the classroom, the home, or the community. Maladaptive behaviors include poor attention, aggression, stereotypic or self-stimulating behaviors, oversensitivity to sensory input, and difficulty with generalization of skills (National Research Council, 2001; Simpson & Miles, 1998). These behaviors can be among the most challenging and stressful factors for professionals and can interfere with learning and development in communication and socialization. Problem behaviors may be triggered or exacerbated by an inability to understand the expectations of the environment (including consequences of their behavior), inability to communicate wants and needs, or difficulty in initiating and maintaining positive social relationships. Aggression towards others, self-injurious behaviors, noncompliance, and disruption of session routines may create difficult and frustrating situations for everyone involved. Table 2 provides examples of the characteristic features of autism and how they might cause difficult behaviors (Adamek & Darrow, 2005, pp. 190–191).

Table 2

Characteristic Features and Examples of Difficult Behaviors

Characteristic Feature	Specific Difficulties	Possible Behavior
Language and communication impairment	Difficulty understanding directions and expressing self	Not following through with directions, aggression to others or self
Social interaction difficulty	Difficulty reading social cues from others, difficulty understanding the perspective of others	Difficulty interacting with others, sharing classroom materials, inflexible in social situations; isolation from peers, minimal spontaneous interaction with peers
Focus of attention problems	Difficulty processing information, focusing on the main feature of instruction; difficulty filtering out auditory/visual distracters	Not following through with directions, tasks, or assignments; engaging in off-task or self-stimulating behaviors; inability to follow multi-step directions
Aggressive, stereotypic or self-stimulating behaviors	Difficulty communicating needs or understanding expectations; frustrations	Acting out towards others; rocking or hand flapping to provide sensory stimulation; visually focusing on lights, fan blades, or shiny objects
Oversensitivity to sensory input	Processing problems that impair tolerance for tactile, visual, or auditory stimuli	Acting out or isolation; holding ears with hands; rejecting touch from others; refusal to play instruments that provide tactile stimulation
Difficulty generalizing behaviors	Difficulty applying skills learned in one situation to another situation	Difficulty with transitions; may act out physically, vocally, or refuse participation; difficulty transferring skills from one setting to another without additional instruction

Fortunately, problematic behaviors can be reduced by setting up a structured environment and through the use of behavioral strategies (providing examples and cues to clarify expectations, reinforcing positive behavior, etc.). Environmental structure (such as a well organized room with consistent work spaces and limited clutter) can help the child organize and focus attention appropriately. Some children derive structure and support by being close to others for structure and support, while others may need more space due to issues such as tactile defensiveness or hyperactivity. Providing instruction in close proximity is important for some children. Close proximity makes it possible for the music therapist to provide physical and gestural prompts when needed and gives the child a clear idea of where he or she should be looking for instruction.

In addition to setting up a structured environment, it is important to understand causes of inappropriate behavior so that strategies for developing appropriate behavior can be devised. For example, some children are more likely to misbehave if they sit next to one another—they either irritate one another or egg each other on. The mere fact of sitting by one another can trigger negative behaviors. A seating chart that places these children away from each other can prevent problems from beginning. For some children, sitting near the therapist may foster calm and focused behavior. It is important to recognize antecedents (what happens before the target behavior) and consequences (what happens as a result of the behavior) in order to determine some possible causes and reinforcing events.

While no single intervention will deal effectively with all problem behaviors, most professionals recommend using a preventative approach to decrease problem behaviors and increase positive behaviors. A proactive approach, such as utilizing **positive behavioral supports** (assessing what maintains the behavior and developing strategies to replace the behavior), can create an environment for success. This approach builds on the strengths of the child and focuses on changing the environment, instructional strategies, and consequences to promote positive behaviors.

MUSIC THERAPY GOALS AND INTERVENTIONS

Music therapy is an effective approach for addressing language and communication skills, social skills, cognitive skills, and behavioral skills for children with autism (Bettison, 1996; Davis, 1990; Edgerton, 1994; Goldstein, 1964; Hairston, 1990; Hermelin, O'Connor, & Lee, 1989; Hollander & Juhrs, 1974; Humpal, 1990; Kostka, 1993; Lim, 2007; Litchman, 1976; Ma, Nagler, & Lee, 2001; Mahlberg, 1973; Nelson, Anderson, & Gonzales, 1984; Reitman, 2006; Saperston, 1973; Schmidt & Edwards, 1976; Staum & Flowers, 1984; Stevens & Clark, 1969; Thaut, 1984, 1988; Umbarger, 2007; Walworth, 2007; Warwick 1995; Whipple, 2004; Wimpory, Chadwick, & Nash, 1995). Music therapy goals for children with autism focus primarily on improving communication, social interactions, and behavior. Secondary areas of focus include improvement of academic skills, physical skills, and leisure skills.

As noted earlier, some children with autism are more attentive and responsive to musical stimuli; thus, music therapy can be a highly motivating medium for addressing these goals. In addition, music is a flexible medium (see Chapter 3); therefore, it can be used for a variety of goals and readily adapted to suit the diverse strengths and limitations found within this population. Music therapy interventions involve the child in listening, singing, playing, moving, or responding verbally and nonverbally. Through goal-directed music therapy interventions, a child can also work on several skills at once. For instance, an intervention that involved participation in a percussion ensemble could focus on communication (nonverbal communication and self-expression through drumming, making choices about what instrument to play), social skills (interacting appropriately with peers, taking turns playing, listening to others, taking leadership) and appropriate behavior (following directions, listening to the leader, following through with tasks).

Music Therapy to Improve Communication Skills

As noted previously, children with autism have deficits in expressive and receptive communication skills. Music therapy provides a rich opportunity for language experiences through age-appropriate and interesting music interventions. Several studies indicate that music therapy can improve communication and language skills (Edgerton, 1994; Litchman, 1976; Mahlberg, 1973; Saperston, 1973). Music therapists use the elements of music (melody, rhythm, pitch, dynamics, form) to develop basic listening skills such as **auditory awareness** (sound vs. no sound), **auditory discrimination** (are two sounds same or different?), **sound identification** (recognition of the sound, such as a flute or a piano), and **localization** (locating the source of the sound). Music therapy interventions can encourage **expressive** (speaking, signing) and **receptive** (listening, understanding signs and gestures) **language**.

Because music is interesting and motivating, it can promote attention, active participation, and verbal and nonverbal response. For instance, action songs, chants, and instrument playing can elicit vocal/verbal and physical responses that promote receptive communication skills. Rhythm paired with speech can encourage verbalizations and appropriate pacing. Call-and-response rhythmic chants can increase imitation skills, first on instruments, then in speech. Songs with repetitive lyrics and melodies can facilitate memory for vocabulary and other information. Pairing songs with visual cues and movement can enhance comprehension of vocabulary and concepts. For instance, a song about winter could be used to introduce and reinforce concepts such as temperature, seasonal changes, appropriate attire (winter coats and mittens), and directions. Music can be a highly motivating tool to encourage imitative and spontaneous language (see Figure 1).

EXAMPLES OF MUSIC THERAPY INTERVENTIONS FOR COMMUNICATION
(Thaut, 1999)

1. **Music interaction to establish communicative intent (facilitate desire or necessity to communicate)**
   - Offer musical interactions (e.g., question-and-answer, imitative) on drum, metallophone, or other instruments.
   - Accompany the child's movements or habitual sounds (crying, laughing) on the piano.
   - Sing an action song to the child and cue the proper physical responses.

2. **Action songs to promote interaction (after communicative intent is established)**
   - Introduce chants or songs that integrate rhythm, body percussion, and vocalization that present instructions for active physical and vocal response.

3. **Oral motor exercises to strengthen awareness and functional use of lips, tongue, jaws, teeth**
   - Play wind instruments.
   - Performing oral motor imitation exercises of the articulators.

4. **Sequence imitation of gross motor, oral motor, and oral vocal motor skills (after perceptual and imitative skills are established)**
   - First, introduce the name of a body part (e.g., "arm") while moving that part.
   - Second, have the child practice oral motor positions of the articulators for that word (e.g., "a" and "m").
   - Third, while the child moves the body part in an imitation exercise, ask him to sound out the parts of that body part (e.g., saying "arm" while moving, or parts of the word as is possible).

5. **Shaping vocal inflection of children who have some speech sounds**
   - Vocal improvisation on vowel and consonant combinations.
   - Sustaining sounds on wind instruments.
   - Producing vocal sounds combined with graphic notations to represent speech inflection.
   - Breathing exercises to improve vocal strength, exercise laryngeal function, and refine oral motor function.

Figure 1. Examples of Music Therapy Interventions for Communication Skills

If a child is using an **alternative and augmentative communication (AAC) system**, the music therapist can collaborate with the speech language pathologist to create responses for use in music. Examples include:

- Icons to represent music, or a picture of the music room
- Pictures or names of teachers, therapists, or peer buddies in music
- Pictures or drawings of instruments or props used in music
- Names of favorite songs sung in music

- Iconic representations of note values, such as whole notes, half notes, quarter notes, eighth notes
- Pictures related to the schedule or order of events in music, such as a "hello song" or opening song," "movement time," "play instruments," or "sing songs"
- Functional signs used for directions such as "stop," "play," "dance"

Because communicative deficits are a key problem area for children with autism, it is important to promote receptive and expressive communication in all aspects of instruction. Many children are more successful when presented with visual cues along with verbal instructions. Visual cues (**icons, photos, functional signs**) can be used for giving directions, offering choices, teaching new skills, or providing structure for an activity. Visual enhancements should be simple and consistent throughout the child's day to encourage generalization of skills and to support comprehension (Scott et al., 2000). Suggested uses for visual cues include:

- Describing rules (listen, hands to self)
- Presenting schedule of interventions, which creates predictability for children
- Modeling movement
- Pairing pictures with songs to allow choice (a picture of a sun for "Mr. Sun")
- Presenting a calming routine for coping with change or anxiety (e.g., take two breaths, squeezing/releasing hands). (Adamek & Darrow, 2005)

Abdi faces several challenges in his education. Not only does he have autism, but his native language spoken at home is not English. Abdi frequently becomes upset and aggressive in the classroom because he is unable to communicate his choices. Music therapy provides a consistent structure and the opportunity for repeated practice of words he needs to communicate choices. A calming song, written by his music therapist, lists six of Abdi's favorite things to do (e.g., rest, read a book). His classroom teacher keeps a copy of Abdi's special song (along with visual cues) in the classroom for use during choice time, or to help calm him when he becomes upset. The songs learned in music therapy are integrated into other instructional times to help hold Abdi's attention, increase his comprehension, and increase his time on task in the group. His ability to communicate choices about songs, instruments, and feelings has also contributed to his improved behaviors in school.

Music Therapy to Improve Social and Emotional Skills

> *Evan, a student with Asperger's Syndrome, entered the school as a 2nd grader. Although he was academically above grade level, he was having difficulty during lunch and recess. Some students found his loud voice and unusually deliberate speech patterns irritating and his social skills awkward. However, Evan was able to shine in a special classroom project, a musical written and produced by the students, about how blood circulates in the human body. A number of students auditioned for the "scientist narrator" position, but most could not be easily understood through the microphone and speakers. Evan, an excellent and precise reader, was perfect for the part. As a lead part in the musical, he was able to utilize his strengths and be seen as an essential member of the group, especially by the students writing the script. The friendships and tolerance that developed during the musical carried over to the creation of a small music group in which social skills training became a part of Friday Fun Time. Evan realized that during music, he understood the rules and could be successful with peers. He later joined band and excelled in that structured experience right up through high school graduation.*

Children with autism and ASD have deficits in social skills, social interaction, and emotional expression. Because autistic children often reject or ignore others' attempts at social interaction, music can function as an attractive mediating object. Music provides a point of mutual interaction between therapist and child. Studies by Goldstein (1964), Stevens and Clark (1969), Hollander and Juhrs (1974), Schmidt and Edwards (1976), and Warwick (1995) have shown improved social behavior and interpersonal relationships as a result of music therapy treatment. In addition, music is an effective medium for eliciting and shaping emotional responses. Different types of music can be associated with different moods and emotions, which can in turn be paired with body language and verbal labeling of moods (Thaut, 1999).

Music making (singing, movement, instrument playing) with the therapist or with peers lends itself to interaction and the use of social skills. In one-to-one sessions with the child, the therapist can make musical contact and set up musical interactions that require social interaction (such as imitation or call and response) (Thaut, 1999). In group music experiences, children can practice responding to others, taking turns, listening, sharing ideas, greeting others, and sharing equipment. Simple skills such as holding hands with a peer, listening to others, or starting and stopping with the group can be difficult but important skills to develop. Below is an example of a social story song about *waiting your turn* (to the tune of ABC song) (Adamek & Darrow, 2005, p. 187):

Wait your turn, wait today, Then you'll have a chance to play.
First it's her, then it's him, Round the circle back to you.
Wait your turn, wait today, Then you'll have a chance to play.

Music therapists can promote meaningful social relationships with peers by providing structured and motivating opportunities for social interaction in the music setting (Adamek & Darrow, 2005; Brown et al., 1979; Jellison, Brooks, & Huck, 1984). Music groups including movement can also provide opportunities to practice appropriate personal space (how close one stands or sits next to others while still feeling comfortable), and socially appropriate touch.

> Jamilia, who has autism, is a very musical child. She is able to learn new lyrics and melodies quickly and follows directions sung in lyrics well. Jamilia really wanted to be a part of the group, but her initiations were often rebuffed by other children because she had no sense of space or boundaries. She would squeeze herself into a classroom line, typically next to students wearing the prettiest dresses. Sometimes, out of the blue, she would lean over and touch or sniff other children's hair and talk about what they were wearing or doing. In music therapy, Jamilia learned songs that taught interactive skills, such as "find a friend and look them in the eye, find a friend and now say Hi."

> For movement activities, the teacher marked the classroom floor with round Velcro pieces that were called "bubbles." These bubbles provided an easy visual reminder of where to stand in relation to others. In an intervention similar to the game Musical Chairs, the children would move as long as the music was playing. Whenever the music stopped, students jumped on to one of the bubbles. Students were praised for "good bubble space." As the children internalized this sense of appropriate social space, the Velcro spots were gradually removed so students needed to "think the space." The concept of bubble space (socially appropriate personal distance) was then integrated into other favorite activities, such as singing a favorite train song, which required the children to keep their social distance while moving. These skills were then successfully generalized to other classroom and social settings.

Music Therapy to Improve Behavior

> Abdi, like many children with autism, does not like change. Sometimes, he has verbal outbursts or becomes physically aggressive when his teachers change the classroom routine. Fortunately, his interest in music and music

activities helps him to tolerate change. For example, Abdi has become accustomed to and enjoys playing drums with mallets; but because the music is so motivating, he is willing to try a different type of drum played only by his hands as requested.

Behavioral difficulties are another key feature of ASD. Just as with all other characteristics of autism, behavior skills vary in severity from one individual to the next. As noted earlier, behavior problems may be related to difficulty communicating or limited comprehension of the expectations and consequences of their behavior.

Music therapy can be structured to provide predictable experiences in which children can practice appropriate behavior. The rules for appropriate participation in a music group (such as following directions, starting and stopping at the correct place) can be practiced step by step, even as the group members engage in attractive musical arrangements. Those students with more advanced musical skills can practice these basic behavioral expectations within the context of more complex and interesting music. For instance, a small group percussion ensemble can learn basic steady beat patterns that can be extended to include more complicated rhythms on a variety of instruments. Children who follow directions, meet expectations, and participate with others may be asked to perform for others. In this way, music can be used to improve self-esteem and leadership skills. Music can also be used as reinforcement for appropriate behavior, offered as a reward for following through with expectations. Extra time playing instruments, listening to music, or making music with others may be highly reinforcing and motivating for some students.

Music therapists can utilize various methods to promote positive behaviors, including the following (Adamek & Darrow, 2005, pp. 188–189):

- Creating a sense of predictability and routine in the session, such as using a visually prominent schedule board, having a predictable room set-up, or using familiar materials.

Mrs. Hawkins' music therapy space is a model of predictability. When the children enter the room, they know exactly where they will find the rhythm instruments, the chairs, and the music board, which spells out the order of musical events for each day's session. Today, the board presents a sequence of pictures that represent (1) the opening song/warm-up, (2) a movement activity, (3) time for singing, (4) playing instruments, (5) surprise to allow for teaching flexibility and student choice, and (6) closing.

Everyone thought James would do well in regular music classes. However, his need for consistency and difficulty with change become clear on the first day. Mrs. Lin, the teacher, looked at the clock and said, "Let's sing

'Five Little Monkeys Jumping on the Bed.' We have just enough time for 2 little monkeys to jump on the bed today." James's response was a major tantrum with screams of "No!! There must be 5." That's because every time he sang this song, they started with the number, 5. Only 2 monkeys! That was just more change than he could handle.

Mrs. Nelson, the music therapist, was contacted to set up a series of sessions to work with James on coping with a change in routine. A "surprise" symbol, selected with the ASD classroom teacher and speech clinician, was introduced. Visuals with choices for changes in how the music was performed including fast/slow, loud/soft, or instrumentation were made and familiar songs were sung with changes. Next, dice were presented and James practiced rolling, saying the number and setting out a matching number of items. "It's a surprise!" was said frequently when the dice were rolled. James was ready to choose a song, roll the dice, and sing using the "surprise" number. A social story song about "No Turn Today—but it's OK" was sung to the numbers that were not chosen.

- Practicing flexibility or tolerance of change by varying a musical element within the song or activity.

  During instrument playing, Mrs. Hawkins integrates small but tolerable changes in the routine by having the children play a favorite well-known rhythm pattern, but then adding a rhythm instrument different from that originally taught.

- Providing positive reinforcement for appropriate behaviors.

  As Jamilia keeps her hands to herself in the "Little Red Caboose" song, Mrs. Hawkins praises her for good bubble behavior, and she asks her to choose which instrument she would like to play during instrument time.

- Providing a means of communication for the child, and making sure that communication system transfers to all environments, including music therapy.

  One of the children in Mrs. Hawkins' ASD group uses basic sign language, while another uses visuals to communicate. Mrs. Hawkins makes sure that she utilizes of these communication systems in song time and all other aspects of her session.

- Teaching peers how to interact in a positive way with the child.

  Before Jamilia started to attend the regular music class, Mrs. Hawkins sat down with the children to discuss practical ideas for getting along with their classmates, such as moving a little bit further away if a classmate moves within your bubble space.

Music Therapy to Improve Academic, Physical/Motor, and Leisure Skills

In addition to the aforementioned areas of difficulty for children with autism (communication skills, social skills, and behavior), other areas of deficit such as academic skills, physical/motor skills, and leisure skills can be addressed through music therapy. Studies indicate that music can be used to enhance memory, attention, executive function, and emotional reasoning (Bettison, 1996; Hermelin et al., 1989; Ma et al., 2001; Reitman, 2006; Thaut, 1988; Wimpory et al., 1995). Figure 2 shows examples of how music therapy can promote preacademic and academic development.

Music as a carrier of nonmusical information
- Songs with lyrics about world facts, math, vocabulary, body parts, and other academic content.

Music listening to promote a learning environment conducive to attention and focused learning (Holland & Juhrs, 1974; Litchman, 1976).

Music as reinforcement (reward) for compliance in academic tasks

Music to teach specific concepts
- Music interventions that require use of numbers
- Music interventions that require following multi-step directions
- Music interventions that present colors, shapes, forms, and other concepts
- Music interventions that require practice of auditory memory or auditory motor memory

Figure 2. Examples of Music Therapy for Preacademic and Academic Development (Thaut, 1999)

Songs, chants, and rhythm activities can be used to reinforce math skills such as counting, 1:1 correspondence, and ordering. Songs with repetitive lyrics, rhythmic patterns, and added movements can give children many opportunities to count, add, subtract, and place items in order in a fun and interesting way. Categorization by size, shape, color, and sound can all be practiced through simple music activities and musical instruments. Other concepts such as high and low, in and out, front and back, slow and fast can be taught and practiced through music therapy interventions combining music and movement. Incorporating movement along with songs and rhythm gives the children different options for understanding and remembering the concepts, making the concepts come to life through music and movement. Music activities can also be developed to enhance focus of attention, memory skills, ordering of tasks, and task completion.

Physical skills and sensorimotor development. Some children with autism have atypical sensorimotor development, physical/motor delay, or disabilities. With regard to sensorimotor development, children can learn to tolerate and integrate auditory, visual, and tactile stimuli through manual exploration of musical instruments and movements to music. An engaging musical sound or instrument may be helpful in reducing self-stimulating behaviors (such as flapping arms, twirling) (Koegel et al., 1982). The therapist should remember, however, that individuals with autism can have unique and maladaptive responses to particular stimuli; consequently, the therapist should be careful to avoid introducing musical sounds or objects that are not well tolerated or that become a new object of **perseveration** (nonproductive persistence in an action or attention to an object) (Thaut, 1999).

Music therapy interventions can focus on improving fine motor skills through instrument playing, such as piano/keyboard, guitar, or other small instruments requiring fine motor control. Gross motor skills can be enhanced through participation in movement to music activities (e.g., stretching, extending limbs, locomotion, crossing the midline, skipping, hopping, etc.) and music making through playing instruments requiring large muscle use, such as hand drums or mallet instruments. In addition, eye-hand coordination can be improved through playing two-handed instruments or reaching to play a percussion instrument that is attached to a stand. Enhanced motor coordination or body image has also been reported as a result of music therapy interventions (Goldstein, 1964; Mahlberg, 1973; Saperston, 1973; Thaut, 1999).

Leisure skills. A child with communication, social, and behavior problems may have difficulty finding appropriate leisure activities. Music therapists can instruct clients on music making/listening as part of leisure time. This could be as simple as learning how to use a radio or CD player, purchasing preferred music, or learning a few current dance steps. Music as a leisure skill could also involve learning to play an instrument such as guitar, keyboard, or drums, or joining in a community choir that is structured to support the needs of individuals with disabilities. Instruments and sheet music can be adapted through color-coding or adaptive playing techniques. Leisure music activities should be age-appropriate, socially acceptable, interesting, and fun. Whenever possible, leisure music activities should involve others to continue to improve social skills while sharing the joy of making music with others.

In conclusion, music is an attractive form of sensory stimulation for many children with autism. Furthermore, many children with autism show greater competence in music-based skills than in other areas. Consequently, music can be a very effective medium for promoting therapeutic and educational goals and objectives. Table 3 provides an overview of several goal areas with sample music therapy strategies (Adamek & Darrow, 2005, pp. 198–199).

Table 3
Summary of Goal Areas and Examples of Music Therapy Interventions

GOAL AREA	SAMPLE MUSIC THERAPY STRATEGY
Communication Skills	• Making choices through instrumental and vocal activities • Echoing verbalizations of therapist through songs • Following directions and being the leader (stop/go)
Social/Emotional Skills	• Practicing sharing/taking turns • Working together as a group to make music in an ensemble • Emotional expression/sharing of feelings through songs, instruments, and movement • Increasing self-esteem by learning new skills • Interacting with peers through music making
Behavior Skills	• Structured music activities to practice following directions • Opportunities to be a leader in the group; opportunities to follow others' lead • Music to reinforce appropriate behavior
Academic Skills	• Counting songs/rhythm activities • Movement to reinforce concepts such as in/out, high/low, in front/behind • Categorization of instruments; colors, size, shapes, sounds
Physical Skills	• Developing gross motor skills through movement to music • Developing fine motor skills through playing instrument • Gait training through rhythmic stimulation
Leisure Skills	• Developing skills playing instruments such as guitar or piano for leisure time • Participating in a vocal music group in preparation for community vocal group

SUMMARY

Autism is a neurological disorder that affects a person's ability to communicate and interact with others. Autism is a developmental disability and is considered to be a spectrum disorder because it affects individuals in different ways and to varying degrees. Autism affects approximately 1 in 150 people in the U.S., which means that approximately 1.5 million Americans today have some form of autism.

Autism is four times more prevalent in boys than in girls, and the rate of children diagnosed with autism is increasing by 10–17% each year.

Autism and Autism Spectrum Disorders (ASD) falls under the umbrella category of Pervasive Developmental Disorders (PDD), listed in the *Diagnostic and Statistical Manual of Mental Disorders* (American Psychiatric Association, 2000). This category includes neurological disorders such as autism, Rett's Syndrome, and Asperger's Syndrome that are characterized by severe and pervasive impairments in many areas of development.

Individuals with autism have qualitative impairment in reciprocal social interaction and communication skills, based on what is typical for their developmental level. They also have restricted repertoire of interests and activities and may display unusual or stereotypical behaviors. Symptoms of autism begin before the age of 3 and continue throughout a person's life. Genetic factors and environmental factors are linked to the causes of autism, yet there is no definitive answer to the question, "What causes autism?" Over 92,000 students with autism and ASD received special education services in the U.S. during the 2001–2002 school year.

Music therapy has been shown to be an effective intervention to improve individual's communication skills, social skills, and behavior, as well as to improve academic, physical/motor, and leisure skills. Music therapists utilize singing, playing instruments, and listening as well as responding to the musical elements such as rhythm, melody, and tempo to work on specific goals and objectives. Music therapy sessions may be 1:1, in small groups of children with autism, or in integrated settings with typically developing peers. Individuals can develop and practice language and communication skills, social skills, and appropriate behaviors in the motivating and engaging music therapy setting.

STUDY QUESTIONS

1. What are the three key areas of functioning in which individuals with ASD differ from their peers?

2. Why is autism considered a spectrum disorder?

3. Give several examples of alternative and augmentative communication (AAC) systems and how a music therapist might use one within a session.

4. Give several examples of how music therapy can be used to support social and peer interactions.

5. How can functional academic skills be taught in a music therapy session?

6. How can a music therapist use a proactive approach to decrease problem behaviors and increase positive behaviors? What might a person think about when planning a session?

7. Considering that many individuals with ASD have sensory processing difficulty, what are some factors a music therapist should think about when planning musical and therapeutic interventions?

8. How might music therapy be used as a reinforcer for a student with ASD?

9. Theories on the causes of autism have changed over the past 40 years. What are some of the current theories on the etiology of autism?

REFERENCES

Adamek, M., & Darrow, A. A. (2005). *Music in special education.* Silver Spring, MD: American Music Therapy Association.

American Psychiatric Association. (2000). *Diagnostic and statistical manual of mental disorders* (4th ed., text revision). Washington, DC: Author.

Applebaum, E., Egel, A., Koegel, R., & Imhoff, B. (1979). Measuring musical abilities of autistic children. *Journal of Autism and Developmental Disorders, 9,* 279–285.

Autism Society of America. (2008). *About autism.* Retrieved from www.autism-society.org

Autism Speaks. (2008). *What is autism?: An overview.* Retrieved from www.autismspeaks.org

Bettison, S. (1996). The long-term effects of auditory training on children with autism. *Journal of Autism and Developmental Disorders, 26,* 361–375.

Blackstock, E. G. (1978). Cerebral asymmetry and the development of early infantile autism. *Journal of Autism and Childhood Schizophrenia, 8,* 339–353.

Bondy, A., & Frost, L. (1994). The Picture Exchange Communication System. *Focus on Autistic Behavior, 9,* 1–19.

Brown, L., Branston, M. B., Hamre-Nietupski, S., Pumplan, I., Certo, N., & Gruenewald, L. (1979). A strategy for developing chronological age appropriate and functional curricular content for severely handicapped adolescents and young adults. *Journal of Special Education, 13,* 81–90.

Centers for Disease Control and Prevention. (2008). *Autism spectrum disorders overview.* Retrieved from www.cdc.gov

Davis, R. K. (1990). A model for the integration of music therapy with preschool classrooms for children with physical disabilities or language delays. *Music Therapy Perspectives, 8,* 82–84.

Edgerton, C. (1994). The effect of improvisational music therapy on the communicative behaviors of autistic children. *Journal of Music Therapy, 31,* 31–62.

Foxton, J. M., Stewart, M. E., Barnard, L., Rodgers, J., Young, A. H., O'Brien, G., & Griffiths, T. D. (2003). Absence of auditory "global interference" in autism. *Brain, 126,* 2703–2709.

Frith, U. (1972). Cognitive mechanisms in autism: Experiments with color and tone sequence production. *Journal of Autism and Childhood Schizophrenia, 2,* 160–173.

Frith, U. (2003). *Autism: Explaining the enigma.* Malden, MA: Blackwell.

Frost, L., & Bondy, A. (1994). PECS: *The Picture Exchange Communication System training manual.* Cherry Hill, NJ: Pyramid Educational Consultants.

Goldstein, C. (1964). Music and creative arts therapy for an autistic child. *Journal of Music Therapy 1,* 135–138.

Gray, C., & Garand, J. (1993) Social stories: Improving responses of students with autism with accurate social information. *Focus on Autistic Behavior, 8,* 1–10.

Hairston, M. (1990). Analysis of responses of mentally retarded autistic and mentally retarded nonautistic children to art therapy and music therapy. *Journal of Music Therapy, 27,* 137–150.

Heaton, P. (2003). Pitch memory, labeling, and disembedding in autism. *Journal of Child Psychology and Psychiatry, 44*, 543–551.

Heaton, P. (2005). Interval and contour processing in autism. *Journal of Autism and Developmental Disorders, 35*, 787–793.

Heaton, P., Hermelin, B., & Pring, L. (1998). Autism and pitch processing: A precursor for savant musical ability. *Music Perception, 15*, 291–305.

Heaton, P., Pring, L., & Hermelin, B. (2001). Music processing in high functioning children with autism. *Annals of the New York Academy of Sciences, 930*, 443–444.

Heflin, L. J., & Alaimo, D. F. (2007). *Students with autism spectrum disorders: Effective instructional practices.* Upper Saddle River, NJ: Pearson Merrill/Prentice Hall.

Hermelin, B., O'Connor, N., & Lee, S. (1989). Intelligence and musical improvisation. *Psychological Medicine, 19*, 447–457.

Hermelin, B., O'Connor, N., & Lee, S. (1997). Musical inventiveness of five idiot-savants. *Psychological Medicine, 17*, 685–694.

Hollander, F. M., & Juhrs, P. D. (1974). Orff-Schulwerk: An effective treatment tool with autistic children. *Journal of Music Therapy, 11*, 1–12.

Humpal, M. (1990). Early intervention: The implications for music therapy. *Music Therapy Perspectives, 8*, 30–35.

Jellison, J. A., Brooks, B. H., & Huck, A. M. (1984). Structuring small groups and music reinforcement to facilitate positive interactions and acceptance of severely handicapped students in regular music classrooms. *Journal of Research in Music Education, 32*, 243–264.

Johnson, C. P. (2004). Early clinical characteristics of children with autism. In V. B. Gupta (Ed.), *Autistic spectrum disorders in children* (pp. 85–123). New York: Marcel Dekker.

Kanner, L. (1943). Autistic disturbances of affective contact. *Nervous Child, 2*, 217–150.

Koegel, R. L., Rincover, A., & Egel, A. L. (1982). *Educating and understanding autistic children.* San Diego, CA: College Hill.

Kostka, M. (1993). A comparison of selected behaviors of a student with autism in special education and regular music classes. *Music Therapy Perspectives, 11*, 57–60.

Kravits, T. R., Kamps, D. M., Kemmerer, K., & Potucek, J. (2002). Brief report: Increasing communication skills for an elementary-aged student with autism using the Picture Exchange Communication System. *Journal of Autism and Developmental Disorders, 32*, 225–230.

Lim, H. A. (2007). *The effect of "developmental speech-language training through music" on speech production in children with autism spectrum disorders.* Unpublished doctoral dissertation, The University of Miami, 2007.

Litchman, M. D. (1976). The use of music in establishing a learning environment for language instruction with autistic children (Doctoral dissertation, State University of New York at Buffalo, 1976). *Dissertation Abstracts International, 37*, 4992A. (UMI No. 773557)

Ma, Y., Nagler, J., & Lee, M. (2001). Impact of music therapy on the communication skills of toddlers with pervasive developmental disorder. *Annals of the New York Academy of Sciences, 930*, 445–447.

Mahlberg, M. (1973). Music therapy in the treatment of an autistic child. *Journal of Music Therapy, 10*, 189–193.

Mastropieri, M., & Scruggs, T. (2000). *The inclusive classroom: Strategies for effective instruction.* Upper Saddle River, NJ: Merrill/Prentice Hall.

Mottron, L., Peretz, I., Belleville, S. & Rouleau, N. (1999). Absolute pitch in autism: A case study. *Neurocase, 5*, 485–502.

Mottron, L., Peretz, I., & Menard, E. (2000). Local and global processing of music in high-functioning persons with autism. *Journal of Child Psychology and Psychiatry, 41*, 1057–1068.

Mundy, P., & Stella, J. (2000). Joint attention, social orienting, and communication in autism. In A. Wetherby & B. Prizant (Eds.), *Autism spectrum disorders: A transactional developmental perspective* (pp. 55–78). Baltimore: Paul H. Brookes.

National Research Council. (2001). *Educating children with autism.* Committee on Educational Interventions for Children with Autism. Division of Behavioral and Social Sciences and Education. Washington, DC: National Academy Press.

Nelson, D., Anderson, V., & Gonzales, A. (1984). Music activities as therapy for children with autism and other pervasive developmental disorders. *Journal of Music Therapy, 21*, 100–116.

Nieto Del Rincon, P. L. (2008). Autism: Alterations in auditory perception. *Reviews in the Neurosciences, 19*, 61.

O'Connell, T. (1974). The musical life of an autistic boy. *Journal of Autism and Childhood Schizophrenia, 4*, 223–229.

Pronovost, W. (1961). The speech behavior and language comprehension of autistic children. *Journal of Chronic Diseases, 13*, 228–233.

Reitman, M. R. (2006). Effectiveness of music therapy interventions on joint attention in children diagnosed with autism: A pilot study. *Dissertation Abstracts International: Section B: The Sciences and Engineering, 66*, 6315.

Rice, C. (2007). *Prevalence of autism spectrum disorders—Autism and developmental disabilities.* Centers for Disease Control and Prevention. Retrieved from www.cdc.gov/mmwr/preview/mmwrhtml/ss5601a1.htm

Rimland, B. (1964). *Infantile autism.* New York: Appleton-Century-Crofts.

Saperston, B. (1973). The use of music in establishing communication with an autistic mentally retarded child. *Journal of Music Therapy, 10*, 184–188.

Schmidt, D., & Edwards, J. (1976). Reinforcement of autistic children's responses to music. *Psychological Reports, 39*, 571–577.

Scott, J., Clark, C., & Brady, M. (2000). *Students with autism: Characteristics and instruction programming.* San Diego, CA: Singular.

Sherwin, A. (1953). Reactions to music of autistic children. *American Journal of Psychiatry, 109*, 823–831.

Simpson, R. L., & Miles, B. S. (1998). *Educating children and youth with autism.* Austin, TX: PRO-ED.

Staum, M., & Flowers, P. (1984). The use of simulated training and music lessons in teaching appropriate shopping skills to an autistic child. *Music Therapy Perspectives, 1*, 14–17.

Stevens, E., & Clark, F. (1969). Music therapy in the treatment of autistic children. *Journal of Music Therapy, 6*, 98–104.

Thaut, M. (1984). A music therapy treatment model for autistic children. *Music Therapy Perspectives, 1*, 7–13.

Thaut, M. H. (1987). Visual vs. auditory (musical) stimulus preferences in autistic children: A pilot study. *Journal of Autism and Developmental Disorders, 17*, 425–432.

Thaut, M. H. (1988). Measuring musical responsiveness in autistic children: A comparative analysis of improvised musical tone sequences of autistic, normal and mentally retarded individuals. *Journal of Autism and Developmental Disorders, 18*, 561–571.

Thaut, M. H. (1999). Music therapy with autistic children. In W. B. Davis, K. E. Gfeller, & M. H. Thait (Eds.), *An introduction to music therapy: Theory and practice* 2nd edition (pp. 163–178). Dubuque, IA: McGraw-Hill College.

Umbarger, G. (2007). State of the evidence regarding complementary and alternative medical treatments for autism spectrum disorders. *Education and Training in Developmental Disabilities, 42*, 437–447.

U.S. Department of Education. (2007). *Twenty-seventh annual report to Congress on the implementation of the Individuals with Disabilities Education Act.* Washington, DC: U.S. Government Printing Office.

Walworth, D. D. (2007). The use of music therapy withn the SCERTS model for children with autism specturm disorder. *Journal of Music Therapy, 44,* 2–22.

Warwick, A. (1995). Music therapy in the education service: Research with autistic children and their mothers. In T. Wigram, B. Saperston, & R. West (Eds.), *The art and science of music therapy: A handbook* (pp. 209–225). Chur, Switzerland: Harwood Academic.

Whipple, J. (2004). Music in intervention for children and adolescents with autism: A meta-analysis. *Journal of Music Therapy, 41,* 90–106.

Wimpory, D., Chadwick, P, & Nash, S. (1995). Brief report: musical interaction therapy for children with autism. An evaluative study with two year follow-up. *Journal of Autism and Developmental Disorders, 25*(5), 541–552.

Young, R. L., & Nettelbeck, T. (1995). The abilities of a musical savant and his family. *Journal of Autism and Developmental Disorders, 25*(3), 231–248.

CHAPTER 6

MUSIC THERAPY FOR CHILDREN AND ADULTS WITH PHYSICAL DISABILITIES

Michael H. Thaut
Kathrin Mertel
Anne K. Leins

CHAPTER OUTLINE

 PHYSICALLY DISABLING CONDITIONS
  Cerebral Palsy
  Muscular Dystrophies
  Spina Bifida
  Clubfoot
  Congenital Dislocation of the Hip
  Arthrogryposis
  Juvenile Rheumatoid Arthritis
  Dwarfism
  Osteogenesis Imperfecta
  Thermal Injuries
  Spinal Cord Injuries
  Acquired Amputations
  Poliomyelitis
 MUSIC THERAPY WITH THE PHYSICALLY DISABLED: AN OUTLINE
  Settings
  Background Knowledge
  The Interdisciplinary Team Member
  Goals

MUSIC THERAPY IN THE TREATMENT OF PHYSICAL DISORDERS
Motor Skills
Communication Skills
Cognitive Skills
Social Skills
Emotional Skills
Musical Skills

Physically disabling conditions in children and adults encompass a wide variety of disorders with different causes and consequences for the afflicted person. The common problem, however, for all conditions discussed in this chapter is an interference with a person's physical abilities. Conditions that impede physical functioning are defined in various ways and include such terms as *orthopedically handicapped, crippled, physically impaired,* or *physically handicapped.* These terms are often used interchangeably. Because most rehabilitation efforts are usually utilized as early as possible, this chapter will emphasize pediatric rehabilitation for children.

Physically disabling conditions can be described according to a person's locomotor abilities (ability to walk). They can also be described as congenital and/or chronic and acquired and/or acute conditions (Sherrill, 1981).

Congenital and/or chronic conditions are caused by birth defects. When bodily or functional abnormalities are present at birth, they are called congenital. When they appear later in life but are genetically caused, they are called chronic. The most common conditions in this category are cerebral palsy, muscular dystrophies, spina bifida, clubfoot, congenital dislocation of the hip, arthrogryposis, juvenile rheumatoid arthritis, dwarfism, and osteogenesis imperfecta.

Acquired and/or acute conditions result from three different causes: trauma, disease, or disorders of growth and development (osteochondroses) (Sherrill, 1981). These conditions encompass thermal injuries (burns), spinal cord injuries (traumatic paraplegia and quadriplegia), acquired amputations, and poliomyelitis.

It is important to realize that physically disabled children often suffer from multiple impairments. The trauma or defect that damages the human nervous system, be it congenital or acquired, rarely affects just one isolated area, but is often widespread and thus impairs more than one function. We often see physical impairment in conjunction with intellectual deficits, speech impairment, or sensory impairments such as blindness or deafness. For example, a cerebral palsy child also may be mentally retarded or may have impaired vision or speech. The opposite case, however, may also be found. A child could be very severely involved physically with a condition such as osteogenesis imperfecta but could have normal intellectual capacities. It is a challenge for the professional caregiver to create an environment for multiply disabled children in which their weaknesses are compensated for and their abilities are strengthened.

PHYSICALLY DISABLING CONDITIONS

Cerebral Palsy

Cerebral palsy is a nonprogressive disorder of movement and posture that is caused by damage to the motor areas of the brain. About 85–90% of such brain damage occurs during pregnancy or birth. Cerebral palsy from such early causes is termed congenital. Injuries to the brain during childhood account for the other 10–15% of cerebral palsy cases that are termed acquired (Bleck & Nagel, 1982). Over 750,000 persons in the United States have been diagnosed as cerebral palsied, one third of whom are under 21 years of age. According to Bleck and Nagel, 7 out of every 1,000 children are born with cerebral palsy. Many of the milder cases, approximately 1 out of those 7, do not require special treatment.

One common way to classify cerebral palsy is by motor abnormality. It is important to recognize in this context that motor abnormalities in cerebral palsy depend on the type of lesion. In spastic lesions, the pyramidal system in the central nervous system has been damaged. In pure athetoid lesions, only the extrapyramidal system is involved. It is important to note that the central control system is damaged in cerebral palsy. The peripheral nervous system and muscles are intact (Gage, 1989). Based on the type of lesion, functional movements may show different abnormalities. Understanding the different impairments associated with different lesions is essential to design effective treatment programs (Malherbe, Breniere, & Bril, 1992). Specifically in gait, several typical features, such as impaired balance, reflex patterns used to ambulate, abnormal muscle tone, imbalance between muscle groups, and loss of selective muscle control, have been well analyzed and described (Sutherland & Davids, 1993).

Seven types of cerebral palsy are commonly described:

Spasticity. In spastic cerebral palsy, the muscles of the arms and legs are tight and contract strongly when one attempts to stretch or move suddenly. Several important muscle reflexes are also disturbed, which leads to abnormal movement patterns and posture. As the child grows older, the contracted muscles become shorter, and deformities of the limbs, pelvis, and spine can occur.

Athetosis. The athetoid child shows involuntary, purposeless movements of the limbs. In addition, purposeful movements are contorted.

Rigidity. Rigidity is a more severe form of spasticity.

Ataxia. Children with ataxia walk slowly, with a swaying trunk, with feet apart and arms held up to maintain balance. Ataxia refers to a lack of balance, a lack of sense of position in space, and uncoordinated movement.

Tremor. This condition refers to a shakiness of limbs, especially when the person tries to move the limb. Tremor in a resting limb is unlikely to be observed.

Mixed Type. Children with this condition usually have both spasticity and athetosis. Also, tremor and ataxia may be seen mixed in with other conditions.

Atonia. This is a condition of no or very flaccid muscle tone, which may be seen in infants. Atonia will usually develop into athetosis.

Another way to categorize cerebral palsy conditions is according to limb involvement. The most common conditions are:

1. Monoplegia—one limb involved
2. Hemiplegia—upper and lower limb on one side of the body
3. Paraplegia—lower limbs only
4. Diplegia—major involvement of lower limbs and only minor involvement of upper limbs
5. Triplegia—involvement of three limbs, usually both lower limbs and one upper limb
6. Quadriplegia—major involvement of all four limbs

Almost all cerebral palsied children have multiple disabilities. Approximately 50–60% are mentally retarded, and about the same percentage have visual impairments. Between 5% and 8% have hearing loss. Approximately one third have seizures at some time in their lives. Most of these children need some form of speech therapy. Learning disabilities are also very common, often accentuated by hyperactivity, distractibility, lack of concentration, and poor attention span.

Muscular Dystrophies

Muscular dystrophy is a progressive weakness of all muscles in the body, which can be attributed to a degeneration of muscle cells and their replacement by fat and fibrous tissue. The most common type of progressive muscular dystrophy is the Duchenne type. Its onset is usually before the age of 3, but symptoms may appear as late as age 10 or 11. The disease is genetically encoded. Inheritance patterns can be demonstrated in family histories. Approximately 250,000 persons suffer from muscular dystrophies in the United States.

Early signs of the disease include awkward and clumsy movements, poor posture, and tiptoeing. Muscle weakness develops from the feet upward to the legs, hips, abdomen, shoulders, and arms. Hands, neck, and face are affected later. In Duchenne type muscular dystrophy, the course of the illness becomes progressively worse. Most children are wheelchair-bound by age 10. Death occurs usually in the late teens. The disease itself is not fatal; however, secondary complications, such as heart failure due to a weakened heart muscle, or overwhelming lung infection because of weakness of the muscles involved in breathing, are the usual cause of death.

Spina Bifida

Spina bifida is an open defect in the spinal column caused by abnormal fetal development. It is the most seriously disabling condition in children. The incidence per 1,000 births ranges from 1.1 to 4.2 (Sherrill, 1981). Spina bifida is caused by a failure of the back arches of the vertebra to close before birth. In spina bifida occulta, the bony defect is covered by skin, but there is no outpouching of the spinal cord. Few, if any, problems are associated with spina bifida occulta.

There are other forms of this disorder that are serious. Meningocele is a condition in which the meninges (spinal cord covering) protrude through the opening at the back of the spinal column. The most serious condition is called myelomeningocele, in which the spinal cord and the meninges develop outside the body.

There are many disabilities associated with spina bifida. The higher the location of the defect along the spinal column, the greater the likelihood that paralysis of the trunk and pelvis will manifest, which results in the inability to walk independently. Defects in the lowermost parts of the back may permit walking with crutches and leg braces. Many children have bony deformities, such as dislocation of the hip, clubfoot, turned-in feet, and so forth. Again, depending on the location of the defect, loss of skin sensation is a common problem. Paralysis of the bladder and the muscles involved in urination is present in all children with this condition; bowel paralysis is present in some children. In 90% of all children with spina bifida, hydrocephalus (water on the brain) occurs, which is caused by an increased amount of cerebrospinal fluid in the brain. Hydrocephalus is frequently associated with mental retardation. Medical attention to the problems of spina bifida, for example, neurosurgery to close the defect in the spinal column, orthopedic surgery to correct bone deformities, or urinalysis to control bladder function, has helped to improve the quality of life of the affected child. However, most children with spina bifida will need extended care throughout their lives.

Clubfoot

According to Sherrill (1981), congenital clubfoot is the most common of all congenital orthopedic disabilities, with an incidence of about 1 in every 700 births. The entire foot is inverted, with the heel drawn up, and the forefoot bent inward (adducted). Clubfoot varies in degrees of severity. Casting, bracing, splinting, and surgery can often correct the condition.

Congenital Dislocation of the Hip

Congenital dislocation of the hip is caused by an abnormal fetal development of the hip bones. It can be so mild that it is not detected until the child begins to walk. Corrective treatment includes surgery, casting, and splinting. In most instances, the child will spend extended periods of time immobilized and hospitalized in casts or splints.

Arthrogryposis

Arthrogryposis is a congenital disease in which affected children are born with rigidly fixed and stiff joints and weak muscles. For example, shoulders may be turned in, elbows are straightened, and wrists are flexed and turned inward. Lower extremities are also frequently affected. Joints are often larger and have a loss of motion. The spinal cord sometimes is curved (scoliosis). Children with this disease may or may not be able to walk. However, within their limited mobility and movement awkwardness, they can function well and have no pain associated with their deformities.

Juvenile Rheumatoid Arthritis

Juvenile rheumatoid arthritis is a disease that affects children, usually before the age of 11, with two peaks of incidence between the ages of 2 and 4, and between 8 and 11. Girls are affected by this disease three to five times more often than boys. The specific cause for this disease is unclear. It appears that the inflammation of joints is a result of abnormal antibodies attacking normal body tissue. However, it is unknown why these antibodies appear. Unlike adult arthritis, most child sufferers will be free from active disease within 10 years after onset.

One or more joints will be inflamed during the disease. Some forms of disease are also associated with fever and skin rashes. Acute episodes of joint inflammations are usually extremely painful and may last from a few days to several weeks. The affected joints are swollen, discolored, and tender. Knees, ankles, feet, wrists, hands, shoulders, elbows, and hips can be affected.

Dwarfism

Dwarfism is a congenital condition that is due to abnormal skeletal development and is characterized by retarded physical growth, which is more than three standard deviations from the mean for the age group. Most dwarfs have relatively normal trunks and heads with disproportionately short arms and legs. Their physical mobility is rarely restricted other than by height, and their intelligence is normal or above average.

Osteogenesis Imperfecta

The common term for *osteogenesis imperfecta* (OI) is brittle bone disease. It is an inherited condition that affects males and females equally. The disorder, which can be present at birth or develop later, is characterized by weak bones and short limbs that deform easily because of repetitive fractures and healing in deformed positions. The joints are excessively mobile because of greater elasticity of muscle tissue and skin. Independent walking ability is rarely attained by children or adults. Children with OI have normal intelligence and achieve well academically. However, physical activities are severely restricted.

Thermal Injuries

Thermal injuries can be caused by fire, chemicals, electricity, radiation, and prolonged contact with extreme degrees of hot or cold liquids (Sherrill, 1981). Thermal injuries are evaluated by extent and degree. The extent of damage to the body is evaluated by the total surface area affected by the injury. Degree is determined in three categories. First-degree burns affect only the outer layer of the skin and will heal quickly, although they appear red and are sensitive to touch. Second-degree burns destroy the outer skin layer and produce severe scarring. They expose nerve endings and are, therefore, very painful. However, second-degree burns can heal spontaneously over several weeks. Third-degree burns involve all skin layers and may involve muscles, tendons, and bones. The affected areas are white and dry and feel like leather. Because nerve endings are destroyed, initially no pain is present. Third-degree burns require skin grafting and prolonged hospitalization. Treatment involves bathing in special solutions, removal of dead skin tissue, dressing changes, and surgical procedures, including skin grafting.

Most treatment procedures associated with thermal injuries are very painful. Especially for younger children, these procedures can have an emotionally traumatizing effect. After hospitalization, long periods of rehabilitation are often necessary. Inevitably, scar tissue will form, which is very sensitive to sunlight. Also, layers of thick scar tissue will restrict the range of motion of joints. Braces, splints, and supportive bandages or masks are used to restrict the growth of scar tissue. One of the most difficult problems for burn victims to cope with is the deformed physical appearance, which sets them apart from other persons.

Spinal Cord Injuries

Severe spinal cord injuries result in different types of paralysis of parts of the body, categorized as paraplegia or quadriplegia. Paraplegia refers to paralysis of the lower part of the body, including motion and sensation. Quadriplegia refers to paralysis of all four limbs. Although these conditions can be caused by congenital abnormalities, more common in rehabilitation settings are traumatic injuries. Frequent causes are motor vehicle accidents, sports accidents, bullet wounds, or injuries from falling from a height. The paralysis is caused by an interruption of the nerve pathways going from the brain to the involved limb via the spinal cord. The higher in the spinal cord the injury occurs, the more severe the resulting paralysis will be. Nerve pathways in the spinal cord that are completely destroyed will not regenerate and cannot be repaired by current medical techniques. Thus, the paralysis will be permanent. Handling of the patient and immediate start of emergency care after the trauma may be critical to the outcome of the injury. Any incomplete nerve damage may still be repairable if emergency procedures can start early.

In rehabilitation, the major emphasis should be on the patient's psychological status in regard to morale, motivation, and attitude to an altered quality of life. Emotional, social, and occupational changes in an injured person's life can be severe. Supportive counseling; emotional support from family, friends, and peers; and adaptive techniques to facilitate activities of daily living and occupational endeavors are necessary.

Acquired Amputations

Most elective amputations in children occur between 12 and 21 years of age. Most common causes for traumatic amputations are motor vehicle accidents, farm accidents, power tool accidents, and gunshot injuries. Other causes for amputations include cancer, infections, bone tumors, or vascular conditions like gangrene.

The loss of a limb in elective amputation is one of the most psychologically traumatizing disabilities a child can experience. Any rehabilitation plan for an amputee child includes strong psychological support for both the child and the family. The main goal for treatment of an amputee child is to enable him or her to develop and grow as normally as possible and enjoy a meaningful quality of life. One of the major aspects of amputee rehabilitation is the use of prosthetic devices as artificial limbs. Today, prosthesis fitting occurs usually within 30 days after the amputation because of advances in surgical techniques. Training in the use of prostheses should include functional activities of daily living as well as leisure and recreational activities as much as possible.

Poliomyelitis

Poliomyelitis is a viral infection that attacks the motor cells in the spinal cord. The virus enters through the intestinal tract, travels through the bloodstream, and settles in the motor cells of the spinal cord. The virus may cause only inflammation and swelling of the cells, in which case full recovery can take place. In severe cases, the motor cells are destroyed, and irreversible muscle paralysis will occur. At the onset of the infection, fever, painful muscle spasms, and muscle stiffness occur. After the acute phase, muscle function will return to normal or muscular paralysis will persist. A complete diagnosis of the extent of permanent damage should be made 18 months after onset of the infection.

Affected children will, for the most part, have moderate to severe paralysis of the lower limbs and, at times, the trunk. Also, spinal curvature (scoliosis) and joint deformities may develop because of muscle weakness. Rehabilitation includes strength training for weakened muscles, the use of braces to support weakened joints, and the use of crutches and wheelchairs for mobility. Poliomyelitis affects only the neuromuscular system. Other bodily functions and intellectual capacities are unaffected. Although poliomyelitis still exists today, cases have become rare in developed countries since the introduction of vaccines.

MUSIC THERAPY WITH THE PHYSICALLY DISABLED: AN OUTLINE

Settings

The music therapist will encounter physically disabled children in a variety of settings. Because of the mainstreaming laws in this country (PL 94-142), most physically disabled children will be part of an educational setting, be it a mainstreamed classroom with normal and disabled children, a special classroom in a normal school setting, or a school for children with special needs. Other settings in which music therapists work with these children include hospital outpatient programs, developmental centers, group homes, or preschool programs. Jellison (2000) provides a comprehensive research survey on the effectiveness of music therapy methods with disabled children in various settings.

Background Knowledge

In order to work efficiently with the physically disabled child, the music therapist must be thoroughly familiar with the particular disabling condition. Each condition has a different cause, diagnosis, and treatment requirements (Toombs-Rudenberg, 1982). For example, conditions such as cerebral palsy require specific knowledge of handling techniques. The music therapist who works with physically disabled persons will need to know how to position a physically involved child on the floor, in a chair, or in a wheelchair, to support and allow for the best range of movement possible or to avoid reinforcing detrimental postures, reflexes, and motions. The music therapist also needs to be familiar with techniques for transferring children from a bed to a chair, or from a lying into a sitting position.

Another important consideration is the developmental course and diagnosis of the condition. Is the impairment a progressive illness that will get worse over time? If this is the case, what level of functioning can the therapist realistically expect from the child at a given stage of the illness? Understanding of the diagnosis of a particular condition will give the music therapist the knowledge of what areas of behavior are affected and what level of functioning can be expected from the child.

Another important area of knowledge for the music therapist includes the steps and progressions of normal development in the areas of motor, social, emotional, and cognitive behavior. Research has shown very clearly that the development of disabled children follows the same progressions as that of normal children. They will, however, develop at a slower pace or their development may be arrested at a certain level (Cratty, 1975). This knowledge is very important for the formulation of appropriate treatment goals in order to move the child, in a developmentally meaningful and attainable way, to higher levels of functioning.

The Interdisciplinary Team Member

From the foregoing discussion, it is quite obvious that the music therapist must be thoroughly familiar with the developmental, psychological, and medical information that pertains to each disabling condition. This background of knowledge is also necessary for the music therapist to function efficiently as a member of an interdisciplinary treatment team, be it as a staff member in a special education program or as a therapist on a hospital staff.

Goals

The music therapist pursues three different types of goals in working with physically disabled children: educational, rehabilitative, and developmental.

Educational goals. Educational goals focus on the academic development of the child, which also includes social, emotional, and physical skill development. Music therapy goals are closely linked to the educational planning for the child, usually in a special education setting. The music therapist uses music activities and related experiences in speech, movement, and other creative arts media, such as drama or visual arts, to support and enhance educational concepts. Examples would be background music to enhance attention span and cognitive learning; songs and chants to teach academic concepts, for example, multiplication tables or knowledge about the world; music group activities to teach social skills; playing instruments to enhance motor skills; and musical activities such as singing and chanting or performing musical dramas to enhance communication skills.

Rehabilitative goals. Rehabilitative goals focus on remedial or compensatory therapy for physical deficits, such as the use of muscles for movement, posture, and respiration, or sensory perception in the auditory, visual, and tactile modes. Other therapeutic efforts may be directed toward disorders of speech, for example, aphasic or apraxic conditions, or problems with speech fluency or proper use of voice. The music therapist works on rehabilitative goals usually in an inpatient or outpatient hospital setting.

Developmental goals. Developmental goals focus on enhancing normal development of a child by enriching his or her life with as many normal social, emotional, and sensorimotor experiences through music as possible. The music therapist develops musical activities that utilize any existing functional ability in the child to provide rewarding recreational and leisure experiences. In other words, the music therapist uses music to enrich and normalize the quality of life for a disabled child as much as possible. For example, it may be possible to teach a child to play a musical instrument, using adaptive devices, or to integrate him or her into an orchestra, band, choir, or musical theater group.

Some settings for physically disabled children with expanded resources will enable music therapists to integrate educational, rehabilitative, and developmental goals in their work. An integrated approach usually has a positive motivational effect on the child because it diminishes the feeling of being a patient or of suffering from deficits that need special treatment.

MUSIC THERAPY IN THE TREATMENT OF PHYSICAL DISORDERS

As we have discussed, the goals of music therapy with physically disabled children can be divided into three major categories: educational goals, rehabilitative goals, and developmental goals. Within each of these goal areas, we can further divide music therapy interventions according to specific behaviors or skills that should be addressed in the treatment program. Six treatment areas for music therapy interventions are recommended: motor skills, communication skills, cognitive skills, social skills, emotional skills, and musical skills.

Motor Skills

Music communicates information to the brain that can have profound effects on development, learning, and recovery of function. Aside from music, few endeavors possess the ability to so widely activate the neural networks of the brain and stimulate such a variety of cognitive modalities.

Throughout the last decade, research efforts have demonstrated that the auditory perception of rhythm is connected to the priming and timing reactions of the motor system. As the main element of chronological organization in music, rhythm has an ability to facilitate sensorimotor reactions by creating stable and well-defined templates for the temporal organization of motor responses. In this way, rhythm can be useful in helping to initialize and regulate motor movements. Music has a multitude of neurologic effects, and playing music leads to an activation of widely distributed cortical and subcortical networks related to motor, sensory, and cognitive aspects of brain function (Penhune, Zatorre, & Evans, 1998; Platel et al., 1997; Schlaug & Chen, 2001). Taken together, music—or especially rhythm—can serve as a model of temporality in the human brain (Harrington & Haaland, 1999; Rao, Mayer, & Harrington, 2001). The fact that cerebellar pathology fails to affect the capacity of auditory rhythms to entrain rhythmic motor responses (Molinari et al., 2001) suggests that sensory rhythms can compensate for damaged brain mechanisms normally responsible for timing.

Neurological music therapy offers a wide variety of techniques for improving the motor performance of the physically disabled child based upon the known structure and function of the neural auditory-motor system. Common goals in this area of therapy are strengthening of muscles; increasing range of motion and mobility; exercising coordination, balance, and gait; enforcing proper muscular positioning; and training functional motor activities.

Therapeutic techniques can be divided into two main categories: movement to music and movement through music. In the first approach, music is used as an accompaniment to guide and structure motor activities. Soothing music with low volume levels may be used to help muscle relaxation in conditions of muscle stiffness or spasticity.

Investigations of the impact of music and rhythm on motor processes suggest that rhythmic stimuli may be used as pacemakers or timekeepers to structure proper timing and spatial coordination, anticipation, and rhythmicity in movement (Cotton, 1974; Thaut, 1985). Further, research has shown that rhythmic musical stimuli are able to influence muscle activity (Thaut, McIntosh, Rice, & Prassas, 1992). These researchers documented that leg muscles became more active and worked more efficiently when their movement was synchronized with a rhythm. For a specific discussion of the effect of rhythmic synchronization on movement, please see Chapter 10 (Music Therapy in Neurological Rehabilitation).

Songs and instrumental music can also be used to structure and pace arm and hand movement, for example, during reaching and grasping exercises. Rhythmic stimuli have also been found to effectively facilitate gait training (Thaut, Hurt, Dragon, & McIntosh, 1998). All music therapy techniques that utilize movement to music can be categorized either as addressing intrinsically rhythmic movements such as gait, or as cuing broad ranges of functional movements that usually consist of single discrete motions.

Neurologic music therapy techniques that address the sensorimotor domain are:

- Rhythmic Auditory Stimulation (RAS)
- Patterned Sensory Enhancement (PSE)
- Therapeutic Instrumental Music Performance (TIMP)

Rhythmic Auditory Stimulation (RAS). RAS is a technique used to facilitate the rehabilitation of movements that are intrinsically and necessarily rhythmic, such as gait. Unfortunately, the majority of physically disabled children have problems with the patterns of their gait, which result in mildly to severely impaired locomotion. Gait training using RAS involves instructing the child to walk to an auditory rhythm while assisted in regulating his or her movements, in this case the alternating leg, heel, and toe movements foundational to walking. Through the input of the auditory rhythm, not only the movement is regulated, but the timing of the sequence of muscle contractions that produce the movement is optimized. The steadily presented auditory rhythm leads to the development of a more functional gait pattern for the patient. Though RAS can be used for any rhythmic movement, the effect on gait performance has thus far been most strongly established for stroke patients (Luft et al., 2004; Mandel, Nymark, Balmer, Grinnell, & O'Riain, 1990; McCombe & Whitall, 2005; Schauer & Mauritz, 2003; Thaut, Kenyon, Hurt, McIntosh, & Hoemberg, 2002; Whitall, McCombe-Waller, Silver, & Macko, 2000); persons suffering from Parkinson's disease (Bernatzky, Bernatzky, Hesse, Staffen, & Ladurner, 2004; Del Olmo & Cudeiro, 2003; Freeland et al., 2002; Howe, Lovgreen, Cody, Ashton, & Oldham, 2003; Lim et al., 2005; McIntosh, Brown, Rice, & Thaut, 1997; Miller, Thaut, McIntosh, & Rice, 1996; Morris et al., 2004; Pacchetti et al., 1998, 2000; Rochester et al., 2005; Thaut, McIntosh, & Rice, 1996) and individuals with traumatic brain injuries (Hurt, Rice, McIntosh, & Thaut, 1998). Practicing walking with RAS will improve both timing and speed of movement. In addition, improvements in spatial aspects of gait, such as length of stride, range of motion, trajectory fluidity, and the associated muscle activation patterns, can be observed.

RAS can be used in two different ways:

- As an immediate entrainment stimulus which provides rhythmic cues during therapy in order to improve walking tempo, balance, and control of muscles and limbs;

- As a facilitating stimulus for a certain training period in order to help the patient achieve a more functional gait pattern that can then be transferred to everyday life without continued rhythmic facilitation.

For a detailed description concerning the application of the RAS gait training manual, please see Chapter 10.

During RAS, the music therapist walks with the patient (often with the assistance of a physical therapist) while either applying a simple metronome click based on the patient's individual cadence, or playing a song in 2/4 or 4/4 meter with a dominant beat in order to cue gait parameters. The music can be pre-recorded or presented live by the therapist using an autoharp, drum, or other appropriate and portable instrument.

One of the more recent investigations into the usefulness of RAS in gait training is E. Kwak's "Effect of Rhythmic Auditory Stimulation on Gait Performance in Children with Spastic Cerebral Palsy" (2007). In her study, Kwak discovered that the use of RAS therapy improved gait performance, specifically through an improvement in velocity and stride length brought about by improved balance, trajectory, and kinematic stability without increasing cadence. This researcher also assessed the efficacy of therapist-facilitated RAS versus self-guided training. Kwak concluded that the therapist-facilitated group demonstrated more improvement in gait, though she also found the motivation level of the patients to be strongly related to therapeutic success.

We can conclude that the physiological effects of rhythm on the motor system lead to improvements of movement control in rehabilitation and the establishment of functional, stable, and adaptive gait patterns in patients with gait deficits due to neurological impairment.

Patterned Sensory Enhancement (PSE). In the second approach (movement through music), playing musical instruments provides an excellent method for exercising muscles and improving both gross and fine motor skills. As discussed in the previous section, motor control mechanisms underlie the effects of temporally based sensory cues (such as rhythm) and result in the improvement of motor function. Rhythm patterns are not the only templates that can be used for the training of motor ability in RAS. Other aspects of music, such as sound patterns (e.g., melodies), can help provide spatial and temporal information about physical movements. The technique of PSE uses the temporal, visual-spatial, and dynamic patterns in music to provide a structure for cuing discrete movements and facilitating longer movement sequences. This technique is especially useful in exercises aimed at improving hand and arm movement. A more detailed discussion of PSE is provided in Chapter 10.

A simple task, such as putting on a shirt, necessitates that one is first able to raise and lower one's arms. In order to practice this task with a patient using PSE, the therapist may lead the child's movement by playing a melody of ascending tones while the child raises his or her arms, and by playing a melody of descending tones while the child lowers his or her arms. In this way, these foundational movements can be facilitated. In PSE, the melody can also serve as a force cue; that is, at the point when the movement is naturally the most strenuous, the chord or melody is played very powerfully in order to musically demonstrate the force needed or desired at that instant in the movement. When the movement is in a stage of conclusion or relaxation, the melody reflects this by becoming gentler and quieter. Basically, the melody or pattern of chords ought to communicate information in real time to the patient about the effort or force appropriate for each instant of the movement. Visuospatial functions, perceptive qualities such as pitch and timbre, and central sensorimotor circuits are all employed in eye-hand and ear-hand coordination. A child who receives repeated and structured training in this form may over time begin to rely on his or her musical memory to provide representations of sequential motor ordering that can be applied to his or her movements. This process is not dependent on conscious attention to the details of the recalled music, and encouraging the development of this method is one of the essential goals of PSE. Therefore, PSE can be used to structure in time, space, and force, any functional movement patterns (e.g., grasping, reaching, or lifting movements) or sequences (e.g., sit-to-stand transfers) involving the whole body.

It must be emphasized that PSE is not accomplished by simply playing random music as a sort of "accompaniment" to the patient's movements. The qualities of the music must be matched to the movement pattern that is to be practiced. In this regard, it is essential for the therapist to be aware of and analyze the kinematic aspects of the particular movement before translating this movement pattern into an effective PSE exercise.

In summary, PSE is able to utilize all musical elements in a multidimensional framework while using sound patterns to cue desired movements.

Therapeutic Instrumental Music Playing (TIMP). The creation and performance of music is able to unite diverse human qualities such as emotion and intellect with rhythm and motor skills. The neurologic music therapy technique that makes use of this integrative effect is called Therapeutic Instrumental Music Playing (TIMP). A detailed discussion of TIMP is given in Chapter 10.

Musical instruments are useful and highly motivational tools in physical rehabilitation, especially when used for the purpose of rehabilitating motor movements in physically disabled children. Participating in TIMP is not only motivating for the patient, but allows the patient and therapist to work on endurance, timing of movements, strength, flexibility, and range of motion. Furthermore, music and sound are used successfully to provide auditory feedback during movement training (Flodmark, 1986; Talbot & Junkala, 1981).

Three elements form the basis of the therapeutic design of TIMP exercises:

1. **The musical structure** is used to facilitate the organization of movement in time and space, as well as to mediate force dynamics. Just think of the PSE mechanisms described above that could be easily integrated into TIMP exercises. For instance, spatial cuing is considerably enhanced by setting up the instruments in a way specific to the needs of the patient.

2. **The choice of instruments** and the method of playing both enhance therapeutically useful movements. Specific instruments may be more appropriate when focusing on a certain part of the body or when working on fine or gross motor skills. A descriptive list will be presented below.

3. **The spatial arrangement** and location of the instruments facilitate desired paths of motion for the limbs as well as positions of the body.

As one can imagine, in a therapeutic setting, the variety of possibilities for instrumental setup is nearly limitless. Musical instruments can serve both to define the parameters of a desired movement and as targets to which movement can be directed. That is, the specific instrumental setup visually defines parameters of the movement, but, as mentioned before, the child also receives both auditory and kinesthetic feedback from successfully contacting the target instrument. Sound provides an additional stimulus to excite the motor system while acoustic feedback informs the patient about his or her timing, strength, and range of motion. Furthermore, participating in functional music-centered exercises can generate feelings of accomplishment and collaboration, perhaps more so than doing other types of exercises such as bicep curls. These feelings complement the intrinsically motivating character of music, and both effects can serve as powerful reinforcing stimuli for the patient to continue working towards his or her therapeutic goals. The musical phrasing and metric organization present during training has a carry-over effect to daily life as the child develops a heightened capacity to remember movement sequences and an ability to refine the quality of these sequences. Lastly, active singing contributes to the development of an inner pacemaker and encourages the patient to maintain an upright position and increase his or her respiratory functions during the exercises.

In summary, TIMP can be used in functional exercises that require the patient to move towards or alternate between several targets. This type of therapy allows the therapist to address functional needs of the patient, such as arm and leg flexion/extension, finger strength and dexterity, or strengthening of specific muscle groups, among other goals.

Some examples of instruments that can be used for TIMP exercises. The therapeutic appropriateness of instrument selection is based on a thorough assessment of the physical abilities and motoric restrictions of the patients, as well as a kinematic analysis of motor functions required to play different instruments.

Percussion instruments are the most accessible group of musical instruments because they are easy to play even for nonmusicians. The fact that these instruments are mostly nonpitched allows flexible arrangement in groups. Percussion instruments can be used to practice gross motor functions like flexion/extension of arms and legs.

Consider the following example. The therapist may choose the tambourine for exercises involving knee extension and flexion. The tambourine would be placed knee-high in front of the seated patient. The patient is then instructed to extend his or her leg and strike the tambourine with the toes in accompaniment to the song. By doing this, the patient is practicing repetitive knee flexion and extension.

Another example of a possible TIMP exercise involves practicing weight-shift. This can be done in a seated as well as a standing position. The therapist would place two waist-high congas on the left and right side of the patient. During the exercise, the patient has to sway from side to side and hit the congas to the rhythm of the song. By doing this, the patient is practicing shifting his or her weight as he or she strikes the congas.

A third example would address arm movement. The therapist could place a drum and a cymbal (on a stand) in front of the patient. By holding a mallet with both hands, the patient plays first the lower positioned drum and then the higher positioned cymbal. By playing in this manner, the patient is able to practice repetitive arm extension.

Strumming the autoharp provides an excellent method for developing wrist and arm control. For example, in order to address the fine motor skills of the hand, the child could strum the autoharp using a pick or a soft stick with thumb, index, and middle finger (tripod grip). This exercise would be a creative way to help preschool children build up the strength and endurance necessary for establishing writing skills.

Due to injury or handicap, the patient is often unable to use bows, picks, or mallets in a traditional way. Therefore, the therapist must adapt many musical instruments for ease of use on a patient-by-patient basis. Clark and Chadwick (1980) have written a comprehensive guide for the clinical adaption of musical instruments for disabled populations. Elliot (1982) has provided an in-depth manual detailing the physical requirements needed (positioning, range of motion, involved muscle groups, etc.) to play a wide variety of musical instruments. This guide allows the therapist to match specific instruments with the individual abilities of the patient, as well as to select instruments based on specific therapeutic goals.

When using songs during exercises with pediatric patients, it is important to select songs with a high degree of familiarity and structural simplicity. However, children often wish to sing along with the familiar tune, which may interfere with their instrumental performance. In this case, a simple repetitive melody with original lyrics may lead to a more effective interaction with the group and a better functional performance for the children. Also, it is important to remain aware of the cognitive level of one's patients. For certain individuals, playing a musical instrument and listening to a song at the same time may be overwhelming. In this case, simply providing rhythmic structure with elements of PSE allows for a more effective therapy and a more enjoyable experience for the child.

Communication Skills

Nonverbal elements of vocalization are based on musical components such as rhythm, timbre, melodic contour, tempo, and pitch. Not only are these components foundational in human language as a whole, but mastery of them is necessary for an individual's normal language development. For the infant, practicing these musical components in the form of monosyllabic utterances represents the first step in the development of vocal communication. This type of proverbial communication often occurs between the infant and caregiver and is commonly known as baby talk. Regardless of the patient's developmental age, musical elements remain an important part of verbal and nonverbal communication. Of course, when one is working on speech and language skills, it is important to consider the child's developmental level.

Early exposure to music as well as active music performance can increase a child's processing of spoken language. According to Gaab et al. (2005), musicians are superior in processing single sounds of spoken language in comparison to nonmusicians. Understanding speech is a complicated and involved neural process. Practicing a musical instrument or participating in active singing helps children more easily distinguish subtle but critical variations in sound, such as "ba" and "da." This increased listening comprehension leads to better verbal performance for those who practice music. Even singing and playing rhythmic games can enhance speech and language comprehension.

For the diagnosis of a developmental speech disorder, a child must present with a delay of six months behind the norms for his or her age group. Knowledge of diagnoses and the severity of a patient's speech or language disorder should be taken into serious consideration when formulating therapeutic plans and goals.

Speech disturbances can occur in different forms and can involve delays or problems with sensory faculties (visual or hearing impairment), motor faculties that affect speech production, or developmental problems related to neglect of the child and subsequent language delay.

Unfortunately, children who have any type of difficulty communicating tend to be more emotionally troubled than their peers, in part because of the frustration relating to their awareness of an inability to communicate, but also due to increased pressure and criticism from their peers and adults. This type of psychological situation often serves to exacerbate the communication problem.

With its motivating and encouraging character, music can facilitate the creation of involuntary sound production. Repeating a child's random sounds and utterances is often encouraging to the child, who may then begin to repeat back to the therapist simple presented patterns of sound. Picking up the child's random sound utterances in a musical intervention has the effect of encouraging the child to continue and imitate presented sound patterns. Secondly, music can serve as an effective reward to reinforce and encourage a child's communication behavior. The child can be rewarded for asking an appropriate question by being given the opportunity to play a musical instrument or listen to a favorite song.

Rhymes, finger games, and songs can help children learn and improve their speech ability at any developmental stage. During these games, the child will experience the use of words, vocabulary, speech melody, and other characteristics of language in an enjoyable way. In these situations, learning through music also enhances both concentration skills as well as memory performance.

Generally, the function of music therapy in language or speech disorders is to help the child develop spontaneous and functional speech as well as improve the child's speech comprehension. More specific targets might consist of working on motor control and muscular coordination (both of which are essential for articulation), fluency of speech, vocal production and sequencing of speech sounds, as well as speech rate and intelligibility.

Neurological music therapy includes several speech therapy techniques that use musical materials to remediate speech deficiencies. Techniques exist that address disorders such as apraxia, aphasia, fluency disorders (stuttering and cluttering), and voice disorders that may result in abnormal pitch, loudness, timbre, breath control, or prosody of speech. Techniques developed for work with aphasic or dyspraxic children are based on melodic intonation therapy and the stimulation approach. For details, please see Chapter 10.

As mentioned above, keep in mind that applied techniques should match the developmental stage and current needs of the child.

Melodic Intonation Therapy (MIT). Sparks, Helm, and Albert (1974) first described MIT as treatment technique developed for the rehabilitation of patients with expressive aphasia. A curious but very common observation of aphasic patients is that they are able to sing despite not being able to speak. During therapy, the patient's unimpaired ability to sing is used to facilitate spontaneous and voluntary speech by using sung and chanted melodies that resemble natural speech intonation patterns. One suggestion as to the mechanism of success seen by applying MIT to patients with aphasia is that MIT facilitates the use of language areas of the right hemisphere, after damage to the language areas in the left hemisphere (Albert, Sparks, & Helm, 1973). Another explanation is that singing increases the role of the right hemisphere in interhemispheric control of language (Sparks et al., 1974). Furthermore, Boucher, Garcia, Fleurant, and Paradis (2001) have recently suggested that a treatment emphasizing the rhythmic attributes of target utterances can improve repetition to a greater degree than one emphasizing their melodic attributes. Similarly, reduction of speech rate, improvement of vocabulary, and maintenance of proper breathing may all contribute to the improvement of spontaneous speech in these patients.

Please see Chapter 10 for a detailed description of the application of MIT. The main purpose of MIT is to translate the speech inflection and the rhythmic patterns of brief sentences into musical prosody. The patient will then be able to sing this pattern and learn to transfer the pattern back to spoken language. It is, of course, most practical to initially teach functional sentences such as "Good morning," "My name is Linda," or any other pertinent details that the patient or his or her family can suggest.

Rhythmic Speech Cuing (RSC). This technique uses rhythmic cuing to control the initiation and rate of speech. RSC can be performed using only a simple metronome or a beat embedded in music, and has demonstrated success in the treatment of individuals affected by fluency disorders such as stuttering, cluttering, and dysarthria (Pilon, McIntosh, & Thaut, 1998; Thaut, McIntosh, McIntosh, & Hoemberg, 2001). Stutterers may increase their fluency by speaking rhythmically or by using strong melodic inflections. Some clutterers may be able to decelerate their rapid and unintelligible utterances by using similar techniques. Further, RSC has been documented to increase the intelligibility of speech in dysarthric patients.

During RSC exercises, the therapist should always use a metronome either to prime speech patterns or to pace the rate of speech. The therapist may also use the client's hand to tap the rhythm of the spoken words or sentences on his or her lap. In this manner, the patient receives the rhythmic stimulus in both an auditory and sensory way. The same procedure can be done with the patient simultaneously speaking and drumming the rhythm of the words and sentences.

Broadly, RSC can be applied using both metric and patterned cuing. Metric cuing refers to rhythmic tapping that is matched to each pronounced syllable in a short sentence such as "Good mor-ning, how are you?" and is useful for the improvement of sequencing and timing. This form is highly effective with stuttering patients or with individuals showing slowed and slurred speech patterns. Specifically in the case of slurred speech patterns, separating the words into syllables can enhance the phoneme articulation as well as improve the timing for initiating the next word or syllable in a sentence.

During patterned cuing, the therapist uses beat patterns that simulate the stress patterns of normal speech inflection. In this way, the patient is practicing bringing his or her speech pattern closer to normal speech prosody. Patterned cuing is more effective with mildly dysarthric patients and can also be used as a higher level of training after patients have successfully mastered metric cuing.

An example of patterned cuing may involve the patient first identifying the stressed words or syllables of the sentence to be practiced. Usually this is done by having the therapist write down the sentence and having the patient underline the stressed items: "Good morning, how are you?" The patient then plays out the rhythm of the sentence while the therapist speaks the words, and then the patient simultaneously speaks the sentence and plays out its rhythm.

As mentioned above, singing has the potential to facilitate word production using strong melodic inflections. One possible explanation for this is that sung words are articulated at a slower rate in singing than they are in speaking. This reduction in speed enables pronunciation of words that would otherwise be spoken too rapidly.

Regarding the use of songs, one must consider that the patient may not be able to process such complicated musical stimuli depending on the extent of brain damage or level of cognitive functioning. In cases where songs are not deemed appropriate, a simple beat from a metronome can provide a clear and suitable stimulus.

Vocal Intonation Therapy (VIT). VIT addresses the rehabilitation of abnormal pitch, loudness, timbre, breathing, and prosody of speech. The exercises are similar to vocal warm-ups used by choir conductors and train all aspects of voice control including inflection, pitch, breathing, timbre, and dynamics.

When dealing with children, it is often helpful to combine these exercises with a story in order to help maintain the child's attention. For example, an exercise geared toward expanding the range of pitch in a child's spoken voice could involve the child drawing a picture of a house in which a mouse must go from the cellar to the top floor in search of some cheese. Each stairway that the mouse ascends represents a five-tone scale beginning with the lowest pitch that the child can sing. As the story goes, once the mouse has ascended the first staircase, it loses its footing and tumbles right back down, a progression that the child expresses as a glissando down. The mouse then recovers and climbs back up the stairs (which the child again expresses by singing the same five-tone scale) and reaches the staircase on the next level. Here, the starting point for the scale begins a half tone higher than the first set of stairs, and the mouse again climbs the staircase, tumbles down, and climbs up again to reach the next staircase. This process is repeated until the top of the child's register is reached, and, of course, the mouse finds the cheese. Naturally this game can also begin at the top floor of the house and progress downwards to the basement in the same manner.

Voice exercises can also be combined with play scenarios involving toys for children. For example, one may set up a "construction zone" with bulldozers, cranes, and dump trucks, and then assign certain sounds to each toy. In this manner, the child is instructed to raise his or her voice in pitch when the bulldozer loads the dump truck, or sing descending tones when the crane lowers material to the ground.

Before the session concludes, singing of simple intoned phrases simulating the prosody, inflection, and pacing of normal speech should be added, such as "Let's go and play."

Therapeutic Singing (TS). This is a technique that involves the unspecified use of singing activities to facilitate initiation, development, and articulation in speech and language as well as to increase the functions of the respiratory apparatus. Therapeutic singing shows positive effects on a variety of neurological and developmental speech and language dysfunctions (Glover, Kalinowski, Rastatter, & Stuart, 1996; Jackson, Treharne, & Boucher, 1997). In singing, both language (the lyrics) and music are merged into one performance. It is probable that syllable chunking and rhythmic anticipation also participate in the advantage of singing over speaking for the rehabilitation of speech and language.

Oral Motor and Respiratory Exercises (OMREX). OMREX addresses the improvement of articulatory control, respiratory strength, and function of the speech apparatus through sound vocalization and wind instrument playing. This technique is often used with patients suffering from developmental disorders, muscular dystrophy, and dysarthria (Haas, Distenfeld, & Axen, 1986). Children suffering from these disorders often lack the ability to close their mouth completely and therefore may exhibit profuse drooling of saliva. Playing wind instruments such as the recorder or harmonica is ideal for encouraging the child to close his or her lips for long periods of time. Exercises directed at facilitating lip closure would also improve the child's ability to pronounce fundamental sounds like "p" and "ma." The song "Old McDonald Had a Farm," with its frequent incorporation of idealized animal noises, is also a fun and useful way for practicing basic speech sounds. Singing in general encourages prolonged voicing and use of multiple tones. Singing songs with simple combinations of syllables (such as "la-la" or "da-do") in place of lyrics can help the patient practice articulatory control by addressing isolated tongue movements.

Another problem patients are frequently faced with is pathologic or dysfunctional respiratory control. Rhythm and music can be included in an exercise to help set appropriate rates of breathing frequency and depth. This inclusion of rhythm then enhances the ability of the exercise to address breath strength and control. Respiratory strength can be improved by consciously inspiring and expiring following the cues of a presented rhythm. For example, the patient can play the flute to a simple musical line sung by the therapist, such as "Lin-da plays the flute," and following the end of the line, the patient is instructed by a predefined cue to inspire deeply and blow a continuous breath into the flute. The length of breath that the child must exhale into the instrument can be modified at the discretion of the therapist, perhaps by instructing the child to continue blowing as long as the therapist plays a single chord on the piano. The point of such an exercise is to gradually increase the length of time the child is able to exhale under voluntary control, therefore allowing for easier pronunciation of longer sentences or multisyllabic words.

Therapeutic exercises with a basis in rhythm create a predictability that facilitates motor planning and execution.

Speech Stimulation (STIM). Musical material such as songs, rhymes, and chants can assist patients with aphasia in stimulating nonpropositional speech patterns. For triggering the initiation of nonpropositional speech, the use of familiar songs is strongly recommended as familiar songs tend to be overlearned and contain nonpropositional language. During STIM exercises, the patient initiates singing song lyrics or is instructed to complete lines of lyrics, such as "Twinkle, twinkle, little ____." Another way to work with familiar lyrics is to have the therapist and patient take turns singing lines from a well-known song. One of the reasons that singing provides a stronger facilitating effect than speaking may be that the reproduction of familiar songs imposes a reduced demand for the formulation of new language (Peretz, Babai, Lussier, Hébert, & Gagnon, 1995; Wallace, 1994). The fact that such songs have been repetitively heard and reproduced means that the patient's mental representation of these songs is tied not only to their musical and lyrical content, but also to their specific motor program as related to the act of singing. This could explain why automatized formulations such as familiar songs, rhymes, or chants, and other similar materials such as months of the year or the alphabet are less vulnerable to loss following brain damage than unfamiliar material.

Songs and other overlearned information are often stored as clear and lasting long-term memories. Therefore, if the patient is able to associate certain words with these memory traces, it follows that these words will also be stored more durably. If asked, the patient may readily bring up various personal experiences or feelings related to a particular song.

STIM can also be applied to encourage the development of functional context-related verbalizations, such as "I want ___" or "This is ___."

Furthermore, STIM can be a useful tool for helping to increase the patient's vocabulary. In this case, using songs with lyrics that tell a coherent story, such as Hansel and Gretel, would be most appropriate. For instance, the therapist may provide a book detailing pictures from the well-known folk tale, and as the therapist sings the song to the child, the child can look at the corresponding pictures. Next, the therapist may employ functional speech patterns such as, "This is a ___," when pointing at a specific object in one of the pictures. Here the child must fill in the word corresponding to the object in the picture. Lastly, the child is then asked to describe the picture on his or her own.

In summary, STIM is often used to elicit functional speech responses through musical phrases and to bring out the association of words with familiar tunes (Basso, Capitani, & Vigndo, 1979).

Developmental Speech and Language Training Through Music (DSLM). Musical activities and experiences can be good motivators and facilitators to encourage children to communicate, be it verbally or nonverbally. DSLM is the specific use of developmentally appropriate musical materials and experiences to enhance speech and language development through singing, chanting, playing musical instruments, and combining music, speech, and movement.

Groups especially are an excellent setting to apply DSLM because just being involved in a rewarding musical activity with others can encourage or motivate the child to engage in communication. A typical group activity could be singing songs that incorporate the child's and other group members' names, saying names when taking turns while playing instruments. Another part could be singing songs to teach the day and time with the typical greetings and gestures.

Symbolic Communication Training Through Music (SYCOM). This is the use of musical performance exercises using structured instrumental or vocal improvisation to train communication behavior, language pragmatics, appropriate speech gestures, and emotional communication in a nonverbal language system that is sensory structured, has strong affective saliency, and can simulate communication structures in social interaction patterns in real time. Examples could be musical dialogues using drums, turn taking through eye contact, or composing patterns for question-answer games.

Cognitive Skills

Musical materials may enhance cognitive learning processes in the physically disabled child. Music can be used very efficiently as a motivating stimulus, reinforcement, and reward for learning efforts. It seems that the brain is attracted to and able to successfully process music beginning in early infancy, which indicates that the influence of music on cognition is an innate rather than a learned phenomenon. Roederer's (1982) statement that "the human brain is instinctively geared toward exercising or entertaining itself with sound processing operations even if they are of no immediate need or of no current survival value but crucial to overall human performance" (pp. 42–43) leads to the conclusion that music is a part of human cognition. In general, studies of cognition have investigated principles of perception, identification, usage, storage, and recall of information, most of which are defined as some sort of sensory stimulation. In addition to these activities, emotional reactions, motivations, affective behaviors, and adaptive motor responses all contribute to cognitive processing. All of these affective aspects of behavior are necessary for the processing of information within a sociocultural context. The function of learning is to develop patterns of behavior that allow the individual to adapt to the changing environment. Neurologically, experiences physically change the microstructure of the nervous system by altering neural circuits that are involved in thinking, perceiving, planning, and performing cognitive skills. In all of its structured forms, music readily lends itself to the integration of perceptual, stimulus-response, relational, and motor learning, as well as both the informative and affective aspects of cognition.

Producing and processing music is a complex human ability that challenges the brain in a holistic way. The results of several studies suggest that active music performance may enhance cognitive abilities. Rauscher et al. (1997) found that preschool children with musical training were better in solving space-time related tasks than children without musical training. Music processing seems to involve systems distributed over large areas of both hemispheres, and musical training has a significant effect on the plasticity of the involved neural structures. Interestingly, the results of numerous studies indicate that the processing of music within the brain is more diversified and complex and requires the activation of a larger number of neural pathways than do verbal or mental arithmetic tasks.

According to these findings, it seems that there are unique neural mechanisms devoted solely to the recognition and processing of music, while verbal or arithmetical tasks are routed through different networks. Furthermore, the various components of music, such as rhythm, tempo, and melody, are processed in different areas of the brain.

Cognitive training must be sequentially ordered, beginning with the most basic skills such as attention and concentration, then progressing to more complex skills like memory, verbal language, executive functioning, and social behavior. Cognitive training methods distinguish between three areas:

1. Auditory attention and perception training
2. Memory training
3. Executive functions training

Music as background stimulus for the learning environment can promote heightened attention and reduce anxiety. Some theories suggest that information learned in a particular mood or associated with an emotional stimulus will be recalled more easily when the previous mood or stimulus is present in the recall situation (Bower, 1981). Thus, music as mood stimulus, provided in the learning environment, may be used to facilitate efficient memory recall.

The following are training techniques to improve attention and perception skills.

Musical Sensory Orientation Training (MSOT). The goal of this method is to facilitate the training of basic cognitive skills such as attention and concentration. The therapist uses music (either live or recorded) to stimulate arousal and recovery of wake states and to encourage the patient's active involvement as well as orientation to person, place, and time. MSOT could be applied with patients in lowered states of consciousness (e.g., coma) in order to facilitate recovery by helping to slowly build up longer spans of concentration. This can be accomplished by letting the patient watch the therapist play an instrument or by composing a song with the therapist consisting of basic personal information (name, age, etc.). In more advanced recovery of developmental stages, training would involve active engagement in simple musical exercises such as striking a drum at a specified moment during a song. This therapy can increase vigilance and train basic attention maintenance with emphasis on the quantity rather than quality of response (Ogata, 1995). MSOT exercises address sensory stimulation, arousal orientation, vigilance, and attention maintenance.

Musical Neglect Training (MNT). This technique addresses patients who, due to injury or disease, neglect one side of their body and/or perceptual field. In order to fully participate in MNT, the patient must acknowledge the entirety of his or her environment and body. This is accomplished through exercises using musical instruments to produce a structured tempo, time, and rhythm, while the spatial configuration of the instruments helps to focus attention to the neglected side of the patient's body or visual field. MNT can also involve receptive music listening to stimulate hemispheric brain arousal while performing nonmusical exercises aimed at correcting visual neglect or inattention (Anderson & Phelps, 2001; Hommel et al., 1990).

Auditory Perception Training (APT). Auditory discrimination is crucial for sharpening cognitive functions and for developing or regaining speech and language. In APT, musical exercises consist of the discrimination and identification of different sound components. These are time, tempo, duration, pitch, timbre, rhythmic patterns, and speech sounds. For example, a child may be asked to identify which of two presented tones is higher in pitch, or he or she could be asked to repeat the faster of two rhythm patterns. APT can also be organized through active musical exercises such as playing from symbolic or graphic notion, using tactile sound transmission, or integrating one's movement to music. In this way, different sensory modalities such as visual, tactile, and kinesthetic are integrated during active musical exercises.

Musical Attention Control Training (MACT). Attention and concentration are skills that are very important for learning and developing new behavioral patterns in both the intellectual and sensorimotor domain. A child's ability to interact with and participate in the environment is fundamentally dependent on his or her attentional skills. Attention forms the foundation of memory, language, spatial skills, executive control, and various other mental functions. While attention and concentration are frequently impaired in an injured or poorly developed brain, these two attributes respond well to training. Therefore, cognitive interventions for attention should include training with different stimulus modalities, levels of complexity, and response demands (Cicerone et al., 2000). MACT addresses these criteria and includes structured active or receptive musical exercises involving rehearsed performance or improvisation in which musical elements cue different musical responses. Each of the five types of attention (focused, sustained, selective, divided, and alternating) can be addressed through therapy with MACT. In the following paragraphs, all five types of attention are introduced with examples of how they might be applied therapeutically. Naturally, each exercise must be adapted to the particular level of cognitive functioning of the child or group.

Focused attention is the ability to direct one's mind to a particular thing at the exclusion of other stimuli. For example, this type of attention could be practiced with a child by focusing his or her attention on one selected instrument in a basket of various instruments.

Selective attention is the ability to avoid distractions while focusing on one point of interest. Practicing this ability with children in a classroom setting could take the form of a game such as "leader against heckler." In this game, the group has to stay focused on the play of the leader/therapist and not be disturbed by the performance of the heckler.

Sustained attention, which is also known by the term *concentration*, refers to the ability to hold attention over time. For example, a therapist may introduce a short rhythm pattern to his or her drum circle of five children. The first player starts to play the pattern and the next person clockwise joins after the first is finished. All group members must hold their attention until the entire group plays the pattern together.

Shifting attention is the ability to alternate one's attention from one object or idea to another. This may be addressed therapeutically by providing a guitar and drum to both the therapist and the child. The task of the child is then to select whichever instrument the therapist is playing at the moment and play along. When the therapist switches his or her instrument, the patient must also switch.

Divided attention is the ability to sustain attention between two different things at the same time. An example of this would be practicing with a child to sing a song while playing the rhythm on a drum.

Memory training. Ashcraft (2002) has described three features of successful mnemonic devices. First, they create a structure for learning. Second, they provide a distinctive memory record so that the material is not easily forgotten, and lastly, they guide the learner in the retrieval process. The rhythm and melody of a familiar song could fulfill these principles by providing a structure for learning unfamiliar information, and a familiar melody could present both distinctive memory records and retrieval cues to assist in recall. Hébert and Peretz's (2001) ultimate conclusion was that music serves as sort of a mnemonic for text recall, based on findings that healthy subjects found it difficult to separate the text and tune of a song, whereas brain-damaged subjects did not have this detriment. Wallace (1994) described which melodic characteristics are critical for facilitation on recall of text. She concluded that music, when repeated, simple and easily learned, can render a text more easily memorized and subject to better recall than when the same text is learned without any melody. A repeating, simple melody can provide a recall aid above and beyond what is provided in the text alone or in the poetic properties of the text, such as rhyme. A sung text is more accurately recalled during initial learning and at delayed recall than is a rhythmically spoken text. Melodies provide an information-rich context that is critically connected to the text. In addition to rhythmical information, the melody can provide information about the lengths of lines and intonation patterns within the lyric line. The melody can assist in positioning and sequencing textual units (chunking principle) and thus decreases the likelihood that units will be misplaced and disrupt memory for succeeding units. It may be that paired music and information becomes a "song" in which the information is associated with the familiar music much in the same way that lyrics are associated with a particular song. To successfully recall stored information, the individual can rely upon the familiar music as a retrieval cue (Rainey & Larsen, 2002).

Musical Mnemonics Training (MMT). With this technique, the therapist uses musical exercises to address various memory encoding or recall functions through educational/instructional songs, chants, or activities that combine speech and movement. Music can facilitate, clarify, and illustrate the acquisition of academic information. For example, immediate recall of sounds or sung words may be used to address echoic memory functions. The melodic and rhythmic structure of songs can also serve well as a memory aid for song contents that emphasize academic concepts. Just think of songs about the alphabet or body parts, rhymes and chants that recite historical dates, computational tables, and so on. Also, more personal information such as one's telephone number or address can be provided in a melody to facilitate recall. By applying MMT, musical stimuli are used as a mnemonic device or memory template in form of a song, rhyme, or chant to facilitate learning of nonmusical information by sequencing and organizing the information in temporally structured patterns or chunks.

Associative Mood and Memory Training (AMMT). This training involves musical mood induction techniques (1) to establish congruent mood states to facilitate memory recall, or (2) to access associative mood and memory function through inducing a positive emotional state in the learning and recall process (Bower, 1981; Dolan, 2002).

Musical Executive Function Training (MEFT). Playing a musical instrument in an orchestra or band or composing a musical piece requires the use of cognitive abilities such as organization, problem solving, decision making, reasoning, and comprehension. Each of these abilities is also required during school activities and activities of daily life. MEFT can help children practice and develop these abilities. During MEFT, the therapist uses improvisation and composition exercises in a group or individual setting to practice the aforementioned executive function skills. Composing a piece of music with one's peers or writing a song with the therapist can help the child gain more confidence in his or her skills. Further, MEFT can help facilitate the transfer of these skills into nonmusical everyday contexts, such as planning or scheduling. The social context provides important therapeutic elements such as performance products in real time, temporal structure, creative process, affective content, sensory structure, and social interaction patterns (Dolan, 2002). Also, the therapist has the possibility to address children with disorders of self-awareness. During the experience of performing, the child is able to gain knowledge of his or her present abilities and limitations and, with therapeutic guidance, can begin to formulate self-improvements. Within a group setting, the child can also receive feedback from peers, which can further facilitate the development of self-awareness.

Social Skills

The physically disabled child is often severely restricted in his or her participation in social activities that require physical mobility. Social activities of children, however, are very commonly built around movement activities. Being left out of these activities will keep the child away from significant experiences of social learning that are fundamental for a healthy personality development. Health professionals, teachers, and parents, therefore, are faced with the challenge of finding activities that integrate the physically disabled child into social experiences.

Results of more recent neurobiology, neuropsychology, and music psychology research have led to an enhanced interest in the social function of music. A discussion of the adaptive value of music has emerged; the most commonly discussed explanatory model is based on the assumption of its group cohesive force, which might be originated in the early mother-infant dialogue (Peretz, 2001).

Music making as a form of nonverbal communication offers unique possibilities for relating, whether between the caregiver/therapist and special child or within a group setting. Children with various disabilities can be included in these groups as the exercises can be tailored according to the individual capacities of each group member, and a meaningful group interaction that strengthens emotional ties can evolve.

In an individual setting, the therapist can immediately mirror even the most minimal musical expression of the child and work with it within a musical framework, providing immediate feedback and transmitting meaning and relating to the outside world. The child experiences himself or herself as an active partner in a musical dialogue, and the motivational properties of music will help him or her to stay in contact.

Meaningful and enjoyable participation in musical group activities can take place on various levels of physical or intellectual abilities. Group singing or instrumental ensembles can be arranged to bring together ambulatory and wheelchair-bound children, or children with skilled or impaired usage of hands and fingers, with or without sensory impairments, and engage them in social interaction through music. Music offers a safe and structured setting for communication.

Identity building through music, which is commonly observed in adolescence, can also be used as a therapeutic tool with this population. It is highly probable that music serves as a supportive agent in identity building also in children and adolescents with physical disabilities. In enhancing this process, experiences of limitation, isolation, and loss can be attenuated. Further social gains from music therapy often discussed in literature include increase of independence, enhancement of feelings of self-confidence, self-worth, and self-esteem.

Excellent resources for adaptive devices and proper selection of musical instruments according to physical ability are the books by Elliot (1982), Clark and Chadwick (1980), and the monograph series on music therapy for disabled children by the National Association for Music Therapy (Lathom & Eagle, 1982).

In a therapeutic setting with severely physically disabled children, a co-therapist facilitating the use of instruments is helpful; otherwise, the therapist can always facilitate himself or herself and use his or her voice to accompany the child's musical expressions. Innovations in computer music technology help children with severe physical disabilities to play and compose music.

Emotional Skills

It is well known that music has the power to arouse and express emotions (Juslin & Sloboda, 2001). Music is commonly used by individuals as a means of self-regulation (DeNora, 2000; Juslin & Sloboda, 2001). Neuroscientific research indicates that music is processed in the emotional brain (e.g., limbic system, gyrus cinguli, paralymbic cortical regions).

Emotional self-expression through music is especially meaningful to persons who have no or little means to express themselves verbally. Innovations in digital music provide a mode of creative expression even for people with severe physical disabilities.

Emotional responsiveness to music seems to be inborn (e.g., Masataka, 1999). Music provides developmentally appropriate sensory stimulation even for newborn infants (De L'Etoile, 2006) and has beneficial influence on the development of preterm babies (Standley, 2002). Infants pay more sustained attention to their mothers when they are singing than when they are speaking, even when they use "baby talk" (Trehub, 2003). Shenfield, Trehub, and Nakata (2003) assume that infants' attraction to parents singing is originated in its positive emotive qualities.

The importance of music in attachment, attention, and affect regulation of children has been underscored by research (e.g., De L'Etoile, 2006; Trehub & Trainor, 1998). Children understand the emotional meaning of music much earlier than the emotional meaning of speech melody/intonation (Doherty, Fitzsimons, Asenbauer, & Staunton, 1999). Long before children can understand specific emotional meaning though, they are capable of mirroring emotions in a process of emotional contagion (Hatfield, Cacioppo, & Rapson, 1994). In the same way as they start to cry when hearing other infants crying, they reach a positive affective state through hearing the expression of a positive emotion by the mother (Trehub, 2002).

Physically disabled children have the same need for healthy emotional development and opportunities to express their feelings as do normal children. Because of the experiences of their disabilities, these children may actually have an increased need to cope with feelings, such as grief, depression, or loneliness. Compounding their emotional needs, their physical limitations may prevent them from using some of the more common channels to express feelings.

Music therapy can play an eminent role in satisfying emotional needs. Access to musical experiences can be provided on many different levels of sensory, physical, and intellectual ability. Thus, the music therapist is well equipped to work for the child's emotional development and also to offer help in coping with emotional problems associated with the child's disability.

Research suggests that music therapy is effective in reducing symptoms of depression (Maratos, Gold, Wang, & Crawford, 2008), and music therapy has a positive effect for children and adolescents with psychopathology (Gold, Voracek, & Wigram, 2004). In musical role play, the disabled child can, for instance, be helped to articulate difficult feelings. Through musically guided imagery with induction of relaxation, cognitive and emotional resources can be activated, improving subjective well-being by reducing stress and stimulating pleasure (Leins, 2006).

Additionally, distraction from anxiety and pain discomfort associated with some physical disabilities can be provided. An older study found that sedative music enhances EMG biofeedback relaxation training when compared to EMG biofeedback relaxation training alone for persons with spastic cerebral palsy (Scartelli, 1982). Robb (1996) suggested song writing for restoring emotional well-being in children and adolescents who have been traumatically injured.

Musical Skills

As part of an overall strategy to normalize a physically disabled child's life, the development of special talents and recreational and leisure skills is very essential. By using proper resources for the selection of instruments and adaptive devices as referenced in the section on social skills, therapists can help these children achieve musically.

Musical skill development will normalize the child's life by facilitating performance-oriented success experiences and providing the emotional, cognitive, social, and physical rewards of aesthetic musical training.

SUMMARY

In this chapter, we have presented an overview of physically disabling conditions in children. We have also introduced you to treatment areas, goals, and clinical methods the music therapist uses when working with these children.

Physically disabling conditions can be categorized as ambulatory or nonambulatory. Furthermore, they can be distinguished as congenital and/or chronic or acquired and/or acute. The congenital and/or chronic conditions discussed in this chapter are cerebral palsy, muscular dystrophies, spina bifida, clubfoot, congenital dislocation of the hip, arthrogryposis, juvenile rheumatoid arthritis, dwarfism, and osteogenesis imperfecta. The acquired and/or acute conditions discussed are thermal injuries, spinal cord injuries, acquired amputations, and poliomyelitis.

Many physically disabled children suffer from multiple disabilities, affecting also intellectual and sensory functions. Music therapists encounter these children in special education settings, hospital programs, developmental centers, group homes, and preschool programs.

Music therapists pursue three different types of treatment goals with physically disabled children: educational goals, rehabilitative goals, and developmental goals. Within each of these large goal areas, music therapists use music-based methods to work on motor skills, communication skills, cognitive skills, social skills, emotional skills, and musical skills. Neurological music therapy methods (Thaut, 2005) for the rehabilitation of motor skills are the RAS gait training, Patterned Sensory Enhancement (PSE), and Therapeutic Instrument Music Playing (TIMP). Techniques addressing cognitive problems are Musical Sensory Orientation Training (MSOT), Musical Neglect Training (MNT), Auditory Perception Training (APT), Musical Attention Control Training (MACT), Musical Mnemonics Training (MMT), Associative Mood and Memory Training (AMMT), and Musical Executive Function Training (MEFT). For socioemotional goals, neurologic music therapy techniques such as group improvisation, duo play, music-assisted relaxation training, or song writing provide opportunities for meaningful interaction and self-expression and enhancement of quality of life. Neurological music therapy techniques to work on speech and language problems can be listed as Melodic Intonation Therapy (MIT), Rhythmic Speech Cuing (RSC), Vocal Intonation Therapy (VIT), Therapeutic Singing (TS), Oral Motor and Respiratory Exercises (OMREX), Speech Stimulation (STIM), Developmental Speech and Language Training Through Music (DSLM), and Symbolic Communication Training Through Music (SYCOM).

STUDY QUESTIONS

1. What are the different ways you can describe and categorize physically disabling conditions in children?

2. What different types of goals can the music therapist set with physically disabled children?

3. Describe the main features of physically disabling conditions according to the categories you answered under study question 1.

4. What are the six skill areas music therapists focus on developing with physically disabled children?

5. List three neurological music therapy methods a music therapist uses to work on motor rehabilitation and motor skill development with musical stimuli.

6. List three methods the music therapist uses to work on communication skills with musical stimuli.

7. What are the five different kinds of attention? Name the neurological music therapy method(s) that can be used to work on attention skills.

8. Describe why music/melodies are an excellent template for remembering items.

9. Why is music a particularly efficient medium to provide rewarding social and emotional experiences for physically disabled children?

10. Which specific music therapy techniques can be used to enhance emotional skills in disabled children?

REFERENCES

Albert, M. L., Sparks, R. W., & Helm, N. A. (1973). Melodic intonation therapy for aphasia. *Archives of Neurology, 29*, 130–131.

Anderson, A. K., & Phelps, E. A. (2001). Lesions of the human amygdala impair enhanced perception of emotionally salient events. *Nature, 411*, 305–309.

Ashcraft, M. H. (2002). *Cognition* (3rd ed.). Upper Saddle River, NJ: Prentice Hall.

Basso, A., Capitani, E., & Vigndo, L. S. (1979). The influence of rehabilitation on language skills in aphasic patients. *Archives of Neurology, 36*, 190–196.

Bernatzky, G., Bernatzky, P., Hesse, H. P., Staffen, W., & Ladurner, G. (2004). Stimulating music increases motor coordination in patients afflicted by Morbus Parkinson. *Neuroscience Letters, 361*, 4–8.

Bleck, E., & Nagel, D. (Eds.). (1982). *Physically handicapped children: A medical atlas for teachers.* New York: Grune and Stratton.

Boucher, V., Garcia, L. J., Fleurant, J., & Paradis, J. (2001). Variable efficacy of rhythm and tone in melody-based interventions: Implications for the assumption of a right-hemisphere facilitation in non-fluent aphasia. *Aphasiology, 15*, 131–149.

Bower, G. H. (1981). Mood and memory. *American Psychologist, 36*, 129–148.

Cicerone, K. D., Dahlberg, C., Kalmar, K., Langenbahn, D. M., Malec, J. F., Bergquist, T. F., et al. (2000). Evidence-based cognitive rehabilitation: Recommendations for clinical practice. *Archives of Physical Medicine and Rehabilitation, 81*, 1596-1615.

Clark, C., & Chadwick, D. (1980). *Clinically adapted instruments for the multiply handicapped.* St. Louis, MO: Magnamusic-Baton.

Cotton, E. (1974). Improvement in motor function with the use of conductive education. *Developmental Medicine and Child Neurology, 16*, 637–643.

Cratty, B. (1975). *Remedial motor activity for children.* Philadelphia: Lea and Febiger.

De L'Etoile, S. K. (2006) Infant directed singing: A theory for clinical intervention. *Music Therapy Perspectives, 24*(1), 22–29.

Del Olmo, M. F., & Cudeiro, J. (2003). A simple procedure using auditory stimuli to improve movement in Parkinson's disease: A pilot study. *Neurology & Clinical Neurophysiology, 2*, 1–7.

DeNora, T. (2000). *Music in everyday life.* Cambridge, UK: Cambridge University Press.

Doherty, C. P., Fitzsimons, M., Asenbauer, B., & Staunton, H. (1999). Discrimination of prosody and music by normal children. *European Journal of Neurology, 6*, 221–226.

Dolan, R. J. (2002). Emotion, cognition, and behavior. *Science, 298*, 1191–1194.

Elliot, B. (1982). *Guide to the selection of musical instruments with respect to physical ability and disability.* St. Louis, MO: Magnamusic-Baton.

Flodmark, A. (1986). Augmented auditory feedback as an aid in gait training of the cerebral-palsied child. *Developmental Medicine and Child Neurology, 28*, 147–155.

Freeland, R. L., Festa, C., Sealy, M., McBean, A., Elghazaly, P., Capan A., Brozycki, L., Nelson, A. J., & Rothman, J. (2002). The effects of auditory stimulation on various gait measurements in persons with Parkinson's disease. *Neurorehabilitation, 17*(1), 81–87.

Gaab, N., Tallal, P., Kim, H., Lakshminarayanan, K., Glover, G. H., & Gabrieli, J. D. E. (2005). Neural correlates spectro-temporal processing in musicians and nonmusicians. *Annals of the New York Academy of Sciences, 1060*, 82–88.

Gage, J. R. (1989). An overview of normal and cerebral palsy gait. *Neurosurgery: State of the Art Reviews, 4*, 379–401.

Glover, H., Kalinowski, J., Rastatter, M., & Stuart, A. (1996). Effect of instruction to sing on stuttering frequency at normal and fast rates. *Perceptual and Motor Skills, 83*, 511–522.

Gold, C., Voracek, M., & Wigram, T. (2004). Effects of music therapy for children and adolescents with psychopathology: A meta-analysis. *Journal of Child Psychology and Psychiatry, 45*(6), 1054–1063.

Haas, F., Distenfeld, S., & Axen, K. (1986). Effects of perceived music rhythm on respiratory patterns. *Journal of Applied Physiology, 61*, 1185–1191.

Harrington, D. L., & Haaland, K.Y. (1999). Neural underpinnings of temporal processing: A review of focal lesion, pharmacological, and functional imaging research. *Reviews in Neuroscience, 10*, 91–116.

Hatfield, E., Cacioppo, J. T., & Rapson, R. L. (1994). *Emotional contagion: Studies in emotion and social interaction.* New York: Cambridge University Press.

Hébert, S., & Peretz, I. (2001). Are text and tune of familiar songs separable by brain damage? *Brain & Cognition, 46*, 169–175.

Hommel, M., Peres, B., Pollak, P., Memin, B., Besson, G., Gaio, J., & Perret, J. (1990). Effects of passive tactile and auditory stimuli on left visual neglect. *Archives of Neurology, 47*, 573.

Howe, T. E., Lovgreen, B., Cody, F. W., Ashton, V. J., & Oldham, J. A. (2003). Auditory cues can modify the gait of persons with early-stage Parkinson's disease: A method for enhancing Parkinsonian walking performance? *Clinical Rehabilitation, 17*(4), 363–367.

Hurt, C. P., Rice, R. R., McIntosh, G. C., & Thaut, M. H. (1998). Rhythmic auditory stimulation in gait training for patients with traumatic brain injury. *Journal of Music Therapy, 35*(4), 228–241.

Jackson, S. A., Treharne, D. A., & Boucher, J. (1997). Rhythm and language in children with moderate learning difficulties. *European Journal of Disorders of Communication, 32*, 99–108.

Jellison, J. A. (2000). A content analysis of music research with disabled children and youth (1975–1999): Applications in special education. In C. E. Furman (Ed.), *Effectiveness of music therapy procedures: Documentation of research and clinical practice* (pp. 199–264). Silver Spring, MD: American Music Therapy Association.

Juslin, P. N., & Sloboda, J. A. (2001). *Music and emotion: Theory and research.* New York: Oxford University Press.

Kwak, E. E. (2007). Effect of rhythmic auditory stimulation on gait performance in children with spastic cerebral palsy. *Journal of Music Therapy, 44*(3), 198–216.

Lathom, W., & Eagle, C. (1982). *Music therapy for handicapped children.* Project Music Monograph Series. Washington DC: National Association for Music Therapy.

Leins, A. K. (2006). *Heidelberger therapiemanual: Migräne bei kindern* [Music therapy for children with migraine headache]. Berlin: Uni-Edition.

Lim, I., Van Wegen, E., de Goede, C., Deutekom, M., Nieuwboer, A., Willems, A., & Jones, D. (2005). Effects of external rhythmical cueing on gait in patients with Parkinson's disease. *Clinical Rehabilitation, 19*(7), 695–713.

Luft, A. R., McCombe-Waller, S., Whitall, J., Forrester, L. W., Macko, R., Sorkin, J. D., et al. (2004). Repetitive bilateral arm training and motor cortex activation in chronic stroke: A randomized controlled trial. *Journal of the American Medical Association, 292*(15), 1853–1861.

Malherbe, V., Breniere, Y., & Bril, B. (1992). How do cerebral palsied children with hemiplegia control their gait. In M. Woollacott & F. Horak (Eds.), *Posture and control mechanisms* (Vol. 2, pp. 102–105). Eugene: University of Oregon Books.

Mandel, A. R., Nymark, J. R., Balmer, S. J., Grinnell, D. M., & O'Riain, M. D. (1990). Electromyographic feedback versus rhythmic positional biofeedback in computerized gait retraining with stroke patients. *Archives of Physical and Medical Rehabilitation, 71*, 649–654.

Maratos, A. S., Gold, C., Wang, X., & Crawford, M. J. (2008). Music therapy for depression. *Cochrane Database of Systematic Reviews*, (1). Art. No.: CD004517. DOI: 10.1002/14651858. CD004517.pub2

Masataka, N. (1999). Preference for infant-directed singing in 2-day-old hearing infants of deaf parents. *Developmental Psychology, 35*, 1001–1005.

McCombe, W. S., & Whitall, J. (2005). Hand dominance and side of stroke affect rehabilitation in chronic stroke. *Clinical Rehabilitation, 19*(5), 544–551.

McIntosh, G. C., Brown, S. H., Rice, R. R., & Thaut, M. H. (1997). Rhythmic auditory-motor facilitation of gait patterns in patients with Parkinson's disease. *Journal of Neurology, Neurosurgery, and Psychiatry, 62*, 122–126.

Miller, R. A., Thaut, M. H., McIntosh, G. C., & Rice, R. R. (1996). Components of EMG symmetry and variability in Parkinsonian and healthy elderly gait. *Electroencephalography and Clinical Neurophysiology, 101*, 1–7.

Molinari, M., Thaut, M. H., Gioia, C., et al. (2001). Motor entrainment to auditory rhythm is not affected by cerebellar pathology. *Proceedings of the Society for Neuroscience, 950.2.*

Morris, G. S., Suteerawattananon, M., Etnyre, B. R., et al. (2004). Effects of visual and auditory cues on gait in individuals with Parkinson's disease. *Journal of the Neurological Sciences, 219,* 63–69.

Ogata, D. (1995). Human EEG responses to classical music and simulated white noise: Effects of a musical loudness component on consciousness. *Perceptual and Motor Skills, 80,* 779–790.

Pacchetti, C., Aglieri, R., Mancini, F., Martignon, E., & Nappi, G. (1998). Active music therapy and Parkinson's disease: Methods. *Functional Neurophysiology, 10,* 1–7.

Pacchetti, C., Mancini, F., Aglieri, R., Fundarò, C., Martignoni, E., & Nappi, G. (2000). Active music therapy in Parkinson's disease: An integrative method for motor and emotional rehabilitation. *Psychosomatic Medicine, 62,* 386–393.

Penhune, V. B., Zartorre, R. J., & Evans, A. (1998). Cerebellar contributions to motor timing: A PET study of auditory and visual rhythm reproduction. *Journal of Cognitive Neuroscience, 10,* 752–765.

Peretz, I. (2001). Listen to the brain: A biological perspective on musical emotions. In P. Juslin & J. A. Sloboda (Eds.), *Music and emotion: Theory and research* (pp. 105–134). Oxford, UK: Oxford University Press.

Peretz, I., Babai, E. M., Lussier, I., Hébert, S., & Gagnon, L. (1995). Corpus d'extraits musicaux: Indices relatifs à la familiarité, à l'âge d'acquisition et aux évocations verbales. *Canadian Journal of Experimental Psychology, 49,* 211–239.

Pilon, M. A., McIntosh, K. W., & Thaut, M. H. (1998). Auditory vs. visual speech timing cues as external rate control to enhance verbal intelligibility in mixed spastic-ataxic dysarthric speakers: A pilot study. *Brain Injury, 12,* 793–803.

Platel, H., Price, C., Baron, J. C., Wise, R., Lambert, J. Frackowiak, R. S., et al. (1997). The structural components of music perception: A functional anatomical study. *Brain, 120,* 229–243.

Rainey, D. W., & Larsen, J. D. (2002). The effect of familiar melodies on initial learning and long-term memory for unconnected test. *Music Perception, 20*(2), 173–186.

Rao, S. M., Mayer, A. R., & Harrington, D. L. (2001). The evolution of brain activation during temporal processing. *Nature Neurosciences, 4,* 317–323.

Rauscher, F. H., Shaw, G. L., Levine, L. J., Wright, E. L., Dennis, W. R., & Newcomb, R. L. (1997). Music training causes long-term enhancement of preschool children's spatial-temporal reasoning. *Neurological Research, 19,* 2–8.

Robb, S. L. (1996). Techniques in song writing: Restoring emotional and physical well being in adolescents who have been traumatically injured. *Music Therapy Perspectives, 14,* 30–37.

Roederer, J. G. (1982). Physical and neuropsychological foundations of music: The basic questions. In M. Clynes (Ed.), *Music, mind, and brain: The neuropsychology of music* (pp. 37–46). New York: Plenum Press.

Rochester, L., Hetherington, V., Jones, D., Nieuwboer, A., Willems, A. M., Kwakkel, G., & Van Wegen, E. (2005). The effect of external rhythmic cues (auditory and visual) on walking during a functional task in homes of people with Parkinson's disease. *Archives of Physical Medicine & Rehabilitation, 86*(5), 999–1006.

Scartelli, J. P. (1982). The effect of sedative music on electromyography biofeedback assisted relaxation training of spastic cerebral palsied adults. *Journal of Music Therapy, 19,* 210–218.

Schauer, M. L., & Mauritz, K. H. (2003). Musical motor feedback (MMF) in walking of hemiparetic stroke patients: Randomized trials of gait improvement. *Clinical Rehabilitation, 17*, 713–722.

Schlaug, G., & Chen, C. (2001). The brain of musicians: A model for functional and structural adaptation. *Annals of the New York Academy of Sciences, 930*, 281–299.

Shenfield, T., Trehub, S., & Nakata, T. (2003). Maternal singing modulates infant arousal. *Psychology of Music, 31*, 365–375.

Sherrill, C. (1981). *Adapted physical education and recreation: A multidisciplinary approach.* Dubuque, IA: William C. Brown.

Sparks, R. W., Helm, N., & Albert, M. (1974). Aphasia rehabilitation resulting from melodic intonation therapy. *Cortex, 10*, 313–316.

Standley, J. M. (2002). A meta-analysis of the efficacy of music therapy for premature infants. *Journal of Pediatric Nursing, 17*(2), 107–113.

Sutherland, D. H., & Davids, J. R. (1993). Common gait abnormalities of the knee in cerebral palsy. *Clinical Orthopaedics and Related Research, 288*, 139–147.

Talbot, M. L., & Junkala, J. (1981). The effects of auditorally augmented feedback on the eye-hand coordination of students with cerebral palsy. *American Journal of Occupational Therapy, 35*, 525–528.

Thaut, M. H. (1985). The use of auditory rhythm and rhythmic speech to aid temporal muscular control in children with gross motor dysfunction. *Journal of Music Therapy, 22*, 108–128.

Thaut, M. H. (2005). *Rhythm, music, and the brain: Scientific foundations and clinical applications.* New York: Routledge Taylor & Francis.

Thaut, M. H., Hurt, C. P., Dragon, D., & McIntosh, G. C. (1998). Rhythmic entrainment of gait patterns in children with cerebral palsy. *Developmental Medicine and Child Neurology, 40*(78), 15.

Thaut, M. H., Kenyon, G. P., Hurt, C. P., McIntosh, G. C., & Hoemberg, V. (2002). Kinematic optimization of spatiotemporal patterns in paretic arm training with stroke patients. *Neuropsychologia, 40*, 1073–1081.

Thaut, M. H., McIntosh, G. C., McIntosh, K. W., & Hoemberg, V. (2001). Auditory rhythmic enhances movement and speech motor control in patients with Parkinson's disease. *Functional Neurology, 16*, 163–172.

Thaut, M. H., McIntosh, G. C., & Rice, R. R. (1996). Rhythmic auditory stimulation in gait training for Parkinson's disease patients. *Movement Disorders, 11*(2), 193–200.

Thaut, M. H., McIntosh, G. C., Rice, R. R., & Prassas, S. G. (1992). Effect of auditory rhythmic cueing on temporal stride parameters an EMG patterns in normal gait. *Journal of Neurologic Rehabilitation, 6*, 185–190.

Toombs-Rudenberg, M. (1982). Music therapy for handicapped children: Orthopedically handicapped. In W. Lathom & C. Eagle (Eds.), *Music therapy for handicapped children*. Project Music Monograph Series. Washington DC: National Association for Music Therapy.

Trehub, S. (2002, September). Mothers are musical mentors. *Zero to Three*, pp. 19–22.

Trehub, S. E. (2003). The developmental origins of musicality. *Nature Neuroscience, 6*, 669–673.

Trehub, S. E., & Trainor, L. J. (1998). Singing to infants: Lullabies and play songs. *Advances in Infancy Research, 12*, 43–77.

Wallace, W. T. (1994). Memory for music: Effect of melody on recall of text. *Journal of Experimental Psychology, 20*(6), 1471–1485.

Whitall, J., McCombe, W. S., Waller, S., Silver, K. H., & Macko, R. F. (2000). Repetitive bilateral arm training with rhythmic auditory cueing improves motor function in chronic hemiparetic stroke. *Stroke, 31*(10), 2390–2395.

CHAPTER 7

Music Therapy and Elderly Populations

Alicia A. Clair
William B. Davis

CHAPTER OUTLINE

AN INTRODUCTION TO AGING
GERONTOLOGY: THE STUDY OF AGING
THE GRAYING OF AMERICA: DEMOGRAPHICS OF OLDER ADULTS
DEFINITIONS OF AGE
    Biological Age
    Psychological Age
    Psychosocial Age
AGE-RELATED DISORDERS
    Age-Related Psychological Disorders
    Age-Related Physical Disorders
AGING AND THE CHANGING WORKFORCE
COMMUNITY INTEGRATION AND THE OLDER ADULT
THE FUNCTIONAL APPROACH TO TREATMENT
CLINICAL PRACTICE IN MUSIC THERAPY
    Assessment Using Music
    An Approach to Music Therapy Treatment Design
    Music Application for Therapeutic Outcomes
    Music Therapy Activities
    Music Therapy and Evidence-Based Practice
    The Therapeutic Relationship in Music Therapy Practice

AN INTRODUCTION TO AGING

Aging seems like a simple concept to define. We know, for example, that the aging process produces observable changes, such as wrinkled skin, stooped posture, graying hair, and often memory loss. Yet, some persons who have good physical and mental health have less pronounced visible indications of older years. As we will learn, growing old is a complex developmental process that involves the interaction of physical, psychological, and social factors (Erber, 2005; Posner, 1995).

Older adults are the fastest growing population in industrialized countries, resulting in a disproportionate number of mature, elderly persons to younger persons in many societies. By the year 2045, the reductions in mortality and fertility will continue the demographic transition around the globe until the number of older persons who are age 60 and older completely surpasses the number of children. The dwindling proportion of younger persons to older persons leads to the needs for optimum health in all populations throughout the world.

Health for older adults is defined in this chapter as cognitive, physical, and psychosocial functions that are sufficient for satisfactory life quality. Health is not, therefore, defined as the absence of disease or disability, but as the ability of individuals to live life as fully and as independently as possible.

This chapter will introduce you to gerontology, or the study of aging, the demographics of aging, normal aging, chronic illness associated with old age, the concept of functional outcomes and community integration, definitions of music therapy and therapeutic music interventions used with older persons, and the concept of the therapeutic relationship. The chapter will also identify some factors that affect life quality in older persons and introduce you to an approach to develop music therapy treatment for evidence-based outcomes.

Betsy has just turned 70 and now realizes that people are likely to view her as an "older adult." With gray hair, glasses, and wrinkles, she is not surprised when grocery clerks give her a senior citizen discount and offer to help carry her purchases to her car. Though Betsy's husband died 10 years ago, Betsy does not feel old; in fact, she will tell you that she does not feel any different than she did when she was 40. She is in good health, eats well, exercises regularly, and is socially active. Betsy is an excellent example of the vast majority of older adults who live in the United States and remain healthy and active well into their 70s, 80s, and even 90s.

Jerome was a successful businessman who traveled internationally for many years as an account executive for a major financial firm. He has always lived alone by choice but has many friends he sees on a regular basis. One special lady friend has been his companion for dinner, theatre, and weekend card parties for over 30 years. By the time Jerome reached the age of 45, however, his health became a concern; he developed arthritis in his hands that became so debilitating that by the age of 55 he was forced to stop working and go on disability. By the age of 60, hypertension (high blood pressure) had developed, and shortly after his 65th birthday, his friends and family noticed that Jerome was forgetting to attend to basic needs such as eating, bathing, and paying his bills and had become socially withdrawn. After a consultation with a neurologist, he was given a probable diagnosis of Alzheimer's disease. Within a matter of months of his diagnosis, Jerome was placed in a facility specially equipped to care for persons with dementia.

Betsy and Jerome represent the extremes in variations in aging found in persons we refer to as elderly. Many persons remain active and in good health like Betsy, while some, like Jerome, are plagued with physical and cognitive disorders at a relatively young age. There is no time table when an individual becomes old, as aging is a gradual process that involves physical, psychosocial, and cognitive changes (Harris, 2007).

GERONTOLOGY: THE STUDY OF AGING

Over the past 40 years, gerontology has been among the fastest growing scientific disciplines. It can be defined as the systematic study of the phenomena of aging, involving the normal biological, social, and psychological processes of growing old. (Ferraro, 2007; Harris, 2007).

A gerontologist is a person who specializes in one or more aspects of aging. Prominent areas of study include medicine, psychology, sociology, occupational therapy, recreation therapy, physical therapy, nursing, and music therapy. In fact, the study of aging should be multidisciplinary, drawing upon research findings and experiences of many different disciplines, including music therapy.

The term *geriatrics* is sometimes used interchangeably (but erroneously) with *gerontology*. Geriatrics is a medical subspecialty concerned with the care of elderly patients and treatment of their medical problems; thus, it is more limited in scope than gerontology (Erber 2005; Papalia, Camp, & Feldman, 1996).

Senescence, another term frequently encountered in discussions of aging, describes the universal and inevitable decline in the efficiency of body systems. It is a normal aspect of aging and not considered dysfunctional. Senescence is slow and progresses at various rates in different people. It leads to a decrease in energy, eventual organ-system failure, and, ultimately, death. On a more positive note, there are strategies, including music therapy, to compensate for senescence that allow elderly persons to live satisfying, useful lives (Erber, 2005; Waters, 2007).

THE GRAYING OF AMERICA: DEMOGRAPHICS OF OLDER ADULTS

The number and proportion of people in the United States over the age of 65 has grown steadily during the 20th and early part of the 21st century. This growth has fostered increased awareness of the unique problems associated with aging, as well as an interest in working with elderly people (Harris, 2007; Papalia et al., 1996).

In 1900, a little more than 3 million people, or slightly more than 3% of the U.S. population, were over the age of 65. By 1940, that number had increased threefold to more than 9 million people, or 6.8%. In 2000, more than 12.5% of the population was over the age of 65 (35 million people). It is estimated that the percentage of elderly Americans will be 20.1% by the year 2030. That translates into an astonishing 70 million adults over the age of 65 (Erber, 2005; Wilmoth & Longino, 2007).

One factor contributing to the rising proportion of elderly people is increased longevity. For example, a man born in 1900 had a life expectancy of 47.3 years; a woman born during this time could expect to live slightly longer, an average of 48.3 years. By 1985, the life expectancy for men had increased to 71.3, while women born in 1985 expect to live an average of 78.3 years (Harris, 2007; Longino, Soldo, & Manton, 1990). In 2004, a female's life expectancy was 80.4 years, while for men the average lifespan was 75.2 years. Increase in life expectancy can be attributed to several factors, including improvements in health care and changes in lifestyle (exercise, dietary modifications, and reduced use of tobacco products). Today, it is not uncommon for people in the United States to live to the age of 80, 90, or even 100. In fact, the fastest growing segment of our population is those individuals who are 85 years and older (Erber, 2005; Rybash, Roodin, & Hoyer, 1995).

As you can see, there has been and will continue to be a trend toward a large elderly population in our society, which could be beneficial to individuals in those age groups. There is strength in numbers, and this group can wield considerable economic, political, and social clout. This growth, however, presents a challenge, because the elderly population requires increased medical, social, and psychological services. Today elderly people comprise nearly 13% of our population but account for about 33% of our total health care expenditures (Harris, 2007). In addition, this growth implies the need for specialized social and leisure activities for elderly individuals.

DEFINITIONS OF AGE

We generally think about age in terms of the number of birthdays that have passed. Chronological age is simply a measure of time usually described in years that have elapsed since birth. Although this is the most common manner in which we gauge age, it does not provide an adequate description of the aging process. We must also look at biological, psychological, and psychosocial age (Erber, 2005).

Biological Age

There are universal characteristics of aging, sometimes referred to as senescence, that occur in everyone. Aging may be viewed as an ongoing process that begins at conception and ultimately ends with death. About the age of 40, a person starts to show physical signs of the aging process, such as a slight decrease in stamina and strength, the appearance of a few wrinkles or gray hair, and changes in weight and body composition. It is important to note that these characteristics do not appear at the same age for all people but vary considerably in the extent and rate at which the occur (Markson, 2003; Whitbourne, 1996).

Concomitant with alterations in our physical appearance are changes in bones, and muscle strength and endurance. Bones become more brittle and are easier to break; muscle mass decreases, resulting in less strength, and it takes longer to recover from physical exertion. As we advance in age, joints become less flexible and lose density, resulting in stooped posture and loss of height by an inch or two. The percentage of body fat increases as we grow older as well (Markson, 2003).

In addition, cellular, molecular, and organ functions become less efficient with age. This decreases the older person's ability to maintain homeostasis, or stability of chemical and physical states within the body. For example, the ability to govern blood pressure and pulse rate declines with advancing years, which eventually contributes to dysfunction of the skeletal, muscular, nervous, and sensory systems (Markson, 2003; Waters, 2007).

Psychological Age

Gerontologists are interested in learning about the impact of growing old on memory, learning, personality, and emotions that defines psychological aging. Psychological aging refers to how well a person responds to a changing environment and how well an individual can adapt to new situations or experiences. Persons who can readily adapt to life changes are viewed as psychologically young compared to an individual who has difficulty adjusting to his or her milieu. For example, Betsy, whom we met earlier in this chapter, varies her routine by shopping in different stores, eating at a variety of restaurants, and taking trips to different interesting places such as museums, the zoo, and other cultural events available in her city. By contrast, a person who does little to vary his or her routine may be considered psychologically old (Erber, 2005; Harris, 2007).

Psychosocial Age

Each society has common notions about how a person at a certain age should act or what he or she should be doing. There is little doubt that our society idealizes youth and discounts much of the experience, wisdom, and knowledge that the elderly population has to offer. Older people are often treated differently simply because of their age. Discrimination against elderly people is called *ageism*. Negative attitudes can begin in early childhood (Anderson, 2003). For example, older adults are often portrayed as insignificant or as a representation of evil or ugliness in children's literature (Leitner, 1983). We hear an older person described as "over-the-hill," "old fool," or "old maid." With some exceptions, older people are often portrayed negatively in movies, television, or music. The Beatles song, "When I'm Sixty-four," for example, even though musically upbeat, describes aging as an unpleasant process.

The emphasis of contemporary American society is on maintaining youthful beauty. We are bombarded with advertisements for hair dyes, wrinkle creams, and vitamins to keep us looking young. Cosmetic surgery is a booming business. The message is clear: the physical effects of aging are undesirable and should be avoided at all costs. It is interesting to note that many other cultures hold their elderly members in esteem and an older person is looked to for wisdom and guidance. Even though Betsy is showing biological signs of aging signified by wrinkled skin and gray hair and takes medication for high blood pressure, she is leading a healthy, active lifestyle that minimizes the effects of premature aging.

To completely understand the natural course of aging, music therapists must recognize that growing old is a natural process and variations in aging are the norm. Although it is easy to understand that biological, psychological, and psychosocial changes occur in all humans, no two people are alike in the way they age. It is useful to remember that differing rates of aging should be understood within the context of physical, social, and environmental influences.

Frequently, aging men and women have chronic or acute diseases concurrent with the normal effects of aging, but, in fact, most elderly persons live a full, independent life and deal effectively with the combination of normal aging and disease (Anderson, 2003).

AGE-RELATED DISORDERS

The presence of chronic disease is not uncommon in elderly people and, frequently, two or more conditions may be present at the same time. The combination of changes due to normal aging and presence of chronic diseases results in an elderly person having less of a capacity to deal with physical and psychological problems. Chronic ailments are usually not an immediate threat to life, but they do increase an older person's limitations in daily function that lead to death over time. According to Wilmoth and Longino (2007), slightly over 100 million Americans have chronic conditions including arthritis, high blood pressure, impairments in sight and hearing, heart disease, and diabetes. Despite medical advances that have reduced the incidence or impact of many debilitating conditions, chronic disease continues to be a major problem for this population. This section will discuss some of the major psychological and physical age-related disorders found in elderly people (Anderson, 2003; Erber, 2005).

Age-Related Psychological Disorders

It has been estimated that up to 25% of people over the age of 75 develop some type of psychological problem (Lewis, 1989). Major disorders in this category include depression and dementia. Paranoid conditions, substance abuse, and anxiety disorders are also prevalent within this age group (Papalia et al., 1996). Since we discussed most of these conditions in detail in Chapter 8, we will present only a brief summary on how depression and dementia relate to the elderly population.

Depression. The incidence of depression increases with advancing age, with estimates that 20–45% of people over the age of 65 suffer from this condition. In fact, the highest suicide rate occurs in white males over the age of 80 (Lewis, 1989). Symptoms of depression include sleep disturbance, loss of self-esteem, chronic fatigue, inability to concentrate, irritability, and social withdrawal. Other characteristics include thought disturbances, deteriorating interpersonal relationships, and a sense of helplessness. Depression in elderly people can be exacerbated by situational factors, including the loss of spouse, relatives, and close friends; displacement from home; and the loss of vitality and ability to do mental and physical tasks that were once routine. Fortunately, depression can usually be treated effectively with medication and psychotherapy (Harris, 2007).

Dementia. Dementia is an illness characterized by multiple cognitive deficits and includes over a dozen similar conditions that have different causes. Dementia may be caused by one or more conditions, such as Alzheimer's disease, substance abuse, Parkinson's disease, or cardiovascular disease. Dementia may have a sudden onset or occur very gradually. Symptoms include the loss of ability to learn new information or to remember previously learned information, or both. Impairment in areas such as speech, writing, gross and fine motor skills, recognition of familiar objects or people, personal hygiene, financial matters, and social skills is common. Dementia is more prevalent in older adults with the rate doubling about every 5 years after the age of 75 (Erber, 2005; Papalia et al., 1996).

Alzheimer's disease. Dementia of the Alzheimer's type is considered to be one of the most devastating diseases of middle and old age (Corain et al., 1993). While not all dementias are of the Alzheimer's type, this disease is the fourth leading cause of death among the elderly in the United States, affecting about 4 million American adults and claiming an estimated 100,000 lives each year. It is the most frequent cause of severe cognitive dysfunction in elderly adults over the age of 65. When initially described by Alois Alzheimer in 1907, the disease was thought to be a rare occurrence, but today it is considered the primary cause of dementia. Prevalence doubles for every half decade for those over the age of 65, and it has been estimated that almost 50% of those individuals 85 and older have symptoms of Alzheimer's (Erber, 2005; Papalia et al., 1996).

Alzheimer's disease causes a steady, gradual decline in cognitive function due to structural changes in the brain. Early symptoms include lapses in judgment, decline in personal hygiene, bizarre thought patterns, changes in personality, disorientation to time and place, anxiety, depression, and general deterioration in overall functioning. In the final stages, the disorder is characterized by the inability to recognize loved ones and by the loss of speech. Alzheimer's disease is always fatal, with death occurring anywhere from 3 to 20 or more years after onset with the average between 4 and 8 years (Erber, 2005; McNeil, 1995).

At this time, the cause of Alzheimer's disease remains unknown, but theories include a genetic link, abnormal protein deposits in the brain, and environmental factors. Diagnosis of the disease is complicated and usually is made only after other conditions (such as brain tumors, metabolic disorders, alcoholism, or infections) have been ruled out. To date, autopsy is the only way to confirm the diagnosis. Brains affected by Alzheimer's disease exhibit neurofibrillary tangles (damaged proteins in the outer layer of nerve cells in the brain) and neuritic plaques (degenerated nerve endings) in areas of the brain responsible for memory and other cognitive functions. Extensive neurological and psychiatric evaluations can help eliminate other conditions such as vascular dementia that is caused by restricted flow of blood to the brain, and Huntington's disease, a serious genetic disorder that causes involuntary motor movements, personality change, and diminished intellectual function (Cutler & Sramek, 1996; Harris, 2007).

Age-Related Physical Disorders

In this section, we examine some of the most important age-related physical disorders. Many people who are elderly will suffer from two or more of these conditions simultaneously.

Disorders of the central nervous system. Most pathological conditions affecting human behavior involve the nervous system. Two common neurological disorders associated with aging include Parkinson's disease and tardive dyskinesia.

Parkinson's disease. This disease is a degenerative disorder of the central nervous system that usually develops after the age of 50. It is characterized by involuntary contractures of the skeletal muscles, resulting in tremors and muscle rigidity. Other symptoms of this chronic and progressive condition include slow and slurred speech, shuffling gait, drooling, and loss of control of facial muscles. There is no known cause, but the drug L-Dopa is effective in controlling most symptoms. Intellectual functioning is usually not impaired until later stages of the disease (Cutler & Sramek, 1996; Mountain, 2004).

Tardive dyskinesia. This increasingly common neurological disorder is a side effect of taking certain medications over a prolonged period of time. It is marked by involuntary facial grimaces, movement of the arms and legs, rocking motions, and bizarre lip and tongue movements. It is usually irreversible, but symptoms can be reduced by taking other medications, or by discontinuing or reducing levels of antidepressants, antihistamines, L-Dopa, and some antipsychotic drugs (Saxon & Etten, 1987).

Musculoskeletal disorders. Elderly individuals can develop pathological conditions associated with changes in muscular function and bone mass and structure.

Osteoarthritis. This common form of arthritis in people over the age of 50 is characterized by inflammation of the joints, cartilage covering, and bone. It causes stiffness, swelling, and pain, which makes movement difficult. During early stages of the disease, the joints in the hands are most often affected, with later involvement of the hips, knees, spine, and shoulders. These changes are irreversible, so treatment consists of managing pain and maintaining flexibility. In severe cases, surgery may be performed to replace the joint (Erber, 2005).

Osteoporosis. Osteoporosis is a common condition that especially affects postmenopausal women (present in about 25% of women over the age of 60). Bones lose mass, become brittle, and are easily fractured. Most frequently affected are the bones in the wrist, hip, and femur (thigh bone). Posture can also be affected by osteoporosis. The cause of the condition is unknown, but contributing factors include estrogen deficiency, calcium deficiency, vitamin D deficiency, lack of exercise, and decreased capability of the body to absorb calcium. Exercise, proper posture, estrogen replacement therapy, vitamin supplements, and calcium are frequently used to reduce the seriousness of osteoporosis (Erber, 2005; Papalia et al., 1996).

Disorders of the blood, heart, and circulatory system. Serious age-related diseases of the blood, heart, and circulatory system include coronary heart disease, arteriosclerosis, myocardial infarction, cerebral vascular accident, and hypertension (Anderson, 2003; Papalia et al., 1996).

Coronary heart disease. Also called **atherosclerosis**, this coronary heart disease results from blockage of the coronary artery due to a buildup of fibrofatty plaques. Plaques stick to the walls of the artery, eventually narrowing the passageway so that the flow of blood is severely restricted, which can result in a heart attack.

Arteriosclerosis. Hardening and thickening of the arteries, or arteriosclerosis, is a major cause of irreversible brain damage. These changes increase the resistance of blood flow through the carotid and coronary arteries, which results in decreased blood flow and/or hypertension (high blood pressure). Lack of blood to the brain causes tissue death, which leads to mental and/or physical impairment.

Myocardial infarction (MI). Myocardial infarction, also called a heart attack, occurs when blockage of an artery interferes with blood supply to the heart. Symptoms include chest pain, decreased blood pressure, difficulty breathing, and a weak pulse. Although sometimes mistaken for heartburn or indigestion, MI is very serious and can lead to heart failure and death.

Cerebrovascular accident (CVA). Commonly referred to as a stroke, a CVA occurs when blood flow to the brain is restricted, or when a blood vessel in the brain ruptures (an aneurism). As with arteriosclerosis, the resultant lack of oxygen to brain cells causes them to die, leaving permanent brain damage. The specific effects of a stroke are determined by extent and location of damage. Affected areas can include speech, memory, vision, motor skills, or personality. CVA can cause paralysis or death.

Disorders of the sensory systems. Humans gather information about their environment through the senses. Changes in the ability to perceive, interpret, and respond to stimuli can affect social interaction, impair safety, and reduce independence. The most common age-related dysfunctions of vision and hearing in the elderly include the following conditions (Erber, 2005).

Glaucoma. This disease of the eye progresses slowly, often without noticeable symptoms. Caused by excessive accumulation of fluid within the eye, it is a leading cause of blindness in the elderly population. Excess fluid causes increased pressure, which can permanently damage the retina and optic nerve. Treatment with medication and laser surgery can return the pressure to normal levels.

Cataracts. Cataracts are the most common age-related dysfunction of the eye, caused by clouding of the lens. As a result, vision becomes increasingly dim and distorted. Surgery to replace the lens is the best treatment.

Presbycusis. The most common age-related dysfunction of hearing, presbycusis is an abnormal physiological deterioration of the auditory system. Higher frequencies are first affected, usually at a relatively young age. This is followed by a decrease in the ability to hear lower frequencies, which is more serious because it affects the ability to understand speech.

Disorders of the respiratory system. Many respiratory problems associated with aging are caused by cumulative exposure to environmental hazards such as smoking, air pollution, or chemical fumes (Erber, 2005).

Chronic obstructive pulmonary disease (COPD). COPD is a disease of the lungs that is caused by long-term exposure to pollutants such as tobacco smoke and air pollution, or by chronic respiratory infections. It develops gradually and results in the lungs' inability to ventilate efficiently. This puts stress on the heart, which must work harder to adequately oxygenate the blood. Persons with emphysema often die from heart failure (Papalia et al., 1996).

Bronchitis. Bronchitis is caused by a bacterial infection or by consistent exposure to environmental hazards. Inflammation of the bronchi interferes with the flow of oxygen in and out of the lungs. This results in excess production of mucus, which can block air passages and cause chronic coughing.

Disorders of the gastrointestinal system. Common diseases that affect the digestive system in older people include ulcers; cancer of the stomach, throat, mouth, and intestines; and diverticulitis (Erber, 2005).

Gastritis and ulcers. Gastritis is an inflammation of the lining of the stomach and can be a precursor to the development of gastric ulcers, the most common form of ulcers in the elderly. Symptoms include pain in the upper abdomen, significant weight loss, and dehydration. Complications from bleeding become more frequent with age and cause more than half of all deaths attributed to ulcers. Treatment involves the use of medication during early stages and surgery for the most severe cases.

Diverticulitis. After the age of 50, it is not uncommon for bulges (called diverticula) to appear in the intestines. These pockets are created by weaknesses in the abdominal wall. If the areas become inflamed, diverticulitis is the result. Symptoms include pain, nausea, and change in bowel habits. Treatment includes diet modification for mild cases or surgery for more advanced forms of the disease.

Disorders of the endocrine system. The most common age-related dysfunction of the endocrine system is diabetes mellitus.

Diabetes. Older people are more likely to contract maturity onset (rather than juvenile onset) diabetes. In general, diabetes is the result of insufficient amounts of insulin being produced by the pancreas. Elderly individuals who are overweight are likely candidates for diabetes. The condition can often be treated with diet, exercise, medication, and weight reduction, but chronic diabetes can lead to ulcers of the skin, weight loss, glaucoma, cataracts, and circulation problems (Erber, 2005).

As we noted at the beginning of this chapter, the scientific study of aging is a 20th-century phenomenon. Only within the past 25 or 30 years have gerontologists begun to discover the normal and pathological changes that occur in the body with age. In most activities, older people do not function as efficiently as they did during their younger years, and things seem to go wrong with their bodies with greater frequency. However, these physiological deviations are only one aspect of the aging process. In the next part of this chapter we discuss the social influences that impact aging.

AGING AND THE CHANGING WORKFORCE

With the passing of the Social Security Act in the United States in 1935, which had parallel counterparts in other countries, older workers became eligible to receive certain benefits that included a continuing income after retirement at the age of 65. This retirement age was common for many years, but increased life expectancy has led to a revision in the Social Security Act to postpone retirement eligibility as late as age 67, depending on an individual's birth year (Lancaster & Stillman, 2002).

It is well-known that the first wave of post-World War II baby boomers, made up of 76 million people born between 1946 and 1964, is about to retire, leaving only 46 million persons born into Generation X between 1965 and 1980 to maintain their workloads. Currently, the millennium generation is entering the work force in large numbers, about 76 million people (Lancaster & Stillman, 2002), yet there is concern regarding their abilities to replace highly skilled employees who will leave employment in the next 10 years. Consequently, older workers will be encouraged to stay in positions far longer than they had planned. It will be important to enhance their abilities to remain productive, thereby assuring their health, well-being, and life satisfaction both on and off the job. To accomplish this end, older workers will require programs that promote their cognitive, physical, and psychosocial functioning.

COMMUNITY INTEGRATION AND THE OLDER ADULT

Many older adults, like Betsy whom we met earlier, live out their lives in great health and complete independence. Others, such as Jerome, require professional interventions to live life to the fullest due to illness, injury, or progressive functional losses that come with advanced age. For those who want to maintain or enhance their current levels of functioning, music therapy interventions promote cognitive, physical, and psychosocial functions that lead to successful community living and good life quality as ultimate treatment outcomes.

The meaning of successful community life varies among individuals who have differing functional abilities that influence the amounts of environmental and care-giving support they require for a satisfying life. Least restrictive communities are those in which individuals have the supports they need without paying for assistance that is not desired or required. Persons with high functional abilities require little to no external support to live independently, while those with low functional abilities require a great deal of support for life within their communities. Within a least restrictive community, individuals are encouraged to use their skills to the fullest extent possible while remaining safe. A least restrictive community, therefore, supports independent functioning and is individualized according to a person's strengths and abilities.

For many older adults, the least restrictive community is a neighborhood in which they live independently in apartments or homes without assistance from anyone. Independent living is a scope of self-care that incorporates a full array of domestic activities, independent self-care, along with mobility within and outside the home, and maintenance of relationships with others (World Health Organization, 2001). Domestic activities include financial management and bill paying, clothes buying, laundry, house cleaning, meal planning, grocery shopping, food preparation and consumption, and the performance of many more household tasks. It may further include the care of a spouse, a pet, or another family member such as a grandchild.

In contrast to independent living, an older adult may have such limited function that complete assistance is required to perform even the basic activities of daily living (ADLs), including bathing, eating, dressing, and toileting. Persons with complete assistance needs will likely reside in a community living center (CLC), formerly called a nursing home, where hired staff members provide continuous care. Most persons in CLCs require a wheelchair for mobility and must have complete assistance when transferring from it to a chair, bed, or toilet. Others are so frail from progressive dementia or from other causes of physical deterioration that they are bound to recliner chairs and beds 24 hours each day. Older persons who move to a community living center have far less functional ability than ever before, likely because they want to postpone the high cost of care for as long as possible.

THE FUNCTIONAL APPROACH TO TREATMENT

The approach to functional outcomes in this chapter is a contemporary approach to eldercare. It is based on the concepts articulated by the *International Classification of Functioning, Disability and Health* (ICF), a descriptive coding system developed by the World Health Organization (WHO, 2001). The ICF provides a description of a wide range of information regarding health that exceeds the limitations imposed by medical diagnoses. The potential for comprehensive description of health and health-relevant components of well-being are presented within the ICF as a unified, standardized language that can be understood across disciplines and throughout the world (WHO, 2001).

A full description of the ICF goes beyond the scope of this chapter; however, the concept of function as a description of ability or disability is pertinent to music therapy practice with older adults. Music therapy interventions are used to treat older individuals who have varying needs for rehabilitation, restoration, and/or support to become fully integrated within their least restrictive communities. The Activities and Participation component of the ICF is applicable to a conceptualization of community integration for persons in late life. It is defined as follows:

Activity is the execution of a task or action by an individual.

Participation is engagement in life situations.

Activity limitations are difficulties an individual may have in executing activities.

Participation restrictions are problems an individual may experience in his or her involvement in life situations. (WHO, 2001)

Within Activities and Participation (WHO, 2001), the role of music therapy becomes the design, implementation, and evaluation of interventions that promote the best functional outcomes possible within the home and the community environments for older adults and their families. Desired functional outcomes are determined by the individuals and their families in consultation with credentialed professionals and form the goals for treatment. Optimal therapeutic outcomes are achieved as music therapy professionals work with older adults and their families as partners in the treatment process, adjusting goals and treatment regimens as outcome assessments indicate. These treatment regimens are positioned within a wellness model that incorporates physical, psychological, social, and environmental factors that contribute to health and well-being. This orientation to wellness differs from a traditional disease model in which the remediation and/or amelioration of isolated physical symptoms is the measure of success.

CLINICAL PRACTICE IN MUSIC THERAPY

Clinical practice in music therapy involves the deliberate and purposeful use of music by a professional, credentialed music therapist who designs interventions that contribute to evidence-based outcomes associated with an individual's life quality within his or her community. Evidence of therapeutic outcomes from music therapy is gathered through assessments of cognitive, physical, and psychosocial skills that transfer to life functions. These skills are those that contribute to life quality through successful experiences in domestic life, self-care, personal satisfaction, spiritual life, and community involvement.

Music therapy interventions require the development, strengthening, and/ or maintenance of skills that transfer readily to "real world" experiences. Music therapy applications effect change, a process that begins with an individual's desire to participate, a critical prerequisite to therapeutic engagement. Music therapy experiences are crafted around individuals' interests in and desires for music. Music activities serve as strong motivators for enduring participation in interventions that are designed to facilitate skill strengthening and new skill development that transfer readily to family and community life. Applications of music therapy occur in supportive environments in which therapeutic relationships with professionally trained music therapy practitioners help individuals learn, adapt, and develop in ways that contribute to their well-being.

The process of music therapy treatment builds and/or enhances functional skills that contribute to each individual's highest level of independence possible and leads to a positive and realistic self-concept, satisfying relationships with friends and family, and the best possible quality of life. When irreversible changes in body structures or systems occur due to injury, disease, or progressive aging, the ultimate goals of music therapy are the achievement of the best possible function and a good understanding of "normal." Through music therapy, the clear understanding of strengths and limitations provides the basis of a new self-concept where individuals are empowered to be all that they can be as they participate in the activities of life (Clair & Memmot, 2008).

Assessment Using Music

Assessment is the measurement of cognitive, physical, and psychosocial functioning levels that pertain to life in the community. Assessment provides the information that indicates physical health, psychological health, independence, meaningful social relations, and ability to deal with the environment. Evaluation of all this information is used to design treatment interventions, set and revise treatment goals, and determine treatment effectiveness at each stage of the treatment process.

The music therapist assesses function in older adults by using music with different media, such as movement, instrumental and vocal improvisation, structured performance, and music listening. Through music, the therapist identifies a person's capabilities and limitations in communication (verbal and nonverbal), affect, attention, behavior, sensory motor perception, and memory (long- and short-term).

Other areas that can be assessed using music are motivation, gross and fine motor skills, and reality orientation (Aldridge & Aldridge, 1992; Clair & Memmot, 2008; Glynn, 1992; Lipe, 1995; Santeramo, 1997). An individual's music preferences, abilities, and skills can also be determined during the assessment process. Once the client's strengths, needs, and preferences have been assessed, the therapist develops an appropriate music therapy treatment program.

An Approach to Music Therapy Treatment Design

To design a music therapy treatment intervention, the music therapist draws upon assessment information regarding an individual's functioning level. Based on this information, the music therapist formulates a plan for treatment. The music therapy treatment design is directed by the desired nonmusical outcomes.

The transformational design model (TDM) (Thaut, 2005) is the framework for the music therapy treatment. Using the TDM model, the music therapist (1) examines an individual's functional assessment of nonmusical behaviors, (2) articulates treatment goals and objectives based on the assessment information, (3) designs functional nonmusical activities, (4) converts the nonmusical activities from step 3 to music activities, and (5) transfers the outcomes of the musical activities into community applications (Thaut, 2005, p. 131). It is often important to assess preference for the music and the preference for the music activity selected, since they can strongly influence a person's willingness to participate.

To illustrate the TDM, a music therapist receives a physician's order to provide an intervention to decrease agitation in our gentleman we met earlier, Jerome, who has late stage dementia.

The music therapist reads the chart to learn that Jerome's agitation consistently occurs during afternoon shift change on the special care unit where he lives.

Step 1: The music therapist goes to the unit for an observational assessment and sees Jerome beginning to pace just before the afternoon CNAs (Certified Nurse Assistants) arrive. As the CNAs meet for report, the pacing becomes faster and Jerome becomes vocal, emitting a crying sound interspersed with screams. After report, he walks quickly away from anyone who approaches him in an attempt to comfort. After 40 minutes, he has quieted vocally but continues to pace. A review of his chart reveals an average weekly weight loss of two pounds.

Step 2: The music therapist determines a decrease in agitation behaviors as the goal for Jerome. She further identifies a decrease in the duration of vocalization and a decrease in the duration of pacing as two treatment objectives for him.

Step 3: The music therapist identifies stress management with deep breathing as a functional, nonmusical activity. She knows from family members that Jerome's preferred music is rhythm and blues. She designs an intervention in which she sings to Jerome using a simple blues melody, followed by some recorded music after he is guided to sit in a recliner.

Step 4: The music therapist goes to the unit before the agitation begins. She finds Jerome in the hallway, greets him, and starts to sing to him. She sings a phrase, pauses, and waits a few seconds for a response. She sings another phrase and Jerome stares at her. She continues to sing as she gestures for him to walk with her into the day room. She gestures for him to sit in a recliner and she fades the singing as she starts the recorded music. She sits beside him until the CNAs come from report.

Step 5: The music therapist continues the music therapy treatment that results in no pacing and no discomforting vocalizations during or after report for five consecutive days. On the fifth day, she provides a protocol for the CNAs to follow and recorded music for them to play as they guide Jerome to his recliner before they go to report. The music therapist fades her treatment and leaves the CNAs to facilitate stress management for Jerome, who continues to remain calm with no signs of agitation during afternoon shift changes.

In a six-week follow-up chart review, the music therapist observes that the agitation has discontinued. Furthermore, Jerome has an average weight gain of one pound per week.

It is important to note that this example is just one illustration of the transformation design model for music therapy treatment. Each treatment is designed specifically for a particular person to achieve a specific outcome. Outcomes must be measureable in order to provide evidence of treatment effectiveness.

Music Applications for Therapeutic Outcomes

Music therapists have demonstrated clinical outcomes with a wide range of music applications. Hand-held percussion and mallet instruments (small drums, tambourines, maracas, xylophones, and glockenspiels) can be effectively used even with participants who function at very low levels. With persons who can produce vocal sounds, singing can provide a wonderful emotional and social outlet if the music is selected with care (pitch not too high, tempo not too fast, volume not too soft or loud). Hanson, Gfeller, Woodworth, Swanson, and Garand (1996) found that movement activities requiring a high level of involvement (such as dancing) can be used across all functioning levels, while Clair, Tebb, and Bernstein (1993) demonstrated that dancing can be used to help married couples rekindle emotional feelings, even after the ability to sing and speak has diminished.

The presentation of music to severely dysfunctional persons, whether live or recorded, can evoke desirable behaviors, including vocal responses, eye contact, motor responses, and affective behavior (smiling, crying). Clair (1996) found that unaccompanied songs were particularly effective with persons affected by late stage dementia. Other useful music experiences involve simple rhythmic activities using hand-held drums and dancing. As dementia progresses, rhythmic and singing experiences must be drastically simplified (e.g., substituting humming for singing or letting the client create an original rhythm rather than try to imitate a predetermined pattern) (Hanson et al., 1996).

In later stages of Alzheimer's disease, severely regressed persons may not recognize place, time, or even the familiar face of a loved one. Attempts to communicate verbally with a client may be met with verbal and/or physical abuse. Validation therapy, developed by Feil (1993), can be an effective way to communicate and interact with this type of individual. This approach is to accept the person as he or she is, be an empathetic listener, and try to understand the client's point of view. Validation therapy can help the therapist understand and interpret important feelings. It is a reliable way to help disoriented people reduce stress and aggression and to restore a sense of worth and well-being.

While we have identified some important uses of music in the treatment of the institutionalized elderly population, much remains to be done. As the number of older people increases in future years, rehabilitation techniques must keep pace. As Gibbons (1988) noted, "The role of music, music development, and music therapy is not clear. It can be defined only by careful research, integrated with competent practice, which are both based on sound theoretical constructs" (p. 39).

Music Therapy Activities

Music activities that provide enjoyment can be therapeutic because they contribute to a person's quality of life. These music activities are pleasant diversions from daily routines or struggles. Diversional activities are valued because they are meaningful, motivating, and enjoyable, and because they provide opportunities to practice skills developed within therapy sessions. Outcomes of diversional activities may be measurable, but these activities differ from music therapy interventions in their design and primary intent for enjoyment, rather than for the development of life functions.

A sing-along with a group of older adults in a community living center can illustrate the difference between music therapy and music activity. Singing can be used for either activity or therapy, depending on the intent for implementation, the number of participants, and the evidence collected to substantiate the outcomes.

For example, if singing is used as a therapeutic intervention to improve the quality of the spoken voice, an individual can be assessed prior to implementation, for example, with ratings for loudness level and/or degree of breathiness, or ratings for duration of vocal sound production. Following the initial measurement, singing would be implemented to encourage progressively louder singing and/or longer sung phrases. Following a 15-minute singing intervention, the quality of the spoken voice would again be assessed to determine changes in vocal quality from the first to the second measure.

For using singing as a diversional activity, the participant would be encouraged to sing along, perhaps in a large group of other singers. Expressions of pleasure would be noted, such as smiles, positive comments about preferred songs, and associated memories described verbally by the participants. This singing experience would provide, in this case, an opportunity to engage in a pleasurable community activity.

Music Therapy and Evidence-Based Practice

Evidence-based practice, which had its beginnings in the push for accountability in healthcare (Shapiro, Laskerk, Bindman, & Lee, 1993), has moved to therapeutic interventions in other disciplines, including music therapy. It stemmed from the insistence of insurance providers to have research data that indicates medical necessity rather than mere clinical authority for medical procedures (Shapiro et al., 1993). The result was an explosion of scientific studies to acquire research data upon which medical decisions could be based, the development of clinical skills to assess and use the information gleaned from research literature, and the applications of research knowledge to interventions to gain the best possible outcomes (Daly, 2005).

Over time, research has shown that persons' ability to function and their quality of life are important factors in the selection of medical interventions and in patients' adherence to treatment regimens. These factors demonstrate the complexities of evidence-based medicine and the need for collaboration across disciplines to facilitate the best patient outcomes (Daly, 2005).

Music therapists have been challenged over the years to provide evidence for interventions and are trained to gather data regarding treatment outcomes. The continued need for measureable, evidence-based outcomes in music therapy remains paramount as music therapists work with other health care providers to contribute to the quality of life for older adults.

The evidence for music therapy outcomes is as follows:

1. Increase upper/lower extremity strength, mobility, balance, gait speed, and range of motion (Cotter, 1959; Hamburg & Clair, 2003; Olson, 1984; Weideman, 1986)

2. Promote social interaction (Bright, 1972; Clair, 1996; Clair & Ebberts, 1997; S. Johnson, personal communication, 1990; Lipe, 1991; Lord & Gardner, 1993; Pollack & Namazi, 1992; Roskam, 1993; Wylie, 1990; Ziv, Granot, Hai, Dassa, & Haimov, 2007)

3. Stimulate long-term memory (S. Johnson, personal communication, 1990; Wylie, 1990)

4. Improve short-term memory and other cognitive abilities (reduce confusion, improve retention of information) (Bruer, Spitznagel, & Cloninger, 2007; Gregory, 2002; Groene, 2001; S. Johnson, personal communication, 1990; Prickett & Moore, 1991; Reigler, 1980)

5. Improve reality orientation (Bumanis & Yoder, 1987; Reigler, 1980; Smith-Marchese, 1994)

6. Improve self-esteem (Bright, 1972; Clair, 1996; S. Johnson, personal communication, 1990; McClosky, 1985)

7. Promote relaxation/reduce stress (Bright, 1972; Clair, 1996: S. Johnson, personal communication, 1990; McClosky, 1985)

8. Improve verbal skills (Brotons & Kroger, 2000; Cotter, 1959; S. Johnson, personal communication, 1990)

9. Improve personal hygiene (Kurz, 1960; Thomas, Alexander, & Heitman, 1997)

10. Strengthen sensory training (Wolfe, 1983)

11. Improve communication skills (Redinbaugh, 1988)

12. Reduce maladaptive behavior (Bright, 1972; Clair, 1996; Clark, Lipe, & Bilbrey, 1998; Gibbons, 1984; Gibbons, 1988)

13. Enhance reminiscence (Bright, 1972; Byrne, 1982; S. Johnson, personal communication, 1990; Olson, 1984; Wylie, 1990)

14. Improve motor and verbal behaviors in Alzheimer's patients (Clair, 1996; Millard & Smith, 1989)

15. Maintain levels of participation in Alzheimer's patients (Brotons & Pickett-Cooper, 1994; Cevasco & Grant, 2003; Clair & Bernstein, 1990; Mathews, Clair, & Koslowski, 2001; Millard & Smith, 1989; Pollock & Namazi, 1992)

16. Decrease wandering (Fitzgerald-Cloutier, 1993; Groene, 1993)

17. Assist in recalling information (Aldridge & Aldridge, 1992; Depperschmidt, 1992; Foster & Valentine, 2001; Lipe, 1995; Prickett & Moore, 1991; Sambandham & Schirm, 1995; Smith, 1986)

18. Reduce agitation (Brotons & Pickett-Cooper, 1996; Casby & Holme, 1994; Clair, 1996; Clair & Bernstein, 1994; Denny, 1997; Gerdner & Swanson, 1993; Goddaer & Abraham, 1994; Lou, 2001; Strick, 1997)

19. Improving adherence to therapy programs (Johnson, Otto, & Clair, 2002)

The Therapeutic Relationship in Music Therapy Practice

Care for older adults by much younger professionals sometimes leads to discomfort for the music therapist, who must assume the role of a care provider. It is essential that older adults be treated with dignity and that they understand how the music therapist will work with them. It is also essential that young practitioners understand the nature of the relationship they must establish to achieve the best possible therapeutic outcomes.

The therapeutic relationship is characterized by a set of clear boundaries for behaviors that serves as a framework in which trust is established, respect is engendered, power is clarified, and personal closeness is not social in nature. It is through the therapeutic relationship that the music therapist clarifies acceptable behaviors, confirms the therapeutic purposes of interventions, and directs individuals' and their families' expectations toward functional outcomes and away from personal or social interactions with the music therapist.

The trust in the therapeutic relationship is based on confidence in the music therapist's competence to use knowledge, skills, and abilities to provide treatment. Confidence is prerequisite to a therapeutic commitment and is integral to ongoing treatment participation. Confidence and trust are also critical to persistence to achieve when treatment demands progressively increase.

The respect component of the therapeutic relationship is best when it is mutual between the music therapist and the care recipient; however, unconditional acceptance of the recipient by the music therapist is essential. Unconditional acceptance is characterized as the professional delivery of services without regard for the recipient's and the recipient's family background, sexual orientation, education level, religious affiliation, financial and other resources, the family's ability to cope, and all aspects of the recipient's life before, during, and after injury, illness, or disability. It honors the recipient's right to decide the level of treatment engagement based on full knowledge of his or her condition, provided the recipient has adequate cognitive functioning to make such decisions.

The power, authority, or control in the therapeutic relationship lies heavily with the music therapist. It is based on the music therapist's unique knowledge of the professional discipline and knowledge of the care recipient's and the family's privileged information. The music therapist's power is always held in check by accountability and treatment decisions focused on enhanced treatment effectiveness. The music therapist's decisions regarding treatment design and implementation makes the music therapist ultimately responsible for treatment outcomes.

Personal closeness inherent within therapeutic relationships can be very confusing for the care recipient and the recipient's family. The nature of music activities lead to further confusion when they evoke expressions of emotions that are very personal. Physical proximity and touch, knowledge of personal information, assistance with functioning, and the amount of time spent together in the treatment setting can easily lead to erroneous assumptions on the part of recipients and their families. It is critical for the music therapist to periodically clarify the boundaries for relationships as stipulated in the Code of Ethics and the Standards of Professional Practice (American Music Therapy Association, 2007) (refer also to Chapter 15).

All music therapists who join the treatment teams for care recipients and their families must demonstrate abilities to form and maintain therapeutic relationships. They must also have skills to build interventions based on recipients' interests and strengths, with considerations and adaptations for their limitations. In the contexts of therapeutic relationships, music therapists must have the capacity to transfer and apply information from treatment to community living settings, and have the ability to work independently, yet collaboratively, within the team context. Table 1, while not exhaustive, identifies some of the personal and professional characteristics of music therapists.

Table 1
Personal and Professional Characteristics of Music Therapists

Personal Characteristics	Professional Characteristics
A problem solver	Knowledgeable and competent
A self-starter and independent worker	Articulate in written and spoken forms
Sensitive to others	Effective and efficient
Tolerant and respectful	Maintains high standards of practice
Appropriate with interpersonal skills	Accountable
Energetic	Ethical
Realistic and forthright	Highly organized
Appropriately assertive	Willing speaker for the team or profession
Trustworthy	Adapts as needed
Committed to self-care	Respects and supports colleagues

SUMMARY

Aging is a lifelong developmental process that begins at conception and ends, ultimately, in death. Due to increased longevity and a surge in population, the United States is experiencing explosive growth in the proportion of elderly people. This increase presents a challenge to gerontologists and society because of the increased medical, social, and psychological services required by this population.

Aging is marked by changes in functional capacity and structural modifications affecting virtually every system in the body, but the rate at which those changes occur varies among individuals due to genetic and environmental factors. As we grow older, we are less efficient at physical and some cognitive tasks, and the body is more susceptible to age-related diseases. We experience psychosocial changes as well, related to roles, relationships, income, status, and activity patterns.

We distinguished between normal aging and age-related dysfunctions. Certain conditions, such as Alzheimer's disease and disorders of the circulatory system, are considered to be age-related diseases, whereas reduced vision and hearing are universal features of aging and not considered pathological.

Elderly people who are institutionalized have a unique set of problems and needs. Music therapy can be an effective means of rehabilitation for these clients in helping them maintain or improve physical, mental, and psychological functions. Research has shown that, as a group, elderly people have both the interest and ability to develop their music skills. A good music therapy program contains opportunities not only to listen to music, but also to create, perform, and move to music if clients are physically and cognitively capable.

STUDY QUESTIONS

1. Define the term *gerontologist*.
2. Discuss why there is such a rapid increase in the numbers of persons over age 65. What are the implications for music therapists?
3. Describe the aging process from a biological, psychological, and psychosocial perspective.
4. What factors play a part in increasing the incidence of depression among the elderly?
5. Define *ageism*.
6. Discuss the type of physical problems that can affect a person as he or she ages.
7. What is meant by a *least restrictive community*?
8. Describe the function of a community living center.

9. Define evidence-based outcomes and explain why this concept is so important for music therapists to be familiar with.

10. Define the *transformational design model* (TDM) then describe the five stages that comprise the model.

11. What are the differences between therapeutic music applications and music therapy activities?

12. Describe the meaning of the therapeutic relationship.

13. List at least seven music therapy goals often used with elderly persons.

REFERENCES

Aldridge, D., & Aldridge, G. (1992). Two epistemologies: Music therapy and medicine in the treatment of dementia. *The Arts in Psychotherapy, 19,* 243–255.

American Music Therapy Association. (2007). Code of ethics. *AMTA member sourcebook* (pp. 24-28). Silver Spring, MD: Author.

Anderson, M. A. (2003). *Caring for older adults holistically* (3rd ed.). Philadelphia: F. A. Davis.

Bright, R. (1972). *Music in geriatric care.* Melville, NY: Belwin-Mills.

Brotons, M., & Kroger, S. (2000). The impact of music therapy on language functioning in dementia. *Journal of Music Therapy, 37,* 183–195.

Brotons, M., & Pickett-Cooper, P. (1994). Preferences of Alzheimer's disease patients for music activities: Singing, instruments, dance/movement, games, and composition/improvisation. *Journal of Music Therapy, 31,* 220–233.

Brotons, M., & Pickett-Cooper, P. (1996). The effects of music therapy intervention on agitation behaviors of Alzheimer's disease patients. *Journal of Music Therapy, 33,* 2–18.

Bruer, A. B., Spitznagel, E., & Cloninger, C. R. (2007). The temporal limits of cognitive change from music therapy in elderly persons with dementia or dementia-like cognitive impairment: A randomized controlled trial. *Journal of Music Therapy, 44*(4), 308–328.

Bumanis, A., & Yoder, J. W. (1987). Music and dance: Tools for reality orientation. *Activities, Adaptation, and Aging, 10,* 25–33.

Byrne, L. A. (1982). Music therapy and reminiscence: A case study. *Clinical Gerontologist, 1,* 76–77.

Casby, J. A., & Holme, M. B. (1994). The effect of music on repetitive disruptive vocalizations in persons with dementia. *The American Journal of Occupational Therapy, 48*(10), 883–889.

Cevasco, A. M., & Grant, R. E. (2003). Comparisons for different methods for eliciting exercise-to-music for clients with Alzheimer's disease. *Journal of Music Therapy, 40,* 41–56.

Clair, A. A. (1996). The effect of singing on alert responses in persons with late stage dementia. *Journal of Music Therapy, 33,* 234–247.

Clair, A. A., & Bernstein, B. (1990). A comparison of singing, vibrotactile and nonvibrotactile instrumental playing responses in severely regressed persons with dementia of the Alzheimer's type. *Journal of Music Therapy, 27,* 119–125.

Clair, A. A., & Bernstein, B. (1994). The effect of no music, simulative background music and sedative background music on agitated behaviors in persons with severe dementia. *Activities, Adaptation, and Aging, 19*(1), 61–70.

Clair, A. A., & Ebberts, G. (1997). The effects of music therapy on interaction between family caregivers and their care receivers with late stage dementia. *Journal of Music Therapy, 34,* 148–164.

Clair, A. A., & Memmot, J. (2008). *Therapeutic uses of music with older adults.* Silver Spring, MD: American Music Therapy Association.

Clair, A. A., Tebb, A., & Bernstein, B. (1993, January/February). The effects of a socialization and music therapy intervention on self-esteem and loneliness in spouse caregivers of those diagnosed with dementia of the Alzheimer's type: A pilot study. *American Journal of Alzheimer's Disease and Related Disorders and Research,* pp. 24–32.

Clark, M. E., Lipe, A. W., & Bilbrey, M. (1998). Use of music to decrease aggressive behaviors in people with dementia. *Journal of Gerontological Nursing, 24*(7), 10–17.

Corain, B., Iqbal, K., Nicolini, M., Winblad, B., Wishiewski, H., & Zatta, P. (1993). *Alzheimer's disease: Advances in clinical and basic research.* West Sussex, England: John Wiley & Sons.

Cotter, V. W. (1959). *Effects of the use of music on the behavior of geriatric patients.* Unpublished master's thesis, University of Kansas, Lawrence.

Cutler, N. R., & Sramek, J. J. (1996). *Understanding Alzheimer's disease.* Jackson: University Press of Mississippi.

Daly, J. (2005). *Evidence-based medicine and the search for a science of clinical care.* Berkeley: University of California Press.

Denny, A. (1997). Quiet music: An intervention for meal-time agitation. *Gerontological Nursing, 23,* 16–23.

Depperschmidt, K. A. (1992). *Musical mnemonics as an aid to memory in patients with dementia of the Alzheimer's type.* Unpublished master's thesis, Colorado State University, Ft. Collins.

Erber, J. T. (2005). *Aging and older adulthood.* Belmont, CA: Thompson Wadsworth.

Feil, N. (1993). *The validation breakthrough: Simple techniques for communicating with people with "Alzheimer's-type dementia."* Baltimore: Health Professions Press.

Ferraro, K. F. (2007). The evolution of gerontology as a scientific field of inquiry. In J. M. Wilmoth & K. F. Ferraro (Eds.), *Gerontology: Perspectives and issues* (pp. 13– 33). New York: Springer.

Fitzgerald-Cloutier, M. L. (1993). The use of music to decrease wandering: an alternative to restraints. *Music Therapy Perspectives, 11,* 32–36.

Foster, N. A., & Valentine, E. R. (2001). The effect of auditory stimulation on auto-biographical recall in dementia. *Experimental Aging Research, 27,* 215–228.

Gerdner, L. A., & Swanson, E. A. (1993). Effects on individualized music on confused and agitated elderly patients. *Archives of Psychiatric Nursing, 7,* 284–291.

Gibbons, A. C. (1984). A program for noninstitutionalized, mature adults: A description. *Activities, Adaptation, and Aging, 6,* 71–80.

Gibbons, A. C. (1988). A review of literature for music development/education and music therapy with the elderly. *Music Therapy Perspectives, 5,* 33–40.

Glynn, N. J. (1992). The music therapy assessment tool in Alzheimer's patients. *Journal of Gerontological Nursing, 18,* 3–9.

Goddaer, J., & Abraham, I. L. (1994). Effects of relaxing music on agitation during meals among nursing home residents with severe cognitive impairment. *Archives of Psychiatric Nursing, 8,* 150–158.

Gregory, D. (2002). Music listening for maintaining attention of older adults with cognitive impairments. *Journal of Music Therapy, 39,* 244–264.

Groene, R. W. (1993). Effectiveness of music therapy 1:1 intervention with individuals having senile dementia of the Alzheimer's type. *Journal of Music Therapy, 30,* 138–157.

Groene, R. W. (2001). The effect of presentation and accompaniment style on attentional and responsive behaviors of participants with dementia diagnoses. *Journal of Music Therapy, 38,* 36–50.

Hamburg, J., & Clair, A. A. (2003). The effects of a movement with music program on measures of balance and gait speed in healthy older adults. *Journal of Music Therapy, 40*(3), 212–226.

Hanson, N., Gfeller, K., Woodworth, G., Swanson, E. A., & Garand, L. (1996). A comparison of the effectiveness of differing types and difficulty of music activities in programming for older adults with Alzheimer's disease and related disorders. *Journal of Music Therapy, 33*, 93–123.

Harris, D. K. (2007). *The sociology of aging* (3rd ed.). New York: Rowman and Littlefield.

Johnson, G., Otto, D., & Clair, A. A. (2002). The effect of instrumental and vocal music on the adherence to a physical rehabilitation exercise program with persons who are elderly. *Journal of Music Therapy, 38*, 82–96.

Kurz, C. E. (1960). *The effects of a planned music program on the day hall sound and personal appearance of geriatric patients.* Unpublished master's thesis, University of Kansas, Lawrence.

Lancaster, L. C., & Stillman, D. (2002). *When generations collide.* New York: Harper Collins.

Leitner, M. J. (1983). The representation of aging in pop/rock music in the 1960s and '70s. *Activities, Adaptation, and Aging, 3*, 49–53.

Lewis, S. C. (1989). *Elder care in occupational therapy.* Thorofare, NJ: Slack.

Lipe, A. (1991). Using music therapy to enhance the quality of life in a client with Alzheimer's dementia: A case study. *Music Therapy Perspectives, 9*, 102–105.

Lipe, A. (1995). The use of music performance tasks in the assessment of cognitive functioning among older adults with dementia. *Journal of Music Therapy, 32*, 137–151.

Longino, C. F., Soldo, B. J., & Manton, K. G. (1990). Demography of aging in the United States. In J. M. Wilmoth & K. F. Ferraro (Eds.), *Gerontology: Perspectives and issues* (pp. 19–41). New York: Springer.

Lord, T. R., & Gardner, J. E. (1993). Effects of music on Alzheimer's patients. *Perceptual and Motor Skills, 76*, 451–455.

Lou, M. F. (2001). The use of music to decrease agitated behavior of the demented elderly. *Scandinavian Journal of Caring Sciences, 15*, 165–173.

Markson, E. W. (2003). *Social gerontology today: An introduction.* Los Angeles: Roxbury.

Mathews, R. M., Clair, A. A., & Kosloski, K. (2001). Keeping the beat: Use of rhythmic music during exercise activities for the elderly with dementia. *American Journal of Alzheimer's Disease and Other Dementias, 16*(6), 377–380.

McClosky, L. J. (1985). Music and the frail elderly. *Activities, Adaptation, and Aging, 7*, 73–75.

McNeil, C. (1995). *Alzheimer's disease: Unraveling the mystery* (NIH Publication No. 95-3782). Bethesda, MD: National Institutes of Health.

Millard, K. O., & Smith, J. M. (1989). The influence of group singing therapy on the behavior of Alzheimer's disease patients. *Journal of Music Therapy, 26*, 58–70.

Mountain, G. (2004). *Occupational therapy with older people.* Philadelphia: Whurr.

Olson, B. K. (1984). Player-piano music as therapy for the elderly. *Journal of Music Therapy, 21*, 35–45.

Papalia, D. E., Camp, C. J., & Feldman, R. D. (1996). *Adult development and aging.* New York: McGraw-Hill.

Pollock, N., & Namazi, K. (1992). The effect of music participation on the social behavior of Alzheimer's patients. *Journal of Music Therapy, 29*, 54–67.

Posner, R. A. (1995). *Aging and old age.* Chicago: The University of Chicago Press.

Prickett, C. A., & Moore, R. S. (1991). The effects of music to aid memory of Alzheimer's patients. *Journal of Music Therapy, 28*, 102–110.

Redinbaugh, E. M. (1988). The use of music therapy in developing a communication system in a withdrawn, depressed older adult resident: A case study. *Music Therapy Perspectives, 5*, 82–85.

Reigler, J. (1980). Comparison of a reality orientation program for geriatric patients with and without music. *Journal of Music Therapy, 17*, 26–33.

Roskam, K. S. (1993). *Feeling the sound: The influence of music on behavior.* San Francisco: San Francisco Press.

Rybash, J. M., Roodin, P. A., & Hoyer, W. J. (1995). *Adult development and aging* (3rd ed.). Madison, WI: Brown and Benchmark.

Sambandham, M., & Schirm, V. (1995). Music as a nursing intervention for residents with Alzheimer's disease in long-term care. *Geriatric Nursing, 16*, 79–83.

Santeramo, B. (1997). *The influence of music versus no music on agitation behaviors of Alzheimer's patients.* Unpublished master's thesis, Colorado State University, Fort Collins.

Saxon, S. V., &. Etten, M. J. (1987). *Physical changes and aging.* New York: Tiresias Press.

Shapiro, D. W., Laskerk R. D., Bindman, A. B., & Lee, P. R. (1993). Containing costs while improving quality of care: The role of profiling and practice guideline. *Annual Review of Public Health, 14*, 219–241.

Smith, G. H. (1986). A comparison of the effects of three treatment interventions on cognitive functioning of Alzheimer's patients. *Music Therapy, 64*, 41–56.

Smith-Marchese, K. (1994). The effects of participatory music on the reality orientation and sociability of Alzheimer's residents in a long-term-care facility. *Activities, Adaptation, and Aging, 18*, 41–55.

Strick, E. (1997). *The use of tactile stimulation in music to influence agitated behaviors in Alzheimer's dementia.* Unpublished master's thesis, Colorado State University, Fort Collins.

Thaut, M. H. (2005). *Rhythm, music and the brain: Scientific foundations and clinical applications.* Florence, KY: Routledge.

Thomas, D., Alexander, T., & Heitman, R. (1997). The effects of music on bathing cooperation for residents with dementia. *Journal of Music Therapy, 34*, 246–259.

Waters, D. J. (2007). Cellular and organismal aspects of senescence and longevity. In J. M. Wilmoth & K. F. Ferraro (Eds.), *Gerontology: Perspectives and issues* (pp. 59–88). New York: Springer.

Weideman, D. A. (1986). *Effect of reminiscence and music on movement participation level of elderly care-home residents.* Unpublished master's thesis, University of Kansas, Lawrence.

Whitbourne, S. K. (1996). *The aging individual.* New York: Springer.

Wilmoth, J. M., & Longino, C. F. (2007). Demographic perspectives on aging. In J. M. Wilmoth & K. F. Ferraro (Eds.), *Gerontology: Perspectives and issues* (pp. 35–56). New York: Springer.

Wolfe, J. R. (1983). The use of music in a group sensory training programs for regressed geriatric patients. *Activities, Adaptation, and Aging, 3*, 49–62.

World Health Organization. (2001). *International classification of functioning, disability and health.* Geneva, Switzerland: Author.

Wylie, M. E. (1990). A comparison of the effects of old familiar songs, antique objects, historical summaries, and general questions on the reminiscence of nursing-home residents. *Journal of Music Therapy, 27*, 2–12.

Ziv, N., Granot, A., Hai, S., Dassa, A., & Haimov, I. (2007). The effect of background stimulative music on behavior in Alzheimer's patients. *Journal of Music Therapy, 44*(4), 329–343.

CHAPTER 8

MUSIC THERAPY IN THE TREATMENT OF BEHAVIORAL-EMOTIONAL DISORDERS

Kate E. Gfeller
Michael H. Thaut

CHAPTER OUTLINE

BEHAVIORAL-EMOTIONAL DISORDERS: AN INTRODUCTION
SOME COMMON CATEGORIES OF BEHAVIORAL-EMOTIONAL DISORDERS
- Schizophrenia
- Mood Disorders
- Anxiety Disorders
- Personality Disorders
- Substance-Related Disorders
- Other Psychiatric Disorders

PHILOSOPHICAL ORIENTATIONS TO PSYCHIATRIC TREATMENT
- Treatments That Focus on Affect
- Treatments That Focus on Behavior
- Treatments That Focus on Cognition
- Treatments That Focus on Physical Factors: Biomedical Model
- Eclectic Orientation

CLINICAL USES OF MUSIC THERAPY IN THE PSYCHIATRIC SETTING
- Considering Individual Differences in Age and Culture
- Categories of Music Activities Used in Therapy

LEVELS OF GROUP THERAPY BASED ON THE CLIENT'S FUNCTIONAL LEVEL
- Supportive, Activity-Oriented Music Therapy
- Reeducative, Insight-and-Process-Oriented Music Therapy
- Reconstructive, Analytically and Catharsis-Oriented Music Therapy

CHANGES IN HEALTH CARE DELIVERY: SHORT-TERM CARE

BEHAVIORAL-EMOTIONAL DISORDERS: AN INTRODUCTION

In everyday life, we come across behaviors that seem odd, eccentric, or horrifying: homeless persons wearing bizarre clothing and hoarding items in a shopping cart; movie stars engaging in risky or attention-getting behaviors; random shooting of innocent victims on college campuses. Though less extreme, we may know of people who feel hopeless or who fear seemingly harmless situations (e.g., riding in an elevator). Are these behaviors normal or abnormal?

The notion of "normalcy" is complex. Within each culture, there is a range of acceptable behavior for particular situations. Some actions, such as killing, are considered illegal within everyday life, but are condoned on the field of battle. Weeping inconsolably is considered normal for a grieving widow, but abnormal if it occurs day after day and without any provocation. Tattered, dirty, and ill-fitting clothing may be considered a sign of abnormality in a homeless person, but would be considered a sad circumstance in the case of political refugees who must flee their homes. Rough-and-tumble behaviors, which we expect on a football field, would be considered unacceptable at a symphony concert. Whether a behavior or emotion is considered acceptable depends upon the situation and societal norms. Thus, social mores will, to a greater or lesser extent, determine what constitutes acceptable or "normal" behavior. Individuals within the same culture will also differ in what they consider to be normal and acceptable.

Even highly trained mental health professionals have differing opinions about what constitutes normalcy and which terms are most appropriate to use in this context. As you read textbooks or articles written by psychologists, psychiatrists, counselors, and other health professionals, you may run across some of the following terms: *mental illness, mental disorders, psychiatric disorders, psychopathology, emotional illness, emotional impairment, behavioral disorders, behavioral-emotional disorders*, or other terms. Some people use these terms interchangeably, while others are very specific in their choice of terms. For example, some refer to problems with a physiological basis as a mental illness, but use the term *behavioral disorder* when describing abnormal behavior believed to result from environmental influences. The concept of normalcy and terms associated with abnormal behaviors and emotions have changed over time and will be subject to ongoing debate; thus, there is not one clearly correct term. However, one term that some professionals consider more "neutral" with regard to cause as well as symptoms is *behavioral-emotional disorder*. Therefore, *behavioral-emotional disorder* is the term that will be used most often throughout this chapter.

At what point is a behavior and/or emotion considered inappropriate or problematic enough to be considered a behavioral-emotional disorder? The assignment of a formal diagnosis is often related to the (1) frequency, (2) duration, and (3) intensity with which a behavior occurs or the emotion is experienced, as well as the circumstances surrounding the behavior or emotion. For example, it is not unusual for an individual to feel discouraged or depressed by events such as the loss of a loved one or failure in school or business. However, if feelings of depression occur quite frequently, last for weeks or months on end (duration), or are of such severity (intensity) that the individual is unable to function or even attempts suicide, that may be the sign of a clinical depression. Another sign of depression is the occurrence of intense and ongoing feelings of dejection or hopelessness, even though there are no obvious reasons for sadness. In short, a wide range of behaviors is considered acceptable within any given society, but when behaviors are not appropriate to the situation, are maladaptive, or are overwhelming, they are considered symptoms of a behavioral-emotional disorder.

Behavioral-emotional disorders are not caused by lack of character or fortitude. They can occur at almost any age and affect people of all races, religions, or incomes. Affected individuals may demonstrate disturbances in mood and thinking, perception of reality, and ability to relate to other persons. Some disorders are characterized by excessive fears, panic, and obsessive or compulsive behaviors. Other problems such as eating disorders or substance abuse are also considered behavioral-emotional disorders.

It is important to realize that a person's mental health can change over time. For example, some people may suffer one episode of depression, and then return to good mental health for the remainder of their lives. Other people may have recurrent episodes of depression, with periods of healthy functioning in between. Still other people, despite the best possible treatments, may have chronic forms of disorders that last for many years. Fortunately, most disorders are treatable, and people can achieve significant relief from their symptoms.

SOME COMMON CATEGORIES OF BEHAVIORAL-EMOTIONAL DISORDERS

A major attempt to collect and organize data to describe objectively and diagnose behavioral-emotional disorders occurred with the 1952 publication of the *Diagnostic and Statistical Manual of Mental Disorders (DSM)*. This important work systematically organized and categorized the many forms of behavioral and emotional disorders into a uniform system. Subsequent revisions of this manual have been published as mental health professionals learn more about the causes and characteristics of various disorders. The *Diagnostic and Statistical Manual of Mental Disorders (4th ed.) (DSM-IV-TR)*, published in 2000 is the most recent version of this important diagnostic tool (American Psychiatric Association [APA], 2000).

The following portions of this chapter present some basic information about several of the major categories of disorders found in the *DSM-IV-TR*. You will learn more in-depth information about these and other disorders in books and in classes such as Abnormal Psychology.

Schizophrenia

> *Susan is a twenty-eight-year-old woman who is living at home with her parents and is currently receiving Social Security disability checks since she has been unable to sustain gainful employment over the past eight years. While Susan's early childhood seemed unremarkable, during her last year of high school her parents noticed a personality change. Susan seemed aloof and uncomfortable with others. At times she expressed fears that other people were against her or trying to "get her," despite the lack of any real evidence. As her condition deteriorated over a period of months, even her grooming and ability to take care of herself deteriorated. She was often so preoccupied that she failed to carry out simple tasks of daily living, such as grocery shopping or making the bed.*

> *Susan's parents were concerned, of course, but it was not until she started to talk about aliens from other planets speaking to her over the radio that they realized Susan needed psychiatric help. An evaluation of Susan's behavior by a psychiatrist confirmed their suspicion that Susan had a psychiatric disorder. The psychiatrist told them that Susan had schizophrenia and recommended hospitalization for Susan where she would be treated with medications and milieu therapy (a structured environment consisting of a host of supportive therapies such as counseling, vocational rehabilitation, and other forms of therapy).*

What is schizophrenia? Schizophrenia is part of a general psychiatric category known as Schizophrenia and Other Psychotic Disorders. It is a serious disorder in which the individual experiences profound alterations in thinking, sensory perception, affect (emotional expression), and behavior. Symptoms can include **hallucinations**, **delusions**, disordered thinking, movement disorders, flat affect, social withdrawal, and cognitive deficits, which occur for a significant period of time. Schizophrenia usually involves impairment in more than one area of functioning and there are usually multiple symptoms (Wilson, Nathan, O'Leary, & Clark, 1996). While two individuals may have the diagnosis of schizophrenia, they may experience somewhat different symptoms, depending upon the type of schizophrenia, the phase of the illness, and the severity of the illness. During some phases of schizophrenia, symptoms may reach **psychotic** proportions, which means that the person will suffer from a loss of contact with reality and self-perception (Scully, 1985). The most common misconception about schizophrenia is that it means "split personality," or "multiple personality," which actually is another disorder called dissociative identity disorder (Wilson et al., 1996). The term *schizophrenia* refers to the "splitting of the mind," meaning disturbances in thinking, feeling, and actions. There are several types of schizophrenia, each characterized by particular and predominant symptoms. You can learn more specific details about various types of schizophrenia as well as the causes of or risks for schizophrenia in courses such as Abnormal Psychology.

Although only a small proportion (approximately 1%) (National Institutes of Mental Health, 2008) of the population develops schizophrenia during their lifetime, the impact of this illness is tremendous. Schizophrenia tends to have a very negative impact on behavior and ability to function in everyday life and can be chronic in nature. People diagnosed with schizophrenia are the major users of psychiatric hospital beds in the U.S. (Wilson et al., 1996). According to the *DSM-IV-TR* (APA, 2000), there are several clinical symptoms typically exhibited by individuals with schizophrenia:

- **delusions**, which are false beliefs that lack a basis in reality and are maintained by the patient despite evidence that they are false. These include delusions of being persecuted; delusions of grandeur (for example, believing that you are a famous person, such as Elvis Presley, or Jesus Christ); delusions of control (for example, thinking that an alien force is controlling one's behavior); and delusions of romance (false belief that someone is in love with you).

- **hallucinations**, which are sensory experiences that occur in the absence actual environmental stimulation, such as hearing voices, or seeing things that don't exist.

- **disorganized speech**, such as shifting from one topic to another with no natural transitions, or responding to questions in a tangential way. The speech often seems illogical or incoherent. At its most severe, such disorganized speech can make effective communication nearly impossible.

- **grossly disorganized behavior** or **catatonic behavior**, which refers to an inability to organize even basic activities of everyday life; in the case of catatonic behavior, there is marked abnormality in motor behavior, such as a long fixed posture.

- **negative symptoms**, such as deficits in facial affect, poverty of speech (little to say in everyday conversation, or brief and empty replies to questions), or the inability to begin and sustain goal-directed activity (*DSM-IV-TR*, APA, 2000; Wilson et al., 1996).

How is schizophrenia treated? One of the most significant changes in the treatment of schizophrenia has been the development of antipsychotic medications during the 20th century. These medications, which help to normalize neurological processes, have transformed the lives of many psychotic individuals who were once exiled to lifelong residency in the back wards of institutions. These medications do not cure the disease, but they can reduce or eliminate the very debilitating symptoms such as delusions or hallucinations in some individuals and help them to think and behave in more adaptive ways. However, some people develop serious side effects as a result of medications, and other people show limited or no improvement.

Other treatments that have helped schizophrenics to cope with the negative effects of the disease are various forms of psychosocial therapies (Silverman, 2003a; 2005; Silverman & Marcionetti, 2004; Houghton & Smeltekop, 2002; Unkefer & Thaut, 2002). Many clinical studies show that pharmacological treatment by itself may be less efficient than a combination of medication and individual and group therapy (Andreason, 2001). Psychosocial therapies are carried out in individual or group settings (Cassity & Cassity, 2006; Silverman, 2007; Silverman & Marcionetti, 2004; Unkefer & Thaut, 2002). A stable therapeutic relationship between client and therapist as well as a stable work and home environment can help the client cope with his or her illness and to find ways to maximize the client's behavioral strengths while changing maladaptive behavior patterns (Silverman, 2003a).

Therapeutic experiences, including music therapy, may help clients to test the reality of their perceptions in a supportive environment as well as reduce the intensity or frequency of auditory hallucinations (Cassity & Cassity, 2006; Silverman, 2003b, 2005). Techniques may be taught to diminish anxiety and induce relaxation (Cassity & Cassity, 2006; Unkefer & Thaut, 2002; Walworth, 2003). Uplifting experiences may help clients to experience positive feeling states and find motivation to cope with their lives. The structure of a daily schedule of therapy and activities (milieu therapy) may make reality more predictable and less threatening for the client. The therapist functions as an outside personality who supports, strengthens, and guides the disturbed personality of the client (Silverman, 2003a). This function includes teaching the client to deal with everyday problems, such as attending to personal hygiene, paying bills, trying to live independently, and taking medication (Houghton & Smeltekop, 2002; Unkefer & Thaut, 2002). Music therapy can be an effective therapeutic option for addressing psychosocial needs and as part of milieu therapy (Cassity & Cassity, 2006; Silverman, 2007; Silverman & Marcionetti, 2004; Unkefer & Thaut, 2002).

Mood Disorders

Bryce is a 25-year-old salesman who was recently admitted to the hospital by his wife, who complained about his crazy spending sprees and grandiose ideas for his hardware business. In particular, within a period of just a few days, he had purchased a fleet of white limousines, a yacht, and 100 paisley tuxedo jackets, all for the purpose of throwing a party for his business associates where he planned to entertain the group by playing the trombone. All of these actions had been carried out despite the fact that his business assets are quite modest, as is his musical talent. Bryce's wife also recounted to the psychiatrist that Bryce often stays up day and night and that he seems to have boundless energy. The energy would be fine if he spent it wisely, but instead, he comes up with harebrained schemes about buying a fleet of jets to transport hardware all around the globe. This boundless energy is a dramatic contrast to Bryce's mood last year, during which he was so depressed and morose that he could barely get out of bed and get dressed. For nearly three months, Bryce had felt hopeless and worthless and had seriously contemplated suicide. This dramatic change in mood became easier to understand once Bryce's psychiatrist told him that he suffers from a mood disorder, called bipolar disorder. His blue mood last year was a major depressive episode, and his more current euphoria is called a manic episode.

What are mood disorders? Mood disorders are a class of behavioral-emotional disorders characterized primarily by disturbance in mood, such as depression or extreme elation (*DSM-IV-TR*, APA, 2000; Wilson et al., 1996). Because periods of depression or elation may recur over time, the *DSM-IV-TR* organizes the various mood disorders around different types of episodes. **Episodes** are discrete periods of time during which a person has a number of specific symptoms that reflect a marked change from previous functioning (Wilson et al., 1996). The marked change in functioning can be a period of depression and diminished interest (depressive episode), or a period of unusually elevated, expansive, or irritable mood, which is referred to as a manic episode.

During a depressive episode, the person has a persistent depressed mood (most of the day and nearly every day) and several other symptoms, such as diminished interest in activities that are generally enjoyable, changes in appetite or weight, changes in sleep patterns, agitation or lack of energy, feelings of worthlessness, difficulty concentrating and thinking clearly, and thoughts of death and/or suicide (*DSM-IV-TR*, APA, 2000). The symptoms may initially develop at a time of personal crisis (such as the loss of a spouse or a divorce) and then persist beyond a normal period of mourning. However, people with clinical depression can also feel depressed for no apparent reason. In the case of Bryce, the trombone player, the time period in which he felt so despondent that he could barely get out of bed would be an example of a depressive episode.

Keep in mind that the diagnostic use of the word *depression* as found in the *DSM-IV-TR* is a specific medical usage of this word. This word usage (also referred to in some circumstances as *clinical depression*) is different from the more informal use of the word that people use in general conversation to describe a short-term feeling of disappointment or sadness in response to an undesirable situation (such as, "I'm having a bad hair day. How depressing!").

During a manic episode, people may be extremely talkative and may have decreased need for sleep, inflated self-esteem, and racing thoughts or distractibility. They may engage in wild spending sprees or risky behavior, or they may take on unrealistic projects. For example, the vignette about Bryce includes extravagant purchases of yachts and paisley tuxedos and an unrealistic appraisal of his own skill as a musician. These symptoms can result in marked impairment in vocational and social functioning. A combination of episodes and other features (such as the course of outcome of the disorder) together make up a mood disorder.

Under the general category of mood disorders, different sequential patterns of episodes and differences in severity of symptoms are described by different specific types of mood disorders (e.g., major depressive disorder, bipolar disorder, etc.). However, all have in common as a primary feature a significant change in mood that occurs with enough frequency, duration, and intensity to be considered maladaptive (*DSM-IV-TR*, APA, 2000). You can learn more specific details about various types of mood disorders as well as the causes of or risks in courses such as Abnormal Psychology.

How are mood disorders treated? Nowadays, a variety of medications can effectively treat depression or manic episodes. For severely depressed persons who do not respond to medication and who are in acute danger of harming themselves, electroconvulsive therapy (ECT) may be used (Andreasen, 1984; Wilson et al., 1996). **Psychotherapy** (talking therapy) is often a useful component of treatment for mood disorders. The best approach to therapy varies depending on those factors believed to contribute to the disorder and the particular needs of the individual. In some instances, supportive guidance and counseling is helpful and may be all that is needed.

Psychotherapy (talking therapy) can help people work through uncomfortable emotions, problem relationships, or situations, or it can alter maladaptive beliefs (such as setting unrealistic goals for perfection), which are thought to contribute to depression. Some patients require more in-depth therapy in which unresolved or unconscious conflicts, problems, or relationships are explored (Goodwin & Guze, 1979). In many instances, an intervention may include a combination of medication and various types of psychotherapy. Music therapy can play a valuable role in psychotherapy for persons with mood disorders, with objectives of normalizing mood, developing coping strategies, altering maladaptive beliefs, and meeting other psychosocial needs (Cassity & Cassity, 2006; Gardiner, 2005; Luce, 2001; Silverman & Marcionetti, 2004; Silverman, 2007; Unkefer & Thaut, 2002).

Anxiety Disorders

> Gina is a computer programmer for a large insurance company. She is bright, capable, and well liked by her friends. However, her daily trip to the office has become a source of anxiety since the company moved its offices last month to the 23rd floor of a high-rise building. Gina has a phobic reaction to elevators. When she starts to anticipate taking the elevator, she feels intense anxiety and fear. Her heart starts to race, and she feels dizzy and short of breath. Although she knows her fears are "silly," she often avoids the elevator by taking the stairs. She tells her friends that she is using stair-climbing as aerobic exercise but knows all too well that her actions are irrational. Gina suffers from an anxiety disorder called specific phobia.

What are anxiety disorders? Anxiety is a normal response to the stresses of everyday life. However, a person may be diagnosed as having an anxiety disorder when anxiety becomes excessive, ongoing, irrational in relation to the actual situation, and debilitating in everyday functioning. The Anxiety Disorders are a group of diagnoses that are all characterized by unrealistic or excessive anxiety, panic attacks, or avoidance behavior. Many of the anxiety disorders include physical symptoms (e.g., racing heart, dizziness, chest pain) that can easily be mistaken for heart attacks or other physical conditions.

The five major types of anxiety disorders are: (1) **generalized anxiety disorder (GAD)**, (2) **obsessive-compulsive disorder (OCD)**, (3) **panic disorder**, (4) **post-traumatic stress disorder (PTSD)**, and (5) **social phobia** (also referred to as social anxiety disorder). According to the National Institutes of Mental Health (2008; http://www.nimh.nih.gov/health/topics/anxiety-disorders/index.shtml), generalized anxiety disorder is characterized by chronic anxiety, exaggerated worry, and tension that occur with little or no provocation. Feelings of anxiety can be accompanied by physical symptoms such as fatigue, headaches, trembling, or sweating. Obsessive-compulsive disorder is characterized by recurring and unwanted thoughts (**obsessions**) and/or repetitive behaviors (**compulsions**). People with OCD may be bothered by the urgent need to engage in certain compulsive rituals to try and cope with the obsessions (e.g., constant hand washing to eradicate germs, repeated checking of locks on doors, etc.).

Panic disorder is characterized by unexpected and repeated episodes of intense fear accompanied by physical symptoms such as chest pain, heart palpitations, shortness of breath, dizziness, or abdominal distress. There may be a sense of unreality, or fear of impending doom or loss of control. These attacks can come on with no precipitating event. Post-traumatic stress disorder (PTSD) can develop after exposure to a terrifying event or ordeal, such as violent personal assaults, natural or human-caused disasters, accidents, or military combat. People with PTSD have persistent frightening thoughts and memories of their ordeal. They may experience sleep problems, flashbacks, feelings of detachment, or numbness, or may be easily startled (http://www.nimh.nih.gov/health/topics/anxiety-disorders/index.shtml).

Social phobia (social anxiety disorder) is characterized by overwhelming anxiety and excessive self-consciousness, fear of being judged by others, and being embarrassed by one's own actions in everyday social situations. Social phobia may occur only in specific situations, such as a fear of public speaking or playing in a recital. In its most severe form, those affected may have unpleasant symptoms almost anytime they are around other people, which interfere with many aspects of everyday life ((http://www.nimh.nih.gov/health/topics/anxiety-disorders/index.shtml).

This level of anxiety is greater than the normal "nerves" or jittery feelings that one might typically feel when getting ready to perform, compete, or engage in other sorts of public behaviors. You can learn more specific details, as well as the causes or risks, of various types of anxiety disorders in courses such as Abnormal Psychology.

How are anxiety disorders treated? Different types of symptoms and multiple causes are associated with particular anxiety disorders; consequently, there are a variety of treatments prescribed. According to the National Institutes of Mental Health (2008), the practitioners who are most helpful with anxiety disorders are those who have training in two specific types of therapy— cognitive-behavioral therapy and/or behavioral therapy—and who are also open to prescribing medication if it is needed. **Cognitive-behavioral therapy** focuses on changing catastrophic or irrational thoughts that trigger anxiety. For example, the individual may be taught techniques to reduce the fear response by using special relaxation techniques during gradual exposure to the fearful stimulus (Corey, 2001). Successful use of medication suggests a link between some forms of anxiety and biological factors, including panic disorder and obsessive-compulsive disorder (Scully, 1985). A combination of cognitive-behavioral therapy and medication has helped many people with anxiety disorders. Some people have found symptom relief from stress management (including relaxation techniques) (Walworth, 2003), from participation in support groups in which they can verbalize their experiences, or from exercise. Treatment choices should be monitored by a therapist. Music therapy can be a helpful intervention in cognitive-behavioral therapy (Bryant, 1987; Hilliard, 2001; Luce, 2001) as well as in promoting relaxation (Cassity & Cassity, 2006, p. 89; Cassity, 2007; Silverman, 2007; Silverman & Marcionetti, 2004; Unkefer & Thaut, 2002).

Personality Disorders

> *Nancy is a 22-year-old checkout clerk at the local discount store. Nancy will tell you, however, that this job is just temporary, for she anticipates that she will soon be spotted by a talent agent who will notice her beauty and charm. Some of her coworkers, however, find Nancy's "charm" a bit tiresome: She often takes extra coffee breaks so that she can "fix her face," assuming that the others can take care of the store. After all, she needs to look her best. When confronted by the manager about her extra breaks, Nancy walks off in huff, baffled by the manager's lack of sensitivity to her talents and charm. As customers go through the checkout line, Nancy often goes into a monologue about her own appearance—her new haircut, her "nice" skin, or her future as a model. Nancy is the sort of person who "wears thin" on others and tends to have unsatisfying relationships. She has one type of personality disorder, which is called a narcissistic personality disorder.*

What are personality disorders? When we are asked to describe someone's personality, we often think about particular traits or characteristics that remain stable over time. Some people generally have an outgoing and talkative personality. Others might be described as shy or introverted. Some people tend to be a bit crabby or cynical. However, most people can modify their behavior to some extent in order to deal successfully with the requirements of each day. For example, a typically shy individual can work up the courage to give a required talk in class, or a talkative person can control his or her chattiness at a quiet event such as a funeral or symphony concert.

In the case of a personality disorder, the individual exhibits personality traits that are so extreme and so inflexible that they cause difficulties in school, at work and in interpersonal relationships (Wilson et al., 1996). According to the *DSM-IV-TR* (APA, 2000), there is an enduring pattern of internal experience (such as thoughts or beliefs) and behavior that is markedly different from the expectations of one's culture. These differences can include deviation in (1) cognition, or how people perceive and interpret themselves, others, and events; (2) affectivity, meaning the range, intensity, and appropriateness of emotional responses; (3) interpersonal functioning; or (d) impulse control (ability to pause and think through consequences of one's actions before acting). These traits are stable, are of long duration, appear across a broad range of situations, and tend to interfere with social and occupational functioning (*DSM-IV-TR*, APA, 2000).

There are a number of different types of personality disorders, but they can be categorized into three clusters based on descriptive similarities (*DSM-IV-TR*, APA, 2000; Wilson et al., 1996). The first cluster, Cluster A, includes personality disorders in which the individuals seem odd or eccentric. The second cluster, Cluster B, includes personality disorders characterized by dramatic, emotional, and erratic personalities (*DSM-IV-TR*, APA, 2000; Wilson et al., 1996). For example, Nancy, the checkout clerk at the beginning of this section, fits within this category. The third cluster, Cluster C, includes personality disorders characterized by anxiety, fearfulness, and avoidance (*DSM-IV-TR*, APA, 2000; Wilson et al., 1996). You can learn more specific details, as well as the causes or risks, of various types of personality disorders in courses such as Abnormal Psychology.

How are personality disorders treated? Because a personality disorder is comprised of an enduring personality trait, change is difficult to attain. Few persons with personality disorders (especially from the odd and eccentric class) seek treatment of their own volition. When seen by professionals, they are often treated in outpatient settings. Clients may seek outpatient treatment in order to complain about problems in their lives. They often lack insight regarding their own limitations, frequently projecting blame onto others. This lack of insight makes therapeutic progress difficult to achieve (Scully, 1985).They will complain about problems in their lives, mood disturbances, or physical illness, but they fail to recognize their own contributions to the problems. Sometimes persons with personality disorders will seek treatment that focuses on a particular problematic aspect of their life, such as chemical dependency or depression.

Because of the enduring pattern of maladaptive behavior and the lack of insight often observed in these diagnoses, individuals with these disorders may benefit little from many traditional forms of treatment. The use of psychoanalysis (with the goal of affecting fundamental changes in the personality structure) has long been a treatment of choice for personality disorders (Corey, 2001; Wilson et al., 1996), but this form of therapy typically requires an extended commitment of time and financial resources in order to achieve positive change. Counseling techniques that facilitate changes in cognition, mood, behavior, or social interaction are now being used with greater frequency (Wilson et al., 1996). Pharmacology (medication) has been used to reduce the negative impact of various symptoms, such as depression, anxiety, impulsiveness, or cognitive distortions, but these medications do not change the fundamental personality traits per se. Consequently, it is common to pair psychotherapy with pharmacological approaches (Wilson et al., 1996). Music therapy may be a therapy of choice in treatment programs that facilitate changes in cognition, mood, behavior, or social interaction (Cassity & Cassity, 2006; Silverman, 2007; Unkefer & Thaut, 2002). Music therapy has also been a successful treatment in conjunction with chemical dependency, which is often co-occurs with personality disorders (Freed, 1987; James, 1988).

Substance-Related Disorders

Jack, a 46-year-old salesman, has consumed large quantities of wine and whiskey daily for over six years. Over this time, poor performance at work has led to a string of short-term jobs and subsequent financial difficulties. Because much of the income he does have goes toward his drinking habit, he is poorly nourished and in generally poor health. Much of Jack's daily routine revolves around the local bar or drinking alone in his small apartment. After a recent drinking binge, he was shaking so badly that he was unable to light his own cigarette. He has had numerous blackouts from drinking. Jack can be charming and chatty, but he is often anxious, disoriented, or angry. A few years ago, his wife tried to get Jack to attend Alcoholics Anonymous, but Jack told her angrily that he can control his drinking and that he is tired of her hounding him. Eventually, she filed for divorce. Jack now uses her "thoughtless abandonment" of him as justification for drinking even more.

What are substance-related disorders? According to the *DSM-IV-TR*, this category includes disorders related to the taking of a drug of abuse (including alcohol), the side effects of a medication, and toxin exposure. Those who fit within this disorder use a variety of substances such as alcohol, amphetamines, cocaine, inhalants, sedatives, or pain killers, to name just a few. The Substance-Related Disorders are divided into (1) substance use disorders (substance dependence and substance abuse) and (2) substance-induced disorders (substance intoxication, substance withdrawal, substance-induced psychotic disorder, etc.). A detailed list of substances of use, symptoms of specific diagnoses, and risks associated with this category are detailed in the *DSM-IV-TR* and are presented in courses such as Abnormal Psychology.

In cases of substance dependence, there is a maladaptive pattern of substance use that leads to significant impairment or distress over a 12-month period. Problems include substance tolerance (markedly increased amounts required to achieve the desired effect); withdrawal; persistent difficulty in controlling substance use; considerable time dedicated to obtaining the substance; and reduction in social, occupational, or recreational activities because of substance use. Intoxication or withdrawal (upon discontinued use of the substance) is also associated with substance-related disorders. Other symptoms include clinically significant problems in physical functioning (such as abnormal heart rate, agitation, nausea, abnormal blood pressure, etc.); poor social interaction; disordered mood, sleep, and sexual functioning; or disturbances in perception (such as hallucinations) and cognition. Some individuals have dual diagnoses in which substance-related disorders co-occur with another type of disorder such as a mood, personality, or anxiety disorder.

How are substance-related disorders treated? There are a number of treatments for substance abuse and dependence, including group, family, and marital therapy (in which social, familial, and emotional factors contributing to use are explored and expressed); behavior therapy; detoxification and inpatient treatment; pharmacological interventions (such as Methadone or Antabuse); and self-help groups (such as Alcoholics Anonymous, AA) (Wilson et al., 1996). These programs may address factors that contribute to abuse, as well as assist persons in managing withdrawal, curbing cravings, and maintaining sobriety. Treatment may take place in a variety of settings, such as community-based programs (e.g., AA or community mental-health centers), private counseling, clinic or hospital-based care, or outpatient programs. Music therapy can be used to assist patients in confronting addiction, regulating mood (such as reduction of anxiety or frustration), coping with and expressing feelings, improving self-esteem, reducing isolation through affiliation with supportive peers, teaching skills and activities that promote sobriety, and developing healthy lifestyle choices (Bednarz & Nikkel,1992; Cevasco, Kennedy, & Generally, 2005; Freed, 1987; Heaney, 1992; James, 1988; Murphy, 1983; Soshensky, 2001; Silverman, 2003c; Walker, 1995).

Other Psychiatric Disorders

While the aforementioned disorders are among those commonly treated in psychiatry (Andreasen 1984, 2001; Cassity & Cassity, 2006; Wilson et al., 1996), there are many other types of disorders frequently seen in psychiatric treatment and counseling. You can learn about other types of behavioral-emotional disorders in psychology courses and more advanced music therapy classes.

As can be seen, different behavioral-emotional disorders have very different symptoms, and they may result from different causes. Some disorders are strongly associated with a physiological cause (such as a genetic predisposition or a biochemical imbalance); other disorders have been associated with environmental stressors (*DSM-IV-TR*; Wilson et al., 1996). Physiological and environmental causes also interact. For this reason, it is not unusual to use medications as well as psychosocial support in the treatment of disorders (Andreason, 2001; Cassity & Cassity, 2006;

Unkefer & Thaut, 2002). Unfortunately, medications do not always fully address negative symptoms, so the individual must also learn to cope with the illness through psychological and social forms of therapy and support (Andreason, 2001; Silverman, 2007; Silverman & Marcionetti, 2004; Wilson et al., 1996).

Behavioral-emotional disorders also vary in severity and duration. Some disorders that are relatively mild can often be managed with short-term outpatient counseling or with medications, and have a limited impact on everyday life. Other disorders are so severe that a person has difficulty in nearly all aspects of daily life (vocation, relationships, everyday life skills, etc.). The impact of a disorder is also related to the course of the illness. Some disorders are brief in duration; they may occur once, with a return to typical functioning. Others, while relatively brief in duration, may be episodic (occur off and on over time, with return to typical function in between episodes). An episodic course of illness may require several short-term hospitalizations or outpatient treatment during recurrence of the disorder. Others disorders are chronic; that is, after the initial diagnosis, the individual never fully regains complete health despite the availability of suitable treatment. Chronic disorders require long-term changes in lifestyle and ongoing symptom management.

In summary, behavioral-emotional disorders vary considerably in type, cause, symptoms, severity, and course. Therefore, the treatment of choice varies from one disorder to the next and from one person to the next. Because music therapists often work as part of a mental health team, it is important for them to understand prominent treatment methods found in contemporary psychiatry so they can use music therapy interventions that will provide a cohesive treatment approach. In the following section of this chapter, we will discuss some of the prominent approaches or philosophies found in current psychiatric treatment and provide a few examples of how music can be used therapeutically in a manner consistent with each treatment philosophy.

Please note that, like the field of psychology, the field of music therapy has different philosophies or approaches specific to our field. Chapter 15 will describe specific music therapy approaches or philosophies, and techniques associated with those orientations.

PHILOSOPHICAL ORIENTATIONS TO PSYCHIATRIC TREATMENT

There is no single approach to psychiatric treatment that is universally accepted for all disorders, or even for a single disorder. Mental health professionals hold a variety of opinions on the primary causes of mental disorders and which approaches are most appropriate and efficacious in treating specific disorders. It is interesting to note, however, that some people with the same basic diagnosis may respond differently to different types of treatments. Effective therapists keep in mind the unique needs and strengths of each client, and they develop individualized treatment plans that should be modified or fine-tuned in response to a client's progress and current functional level.

While there is no single accepted therapeutic approach within the field of mental health, it is true that some treatment approaches are more commonly used in contemporary therapy. For example, in recent years, many professionals and research studies have noted the efficacy (effectiveness) of cognitive-behavioral therapy, biomedical, and multi-modal approaches for a number of behavioral-emotional disorders (Cassity, 2007; National Institutes of Mental Health, 2008; Silverman, 2007). In addition, it is not unusual for clinicians to use or combine a variety of treatment approaches (known as an **eclectic** approach). The following section gives a very brief overview of several prominent orientations to therapy within the field of mental health. You can learn more about these and other treatment approaches in other books or in courses such as Abnormal Psychology, Clinical Psychology, or Psychopathology.

Treatments That Focus on Affect

Some types of psychiatric treatment (e.g., psychodynamic, Gestalt) emphasize **affect** (that is, feelings, moods, emotions) and the motivation behind the emotion. Sigmund Freud (1856–1939), who was the first and most prominent psychodynamic theorist, developed an approach to therapy that focused on unconscious psychological processes (e.g., internal conflicts, impulses, desires) that could be made conscious through talking (known as psychotherapy). Subsequently, other theorists also developed approaches to mental health that emphasized the affective (feelings and emotions) realm of human existence.

Within this orientation, emotional and behavioral disorders are attributed to unresolved or conflictual feelings (affect) and the motivation behind those feelings. Current feelings or behaviors that are maladaptive are examined in relation to past conflicts or difficulties. Treatments are designed to help clients explore past conflicts, bring unresolved conflicts (such as traumas or negative events in childhood) into present awareness, and find appropriate expression of emotions. Therapy may include exploration of dreams, the use of a technique called "free associations," talking about events in the past, and exploring one's defense mechanisms, sometimes as they emerge during the therapist–client interaction. Through this process of personal exploration, individuals are believed to develop greater insight into emotional barriers, increase their self-esteem (stronger ego), and improve their ability to relate with others in a more satisfactory and healthy manner. In conventional psychotherapy, the conversation between the patient and the therapist is the primary form of treatment.

In music therapy, music, which has often been called the language of emotions, becomes an important form of communication for exploring and expressing feelings (Cassity & Cassity, 2006; Gardiner, 2005; Ruud, 1980; Unkefer & Thaut, 2002). In some therapy sessions, music may be the primary form of interaction. In some sessions, verbal interchange between the therapist and patient may follow the musical interaction.

Musical activities such as guided music listening, guided imagery (using music to evoke images), or improvisation may be used to explore unconscious material (Blake & Bishop, 1994; Bonny, 1994; Cassity & Cassity, 2006; Goldberg, 1989; Nolan, 1994; Unkefer & Thaut, 2002; Warja, 1994; Wheeler, 1983). The individual may play music on an instrument as an alternative expression for uncomfortable or conflictual thoughts and feelings (Ruud, 1980). Toward the objective of an increased sense of mastery, the music therapist selects musical tasks (such as learning a new musical instrument or reviving old musical skills) that provide a realistic challenge for the client. Through this process, the individual develops a sense of control over his or her own actions and increased self-worth (Ruud, 1980).

Treatments That Focus on Behavior

Early in the 20th century, John B. Watson, Wilhelm Wundt, B. F. Skinner, and other founders of behaviorism sought to redirect psychology away from the introspective emphasis on feelings (as emphasized in Freud's psychoanalysis) and emphasize an objective measurement and modification of observable behavior (Wilson et al., 1996). Behaviorists believe that human behavior is shaped through **conditioning** (behaviors that are rewarded are more likely to reoccur) and **observational learning** (Corey, 2001; Hall, 1971). Within this orientation, not only do we learn our ABCs and other academic information, but we learn how to relate to others, how to behave in different situations (i.e., how to act in church as opposed to how to act at a football game), and how to express our feelings.

For example, at bedtime, many children resist the idea of giving up their playtime to go to sleep. Sometimes children will cry, scream, or ask for more stories, water, or other forms of attention. If 3-year-old Jason does not get his way upon the first verbal request, he may decide to get mom's attention by crying or screaming. It is not unusual for a parent to succumb to the child's screams, allowing another story or an extra glass of water in order to stop the loud wailing. When this happens, the child discovers that when he screams and creates a commotion, he may get to stay up longer. His screaming becomes reinforced (rewarded) by getting his way. As a result, Jason is more likely to scream the next time he wants to stay up longer.

In much the same way that Jason's screaming behavior was learned, more serious behaviors such as physical aggressiveness, antisocial acts, and other characteristics of behavioral-emotional disorders can be learned through reinforcement. For example, an adolescent from a poor home environment may get little attention in the form of love and nurturing from Mom and Dad; however, the same teenager may gain the admiration of peers for having an expensive iPod that he shoplifted from a store. In short, the reinforcement for the antisocial behavior may be strong enough, especially in the face of an unsatisfactory family environment, to encourage future illegal acts.

The fundamental role of the therapist in the behavioral model is to create an environment in which positive, desirable behaviors are rewarded (reinforced), and negative behaviors are reduced by eliminating reinforcement of those negative actions (Corey, 2001). In order to do this, the therapist, sometimes in conjunction with the client, will evaluate the client's present behaviors. Problem behaviors are identified, and the extent to which they occur is noted (see Chapter 15 regarding clinical assessment). Then the therapist works with the client to explore how these behaviors should be changed. For example, if a child is easily distracted, the therapist will reinforce (reward) the child through praise or some other form of reward when he pays attention and participates in the activity as he is supposed to (Hall, 1971).

There are many ways in which a treatment team might use behavioral approaches. One key in effective therapy is finding a reinforcement that is truly meaningful to the particular client. Some people respond well to praise. Some people may prefer time spent at a favorite hobby or game. Some find money or food very reinforcing. Many different things can be used as reinforcement in a behavioral program (Hall, 1971). One of the special tools that music therapists use for reinforcement is music itself. Because most everyone has some type of music they enjoy listening to, and because music activities can be gratifying, music listening or participation can be used as a reward to help change behavior in the desired direction (Lathom & Eagle, 1984). If the music therapist has been successful in establishing good rapport with the client, the therapist's time and attention as well as the music therapy activities can be rewarding.

For example, many teenagers are attracted to guitar music, since rock music is an important part of adolescent culture (Cassity & Cassity, 2006; Paul, 1982).

> Joshua is enrolled in an alternative school for adolescents who have had done poorly in regular school programs because of aggressive behavior, truancy, poor study habits, and petty crimes. Joshua says he doesn't want to do his math assignments because "they are so boring," but this is just his excuse for avoiding school work that is extremely difficult for him and that makes him feel stupid. He would rather goof off and create diversions than stick to his math assignments. Knowing that Josh really loves music, his teacher has worked out a contract with Josh: each class period during

which Josh finishes his math assignment by the end of class and without creating a problem, he earns 5 points. When Josh earns 25 points, he can "cash" them in for a guitar lesson with Aaron, the music therapist at the school. Josh thinks Aaron is a pretty cool guy, because he has awesome guitar skills. During music therapy, Josh learns guitar skills, and Aaron provides an excellent role model for appropriate expression of feelings and social manners. During the course of the guitar lessons, Aaron works with Josh on learning how to set realistic goals and coping with frustration. Because Josh handled himself so well in music therapy over a period of 5 lessons, he "earned" the opportunity to accompany Aaron to the guitar store to pick up class supplies for the school.

Behavioral therapy can be used to change a wide variety of behaviors, including antisocial behaviors, poor social skills, underdeveloped communication, muscular tension phobias (unrealistic fears), and passive or unproductive ways of relating to others, to name just a few. Behavioral therapy is very flexible and can be used with clients of all ages and with a variety of functional levels (Corey, 2001). However, some psychologists believe that behavioral theories explain only partially or inadequately many types of human behavior. For that reason, some therapists combine behavioral approaches with those that emphasize cognition (see the following section). This focus on both behavioral and cognitive aspects of functioning is referred to as cognitive-behavioral therapy, which takes into account internal thoughts or meaning of events as they influence mood or behavior (Cassity & Cassity, 2006).

Treatments That Focus on Cognition

Some types of treatment emphasize the internal mental (cognitive) life of the individual rather than feelings or overt behaviors. Cognitive therapies (e.g., Cognitive Therapy, Rational Emotive Therapy, Cognitive-Behavioral Therapy [Corey, 2001]) are based upon the premise that what we think about an event, object, or person has an enormous influence on what we feel and how we act (Cassity & Cassity, 2006; Corey, 2001; Gardiner, 2005; Hilliard, 2001; Luce, 2001; Unkefer & Thaut, 2002). According to Cassity (2007), the use of cognitive-behavioral therapy has recently grown, and will continue to increase, as a philosophical orientation in psychiatric care and, consequently, also in music therapy.

Rather than emphasizing how people feel about their past or current circumstances, cognitive approaches emphasize the importance of cognitive (mental) processes as determinants of behavior. When people have thoughts that are considered "irrational"—that is, not realistic or sensible—they are more like to feel stress, anxiety, and feelings of inadequacy. What is irrational thinking?

Kari is a 32-year-old stock broker who seems a model of the successful business woman that has it all. She has a lovely figure, is perfectly groomed, and her many talents in tennis, singing, and gourmet cooking are enviable. Kari makes this all look easy, but in reality, she spends hours per week at the gym and watches every bite she eats in order to avoid gaining any weight. She feels like she has failed if she does not win all her tennis matches, and she has to get up extra early each morning in order to look beautifully groomed and to have a perfectly kept apartment. Because she wants to be liked by everyone, Kari puts immense effort into being friendly and helpful; even small social slights can send her into a spiral of self-doubt. Few would imagine that when Kari goes home to her spotless apartment at night, she is sometimes overwhelmed by feelings of anxiety, loneliness, and inadequacy that are generated in part by her irrational beliefs that she must be perfect in order to be "okay." Not infrequently, Kari sits on the couch alone weeping, wondering if she would be better off dead.

Although hard work and talent are basically positive attributes, in Kari's case, she has set the bar too high: she expects herself to be perfect in all things in order to be a "good person." Realistically, no one human being can expect to achieve excellence in all things. Some people are great cooks; other people have aptitude in sports or in music; some people have a knack for math or for sewing. And all of us find some things that are difficult or frustrating. Consequently, the idea of excelling in all things would be considered an **irrational thought**. In her quest to feel adequate (which, to Kari, means being excellent at all things), Kari has contributed to her own sense of inadequacy and depression.

A cognitive therapist acts as a guide or instructor of sorts to help the client realize and confront irrational thoughts and then adopt new and healthy responses. For example, after the therapist has established a working relationship with Kari, he or she would guide her in the following steps: (1) help Kari to become aware of her beliefs, (2) confront the irrational nature of her perfectionism, (3) identify experiences in life during which this irrational belief system has been at work, and (4) take steps toward altering her behaviors (Corey, 2001).

One example of a music therapy intervention that reflects this orientation might be the use of lyrics and musical content of songs, or songwriting in group or individual therapy to help explore irrational beliefs and the subsequent emotions produced as a result of disordered thinking (Bryant, 1987; Cassity & Cassity, 2006; Luce, 2001; Dileo Maranto, 1996; Hilliard, 2001; Maultsby 1977; Unkefer & Thaut, 2002).

Kari's psychologist has referred her to an outpatient music therapy group at a local mental health center in order to help Kari gain greater insights into her irrational thoughts and to gain social support for changing her belief system. Because many of the clients in this group are working on setting realistic goals, the music therapist has chosen to play for the group a song by Billy Joel named "Pressure." This song portrays the emotional tension that builds up when people try to accomplish more than is humanly possible. After the song is played, the music therapist leads a group discussion about what the song lyrics mean (in an activity called lyric analysis [Unkefer & Thaut, 2002]); group members then relate the song lyrics to their own situations. As Kari joins in on the discussion, she may develop some insights into her own self-imposed pressures. The comments of other group members can help her to realize that she is not the only person struggling with this problem; that realization may help her to open up to others more easily when she needs support.

Treatments That Focus on Physical Factors: Biomedical Model

The use of the biomedical model, along with cognitive therapies, has increased over the past few decades and is likely to remain at the forefront of psychiatric care in the coming decade (Cassity, 2007). This model, which examines the role of brain function in all aspects of behavior, including mental disorders, attributes emotional and behavioral disturbances to biological factors such as biochemical imbalances, neurological abnormalities or deficits, genetic problems, or physical illnesses like infections (Andreasen, 1984, 2001; Gardiner, 2005; Unkefer & Thaut, 2002; Wilson et al., 1996).

Recent advances in technology and assessment (e.g., x-ray images, tests of the brain's biochemistry, assessments of neurological functioning) have made it possible to identify biological changes or features associated with some types of mental illness such as mood disorders or schizophrenia (Andreason, 2001; Gardiner, 2005; Wilson et al., 1996). The development of brain scanning technology (which allows examination of the living brain while the person in the scanner carries out cognitive or motor tasks) has been instrumental in the establishment of the new field of cognitive neuroscience. In this field, cognitive and affective behaviors are studied in relationship to their neurobiological foundations and mechanisms, integrating a biological and a behavioral/cognitive view on mental function.

Cognitive neuroscience (as an important subdivision of the biomedical model) offers new insights regarding neurological mechanisms associated with behavioral-emotional disorders, and characteristic disturbances in thinking, feeling, perception, and behavior. Cognitive neuroscience illuminates the disease process, which, in turn, leads to better pharmacological and behavioral treatments. Neuropsychiatry, as the clinical sister of cognitive neuroscience, builds on knowledge of brain function to develop treatment strategies that combine learning and training techniques in cognitive rehabilitation with medication (Halligan & David, 2001).

While some physically-based disorders can be clearly attributed to biological origins such as genetic predisposition, in some cases it is difficult to determine the **etiology** (cause or basis) of the mental disorder. For example, we know that physical changes (i.e., change in appetite, lethargy, poor sleep patterns) may accompany depression, but it is not always clear whether the biological change occurred first and actually brought on the depression, or whether environmental stressors precipitated subsequent physical changes. The mind and the body work together closely in reaction to the environment (Andreasen, 1984, 2001).

Some disorders believed to have biological origins are treated primarily through pharmacological means (medication) or through special types of treatments (such as electroconvulsive therapy) (Andreasen, 1984, 2001). In other instances, particularly where environmental stressors are believed to be a factor, changes in the environment or therapies to improve coping with stress may be used in conjunction with or in lieu of medication (Cassity & Cassity, 2006; Gardiner, 2005; Hanser, 1985; Silverman, 2007; Unkefer & Thaut, 2002; Wilson et al., 1996). For example, depression or anxiety related to stressors might be treated in part through a program of muscle relaxation training (Byrnes, 1996).

> *Juan, a business executive for a large corporation, has been feeling immense pressure at work and subsequent feelings of anxiety and depression. His treatment team has recommended, in addition to psychotherapy, relaxation training. The music therapist may assist Juan in relaxation response by selecting appropriate musical stimuli for use during relaxation training sessions. Since Juan also indicated to his psychologist that he used to enjoy playing in a jazz ensemble, the music therapist might explore with Juan the possibility of reviving music as a positive leisure-time skill. By helping Juan to relax and reduce his stress, he has a more positive attitude toward life, and he's learning to cope more effectively with the grind of daily life.*

In addition to assisting with relaxation training, the music therapist may work with clients who are on medication for the primary symptoms of a disorder, but who still need additional support in order to return to a normal life. For example, some clients with serious, chronic disorders such as schizophrenia may respond only partially to medication (Silverman, 2003b). Even with medication, some patients may need a structured milieu and some assistance in developing more appropriate interpersonal skills (Cassity & Cassity, 2006; Scartelli, 1989; Silverman, 2003a, 2003b; Silverman & Marcionetti, 2004; Unkefer & Thaut, 2002). The following vignette is an example of milieu therapy.

> *Paul was diagnosed with paranoid schizophrenia at the age of 18. Although medications help to reduce the number and intensity of his hallucinations, the medication controls his symptoms only partially. Furthermore, when he is feeling a little better, he sometimes stops taking his medications, and then the symptoms get worse. Paul tends to be reclusive and he has difficulty maintaining the basic routines of everyday life, such as his personal hygiene, shopping for groceries, and interacting with others. Paul's psychiatrist knows that Paul needs some ongoing support to keep him functioning at his optimal level—support to take his medication, counseling to maintain his basic skills of daily living (cooking meals, cleaning his room, shopping, doing laundry, maintaining his grooming, etc.), and opportunity to practice and maintain social interactions. Therefore, Dr. Raheim has Paul attend a weekly outpatient session at the local mental health clinic. Each week, Paul meets with the nurse to talk about any problems with his medications. Then he checks in with the social worker to work out any problems with housing or work. After those visits, he walks down the hall of the mental health center where the music therapist holds a weekly jam session for a small group of persons with chronic behavioral-emotional disorders.*

> *At first glance, this music therapy session looks like any other garage band, but Steve, the music therapist, has take special care to choose music that is preferred by the band members and is relatively easy to play (given the limited technical skills of the group members). Steve is alert to any negative side effects of medications, such as slower response, or motoric stiffness that may impede successful participation. Some of the main goals of this session are to help the clients maintain connections within their community, to practice simple social interactions, to stay focused on a structured task of playing the music, to develop healthy leisure skills that can add quality to everyday life, and to enhance self-esteem. Because the five members of the band have very different musical skills as well as functional levels, Steve designs music activities that offer varying levels of structure and require lesser or greater response difficulty (Cassity & Cassity, 2006; Unkefer & Thaut, 2002). Within the context of this session, the band members practice and role play social interaction, maintain good*

reality orientation, follow through on requests, and practice appropriate expression of feelings and other important behaviors.

Some behavioral-emotional disorders have a neurological component—that is, the person's problems in regulating their behaviors and moods are clearly related to neurological deficits that impair attention, memory, and other aspects of cognitive functioning. In such cases, the music therapist may use techniques associated with a type of music therapy called Neurologic Music Therapy (NMT) that uses specific techniques such as Music Attention Control Training or Musical Mnemonics Training (Gardiner, 2005). You will learn more about NMT in other chapters of this book.

Eclectic Orientation

While these orientations may all seem very different, in actuality many of them share some common features. Furthermore, many therapists believe that no existing treatment approach is effective for all clients in all situations. Therefore, while a particular therapist or clinical setting may favor one model or another (e.g., some clinics use primarily behavioral models, while others adopt a biomedical approaches), more often, therapy teams will draw from a variety of models, integrating the benefits of several approaches in order to serve a particular client's needs. This is called an **eclectic** orientation or approach (Corey, 2001; Silverman, 2007).

Within the psychiatric setting, the music therapist must take into consideration the philosophical orientation of treatment recommended for each client. By cooperating with the rest of the treatment team (e.g., psychiatrists, psychologists, nurses, and social workers) on the treatment approach, the client will benefit from a more cohesive and coordinated treatment program. On a treatment team, each professional contributes particular expertise and treatment methods. For example, the psychiatrist is the team member responsible for prescribing medications. A psychiatric social worker may use his or her knowledge of the health and welfare systems to assist the individual in finding stable housing and work. The music therapist plans and implements musical experiences to facilitate emotional and behavioral change. Music can be a particularly powerful art form for helping people to develop new insights and to establish positive social relationships. In addition, music therapy can be an important tool in helping clients to persist in maintaining their treatment regimens, such as attending outpatient therapy. Several studies indicate that many clients find music therapy to be motivating, enjoyable, as well as helpful in working on a variety of objectives; thus, music therapy can foster ongoing participation and commitment to therapy goals and the therapeutic milieu (e.g., Heaney, 1992; Silverman, 2003a, 2006, 2007; Silverman & Marcionetti, 2004).

Now that we've introduced some common approaches to psychiatric treatment, we'll focus on some categories of music therapy interventions that are commonly used in programs that serve persons with behavioral-emotional disorders.

CLINICAL USES OF MUSIC THERAPY IN THE PSYCHIATRIC SETTING

Considering Individual Differences in Age and Culture

Just as there is no single accepted orientation to psychiatric treatment, there is no single music therapy intervention that will be appropriate for all clients who have behavioral-emotional disorders. One reason is that these types of disorders can span a wide age range, with some problems appearing in childhood, while other problems may occur well into adulthood. The sorts of music and interventions that would be appropriate for a 5-year-old child likely will not be suitable for an adult.

Musical activities are a natural part of childhood and can be tailored to the suit the abilities and needs of children at all stages of development (Cassity & Cassity, 2006); thus, music is a wonderful therapeutic tool for children. Puppets, toys, and other children's games may be incorporated into therapy interventions. A music therapist working with adolescents is likely to draw heavily on music from the rock music genre, since that style of music is such an important part of adolescent culture (Brooks, 1989; Cassity & Cassity, 2006).

With maturity, adults tend to develop a range of preferred styles such as classical, popular, rock, and jazz. The music therapist working with elderly clients will need to address the musical tastes as well as some of the unique physical and psychosocial changes that occur as a result of the aging process (Cassity & Cassity, 2006; Corey & Corey, 1987).

Clients vary in culture as well as in age. Different cultures hold different values and have different musical heritages; therefore, musical tastes and experiences will vary from one person to the next. Even within one culture, individuals have their own personal tastes with regard to preferred music and music that is meaningful (Unkefer & Thaut, 2002). For example, a client whose is Muslim and grew up in the Middle East may find no particular emotional satisfaction from a song such as "Amazing Grace," which has particular meaning to many Christians who grew up in the United States. Furthermore, there are important cultural differences with regard to values and acceptable behaviors that require consideration. For example, making direct eye contact is a sign of positive self-esteem and good social skills in some cultures. In others, direct eye contact with an elder or with a stranger can be considered inappropriate. These cultural differences must be incorporated into treatment objectives (Brooks, 1989).

Fortunately, music can be meaningful to a wide range of ages and to people from diverse cultures (see Chapter 3). Structurally, music varies greatly in style and complexity. Consider the difference between the nursery song "The Itsy-bitsy Spider," the country-western song "The Gambler," and Beethoven's "Fifth Symphony." Almost everyone can find some type of music that is enjoyable and interesting. This wide range in style and complexity contributes to music's accessibility and flexibility as a therapeutic tool.

As the following section indicates, people can be involved in music in so many different ways. Music can be enjoyed passively by listening or through direct involvement in music making (Unkefer & Thaut, 2002). The following section outlines some categories of how music is commonly used as a therapeutic intervention with psychiatric clients.

Categories of Music Activities Used in Therapy

Listening and responding to music. As we noted in Chapter 3, music can arouse emotions and thoughts in people (Cassity & Cassity, 2006; Gardiner, 2005; Unkefer & Thaut, 2002). Sometimes, people describe music as sounding like a particular feeling, such as mournful or perhaps happy. Music may also bring to mind particular memories or thoughts. For example, a song such as "Pomp and Circumstance" might remind us of graduation. Because music is an emotional language that elicits thoughts and feelings, it can be a powerful tool toward increasing emotional expression and self-awareness.

> *John, a client in music therapy, has gone through a devastating series of personal losses throughout his lifetime. As a child, his father abandoned the family. Later, his mother became ill and died while he was in high school. In his adolescence and young adulthood, he found it difficult to meet and establish a comfortable relationship with women. Hal, the music therapist, decided to focus today's group therapy session on the topic of relationships, and he started the group discussion with Simon and Garfunkel's classic song, "I Am Rock," which describes a person who is afraid to get close to others for fear of being hurt. After the song is finished, John tells Hal that he feels just like the singer—that he, too, is afraid to get close to others for fear that the person will abandon him and he'll get hurt all over again. The rest of the group then offers Hal feedback and support.*

As this example illustrates, a music therapist can use the emotional language of music to help clients become more aware of their feelings and thoughts, or to promote discussion, social interaction, or insights (Blake & Bishop, 1994; Bryant, 1986; Cassity & Cassity, 2006; Gardiner, 2005; Hilliard, 2001; Luce, 2001; Plach,

1980; Silverman 2003a, 2003b, 2005, 2007; Silverman & Marcionetti, 2004; Unkefer & Thaut, 2002). In the example above, music is used in conjunction with verbal forms of psychotherapy.

Playing and composing music. Music therapists are trained to help even people with no musical training to sing, play instruments, or compose music. The act of playing music can include improvisation, where members of the group make up music and interact with one another. In other cases, music performing will consist of the playing of precomposed works. Sometimes music performing will entail the creation of a new composition by an individual or group of clients (Cassity, 2007; Cassity & Cassity, 2006; Ficken, 1976; Freed, 1987; Silverman, 2003a, 2005; Unkefer & Thaut, 2002). Adaptive teaching techniques and specially arranged musical compositions can facilitate participation by people with a wide range of skills and functional levels.

Oftentimes, clients will exhibit the same sorts of behaviors in music making (both healthy and maladaptive) that they show in other aspects of their lives. For example, during group singing, a shy and withdrawn client may find it very difficult to take the initiative to select a song that she likes. She may also feel quite self-conscious, thus finding it difficult to actually stick with the group from beginning to end. In contrast, a client who is in a manic episode may be expansive and dominate the group, trying to "run the show." Within the music-making activity, the therapist encourages each client to try more healthy and adaptive behaviors and sets limits to maladaptive behaviors. Healthy interaction and on-task behaviors are the predominant objectives in this type of activity.

Moving to music. Music and movement have been paired throughout history. Movement can be a powerful tool for personal expression or to enhance self-awareness. For example, a group of clients may transform the lyrics of the song "You'll Never Walk Alone" into expressive movement. In addition, more structured types of social dances can be used to promote appropriate social interaction and active participation. In some instances, music can be used to promote physical exercises, as in an aerobics class. In each of these instances, music acts as a stimulus to movement whether it is a supportive activity such as folk dance, or an insight-oriented activity such as expressive movement (Cassity & Cassity, 2006; Cevasco et al., 2005; Silverman, 2003c, 2006, 2007; Unkefer & Thaut, 2002).

Music combined with other expressive arts. Music can be paired effectively not only with movement and dance, but with visual and written arts. Musical stimuli can act as a catalyst for expression of thoughts and feelings in an art or literary medium.

For example, in group therapy, clients may cooperate to draw a picture and write a poem that reflects the music heard in a recording of Tchaikovsky's "Nutcracker Suite." This activity has at least two therapeutic objectives: first, individuals in this group are encouraged to express themselves through an artistic medium; second, the group members must cooperate with one another, solving problems and working out interpersonal differences in order to create a final product. The qualities of the music, whether the music is rhythmic and brisk or quiet and contemplative, will help generate ideas and structure the visual and literary art (Cassity & Cassity, 2006; Plach 1980; Unkefer & Thaut, 2002).

Music for recreation and enjoyment. People often assume that therapy consists entirely of somber, thought-provoking events. However, in actuality, many clients also benefit from opportunities to relax and have fun, especially in structured social events (Cassity & Cassity, 2006; Cevasco et al., 2005; Plach, 1980; Silverman, 2006, 2007; Silverman & Marcionetti, 2004; Unkefer & Thaut, 2002). For example, some high-functioning business executives may suffer primarily from an inability to unwind and enjoy themselves. Recreation through making music or musical games (such as "Name That Tune") may also be valuable for some low-functioning, psychotic individuals who have difficulty organizing their own thoughts and actions enough to participate effectively in leisure-time events. Some chemically dependent clients may have spent a good proportion of their free time getting "high" on drugs. Following detoxification, these individuals may need appropriate leisure-time skills to fill those now-empty hours. In short, recreational music can be a useful therapeutic option.

Music and relaxation. In music therapy sessions, music is used to promote relaxation, not so much in the incidental manner that occurs during leisure hours, but rather in the provision of structured techniques that promote mental and physical relaxation. For example, music can be introduced along with various types of muscle relaxation training in order to promote physical relaxation (Cassity & Cassity, 2006; Hanser, 1985; Unkefer & Thaut, 2002). With enough training, sometimes even the sound of a particular musical selection that has been used consistently in relaxation training can trigger a relaxation response. Music can also be used to evoke images in a process called music imagery (Bonny, 1994). For example, the music therapist may select an instrumental piece that tends to remind listeners of ethereal events or the peacefulness of a meadow. These images can help the client to reduce tension and focus on positive thoughts and feelings (Scartelli, 1989). On a more superficial level, listening to favorite music of a relaxing nature can temporarily distract the client from a barrage of anxious thoughts and feelings.

The previous uses of music therapy techniques should not be interpreted as a "cookbook" for how to do music therapy. Rather, these categories provide a brief overview of different ways in which music can be used as a therapeutic tool. The effectiveness of the activity or musical stimulus requires appropriate application and implementation. The best potential activity can be a disaster if used with the wrong client or if it is not effectively facilitated. Successful implementation of an activity requires the sensitivity and knowledge of an adequately trained professional. In addition, the selection of an intervention should be based on the treatment needs of the individual and group as determined in assessment. One important consideration is the present functional level of the client. The following section will provide an overview of music therapy interventions broken down by levels of group therapy, based on the client's functional level and need.

LEVELS OF GROUP THERAPY BASED ON THE CLIENT'S FUNCTIONAL LEVEL

As you have already learned, the symptoms and behaviors of clients with different disorders can vary considerably. Symptoms can range from social withdrawal to aggression, or from euphoria to depression. For example, a person having a psychotic episode may be confused about who and where he or she is (poor **reality orientation**) and have difficulty with even the most basic self-help skills (i.e., eating or dressing). In contrast, some individuals, while possibly suffering from a change in mood, may be fully cognizant of reality and capable of personal insights concerning their own problems (Cassity & Cassity, 2006; *DSM-IV-TR*, APA, 2000; Unkefer & Thaut, 2002; Wilson et al., 1996).

Furthermore, the course of treatment and functional level can vary considerably from one client to the next. For example, in the first few days following admission to a hospital, a client with a biologically-based disorder may be confused and have difficulty doing even simple tasks. After several days of successful pharmacotherapy and a structured milieu of individual and group therapy, the same individual may be lucid and readily able to follow through on daily responsibilities. With regard to treatment regimes, one client may be hospitalized for only a day or two, and during that time attend only one music therapy session. In contrast, a person with chronic mental illness who is living in a group home may participate in an outpatient music therapy support group one time per week over many weeks or months.

In short, clients with emotional or behavioral disorders demonstrate a wide range of characteristics and function more or less effectively in everyday life. Therefore, music therapy interventions must be applied in a suitable manner for the individual's present level of functioning and treatment needs. Wheeler (1983) has proposed three levels of clinical practice in music therapy in order to meet the widely divergent needs of psychiatric clients: (1) **supportive, activity-oriented** music therapy; (2)

reeducative, insight-and-process-oriented music therapy; and (3) **reconstructive**, analytically and catharsis-oriented music therapy.

Supportive, Activity-Oriented Music Therapy

On this level, the music therapist designs activities that promote healthy behavior and foster participation. The music activity requires active involvement and awareness of the here-and-now (Unkefer & Thaut, 2002; Wheeler, 1983). The types of activities used at this level may appear similar to those initiated informally in everyday life, such as group singing, playing musical instruments, or musical games.

There are, however, some important differences. These activities are carefully structured by the therapist in order to maximize participation by clients who may vary greatly in functional level and musical ability. For example, clients who are disoriented, withdrawn, or anxious may have difficulty initiating or sustaining even the simplest interactions and involvement with others. The music therapist can design the activity so that these types of individuals can experience some level of success and appropriate participation in a social event. This level of activity may also be appropriate for some individuals who, as a result of an acute emotional problem, may be temporarily functioning at a lower level than usual. Even higher functioning clients, however, can benefit from leisure skills that can be developed during activity-oriented sessions.

A number of therapeutic objectives can be realized in activity-oriented music therapy: (1) improved social interaction and awareness of others; (2) maintaining reality orientation, or awareness of the here-and-now; (3) diversion from neurotic concerns or obsessions; (4) appropriate and successful involvement in a group activity; (5) controlling impulsive behaviors; and (6) healthy use of leisure time (Unkefer & Thaut, 2002; Wheeler, 1983). Let us consider one example of an activity-oriented music therapy session.

Patricia's music therapy clients tend to have chronic mental illness and often have difficulty with concentration, simple social interaction, and completing a task. Today she has chosen the song, "My Favorite Things" from The Sound of Music to start her session. First, she puts up a chart with the words to the song and plays the guitar as the group sings the song all together. After singing the song as a group, she asks each group member to turn to his or her neighbor and ask that person about his or her favorite kind of music, favorite sport, and favorite season of the year. After a few minutes, Patricia puts up a copy of the song "My Favorite Things," but there are words missing from the song. Patricia asks each member to share one of the favorite things that their neighbor talked about, and she will then put those ideas into the song. Finally, the group sings together their own version of "My Favorite Things," which now includes their own ideas, rather than "raindrops on roses and whiskers on kittens" as occurs in the original song. From time to time during this session, various group members are very reluctant to participate or have difficulty staying with the group. Other people make comments that might seem odd or irrelevant to the topic at hand. Patricia encourages or redirectes each person in keeping with the treatment team's therapy plan.

Although this looks basically like a fun sing-along, much more is going on. The participants in this group have serious mental disorders that interfere with their concentration, with talking to others, or with completing even simple tasks (Cassity & Cassity, 2006; Unkefer & Thaut, 2002; Wilson et al., 1996). During this activity, Patricia first encourages purposeful participation in a structured, reality-oriented task by getting the clients involved in group singing. Then, she facilitates appropriate social interaction on a reality-based topic of "favorite things." The structure of a simple topic can assist withdrawn or psychotic individuals to interact more effectively. As she filled in the new lyrics to the song, Patricia helped the clients to contribute ideas that are related to the topic of "favorite things."

During supportive group therapy, the therapist may reflect back to the client when a negative behavior occurs (such as interrupting others, talking about things unrelated to the group discussion, failing to comply with instructions, etc.) and help the client to try healthy alternatives. However, at this level of intervention, the therapist usually does not delve into the reason for maladaptive behaviors. That type of intervention is more likely to occur at the next level of treatment: reeducative, insight-and-process-oriented music therapy.

Reeducative, Insight-and-Process-Oriented Music Therapy

At this level, active involvement is still important, but there is greater emphasis on verbal reflection and processing about interpersonal relationships and emotions. Therefore, activities are designed that foster (1) identification and expression of feelings, (2) problem solving, (3) awareness of one's own behaviors, and (4) facilitation of behavioral changes. At this level, the client is capable of gaining insights into feelings and behaviors and reorganizing values and behavioral patterns (Bryant, 1987; Ficken, 1976; Freed, 1987; Hilliard, 2001; Luce, 2001; Unkefer & Thaut, 2002; Wheeler, 1983). How is music used at this level? Let's consider one example.

Patricia has a weekly outpatient group for clients who no longer need hospitalization, but who still need some ongoing support and therapy at this stage in their treatment. Patricia starts the session out with what appears to be a sing-a-long. Each group member receives a song book with many popular songs. If Patricia were planning this activity for lower-functioning clients, she might simply ask each client to pick a song to sing with the rest of the group. The objective would be appropriate group participation. However, at the reeducative level, she will set higher expectations. For this group, she has asked each client to pick one song that best expresses how he or she feels today. After the group sings the songs together, Patricia encourages each client to share how the song reflects his or her feelings. Then she asks each person to share what events have possibly contributed to those feelings. In the case of negative emotions, the group will talk about possible coping strategies for eliminating the problem or for managing the negative feelings.

This level of therapy generally requires that the clients are well oriented to reality and are able to communicate with others more than superficially. Within this sample activity, the therapist may wish the clients to (1) identify one feeling that they have, (2) share that feeling with the group, and (3) try to determine one event that has possibly contributed to that feeling. While the therapist may facilitate awareness of and insights regarding emotions or behaviors, at this level the focus still tends to be on present events rather than unconscious conflicts that may contribute to emotional distress. That sort of in-depth probing occurs at the next level: reconstructive, analytically and catharsis-oriented music therapy.

Reconstructive, Analytically and Catharsis-Oriented Music Therapy

On this level, music activities are used to uncover, relive, or resolve subconscious conflicts, such as traumas experienced as far back as early childhood, that continue to hamper personality development (Corey, 2001).

Harold, an adult male of 40 years of age, has difficulty interacting comfortably with women. According to Harold's psychotherapist, this difficulty might be attributed to his relationship with his mother, who was a punitive, intimidating woman. In outpatient music therapy, Patricia chooses activities for Harold (such as Guided Imagery and Music) that elicit images or feelings associated with the client's present or past. Through the process of bringing unconscious feelings and conflicts (i.e., Harold's feelings of frustration and hostility toward his mother) to conscious awareness, the client can achieve the insights necessary to work out maladaptive behaviors and anxieties (Bonny, 1994; Corey, 2001; Nolan, 1994; Ruud, 1980; Unkefer & Thaut, 2002; Warja, 1994; Wheeler, 1983). Thus, the neurotic elements of the client's behavior can actually be restructured to reduce dysfunctional behavior. For example,

Harold may, as a result of therapy, feel less intimidated when he interacts with women.

The music therapist who provides reconstructive therapy requires advanced training and supervision (Bonny, 1994; Goldberg, 1989; Nolan, 1994; Unkefer & Thaut, 2002; Wheeler, 1983). The client who engages in this level of treatment needs to have good reality orientation and a high level of motivation for personal change. In reconstructive therapy, music is often used to help elicit images or reconstruct past conflicts. For example, many people have heard music and have described it as reminding them of a scene (i.e., a peaceful meadow or a thunderstorm), or as representative of different kinds of emotions. The music therapist selects music that is particularly effective at eliciting images. Another type of activity often used at this level is improvisation (Unkefer & Thaut, 2002; Wheeler, 1983). Through the process of interacting with musical instruments, the client may nonverbally express feelings or act out relationships with significant people from the past.

The techniques used in **psychodynamic** music therapy are typically reconstructive, that is, they result in major changes in the personality structure. Therefore, these techniques require specialized professional training beyond the undergraduate music therapy degree (Bonny, 1994; Wheeler, 1983). Furthermore, since reconstructive therapy typically requires extended time for meaningful change, the client must be willing to commit extensive personal energy and financial resources. Some people argue that the necessary financial and personal commitment is unrealistic, or that some people (especially low-functioning or nonverbal clients) may realize minimal benefits from this model (Corey, 2001; Wilson et al., 1996). In addition, some therapists are uncomfortable with the basic philosophical views of the psychodynamic model. One model that has developed in reaction to psychodynamic philosophy is the behavioral model of therapy (Corey, 2001).

The client's diagnosis, the philosophical approach of the treatment team, and the level of psychosocial functioning and therapeutic need are all important considerations in designing an appropriate intervention at the appropriate level (Unkefer & Thaut, 2002). It is also important to consider the maturational development, chronological age, and cultural background of the clients (Cassity, 2007). That is why the American Music Therapy Association has established standards for the instruction and clinical training required for professional certification.

CHANGES IN HEALTH CARE DELIVERY: SHORT-TERM CARE

The manner in which psychiatric treatment is provided has changed dramatically over the past few decades. In the mid-20th century, as the profession of music therapy was becoming formally organized, people with chronic psychiatric disorders such as schizophrenia or chronic mood disorders spent much of their lives in remote psychiatric institutions. Music therapists helped to enhance the quality of life and maximize on-task functioning by establishing hospital bands, orchestras, and choirs. After the discovery of antipsychotic medications, many people with severe and chronic mental illnesses were able to function more normally, but may have required intermittent hospitalization for several weeks or months.

By the end of the 20th century, in response to more effective pharmacological treatments and changes in health-care policy (Sarafino, 1997), hospitalization for a mental disorder was more commonly quite short in duration. An individual may be admitted to a hospital because of a severe psychotic episode or in response to a suicide attempt. However, the person may be hospitalized only long enough for a psychiatric evaluation, to stabilize the behavior of the individual through pharmacological treatment and milieu therapy, and to plan an outpatient treatment protocol, such as individual psychotherapy or group therapy at a community mental health drop-in center (Cassity, 2007; Cassity & Cassity, 2006; Silverman, 2006, 2007; Silverman & Marcionetti, 2004; Unkefer & Thaut, 2002).

The emphasis on short-term hospitalization has changed the manner in which music therapy is delivered (Cassity, 2007; Cassity & Cassity, 2006; Silverman, 2007; Unkefer & Thaut, 2002). Music therapists are more likely to provide activities that help stabilize the behaviors of the individual (supportive, activity-oriented therapy) while the client is hospitalized. A music therapist may provide reeducative or reconstructive music therapy programming for higher functioning clients who attend outpatient therapy.

In short, there are no simple formulas for selecting music therapy activities. The music therapist needs to consider each client's diagnosis; the developmental level, chronological age, and cultural background; the philosophical approach of the treatment team; and the level of functioning and therapeutic needs of the clients attending music therapy. Oftentimes, participants in group therapy will represent a variety of diagnoses, age levels, functional abilities, and cultural backgrounds. This poses an interesting challenge for the therapist, who must find ways to accommodate each client's needs within a single session. Given these complexities, music therapists need considerable training, both in basic therapeutic interaction as well as specific uses of music, in order to best meet the needs of clients with mental disorders.

SUMMARY

Behavioral-emotional disorders are manifested in a variety of ways. Psychiatric symptoms can be observed at all ages with many different aspects of a person's personality functioning affected, including thinking, feeling, perception of reality, and the ability to master the tasks of daily life. Also, we have seen that most disorders consist of different phases in which symptoms may be amplified or may be more moderate, allowing the patient to lead a nearly normal life.

Many advances have been made in the last 30 years toward an understanding of the causes of behavioral-emotional disorders and the development of better treatment methods in pharmacological and psychosocial therapies. Music therapy is one of the therapies frequently used to eliminate or reduce the impact of maladaptive behaviors. Music therapists serve children and adults with mental disorders. Because music is a flexible art form that appeals to many people, it has great potential as a treatment tool with widely divergent therapeutic needs. Music will be used in different ways, however, depending upon the functional level of the client.

Music therapy can act as a supportive, activity-oriented therapy, as a reeducative, insight-oriented therapy, or as a reconstructive, analytic tool. In addition to being adapted for the different functional levels of clients, music therapy interventions should also reflect the philosophical orientation of the treatment. Treatment may be focused on affect, behavior, cognition, or biological functioning or an eclectic approach may be used.

Music therapy can take a variety of forms, including listening and responding to music, playing and composing music, music and movement, music combined with expressive arts, recreational music, and music and relaxation. The application of various interventions should be adapted for the chronological and developmental age of the client. In addition, it should be based on information gathered in a music therapy assessment and from other existing information found in the client's records.

STUDY QUESTIONS

1. What are the major diagnostic features of schizophrenia?
2. Describe different treatment approaches to schizophrenia.
3. What are the major diagnostic features of mood disorders?
4. Describe different treatment approaches to mood disorders.
5. What is the definition of a personality disorder?
6. Why are personality disorders considered by many as difficult to treat?
7. What are the diagnostic classifications of anxiety disorder, and which treatment approach works best with which disorder type?
8. What are some symptoms associated with a substance-related disorder?
9. List the three levels of therapy described by Wheeler.
10. Describe different categories of music therapy interventions commonly used in psychiatric care.

REFERENCES

American Psychiatric Association. (2000). *Diagnostic and statistical manual of mental disorders* (4th ed., text revision) (*DSM IV-TR*). Washington, DC: Author.

Andreasen, N. (1984). *The broken brain.* New York: Harper and Row.

Andreasen, N. (2001). *Brave new brain (pp. 25–40).* New York: Oxford University Press.

Bednarz, C. F., & Nikkel, B. (1992). The role of music therapy in the treatment of young adults diagnosed with mental illness and substance abuse. *Music Therapy Perspectives, 10*(1), 21–26.

Blake, R., & Bishop, S. (1994). Bonny method of guided imagery and music (GIM) in the treatment of post-traumatic stress disorder with adults in the psychiatric setting. *Music Therapy Perspectives, 12*(2), 125–129.

Bonny, H. (1994). Twenty-one years later: A GIM update. *Music Therapy Perspectives, 12*(2), 70–74.

Brooks, D. (1989). Music therapy enhances treatment with adolescents. *Music Therapy Perspectives, 6*, 37–39.

Bryant, D. (1987). A cognitive approach to therapy through music. *Journal of Music Therapy, 24*(1), 27–34.

Byrnes, S.R. (1996). The effect of audio, video, and paired audio-video stimuli on the experience of stress. *Journal of Music Therapy 33*(4), 248–260.

Cassity, M. (2007). Psychiatric music therapy in 2016: A Delphi poll of the future. *Music Therapy Perspectives, 25*(2), 86–93.

Cassity, M., & Cassity, J. (2006). *Multimodal psychiatric music therapy for adults, adolescents, and children: A clinical manual* (3rd ed.). Philadelphia: Jessica Kingsley.

Cevasco, A., Kennedy, R., & Generally, N. (2005). Comparison of movement-to-music, rhythm activities, and competitive games on depression, stress, anxiety, and anger of females in substance abuse rehabilitation. *Journal of Music Therapy, 42*(1), 64–80.

Corey, G. (2001). *Theory and practice of counseling and psychotherapy* (6th ed.). Pacific Grove, CA: Brooks/Cole.

Corey, M., & Corey, G. (1987). *Groups: Process and practice* (3rd ed.). Monterey, CA: Brooks/Cole.

Dileo Maranto, C. (1996). A cognitive model of music in medicine. In R. R. Pratt & R. Spintge (Eds.), *Music medicine II* (pp. 327–332). St. Louis, MO: MMB Music.

Ficken, T. (1976). The use of songwriting in a psychiatric setting. *Journal of Music Therapy, 13*(4), 163–172.

Freed, B. S. (1987). Songwriting with the chemically dependent. *Music Therapy Perspectives, 4*, 13–18.

Gardiner, J. C. (2005). Neurologic music therapy in cognitive rehabilitation. In M. Thaut (Ed.), *Rhythm, music, and the brain* (pp. 179–202). New York: Routledge.

Goldberg, F. S. (1989). Music psychotherapy in acute psychiatric inpatient and private practice settings. *Music Therapy Perspectives, 6*, 40–43.

Goodwin, D., & Guze, S. (1979). *Psychiatric diagnosis.* New York: Oxford University Press.

Hall, V. (1971). *Managing behavior.* Lawrence, KS: H & H Enterprises.

Halligan, P. W., & David, A. S. (2001). Cognitive neuropsychiatry: Towards a scientific psychopathology. *Nature Reviews Neuroscience, 2*, 209–214.

Hanser, S. (1985). Music therapy and stress reduction research. *Journal of Music Therapy, 22*(4), 193–201.

Hanser, S. (1987). *Music therapist's handbook.* St. Louis, MO: Warren H. Green.

Heaney, C. J. (1992). Evaluation of music therapy and other treatment modalities by adult psychiatric inpatients. *Journal of Music Therapy, 29*(2), 70–86.

Hilliard, R. (2001). The use of cognitive-behavioral music therapy in the treatment of women with eating disorders. *Music Therapy Perspectives, 19*(2), 109–113.

Houghton, B. A., & Smeltekop, R. A. (2002). Music therapy and psychopharmacology. In R. Unkefer & M. Thaut (Eds.), *Music therapy in the treatment of adults with mental disorders* (pp. 133–154). St. Louis, MO: MMB.

James, M. R. (1988). Music therapy and alcoholism, part II: Treatment services. *Music Therapy Perspectives, 5*, 65–68.

Lathom, W., & Eagle, C. (1984). *Music therapy for handicapped children.* Lawrence, KS: Meseraull.

Luce, D. (2001). Cognitive therapy and music therapy. *Music Therapy Perspectives, 19*(2), 96–103.

Maultsby, M. (1977). Combining music therapy and rational behavior therapy. *Journal of Music Therapy, 14*(2), 89–97.

Murphy, M. (1983). Music therapy: A self-help group experience for substance abuse patients. *Music Therapy, 3*(1), 52–62.

National Institutes of Mental Health. (2008). Retrieved March 24, 2008, from http://www.nimh.nih.gov/health/topics/anxiety-disorders/index.shtml

Nolan, P. (1994). The therapeutic response in improvisation music therapy: What goes on inside? *Music Therapy Perspectives, 12*(2), 84–91.

Paul, D. (1982). *Music therapy for handicapped children: Emotionally disturbed.* Washington, DC: National Association for Music Therapy.

Plach, T. (1980). *The creative use of music in group therapy.* Springfield, IL: Charles C. Thomas.

Ruud, E. (1980). *Music therapy and its relationship to current treatment theories.* St. Louis, MO: Magnamusic-Baton.

Sarafino, E. (1997). *Health psychology: Biopsychosocial interaction* (3rd ed.). New York: John Wiley & Sons.

Scartelli, J. P. (1989). *Music and self-management methods.* St. Louis, MO: Magnamusic-Baton.

Scully, J. H. (1985). *Psychiatry.* New York: John Wiley and Sons.

Silverman, M. J. (2003a). Contingency songwriting to reduce combativeness and non-cooperation in a client with schizophrenia: A case study. *The Arts in Psychotherapy, 30*(1), 25-33.

Silverman, M. J. (2003b). The influence of music on the symptoms of psychosis: A meta-analysis. *Journal of Music Therapy, 40*(1), 27–40.

Silverman, M. J. (2003c). Music therapy and clients who are chemically dependent: A review of literature and pilot study. *The Arts in Psychotherapy, 30*, 273-281.

Silverman, M. J. (2005). The effects of reading, interactive live music making, and recorded music on auditory hallucinations: A pilot study. *Music Therapy Perspectives, 23*(2), 106–110.

Silverman, M. J. (2006). Psychiatric patients' perception of music therapy and other psychoeducation programming. *Journal of Music Therapy, 43*(2), 111-122.

Silverman, M. J. (2007). Evaluating current trends in psychiatric music therapy: A descriptive analysis. *Journal of Music Therapy, 44*(4), 388–414.

Silverman, M. J., & Marcionetti, M. J. (2004). Immediate effects of a single music therapy intervention with persons who are severely mentally ill. *The Arts in Psychotherapy, 31*(5), 291–301.

Soshensky, R. (2001). Music therapy and addiction. *Music Therapy Perspectives, 19*(1), 45–52.

Unkefer, R., & Thaut, M. (2002). *Music therapy in the treatment of adults with mental disorders.* St. Louis, MO: MMB.

Walker, J. (1995). Music therapy, spirituality, and chemically dependent clients. *Journal of Chemical Dependency Treatment, 5*(2), 145–166.

Walworth, D. (2003). The effect of preferred music genre selection versus preferred song selection on experimentally induced anxiety levels. *Journal of Music Therapy, 40*(1), 2–14.

Warja, M. (1994). Sounds of music through the spiraling path of individuation: A Jungian approach to music psychotherapy. *Music Therapy Perspectives, 12*(2), 75–83.

Wheeler, B. (1983). A psychotherapeutic classification of music therapy practices: A continuum of procedures. *Music Therapy Perspectives, 1*(2), 8–16.

Wilson, G. T., Nathan, P. E., O'Leary, K. D., & Clark, L. A. (1996). *Abnormal psychology: Integrating perspectives.* Boston: Allyn and Bacon.

CHAPTER 9

GROUP MUSIC PSYCHOTHERAPY IN CORRECTIONAL PSYCHIATRY

Michael H. Thaut

CHAPTER OUTLINE

MUSIC THERAPY IN CORRECTIONAL PSYCHIATRY: RATIONALES AND GOALS
PROFESSIONAL CONSIDERATIONS FOR THE CORRECTIONAL MUSIC THERAPIST
THREE TYPES OF GROUP MUSIC PSYCHOTHERAPY
    Guided Music Listening and Counseling
    Therapeutic Music Improvisation
    Music and Relaxation
A "MUSICAL SEMANTICS" MODEL OF THERAPEUTIC MUSIC IMPROVISATION
CLINICAL CONSIDERATIONS

Penal institutions in the United States are in pressing need of psychiatric services. Many studies have documented the growing number of prisoners with severe mental problems. For example, a study of the Alabama prison system reported 10% of all inmates to be psychotic, and 60% having severe psychiatric disturbances (Leuchter, 1981). One of the contributing factors may be that the deinstitutionalization of many psychiatric patients over the last 20 years and the lack of community-based outpatient psychiatric programs have victimized many patients by driving them into criminal activity, due to lack of adequate health and welfare services.

Psychiatric services are one of the least available health services for prisoners (Valdiserri, 1984). Two reasons may account for this. First, correctional psychiatry often stands in conflict with penal philosophies, which do not support the concept of rehabilitation and treatment in prisons. Second, the prison environment presents a very stressful and uninviting professional environment that may deter qualified professionals from working there.

Correctional psychiatry should be distinguished from the more popular field of forensic psychiatry. Whereas a correctional mental health professional works in prisons with prisoners who have been found guilty and sentenced by the courts but have a psychiatric diagnosis, forensic psychiatry involves psychiatric evaluations of prisoners and treating patients with criminal records who have been found not guilty by reason of insanity. Forensic psychiatry usually works outside of prisons in special wards of regular state hospitals. In this chapter, we will discuss the role of psychiatric services in corrections, professional considerations for the music therapist, three styles of group music psychotherapy, and a specific model for therapeutic music improvisation called the "musical semantics" model. The reader should keep in mind that the information provided here specifically for corrections can be applied to the forensic setting when adapted to the differences in institutional rules, goals, therapeutic milieu, and background of the patients. Furthermore, much of the information on group music psychotherapy and the model of therapeutic improvisation is relevant for music therapists in general who work in psychiatric settings.

MUSIC THERAPY IN CORRECTIONAL PSYCHIATRY: RATIONALES AND GOALS

Music therapy can be a very successful psychosocial treatment modality in the prison system (Thaut, 1987). Involvement in music therapy may, for two reasons, provide an incarcerated psychiatric patient with strong emotional and motivational ties to reality. One, the musical experience may become a surrogate for healthy "real-life" experiences, which do not exist in the individual's incarcerated environment. Two, the musically induced mood and emotional response of the patient can facilitate a learning process in thinking, feeling, and behavior that is therapeutically meaningful.

Music therapy interventions provide the imprisoned psychiatric patient with an adaptive and enjoyable medium to express and release personal thoughts and feelings in a constructive, structured manner. Through musical experiences, the individual may learn to properly formulate and organize personal feelings and thoughts. The prisoner may also learn discipline, impulse control, and social skills in individual and group settings (Thaut, 1987). Music-based therapy experiences may be used to motivate the severely disturbed patient to reenter reality through a nonthreatening medium. Reducing anxiety, stress, hostility, and combativeness, and using music for positive mood induction are also essential goals for the correctional music therapist.

Since the 1990s, the number of music therapy programs in correctional settings has been growing, although music therapy in corrections remains a small specialized field. In a recent survey, 132 music therapists were identified as working in either corrections or forensic settings (Codding, 2002). Important subsettings related to corrections and forensics can be found in institutions for juvenile offenders or in substance programs (Gallagher & Steele, 2002; Rio & Tenney, 2002; Wyatt, 2002).

Research in correctional settings has shown that music experiences can be used as a therapeutic tool to alter mood, anxiety, and thoughts about self in psychiatric prisoner-patients (Thaut, 1989a, 1989b). Some of the major goal areas in correctional music therapy are to:

1. Increase self-esteem, learn respect for others.
2. Provide a means of self-expression for feelings, thoughts, and memories.
3. Provide theme-centered structures for social interaction in group therapy, improve group cohesiveness, and increase awareness of others.
4. Reduce aggressive and hostile behavior.
5. Facilitate psychosocial development and adjustment.
6. Provide a nonthreatening and motivating reality focus.
7. Induce mood change.
8. Promote social interaction and interpersonal support.
9. Promote emotional learning in the following steps:
   a) experience emotions
   b) identify emotions
   c) express emotions appropriately
   d) perceive emotions of others
   e) modulate own emotional experiences through feedback from others.

In summary, in music, as an affective and pervasive sensory stimulus, real-life experiences and feelings can be recreated. Reality contact can be made attractive and rewarding. Healthy and appropriate structures of social feedback and interaction can be built. Tension, stress, and anxiety can be channeled and diffused constructively. All of this is possible through music in an environment that has very few tangible and physical means to produce these experiences, which are indispensable for a therapeutic milieu.

PROFESSIONAL CONSIDERATIONS FOR THE CORRECTIONAL MUSIC THERAPIST

The correctional music therapist needs to understand the prison-specific rules of conduct and social dynamics of a penal institution. Prisons are societies within our society with their own rules, values, and behavior codes. The music therapist, in order to be efficient, must have knowledge about typical prisoner behaviors, power structures among inmates, manipulative behavior, prison jargon, and the development of different prisoner personalities formed during incarceration. Otherwise, the therapist will fail in his or her attempt to develop a therapeutic relationship with the prisoner-patient, or worse, may become a victim of the prisoner's manipulations.

Every institutional regulation in a prison is made to support and strengthen institutional security, which is the main rule that overrules every other concern and program. The music therapist is responsible for security in his or her working area. Competence and responsibility in handling security issues will enhance the respect shown to the therapist by the inmates and security staff. Good communication and cooperation with the security staff is necessary to build a successful music therapy program.

There are several other prison-specific professional concerns with which the music therapist must deal. For one, the hierarchical and security-dominated organization of a penal psychiatric unit seems, at first, largely contradictory with a desirable therapeutic milieu. The music therapist needs to accept the reality of a prison setting and develop adapted techniques within the institutional framework. Less equipment may be available than in other clinical settings. Hours of programming may be restricted. At times, the music therapist may feel more like a guard than a therapist. Emotional sharing and openness, between prisoners themselves and between the therapist and the prisoners, have to be handled cautiously and may not always be therapeutic goals.

Imprisonment may exacerbate psychiatric symptoms in a patient, which may make the therapist feel that efforts to create a therapeutic environment are in vain. On the other hand, malingering and other forms of manipulation to exploit their illnesses to their benefit are also frequently seen in prisoner-patients.

The music therapist should be familiar with the criminal record of the patient. However, the therapist must learn to separate treatment issues from criminal issues. The music therapist will very likely experience ambivalent feelings toward the prisoner, such as anger or cynical and punitive attitudes and overwhelming empathy, at some time during his or her employment. Those attitudes will make the therapist less efficient.

Three steps will help the music therapist to maintain an efficient professional attitude. First, the therapist needs to constantly realize that even small therapeutic contributions can make a dramatic difference in a prisoner-patient's therapeutic progress. Second, the music therapist needs to establish him- or herself firmly as an integral part of the treatment team and develop supportive interpersonal relationships with other staff members. Third, therapeutic interventions should be brief, time-limited, focusing on the here and now, and guided by realistic and attainable treatment goals and objectives.

Therapy should be presented as an opportunity for the prisoner to work on specific therapeutic goals. However, the responsibility for appropriate improvement in therapy has to remain with the prisoner-patient. In building relationships with prisoner-patients, the therapist should develop a firm and friendly rapport. It is advantageous to spell out to the patient the terms of the relationship, that is, the specific limitations the therapist wishes to set or the environment dictates, as well as the interpersonal rapport that can be achieved.

THREE TYPES OF GROUP MUSIC PSYCHOTHERAPY

Three different types of group music psychotherapy have been found to be highly successful in working with psychiatric prisoner-patients: supportive group music therapy using guided music listening and counseling techniques, therapeutic music improvisation, and music and relaxation (Fulford, 2002; Hakvoort, 2002; Reed, 2002; Thaut, 1987, 1989a).

Guided Music Listening and Counseling

In this technique, the patients spend the initial part of the session describing their current moods, feelings, and concerns. In a second step, each patient is asked to formulate a personal agenda, which should spell out a behavioral goal or an area of concern the patient wishes to work on during the session. The third phase of the session involves listening to recordings of music pieces that each patient selects. The music should relate to the personal agenda of the patient, for example, by matching the current mood, by altering the mood in desired directions, by working on cognitive learning strategies (such as in anger management) (Hakvoort, 2002), by expressing important personal feelings and thoughts, by facilitating positive associations or recall of important memories, or by providing a source of motivation for the patient to make therapeutic progress.

Following each musical excerpt, the patients are encouraged to discuss the feelings and thoughts provoked by the music. These may include joy, nostalgia, loneliness, struggle, depression, love, thoughts about the past and loved ones, or concerns about the future. In the next phase, personal interpretations of the musical experience as to its meaning for each patient's personal agenda are encouraged and guided by the therapist. Following these interpretations, therapeutic goals are formulated for each patient for the following days or weeks.

Therapeutic Music Improvisation

Instrumental group improvisation sessions permit communication between patients through a variety of chosen or assigned pitched and nonpitched percussion instruments. The patients learn to appropriately express and communicate feelings such as anger, joy, celebration, relief, grief, etc., on their instruments. The therapist sets up simple jazz-type improvisational structures in which the patients learn to alternate between playing as a group and individual free playing. Often, patients who cannot appropriately communicate verbally interact and express themselves in an organized and coherent manner on musical instruments. After the instrumental improvisations, the ensuing group discussion focuses on the musical experience as a behavioral learning experience to practice social interaction, to experience and communicate emotions, to experience success, to release tension and reduce anxiety, and to experience reality in a nonthreatening and rewarding manner.

Music and Relaxation

In music and relaxation sessions, the initial phase is spent with the patients to identify feelings of anxiety, stress, or tension, as well as the sources of these experiences in the prisoners' lives. This phase is followed by teaching and applying stress management techniques. A technique that can be taught quickly and gives the patient a successful relaxation experience is progressive muscle relaxation (Jacobson, 1974). Progressive muscle relaxation requires no imagery, will power, or suggestion, and is therefore especially suited for severely mentally ill patients. While going through the relaxation exercises, the patients listen to soft background music, which they can choose according to their preferences, to enhance the state of psychological and physiological relaxation (Unkefer & Thaut, 2005). After the exercise portion, the patients are given the opportunity to discuss their experiences during the session as well as ways to apply music and relaxation outside of music therapy.

A "MUSICAL SEMANTICS" MODEL OF THERAPEUTIC MUSIC IMPROVISATION

One of the most effective ways to facilitate group psychotherapy experiences in music therapy is through therapeutic music improvisation. In this modality, patients actively engage in music performance on instruments using musical elements and forms that can be quickly mastered by musically untrained individuals. The basic goal in all forms of therapeutic improvisation is the use of active music making to experience and communicate nonmusical thoughts and feelings that are related to important therapeutic issues.

Although therapeutic music improvisation is widely used clinically and often described in the literature in great technical detail (Watson, 2002), several key issues in the therapeutic understanding of this technique are unresolved. This may be one of the reasons that this technique has not been widely accepted by the general psychotherapy community as a viable form of intervention. One of the major unresolved issues refers to the question of "meaning" in music when the music therapist asks the patient to play music, or when the music therapist tries to respond to or interpret the patient's musical utterance.

The model described here has been found to be very useful for applying therapeutic music improvisation to psychotherapy in many settings. The model is based on the recognition that music does not communicate directly referential information as verbal language does. The meaning or "semantics" of language are based on the fact that in speech we use sound patterns as words that stand for concepts known to us by definition or experience. The word *ball*, for example, refers to a round object, an object for certain games, or a colloquial expression for an experience ("having a ball"). Sound patterns in music, it is generally agreed in the study of music theory and aesthetics (Raffman, 1992), do not have these meanings. Therefore, inherent conceptual problems arise immediately when the therapist asks the patient to improvise music for nonmusical goals, for example, by expressing a feeling word or an emotional experience, or when the patient's musical expressions are interpreted in nonmusical terms. Such a way of looking at a patient's musical performance cannot result in satisfactory results, because it assumes that there is a way for literal and referential meanings of musical patterns to be translated into nonmusical "language." Therefore, a frequent observation in therapeutic improvisation is that literal translations or interpretations are neither musically satisfactory nor therapeutically meaningful. The music suffers from the patient trying to create direct analogies between musical events and feelings and thoughts. The therapeutic understanding suffers, because the therapeutic meaning of a patient's musical response has to be interpreted by creating analogies between musical events and nonmusical events.

The musical semantics model holds that these analogies are musically restraining as well as arbitrary in therapeutic interpretation because they are based on an impossibility, that is, asking music to express referential meaning similar to language. Even the emphasis on expressing feeling states through music does not solve that dilemma because it is still assumed that music can communicate directly stereotyped emotional responses such as joy, jealousy, love, fear, anger, etc.

Therapeutic music improvisation based on the musical semantics model evolves within a hierarchy of three levels. The musical semantics model states that the meaning and validity of musical expressions, even in a therapeutic setting, is initially determined entirely within the music itself. Therefore, on the first level, a patient's musical playing, regardless of whether the performance level is very simple or rather sophisticated, always represents primarily his or her musical thoughts rather than nonmusical thoughts. Therefore, as a first step, the therapist tries to encourage good musical expression in the patient's or the group's improvisation. The patient is asked to improvise music in a rhetorical style reminiscent of Baroque schools of improvisation (Schulenburg, 1995), that is, to communicate musical thoughts through musical improvisation, for example, by improvising on a brief melody, a change in timbre, or a rhythmic pattern. The meaning of this improvisation is found in the particular expression of a musical feeling or thought and should not be interpreted immediately as a referential expression of a nonmusical thought or emotion. The therapeutic value of the musical response develops in the expression of musical coherence, for example, through a simple musical phrase expressing tension and stability, a beginning and an ending, a variation on a previous motive, a surprise turn in a melody, a sensitive and controlled change in tempo or dynamic level, etc.

On the first level, the therapist encourages and evaluates musical expression in improvisation by the criterion of musical coherence as one aspect of the general state of cognitive or emotional coherence of the patient. It is important to remember that musical coherence is not defined by the sophistication of the music. Very simple musical responses can be coherent or incoherent. The therapist tries to help the patient achieve satisfactory musical expressions, that is, musical coherence, not as a literal translation of a nonmusical thought or feeling experience but as a means to help the patient achieve cognitive and emotional coherence in one area of his or her general behavior and mental status. Thus, musical improvisation can be used as a diagnostic tool in the therapy process or as a training tool for improvement in cognitive and affective coherence prototypical for nonmusical cognitive or affective behavior and as a critical element in cognitive rehabilitation (Perilli, 1996).

The counseling process that embeds any therapeutic music experience will provide the appropriate direction and understanding of this therapeutic process for the patient. The patient understands that musical improvisation is not an end in itself. Yet the patient interprets and analyzes his or her musical expressions initially in terms of creating music. This analysis leads naturally to an analysis of general issues of behavioral coherence, for example, by discussing how the patient was able to create, communicate, and adapt coherent thoughts in music and how that process relates to general issues of behavioral coherence. Thus, the musical improvisation is structured musically yet is also a functional therapeutic experience. However, this counseling process is meaningful only if the process of creating musical coherence was fully explored and experienced by the patient. Therefore, the emphasis in the improvisation must be placed on the coherence of musical process in order to create therapeutic relevance that is congruent with the capacity of musical communication.

On the second level, appropriate "coherent" musical expressions are considered to reflect appropriately ordered sensory behavior that can be molded into appropriate social interactions and group experiences. Musical forms can express and simulate an infinite variety of interactive relationships, for example, playing solos, playing as a group, creating musical dialogs, alternating individual versus group playing, etc. Thus, the structure of the therapeutic improvisation facilitates appropriate interactive behavior based on the appropriateness of the musical behavior. The appropriate expression of musical thoughts and feelings becomes the avenue to enter the reality of an appropriate social experience.

It is important to recognize that on both levels of therapeutic music improvisation patients will report emotional experiences that already go beyond the musical emotion. Two frequent types of responses comment on the musical experience as: (a) a change agent, offering a different perspective on a person's thinking and feeling about self; (b) an intensification, accessing, or release of existing emotion (Thaut, 1989a). Those emotional or cognitive responses are therapeutically very useful because they reflect an introspective thinking and feeling process on the part of the patient. It is important to realize, however, that these responses are not reflecting a literal translation of music in which a musical response directly expresses a nonmusical thought or emotion. Actually, asking patients to use music as a referential expression of thoughts and feelings may stifle their emotional development of the music because they can never experience the full communicative quality of the music, which can only unfold within its own "semantic" value, that is, the communication of musical patterns. Rather, the coherence of the musical experience creates a cognitive and affective state in which more general inner reflections about self are possible (Sloboda, 1992).

It has been an interesting clinical observation that prisoner-patients, when given a choice list of "feeling" words (*happy, sad, angry*, etc.) and one "nonfeeling" word (*memory*) to improvise on, very consistently chose the "nonfeeling" word *memory*. However, the musical improvisations were richer in musical content than when trying "to play a feeling word," possibly because it gave them fewer constraints than trying to literally and awkwardly translate to a musical instrument what it sounds like to feel angry. Using the musical semantics model for musical expression, this fact comes as no surprise because, according to this model, music cannot communicate such concepts directly.

The first two levels of therapeutic music improvisation are prerequisites for the introduction of the third level in which a patient can make referential or inferential transformations from a musical statement to a nonmusical statement. On this level, patients may be able to improvise musical patterns that they experience as representative of a nonmusical thought or feeling, thus using music effectively to communicate in analogy to "language." However, this process is a translation of music into a nonmusical, more linguistic understanding of a musical event, which is meaningful only if the musical expression is fully appreciated in musical terms first. Two examples may illustrate this point. The first example tries to illustrate by analogy: a meaningful translation of a text from one language into another can be accomplished only if the original text is intelligible and meaningful. The second example refers to musical experiences: a patient may repeat a certain rhythmic phrase over and over during an improvisation. Without an understanding of musical semantics, the therapist may be tempted to interpret this as maladaptive, for example, a translation of compulsive behavior into music. However, a musical analysis may yield this as the emergence of musical coherence reflective of a general improvement in mental functioning because the patient tries to create musically meaningful patterns. In another scenario, a therapist may ask a patient to express a feeling word in music and then use this experience to generate insight in emotional experiences. However, the musical task, due to its literal "translating" character, restrains the patient's musical expression so that the ensuing discussion lacks depth because the foundational musical experience lacked cognitive and affective musical significance to the patient. Therefore, the basis of transformatory adaptations of music, which can be very effective in the therapeutic process, is the therapeutic emphasis on musical coherence as a tool for behavior learning and change in the patient.

In summary, the musical semantics model emphasizes a hierarchy of three steps in the therapeutic process related to music improvisation:

1. The development of music coherence
2. The development of appropriate behavior
3. The development of transformations of music to "language" expressions

CLINICAL CONSIDERATIONS

Clinical reality in a psychiatric prison hospital is characterized by several factors that need to be taken into account in the clinical practice of correctional music therapy. First, many prisoners function on a low intellectual level, especially as far as verbal skills are concerned. Second, prisoners crave immediate tangible rewards and gratification in an environment where only the basic necessities of daily life are provided and where emotional and physical survival is a daily challenge. Third, a therapeutic program must not contradict basic prison structures regarding security and codes of behavior conduct. If it does, it will become a source of behavior confusion for the inmates, and it will put at risk the physical safety of the inmates as well as the staff. Fourth, normal emphasis in group and individual therapy on self-disclosure, empathy, and sharing can find only limited application in a prison setting.

Power hierarchies among inmates, exploitation of weaker inmates, and use of private information for extortion, control, and manipulation of others require a selective and prudent use of self-disclosure, empathy, and sharing in therapy. However, a therapeutic program that, within these limitations, can offer therapeutic support and meaningful choices and thus return self-respect, identity, and responsibility to its patients, will be greeted with enthusiasm and support by the patients and the staff.

The personal agenda technique (Yalom, 1983), as discussed in the previous sections of this chapter in conjunction with guided music listening, is a safe and efficient approach to therapy in the prison setting. Its here-and-now focus and emphasis on individual goal setting are very adaptable to the specific requirements of a correctional music therapy group. It also requires cooperative behavior within a group and offers opportunities to become socially involved without forcing everybody's involvement in an individual's therapeutic issues. However, in order to have his or her own personal agenda met, a patient has to tolerate and respect everyone else's agenda in the session.

In selecting the music for therapy, three factors need to be considered. First, the therapist has to allow for individual choices as much as possible to maintain a patient's interest and motivation. The use of popular music in this regard is important but must be considered therapeutically in the context of positive outcomes for the patient. Popular music is an important part of the social discourse of a patient, but it may exacerbate a prisoner-patient's attitudes, values, and behavior, either positively or negatively (Bushong, 2002; Gowensmith & Bloom, 1997). When using the personal agenda technique, individual music selections should match individual agendas. Second, a survey of theories of music perception regarding emotion and meaning in music (Unkefer & Thaut, 2005) suggests that meaningful responses to music, whether in listening or performing, can occur only within a person's preference for and familiarity with a musical style. It is therefore imperative for the music therapist to offer therapeutic music experiences in musical styles that are familiar to and preferred by the patients. Third, in order to facilitate a patient's response to the therapeutic music experience, the therapist needs to explain to the patient the ways in which music can evoke emotional and motivational responses, stimulate thoughts and memories, give a feeling of energy and activation, or provide the activity structure for performance-based therapeutic experiences.

Verbal responses of prisoner-patients are varied and range from monosyllabic and noncommittal utterances to brief answers and interpretations in response to events in the group, to responses that show insight into the patient's own behavior and express the desire to change. Some patients may be so acutely confused that meaningful verbal participation is not possible. However, musical experiences can be perceived on very different levels of emotional or intellectual functioning and can evoke meaningful responses on different levels of behavioral functioning. Thus, music therapy offers graded opportunities for the mentally ill prisoner to reenter reality and engage in a rewarding behavioral learning process at his or her level of functioning. The uniqueness of music therapy as a performance-based therapy with strong affective-motivational qualities makes it an effective treatment modality in correctional psychiatry.

SUMMARY

As we have learned, correctional music therapy is a rewarding but difficult field. Psychiatric services in the penal system are much needed and not always sufficiently available. The penal environment poses unique challenges to psychiatric treatment. Clinical practice must adapt to many limitations and restrictions that are inherent in the structure of a prison system.

We have outlined how music therapy can meet the challenge of the penal environment and provide meaningful therapeutic interventions for the incarcerated mentally ill. We have also discussed what special personal and professional challenges the correctional music therapist faces. Therapeutic music experiences can be one of the strongest emotional ties to reality for the incarcerated mentally ill.

Three types of therapy groups have been found to be highly successful at providing meaningful therapeutic music experiences for penal patients: supportive group therapy incorporating counseling techniques and guided music listening, therapeutic music improvisation, and music and relaxation. A new model for therapeutic music improvisation was introduced that emphasizes the inherent attributes of music in providing for therapeutic change.

In conclusion, we have addressed some clinical considerations that are specific to correctional music therapy. A thorough understanding of the prison environment is necessary as well as adaptive approaches to conducting therapy. However, music therapy is a modality that can exert a far-reaching influence on the psychiatric prisoner-patient's behavior.

STUDY QUESTIONS

1. What are the three steps of the "musical semantics" model in therapeutic music improvisation?

2. Three types of group music psychotherapy discussed in this chapter are
   _____, _____ , and _____ .

3. What steps can the correctional music therapist take to maintain an effective professional attitude?

4. What are some of the major goal areas in correctional music therapy interventions?

5. What is the personal agenda technique?

6. Discuss some of the clinical considerations for the correctional music therapist in regard to prisoner behavior and music choices.

REFERENCES

Bushong, D. J. (2002). Good music/bad music: Extant literature on popular music media and antisocial behavior. *Music Therapy Perspectives, 20*, 69–79.

Codding, P. A. (2002). A comprehensive survey of music therapists practicing in correctional psychiatry. *Music Therapy Perspectives, 20*, 56–68.

Fulford, M. (2002). Overview of a music therapy program at a maximum security unit of a state psychiatric facility. *Music Therapy Perspectives, 20*, 112–116.

Gallagher, L. M., & Steele, A. L. (2002). Music therapy with offenders in a substance abuse/mental illness treatment program. *Music Therapy Perspectives, 20*, 117–122.

Gowensmith, W. N., & Bloom, L. J. (1997). The effects of heavy metal music on arousal and anger. *Journal of Music Therapy, 24*, 33–45.

Hakvoort, L. (2002). A music therapy anger management program for forensic offenders. *Music Therapy Perspectives, 20*, 123–132.

Jacobson, E. (1974). *Progressive muscle relaxation.* Chicago: University of Chicago Press, Midway Reprint.

Leuchter, A. F. (1981). The responsibilities of the state for the prevention and treatment of mental illness among prisoners. *Journal of Forensic Science, 26*, 134–141.

Perilli, G. G. (1996). Music therapy in a psychiatric rehabilitation program: From deficit to psycho-social integration. In I. N. Pedersen & L. O. Bonde (Eds.), *Music therapy within multidisciplinary teams* (pp. 25–37). Aalborg, Denmark: Aalborg University Press.

Raffman, D. (1992). Proposal for a musical semantics. In M. Riess Jones & S. Holleran (Eds.), *Cognitive bases of musical communication* (pp. 23–32). Washington, DC: American Psychological Association.

Reed, K. J. (2002). Music therapy treatment groups for mentally disordered offenders (MDO) in a state hospital setting. *Music Therapy Perspectives, 20*, 98–104.

Rio, R. E., & Tenney, K. S. (2002). Music therapy for juvenile offenders in residential treatment. *Music Therapy Perspectives, 20*, 89–97.

Schulenburg, D. (1995). Composition and improvisation in the school of J. S. Bach. In R. Stinson (Ed.), *Bach perspectives* (pp. 1–42). Lincoln: University of Nebraska Press.

Sloboda, J. A. (1992). Empirical studies of emotional response to music. In M. Riess Jones & S. Holleran (Eds.), *Cognitive bases of musical communication* (pp. 33–50). Washington, DC: American Psychological Association.

Thaut, M. H. (1987). A new challenge for music therapy: the correctional setting. *Music Therapy Perspectives, 4*, 44–50.

Thaut, M. H. (1989a). The influence of music therapy interventions on self-rated changes in relaxation, affect, and thought in psychiatric prisoner-patients. *Journal of Music Therapy, 26*, 155–166.

Thaut, M. H. (1989b). Music therapy, affect modification, and therapeutic change. *Music Therapy Perspectives, 7*, 55–62.

Thaut, M. H. (2005). *Rhythm, music, and the brain.* New York: Routledge.

Unkefer, R. F., & Thaut, M. H. (Eds). (2005). *Music therapy in the treatment of adults with mental disorders.* Philadelphia: Barcelona.

Valdiserri, E. V. (1984). Psychiatry behind bars. *Bulletin of the American Academy of Psychiatry Law, 12*, 93–99.

Watson, D. M. (2002). Drumming and improvisation with adult male sexual offenders. *Music Therapy Perspectives, 20*, 105–111.

Wyatt, J. G. (2002). From the field: Clinical resources for music therapy with juvenile offenders. *Music Therapy Perspectives, 20*, 80–88.

Yalom, I. (1983). *Inpatient group psychotherapy.* New York: Basic Books.

CHAPTER 10

MUSIC THERAPY IN NEUROLOGIC REHABILITATION

Michael H. Thaut
Corene Thaut
Blythe LaGasse

CHAPTER OUTLINE

REHABILITATION TECHNIQUES IN NEUROLOGIC REHABILITATION
Principles of Neurologic Rehabilitation
Cognitive Deficits
Communication Deficits
Physical Deficits
Socioemotional Deficits
NEUROLOGIC MUSIC THERAPY
Neurologic Music Therapy with Cognitive Deficits
Neurologic Music Therapy with Speech and Language Deficits
Neurologic Music Therapy with Sensorimotor Deficits
STROKE
Prevalence
Definition
Etiology and Diagnosis
Assessment
TRAUMATIC BRAIN INJURY
Prevalence
Definition
Etiology and Diagnosis
Assessment
Treatment for Stroke and Traumatic Brain Injury

NEUROLOGIC MUSIC THERAPY FOR PATIENTS WITH STROKE AND TRAUMATIC
    BRAIN INJURY
    Neurologic Music Therapy with Cognitive Deficits
    Neurologic Music Therapy with Communication Deficits
    Neurologic Music Therapy with Physical Deficits
    Music Therapy with Socioemotional Deficits
PARKINSON'S AND HUNTINGTON'S DISEASE
    Prevalence
    Definition
    Etiology and Diagnosis
    Assessment
    Treatment for Patients with Parkinson's or Huntington's Disease
NEUROLOGIC MUSIC THERAPY FOR PATIENTS WITH PARKINSON'S OR
    HUNTINGTON'S DISEASE
    Neurologic Music Therapy with Cognitive Deficits
    Neurologic Music Therapy with Communication Deficits
    Neurologic Music Therapy with Physical Deficits
MULTIPLE SCLEROSIS
    Prevalence
    Definition
    Etiology and Diagnosis
    Assessment
    Treatment for Patients with Multiple Sclerosis
NEUROLOGIC MUSIC THERAPY FOR PATIENTS WITH MULTIPLE SCLEROSIS

REHABILITATION TECHNIQUES IN NEUROLOGIC REHABILITATION

Principles of Neurologic Rehabilitation

Several distinct treatment approaches have been developed over the last 40 years in neurologic rehabilitation. They are based on different models of understanding how the brain works regarding, for example, the control of movement, speech, and cognitive functions. A detailed discussion would exceed the scope of this text, but some brief examples of three major models in motor control will be useful to introduce some key concepts (Shumway-Cook & Woollacott, 1995).

The oldest model in therapy is based on the reflex model. The reflex model originated in the earlier part of the 20th century from the work of neurophysiologists who studied the nerve pathways of motor reflexes in order to understand the basic mechanisms of the motor system. The reflex model emphasizes for therapy the importance of stimulating normal reflex patterns from the outside, such as through sensory stimulation, to facilitate normal motor behavior because reflexes are considered the basis for all movement.

The hierarchical model of motor control emerged in the 1930s and has dominated the understanding of movement control for many decades. This model states that control of movement is organized hierarchically from lowest levels in the spinal cord to intermediate levels to highest levels in the neocortex. Internal motor programs drive movement patterns. These programs are built by contributions from different brain and spinal cord systems, ranging from "most automatic control" on lower brain centers to "most volitional" in higher brain regions. The hierarchical model suggests that damage interrupts the control hierarchy at some level and that therapy should, for example, emphasize the inhibition of lower level reflex patterns so that higher brain areas can regain control. This model also implies that normal motor function will reappear only in a step-like fashion after damage, from lower, mostly reflexive, to higher, more volitional, levels. Approaches in physical therapy based on this model are, for example, the Bobath or NDT (Neurodevelopmental Treatment) methods.

The most recent model assumes a systems approach in motor control where movement arises out of the interaction between different systems in the central nervous system and the environment without a necessary distinction between higher or lower levels. Control is not based on reflex stimulation or hierarchically organized muscle activation patterns, but rather on strategies that are generated to achieve movement goals. The most persuasive evidence in recent research supports the systems approach because, for example, (1) the development of motor skills in children (e.g., kicking, reaching, walking) does not necessarily show a developmental sequence from reflexive to internally commanded movement, and (2) in complex movements the distinctions between automatic and volitional commands are becoming increasingly blurred. When planning and executing a movement, it may be more useful to speak about both aware and unaware adjustments in, for example, posture, direction of reaching, speed of walking, or strength of muscle activation. However, both adjustment processes are equally complex. The systems model leads to two principles for the development of treatment techniques. First, therapy should emphasize functional, task, and goal-oriented activities and exercises. Second, the therapist should use effective learning and training strategies by, for example, emphasizing the training of functional movements in a highly repetitive, patterned, and rhythmic manner.

Efforts in neurologic rehabilitation generally can be grouped into four deficit areas: cognitive deficits, communication deficits, physical deficits, and socioemotional deficits. In the following section, we will give a brief overview of the major focus of therapy in each deficit area.

Cognitive Deficits

In cognitive rehabilitation, two major efforts stand out in the clinical setting: memory and attention/perception training. In memory training, therapy methods can be divided into compensatory external aids (diaries, wristwatch alarms, computers, etc.) that assist the patient in memory deficits, and compensatory internal aids that provide the patient with strategies to remember information, recall performance, etc.

Examples of internal aids are visual imagery, rhymes or songs that structure the sequence of information and facilitate memorization, simple repetition, grouping related information (chunking), or relating new information to previously learned and well-consolidated material.

Attention/perception training focuses on the accurate use of the senses in perception as well as the ability to attend to important events and stimuli in an appropriate manner. Of concern in this area are problems such as visual inattention and visual or other sensory neglect syndromes of one side of the body. Individuals may read only one half of a newspaper page or eat the food on only one half of a plate. Cognitive training, making patients aware of their deficits as well as methods such as picture completion and object assembly, has proven useful.

Auditory, visual, and tactile training and body awareness training are also important components of a perceptual training program. Attention training may also focus on using proper attention span and adapting appropriate attention strategies, for example, to maintain attention or to sustain, select, alternate, and divide attentional focus between important events.

Communication Deficits

Because aphasia is the most common disorder of communication in brain-injured persons, it has received the most attention in developing therapy techniques. Depending on the site of the brain lesion, expressive or receptive channels of verbal communication may be damaged. Many techniques have been developed to treat aphasia. Some of the more general techniques to improve overall communicative ability are Promoting Aphasics Communicative Effectiveness (PACE), Functional Communication Therapy (FCT), gestural systems (Sign Language or Amerind), Bliss (visual symbol system), and visual communication systems. The above-mentioned techniques emphasize communication (including verbal, nonverbal, and/or gestural communication) rather than the training of spoken language.

More direct techniques foster the use of spoken language. For example, deblocking tries to unlock communicative channels by presenting the information in an undamaged mode before using it in the damaged mode. A patient who has difficulty in understanding what he or she reads may be presented with the written material in spoken form before seeing it written down.

A second technique emphasizing the recovery of spoken language is Melodic Intonation Therapy (MIT), which will be discussed in detail in the section on neurologic music therapy methods. A third technique is the stimulation approach, which attempts to trigger reflex-like speech by encouraging patients to complete automatic phrases, such as "good _____ [morning]," or to complete previously learned songs or rhymes.

Dyspraxia is a disturbance in the ability to sequence spoken language due to an inability to perform complex motor acts despite normal muscle strength, sensation, and coordination. In dyspraxia, two different approaches exist. One emphasizes the use of automatic or reflex-like speech, MIT, or the stimulation approach. The other approach encourages direct work on articulation and sequencing of sounds.

Dysarthria is slow, slurred speech that results from a lesion disrupting the control of the muscles needed for articulation. Therapy for dysarthria focuses on breath control, rate of speech, oral motor control, and intonation exercises that improve vocal power, melodic and rhythmic inflection, and clarity of articulation. Severely dysarthric patients will also need help with eating because swallowing and tongue movement may be impaired.

Physical Deficits

Many specific techniques for treating movement disability and muscle dysfunction have been developed by physical and occupational therapists. These techniques, such as the Bobath approach, Rood method, and Brunnstrom approach, rely on different physical exercise programs to normalize muscle tone and posture, to work through abnormal movement reflexes, to regain range of motion and muscle strength, and to develop movement coordination. A more recent approach in therapy has been the introduction of biofeedback methods (Basmajian, 1984). By using visual or auditory feedback to indicate unconscious muscle activity, patients can be helped to regain control over weak muscles. In general, current theory favors active and repetitive training exercises of functional movements. A systems approach in motor control has changed some of the more traditional views on how to rehabilitate motor functions.

Experimental studies have shown that therapy administered during the early stages of recovery after a brain injury can significantly improve and sustain gains in physical functioning. However, it is difficult to demonstrate the superiority of one method over another. One very important factor frequently mentioned by professionals is patient motivation, which seems to have a considerable influence on the success of therapy. However, little research data are available in this area (Wade, Langton-Hewer, Skilbeck, & David, 1985).

Socioemotional Deficits

Life after a severe brain injury often requires extensive adaptations to new roles by the patients and their caregivers. Four stages in adapting to the brain injury have been identified by Holbrook (1982). The first stage, crisis, is characterized by shock, confusion, and a high level of anxiety. In the second stage, treatment, patient and family usually develop high expectations of recovery coupled with the denial that the disability is permanent. In this stage, which usually takes place during hospitalization, patients and family may be highly motivated and enthusiastic about treatment progress. However, therapy staff should try to develop realistic expectations without dampening hope or enthusiasm. The third stage, realization of disability, usually coincides with discharge from the hospital or active treatment. During this period, there is often grief and bereavement over the disability, which may lead to feelings of despair and frustration. The experience of an altered and diminished quality of life very frequently leads to depression. Supportive counseling by professionals usually helps to assist the patient and the family through this stage. In the fourth stage, adjustment, the patient ideally has adopted and adjusted to a new lifestyle where he or she finds ways to contribute meaningfully to the family life and to participate in occupational and leisure activities. Depending on the severity of the injury, however, many patients never reach this stage, or may take years to do so.

NEUROLOGIC MUSIC THERAPY

Neurologic Music Therapy (NMT) is defined as the therapeutic application of music to cognitive, sensory, and motor dysfunctions due to neurologic disease of the human nervous system. NMT is a research-based system of standardized clinical techniques for sensorimotor, speech and language, and cognitive training. NMT is based on the **Rational Scientific Mediating Model, (R-SMM)**, a neuroscience model of music perception and production and the influence of music on functional changes in nonmusical brain and behavior function. Treatment techniques in NMT are based on scientific research and are applied as **Therapeutic Music Interventions (TMI)**, which are adaptable to patient needs and functional therapeutic goals.

Neurological rehabilitation is an area in music therapy that is strongly substantiated by the basic science and clinical research coming from scientists in and out of the field of music therapy since the middle 1990s. Advanced training is strongly recommended when working with these populations due to the knowledge of neuroanatomy, brain pathology, and medical terminology that is required by the therapist. A wide variety of techniques are used to address sensorimotor, speech and language, cognitive, and psychosocial behavior with neurological disorders such as stroke, traumatic brain injury, Parkinson's disease, Huntington's disease, and multiple sclerosis.

Neurologic Music Therapy with Cognitive Deficits

Neurologic music therapy techniques in this area of treatment can be grouped into the following categories: attention and perception, memory, and executive function.

Musical Sensory Orientation Training (MSOT) is the use of music, presented live or recorded, to stimulate arousal and recovery of wake states and facilitate meaningful responsiveness and orientation to time, place, and person. In more advanced recovery of developmental stages, training would involve active engagement in simple musical exercises to increase vigilance and train basic attention maintenance with emphasis on quantity rather than quality of response (Ogata, 1995).

Musical Neglect Training (MNT) involves active performance exercises on musical instruments, which are structured in time, tempo, and rhythm, with an appropriate spatial configuration of instruments to focus attention to a neglected or unattended visual field. Musical Neglect Training may also involve receptive music listening to stimulate hemispheric brain arousal while engaging in exercises addressing visual neglect or inattention (Anderson & Phelps, 2001; Frasinetti, Pavani, & Ladavos, 2002; Hommel et al., 1990).

Auditory Perception Training (APT) is the use of musical exercises to discriminate and identify different components of sound, such as time, tempo, duration, pitch, timbre, rhythmic patterns, as well as speech sounds. Integration of different sensory modalities such as visual, tactile, and kinesthetic input is used during active musical exercises such as playing from symbolic or graphic notion, using tactile sound transmission, or integrating movement to music (Bettison, 1996; Gfeller, Woodworth, Robin, Witt, & Knutson, 1997; Heaton, Pring, & Hermelin, 2001).

Musical Attention Control Training (MACT) involves structured active or receptive musical exercises, using precomposed performance or improvisation, in which musical elements cue different musical responses in order to practice sustained, selective, divided, and alternating attention functions (Thaut, 2005).

Musical Mnemonics Training (MMT) is the use of musical exercises to address various memory encoding and decoding/recall functions. Immediate recall of sounds or sung words using musical stimuli may be used to address echoic functions. Musical stimuli may be used as a mnemonic device or memory template in a song, rhyme, or chant, or to facilitate learning of nonmusical information by sequencing and organizing the information in temporally structured patterns or chunks (Claussen & Thaut, 1997; Deutsch, 1982; Gfeller, 1983; Maeller, 1996; Wallace, 1994).

Associative Mood and Memory Training (AMMT) involves musical mood induction techniques (1) to instate a mood congruent mood state to facilitate memory recall, or (2) to access associative mood and memory function through inducing a positive emotional state in the learning and recall process (Bower, 1981; Cahill et al., 1996; Dolan, 2002).

Musical Executive Function Training (MEFT) is the use of improvisation and composition exercises, individually or in a group, to practice executive function skills such as organization, problem solving, decision making, reasoning, and comprehension, within a social context that provides important therapeutic elements such as performance products in real time, temporal structure, creative process, affective content, sensory structure, and social interaction patterns (Dolan, 2002).

Neurologic Music Therapy with Speech and Language Deficits

The Neurologic Music Therapy taxonomy includes eight techniques that address speech disorders, based on the current research in this area. These techniques can be used to address disorders such as apraxia; dysarthria; fluency disorders such as stuttering and cluttering; aphasia; and voice disorders that may result in abnormal pitch, loudness, timbre, breath control, or prosody of speech. Goals in the area of speech and communication address issues such as functional and spontaneous speech, speech comprehension, motor control and coordination essential for articulation, fluency of speech, vocal production and sequencing of speech sounds, and rate and intelligibility.

Melodic Intonation Therapy (MIT) is a treatment technique developed for expressive aphasia rehabilitation that utilizes a patient's unimpaired ability to sing in order to facilitate spontaneous and voluntary speech through sung and chanted melodies that resemble natural speech intonation patterns (Sparks, Helm, & Martin, 1974). When using MIT with aphasia, the emphasis is to increase the linguistic or semantic aspects of verbal utterances. It is important to remember that MIT is appropriate only for a very small patient population; however, it can be very effective when appropriately applied. Since the MIT protocol is very specific and requires a patient to be seen over an extended period of time (six or more months), modified versions of this technique have also proven to be effective with acute patients as long as the seven principles of language therapy involved in MIT are maintained.

Musical Speech Stimulation (MUSTIM) is the use of musical materials such as songs, rhymes, chants, and musical phrases simulating prosodic speech gestures to stimulate nonpropositional speech. MUSTIM uses completion or initiation of overlearned familiar song lyrics, association of words with familiar tunes, or musical phrases to elicit functional speech responses (Basso, Capatini, & Vignolo, 1979). For example, spontaneous completion of familiar sentences is stimulated through familiar tunes or obvious melodic phrases (e.g., "You are my _____", or "How are you _____?"). MUSTIM is most often used with apraxic and aphasic patients. It can be used as a follow-up to Melodic Intonation Therapy in order to increase the number of functional verbal utterances that a patient is able to produce (e.g., "I want _____" or "I don't want _____").

Rhythmic Speech Cuing (RSC) is the use of rhythmic cuing to control the initiation and rate of speech through cuing and pacing. The therapist may use the client's hand, a drum, or possibly a metronome to prime speech patterns or pace the rate of speech. This technique can be useful to facilitate motor planning for an apraxic patient, cue muscular coordination for dysarthria, or assist in pacing with fluency disorders.

Vocal Intonation Therapy (VIT) is the use of intoned phrases simulating the prosody, inflection, and pacing of normal speech. This is done through vocal exercises that train all aspects of voice control, including inflection, pitch, breath control, timbre, and dynamics. An example would be to sing a five-note scale and gradually move the starting pitch up or down by half steps with an individual who has a limited pitch range in his or her normal speaking voice. This exercise could be further expanded by adding a functional sentence, such as "Let's go to the store."

Therapeutic Singing (TS) is a technique that involves the unspecified use of singing activities to facilitate initiation, development, and articulation in speech and language as well as to increase functions of the respiratory apparatus. Therapeutic singing can be used with a variety of neurological or developmental speech and language dysfunctions (Glover, Kalinowski, Rastatter, & Stuart, 1996; Jackson, Treharne, & Boucher, 1997).

Oral Motor and Respiratory Exercises (OMREX) involves the use of musical materials and exercises, mainly through sound vocalization and wind instrument playing, to enhance articulatory control and respiratory strength and function of the speech apparatus. This technique would be used with such populations as developmental disorders, dysarthria, and muscular dystrophy (Haas, Distenfeld, & Axen, 1986).

Symbolic Communication Training Through Music (SYCOM) is the use of musical performance exercises using structured instrumental or vocal improvisation to train communication behavior, language pragmatics, appropriate speech gestures, and emotional communication in nonverbal language system. SYCOM is sensory structured, has strong affective saliency, and can simulate communication structures in social interaction patterns in real time.

Neurologic Music Therapy with Sensorimotor Deficits

Neurologic music therapy offers a variety of musical interventions and experiences to address gait and mobility, strength and endurance, coordination, balance and posture, and range of motion.

Rhythmic Auditory Stimulation (RAS) is a neurologic technique used to facilitate the rehabilitation of movements that are intrinsically biologically rhythmical, most importantly, gait. RAS uses the physiological effects of auditory rhythm on the motor system to improve the control of movement in rehabilitation of functional, stable, and adaptive gait patterns in patients with significant gait deficits due to neurological impairment. RAS can be used in two different ways: (1) as an immediate entrainment stimulus providing rhythmic cues during movement, and (2) as a facilitating stimulus for training in order to achieve more functional gait patterns.

Clinical research has shown that auditory rhythm affects not only temporal organization of gait movements but also spatial control, and thus is thought to act more centrally to mediate changes in motor control (Thaut, Miller, & Schauer, 1998).

When using RAS in the treatment of gait disorders, protocol suggests using a process called step-wise limit cycle entrainment (SLICE). Using this optimization strategy, the therapist begins by setting the RAS frequency at the patient's current limit cycle, or preferred step cadence. Once the patient has entrained to the rhythmic stimulus, the RAS frequency is increased, working towards approximating the patient's pre-injury step cadence. A more normal gait pattern may result as long as the neurological and mechanical constraints of the motor system are not violated, that is, the tempo of the RAS must not exceed the patient's capabilities (Thaut, Kenyon, Schauer, & McIntosh, 1999.)

Patterned Sensory Enhancement (PSE) is a technique that uses the rhythmic, melodic, harmonic and dynamic-acoustical elements of music to provide temporal, spatial, and force cues for movements that reflect functional exercises and activities of daily living. PSE is broader in application than RAS, because (1) it is applied to movements that are not rhythmical by nature (e.g., most arm and hand movements, functional movement sequences such as dressing or sit-to-stand transfers), and (2) it provides more than just temporal cues. PSE uses musical patterns to assemble single, discrete motions (e.g., arm and hand movements during reaching and grasping) into functional movement patterns and sequences. PSE also cues them temporally, spatially, and dynamically during training exercises (Thaut, 2005). PSE is often used to work toward goals to increase physical strength and endurance, improve balance and posture, and increase functional motor skills of the upper limbs.

Therapeutic Instrumental Music Performance (TIMP) is the playing of musical instruments in order to exercise and stimulate functional movement patterns. Appropriate musical instruments are selected in a therapeutically meaningful way in order to emphasize range of motion, endurance, strength, functional hand movements, finger dexterity, and limb coordination (Clark & Chadwick, 1980; Elliot,

1982). During TIMP, instruments are not typically played in the traditional manner, but are placed in different locations to facilitate practice of the desired functional movements. Naturally, instruments are played utilizing adaptive equipment in order to meet the patient's needs and skill level.

STROKE

Prevalence

Stroke constitutes one of the most common and disabling neurological diseases in adult life. It is estimated that annually approximately 750,000 Americans have an initial or recurrent ischemic stroke, while the estimated economic costs of a stroke exceed $30 billion per year. The majority of stroke victims survive over an appreciable time, although 150,000 Americans die of stroke annually, and it will contribute to the death of another 140,000. Since the late 1990s, advances in treatment have helped increase the survival rate of stroke victims, resulting in over 4.4 million stroke survivors in the United States (Adams, Vladimir, Hachinski, & Norris, 2001).

Definition

The technical term for stroke is *cerebralvascular accident* (CVA). A stroke occurs when blood supply to a part of the brain is suddenly interrupted. The cells in the affected part of the brain do not receive the necessary supply of oxygen to function and consequently die or become damaged (Wade et al., 1985).

Etiology and Diagnosis

Several causes of stroke have been identified at various frequencies among stroke victims. The different causes are usually categorized into two main groups: ischemia and intracranial hemorrhage.

Ischemic strokes are caused by blockage of an artery (blood vessel) that supplies blood to the brain. For example, arteriosclerosis (a disease causing thickening and hardening of the walls of the arteries that supply the brain with blood) or fatty deposits on the inner walls of the arteries may obstruct blood flow to the brain. If the obstruction is only temporary, an incomplete stroke or transient ischemic attack (TIA) may occur, which can last from a few seconds to several minutes. A TIA must be considered a signal for an impending complete stroke in the future. Other ischemic strokes may be caused by a blood clot, also called thrombus, which may develop on the arteriosclerotic deposits within an artery, closing off an artery and resulting in a condition called cerebral (brain) thrombosis. A third type of arterial blockage, embolism, is caused by a moving blood clot, called an embolus, which has broken away from a thrombus, usually in the heart, and lodges in an artery, cutting off blood supply to the brain.

The most common causes of stroke due to intracranial hemorrhage are hypertension (high blood pressure) and cerebral aneurysm. Strokes due to hypertensive hemorrhage are usually caused by a sudden increase in blood pressure that leads to a rupture of arteries and bleeding inside the brain. Cerebral aneurysm refers to a condition where the wall of an artery bulges, due to a weakness in the tissue of the artery, then breaks, leading to interruption of blood flow and bleeding inside the brain.

Less frequent than ischemia or hemorrhage are brain tumors, which may cause a stroke by pressing on a blood vessel and shutting off blood supply to the brain, or by pressing on the brain tissue itself and causing damage (Brookshire, 1978; Johns, 1978; Pedretti, 1985).

Some of the factors that predispose an individual to a CVA besides arteriosclerosis and hypertension are obesity, diabetes, physical inactivity, or congenital vascular weakness. Unfortunately, at this time there is no proven medical treatment for stroke. The death of brain tissue due to lack of blood supply occurs very rapidly, which makes it impossible to administer treatment quickly enough to alter the situation (Wade et al., 1985). In some cases, surgery has been found to be helpful if bleeding in the brain occurs due to hemorrhage. If the stroke is progressing over several hours or days, some physicians favor the use of medication that prevents blood clotting (Wade et al., 1985).

According to Swenson (1984), the severity of a stroke is dependent on five factors: (1) the cause of the stroke, (2) the location of the stroke, (3) the quantity of brain tissue involved (sometimes a large quantity of actual tissue damage results in a relatively minimal dysfunction or vice versa), (4) the health status of the patient before the stroke, and (5) the number and type of complications occurring after the initial CVA. The actual neurological effects are dependent on the site of the lesion in the brain.

Recovery of physical and cognitive functions after brain damage is a very important but complicated matter. Following the injury to the brain, the victim may lose consciousness and may remain unconscious for a substantial length of time. Once consciousness is regained, a phase of confusion, disorientation, and memory loss usually follows. In this phase, more or less specific symptoms become apparent, too, such as impairment of movement (paralysis), speech, or vision. After this acute phase, a period of recovery begins that can last from several weeks to several months. During this time, lost physical, intellectual, or sensory functions may spontaneously return in the patient. Most of the spontaneous recovery occurs within three to six months after the injury to the brain.

The degree of deficit and recovery are influenced in all types of brain injury by the extent and placement of the lesion and by the rapidity with which the lesion is produced. Generally, the smaller the lesion, the smaller will be the resulting deficit. However, the location in the brain and the distribution of the lesion between the brain hemispheres will also affect the recovery outcome. It is also generally accepted that slower developing lesions frequently result in smaller disruptions of functions than sudden damage (Cohen, 1993).

There is much conjecture about why a patient can regain, seemingly without medical intervention, lost functions that were controlled by damaged areas in the brain. The more reasonable explanations are based on the general concept that intact brain tissue surrounding the damaged area takes over for the destroyed tissue. More recent neuroscience research on brain plasticity has begun to show that networks of brain areas responsible for specific functions can change and become reorganized due to spontaneous mechanisms or due to external influences, such as training and learning experiences. The exact understanding of these neurophysiological processes, however, is still subject to much research and remains a challenge for our understanding of brain mechanisms.

Recent advances in pharmacological treatments may also help to reduce the effects of lesions on functional impairments in patients by, for example, limiting the amount of cell death after the brain accident in areas immediately surrounding the damaged brain tissue.

Assessment

Assessment of stroke patients involves the identification and description of lost functions and the severity of any loss. Four major areas are commonly assessed: cognitive function, communication, physical function, and socioemotional function.

Cognitive function. The term *cognitive function* is usually used to describe a wide variety of mental and intellectual abilities including memory, attention, perception, reasoning, and general state of consciousness. In the initial stages of a stroke, almost 50% of all patients suffer from some alteration of the level of consciousness (Wade et al., 1985). Some patients may be unconscious for a prolonged period of time (comatose), while others may just suffer from confusion or disorientation, or may appear apathetic and lethargic for a few hours or days.

To test for impairments in intellectual and reasoning abilities, IQ tests are often administered. These tests can be used by the neuropsychologist to help determine the level of functioning in areas such as the comprehension of written and spoken information, retention of general knowledge, math, reasoning and understanding abstract information ("How are an axe and a saw alike?"), attention span, memory, and visual perception.

Almost any injury to the brain produces memory problems (Hayden & Hart, 1986). Memory skills that are often affected in stroke patients are retention of information, ability to learn new material, and the ability to remember and generalize knowledge from one setting to another.

Neglecting one side of the body is a problem that highlights some of the perceptual problems stroke patients experience. Our central nervous system is crosswired, that is, one side of the body is controlled by the opposite side (hemisphere) of the brain. Therefore, for example, damage to the visual control centers on the left side of the brain will lead to restricted or completely lost visual perception in the right visual field. It is important to note that the patient is not visually impaired in the right eye; rather, the brain centers that receive visual information from the eye are destroyed. Sometimes visual, auditory, and tactile sensory signals from an entire side are disregarded. A patient may ignore you when you speak if you are standing on the affected side of the body. When patients get dressed, they may forget to put the shoe on the foot of the affected side of the body. Eating the food on only one half of a plate, or reading only one half of a page vertically are other examples of this perceptual neglect.

Communication. Most stroke victims will suffer from some form of communication disorder. Problems with communication abilities can range from understanding spoken language, producing speech, and reading and writing, to using any symbol system for communication such as gestures, sign language, or selecting pictures from visual communication charts. Especially susceptible to severe communication problems are stroke victims with damage to the left side of the brain; it is estimated that in 90% of all right-handed and 75% of all left-handed people, the major language centers are located in the left brain hemisphere (Springer & Deutsch, 1985).

Three distinct kinds of communication disorders may be encountered as a result of stroke. The first, aphasia, is defined as an impairment of the ability to use language as a result of brain damage (Wade et al., 1985). More specifically, aphasia refers to the inability to understand and interpret language symbols and formulate language in symbols. For example, an aphasic patient may be unable to understand spoken language (receptive aphasia), or may be unable to formulate his or her thoughts in spoken words (expressive aphasia). If receptive and expressive problems coexist in a patient, the disorder is referred to as global aphasia.

The second communication disorder, dysarthria, is a speech disorder that results from damage to the neuromuscular systems that control the mechanism of speech production. These include the structures required for breathing, swallowing, vocalizing, and movements of the jaw, lips, tongue, and palate, which are necessary for articulation and resonance in speech production. Dysarthric speech is slow and slurred. The patient speaks in a monotonous, nasal voice. Often, the flow and phrasing of speech is disrupted because the patient has difficulties coordinating breathing and speaking.

The last disorder we shall discuss, apraxia of speech, is a disorder of planning and positioning, in proper sequence, the speech muscles involved in articulation of words. Thus, the sound sequence of spoken language is severely disturbed. In other words, the patient is trying to say one sequence of sounds, and another comes out. Apraxia of speech affects voluntary speech activity. Involuntary activities, such as automatic, reflexlike speech, are not affected. For example, the speech therapist may, without any success, ask the patient to say "good morning" during the therapy session. A little while later, the patient may say "good morning" fluently in response to somebody greeting him in passing in a hospital hallway.

Physical function. One of the most common physically disabling conditions, as a result of stroke, is paralysis—the loss of voluntary control over movement of the limbs (Wade et al., 1985). Most frequently seen in stroke patients are paralysis conditions of the right or left side of the body, which are called right- or left-sided hemiplegia, respectively. Since the central nervous system is "crosswired" to a large extent, that is, nerves originating on one side of the brain cross over to the other side of the body on the cranial and spinal level, damage to the motor areas of the left brain hemisphere will result in right-sided hemiplegia and vice versa.

The physical disability of stroke victims can be described in four categories: strength and endurance, flexibility, muscle tone, and coordination. Muscular strength and endurance is initially greatly diminished and will prohibit or limit purposeful movement. As part of the overall physical recovery, strength usually returns to the unaffected side. However, the affected side of the body will almost always remain weaker.

Flexibility refers to the range of motion of muscles around a joint. Flexibility of the elbow, wrist, shoulder, knee, ankles, etc., may be affected by a stroke. Limited range of motion can be a result of poor muscle strength or disturbed muscle tone. Normal muscle tone constitutes a "background level" of muscular contraction that allows us to move our body against the forces of gravity. Motor recovery in hemiplegia usually progresses through different stages of muscle tone impairment. In the period immediately following the brain injury, muscle tone is usually very flaccid, that is, weak, so no limb movement or very limited movement can be initiated. In the next stage, the beginning of muscle tone recovery, a state of spasticity develops in which the muscles are stiff and contracted, making movements awkward, uncoordinated, and limited in range.

Synergistic mass movements dominate discrete limb movements in this stage; for example, when trying to reach forward with the hemiplegic arm, the patient will move the whole arm, trunk, and shoulder forward in one pushing motion to compensate for the flexor spasticity that limits the normal ability to extend elbow, wrist, and fingers. In the final stages of motor recovery, normal muscle tone reappears and smooth motor coordination becomes possible again. The stages of recovery of muscle tone are well described by Brunnstrom (1970).

The term *motor coordination* is used to describe the well-timed and well-planned execution of complex movements in time and space, and with proper muscle force. Well-coordinated movement usually involves movement patterns that consist of various combinations of sequential, alternating, simultaneous, unilateral (one-sided), or bilateral (two-sided) limb motions.

Socioemotional function. Stroke patients not only experience severe cognitive and physical problems, but are also confronted with many serious social and emotional consequences of their medical condition. The experience of a sudden and very severe loss of physical and intellectual abilities can be emotionally devastating and may lead to depression, feelings of hopelessness, and anxiety states. These emotional reactions can be compounded by confusion, restlessness, or irritability of the patient as a result of memory failure, or inaccurate and distorted sensory input due to, for instance, impaired hearing or vision.

Immediately after the CVA, many patients go through a stage of emotional lability where they suffer from mood swings, extreme emotional reactions, etc. This loss of emotional control is often embarrassing and frustrating to the patient as well as the caregivers.

Social concerns of a stroke patient center around an often dramatic change in living conditions. The patient may not regain the ability to live independently and may require hospitalization and extended care in a nursing home. Even if the patient can return to his or her normal living environment, activities of daily living may pose a major problem. The spouse or children may have to take over many functions, and adaptations of the physical environment may have to be made, such as making the house wheelchair-accessible, etc. Another source of frustration and experience of loss may occur in the area of leisure activities. The patient may no longer be able to pursue previous activities that have given him or her a sense of fulfillment and were an important part of his or her social life with friends and family.

TRAUMATIC BRAIN INJURY

Prevalence

Traumatic brain injury is the major cause of death and disability in the United States for persons under the age of 35, killing more people than all other diseases combined. Approximately 700,000 Americans suffer a head injury each year. Ten to 15% of those injured will never return to their pre-accident lifestyle.

Definition

Head injuries, due to accident, occur without warning. The sudden and often severely disabling change in one's life causes many problems, not only for the injured victim but also for family and professional caregivers. A traumatic head injury results in many and complex physical, linguistic, cognitive, social, emotional, and behavioral changes in an individual. When the brain is injured without penetration of the skull, it is called a closed head injury. An injury of this type usually causes widespread and diffuse damage to the brain. Brain damage due to stroke or penetrating head injuries is usually more localized and causes more specific behavioral deficits.

Etiology and Diagnosis

Closed head injuries can be the result of three external forces, acting simultaneously or successively on the brain during an accident situation: (1) compression of brain tissue; (2) tearing of brain tissue; and (3) shearing, as areas of the brain slide over other areas. For example, such damage can occur when the head in motion is suddenly stopped, such as when hitting the windshield in a car accident. The head will continue forward and smash into the windshield, thereby causing the brain to impact the front of the skull. After collision, the head will rebound, and the brain will hit the back of the skull. This injury is termed *coup-contrecoup* injury (National Head Injury Foundation, 1984). During the back-and-forth head motion of this type of injury, the brain moves over the rough bones at the base of the skull. This motion causes damage to the brain stem, which usually results in a coma state (a prolonged state of unconsciousness where there is no meaningful response to outside stimuli).

Further complications during closed head injury can occur due to swelling of the brain or bleeding in or around the brain. If not medically corrected, these conditions can cause further brain damage or lead to the death of the accident victim. Twenty years ago, 90% of all patients with severe head injuries died. Due to advances in emergency care, such as surgical treatments, medical technology to preserve vital functions, and speedier rescue procedures, today at least 50% of all brain injury victims survive. However, the quality of life for the accident victim is very often seriously diminished.

One of the major factors affecting a person's chances for recovery is the time spent in coma. The longer the person is comatose, the more likely the existence of severe and widespread brain damage.

Assessment

One of the most reliable and most frequently used measurement tools to assess comatose states is the Glasgow Coma Scale (GCS) (O'Shanick, 1986). The GCS measures three clinical features: eye movement, motor response to pain stimuli or command, and verbal response. A numerical rating scale gives an assessment of the severity of the coma state (mild = 13 or more, moderate = 9 to 12, severe = 8 and below).

Glasgow Coma Scale
Eye Opening:

1. None (not due to facial edema)
2. To pain (stimulation to chest/limb)
3. To speech (nonspecific response)
4. Spontaneous

Motor Response to Pain Stimulus or Command

1. No response (flaccid)
2. Extension ("decerebrate")
3. Abnormal flexion ("decorticate")
4. Withdrawal (normal flexor response)
5. Localizes pain (purposeful movement)
6. Obeys command

Verbal Response

1. None
2. Incomprehensible (moans)
3. Inappropriate ("loose associations")
4. Confused ("delirious")
5. Oriented fully

The Rancho Los Amigos Hospital located in Downey, California, has developed an assessment tool to describe and categorize the behavior of patients as they emerge from coma. This *Levels of Cognitive Functioning Scale* (Hagen, Malkmus, & Durham, 1979) is organized into eight stages:

1. **No Response:** Unresponsive to any stimulus.

2. **Generalized Response:** Limited, inconsistent, nonpurposeful responses, often to pain only.

3. **Localized Response:** Purposeful responses; may follow simple commands; may focus on presented object.

4. **Confused, Agitated:** Heightened state of activity; confusion, disorientation, aggressive behavior; unable to self-care; unaware of present events; agitation appears related to internal confusion.

5. **Confused, Inappropriate, Non-Agitated:** Appears alert; responds to commands; distractible; does not concentrate on task; agitated responses to external stimuli; verbally inappropriate; does not learn new information.

6. **Confused, Appropriate:** Good directed behavior; needs cuing; can relearn previously known activities of daily living; serious memory problems; some awareness of self and others.

7. **Automatic, Appropriate:** Robot-like appropriate behavior; minimal confusion; poor insight into own condition; initiates tasks but needs structure; poor judgment, problem-solving, and planning skills.

8. **Purposeful, appropriate:** Alert and oriented; recalls past events; learns new activities and can continue without supervision; independent living skills at home; capable of driving; weaknesses in stress tolerance, judgment, abstract reasoning will persist; may function socially and professionally at reduced levels in society (Hagen et al., 1979).

The behavioral deficits of head-injured patients are usually evaluated in four areas during the rehabilitation process: (1) cognitive problems, (2) sensorimotor problems, (3) medical problems, and (4) socioemotional problems.

Cognitive problems. According to Pedretti (1985) the cognitive problems a head-injured patient experiences involve problems with memory, expressive and receptive language abilities, attention and concentration, and the use of cognitive strategies to solve problems. An individual may have difficulties in learning and retaining new information, as well as maintaining attention and focus on a given task, and may be easily frustrated. The ability to comprehend spoken or written language or follow complex, sequential directions may also be impaired. Left hemispheric brain injuries frequently affect verbal memory skills, whereas right hemispheric damage frequently affects spatial/perceptual skills. Often, head-injured patients have great difficulties in analyzing and integrating information to solve problems (Ashley & Krych, 1995).

Sensorimotor problems. Closed head-injured patients usually show a wide variety of physical and sensory deficits. Damage to the auditory or visual nerve is frequent and results in impaired perceptual skills in hearing and vision. Motor impairment may affect all four limbs in regard to coordination, balance, range of motion, endurance, muscle tone, and body awareness. Due to the more widespread and diffuse localization of closed head injury, affected individuals show motor problems more frequently on both sides of the body compared to stroke patients, where hemi- (one-sided) paresis is the common clinical picture. Also, due to damage to the lower levels of the brain, primitive reflexes, such as seen in normal infants, may reappear, and protective reflexes, such as maintaining balance, may be disturbed, thus limiting voluntary and skilled motor performance.

Medical problems. Head-injured patients may develop associated medical conditions that further complicate the rehabilitation process. Frequently seen in affected individuals are heart conditions, seizures, hypertension, diabetes, or lung diseases. Also, some individuals may develop substance abuse problems (Lynch & Maus 1981).

Socioemotional problems. The sudden and severe alteration of lifestyle may increase the risk of serious emotional and social problems for the head-injured individual. Depression, anxiety, low self-esteem, sexual dysfunction, or aggressive behaviors will interrupt the social and emotional relationships the patient has with his or her family and friends. Furthermore, the patient and his or her caregivers will have to deal with impaired self-care skills with regard to independent living, personal hygiene, dressing, feeding, employment, use of transportation, etc. Many closed head-injured patients exhibit a personality change. Lezak (1976) lists some of these behavior features of personality change:

1. Lack of initiative
2. Rigidity, as manifested in the inability to adapt behavior to changing demands of social or professional situations in daily life
3. Impulsiveness and overactivity, as manifested in the inability to stop ongoing behavior
4. Poor self-awareness, inappropriate social behavior, lack of anxiety over situations
5. Lack of foresight and social judgment

Frequently seen are also combativeness and emotional lability. These changes in personality are considered a result of damage to the frontal lobe, an area of the neocortical part of the human brain responsible for high-level intellectual, sensory, and motor functions.

Treatment for Stroke and Traumatic Brain Injury

Most individuals who suffer from stroke and traumatic brain injury will usually show some degree of spontaneous recovery of lost function during the first weeks or months after the accident. Recovery is fastest in the early weeks, and most measurable recovery is complete within three to six months. However, it is accepted now that long-term training can still significantly improve a patient's functional abilities (Bach-y-Rita, 1992). Many branches of medicine have developed treatments to accelerate or improve the natural recovery process. Although it is often difficult to discern and evaluate separately the distinct contributions of treatment and the spontaneous recovery process to the improvement of the patient, it is widely accepted that therapy can help to make the recovery process more efficient.

Wade et al. (1985) discuss five general ways in which therapy can help the rehabilitation process. First, therapy should help prevent complications, such as illness, muscle weakness, or contractures, which can obstruct the natural recovery process. Second, the therapist may teach adaptive strategies so that the patient can learn to use the unaffected part of the body in place of the affected one. Third, therapy is directed at retraining the affected parts of the nervous system through specific exercise techniques, for example, in the areas of motor performance, speech, etc. Fourth, therapy should ensure the availability and proper use of correct physical aids (sticks, wheelchairs, lifts, ramps) in the patient's daily environment. Fifth, many rehabilitation specialists claim that some long-term disabilities seen in brain-injured individuals are not due to the original loss but rather to learned non-use that results in the patient not using the affected limb even though movement is possible (Taub, 1980).

Recovery of physical abilities is a primary concern of therapists who work with brain-injured patients. It is a general observation that some degree of muscle function is recovered during the first weeks after the accident. Most consideration in therapy is given to the recovery of walking ability and the independent use of arms and hands.

NEUROLOGIC MUSIC THERAPY FOR PATIENTS WITH STROKE AND TRAUMATIC BRAIN INJURY

Our previous discussion makes it clear that stroke and traumatic brain injury affect many different aspects of an individual's lifestyle, behavior, and level of functioning. A brain-injured individual has emotional, physical, social, and cognitive problems that need to be addressed in the rehabilitation process. Therefore, brain injury rehabilitation is carried out by an interdisciplinary treatment team that usually consists of physicians, psychologists, social workers, and rehabilitation specialists in physical therapy, speech therapy, occupational therapy, and related disciplines. A neurologic music therapist will often be a member of such a team and will frequently be asked to collaborate with other therapy disciplines in a client's treatment. Neurologic music therapy offers a specialized set of techniques and activities that address rehabilitation needs of the patient in the areas of cognitive, communication, physical, and socioemotional deficits.

Additionally, musical exercises offer a wide range of structural options to integrate patients into a group therapy setting where music applications can be scaled to each patient's level of functioning and yet contribute to a meaningful, musical group experience. The neurologic music therapist thus can become a very effective transdisciplinary and patient-oriented therapy facilitator in an inpatient or outpatient rehabilitation setting.

Neurologic Music Therapy with Cognitive Deficits

Neurologic music therapy techniques address a variety of cognitive goals with brain-injured patients. **Musical Sensory Orientation Training (MSOT)** uses musical materials to activate a maximum of sensory channels when trying to trigger responses from comatose patients in a sensory stimulation program. Often, songs or instrumental pieces with which the patient was familiar before the accident are used to evoke reactions.

In the early stages of recovery, brain-injury patients are often confused and agitated. MSOT, using familiar and patient-preferred pieces, can be used to relax the patient and provide nonthreatening, pleasant, and familiar sensory stimulation to decrease anxiety and help orient the patient to his or her environment.

Many studies have shown that background music or the use of music to present nonmusical information can improve attention span, reduce distractibility, and ascertain task focus (Jellison, 2000).

The perception of the rhythmic, melodic, harmonic, and dynamic patterns in music is very effective in consciously and subliminally focusing and organizing the flow of our attention. Even untrained musical listeners are immediately attracted to and pay attention to music they like, as well as recognize and remember significant parts of the music, such as melodic or rhythmic phrases, almost instantaneously. **Musical Attention Control Training (MACT)** utilizes these attributes of music to retrain general attentional and perceptual abilities with brain-injured patients. For example, during a musical task the rhythmic, dynamic, melodic, and harmonic structure of the music can be used to train a patient's ability to recognize and discriminate temporal, spatial, or visual cues. An attentional task in music may require the patient to recognize rhythmic or melodic patterns, or to remember spatial patterns of tone sequences on a keyboard or percussion set. These training experiences may be a first important step for the patient to regain attentional abilities, which may be then extended to nonmusical events. Music can also be used to help control attention of patients by focusing them on important nonmusical functional information presented in song form.

In **Musical Neglect Training (MNT)**, musical tasks and cues can be used effectively to train awareness of the neglected body side by playing instruments bilaterally or to practice visual scanning by turning to sounds from different directions during a music and movement exercise. Thus, music can be used more nonspecifically as background stimulus to improve motivation and attention during the relearning process of activities of daily living. However, elements and perceptual features in musical patterns can also be used in a very specific and functional manner to train attentional control. For example, an NMT may help a stroke patient with left-sided neglect practice visual scanning to the left side of his or her body by having the patient play a scale on the marimba. Using MNT, the patient is required to start by playing notes in the right visual field and move to notes in the left visual field. As the patient becomes more aware of the left hemisphere, the therapist would move the marimba further over to the left. Because the patient knows what the scale should sound like, he or she continues to scan the left side until the scale has been completed.

Musical Mnemonic Training (MMT) is a very useful technique for memory retraining programs. The efficiency of music as a mnemonic (memory) device has been well documented in research (Claussen & Thaut, 1997; Gfeller, 1983; Wallace, 1994). Rhythm and melody provide excellent structures to organize, sequence, and remember verbal information. Rhythm and melody can become strongly associated with a verbal text, for example, in a song, and recalling a short melodic excerpt can trigger recall of long lines of words and sentences. Rhyme is another structure often used in music that helps memory recall. Melodic and rhythmic phrasing in a song or chant also helps to "chunk" verbal information. Rhythmic, melodic, and harmonic elements are used in music to create larger patterns that are easily recognizable. In fact, phrase pattern organization is probably one of the most important organizational elements when creating or remembering music (Deutsch, 1983). Chunking refers to organizing single small pieces of information into larger units that are remembered as a whole. To better understand this important concept of efficient memory storage, think of how we recall telephone numbers. We tend to recall them as one "chunk" rather than remembering seven separate numbers. A simple illustration of the phrasing process in music to create more manageable memory chunks is the ABC song. Musical phrasing creates 4 easily remembered "bits" of information out of 26 letters. Remembering 26 separate "bits" of information that are ordered in a rather arbitrary fashion is a considerable challenge for our capacity of memory storage. Therefore, songs, chants, rhymes, etc., are used very efficiently by the neurologic music therapist to train memory function. For example, instructional songs or chants may help the patient remember important information. Rehearsing familiar or new songs and chants may help the patient train memory function.

If auditory perception is impaired due to brain injury, the neurologic music therapist may assist using musical materials to facilitate **Auditory Perception Training (APT)**. Auditory sensory acuity, that is, the discrimination of pitch, loudness, timbre, and time in single tones or sound patterns, may be trained within musical tasks to improve memory and discrimination in general auditory perception important for the perception of speech or environmental sounds. It is no surprise, therefore, that the rhythm section of the *Seashore Test of Musical Aptitude* is still used as a part of the *Halstad-Reitan* test, a neuropsychological assessment tool widely used with brain-injured patients.

Neurologic Music Therapy with Communication Deficits

Neurologic music therapists assist with musical materials and methods in two treatment approaches to aphasia rehabilitation. One form of treatment is **Melodic Intonation Therapy (MIT)** (Sparks et al., 1974). Simple phrases and sentences, which should pertain to the patient's activities of daily living, are sung and chanted to melodies that resemble natural speech intonation patterns. Therapy starts with the patient and therapist singing in unison and progresses to a level at which the patient is able to sing answers to simple questions. Subsequently, the patient moves from singing to chanting, where the melodic and rhythmic inflection is closer to normal speech prosody. In a final step, the patient's intonations are moved back into normal speech inflection. MIT is most successful with aphasic patients who have good auditory comprehension but impaired verbal expression (expressive aphasia). The neurological theory explaining the effectiveness of MIT was based on the assumption that singing, by activating the unaffected right brain hemisphere, bypasses the damaged motor speech function of the left brain hemisphere (Kandel & Schwarz, 1985). However, some recent brain-imaging studies have found that after the completion of MIT training, the normal speech areas in the left hemisphere had been reactivated (Belin et al., 1996).

The other form of aphasia treatment where musical materials can play a beneficial role is **Musical Speech Stimulation (MUSTIM)** (Basso et al., 1979). This approach is based on the observation that aphasics, while unable to give an intentional and voluntary language response, can sometimes produce it automatically in response to a facilitating stimulus. To understand this rationale, we have to realize that in daily life we use many speech phrases almost automatically in conversation with others. For example, we respond verbally to phrases like "Hi," "How are you?" and "Good morning" with little thinking, because in daily use these phrases have become overlearned. In certain frustrating situations, an angry word or exclamation such as "damn" may slip across our tongue without us consciously noticing it. Musical materials, such as song texts, can also become overlearned and thus easy to recall. If somebody intones "Silent Night" or "God Bless America," we may automatically join in and continue with the appropriate words. The stimulation approach uses musical materials among other materials to trigger automatic speech, for example, by singing with the patient and using song lyrics completion ("Silent night, holy_____"; "God bless _____"), or rhythmic chanting in question/answer format to evoke overlearned verbal responses. The stimulation approach tries to trigger a response first in a more automatic way, and later in a more voluntary, intentional way by gradually removing the facilitating stimuli.

Since the rehabilitation of dyspraxia is less understood than that of aphasia, neurologic music therapy methods are less clear-cut than in aphasia. Some clinicians find it useful to adapt MIT and stimulation approach techniques with dyspraxic patients. **Oral Motor and Respiratory Exercises (OMREX)** is a treatment approach that allows for the isolated practice for specific components of the oral apparatus and muscle positions (lips, jaw, tongue, etc.) with and without sound before proceeding to speech–sound production. The neurologic music therapist can support this approach by using wind instruments and vocal exercises with the desired vowel and consonant combinations to practice and reinforce oral motor movements, positions, and sound production.

With dysarthric patients, the neurologic music therapist can support rehabilitation efforts by applying relaxation exercises, especially in the upper trunk, neck, shoulder, and head regions. An important contribution to dysarthria rehabilitation can be made through **Rhythmic Speech Cuing (RSC)** to control the rate of speech. Many dysarthric patients can benefit in intelligibility from slowing their speech rate. This may seem counterintuitive because dysarthric speech is already very slow. However, articulatory clarity, prosodic patterns, and muscular and breath control do benefit from decelerated rhythmic cuing (Pilon, McIntosh, & Thaut, 1998). Furthermore, dysarthric patients also benefit from Oral Motor and Respiratory Exercises (OMREX) to develop good breath support and regular synchronization of breathing and speech phrases. **Vocal Intonation Therapy (VIT)** also utilizes vocal exercises to attain good phonation and resonance in voice control for dysarthria.

In summary, applications to speech and language rehabilitation in neurologic music therapy comprise the following techniques: (1) Melodic Intonation Therapy (MIT), (2) Musical Speech Stimulation (MUSTIM), (3) Rhythmic Speech Cuing

(RSC), (4) Vocal Intonation Therapy (VIT), (5) Therapeutic Singing (TS), and (6) Oral Motor and Respiratory Exercises (OMREX).

Neurologic Music Therapy with Physical Deficits

Neurologic music therapists integrate movement and music when working in physical rehabilitation to provide motivation, purpose and structure, and physiological facilitation to the therapeutic exercises and activities of the patient (Thaut, 1988). Two basic concepts help clients to meet their goals: movement to music and movement through music. In methods using movement to music, music is used as a movement facilitator to provide a timekeeper, or pacemaker, and muscular entrainment signal. One very important aspect of well-coordinated movement is proper timing. The muscles of our body have to move at the right time in relationship to one another. Even simple motions, which we take for granted, such as bringing a coffee cup from the saucer to the mouth and tilting it properly so the coffee can be drunk, require an enormous amount of complex muscular control. Any physical rehabilitation program is therefore most concerned with restoring the capacity for functional movement. Neurologic music therapists can support these efforts very efficiently using music and movement techniques. Using music as a facilitating stimulus in physical exercise is based on three physiological mechanisms:

1. **Patterned Sensory Stimulation:** Music is organized in rhythmic patterns. Rhythmic accents and phrases are predictable timing cues because they occur regularly in the same sequence and in predictable proportional time relationships. Thus, learning to follow a rhythm not only helps to synchronize the timing of a movement to a beat, but helps to plan, program, and execute in a well-organized fashion longer sequences of complex movement patterns, such as reaching for, grasping, and lifting a cup.

2. **Rhythmic Entrainment:** Music is perceived via the auditory sense. Hearing, moreover, is the sense in which the comprehension of timing develops earliest and most efficiently (Gallahue, 1982). For example, when we try to tap our hand along with a rhythmic pattern of sounds or flashing lights, our rhythmic accuracy will always be better when following sounds. The motor system is very sensitive to the input of time information from the auditory system. Timing signals in the auditory system can entrain movement responses very quickly and accurately, even at levels below the perceptual threshold (Thaut et al., 1998). Rhythmic entrainment occurs when the frequency and pattern sequence of movements become locked to the frequency and pattern of an auditory rhythmic stimulus, such as in metronome pulses or the metric and rhythmic patterns in music. Recent research has shown that, when one moves in synchrony with a rhythmic beat, the primary synchronization strategy of

the brain is not to synchronize the motor response to the beat event, but to scale the duration of the movement to the duration of the beat interval (Thaut et al., 1998). This means, for therapeutic applications of rhythmic entrainment, that auditory rhythm enhances time stability and movement planning and execution during the whole duration of the movement and not just at the endpoints of the movement. For example, when moving the arm in synchrony with a beat from one point on a table surface to another, the brain synchronizes the movement by scaling the duration of the arm movement between reaching the points to the time interval between the beats. Therefore, rhythmic cuing of movement is not just a pacemaker, cuing the coincidence of a movement event—for example, tapping the table surface with the finger—to a beat, but a cue to give time stability to the whole movement trajectory, such as the travel path of the arm through space. This finding is extremely important in order to understand why auditory rhythm improves the temporal, spatial, and force aspects of the total movement pattern in therapy and not just the timing of movement endpoints in coincidence with a beat.

3. **Audio-Spinal Facilitation:** Sound activates the motor system in our central nervous system. In order to perceive a sound, first the nerve cells (neurons) in the auditory system have to become activated. However, through the reticular formation, a structure in the brain stem, the excitation patterns in the auditory nerve are passed on to the neurons of the motor system in the spinal cord, which are set into a state of raised excitability and readiness for action. The most dramatic effect of sound to trigger the motor system is the startle reflex. However, the auditory priming effect of the motor system to facilitate functional movement works most effectively when sound is below the intensity level of the startle reflex, and when sound is organized in rhythmic patterns (Rossignol & Melvill Jones, 1976). The muscles will become activated in synchrony with the rhythm, which helps the muscles to anticipate and time the movement properly.

The concept of movement through music refers to playing musical instruments to exercise physical functions, such as fingers, hands, arms, shoulders, legs, and oral motor muscles. By selecting the appropriate musical instrument, specific physical movements that are damaged in a patient (such as the ability to move fingers independently) can be exercised. Since the patient produces musical patterns during the exercise, the above-mentioned three mechanisms of movement to music are also true in this application. However, there are three additional therapeutic mechanisms in using musical instruments:

1. **Auditory Feedback and Purposeful Movement:** When patients perform therapeutic movements using musical instruments, they receive immediate feedback if the movement has been performed properly, because they will have produced a musical tone or beat alone or appropriately placed within a whole sound pattern. This feedback process gives the patient immediate and rewarding knowledge of the results of his or her efforts, thus reinforcing goal-oriented movement performance.

2. **Affective/Motivational Arousal:** Most patients, if appropriate instruments are selected within a well-crafted therapeutic music experience (TME), will enjoy playing musical instruments. Thus, musical instruments can be an important tool to stimulate and maintain a patient's motivation for a physical rehabilitation program.

3. **Motor Memory:** The rhythmic and melodic patterns that a patient produces while exercising with a musical instrument will also help him or her to remember the muscular movements that produced these patterns. So, again, we discover music as a mnemonic device, however, in this context, facilitating motor memory. An example is the pianist who can play, sequentially and simultaneously, many notes in a few seconds without having to remember every single note (the attempt of which would actually prevent his or her performance). What the admiring layperson may refer to as "the fingers remember the music" alludes to the process where the melodic and rhythmic patterns actually have helped the finger and hand motions to be committed to a specific type of memory in our nervous system, the motor memory or ability to remember movement sequences. On a more elementary level, the same mnemonic process can help a patient to perform and remember more efficiently longer and more difficult sequences of movement, for example, combining different finger movements, or using hands and arms in a coordinated way.

In clinical practice, neurologic music therapists use the above-discussed therapeutic mechanisms as rationales to develop scientifically valid and effective treatment techniques. An NMT may use **Rhythmic Auditory Stimulation (RAS)** to provide rhythmic stimuli to improve walking patterns of patients. For example, a stroke patient is walking at a decreased cadence and velocity and exhibits decreased symmetry in the left and right sides of his body. The NMT may practice rhythmic exercises to increase balance, strength, and stability on the affected side and then begin step-wise limit cycle entrainment to gradually increase the speed and cadence of the patient to more normal levels.

Patterned Sensory Enhancement (PSE) is a useful tool to help facilitate physical therapy exercises, such as rotating shoulders, moving arms, and hands, etc., with appropriate music. A patient suffering from a traumatic brain injury can benefit from having a musical cue that provides rhythmic stability as well as spatial and force parameters for his or her movements.

More specifically, neurologic music therapists can retrain functional movements through **Therapeutic Instrumental Music Performance (TIMP)**. For example, keyboard exercises can benefit finger dexterity. Playing percussion instruments can train eye-hand coordination; improve coordination of hands and arms on both sides of the body; improve range of motion of the elbow, shoulder, or wrist; or increase muscular strength. It is important to analyze the physical strengths and weaknesses of the patient and then match the patient with an instrument that requires positioning and motions appropriate to his or her physical ability.

Music Therapy with Socioemotional Deficits

As we have discussed earlier, the social and emotional consequences of brain injury are very serious and require attention in the rehabilitation process. Music therapists can help to meet the social and emotional needs of brain-injured patients in three ways.

One way is to reduce anxiety and alter depressed feelings in the patient who has experienced traumatic changes in the quality of life. Pleasant and rewarding music experiences can be helpful in promoting relaxation, alleviating anxiety, and providing uplifting mood experiences.

Second, music experiences can be used to help the patient cope with the new lifestyle to which he or she must become accustomed. Rather than succumb to functional deficits, the patient should compensate for them by finding meaningful new ways to do things. The patient can accomplish this only if stages of denial or hopelessness are overcome. The patient, in other words, must come to terms with a new lifestyle by accepting the disabilities and developing new ways of adapting. This process of acceptance can be helped along by talking to counselors or other supportive persons about feelings and thoughts of grief, pain, and despair. The music therapist, by using music experiences in the process of therapy, can effectively serve as a facilitator and catalyst in encouraging the patient to experience and express some of these feelings and thoughts, and to induce hope and motivation.

Finally, music experiences can be used to fulfill the patient's needs for social interaction and support. It is important for the patient to become a member of support groups that assist in recovery efforts. Also, family support groups, composed of the patient and family members, have proven to be helpful as well. The music therapist can help clients to experience social interaction through musical group activities that are enjoyable and emotionally uplifting.

PARKINSON'S AND HUNTINGTON'S DISEASE

We will discuss Parkinson's and Huntington's disease together in this section of the chapter because they are both disorders of the basal ganglia, a subcortical brain structure essential for normal cognitive and motor function. In addition to a common location, both diseases are manifested by severe disturbances of movement. However, the malfunctioning neurological systems in the basal ganglia, the cause and progression of the disease, and the nature of the disease symptoms have certain features in common and are quite different in others.

Prevalence

Parkinson's disease (PD) is a neurological disease whose prevalence increases with older age. The estimated worldwide prevalence ranges from 31–328 per 100,000 people (Levine et al., 2003). It is estimated that at least 1% of the population over 65 have PD. The median age for onset reported in most epidemiological studies is in the late 60s. However, the disease can appear in persons below the age of 50. The prevalence of PD is equally distributed across the world, and gender incidence is virtually equal between men and women; however, some studies report a higher prevalence in men (Rajput, Rajput, & Rajput, 2003). The prevalence pattern of PD thus gives very few clues about its possible causes.

Huntington's disease (HD), on the other hand, is an inherited neurodegenerative disease that is fairly rare compared to other neurological disease. The prevalence of HD in Caucasian populations is reported to be 5–7 per 100,000, whereas prevalence in some Asian and African populations is reported to be 0–5 per 100,000 (Walker, 2007). The onset of HD is usually between the ages of 40 and 50. Although any onset age is possible, very early or late onset ages are comparatively rare (before age 20 = < 10%; after age 60 = 15%).

Definition

In Parkinson's disease, it is important to differentiate between the idiopathic form and other forms, usually called Parkinsonism or Parkinsonian symptoms. All Parkinsonian disease states are characterized by four features: (1) tremor in certain body parts, (2) muscular rigidity, (3) slowness and poverty of movement (bradykinesia or hypokinesia), and (4) postural instability (Caird, 1991). Parkinson's disease that occurs by itself, that is, it is not associated with the simultaneous occurrence of other diseases or degenerative brain states, is called idiopathic and is by far the most common form of Parkinson's disease. Other forms of Parkinsonism can be induced by drugs, post-encephalitis, head injuries (e.g., in boxers), Alzheimer's disease, or various forms of brain atrophy, that is, deterioration or degeneration of areas in the brain.

Huntington's disease is an inherited neurodegenerative disease that is transmitted by a dominant genetic defect. The mother or the father can transmit the deficient gene to the child. Thus, almost all patients with HD have a long family history of the disease.

Etiology and Diagnosis

Both PD and HD are diseases of the basal ganglia, a brain structure centrally located below higher cortical areas and above the brainstem. The basal ganglia has close connections to the neorcortex from where it receives and sends sensory and motor information. The basal ganglia plays a critical role in processing sensory information and in controlling movement, especially in initiating, maintaining, and sequencing movement patterns. In idiopathic PD, dopamine, which is an important neurotransmitter for normal basal ganglia function, is depleted. The basal ganglia receives the neurotransmitter from dopamine-producing cells in an area of the brain stem called the substantia nigra. In idiopathic PD, more and more substantia nigra cells die, and thus the basal ganglia receives less and less dopamine necessary for normal functioning. The cause of cell death in the substantia nigra is unknown. Eighty percent of the normal dopamine level has to be lost before Parkinsonian symptoms develop. However, the dopamine concentration in the brain and the number of cells in the substantia nigra decrease as part of the normal aging process anyway. Therefore, it may be difficult to decide in very old age if Parkinsonian symptoms are due to the advanced age of the person or the onset of idiopathic PD.

HD is an inherited disease that is almost completely dominant in genetic transmission. In 1993, a research group located the HD gene on chromosome 4. Genetic testing can identify with very strong reliability if a person has inherited the Huntington gene. The causes for the genetic defect are not well understood at this time. Unlike in PD, dopamine deficiency is not the cause of the disease process in HD. Rather, there is a strong assumption that faulty metabolic processes in the brain chemistry (glucose) of the basal ganglia itself may play a significant role. The errant chemical process leads ultimately to cell death in the basal ganglia.

Assessment

In PD, frequently one of the first symptoms is a tremor in one hand, which may spread to the other hand and other parts of the body. The tremor frequency in PD is characteristically around 5 per second (5 Hertz). Limbs are usually rigid and show resistance to movement when pushed from the outside. Poverty of movement is one of the most debilitating problems in PD. Patients have great difficulty initiating or stopping movement. Walking and arm movements are very slow. Alternating limb movements are especially affected. The slowness of movement, called "bradykinesia," may increase to a state of complete lack of movement, called "freezing" or "akinesia." Sequencing different movements together, for example, changing directions while walking, can trigger freezing episodes. Postural instability is evident in stooped posture, stiff movement of the joints (e.g., the knee or hip), and poor righting reflexes. All these factors put the PD patient at a high risk of falling, especially during walking. Speech may also be affected in PD patients. A frequent symptom is slurring and poor articulation characteristic of dysarthria (see previous section on Treatment for Stroke and Traumatic Brain Injury). In the later stages of PD, cognitive impairments and dementia can develop in addition to the original movement disorder. Two of the most frequently used assessment tools in PD are the Hoehn & Yahr Scale (Hoehn & Yahr, 1967) and the Unified Parkinson's Disease Rating Scale (Fahn, Marsden, Calne, & Goldstein, 1987).

In HD, one of the most visible disease symptoms is the onset of chorea, or involuntary jerking movements involving the whole body. Abnormal movements may initially present as a lack of coordination or unsteady gait; however, these movements will worsen as the disease progresses. Choreitic movements can interfere severely with normal activities of daily life. However, although most noticeable to the observer, they are not the most detrimental aspect of the disease. Higher functioning patients may have very strong chorea, whereas more severely affected patients in the later stages of the disease may actually show fewer chorea symptoms. HD affects a person's overall ability to control voluntary movement, which becomes progressively worse during the disease. Swallowing and speech are frequently affected, too. Furthermore, HD will affect the psychological and cognitive abilities of the patient. Patients with HD often experience depression, anxiety, emotional instability, and blunted affect. Cognitive deterioration may lead to dementia, perceptual deficits, poor attention and memory, poor executive function, and decreasing motivation.

Treatment for Patients with Parkinson's or Huntington's Disease

A difference in rehabilitation strategies exists between plateau diseases such as stroke or TBI, in which the disease does not continually progress after the initial damage, and neurological disorders such PD and HD, which show a progressive worsening of the patient's status. Whereas in nondegenerative disease relearning, retraining, and compensatory strategies are important, maintaining and facilitating functions as long as possible is the primary strategy with degenerative diseases.

The most common and very beneficial basis of treatment in PD is pharmacological, using drugs (L-Dopa) to replace the lost dopamine in the basal ganglia. However, the beneficial effect of drugs tends to diminish over the course of the disease. New advances in treatment research are studying surgical interventions in the basal ganglia, dopamine-producing cell implants in the brain stem, and facilitation of movement through sensory stimulation, most commonly in the auditory or visual modality. Surgery in areas of the basal ganglia, including deep brain stimulation, seems to be most promising in reducing tremors. Deep brain stimulation involves the insertion of a neurostimulator that targets specific brain regions and can be adjusted to provide more or less stimulation. Auditory and visual stimuli seem to be effective in substituting for or enhancing missing or faulty internal neural signals of the basal ganglia necessary for movements that are not generated due to a lack of dopamine.

No single treatment has been found to make a substantial difference in the course of HD so far. Medication can alleviate some of the symptoms of restlessness, chorea, movement slowing, anxiety, depression, fear, or cognitive deterioration. However, the severity of the disease symptoms, unlike in PD, can be only moderately alleviated. Therapeutic exercise in the areas of physical, cognitive, and speech function, as well as relaxation training, psychological counseling, and nutritional regimens are considered useful components in a therapy program for patients with HD.

NEUROLOGIC MUSIC THERAPY FOR PATIENTS WITH PARKINSON'S OR HUNTINGTON'S DISEASE

Neurologic Music Therapy with Cognitive Deficits

Cognitive impairments, including loss of executive functions and attention, are often exhibited by persons with PD and HD, particularly as age and duration of the disease increases. Cognitive treatment of persons with HD and PD is in its relative infancy, with little research to support cognitive therapy with persons with HD. Cognitive training has, however, been shown to be effective in improving executive functioning in adults with PD (Sammer, Reuter, Hullmann, Kaps, & Vaitl, 2006). Training with **Music Executive Function Training (MEFT)** provides a structured environment in which persons can practice executive function skills. **Music Attention Control Training (MACT)** can be useful for practicing attentional skills that may transfer into nonmusical activities. An important aspect to cognitive treatment in neurologic music therapy is the transfer of skills into the typical environment; therefore, generalizations to lifelike exercises are essential for improvements in cognitive skills (Gardiner, 2005).

Neurologic Music Therapy with Communication Deficits

Persons with PD will often develop hypokenetic dysarthria due to damage to cortical and brainstem regions involved in speech. Characteristics of hypokenetic dysarthria include monopitch, harsh vocal quality, breathy voice, decreased pitch range, and variable speech rate (Duffy, 1995). Some of these speech characteristics may improve with pharmaceutical and surgical treatments. Speech therapy (ST) services for persons with PD focus on increasing speech intelligibility, pitch, and loudness. Neurologic music therapy is also effective in the treatment of speech and voice. **Rhythmic Speech Cuing (RSC)** for patients with PD who have dysarthric speech has been successful in controlling speech rate and enhancing intelligibility (Thaut, McIntosh, McIntosh, & Hoemberg, 2001). Neurologic music therapy has also been effective in increasing vocal intensity (Haneishi, 2001). Techniques to facilitate respiration and pitch changes include **Oral Motor and Respiratory Exercises (OMREX)** and **Vocal Intonation Therapy (VIT)**. Further practice of respiration and pitch can be emphasized with **Therapeutic Singing (TS)**.

Neurologic Music Therapy with Physical Deficits

In addition to pharmaceutical and/or surgical treatments, sensorimotor training for persons with PD will focus on functional exercises that facilitate the maintenance of existing skills and activities of daily living. Training in physical therapy and occupational therapy will focus on maintaining maximal independence and safety. Exercise programs are designed to increase muscle and core strength, maintain flexibility, maintain or facilitate ambulation, and decrease fall risk. Neurologic music therapists have a very effective tool in music to facilitate movement in PD. Several studies have demonstrated that PD patients can synchronize their gait movements to rhythmic stimuli, and through **Rhythmic Auditory Stimulation (RAS)** can improve their walking patterns through better posture, more appropriate step rates (step cadence) and stride length, and more efficient and symmetric muscle activation patterns in their legs (Richards, Malouin, Bedard, & Cioni, 1992; Thaut et al., 1996; McIntosh, Brown, Rice, & Thaut, 1997; Miller, Thaut, McIntosh, & Rice, 1996; Nieuwboer et al., 2007). In case of walking patterns that are unsafe due to very fast yet short and shuffling stride, rhythmic cuing can also be used to entrain slower, safer gait patterns. Furthermore, RAS can cue effectively advanced gait exercises, such as walking on inclines, stopping and starting, stair stepping, and turning (Willems et al., 2007). Functional arm and hand movements can also be effectively cued with **Patterned Sensory Enhancement (PSE)** or **Therapeutic Instrumental Music Playing (TIMP)** applications. Arm and hand tremors may be reduced during musical TIMP and PSE applications; however, music performance may not always have a lasting effect on tremor reduction.

Sensorimotor training for persons with HD is similar to treatment in PD, with emphasis on maintaining function. Research has shown that patients with HD can benefit from RAS in improving slowness of movement, especially in walking (Thaut,

Lange, Miltner, Hurt, & Hoemberg, 1999). Thus, neurologic music therapy can play a beneficial role in maintaining functional movement abilities as long as possible. However, the selection of appropriate musical materials is crucial for therapeutic success. Research has shown that patients with HD respond better to metronome rhythm than musical-rhythmic cues when trying to synchronize their movement, especially in more severe stages of the disease. This is probably caused by the cognitive decline and the disturbances in sensory perception that commonly occur in HD, especially in the more advanced stages of the disease.

MULTIPLE SCLEROSIS

Prevalence

Multiple sclerosis (MS) is a disease of the central nervous system that is estimated to affect over 400,000 people in the United States and 2.5 million people worldwide. Multiple sclerosis is 2 to 3 times more common in women than men and is typically diagnosed between the ages of 20 and 50; however, early and late onset are possible. The prevalence of MS is more common among people who live further from the equator during childhood and people who are Caucasians of northern European ancestry. Although MS is not hereditary, genetic factors can increase the risk of developing it.

Definition

Multiple sclerosis is a chronic inflammatory disease of the central nervous system (CNS) that causes lesions of the white matter due to demyelination and inflammation in the brain, spinal chord, and optic nerves (Miller, 2001). Damage to myelin causes disturbances in the ability of nerves to conduct nerve impulses, resulting in the symptoms of MS. Common clinical symptoms include disruption in vision, motor function, and sensory function.

Etiology and Diagnosis

The exact cause of MS is unknown; however, it is generally accepted that MS is an autoimmune disease. In MS, the body's defense system attacks the myelin sheath, the fatty substance that surrounds and protects nerve fibers in the central nervous system. Damaged myelin in persons with MS forms scar tissue, referred to as sclerosis, disrupting the natural transmission from the brain to the spinal cord.

Multiple sclerosis can be mild to severe and is categorized into four disease courses: relapsing-remitting, primary-progressive, secondary-progressive, and progressive-relapsing. Relapsing-remitting MS is the most commonly diagnosed and is characterized by a cycle of attacks and remission periods. Primary-progressive MS involves a slow worsening of neurologic functioning without any apparent remission or exacerbations. Persons with secondary-progressive MS experience an initial period of relapsing-remitting MS followed by a secondary disease course in which the disease develops more rapidly. Persons with progressive-relapsing MS experience a disease course that steadily worsens from the beginning, with clear exacerbations throughout the course of the disease.

Persons with MS have a range of symptoms that can come and go over the course of the disease. Common symptoms include gait difficulties, coordination and balance problems, bladder and bowel dysfunction, numbness, fatigue, dizziness, and vision problems. Individuals with MS may also experience pain, sexual dysfunction, emotional changes, and depression.

Due to the range of clinical symptoms experienced in MS and the absence of a single conclusive testing measure, diagnosing this disease is often difficult and can be delayed for years from initial onset of symptoms. After neurological examination, diagnostic measures for MS often involve numerous tests, including magnetic resonance imaging (MRI), visual evoked potentials (VEP), and testing of the cerebrospinal fluid (Miller, 2001). Although there have been many proposed criteria for diagnosing MS, none has been specifically adopted. However, one diagnostic tool, initially proposed in 2001 by McDonald and colleagues, integrates MRI testing with other clinical assessment measures (Polman et al., 2005). The "McDonald Criteria" was updated in 2005 and has been used extensively as a tool to diagnose MS. A diagnosis of MS includes evidence of damage in at least two areas of the CNS, evidence that damage has occurred at different points in time, and no other explanation for the symptoms. Diagnosing MS quickly and efficiently is considered extremely important due to the benefit of early treatment interventions.

Assessment

Ongoing evaluation of symptoms is important in MS due to the unpredictable and highly variable nature of the disorder. Several different scales have been developed in an attempt to quantify impairments, track treatment response, and predict treatment needs. One of the most widely used assessment tools is the Minimal Record of Disability (MRD). The MRD is based on the World Heath Organization classification of dysfunction, which includes measures of impairment, disability, and handicap. The intent of the assessment is to manage symptoms, prevent secondary complications, and maintain and improve life quality throughout the course of the disease (Smith & Scheinberg, 2001).

Each individual's symptoms of MS can be extremely varied; however, there are certain systems that are more vulnerable and therefore often appear as the first symptoms of MS. Some of the most common symptoms originate in the motor system, somatosensory system, and visual system. Major motor symptoms often start in the legs and may include a still or heavy feeling, abnormal reflexes, pain, and/or muscular spasticity. Motor symptoms in the upper extremities often begin in the distal musculature and may be accompanied by atrophy due to demeylination in the spinal cord (Miller, 2001). Upper extremities symptoms include weakness and spasticity. Persons with MS may have symptoms in the facial musculature, leading to articulatory problems, disruption of speech rhythm (scanning speech), or dysarthria. Lesions that affect the motor symptoms may lead to paralysis as the course of the disease progresses.

Somatosensory symptoms include numbness, burning sensations, tightness, or a tingling sensation. These symptoms may be intermittent or persistent. Abnormal sensations are often tested with vibration and pinprick. Somatosensory deficits may lead to motor difficulties due to the inability to feel extremities (sensory ataxia). Another common symptom is pain, which may be acute or chronic. Pain symptoms may include a stabbing pain, burning pain, feeling of electric shock, "pins and needles," or musculoskeletal pain. Persons with MS also have a greater risk of developing osteoporosis, which can also cause pain (Miller, 2001).

Disturbance of the visual system may be the result of lesions or optic neuritis (inflammation of the optic nerve). Visual system symptoms often include visual disturbances (such as unilateral dimming or blurring), diminished visual acuity, double vision, eye pain, or poor visual contrast. In some cases, vision will be completely lost for a period of time; however, this is usually followed by full recovery of visual abilities (Miller, 2001). Uncontrolled horizontal eye movement, or nystagmus, is another common symptom of MS.

There are many other symptoms that persons with MS may experience. Some people with MS will experience fatigue, depression, mood swings, and irritability. Persons with MS may also experience changes in cognitive abilities including memory, attention, verbal fluency, and executive function skills (Fisher, 2001). Bladder and bowel problems are also common in persons with MS, as well as sexual dysfunction. Less common symptoms include hearing loss, seizures, tremor, breathing problems, and headache.

Treatment for Patients with Multiple Sclerosis

Although there is no cure for MS, many treatment options can help manage exacerbations and symptoms. Medications are very effective in managing symptoms such as bladder and bowel dysfunction, sexual dysfunction, depression, pain, and some motor symptoms such as spasticity. Medication may also be effective in slowing the progression of MS by lessening the severity and frequency of attacks and reducing the accumulation of lesions in the CNS. Physical therapy can be effective in maintaining optimal motor function with gait training, exercise programs, and appropriate assistive devices. Lifestyle changes, such as modifications to diet, can also be useful for managing symptoms such as bladder and bowel dysfunction, fatigue, and mood.

NEUROLOGIC MUSIC THERAPY FOR PATIENTS WITH MULTIPLE SCLEROSIS

The treatment focus in MS is similar to treatment with the other neurodegenerative diseases, with emphasis on maintenance of functional skills and development of safe accommodations. There is a small but growing evidence-base supporting the use of music for cognitive, reparatory, and socioemotional function in persons with MS.

Cognitive deficits are becoming more recognized as a symptom of MS, particularly problems with memory and attention. Musical Mnemonic Training **(MMT)** has been shown to be a useful tool for learning due to increased neural synchronization in cells necessary for learning and memory (Thaut, Peterson, & McIntosh, 2005). The neurologic music therapist can use MMT for training of relevant information with persons with memory loss due to MS. This is supported by evidence that a musical template can increase word order memory in persons with MS (Thaut et al., 2008). This evidence suggests that, despite damage due to the underlying disease process, melodic-rhythmic templates may support memory and learning (Thaut, Peterson, Sena, & McIntosh, 2008). Considering the cognitive complications of MS, neurologic music therapy treatment could be used as an effective tool for maintaining cognitive function.

The muscles of respiration in persons with MS can become weak as the disease progresses. Neurologic music therapists can use techniques such as **Therapeutic Singing (TS)** or **Vocal Intonation Therapy (VIT)** to increase respiratory strength in persons with MS. These exercises allow for structured expansion and release of respiratory muscles, which has been shown to increase respiratory muscle strength (Wiens, Reimer, & Guyn, 1999). Increased muscle strength may allow for controlled inhalation and exhalation, which is necessary for speech production.

The diagnosis of a neurodegenerative disease can be devastating for an individual and his or her family. Music therapy interventions can effectively address issues of depression and anxiety (Ostermann & Schmid, 2006; Schmid & Aldridge, 2004). Music therapy can also be used to increase coping skills (Steele, 2005). Improvements in these areas can be beneficial to the improvement of physical functioning and feeling of wellness, which may aid in the ongoing maintenance of emotional, cognitive, and physical function.

SUMMARY

This chapter has provided rationales and techniques for rehabilitation and the specific role of neurologic music therapy in the treatment process, as well as an overview of diseases frequently encountered in neurologic rehabilitation.

Strokes (cerebrovascular accidents) are caused by an interruption of the blood supply to the brain either by blockage (ischemia) or rupture (intracranial hemorrhage) of blood vessels. The damage to the brain that results is dependent on the location of the stroke and can result in cognitive, communication, physical, and socioemotional dysfunction. Spontaneous recovery of some or all abilities will occur in most cases during the first three months after the stroke. During this time, rehabilitation efforts are the most effective.

Traumatic head injuries are the leading cause of death and disability for Americans under the age of 35. Head injuries due to external trauma cause diffuse brain damage and often damage the brain stem, which can lead to a state of prolonged unconsciousness (coma). Once the client begins to awaken from the coma, a long and complicated recovery process begins, often lasting six months or more. Problems associated with head injury include deficits in cognitive, communicative, sensorimotor, and socioemotional abilities.

Parkinson's disease and Huntington's disease are disorders of movement caused by basal ganglia dysfunctions. In both diseases, cognitive and perceptual deficits will appear in the later, more advanced stages of the disease process. Patients with Parkinson's disease suffer from tremors, especially in the upper limbs, and slowing or akinesia of movement. Gait is especially affected by the poverty of movement, which increases with disease duration. Pharmacological treatment (L-Dopa) is very effective, but the benefits diminish with prolonged use of medication. New treatment approaches include surgical interventions and sensory-based training and facilitation techniques.

Huntington's disease is a genetically dominant disorder that is characterized by choreitic movements and a severe deterioration of functional movement and cognitive abilities.

Multiple sclerosis is a chronic inflammatory disease of the central nervous system (CNS) that causes lesions of the white matter, which leads to disturbances in the ability of nerves to conduct nerve impulses. This disease causes progressive loss or disruption of vision, motor function, and sensory function

Neurologic music therapy (NMT) is research-based system of standardized clinical techniques for sensorimotor, speech and language, and cognitive training. A wide variety of techniques are effectively used in NMT to address sensorimotor, speech and language, cognitive, and psychosocial behavior with neurological disorders such as stroke, traumatic brain injury, Parkinson's disease, Huntington's disease, and multiple sclerosis.

STUDY QUESTIONS

1. The two most common causes of cerebralvascular accidents are _____ and _____.

2. What are the four areas of lost function most commonly assessed in stroke patients? Give an example of a lost function for each area.

3. How does the type of brain damage often differ between closed head injury and stroke?

4. Name and describe the two commonly used measurement instruments that assess comatose and postcomatose states in brain-injured patients.

5. What are the five ways in which therapy can help in rehabilitating brain-injured patients?

6. What are the methods a neurologic music therapist can use when rehabilitating cognitive deficits of brain-injured patients?

7. What are the methods in neurologic music therapy to remediate communication deficits of stroke patients?

8. Describe three methods, musical materials, and rationales for music therapy in physical rehabilitation.

9. How can the neurologic music therapist meet the social and emotional needs of the brain-injured patient through music-based methods?

10. What are some of the techniques the neurologic music therapist can apply to therapy for patients with Parkinson's and Huntington's disease?

11. What are some techniques that can be used in neurologic music therapy for patients with multiple sclerosis?

REFERENCES

Adams, H., Vladimir H., Hachinski, V., & Norris, J. W. (2001). *Ischemic cerebrovascular disease.* New York: Oxford University Press.

Anderson, A. K., & Phelps, E. A. (2001). Lesions of the human amygdale impair enhanced perception of emotionally salient events. *Nature, 411*, 305–309.

Ashley, M. J., & D. K. Krych. (1995). *Traumatic brain injury rehabilitation.* New York: Appleton-Century-Crofts.

Bach-y-Rita, P. (1992). Recovery from brain damage. *Journal of Neurologic Rehabilitation, 6*, 191–200.

Basmajian, J. V. (Ed.). (1984). *Therapeutic exercise.* Baltimore: Williams and Wilkins.

Basso, A., Capatini, E., & Vignolo, L. A. (1979). Influence of rehabilitation on language skills in aphasic patients. *Archives of Neurology, 36*, 190–196.

Belin P., Van Eeckhout, P. Zilbovicius, M., Remy, P., Francois, C., Guillaume, S., Chain, F., Rancurel, G., & Sampson, Y. (1996). Recovery from nonfluent aphasia after melodic intonation therapy. *Neurology, 47*, 1504–1511.

Bettison, S. (1996). The long-term effects of auditory training on children with autism. *Journal of Autism and Developmental Disorders, 26*, 361–375.

Bower, G. H. (1981). Mood and memory. *American Psychologist, 36*(2), 129–148.

Brookshire, R. H. (1978). *An introduction to aphasia*. Minneapolis, MN: BRK.

Brunnstrom, S. (1970). *Movement therapy in hemiplegia*. New York: Harper & Row.

Cahill, L., Haier, R. J., Fallon, J., Alkire, M. T., Tang, C. & Keator, D. (1996). Amygdala activity at encoding correlated with long-term, free recall of emotional information. *Proceedings of the National Academy of Sciences USA, 93*, 8016–8021.

Caird, F. I. (1991). *Rehabilitation in Parkinson's disease*. New York: Chapman & Hall.

Clark, C., & Chadwick, D. (1980). *Clinically adapted instruments for the multiply handicapped*. St. Louis, MO: Magnamusic-Baton.

Claussen, D., & Thaut, M. H. (1997). Music as a mnemonic device for children with learning disabilities. *Canadian Journal of Music Therapy, 5*, 55–66.

Cohen, H. (Ed.). (1993). *Neuroscience for rehabilitation*. Philadelphia: Lippincott.

Deutsch, D. (1982). Organizational processes in music. In M. Clynes (Ed.), *Music, mind, and brain* (pp. 119–136). New York: Plenum.

Dolan, R. J. (2002). Emotion, cognition, and behavior. *Science, 298*, 1191–1194.

Duffy, J. R. (1995). *Motor speech disorders. Substrates, differential diagnosis and management*. St. Louis, MO: Mosby.

Elliot, B. (1982). *Guide to the selection of musical instruments with respect to physical ability and disability*. St. Louis, MO: Magnamusic-Baton.

Fahn, S., Marsden, C. D., Calne, D. B., & Goldstein, M. (Eds.). (1987). United Parkinson's Disease Rating Scale. In *Recent developments in Parkinson's disease* (Vol. 2, pp. 153–163, 293–304). Florham Park, NJ: Macmillan Health Care Information.

Fisher, J. (2001). Cognitive impairment in multiple sclerosis. In S. Cook (Ed.), *Handbook of multiple sclerosis* (3rd ed., pp. 233–256). New York: Marcel Dekker.

Frasinetti, F., Pavani, F., & Ladavos, E. (2002). Acoustical vision of neglected stimuli: Interaction among spatially convergent audio-visual imputs in neglect patients. *Journal of Cognitive Neuroscience, 14*, 62–69.

Gallahue, D. (1982). *Understanding motor development in children*. New York: John Wiley and Sons.

Gardiner, J. (2005). Neurologic music therapy in cognitive rehabilitation. In M. H. Thaut (Ed.), *Rhythm, music, and the brain: Scientific foundation and clinical application* (pp. 179–201). New York: Routledge.

Gfeller, K. E. (1983). Musical mnemonics as an aid to retention with normal and learning disabled students. *Journal of Music Therapy, 20*, 179–189.

Gfeller, K. E., Woodworth, G., Robin, D. A., Witt, S., & Knutson, J. F. (1997). Perception of rhythmic and sequential pitch patterns by normally hearing adults and adult cochlear implant users. *Ear and Hearing, 18*, 252–260.

Glover, H., Kalinowski, J., Rastatter, M. & Stuart, A. (1996). Effect of instruction to sing on stuttering frequency at normal and fast rates. *Perceptual and Motor Skills, 83*, 511–522.

Haas, E., Distenfeld, S., & Axen, K. (1986). Effects of perceived music rhythm on respiratory patterns. *Journal of Applied Physiology, 61*, 1185–1191.

Hagen, C., Malkmus, D., & Durham, P. (1979). Levels of cognitive functioning. In Professional Staff Association of Rancho Los Amigos Hospital (Ed.), *Rehabilitation of the head-injured adult: Comprehensive physical management*. Downey, CA: Rancho Los Amigos Hospital.

Haneishi, E. (2001). Effects of a music therapy voice protocol on speech intelligibility, vocal acoustic measures, and mood of individuals with Parkinson's disease. *Journal of Music Therapy, 38*, 273–290.

Hayden, M., & Hart, T. (1986). Rehabilitation of cognitive and behavioral dysfunction in head injury. *Advanced Psychosomatic Medicine, 16*, 194–229.

Heaton, P., Pring, L., & Hermelin, B. (2001). Musical processing in high functioning children with autism. *Annals of the New York Academy of Sciences, 930*, 443–444.

Hoehn, M. M., & Yahr, M. D. (1967). Parkinsonism: Onset, progression, and mortality. *Neurology, 17*, 427–442.

Holbrook, M. (1982). Stroke: Social and emotional outcome. *Journal of the Royal College of Physics, 16*, 100–104.

Hommel, M., Peres, B., Pollak, P., Memin, B., et al. (1990). Effects of passive tactile and auditory stimuli on left visual neglect. *Archives of Neurology, 47*, 573–576.

Jackson, S. A., Treharne, D. A., & Boucher, J. (1997). Rhythm and language in children with moderate learning difficulties. *European Journal of Disorders of Communication, 32*, 99–108.

Jellison, J. A. (2000). A content analysis of music research with disabled children and youth (1975–1999): Applications in special education. In AMTA (Ed.), *Effectiveness of music therapy procedures: Documentation of research and clinical practice* (3rd ed., pp. 199–264). Silver Spring, MD: American Music Therapy Association.

Johns, D. F. (1978). *Clinical management of neurogenic communicative disorders*. Boston: Little, Brown.

Kandel, E., & Schwarz, J. (1985). *Principles of neural science*. New York: Elsevier.

Levine, C. B., Fahrbach, K. R., Siderowf, A. D., et al. (2003). *Diagnosis and treatment of Parkinson's disease: A systematic review of the literature*. Evidence Report/Technology Assessment Number 57. Rockville, MD: Agency for Healthcare Research and Quality.

Lezak, M. D. (1976). *Neuropsychological assessment*. New York: Oxford University Press.

Lynch, W. J., & Maus, N. K. (1981). Brain injury rehabilitation: Standard problem list. *Archives of Physical Medicine and Rehabilitation, 62*, 223–227.

Maeller, D. H. (1996). *Rehearsal strategies and verbal working memory in multiple sclerosis*. Unpublished master thesis, Colorado State University, Fort Collins.

McDonald, W. I., Compston, A., Edan, G., et al. (2001). Recommended diagnostic criteria for multiple sclerosis: Guidelines from the International Panel on the Diagnosis of Multiple Sclerosis. *Annals of Neurology, 50*, 121–127.

McIntosh, G. C., Brown, S. H., Rice, R. R., & Thaut, M.H. (1997). Rhythmic auditory-motor facilitation of gait patterns in patients with Parkinson's disease. *Journal of Neurology, Neurosurgery, and Psychiatry, 62*, 22–26.

Miller, A. (2001). Clinical features. In S. Cook (Ed.), *Handbook of multiple sclerosis* (3rd ed., pp. 213–232). New York: Marcel Dekker.

Miller, R. A., Thaut, M. H., McIntosh, G. C., & Rice, R. R. (1996). Components of EMG symmetry and variability in Parkinsonian and healthy elderly gait. *Electroencephalography and Clinical Neurophysiology, 101*, 1–7.

National Head Injury Foundation. (1984). *Coma: Its treatment and consequences*. Framingham, MA: National Head Injury Foundation.

Nieuwboer, A., Kwakkel, G., Rochester, L., Jones, D., van Wegen, E., Willems, A., et al. (2007). Cueing training in the home improves gait-related mobility in Parkinson's disease: The Rescue trial. *Journal of Neurology, Neurosurgery & Psychiatry, 78*, 134–140.

Ogata, S. (1995). Human EEG responses to classical music and simulated white noise: Effects of a musical loudness component on consciousness. *Perceptual & Motor Skills, 80*, 779–790.

O'Shanick, G. J. (1986). Neuropsychiatric complications in head injury. *Advanced Psychosomatic Medicine, 16*, 173–193.

Ostermann, T., & Schmid, W. (2006). Music therapy in the treatment of multiple sclerosis: A comprehensive literature review. *Expert Review of Neurotherapeutics, 6*, 469–477.

Pedretti, L. W. (1985). *Occupational therapy practice skills for physical dysfunction.* St. Louis, MO: C. V. Mosby.

Pilon, M. A., McIntosh, K. W., & Thaut, M. H. (1998). Auditory vs. visual speech timing cues as external rate control to enhance verbal intelligibility in mixed spastic-ataxic dysarthric speakers: A pilot study. *Brain Injury, 12*, 793–803.

Polman, C. H., Reingold, S. C., Edan, G., Filippi, M., Hartung, H., Kappos, L., et al. (2005). Diagnostic criteria for multiple sclerosis: 2005 revisions to the "McDonald Criteria." *Annals of Neurology, 58*, 840–846.

Rajput, A. H., Rajput, A., & Rajput, M. (2003). Epidemiology in Parkinsonism. In R. Pahwa, K. Lyons, & W. Koller (Eds.), *Handbook of Parkinson's disease* (3rd ed., pp. 17–42). New York: Marcel Dekker.

Richards, C. L., Malouin, F., Bedard, P. J., & Cioni, M. (1992). Changes induced by L-Dopa and sensory cues on the gait of Parkinsonian patients. In M. Woollacott & F. Horak (Eds.), *Posture and gait: Control mechanisms* (Vol. II). Eugene: University of Oregon Books.

Rossignol, S., & Melvill Jones, G. (1976). Audio-spinal influences in man studied by the H-reflex and its possible role in rhythmic movement synchronized to sound. *Electroencephalography and Clinical Neurophysiology, 41*, 83–92.

Sammer, G., Reuter, I., Hullmann, K., Kaps, M., & Vaitl, D. (2006). Training of executive functions in Parkinson's disease. *Journal of the Neurological Sciences, 248*, 115–119.

Schmid, W., & Aldridge, D. (2004). Active music therapy in the treatment of multiple sclerosis patients: A matched control study. *Journal of Music Therapy, 41*, 225–240.

Shumway-Cook, A., & Woollacott, M. H. (1995). *Motor control: Theory and practical applications.* Baltimore: Williams & Wilkins.

Smith, C., & Scheinberg, L. (2001). Symptomatic treatment and rehabilitation in multiple sclerosis. In S. Cook (Ed.), *Handbook of multiple sclerosis* (3rd ed., pp. 609–634). New York: Marcel Dekker.

Sparks, R., Helm, N., & Martin, A. (1974). Aphasia rehabilitation resulting from melodic intonation therapy. *Cortex, 10*, 303–316.

Springer, S. P., & Deutsch, G. (1985). *Left brain, right brain.* New York: Freeman.

Steele, M. (2005). Coping with multiple sclerosis: A music therapy viewpoint. *Australian Journal of Music Therapy, 16*, 70–87.

Swenson, J. R. (1984). Therapeutic exercise in hemiplegia. In J. V. Basmajian (Ed.), *Therapeutic exercise.* Baltimore: Williams and Wilkins.

Taub, E. (1980). Somatosensory differentiation research with monkeys: Implications for rehabilitation medicine. In L. P. Ince (Ed.), *Behavioral psychology in rehabilitation medicine* (pp. 371–401). Baltimore: Williams and Wilkins.

Thaut, M. H. (1988). Rhythmic intervention techniques in music therapy with gross motor dysfunction. *Arts in Psychotherapy, 15*, 127–137.

Thaut, M. H. (2005). *Rhythm, music and the brain.* New York: Taylor and Francis.

Thaut, M. H., Kenyon, G. P., Schauer, M. L., & McIntosh, G. C. (1999). Rhythmicity and brain function: Implication for therapy of movement disorders. *IEEE Engineering in Medicine and Biology, 18*, 101–108.

Thaut, M. H., Lange, H. W., Miltner, R., Hurt, C. P., & Hoemberg V. (1999). Velocity modulation and rhythmic synchronization in gait of Huntington's disease patients. *Movement Disorders, 14*, 808–819.

Thaut, M. H., McIntosh, G. C., Rice, R. R., Miller, R. A., Rathbun, J., & Brault, J. M. (1996). Rhythmic auditory stimulation in gait training for Parkinson's disease patients. *Movement Disorders, 11*, 193–200.

Thaut, M. H., McIntosh, K. W., McIntosh, G. C., & Hoemberg, V. (2001). Auditory rhythmicity enhances movement and speech motor control in patients with Parkinson's disease. *Functional Neurology, 16*, 163–172.

Thaut, M. H., Miller, R. A., & Schauer, L. M. (1998). Multiple synchronization strategies in rhythmic sensorimotor tasks: Phase versus period corrections. *Biological Cybernetics, 79*, 241–250.

Thaut, M. H., Peterson, D. A., & McIntosh, G. C. (2005). Temporal entrainment of cognitive functions: Musical mnemonics induce brain plasticity and oscillatory synchrony in neural networks underlying memory. *Annals of the New York Academy of Sciences, 1060*, 243–254.

Thaut, M. H., Peterson, D. A., Sena, K. M., & McIntosh, G. C. (2008). Musical structure facilitates verbal learning in multiple sclerosis. *Music Perception, 25*, 325–330.

Wade, D. T., Langton-Hewer, R., Skilbeck, C. E., & David, R. M. (1985). *Stroke: A critical approach to diagnosis, treatment, and management.* Chicago: Yearbook Medical.

Walker, F. (2007). Huntington's disease. *Lancet, 369*, 218–228.

Wallace, W. T. (1994). Memory for music: Effect of melody on recall of text. *Journal of Experimental Psychology, 20*, 1471–1485.

Wiens, M. E., Reimer, M. A., & Guyn, L. H. (1999). Music therapy as a treatment method for improving respiratory muscle strength in patients with advanced multiple sclerosis: A pilot study. *Rehabilitation Nursing, 24*, 74–80.

Willems, A. M., Nieuwboer, A., Chavret, F., Desloovere, K., Dom, R., Rochester, L., Kwakkel, G., van Wegen, E., & Jones, D. (2007). Turning in Parkinson's disease patients and controls: The effect of auditory cues. *Movement Disorders, 22*, 1871–1878.

CHAPTER 11

MUSIC THERAPY, MEDICINE, AND WELL-BEING

Kate Gfeller

CHAPTER OUTLINE

A BIOPSYCHOSOCIAL PERSPECTIVE OF HEALTH AND ILLNESS
MUSIC IN THE PROMOTION OF HEALTH AND WELL-BEING
MEDICAL APPLICATIONS OF MUSIC THERAPY
    Biological Needs
    Psychological and Social Needs
ASSESSMENT PROCEDURES
    Self-Report Measures
    Observation of Behavioral Responses
    Clinical Measures

Kirsten, a music therapist in a large medical hospital, has been invited to talk about her work at the West High Career Fair. One of the students asks, "What's a typical day like in your job?" "A typical day?" Kirsten thinks to herself. "Just about the only thing that is typical about my work is that I do many different things each day." Because variety seems to characterize her work, Kirsten decides that she should illustrate her varied responsibilities by describing the different sessions she completed the day before. "I'm going to tell you about what I did yesterday, to give you a little glimpse into my work. However, I'm going to 'make up' the names of the patients I work with, for I need to protect the confidentiality of all the patients—that is, I must not share their identity outside of the treatment team. OK, I'll get started.

"Although music therapists at the hospital work with many types of patients, my case load is typically on the Pediatric Unit. Things change

quickly in the hospital—from minute to minute, and from day to day, so one of the first things I do each morning is to find out the current status of the children, and what procedures they'll face that day. In order to do this, I attend the inpatient pediatric interdisciplinary report on two different floors. The charge nurse gives a quick verbal accounting of the status of all inpatients, discharges, surgical schedules, and transfers. That information helps me plan for the many different sessions I'll provide that day.

"One of the sessions I provide is a music therapy group for preschoolers in the pediatric playroom. This is available for all the patients who are well enough to leave their rooms, and their families are encouraged to attend. If you were to observe this session, you might think it's just like any preschool activity. That's exactly how it should look—fun and relaxed. But the reason it looks so relaxed is that the activities have been planned around the medical needs and functional levels of the kids in the group. For example, if one of the kids is hooked to an IV, we make sure that each activity is modified so that his IV doesn't prevent active participation. During this play time, we encourage social interaction and involvement in the sorts of 'normal' activities that kids their age would have if they weren't in the hospital. We sing songs like 'Mary Has a Red Dress,' 'Old MacDonald,' or 'Five Little Ducks,' which teach or reinforce colors, numbers, and other things that toddlers need to know. These fun childhood activities also comfort the children and improve their moods. After all, it can be pretty scary to be in the hospital. When the parents join their kids in something fun and 'normal,' they relax a little bit, too. As soon as the session is over, it's time to clean up and sanitize all the toys and musical instruments, and head over to the nurses station to chart.

"Unfortunately, little Miranda, a toddler on the burn unit, was medically too unstable to join the morning group, so we had music therapy in her room during the early afternoon. Because of her burns, Miranda is at risk for infection. That means I have to wear a gown and gloves, and follow special procedures for infection control whenever I work with her. Miranda is pretty shy and withdrawn, so I started with one of her favorite songs to engage her in interaction, and to allow more work on her rehabilitative goals.

"After working with Miranda, I headed off to do several individual music therapy sessions on the Pediatric Intensive Care Unit for patients who *need calming or pain control. Before I meet with each one, I check with family members to find out favorite songs and pastimes. In some cases, I play guitar or Q Chord and sing with them. Sometimes, I put together an iPod with their favorite music that they can play on their own. Keeping the children calm and distracted helps to reduce the amount of pain medication required, and it makes things much easier for the rest of the medical team and parents. It's tough to watch little kids suffer.*

"Sometimes, I work directly with the parents. Having your child in the hospital is really stressful. Yesterday, I met with Jacob's parents to teach them musical ways to interact with their tiny little 3-month old. Jake is awake, but he can't express himself with his voice—you know, cooing and crying like other babies do—because of being on a ventilator. Those parents feel pretty helpless, and they feel much better when they have something concrete and useful they can do with their new baby.

"So what happened next—I went to the bedside of a 12-year old, Rosa, who is in a coma as a result of a motor vehicle accident. The staff hopes that Rosa will show some physiological responses to familiar and appropriate musical stimulation. I checked with the family regarding Rosa's favorite music—she loves J. Lo—and I play my guitar and sing music that Rosa likes in order to provide meaningful and calming stimulation. It's really pretty amazing. Rosa doesn't sing along or show any obvious response to my music, but the nursing staff has told me that they see a beneficial drop in heart rate and blood pressure as I sing and play. She responds to the music physically, even though she can't talk to us.

"So what happened next? Well, I met with Derrick, a 14-year-old, who has the very scary, lonely, and grown-up job of waiting for a heart transplant. He's been waiting six months for a heart donor, and staying in the hospital can be a real drag. So I helped Derrick write his own song, 'The Hospital Blues,' to encourage and validate his expression of feelings.

"After my last session, I finished up the day by doing my charting, wrapping up correspondence and planning, and it was time to head home to my family. Tomorrow, I may see some of the same kids, as well as some different children. Each day brings new challenges and new opportunities."

In the example above, Kirsten's work reflects a contemporary view of health and illness, a **biopsychosocial model**, which addresses the role of biological, psychological, and social factors in the human "system" (Sarafino, 2006). Previously, medical practitioners tended to focus only on the physical (biological) aspects of health and illness. In contrast, within the biopsychosocial perspective, all three factors—biological, psychological, and social factors—affect and are affected by the person's health.

A BIOPSYCHOSOCIAL MODEL OF HEALTH AND ILLNESS

Biological factors include inherited physical characteristics, as well as the function and structure of our body (such as a malformed heart valve or allergies). **Psychological** factors include cognition (mental activity), emotions, and motivation. **Social** factors include values of our culture (such as media representation of ideal body weight), our family (such as parental or spousal attitudes about nutrition), and community influences (such as recreation systems or biking trails that promote exercise). Within the dynamic entity of the human system, all three factors interact (Sarafino, 2006).

There are many examples in everyday life that illustrate this dynamic relationship. Consider the stress associated with final exams.

> It's Friday morning of finals week and Josh rolls out of bed after 2 hours of sleep. His throat feels scratchy, his head feels like it's about to explode from sinus congestion, his complexion looks like a "before" picture for an acne cream commercial, and there isn't a muscle or joint in his body that doesn't ache. "I don't need the flu!" Josh moans, as he drags himself to the medicine cabinet for some cold medicine. It's been the usual ordeal of finals week: an average of 2 to 3 hours of sleep per night, loading up on junk food and coffee, absolutely no exercise other than moving his fingers at the computer, petty arguments with his girlfriend, and plenty of worry about exams. His parents are breathing down his neck—"It's about time we see some decent grades for all that tuition we pay!" Josh was looking forward to some heavy partying tonight after the last exam, but his body has basically revolted—it looks like he'll be celebrating the end of finals in bed with a box of Kleenex and some chicken soup.

During exam time, college dorms are basically stress colonies filled with exhausted and irritable students coughing and sneezing, dealing with acne breakouts, dermatitis, queasy stomachs, and other stress-related maladies. Fortunately, exams are a temporary stress shared among friends, and there is a definite and predictable ending to finals. Once exams are over, many students can look forward to a break at home, or partying with friends to celebrate the semester's conclusion.

For persons who provide care for loved ones with chronic conditions such as Alzheimer's disease or terminal cancer, there is limited relief along the way, and no party to anticipate. The physical and psychological stresses compound as the loved one's condition continues to deteriorate over weeks, months, or even years. As the patient declines, socializing and leaving the home becomes more difficult, and caregivers often become isolated from their social network. Ongoing stress contributes to a higher incident of health problems among long-term caregivers, who are sometimes referred to as the "second victim" (Kiecolt-Glaser, Dura, Speicher, Trask, & Glaser, 1991). The heavy toll on physical, psychological, and social well-being in this scenario is a clear example of the dynamic interplay of the biopsychosocial model of health and illness.

The biopsychosocial model of health and illness helps us understand factors that promote and maintain health and well-being. This model also assists us in developing and selecting effective strategies for coping with and recovering from illness. For example, medical research has revealed that people who enjoy a high degree of social support from family and friends and who engage in healthy lifestyle habits (regular exercise and good nutrition) tend to be healthier and live longer than people who do not. Scientists also realize that psychological factors can play a role in illness. For example, ongoing stress impairs functioning of the immune system and makes people more vulnerable to **opportunistic diseases** (infections that do not affect healthy individuals, but that cause illness in a person with a weakened immune system). Consequently, with regard to promoting and maintaining well-being, a person who has a strong social network, good lifestyle habits, and who is effective at managing stress is more likely to enjoy good health (Sarafino, 2006).

In addition to influencing one's general health, psychological and social factors influence coping with or recovery from illnesses or medical conditions. For example, research indicates that reduction of anxiety in patients awaiting surgery enables faster recovery and discharge (Good et al., 2001; Sarafino, 2006). Psychological techniques can assist in pain management, reduce depression, and boost immune function in persons with conditions such as cancer (McKinney, Antoni, Kumar, Tims, & McCabe, 1997; McKinney, Tims, Kumar, & Kumar, 1997; Sarafino, 2006). This relationship between recovery and psychosocial factors is not only associated with quality of patient care, but also has implications for the containment of healthcare costs; faster recovery is typically associated with smaller medical bills.

A biopsychosocial model requires attention to psychological and social as well as biological factors; therefore, an interdisciplinary approach to health promotion and medical care is warranted. Music therapy can contribute to the treatment team's valuable interventions that promote healthy habits as well as alleviate the negative impact of uncomfortable treatment regimens, diseases, or debilitating conditions. This chapter will (1) provide a brief overview of music therapy in the promotion of health and well-being, and (2) describe uses of music therapy to address physical, psychological, and social needs of persons with acute and chronic medical conditions.

MUSIC IN THE PROMOTION OF HEALTH AND WELL-BEING

As noted in Chapter 3, music is associated with emotions (Gfeller, 2002a, 2002b, 2002c; Kwoun, 2005; Langer, 1942; Sloboda & O'Neill, 2001; Zatorre, 2005) and contributes to the integration of society (Gfeller, 2002a; Merriam, 1964). Regular involvement in activities such as music groups, which encourages social involvement and personal control and provides opportunities to increase knowledge, contributes to a sense of well-being and greater cognitive and physical health (Bolton, 1985; Clair, 1996; Coffman & Adamek, 1999; Okun, Olding, & Cohn, 1990).

Wellness programs include an interplay of self-responsibility, nutritional awareness, physical fitness, stress management, and environmental sensitivity (Ghetti, Hama, & Woolrich, 2004; Reuer, 2007). Music therapy and music-based activities (such as participation in community bands, choirs, dances, etc.) can contribute to wellness programming with a variety of populations, including older adults, within the workplace and in schools. Music therapy wellness programs for persons nearing or beyond retirement help maintain quality of life by (1) increasing motivation for and compliance with physical exercise, (2) providing opportunities for meaningful interaction with peers (such as involvement in bands, choirs, and other musical activities), (3) providing an outlet for emotional expression (which can reduce anxiety and stress), and (4) stimulating cognitive functioning (Clair, 1996; Coffman, 2002; Coffman & Adamek, 1999; Ghetti et al., 2004; Reuer, 2007). In addition to helping maintain robust health, wellness programs can also reduce the negative impact of ongoing stress experienced as a result of bereavement, long-term caregiving, or other stressful life events (Clair, 1996; Pelletier, 2004).

In corporations, wellness programs have been initiated to promote healthy lifestyle choices, which can, in turn, increase employee stamina, productivity, and job satisfaction; boost employee morale and creativity; decrease absenteeism and sick leave; and reduce medical costs and insurance premiums. Music in conjunction with exercise can help with persistence of effort. Work-place programs such as group drumming, instrumental and vocal ensembles, and other forms of recreational music can contribute to relaxation, group cohesion, and self-expression, and can reduce stress (Ghetti et al., 2004; Reuer, 2007). Within schools, music therapy programs can be used to encourage physical activity, can act as a carrier of information (such as learning wellness concepts), and can support positive social interaction and cooperation (Ghetti et al., 2004).

A number of studies have investigated the effect of music engagement or listening on wellness. A longitudinal study examining the lifestyles of older adults and incidence of dementia found that ongoing engagement in activities such as playing musical instruments and dancing is associated with lower risk of Alzheimer's disease and other forms of dementia. The authors of the study hypothesized that playing music and dancing provided novel and challenging mental and physical activity that help maintain neurological integrity (Verghese et al., 2003). Older adults who participate in musical activities such as choir, band, or music appreciation have reported enhanced quality of life and social connection (Clair, 1996; Coffman, 2002; Coffman & Adamek, 1999).

Several studies have examined the responses of adults to music listening in conjunction with imagery or cognitive-behavioral strategies (reframing, see Chapter 8). McKinney, Antoni, et al. (1997) and McKinney, Tims, et al. (1997) found that well adults who participated in Guided Imagery and Music (GIM) experienced elevation in depressed mood, reduced blood pressure and levels of hormones associated with stress, and improved immune functioning. Another study revealed that university students and employees reporting some state anxiety, who participated in music-assisted reframing of stress, experienced reduction in anxiety and improved mood state (Kerr, Walsh, & Marshall, 2001). Smith and Joyce (2004) compared relaxation states of college-aged students who were given the choice to (1) listen to music by Mozart, (2) listen to New Age music, or (3) read a popular magazine during three half-hour sessions over three consecutive days. Those in the Mozart listening group reported greater psychological relaxation and less stress than those in the New Age or reading groups.

In conclusion, music listening and music engagement can be a viable part of wellness programs to promote persistence in exercise, expression of emotions, relaxation, stress reduction, and social affiliation. This can support health maintenance, as well as assist persons with stressful life circumstances in coping and maintaining optimal functioning.

While the wellness movement has gained momentum over the past decade, at present, many more music therapists work within hospitals, clinics, and rehabilitation centers that serve persons with acute and chronic medical conditions. The remainder of this chapter addresses music therapy in medical settings.

MEDICAL APPLICATIONS OF MUSIC THERAPY

Over the past half century, there has been a burgeoning interest in music therapy in medical treatment, including numerous research studies. Readers wishing to examine this body of research are encouraged to review documents such as Jayne Standley's "Music Research in Medical Treatment" in the third edition of *Effectiveness of Music Therapy Procedures: Documentation of Research and Clinical Practice* (Standley, 2000b) published by the American Music Therapy Association. Standley's chapter presents a comprehensive listing and analysis of research studies regarding music and medicine up to the 21st century. As that listing of studies and continuing research cited in this chapter indicate, music therapists serve a variety of patients, young and old, in different types of medical settings. In a general hospital, the therapist may work with premature infants, patients undergoing surgical procedures or chemotherapy, women in labor and delivery, burn victims, and persons with acute or chronic illness. In an outpatient facility, a music therapist may assist clients suffering from chronic pain or undergoing tedious or uncomfortable rehabilitation.

Although patient needs vary, depending upon their diagnosis and individual circumstances, within a biopsychosocial approach to medicine, patient needs can be grouped into (1) biological factors, (2) psychological factors, and (3) social factors that are interrelated in a dynamic human system (Sarafino, 2006).

Biological Needs

While this section will focus primarily on physical indicators of health and illness, such as blood pressure or measures of physical pain, it is impossible to establish a neat and tidy distinction between physical health and psychological and social factors; as noted previously, these factors all influence once another. While psychological and social factors will be emphasized to a greater extent later in this chapter, you will notice interactions among these factors throughout this chapter.

The biological needs of medical patients differ depending on their specific diagnosis. However, there are several common foci for music therapy services: (1) improved functioning of the body's physical system (e.g., respiratory, cardiac functioning), and (2) pain management, including physical tolerance for uncomfortable treatment procedures.

Improved functioning of physical systems. Several studies have examined the effects of music therapy in cardiac or pulmonary rehabilitation. Reduced endurance, muscular tension, elevated heart rate and blood pressure, and impaired respiratory functioning are some of the physical characteristics associated with chronic illnesses such as cardiac disease, congestive obstructive pulmonary disease (COPD, which includes emphysema and chronic bronchitis), or asthma. Proper breathing patterns and expansion of the lungs are essential to basic respiratory function, including transmission of adequate oxygen supply to the vital organs. Compromised cardiac and pulmonary function is associated with congestion as well as lack of vitality and endurance. Even a short walk across the room or maintaining the breath support needed for a conversation can be challenging. For some individuals, playing wind instruments or singing can help increase or maintain the level of respiratory function (Behrens, 1982; Bolger, 1984; Engen, 2005; Rudenberg & Royka, 1989; Schwankovsky & Guthrie, 1985; Standley, 1986; Wade, 2002). Studies examining the effect of music plus exercise, vocal exercises and group singing, and music-assisted relaxation training indicate improved persistence in physical exercise, reduced blood pressure, and improved breath management and support (Engen, 2005; Mandel, 1996; Mandel, Hanser, Secic, & Davis, 2007; Metzger, 2004a, 2004b; Wade, 2002).

In some instances, medical treatment includes or is followed by a period of physical therapy and other forms of rehabilitation. For example, initial recovery from a stroke may be followed by many hours of tedious, tiring exercise. Music can enhance the rehabilitation process. Enjoyable or inspirational music can reduce the patient's awareness of the negative aspects of therapy, such as discomfort and monotony. In addition, a strong, rhythmic beat provides a steady auditory cue to help with motor planning (Lucia, 1987; Rudenberg & Royka, 1989; Standley, 1986, 2000b; Staum, 1983; Thaut, 1985). Chapters 6 and 10 describe in detail uses of music in neuromotor rehabilitation. Psychosocial factors associated with chronic disease will be addressed later in this chapter.

The Neonatal Intensive Care Unit (NICU) is another medical setting in which music therapists deal with compromised physical functioning. Premature and high-risk infants, who have immature and highly reactive neurological systems, live in a physical environment (NICU) with a high level of adverse stimulation. While one might presume that a hospital is a quiet and restful place, in fact, medical equipment essential to sustaining life is often noisy, and the lighting required for the medical staff is a far cry from the darkness of the womb. Furthermore, because of numerous physical problems, invasive or uncomfortable medical procedures (such as blood draws or injections), while necessary, result in stress (Hanson-Abromeit, 2003; Standley & Whipple, 2003).

One of the tools that music therapists use to counterbalance the cacophony of beeps, buzzes, and staff conversations in the NICU is music. Music has rhythmic, melodic, and harmonic organization that makes it more pleasant and soothing for infants than many other sounds (Standley, 2001a, 2001b, 2001c). An appropriate choice of music can promote neurological development, as well as mask the aversive sounds of the NICU. In cultures worldwide, caregivers use rhythmic lullabies paired with rocking and cuddling to sooth infants and to establish a parent-child bond. Music therapists select music with appropriate structural features, such as those found in lullabies (relatively consistent tempo, melodic range, and dynamics played at a suitable decibel level), that do not overstimulate the fragile infant. The interventions must be individualized for each infant's needs and responses, and comfort and calming stimulation should be balanced with stimuli that encourage developmental growth (Hanson-Abromeit, 2003). Standley (2001a, 2001b, 2001c) advocates three primary uses of music therapy in the NICU, which promote growth and development: (1) music to mask (cover up) stress-inducing environmental stimuli; (2) music to assist neurological maturation and teach tolerance to stimulation; and (3) music to reinforce nonnutritive sucking, which helps the baby prepare for feeding (Standley & Whipple, 2003).

> Kim, the music therapist on the NICU, has been called in to assist one of the nurses who is going to take a blood draw from Collin, a premature infant of 30 weeks gestational age. Kim's job is to help Collin, who is already pretty reactive and fragile, to tolerate this procedure. Kim begins quietly humming and singing prior to the blood draw and continues the music, along with firm touch to the infant's head, feet, or trunk. This helps soothe little Collin and also provides a calming environment for the staff completing the blood draw. Kim remains with Collin during and after the procedure, providing the live auditory and tactile stimulation based on Collin's responses (behavioral cues), until he becomes calm and progresses to a sleep state.

Carefully selected music is an appropriate form of stimulation that can help babies to self-regulate and improve on a number of physiological and behavioral variables (Hanson-Abromeit, 2003; Standley & Whipple, 2003). Research examining the use of sung or recorded lullabies indicates significant improvements for length of hospital stay, weight gain, behavior state, oxygen saturation, heart rate, nonnutritive sucking rate, and feeding rate (Caine, 1991; Cassidy & Standley, 1995; Coleman, Pratt, Stoddard, Gerstmann, & Abel, 1997; Collins & Kuck, 1991; Hanson-Abromeit, 2003; Standley, 1998a, 1998b, 2000a, 2001a, 2001b, 2001c, 2003; Standley & Whipple, 2003). It is important to note, however, that premature infants are hypersensitive to stimuli, and therefore the therapist needs to be alert to cues of overstimulations, such as disengagement or particular gestures and facial movements (Hanson-Abromeit, 2003; Standley, 2001a, 2001b).

Giving birth to a premature or high-risk infant results in considerable stress for the parents, who may feel guilt, helplessness, anxiety, grief, and lack of preparation for the financial and parental challenges that lie ahead. The noisy, sterile, and unfamiliar atmosphere of the NICU can add to feelings of disorientation and alienation. Parents may also feel insecure about how to handle or interact with their tiny, fragile baby (Whipple, 2000). Music therapists may work with families to help them interact more positively and confidently with their babies. This can include encouraging parents who may be self-conscious about their voices to hum or sing favorite songs and lullabies, while also coaching them on proper tactile stimulation. The therapist may also assist the mother in recording her own lullabies, which can be used to sooth her baby when she is away from the NICU (Hanson-Abromeit, 2003; Standley, 2001a, 2001b, 2001c).

The music therapist can also counsel the parents on the transition to the home environment and uses of music for comfort and bonding at home (Hanson-Abromeit, 2003). Whipple (2000) examined the effect of parent training in music and multimodal stimulation on the quantity and quality of parent-neonate interactions. The infants of those parents who received training demonstrated fewer stress behaviors, and the appropriateness of parent actions and responses were significantly greater than for parents without training. The infants in the parent-training group also had shorter length of hospitalization; average daily weight gain was greater (though not statistically significant).

> *Kim, the music therapist for NICU, works directly with the premature infants to provide appropriate stimulation and to help them achieve calm behavioral states. She also provides consultation and support to the families, who are often anxious and worried about how to interact with their tiny offspring. Today, Kim noticed a grandmother holding her granddaughter, now 35 weeks gestational age. Although Mrs. Barrigan was trying to calm her hungry granddaughter, Kylie, both baby and grandma appeared stressed; Mrs. Barrigan kept shifting Kylie in her arms as she sought a comfortable position. In response to grandmother's actions, Kylie was fussing, extending her arms, and experiencing oxygen desaturation. Kim introduced some humming, gradually progressing to lullabies to facilitate infant calming. Kylie responded by tucking closer to her grandmother, bringing her hands to her face, opening her eyes, and quietly attending to the stimulation. In turn, Mrs. Barrigan responded by holding the infant quietly, gently rocking the child, smiling, and engaging in quiet singing, too. What a special moment for grandma and grandchild.*

Pain reduction and tolerance for treatment procedures. Pain is a complex phenomenon (Sarafino, 2006). It can be acute (i.e., of short duration) or chronic, sudden, or gradual. It may be sensed in a location far removed from the location of injury, and it can vary in quality (stabbing, dull, throbbing, searing, etc.). Pain may stem from tissue damage and insult to nerve endings, but some pain cannot be explained simply in physical terms. Therefore, although it is considered a biological aspect of health care, pain is an excellent example of the biopsychosocial model of illness, for psychological (emotional and cognitive) and social factors are known to contribute to the severity of perceived pain (Anderson & Masur, 1983; Gracely, McGrath, & Dubner, 1978; Jacox, 1977; Sarafino, 2006). For example, pain that is associated with a life-threatening illness can be more difficult to tolerate than pain associated with a nonmalignant disorder or discomfort associated with beneficial treatment.

Anxiety, tension, fear, and perceived loss of control can accompany and exacerbate feelings of distress and pain. Anxiety and tension contribute to the perception of pain in several ways. These negative emotions can lead to increased muscle tension, which, in turn, can create greater pressure on already sensitive nerve endings (Jacox, 1977). Tension can also interfere with normally relaxed breathing patterns and cause deoxygenation (oxygen deficits) in muscle tissue (Clark, McCorkle, & Williams, 1981). Moreover, anxiety or fear can heighten a person's attention to the pain, thus increasing its perceived severity.

Many aspects of pain perception can be explained by a principle known as the Gate Control Theory of Pain (Melzack & Wall, 1965, 1982; Sarafino, 2006). According to this theory, actual physical insult occurs in nerve endings throughout the body, but awareness and interpretation of the stimulation takes place in the central nervous system (CNS). A neural "gate" can be opened or closed to varying degrees, thus modulating the incoming pain signals before they reach the brain (Sarafino, 2006). When a pain signal enters the spinal cord and the gate is open, transmission cells send the pain impulses freely. But if the gate is closed, the strength of the pain signal to the brain will be modulated. The extent to which the gate is open or closed depends on (1) the amount of noxious stimulation (the more pain, the more active the pain fibers), (2) the amount of sensation in other peripheral fibers (competing stimuli such as massage or rubbing), and (3) the messages that descend from the brain. The effects of some brain processes, such as anxiety, tension, or depression, can open or close the gate for all or some types of inputs.

The Gate Control Theory of Pain, developed in the 1960s, has been upheld by numerous research studies over the past few decades and continues to be one of the most influential and important theories of pain perception. In particular, it helps explain the tremendous importance of psychosocial variables, as well as addressing biological aspects of pain (Sarafino, 2006).

How might this theory be illustrated in everyday life? Even while pain stimuli are occurring, the central nervous system is taking in other stimuli as well: the sound of people talking, the smells in the room, a program on television, and car horns honking in the street. Because the CNS can process only limited amounts of information at any given time, these sensations compete with the pain stimulus for attention. As a result of the limited capacity of conscious awareness, our perception of pain is reduced to the extent that we direct attention to other internal or external stimuli (i.e., conversation, music, etc.) (Farthing, Venturino, & Brown, 1984). In other words, if conscious awareness (attention) can be focused on a strong, positive stimulus rather than the pain, the perception of pain can thus be attenuated (Anderson & Masur, 1983; Farthing et al., 1984; Jacox, 1977; Melzack & Wall, 1982; Sarafino, 2006).

> *Nine-year old Carlos is home from school today because he has strep throat. He hates being sick! He hates the fiery feeling in his throat and it hurts whenever he swallows. His forehead is pounding, and he feels rotten all over. How can he possibly endure this for another minute? After school, his friend George stops by to visit and tells him all about the big event at school today. Evidently some of the frogs got out of the classroom terrarium and started jumping all around the room. The girls were all screaming, and the teacher was racing around in her high heels and nice dress, trying to catch the frogs. It was complete chaos!*

> *Carlos's mother has just stopped by his room to see how he is feeling and is surprised to see her suffering son giggling and enjoying his company. His pain, for now, seems bearable. The stronger and entertaining stimulus of George's story of the frogs at school (which acts as a form of distraction) has won the battle for attention from Carlos's central nervous system.*

A number of methods of pain management based on the Gate Control Theory of Pain have been developed, including distraction (e.g., video games, movies, stories), focus on positive stimuli or interesting activities (e.g., conversation, mental tasks such as solving a puzzle), massage, relaxation, biofeedback, exercise, and rest (Anderson & Masur, 1983; Jacox, 1977; Sarafino, 2006). In the clinical setting, some methods for managing pain are more easily provided than others.

Music is one stimulus that can be used in conjunction with all of these methods with little expense or inconvenience (Gfeller, Logan, & Walker, 1990; Standley, 2000b). Music therapists work with clients to manage or alleviate pain that is either acute (occurs suddenly and is short in duration) or chronic. In addition, the source of pain may be a disease or condition, or a treatment procedure that, while necessary for well-being, inflicts pain or discomfort.

Music therapy interventions for pain control. One of the common uses of music therapy in medical care is pain management. Pain is a symptom of many acute and chronic illnesses or conditions, but it can also be an undesirable side effect of life-saving treatments. While pain can be an important warning that medical help is needed, pain can also interfere with compliance with medical procedures (Skole & Krevsky, 2006) and rehabilitation, and it can slow recovery (Good et al., 2001).

Uncontrolled pain that is prolonged can dominate the lives of individuals, impairing their general functioning, ability to work, and social and emotional adjustment (Sarafino, 2006).

In today's world of sophisticated medications and treatments, why would the use of music as an aid to pain control be of value? First, because perception of pain is influenced by psychological and social as well as physical factors, it is important to address all factors (Colwell, 1997; Gfeller et al., 1990; Godley, 1987; Jacox, 1977; Sarafino, 2006; Standley, 1986). Research indicates that the music can reduce patient anxiety, which in turn can enhance the effectiveness of **anesthetics** (a drug that results in loss of sensation) and **analgesics** (pain killers). This translates to fewer or smaller doses of sedatives or pain killers, which in turn can facilitate recovery. This can translate into reduced length of hospitalization (Good et al., 2001; Skole & Krevsky, 2006; Standley, 1986, 2000b).

Another reason that music therapy may be used to help control pain is that some medical conditions cannot be remedied through surgical methods, and analgesics may not provide adequate relief over extended periods of time. For example, someone with cancer may suffer severe pain and receive only partial relief from medication (Sarafino, 2006). Furthermore, some patients object to the confusion or other negative side effects that accompany strong narcotics.

Maintaining mental clarity is of particular concern for patients in hospice care (for more information about hospice, see Chapter 12). Hospice or palliative care consists of the reduction or abatement of pain and other troubling symptoms experienced by terminally ill patients (Munro, 1984). In preparation for death, many individuals feel the need to secure the financial welfare of their families and to come to terms with feelings about their own mortality. In order to attend to these issues, mental clarity is important. Therefore, the use of heavy medication may be undesirable.

In some instances, it is important to reduce the amount of anesthesia administered during surgery, especially if the standard dose might suppress respiratory functioning or cause mental sluggishness. For example, it is important to avoid the latter problem in outpatient surgeries. Childbirth is another area for which an adjustment is indicated, because less anesthesia is considered preferable for the baby's well-being (Browning, 2001; Clark, 1986; Clark et al., 1981; Hanser, Larson, & O'Connell, 1983; Pelletier, 2004).

Techniques that make use of the power of the human mind to reduce the perception of pain are called **cognitive pain control strategies** (Sarafino, 2006). Cognitive pain control methods are not intended to eliminate traditional pharmacological painkillers. However, these strategies can help reduce the required dosage, which is generally preferable; there are also circumstances in which medication is contraindicated (Scartelli, 1989). Consequently, cognitive means for reducing pain are often beneficial.

There are several ways that music can be used in conjunction with cognitive pain control strategies to reduce the perception of pain: (1) as a stimulus for active focus or distraction, (2) to facilitate a relaxation response, (3) as a masking agent, (4) as an information agent, and (5) as a positive environmental stimulus.

Music as a stimulus for active focus or distraction is a common method of reducing pain perception. Active focus requires to a positive stimulus, while distraction is the drawing of attention away from an aversive stimulus. Music can be used as a positive and competing stimulus to reduce attention to the negative aspects of pain or an uncomfortable medical procedure (such as outpatient surgery, injections, cardiac testing, or dental procedures), and to put focus onto positive stimuli. This approach is based on the Gate Control Theory of Pain. According to Clark et al. (1981), the music is an active focal point, and the patient is coached and encouraged to focus on and follow the music, thereby taking a more active role in his or her pain management. When used as a distracter or focal point, the selected music must hold the interest and attention of the patient. It should be age-appropriate and reflect the patient's preferred repertoire or general musical styles (Clark et al., 1981; Gfeller et al., 1990; Godley, 1987; Mitchell & MacDonald, 2006; Noguchi, 2006; Standley, 1986, 2000b; Whipple, 2003).

> *Kate is a music therapist at Mercy Hospital. One of the services she provides is helping expectant mothers to prepare for childbirth. She joins the Lamaze teacher at a number of Lamaze classes and explains to the mothers-to-be how they can use music to help manage their pain during labor and delivery. Kate explains that music can act as a distracter or focal point to help reduce the intensity of the pain. Because each of the expectant mothers in the class has different musical tastes, Kate knows that one kind of music will not work for everyone. If the music is being used as a focal point or for distraction, it needs to hold the attention of the individual. That might mean upbeat music rather than slow or relaxing music.*

> *Kate meets with each mother and has them fill out an inventory that describes what kinds of music they enjoy, including particular favorites. Then Kate works with each mother to select music for an individualized tape for the delivery room. After each of the expectant mothers has her childbirth tape ready, Kate works with the group to practice how they can use distraction or focus as a pain management strategy in preparation for the big event.*

Undergoing medical procedures can be anxiety-provoking for individuals, even when there is no clear threat to life (Lepage, Drolet, Girard, Grenier, & DeGagne, 2001). In some cases, the procedure itself is awkward and uncomfortable, or results in pain. In addition, procedures often take place in settings that are unfamiliar or sterile, and the medical procedures may undermine one's sense of control. There may also be uncertainty regarding the outcome. These issues can contribute to fear, anxiety, and stress.

The use of music to reduce the pain or discomfort in surgery or a treatment procedure has been documented in a number of medical settings, including dental treatment (Gardener & Licklider, 1959; Gfeller et al., 1990; Monsey, 1960; Standley, 1986); labor and delivery (Browning, 2001; Burt & Korn, 1964; Clark, 1986; Clark et al., 1981; Hanser et al., 1983; Standley, 1986, 2000b); during colonoscopies (Skole & Krevsky, 2006); blood donation (Bonk, France, & Taylor, 2001); debridement (cleaning and dressing of burn wounds, which can be very painful) in burn units (Daveson, 1999; Fratianne et al., 2001; Tan, Yowler, Super, & Fratianne, 2008); in chronic pain programs (Colwell, 1997; Godley, 1987; Siedlecki & Good, 2006); in pediatric units to reduce distress response to injections and other procedures (Daveson, 1999; Malone, 1996; Whitehead-Pleaux, Zebrowski, Baryza, & Sheridan, 2007; Whipple, 2003); and in surgical units (Allen et al., 2001; Ayoub, Rizk, Yaacoub, Gaal, & Kain, 2005; Lepage et al., 2001; Standley, 2000b; Walters, 1996).

Research shows that music, when used in the postsurgical unit, was more effective than pain medication alone, and it reduced required dosage of pain medication (Good et al., 2001; Locsin, 1981). The benefits of using music included physical benefits such as decreased use of sedatives (Ayoub et al., 2005; Good et al., 2001; Lepage et al., 2001; Locsin, 1981; Skole & Krevsky, 2006; Standley, 1986, 2000b); lower heart rate, blood pressure, or cardiac work load (Allen et al., 2001; Standley, 2000b); as well as psychological effects such as reduced anxiety or distress (Lepage et al., 2001; Skole & Krevsky, 2006; Standley, 2000b; Whitehead-Pleaux et al., 2007), and reduction in dizziness, nausea, or other negative symptoms (Bonk et al., 2001). Reduced anxiety helps patients to relax, which can reduce the required dosage for sedatives.

Although music as a distraction or focal point can be effective, research has shown that no single pain control technique works for every person in every circumstance (Anderson & Masur, 1983; Jacox, 1977; Sarafino, 2006; Standley, 2000b). For example, distraction can be especially useful as a technique for people who like to ignore or avoid the procedure as it occurs. However, other people referred to in pain research as "monitors," tend to feel less anxious if they can receive continual information about what is happening and why (Sarafino, 2006). For that kind of individual, distraction may be less effective. Another limitation of active focusing is that it requires sustained concentration. If the patient experiences severe or prolonged pain, fatigue eventually sets in and reduces the effectiveness (Standley, 2000b). Other strategies must then be engaged (Jacox, 1977). Therefore, therapists assisting in pain management should be skilled in a variety of pain control methods (Sarafino, 2006; Standley, 2000b).

Music as a cue for relaxation response is another way that music can be used to manage pain. Because relaxation as a response is considered incompatible with tension, muscular relaxation is another approach that can reduce pain (Browning, 2001; Clark et al., 1981; Colwell, 1997; Godley, 1987; Jacox, 1977; Scartelli, 1989; Standley, 1986, 2000b). As relaxation occurs, the patient experiences reduced muscle tension, along with deeper and more even respiration. This reduces muscular pressure on nerve endings and reinstates a steady supply of oxygen to muscle tissue. In addition, relaxation can reduce anxiety and fear, psychological correlates that can make the pain or treatment seem more intolerable (Godley, 1987; Jacox, 1977; Pelletier, 2004; Robb, Nichols, Rutan, Bishop, & Parker, 1995; Standley, 1986, 2000b).

Music can be used in conjunction with relaxation techniques, both with or without imagery (Bonny, 1989; Browning, 2001; Clark et al., 1981; Colwell, 1997; Daveson, 1999; Edwards, 1998; Fratianne et al., 2001; Godley, 1987; Good et al., 2001; Jacobsen, 1934; Robb et al., 1995; Scartelli 1989; Sahler, Hunter, & Liesveld, 2003; Standley, 2000b; Tan et al., 2008). The music therapist assesses the patient's musical preference, and together they select music that is pleasurable and promotes relaxation. For example, a slow, steady beat can prompt even, deep respiration. Music that evokes vivid images can guide thoughts to pleasant scenes such as serene meadows or a bank of fluffy white clouds.

One limitation to relaxation strategies is that the techniques must be learned and practiced over a period of time in order to be effective (Clark et al., 1981; Godley, 1987; Jacox, 1977; Pelletier, 2004; Scartelli, 1989). Therefore, these strategies are used less frequently in cases of acute pain or singular treatment procedures (such as a tooth extraction). If, however, lingering pain (as in cases of cancer or chronic back pain) or repeated treatments are anticipated, or if adequate preparation time is available (as in childbirth), the patient can learn to relax using music in conjunction with other methods, such as progressive relaxation or guided imagery. The role of the music therapist includes not only selecting and providing music, but also training and coaching the client on relaxation techniques (Browning, 2001; Clark et al., 1981; Godley, 1987; Standley, 1986, 2000b).

Music as a cue for relaxation can be beneficial in a variety of treatment settings, including chronic pain control (Colwell, 1997; Godley, 1987; Kruse, 2003; Standley,

2000b); rehabilitation programs for physically disabled clients with muscle tension (Scartelli, 1982, 1984); labor and delivery (Browning, 2001; Clark, 1986; Clark et al., 1981; Hanser et al., 1983; Pelletier, 2004; Standley, 2000b); medical-surgical units, including pediatric surgical units (Robb et al., 1995; Siegel, 1983; Standley, 2000b); and in burn units during debridement (Daveson, 1999; Edwards, 1998; Fratianne et al., 2001; Tan et al., 2008).

Let's go back to Kate's program for expectant mothers.

In addition to teaching them about music as a distracter or focal point, Kate also explains that music can be used in conjunction with relaxation techniques. Kate will work with the patient to identify music that will be relaxing, which can help to induce steady and deep breathing, and that may be useful in eliciting beautiful and relaxing images. Because no single pain management technique works for all people in all situations, Kate's two-pronged approach—giving the mothers music for distraction or focus, and other music to promote relaxation—gives the expectant mothers a menu of pain control strategies they can chose from as needed during delivery.

Music as a masking agent is yet another way that music can help manage pain. A number of factors contribute to fear and anxiety during medical treatment. Some are external elements, such as the sounds produced by equipment, or cries of pain from other patients. For example, some people find the sound of the dental drill anxiety-producing (Gfeller et al., 1990; Rankin & Harris, 1984). As the drill whirs and whines, the patient's tension mounts. In hospital settings, the clanging, buzzing, or beeping of equipment or the cries of other patients can be unnerving (Clark et al., 1981). Music played through headphones can mask some of these unpleasant sounds and therefore avert some of the patient's anxiety that is caused by outside agents (Gfeller et al., 1990; Standley, 1986, 2000b). Music has also been used effectively in pediatric units to assist tired and anxious parents trying to relax and cope as their youngsters undergo long and uncertain days of testing and treatment (Wolfe & Woolsey, 2003).

Music as an information agent has been documented as an effective strategy for pain control. One of the cognitive interventions believed to reduce negative psychological correlates of pain is the provision of information regarding the experience of pain during medical procedures (Anderson & Masur, 1983; Jacox, 1977; Sarafino, 2006; Standley, 2000b). For example, it is common for nurses or doctors to explain or interpret physical sensations (e.g., "You will feel a short sting, followed by some pressure") when they administer injections as a way of reducing the anxiety about the procedure. Preparing an individual for a medical procedure such as surgery can assist in alleviation of fear and can facilitate postprocedural recovery (Sarafino, 2006).

Music as a carrier of information has proven beneficial toward this end (Chetta, 1981; Whipple, 2003). For example, preoperative teaching sessions for hospitalized children can include songs imparting information about surgery and the various people (doctors, nurses) who will be encountered.

> *One of Ginny's responsibilities at the hospital is to help children in pediatrics to prepare for surgery or other uncomfortable procedures. In her music therapy cart that she wheels to pediatrics, she has some musical instruments as well as puppets dressed liked doctors, nurses, and other kinds of medical personnel. Kyle, a 4-year-old who is scheduled for surgery the next day, is on Ginny's list to receive music therapy today. She goes to his room and puts on a puppet show with the medical puppets, in which she introduces the primary personnel that Kyle will meet, and the sorts of basic procedures they will do as they prepare Kyle for surgery. Ginny sings the song, "Who Are the People in the Hospital?" as she introduces each puppet, and each special puppet is introduced with a particular song that Ginny has written. Although this looks like play time, specialists in pediatric care have found that such play can make a significant difference in helping children adjust to the hospital and procedures.*

Music as a positive environmental stimulus brings warmth and a sense of normalcy to medical settings. A treatment room may be filled with unpleasant smells (such as the odor of disinfectant), large ominous-looking equipment, and bustling medical personnel who do not always have the time to establish a rapport with and address the psychological concerns of each patient. Especially for young children, an environment so radically different from home and school can create fears and anxiety (Barrickman, 1989; Clark et al., 2006; Ferrer, 2007; Kruse, 2003; Marley, 1984; Robb, 2003; Rudenberg, 1985; Sarafino, 2006; Schwankovsky & Guthrie, 1985; Whipple, 2003). Furthermore, the patients are frequently the passive recipients of treatment intervention, with little control over their schedules or even their own bodies. This lack of control is another source of stress and can exacerbate perception of pain (Gfeller et al., 1990; Langer, 1983; Lefcourt, 1982; Meinhart & McCaffery, 1983; Sarafino, 2006).

Even though perceived loss of control may be unavoidable in some medical circumstances, such as during chemotherapy or other medical procedures, patients can reestablish some control and introduce familiarity into the environment with access to preferred music (Barrickman, 1989; Clark et al., 2006; Ferrer, 2007; Gfeller et al., 1990; Robb, 2003; Whipple, 2003; Whitehead-Pleaux et al., 2007). In addition, music as an aesthetic medium provides positive sensory stimulation in an otherwise sterile, isolated, or seemingly hostile environment. For example, Christenberry (1979) reported that burn patients, as a result of isolation policies aimed at infection control, often lack appropriate sensory stimulation. As a result, patients may turn to inappropriate internal self-stimulation (i.e., hallucinations) or become less tolerant of the medical procedures. Song writing as well as music engagement has been helpful to pediatric patients in burn units who are in isolation, or during the stress and pain of debridement (Daveson, 1999; Edwards, 1998; Fratianne et al., 2001; Tan et al., 2008). Music provides a positive form of sensory stimulation, an agent for relaxation, and engagement in this sterile, isolated environment.

The positive influence of music in a medical environment can be demonstrated not only through psychological measures of perceived well-being, but also through physiological changes. Several studies comparing medical treatment with and without music have demonstrated reduction in blood pressure or heart rate in the music condition (Allen et al., 2001; Bonny, 1983; Locsin, 1981; Oyama et al., 1983).

Biochemical aspects of the pain experience are being researched to better understand how pain functions and how it can be reduced. Recent studies have shown that the human body responds to pain or stress by producing various chemicals. Some of these substances are a byproduct of pain or stress. Others, like endogenous opioids (such as endorphins), are chemicals that the body produces that actually help to reduce discomfort (Sarafino, 2006; Scartelli, 1989). These chemicals seem to function in a similar way to reduce pain as do drugs such as morphine. Preliminary research (Goldstein, 1980; Rider, Floyd, & Kirkpatrick, 1985; Tanioka et al., 1985) suggests that musical stimuli may influence biochemical production and subsequently reduce discomfort. While further research is needed to better understand this avenue of inquiry, this avenue of inquiry holds important implications for future treatment interventions.

In summary, there are a number of ways that music therapy can be used in managing pain and the psychological stress that accompanies some medical conditions or procedures. As noted earlier, one strategy will not be equally effective with all patients, or even under different circumstances with the same person. Some pain management strategies are more or less effective with particular types of pain (e.g., severe vs. moderate, sudden vs. slow onset, acute vs. chronic, etc.), in particular circumstances, or with particular types of patients, and should therefore be used judiciously in order to provide greatest benefit (Pelletier, 2004; Sarafino, 2006; Standley, 2000b).

To illustrate this point, the medical team of a comprehensive burn care center conducted several research studies to compare the effectiveness of different music therapy interventions at different points in debridement, the process in which the old dressings covering burned skin are removed, dead skin is removed from the burn site, and fresh dressings are applied. The process of debridement, while medically necessary, is associated with significant pain and anxiety (Fratianne et al., 2001; Tan et al., 2008). Some questions were answered in an initial study (Fratianne et al., 2001), which paved the way for more refined analyses in a follow-up study (Tan et al., 2008).

More specifically, the studies (Fratianne et al., 2001; Tan et al., 2008) were designed to assess the relative benefits of (1) Music Based Imagery (MBI), which involves relaxation techniques paired with music and other sensory imagery; and (2) Music Alternate Engagement (MAE), which engages the patient in active music making (such as active listening, singing, and instrumental playing). These two types of music therapy were applied at three points in the debridement process: (1) preparation for the dressing change, (2) during the dressing change, and (3) after the dressing change. Because pain and tolerance for a procedure is a complex phenomenon, the research team used multiple measures to assess the effectiveness of these interventions on three different aspects that reflect tolerance for the procedure: (1) self-report of pain, (2) self-report of anxiety, and (3) a muscle tension inventory (as collected through behavioral observation). Through these two studies of music-based pain management (Fratianne et al., 2001; Tan et al., 2008), the researchers learned that particular types of MAE might be more effective in reducing pain, anxiety, and muscle tension during debridement, and that MBI was most efficient in decreasing pain and muscle tension after debridement.

Most clinicians will not be engaged in systematic research each time they use music-based pain control. However, these and other studies emphasize the importance of selecting interventions carefully and using sensitive clinical measures to evaluate treatment benefit for individual patients.

Psychological and Social Needs

Acute and chronic medical conditions have an impact not only on a person's physical well-being, but also on psychological and social functioning. This, in turn, can influence recovery from and ability to cope with the illness (Christenberry 1979; Colwell, 1997; Godley, 1987; Munro, 1984; Rudenberg & Royka, 1989; Robb, 1999, 2003; Sarafino, 2006; Schwankovsky & Guthrie, 1985). According to Schwankovsky and Guthrie (1985), a person with an acute or chronic medical condition characteristically has a number of psychological and social needs:

1. Adapting to the illness and its limitations
2. Making adjustments within the family unit
3. Adjusting to the medical environment
4. Learning and using appropriate coping mechanisms

5. Reducing fear and anxiety about the illness and prescribed treatment
6. Maintaining an environment as close to normal as possible (normalization)
7. Continuing cognitive and social development
8. Preventing or overcoming developmental delays resulting from the illness or the treatment
9. Engaging in physical activity
10. Facing issues related to one's own mortality

Some of these concerns are direct byproducts of the illness itself. For example, a patient with a respiratory illness may have difficulty maintaining enough breath to converse or walk even small distances (Engen, 2005; Mandel, 1996, Mandel et al., 2007; Metzger, 2004a, 2004b). Other needs result from the subsequent loss of independence, normal routine, and quality of life that accompany hospitalization or convalescence (Engen, 2005; Robb, 2003). For example, a patient hospitalized for eye surgery may be unable to read, drive, or work. These limitations could lead to increased dependence on others for financial support, transportation, and activities of daily living (Sarafino, 2006).

The music therapist can help the patient adjust to these limitations through (1) provision of normalizing activities that promote social, motor, and cognitive development; and (2) provision of psychological and social support through music activities that explore expression of feelings related to the illness and that foster social interaction with staff, peers, and family.

Normalization. Normalization is the process of integrating objects, events, and interactions that resemble everyday life (are normal) into the medical environment. Patients both young and old can benefit from normalization of the hospital environment. However, given the developmental differences between children and adults, the types of intervention will differ. First, let us consider normalization in the pediatric (children's medicine) setting.

Normalization in pediatric care is an important element of quality care for children. In a normal environment, a child's typical day includes school, playtime, other social events, and household responsibilities. Children interact with their parents, teachers, siblings, and peers. In contrast, a hospitalized child spends many hours in an unfamiliar bed in an unfamiliar room with unfamiliar adults who administer injections, intravenous (IV) lines, and x-rays (Robb, 2003). The pediatric environment often has many unfamiliar noises (such as the sounds of medical equipment and ringing phones), and there can be long hours of waiting and worry for children and their parents, as well as anxiety associated with unforeseeable outcomes of treatment (Robb, 2003; Whipple, 2003; Wolfe & Woolsey, 2003). When medical care extends over many weeks or months, the youngster may have limited exposure to family members and other children. The typical routine such as going to school, participating in soccer, and feeding the dog is disrupted.

According to Robb (2003), the hospital setting can undermine a child's feeling of competence (successful mastery over the environment), need for autonomy (self-determination), and relatedness (feeling securely connected with others). The unfamiliar and seemingly unpredictable hospital environment restricts the child's normal opportunities to make choices and act as his or her own agent. Children may be unavoidably separated from the support of family and friends. In response to these stressors, children may respond with disaffection (withdrawal, avoidance, passivity, resistance, alienation) and negative emotions such as boredom, anxiety, fear, and anger (Barrickman, 1989; Robb, 2003; Schwankovsky & Guthrie, 1985; Whipple, 2003). The disruption in normal life can interrupt cognitive, personality, and social development (Robb, 2003).

Robb (2003) has proposed a Contextual Support Model of Music Therapy, which could influence coping in two ways: 1) buffer the effects of stress and reduce psychological distress, and (2) influence how effectively a child copes. Through appropriately structured sessions, music therapy interventions can increase successful mastery over the environment, support a sense of autonomy by providing opportunities for choice and direct involvement, and promote relatedness and rapport.

Hospitalization is not a typical childhood experience, but musical activity is. Music is not only a part of normal childhood, but it can provide order and predictability. Familiar songs and musical games from the child's home environment can bring a known entity into an unfamiliar environment. The predictable structure of music (such as repeating choruses in songs) can be balanced with ample opportunity for the child to make choices and decisions about the musical instruments, tempo, lyrics, rhythm, and other elements of the session. Making music with peers, family, and staff encourages relatedness and an opportunity for self-expression and genuine acceptance (Daveson, 2001; Edwards, 1998; Froelich, 1984; Kennelly, 2001; Robb, 2003; Whipple, 2003).

As music therapy interventions are developed, they should take into account the cognitive development, psychosocial development, and coping style of each child. For example, preschool children, in particular, can be susceptible to the rigors of hospitalization (Robb, 1999). Children in this age range tend to have many misconceptions about illness and medical treatment. Separation and stranger anxiety are also problematic. For adolescents, medical restrictions can conflict with much-desired independence and autonomy (Kennelly, 2001). Music therapists need to consider the developmental levels of each child when establishing treatment goals, objectives, and interventions. Because music can be enjoyed by any age group, and because it can be used in a flexible manner, music is a valuable tool for normalization of the medical environment. Activities designed to promote normalization can be categorized into several areas of a typical childhood experience: (1) play and physical activity, (2) social interaction with peers, and (3) cognitive growth. Each of these areas is briefly discussed in the following section.

Play and physical activities are natural means through which young children explore the environment, express thoughts and feelings, and learn new skills (Froelich, 1984; Robb, 1999, 2003; Schwankovsky & Guthrie, 1985). Learning musical games, playing with musical toys (windup animals, mobiles, and rhythm band instruments), singing, and moving to music are all common childhood activities (Barrickman, 1989; Robb, 2003). Even toddlers can enjoy these experiences, given that music involves sensory and motor experiences within the developmental capability of the young child (Barrickman, 1989; McDonald & Simons, 1989; Robb, 1999). Familiar childhood songs, such as "Old MacDonald," the "Itsy-bitsy Spider," and "London Bridge," seem like old friends in a strange environment (Whipple, 2000). According to Marley (1984), musical games and activities reduce stress-related behaviors in infants and toddlers.

Unfortunately, illness or medical treatments can impede normal childhood motor activity. Children with chronic respiratory or heart conditions may lack the physical strength and vitality to run and play. Children recovering from surgery or orthopedic interventions may have diminished mobility due to IV tubes, traction, or casts. But physical activity need not end altogether. The music therapist can involve the child in music and movement activities to the extent physically possible. For example, a patient with one arm immobilized because of a cast or an IV can play a rhythm instrument vigorously with the other arm. Children confined to bed or wheelchairs can participate in action songs or finger plays (children's songs that use finger motions to help illustrate the story in the song, such as "Where Is Thumbkin?" or "Two Little Blackbirds") that encourage upper body or facial movement (Barrickman, 1989).

Music therapy also provides **structured social interaction.** In nursery schools all over the world, children hold hands, sing, and move together during music activities. Even a strong-willed 2-year-old can be drawn into a group activity featuring a favorite musical game (McDonald & Simons, 1989). Music, traditionally a medium for social involvement, when introduced into the medical milieu, can increase social interaction (Gfeller, 2002a, 2002b, 2002c). Group singing, rhythm band activities, action songs, and finger plays provide opportunities to cooperate, become aware of others, and share ideas. Even shy children can participate nonverbally by playing rhythm instruments, clapping, or performing actions to songs (Barrickman, 1989; Robb, 2003; Whipple, 2003).

Because a serious illness can interfere with psychosocial development and disrupt regular school attendance, **cognitive and academic development** can suffer. The music therapist can introduce or reinforcing academic and pre-academic concepts (colors, numbers, shapes, and other knowledge learned prior to kindergarten) through music activities that are fun and age-appropriate. Many childhood songs ("Mary Has a Red Dress," "The Wheels on the Bus," "Old MacDonald," etc.) teach information about colors, shapes, community helpers, animals, and other concepts learned in preschool and elementary classrooms (Barrickman, 1989; Robb, 2003; Schwankovsky & Guthrie, 1985).

Normalization is also important for adult patients. The cries and screams of a young child that can accompany medical treatment are clear indicators that the child is afraid. But we should not assume from the relatively quiet demeanor of an adult that all is well. Adults, too, have negative reactions to a sterile hospital room, unfamiliar medical procedures, and disruption in lifestyle (Clark et al., 2006; Engen, 2005; Ferrer, 2007; Mandel, 1996; Sarafino, 2006). Normalization of the hospital or rehabilitation environment for adult patients is fostered by providing social opportunities and meaningful leisure activities adapted to fit the individual's level of functioning. For example, group singing or improvisation on musical instruments encourages socialization among patients or between a patient and his or her family (Engen, 2005; Mandel, 1996; Munro, 1984; Standley, 1986). The tedium of long-term hospitalization or restricted movement can be ameliorated through involvement in musical leisure activities. Small, portable instruments, such as synthesizers, autoharps, or kalimbas, can be learned in a short period of time, even by patients with minimal musical training (Munro, 1984).

Psychological and social support for chronic and life-threatening health problems. Chronic or life-threatening diseases such as **heart or pulmonary diseases** and **cancer** can be psychologically devastating and require patients and their families to make permanent behavioral, social, and emotional adjustments. Patients have to adjust to physical threats such as pain, disfigurement, and functional ability. They also experience psychological distress such as anxiety about the future, depression, and anger. Furthermore, the restrictions imposed by their condition can alter normal social routines and environmental circumstances (Sarafino, 2006).

Music therapy can be used to promote recovery and lifestyle changes required for adjustment. Because ongoing anxiety or depression is associated with poor adaptation, problems with compliance, and deterioration, management of stress and anxiety are important outcomes for therapy. Music therapy can be used to explore and express moods, to foster cognitive functioning, to provide social support, and to facilitate social cohesion. Studies of psychoneuroimmunology (Kruse, 2003;

McKinney, Antoni, et al., 1997; McKinney, Tims, et al., 1997) indicate that improved psychological state and social support can have a positive influence on patients' immune functioning, which has important implications for recovery of optimal health (Kruse, 2003).

Research and clinical studies have documented the benefits of music therapy with several specific populations. **Cancer** often causes psychological and social distress to the patient and their loved ones. Kruse (2003) found, from surveying 99 music therapists, that psychosocial needs (100%), anxiety management (98%), and pain management (95%) were the three goal areas most commonly addressed by music therapists with patients in chemotherapy. Common psychosocial problems include depression, anxiety, stress, anger, coping with grief and loss, maintaining a sense of life control, fears of recurrence, changes in self-identity, dealing with body image, and isolation. Music was commonly used to aid expression of feeling or emotions (100%), to support relaxation (91%), to aid spirituality and end-of-life concerns (86%), and to promote cognitive processing and self-expression (76%). Those music therapy interventions most frequently used were music and relaxation (95%), songwriting (89%), instrument playing (82%), and song-leading (70%) (Kruse, 2003).

A number of research and clinical studies have examined the effectiveness of music therapy on psychological and social needs of persons with cancer. Music therapy can result in improved mood, coping behaviors, cognitive functioning, self-expression, addressing spiritual and end-of-life concerns, relaxation, quality of life, and social interaction and affiliation. Music therapy has also been found to reduce stress, boredom, and anxiety (Bailey, 1983; Boldt, 1996; Burns, 2001; Cassileth, Vickers, & Magill, 2003; Kenney & Faunce, 2004; Kruse, 2003; O'Callaghan & McDermott, 2004; Sahler et al., 2003; Smith, Casey, Johnson, Gwede, & Riggin, 2001; Waldon, 2001).

Stress, anxiety, and social isolation are also associated with **heart disease.** Chronic stress and anxiety, which elevate heart rate and blood pressure, are known to increase one's risk for the initial development of heart disease. Furthermore, stress and anxiety, if left unabated, increase vulnerability for future problems (Mandel, 1996). Thus, music therapy may be a useful modality for assisting patients in cardiac rehabilitation in stress management, expression of feelings, relaxation, and reduction of stress through exercise. Group music therapy can expand social support beyond the immediate family and treatment team (Mandel, 1996). Mandel et al. (2007) examined the effectiveness of music therapy in improving health-related outcomes of cardiac rehabilitation over a 7-week time period. Interventions included improvisation, percussion activities, song lyric writing and interpretation, music listening, and music-assisted relaxation and imagery. The interventions were designed to provide social support, relaxation, development of coping strategies, and opportunities to express feelings. In comparison with a group receiving conventional treatment without music therapy, the music therapy group showed a significantly larger decrease in systolic blood pressure and trait anxiety 4 months after treatment, and general improvement in health and social functioning.

Chronic obstructive pulmonary disease (COPD) severely limits daily activity and has many negative effects on quality of life (Engen, 2005). A clinically-based research study by Engen (2005) examined the effect of music therapy on the physical health and general wellness of older adults with emphysema. The music therapy sessions emphasized exercises in posture, breath management, vocal exercises, and group singing. The sessions also included a social component during which participants could share life experiences and benefit from social support. Engen documented a significant improvement in measures of mental health and social health as well as improved breath management, as noted earlier.

In conclusion, music has long been regarded as a powerful form of communication through which we express our deepest emotions and establish social affiliation. Music therapy can be a powerful modality for helping children and adults with acute, chronic, and life-threatening illnesses to cope with their illness and to re-establish satisfying relationships (Colwell, 1997; Engen, 2005; Mandel, 1996; Mandel et al., 2007; Robb, 2003; Whipple, 2003).

ASSESSMENT PROCEDURES

The needs and physical characteristics of medical patients vary greatly from one person to the next. Therefore, the music therapist is challenged to select realistic, appropriate tools for assessing the patient's condition. In so doing, we must not underestimate the importance of sensitive, subjective evaluation by the therapist along with more standardized measurement tools. Subtle changes in behavior or seemingly incidental remarks by the patient can provide important clues about the physical and emotional status. Careful documentation of progress is best achieved with a variety of objective assessment tools applicable to short- or long-term treatment.

Self-Report Measures

One valuable source of information is the patient, who can provide input on physical distress, anxiety, tension, and satisfaction with treatment through interviews or written forms (Douglass, 2006; Fratianne et al., 2001; Gfeller et al., 1990; Sarafino, 2006; Standley, 2000b; Tan et al., 2008; Whitehead-Pleaux et al., 2007). The extent of physical discomfort can be reported on descriptive or numerical scales, in which the patient indicates the intensity of pain on a horizontal or vertical line. Other types of standardized scales, such as the McGill-Melzack Pain Questionnaire or the Stewart Pain-Color Scale provide qualitative information about pain (Stewart, 1977). Similar inventories can measure anxiety or emotional well-being. For example, the State-Trait Anxiety Inventory assesses the patient's level of anxiety (Spielberger, Gorsuch, & Luschene, 1970). Because children differ from adults with regard to cognitive abilities and language, special measures specifically designed for children should be used for young patients (Douglass, 2006; Sarafino, 2006).

Observation of Behavioral Responses

Observational ratings can also document patient status (Douglass, 2006; Sarafino, 2006; Standley, 2000b). For example, muscle relaxation inventories have been used in music therapy programs during childbirth by Codding (1982) and Winokur (1984), and during debridement (Fratianne et al., 2001; Tan et al., 2008). Such an inventory requires the observer to indicate the level of relaxation for specific body areas, such as the forehead, jaw, neck and shoulders, and arms. Observational data on intensity, frequency and duration of such behaviors as crying, facial distortions, restlessness, or treatment resistance can signify the patient's level of comfort or anxiety (Chetta, 1981; Standley, 1986, 2000b). Children may demonstrate different types of behavior in response to pain than do adults, so the age of the patient should be taken into account when selecting behaviors for observation (Douglass, 2006; Sarafino, 2006). Because pain is a subjective phenomenon, it may be advisable to gather both self-report and observational data to get a reliable measure of patient status.

Clinical Measures

Physiological and clinical measures can also provide insight into patient progress. Blood pressure, pulse, and forced expiratory volume (FEV) (exhalation ability) are a few indicators of patient status (Allen et al., 2001; Engen, 2005; Ferrer, 2007; Standley & Whipple, 2003; Wade, 2002). The amount of medication needed for pain control or the length of hospitalization are sometimes appropriate measures of patient satisfaction and treatment effectiveness (Ayoub et al., 2005; Good et al., 2001; Lepage et al., 2001; Sarafino, 2006; Skole & Krevsky, 2006; Standley, 1986, 2000b).

A number of measures can be used in a medical setting to determine physical or psychosocial condition. The developmental level of the patient as well as his or her specific diagnosis should be considered in selecting a suitable assessment tool (Douglass, 2006). Additional assessment measures, some of which are specific to music therapy practice, appear in Jayne Standley's "Music Research in Medical Treatment" in the third edition of *Effectiveness of Music Therapy Procedures: Documentation of Research and Clinical Practice* (Standley, 2000b) published by the American Music Therapy Association. The relative merits and limitations of numerous measures of pain and anxiety are outlined in Kara Groen's (2007) article, "Pain Assessment and Management of End of Life Care: A Survey of Assessment and Treatment Practices of Hospice Music Therapy and Nursing Professionals" (*Journal of Music Therapy,* volume 44, issue 2, pages 90–112). Although this article focuses on hospice care, many of the assessment tools and principles are also relevant to medical care.

Additional information regarding assessment and the assessment process appears in Chapter 15. Selection of a specific assessment tool should reflect its potential as a meaningful indicator of the patient's condition and its ease of use in the clinical milieu. Assessment should neither interfere with treatment nor inflict further distress on an already vulnerable client.

In conclusion, the music therapist employed in a medical setting will work with patients of all ages and with a wide variety of conditions. The problems he or she encounters will depend upon the nature of the condition or illness, the patients' ages, the types of procedures required, and a host of personal circumstances. All these factors need to be considered in determining the patients' needs, the appropriate sorts of interventions, what kinds of music will be acceptable, and the sorts of measures that will provide reliable information about progress. Further, the music therapist must be flexible and cooperative in working with the entire medical team, since most patients benefit from a well-coordinated treatment plan that takes into account physical, psychological, and social factors.

SUMMARY

Music therapists serve individuals who suffer from chronic or acute medical illnesses in a variety of settings, including hospitals, clinics, and rehabilitation programs. While the specific symptoms and problems of clients vary, music therapists generally use music to reduce the impact of physical, psychological, and social problems related to the patient's illness. In contemporary medical practice, a biopsychosocial model informs treatment goals and interventions. Music therapy may be used for the following objectives:

1. *To reduce perception of pain.* Music is used as a cognitive pain control strategy in the following ways: (1) as an active focal point or distracter to reduce awareness of pain, (2) as a cue for relaxation response, (3) as a masking agent for anxiety-producing sounds in the environment, (4) as an information agent, and (5) as a positive stimulus in the environment.

2. *To use music as motivation and structure for physical activity* required in rehabilitation, including mobility and cardiopulmonary functioning.

3. *To normalize the medical environment.* Musical activities provide opportunities for play and physical activity, social interaction, leisure, and academic development. Normalization can reduce the impact of hospitalization on the development of young children and enhance the emotional well-being of adults.

4. *To provide emotional support.* Music, a form of communication associated with emotions, can provide an outlet for emotional expression and can be a source of comfort.

STUDY QUESTIONS

1. Describe the biopsychosocial model of health and illness.
2. What is the basic principle behind the Gate Control Theory of Pain?
3. Why is music used to help relieve pain, despite the sophistication of today's medications and painkillers?
4. List and describe five ways in which music is used to reduce the perception of pain.
5. Give several examples of how music might be used toward improved physical functioning.
6. What are some of the psychosocial needs of persons with acute or chronic medical conditions?
7. What does the term *normalization* mean?
8. Describe ways in which music is used as play and as a physical outlet for children with chronic or acute illness.
9. Describe ways in which music is used to foster social interaction among clients with chronic or acute illness.
10. Describe ways in which music is used to support pre-academic progress of children with acute or chronic illness.
11. Describe ways in which music is used to provide emotional support.
12. Describe several types of assessment methods that a music therapist might use to measure progress of patients with chronic or acute medical conditions.

REFERENCES

Allen, K., Golden, L. H., Izzo, J. L., Jr., Ching, M. I., Forrest, A., Niles, C. R., et al. (2001). Normalization of hypertensive responses during ambulatory surgical stress by perioperative music. *Psychosomatic Medicine, 63*(3), 487–492.

Anderson, K. O., & Masur, F. T. (1983). Psychological preparation for invasive medical and dental procedures. *Journal of Behavioral Medicine, 6*, 1–41.

Ayoub, C. M., Rizk, L. B., Yaacoub, C. I., Gaal, D., & Kain, Z. N. (2005). Music and ambient operating room noise in patients undergoing spinal anesthesia. *Anesthesia & Analgesia, 100*(5), 1316–1319.

Bailey, L. (1983). The effects of live music versus tape-recorded music on hospitalized cancer patients. *Music Therapy, 3,* 17–28.

Barrickman, J. (1989). A developmental music therapy approach for preschool hospitalized children. *Music Therapy Perspectives, 7,* 10–16.

Behrens, G. A. (1982). *The use of music activities to improve the capacity inhalation, and exhalation capabilities of handicapped children's respiration.* Unpublished master's thesis, Kent State University, Kent, OH.

Boldt, S. (1996). The effects of music therapy on motivation, psychological well being, physical comfort and exercise endurance in bone marrow transplant patients. *Journal of Music Therapy, 33,* 164–188.

Bolger, E. P. (1984). The therapeutic value of singing. *New England Journal of Medicine, 311,* 1704.

Bolton, C. (1985). Lifestyle management, proaction, and education efficacy. *Educational Gerontology, 11,* 181–190.

Bonk, V. A., France, C. R., & Taylor, B. K. (2001). Distraction reduces self-reported physiological reactions to blood donation in novice donors with a blunting coping style. *Psychosomatic Medicine, 63*(3), 447–452.

Bonny, H. L. (1983). Music listening for intensive coronary care units: A pilot project. *Music Therapy, 3,* 4–16.

Bonny, H. L. (1989). Sound as symbol: Guided imagery and music in clinical practice. *Music Therapy Perspectives, 6,* 7–10.

Browning, C. A. (2001). Music therapy in childbirth: Research in practice. *Music Therapy Perspectives, 19*(2), 74–81.

Burns, D. S. (2001). The effect of the Bonny Method of Guided Imagery and Music on the mood and life quality of cancer patients. *Journal of Music Therapy, 38*(1), 51–65.

Burt, R. K., & Korn, G. W. (1964). Audioanalgesia in obstetrics: White noise analgesia during labor. *American Journal of Obstetrics and Gynecology, 88,* 361–366.

Caine, J. (1991). The effects of music on the selected stress behaviors, weight, caloric and formula intake, and length of hospital stay of premature and low birth weight neonates in a newborn intensive care unit. *Journal of Music Therapy, 33,* 180–192.

Cassidy, J. W., & Standley, J. M. (1995). The effect of music listening on physiological responses of premature infants in the NICU. *Journal of Music Therapy, 32,* 208–227.

Cassileth, B. R., Vickers, A. J., & Magill, L. A. (2003). Music therapy for mood disturbance during hospitalization for autologous stem cell transplantation: A randomized controlled trial. *Cancer, 98*(12), 2723–2729.

Chetta, H. (1981). The effect of music and desensitization on preoperative anxiety in children. *Journal of Music Therapy, 23,* 74–87.

Christenberry, E. (1979). The use of music therapy with burn patients. *Journal of Music Therapy, 16,* 138–148.

Clair, A. A. (1996). *Therapeutic uses of music with older adults.* Baltimore: Health Professions Press.

Clark, M., Isaacks-Downton, G., Wells, N., Redline-Grazier, S., Eck, C., Hepworth, J. T., et al. (2006). Use of preferred music to reduce emotional distress and symptom activity during radiation therapy. *Journal of Music Therapy, 43*(3), 247–265.

Clark, M. E. (1986). Music-therapy-assisted childbirth: A practical guide. *Music Therapy Perspectives, 3,* 34–41.

Clark, M. E., McCorkle, R. R., & Williams, S. B. (1981). Music-therapy-assisted labor and delivery. *Journal of Music Therapy, 18,* 88–109.

Codding, P. A. (1982). *An exploration of the uses of music in the birthing process.* Unpublished master's thesis, Florida State University, Tallahassee.

Coffman, D., & Adamek, M. (1999). The contributions of wind band participation to quality of life of senior adults. *Music Therapy Perspectives, 17,* 27–31.

Coffman, D. D. (2002). Music and quality of life in older adults. *Psychomusicology, 18*(1–2), 76–88.

Coleman, J. M., Pratt, R. R., Stoddard, R. A., Gerstmann, D. R., & Abel, H. H. (1997). The effects of the male and female singing and speaking voices on selected physiological and behavioral measures of premature infants in the intensive care unit. *International Journal of Arts Medicine, 5*(2), 4–11.

Collins, S. K., & Kuck, K. (1991). Music therapy in the neonatal intensive care unit. *Neonatal Network, 9*(6), 23–26.

Colwell, C. M. (1997). Music as distraction and relaxation to reduce chronic pain and narcotic ingestion: A case study. *Music Therapy Perspectives, 15*(1), 24–31.

Daveson, B. A. (1999). A model of response: Coping mechanisms and music therapy techniques during debridement. *Music Therapy Perspectives, 17*(2), 92–98.

Daveson, B. A. (2001). Music therapy in childhood cancer: Goals, methods, patient choice and control during diagnosis, intensive treatment, transplant and palliative care. *Music Therapy Perspectives, 19*(2), 114–120.

Douglass, E. T. (2006). The development of a music therapy assessment tool for hospitalized children. *Music Therapy Perspectives 24*(2), 73–79.

Edwards, J. (1998). Music therapy for children with severe burn injury. *Music Therapy Perspectives, 16*(1), 21–26.

Engen, R. L. (2005). The singer's breath: Implications for treatment of persons with emphysema. *Journal of Music Therapy, 42*(1), 20–48.

Farthing, G. W., Venturino, M., & Brown, S. W. (1984). Suggestions and distraction in the control of pain: Test of two hypothesis. *Journal of Abnormal Psychology, 93,* 266–276.

Ferrer, A. J. (2007). The effect of live music on decreasing anxiety in patients undergoing chemotherapy treatment. *Journal of Music Therapy, 44*(3), 242–255.

Fratianne, R., Prensner, J., Huston, M., Super, D., Yowler, C., & Standley, J. (2001). The effect of music based imagery and musical alternate engagement on the burn debridement process. *Journal of Burn Care and Rehabilitation, 22*(1), 47–53.

Froelich, M. A. (1984). A comparison of the effect of music therapy and medical play therapy on the verbalization of pediatric patients. *Journal of Music Therapy, 21,* 2–15.

Gardener, E., & Licklider, J. C. (1959). Auditory analgesia in dental operation. *Journal of the American Dental Association, 59,* 1144–1150.

Gfeller, K. E. (2002a). The function of aesthetic stimuli in the therapeutic process. In R. F. Unkefer & M. H. Thaut (Eds.), *Music therapy in the treatment of adults with mental disorders* (pp. 68–84). St. Louis, MO: MMB.

Gfeller, K. E. (2002b). Music as a therapeutic agent: Historical and sociocultural perspectives. In R. F. Unkefer & M. H. Thaut (Eds.), *Music therapy in the treatment of adults with mental disorders* (pp. 60–67). St. Louis, MO: MMB.

Gfeller, K. E. (2002c). Music as communication. In R. F. Unkefer & M. H. Thaut (Eds.), *Music therapy in the treatment of adults with mental disorders* (pp. 42–59). St. Louis, MO: MMB.

Gfeller, K. E., Logan, E. H., & Walker, J. (1990). The effect of auditory distraction and suggestion on tolerance for dental restoration in adolescents and young adults. *Journal of Music Therapy, 27*, 13–23.

Ghetti, C. M., Hama, M., & Woolrich, J. (2004). Music therapy in wellness. In A. A. Darrow (Ed.), *Introduction to approaches in music therapy* (pp. 127–142). Silver Spring, MD: American Music Therapy Association.

Godley, C. A. (1987). The use of music therapy in pain clinics. *Music Therapy Perspectives, 4*, 24–28.

Goldstein, A. (1980). Thrills in response to music and other stimuli. *Physiological Psychology, 8*, 126–129.

Good, M., Stanton-Hicks, M., Grass, J. A., Anderson, G. C., Lai, H. L., Roykulcharoen, V., et al. (2001). Relaxation and music to reduce postsurgical pain. *Journal of Advanced Nursing, 33*(2), 208–215.

Gracely, R. H., McGrath, P., & Dubner, R. (1978). Validity and sensitivity of ratio scales of sensory and affective verbal pain descriptors: Manipulation of affect by diazepam. *Pain, 5*, 768–769.

Groen, K. M. (2007). Pain assessment and management of end of life care: A survey of assessment and treatment practices of hospice music therapy and nursing professionals. *Journal of Music Therapy, 44*(2), 90–112.

Hanser, S. B., Larson, S. C., & O'Connell, A. S. (1983). The effect of music on relaxation of expectant mothers during labor. *Journal of Music Therapy, 20*, 50–58.

Hanson-Abromeit, D. (2003). The newborn individualized development care and assessment program (NIDCAP) as a model for clinical music therapy interventions with premature infants. *Music Therapy Perspectives, 24*, 60–68.

Jacobson, E. (1934). *You must relax.* New York: McGraw Hill.

Jacox, A. D. (1977). *Pain: A source book for nurses and other health professionals.* Boston: Little, Brown.

Kennelly, J. (2001). Music therapy in the bone marrow transplant unit: Providing emotional support during adolescence. *Music Therapy Perspectives, 19*(2), 104–108.

Kenny, D. T., & Faunce, G. (2004). The impact of group singing on mood, coping, and perceived pain in chronic pain patients attending a multidisciplinary pain clinic. *Journal of Music Therapy, 41*(3), 215–224.

Kerr, T., Walsh, J., & Marshall, A. (2001). Emotional chance processes in music-assisted reframing. *Journal of Music Therapy, 38*(3), 193–211.

Kiecolt-Glaser, J. K., Dura, J. R., Speicher, C. E., Trask, O. J., & Glaser, R. (1991). Spousal caregivers of dementia victims: Longitudinal changes in immunity and health. *Psychosomatic Medicine, 53*, 345–362.

Kruse, J. (2003). Music therapy in the United States cancer setting: Recent trends in practice. *Music Therapy Perspectives, 21*(2), 89–98.

Kwoun, S. (2005). *An examination of cue redundancy theory in cross-cultural decoding of emotion in music.* Unpublished doctoral dissertation, University of Iowa, Iowa City.

Langer, E. (1983). *The psychology of control.* London: Lawrence Erlbaum Associates.

Langer, S. (1942). *Philosophy in a new key.* New York: Mentor Books.

Lefcourt, H. (1982). *Locus of control.* London: Lawrence Erlbaum Associates.

Lepage, C., Drolet, P., Girard, M., Grenier, Y., & DeGagne, R. (2001). Music decreases sedative requirements during spinal anesthesia. *Anesthesia & Analgesia, 93*(4), 912–916.

Locsin, R. (1981). The effect of music on the pain of selected postoperative patients. *Journal of Advanced Nursing, 6*, 19–25.

Lucia, C. M. (1987). Toward developing a model of music therapy intervention in the rehabilitation of head and trauma patients. *Music Therapy Perspectives, 4*, 34–39.

Malone, A. (1996). The effects of live music on the distress of pediatric patients receiving intravenous starts, venipunctures, injections, and heel sticks. *Journal of Music Therapy, 33*, 19–33.

Mandel, S. E. (1996). Special features--music for wellness: Music therapy for stress management in a rehabilitation program. *Music Therapy Perspectives, 14*(1), 38–43.

Mandel, S. E., Hanser, S. B., Secic, M., & Davis, B. A. (2007). Effects of music therapy on health-related outcomes in cardiac rehabilitation: A randomized controlled trial. *Journal of Music Therapy, 44*(3), 176–197.

Marley, L. S. (1984). The use of music with hospitalized infants and toddlers: A descriptive study. *Journal of Music Therapy, 21*, 126–132.

McDonald, D. T., & Simons, G. M. (1989). *Musical growth and development: Birth through six*. New York: Schirmer Books.

McKinney, C. H., Antoni, M. H., Kumar, M., Tims, F. C., & McCabe, P. M. (1997). Effects of guided imagery and music (GIM) therapy on mood and cortisol in healthy adults. *Health Psychology, 16*, 1–12.

McKinney, C. H., Tims, F. C., Kumar, A., & Kumar, M. (1997). The effect of selected classical music and spontaneous imagery on plasma beta-endorphin. *Journal of Behavior Medicine, 20*, 85–99.

Meinhart, N. T., & McCaffery, M. (1983). *Pain: A nursing approach to assessment and analysis*. Norwalk, CT: Appleton-Century-Crofts.

Melzack, R., & Wall, P. D. (1965). Pain mechanisms: A new theory. *Science, 150*, 971–979.

Melzack, R., & Wall, P. D. (1982). *The challenge of pain*. New York: Basic Books.

Merriam, A. P. (1964). *The anthropology of music*. Evanston, IL: Northwestern University Press.

Metzger, L. K. (2004a). Assessment of use of music by patients participating in cardiac rehabilitation. *Journal of Music Therapy, 41*(1), 55–69.

Metzger, L. K. (2004b). Heart health and music: A steady beat or irregular rhythm? *Music Therapy Perspectives, 22*(1), 21–25.

Mitchell, L. A., & MacDonald, R. A. R. (2006). An experimental investigation of the effects of preferred and relaxing music listening on pain perception. *Journal of Music Therapy, 43*(4), 295–316.

Monsey, H. L. (1960). Preliminary report of the clinical efficacy of audioanalgesia. *Journal of the California State Dental Association, 36*, 432–437.

Munro, S. (1984). *Music therapy in palliative/hospice care*. St. Louis, MO: Magnamusic-Baton.

Noguchi, L. K. (2006). The effect of music versus nonmusic on behavioral signs of distress and self-report of pain in pediatric injection patients. *Journal of Music Therapy, 43*(1), 16–38.

O'Callaghan, C., & McDermott, F. (2004). Music therapy's relevance in a cancer hospital researched through a constructivist lens. *Journal of Music Therapy, 41*(2), 151–185.

Okun, M., Olding, R., & Cohn, C. (1990). A meta-analysis of subjective well-being among elders. *Psychological Bulletin, 108*, 257–266.

Oyama, T., Hataon, K., Sato, Y., Kudo, M., Spintge, R., & Droh, R. (1983). Endocrine effect of anxiolytic music in dental patients. In R. Droh & R. Spintge (Eds.), *Angst, schmerz, musik in der anasthesie* (pp. 143–146). Basel, Switzerland: Editiones Roche.

Pelletier, C. L. (2004). The effect of music on decreasing arousal due to stress: A meta-analysis. *Journal of Music Therapy, 41*(3), 192–214.

Rankin, J. A., & Harris, M. R. (1984). Dental anxiety: The patient's point of view. *The Journal of American Dental Association, 109*, 43–47.

Reuer, B. (2007). An entrepreneurial journey: A music therapist's story—Personal reflections. *Music Therapy Perspectives, 25*(2), 108–114.

Rider, M., Floyd, J., & Kirkpatrick, J. (1985). The effects of music, imagery, and relaxation on adrenal corticosteroids and the re-entrainment of circadian rhythms. *Journal of Music Therapy, 22*, 46–58.

Robb, S. L. (1999). Piaget, Erikson, and coping styles: Implications for music therapy and the hospitalized preschool child. *Music Therapy Perspectives, 17*, 14–19.

Robb, S. L. (2003). Designing music therapy interventions for hospitalized children and adolescents using a contextual support model of music therapy. *Music Therapy Perspectives, 21*(1), 41–45.

Robb, S. L., Nichols, R. J., Rutan, R. L., Bishop, B. L., & Parker, J. C. (1995). The effects of music assisted relaxation on preoperative anxiety. *Journal of Music Therapy, 32*, 2–21.

Rudenberg, M. T. (1985). Music therapy for orthopedically handicapped children. In W. Lathom & C. Eagle (Eds.), *Music therapy for handicapped children* (pp. 37–116). Lawrence, KS: Meseraull Printing.

Rudenberg, M. T., & Royka, A. M. (1989). Promoting psychosocial adjustment in pediatric burn patients through music therapy and child life therapy. *Music Therapy Perspectives, 7*, 40–43.

Sahler, O. J., Hunter, B. C., & Liesveld, J. L. (2003). The effect of using music therapy with relaxation imagery in the management of patients undergoing bone marrow transplantation: A pilot feasibility study. *Alternative Therapies in Health and Medicine, 9*(6), 70–74.

Sarafino, E. P. (2006). *Health psychology: Biopsychosocial interactions* (5th ed.). New York: John Wiley & Sons.

Scartelli, J. P. (1982). The effect of sedative music on electromyographic-biofeedback-assisted relaxation training of spastic cerebral-palsied adults. *Journal of Music Therapy, 19*, 210–218.

Scartelli, J. P. (1984). The effect of EMG biofeedback and sedative music, EMG biofeedback only, and sedative music only on frontalis muscle relaxation ability. *Journal of Music Therapy, 21*, 67–78.

Scartelli, J. P. (1989). *Music and self-management methods*. St. Louis, MO: Magnamusic-Baton.

Schwankovsky, L. M., & Guthrie, P. T. (1985). Music therapy for other health-impaired children. In W. Lathom & C. Eagle (Eds.), *Music therapy for handicapped children* (pp. 119–167). Lawrence, KS: Meseraull Printing.

Siedliecki, S.L. & Good, M. (2006). Effect of music on power, pain, depression and disability *Journal of Advanced Nursing, 54*(5), 553–562.

Siegel, S. L. (1983). *The use of music as a treatment in pain perception with post-surgical patients in a pediatric hospital*. Unpublished master's thesis, University of Miami, Coral Gables, FL.

Skole, K. S., & Krevsky, B. (2006). The impact of patient-selected music on the tolerability of colonoscopy: A prospective, randomized, double-blind, placebo-controlled study. *Gastrointestinal Endoscopy, 63*(5), AB194.

Sloboda, J. A., & O'Neill, S. A. (2001). Emotions in everyday listening to music. In P. N. Juslin & J. A. Sloboda (Eds.), *Music and emotion: Theory and research* (pp. 415–430). Oxford, England: Oxford University Press.

Smith, J. C., & Joyce, C. A. (2004). Mozart versus New Age music: Relaxation states, stress, and ABC relaxation theory. *Journal of Music Therapy, 41*(3), 215–224.

Smith, M., Casey, L., Johnson, D., Gwede, C., & Riggin, O. Z. (2001). Music as a therapeutic agent for anxiety in patients receiving radiation therapy. *Oncology Nursing Forum, 28*(5), 855–862.

Spielberger, D. D., Gorsuch, R. L., & Luschene, R. (1970). *State-trait anxiety inventory*. Palo Alto, CA: Consulting Psychologist Press.

Standley, J. M. (1986). Music research in medical/dental treatment: Meta-analysis and clinical applications. *Journal of Music Therapy, 21*, 184–193.

Standley, J. M. (1998a). The effect of music and multimodal stimulation on physiologic and developmental responses of premature infants in neonatal intensive care. *Pediatric Nursing, 21*(6), 532–539.

Standley, J. M. (1998b). Pre and perinatal growth and development: Implications of music benefits for premature infants. *International Journal of Music Education, 31*, 1–13.

Standley, J. M. (2000a). The effect of contingent music to increase non-nutritive sucking of premature infants. *Pediatric Nursing, 26*(5), 493–495, 498–499.

Standley, J. M. (2000b). Music research in medical treatment. In AMTA (Ed.), *Effectiveness of music therapy procedures: Documentation of research and clinical practice* (3rd ed., pp. 1–64). Silver Spring, MD: American Music Therapy Association.

Standley, J. M. (2001a). Music therapy for premature infants in neonatal intensive care: Physiological and developmental benefits. *Early Childhood Connections, 7*(2), 18–25.

Standley, J. M. (2001b). Music therapy for the neonate. *Newborn and Infant Nursing Reviews, 1*(4), 211–216.

Standley, J. M. (2001c). The power of contingent music for infant learning. *Bulletin of the Council for Research in Music Education, 149*, 65–71.

Standley, J. M. (2003). The effect of music-reinforced non-nutritive sucking on feeding rate of premature infants. *Journal of Pediatric Nursing, 18*(3), 169–173.

Standley, J. M., & Whipple, J. (2003). Music therapy for premature infants in the neonatal intensive care unit: Health and developmental benefits. In S. Robb (Ed.), *Music therapy in pediatric healthcare: Research and evidence-based practice* (pp. 19–30). Silver Spring, MD: American Music Therapy Association.

Staum, M. (1983). Music and rhythmic stimuli in the rehabilitation of gait disorders. *Journal of Music Therapy, 20*, 69–87.

Stewart, M. L. (1977). Measurement of clinical pain. In A. K. Jacox (Ed.), *Pain: A source book for nurses and other health professionals* (pp. 107–137). Boston: Little, Brown.

Tan, X., Yowler, C. J., Super, D. M., & Fratianne, R. (2008). Music therapy significantly reduces pain, anxiety, and muscle tension involved with burn debridement. *Journal of Burn Care and Research, 29*(2), S83.

Tanioka, F., Takzawa, T., Kamata, S., Kudo, M., Matsuki, A., & Oyama, T. (1985). Hormonal effect of anxiolytic music in patients during surgical operation under epidural anesthesia. In R. Groh & R. Spintge (Eds.), *Angst, schmerz, musik in der anasthesie* (pp. 285–290). Basel, Switzerland: Editiones Roche.

Thaut, M. (1985). The use of auditory rhythm and rhythmic speech to aide temporal muscular control in children with gross motor dysfunction. *Journal of Music Therapy, 22*, 108–128.

Verghese, M., Lipton, R. B., Katz, M. J., Hail, C. B., Derby, C. A., Kulslansky, G., et al. (2003). Leisure activities and the risk of dementia in the elderly. *The New England Journal of Medicine, 248*, 2508–2516.

Wade, L. M. (2002). A comparison of the effects of vocal exercises/singing versus music-assisted relaxation on peak expiratory flow rates of children with asthma. *Music Therapy Perspectives, 20*(1), 31–37.

Waldon, E. G. (2001). The effects of group music therapy on mood states and cohesiveness in adult oncology patients. *Journal of Music Therapy, 38*(3), 212–238.

Walters, C. (1996). The psychological and physiological effects of vibrotactile stimulation, via a Somatron, on patients awaiting scheduled gynecological surgery. *Journal of Music Therapy, 33*, 261–267.

Whipple, J. (2000). The effect of parent training in music and multimodal stimulation on parent-neonate interactions in the neonatal intensive care unit. *Journal of Music Therapy, 37*(4), 250–268.

Whipple, J. (2003). Surgery buddies: A music therapy program for pediatric surgical patients. *Music Therapy Perspectives, 21*(2), 77–83.

Whitehead-Pleaux, A. M., Zebrowski, N., Baryza, M. J., & Sheridan, R. L. (2007). Exploring the effects of music therapy on pediatric pain: Phase 1. *Journal of Music Therapy, 44*(3), 217–241.

Winokur, M. A. (1984). *The use of music as an audio-analgesia during childbirth.* Unpublished master's thesis, Florida State University, Tallahassee.

Wolfe, D., & Woolsey, W. (2003). Information sharing: Developing a music listening/relaxation program for parents of children in pediatric care. *Music Therapy Perspectives, 21*(1), 41–45.

Zatorre, R. (2005). Music, the food of neuroscience? *Nature, 434*, 312–315.

CHAPTER 12

MUSIC THERAPY IN HOSPICE AND PALLIATIVE CARE

Joey Walker
Mary Adamek

CHAPTER OUTLINE

HOSPICE AND PALLIATIVE CARE: WHAT ARE THEY?
WHO BENEFITS FROM HOSPICE OR PALLIATIVE CARE?
MUSIC THERAPIST AS PART OF THE HOSPICE TEAM
ISSUES AT END-OF-LIFE, TYPICALLY ADDRESSED BY MUSIC THERAPISTS
    Physical Issues
    Psychosocial Issues
MUSIC THERAPY GOALS AND INTERVENTIONS COMMONLY USED IN HOSPICE
    AND PALLIATIVE CARE
    Music Therapy to Alleviate Physical Symptoms
    Music Therapy for Psychosocial Support

Mike, a 60-year-old male, had recently moved into a long-term care facility because of complications with his cancer. He was no longer able to care for himself at home. The home health aide had reported that Mike did not want to bathe, get dressed, or do his other activities of daily living. When the music therapist visited late one morning, Mike was lying in bed, unshaven, and he had not put his false teeth in his mouth. He was unkempt and not dressed. He agreed to a music therapy session, and 45 minutes later he was energetic and reminiscing about good times when he and his significant other would dance together in numerous small towns around the area. He asked the music therapist to return the same time the next week. Upon returning the next week, Mike was clean, dressed, and lying on the top of his bed. Soon his significant other entered the room and slid onto the bed with Mike. They were able to share a songbook together, sing, talk about dancing, and express their love for each other.

HOSPICE AND PALLIATIVE CARE: WHAT ARE THEY?

The terms *hospice* and *palliative care* refer to a philosophy of care for people at end-of-life. This **team-oriented approach** provides compassionate **end-of-life care** to enhance comfort and improve quality of life for individuals who have **terminal illness** and for their families. The goals are to prevent suffering, relieve pain, and optimize each person's functioning. The individual's decisions about care are central to the hospice and palliative care philosophy, and the team is guided by the wishes of the patient and family.

People are eligible for hospice treatment when their death is anticipated in six months or less. Palliative care can be provided for persons who are dealing with terminal illness whether or not they have a six-month prognosis. The terms *hospice* and *palliative care* are closely related. Both are concerned with providing relief but not cure, and in some parts of the world the terms are used interchangeably. The term *hospice* will be used throughout this chapter to indicate a model of care to improve quality of life for people with life-limiting illness and for their families.

WHO BENEFITS FROM HOSPICE OR PALLIATIVE CARE?

Adults and children with terminal illness can be admitted to hospice care. The largest number of patients have a cancer diagnosis, while others are admitted with heart, lung, or **neuromuscular disease; Alzheimer's/dementia;** organ failure; HIV/AIDS; or other disorders. Adults and children may have developmental delays concomitant with their medical diagnosis. Children have different physical and psychosocial needs than adults, based on their ages and developmental levels. The family is also a recipient of hospice care while the patient is dying and during **bereavement** after the family member's death. The interdisciplinary team addresses the unique needs of each family unit throughout the dying and bereavement process.

MUSIC THERAPIST AS PART OF THE HOSPICE TEAM

The goal of hospice is to care for each person in a holistic manner. This requires an interdisciplinary team to address patients' physical, psychological, spiritual, and social needs. The interdisciplinary team plans coordinated care, holds regular team meetings, and continues ongoing communication to ensure that goals are met and frequently reassessed. The team includes the primary physician, hospice physician, nurse, social worker, chaplain, home health aide, bereavement counselor, and volunteers. Additional team members may include a music, occupational, or physical therapist; psychologist; pharmacist; and nutritionist, among others. Patients and families are considered part of the team and are able to direct their desired care by communicating specific needs to the rest of the team (National Hospice & Palliative Care Organization, 2008).

Music therapists utilize comprehensive skills to observe, report, document, and provide effective interventions. A music therapist may provide treatment for physical, emotional, spiritual, cognitive, or social needs. Viewing the whole person as the interaction of mind, body, and spirit, the music therapist has a unique place among other professionals on the team. Other team members may concentrate their efforts mostly in one area of expertise, such as with physical or spiritual needs. The music therapist may be able to offer insight for team members concerning the multidimensional needs of each patient.

Hospices are becoming more aware of the benefits of providing music therapy services. Music therapists provide support in a noninvasive, cost-effective approach. Music therapy in hospice care is one of the fastest growing areas in the field of music therapy, with the creation of many new employment opportunities in the last few years (American Music Therapy Association, 2007).

ISSUES AT END-OF-LIFE, TYPICALLY ADDRESSED BY MUSIC THERAPISTS

The needs of hospice patients and families vary greatly, and these needs may rapidly change from day to day, hour to hour, and within a single session (Krout, 2000). Therefore, the music therapist will provide services that concentrate on physical, **psychosocial**, spiritual, and bereavement needs of the moment for each session. For example, the music therapist may have concentrated efforts on a spiritual issue during a past session, and in a present situation may focus on pain control. A session in the future could consist of using music to stimulate memories and life review, or perhaps any combination may take place within a single session. Ongoing assessment is critical to ensure that the patient and family are receiving the care that they desire.

Physical Issues

Pain management. Pain management is a primary focus for the hospice team. Although not every patient in hospice care has pain management needs, pain is still the most common symptom experienced by hospice patients (Kastenbaum, 2001). Patients sometimes improve in hospice care because the team is able to find effective ways of treating the **total pain** of each patient. Cicely Saunders, who is considered the modern founder of hospice, created this concept of "total pain" in order to ensure that psychological, emotional, social, spiritual, as well as physical pain of patients and their loved ones is included in treatment (Hilliard, 2005). This concentration on the whole person interfaces easily with music therapy, as the music therapist can simultaneously address several goal areas with specific interventions.

Hospice care takes into account the desired level of pain management for each patient and family. Because pain is subjective and complex, each person's experience differs from another. For a variety of reasons, people also have different levels of pain that they will tolerate at any given time. One patient may want to be alert and thinking clearly when making legal or financial decisions, while another patient may want to be able to be fully awake to visit with a long unseen family member. Some families do not want to use pain medications for their loved one due to fears of addiction or sedation, and other patients are unable to use medications because of certain symptoms, disease process, allergic reaction, or other undesirable side effects. Some patients may not receive pain medication in a timely fashion, if at all. For others, generational, spiritual, or cultural considerations or stoicism may contribute to reluctance in admitting that pain is actually present. If untreated, unrelieved pain may lead to the following:

- Fatigue
- Stress
- Nausea
- Loss of appetite
- Isolation
- Anxiety

- Difficulties with daily activities
- Disrupted sleep patterns
- Depression
- Relationship difficulties
- Anger
- Thoughts of suicide

(National Foundation for the Treatment of Pain, 2008)

In addition to the problems listed above, patients may use much of their energy to deal with unrelieved pain. They may have little energy remaining to take care of other essential end-of-life issues like emotional problems or spiritual pain. Conversely, Trauger-Querry and Haghighi (1999) discuss the fact that treatment for pain can be resistant if psychosocial, emotional, or spiritual issues are disregarded.

Pain assessment. It can be challenging for adults to admit, describe, and discuss issues of pain. Children's expression and understanding of pain is compounded by their level of development. Instead of verbalizing about pain, children may exhibit behavioral distress, which may involve changes in behavior, sleep, or eating patterns; becoming withdrawn; decreased physical activity; increased irritability; or an increased need to seek comfort (Barrickman, 1989). Preschool children may not be able to verbally describe their pain or anxiety and may act out behaviorally, for example, by screaming, hitting, or having a tantrum. Older children may withdraw and become quiet as a means of control and may not verbally express pain because of fear of receiving painful procedures or treatment. Adolescents may have difficulty communicating their needs in general, and admitting to pain may keep them from spending time with peers or may curb their independence. Within a normalized musical environment, children may demonstrate more congruence with feeling and verbalization and may also express themselves on an emotional level more easily with music as the stimulus (Ghetti & Walker, in press).

Chapter 10 described a number of **assessment tools** that may be useful in a hospice or palliative care setting. Because of the nature of hospice care, the choice of a suitable assessment tool should take into account a number of factors: the functional level of the patient, an assessment that is as nonintrusive as possible, and an assessment that can be completed quickly, given what is sometimes a rapid change in patient status.

Music therapists have access to a variety of formal assessment tools with regard to pain and discomfort. Pain assessment tools such as **Numeric Rating Scale (NRS)** and Faces are recommended for use by nonnursing team members (Mills-Groen, 2007). The patients rate their perceived pain by choosing a number from the scale (NRS) or a picture/line drawing (Faces) of a face of a person experiencing different levels of pain severity. These assessment tools are easy to use and take little time to determine the patient's pain intensity at the moment.

A music therapist must be able to continuously observe in a less formal manner these possible indicators of pain:

- Vocal and verbal complaints
- Rubbing, holding a body part
- Bracing
- Facial grimacing/winces
- Furrowed brow, frown
- Irritability

- Anxiety
- Restlessness
- Physical repetitive movements
- Repeating words or phrases
- Change in behavior from the norm

(Cohen-Mansfield & Creedon, 2002;
Maue-Johnson & Tanguay, 2006;
Warden, Hurley, & Volicer, 2003)

Lower functioning patients may be unable to verbally express their pain and its symptoms; therefore, music therapists carefully observe for the indications listed above and monitor changes in behavior. Often the anxious or restless behavior of a patient in a long-term care facility may appear to be related to a medical condition such as dementia; however, it may be caused by unresolved pain. Other indicators of unaddressed pain in lower functioning patients may include:

- Eyes tightly closed
- Tense muscles, clenched fists
- Increased pacing
- Changes in sleep patterns

- Wanting to exit home or facility
- Increased agitation
- Pulling away or hitting when touched
- Decreased appetite

(Warden et al., 2003)

Symptom management. Symptom management is an integral part of hospice care. Similar to pain management, symptoms may not be eliminated but managed at a level desired by the patient or family.

Dyspnea. **Dyspnea** is shortness of breath that occurs in patients with a variety of life-limiting conditions, but commonly occurs in **chronic obstructive pulmonary disorder (COPD)** and with some cancers. This feeling of not being able to get enough breath or suffocating causes anxiety, which may lead to increased dyspnea which subsequently may lead to increased anxiety in an unlimited cycle (Hilliard, 2005).

Agitation. Agitation can be a significant problem for patients and families. While there are many causes of agitation such as pain or disease process, agitation can lead to safety issues and be distressing for staff or caregivers.

Sleep difficulties. Patients may have problems regulating their sleep cycles. They might sleep during the day, making it difficult to fall asleep at night. Sleep problems can contribute to increase in anxiety and agitation.

Restlessness. Near the end-of-life when multiple body systems are shutting down, some patients (even those who have previously been calm) may experience terminal restlessness. This may include anxiety, thrashing or agitation, palpitations, shortness of breath, insomnia, pain, moaning, yelling, involuntary muscle twitching or jerks, fidgeting, or tossing and turning (Hospice Patient Alliance, 2008). This can be upsetting for the patient, family, and staff who are also coping with other end-of-life issues.

Psychosocial Issues

In hospice care, patients also face end-of-life psychosocial and spiritual issues. As noted in Chapter 10, medical conditions greatly impact a person's psychological, social, and emotional functioning. This impact on quality of life, according to Krout (2000) and Hilliard (2003), can be improved through music therapy psychosocial support. When patients reach a desired or tolerable level of physical comfort, they may have the basic energy or need for emotional support and comfort. Due to the sizeable amount of end-of-life psychosocial needs, concentration will be given to coping with illness and loss through the following areas: (1) anxiety reduction, (2) emotional support, (3) autonomy and control, (4) reduction of isolation, and (5) family cohesion.

Anxiety. Anxiety related to dyspnea was previously discussed; however, anxiety can also be caused by psychological, social, or spiritual factors. A terminal prognosis can create fear of the unknown and manifest in tension and anxiety (Hilliard, 2005). Patients and families may want to know why or how someone will die, if it will be painful, and when it will occur, etc. Family members may not agree on the plan of care (e.g., withholding aggressive treatment or measures given for comfort only), where to spend the last part of life, or merely how to care for the patient. This may compound stress and tension in an already unstable situation and cause more anxiety for the patient as well. Family members may have additional anxiety thinking about and dealing with unknown issues.

Emotional needs related to losses and spirituality. People experience many losses throughout the dying process. Patients may have the role loss that may have helped define who they were. For example, a mother who was the constant caretaker of everyone in the family who can no longer fulfill that role, or a child who cannot attend school, may feel the loss of who he or she is. Patients may also physically appear different and may have lost home and family; they may need an outlet that helps them feel serene, one that can help them express who they are. Patients and families need a way to express their personal identity, search for meaning, understand their relationship to God or Higher Power, and complete unfinished business (Trauger-Querry & Haghighi, 1999).

Each patient guides the depth of emotional involvement for the team according to his or her own individual needs. Patients may need someone who will take time to listen and validate their feelings, and at times they may feel more comfortable expressing feelings to hospice staff instead of a family member. Patients may not want to upset someone in their family or may feel that they shouldn't be feeling a certain way, or that it is wrong to feel an emotion that might be considered negative. It is also possible that they may be unable to verbally express emotions or they may not know what they are feeling.

In general, people of all ages and levels of functioning need help when coping with illness or loss. At end-of-life the problems may be magnified and may feel overwhelming. At times patients may experience a series of losses that appear to never end. Patients may lose independence with the inability to physically or mentally do what they desire, may have chronic and acute pain, may have moved to a different environment and are mourning the loss of a familiar place, may have to adjust to new caregivers and the stress that accompanies loss of privacy or dignity, may have financial concerns or feel like they are a burden, or may be separated from friends or loved ones. In addition to adjusting to a medical condition and their own mortality, patients may have these and other losses that make coping more difficult and contribute to emotional and spiritual pain.

Many people find a need for spiritual comfort at end-of life. If a hospice is **Medicare-certified,** it is required to provide a chaplain for spiritual support. However, the music therapist also provides comfort and additional spiritual support.

Autonomy and control. In some patients, feelings of helplessness and low self-esteem surface with the loss of normalcy and independence. Motivation to attempt straightforward daily responsibilities may decrease and depression may become more likely when people are unable to accomplish simple tasks. Patients who have developed dependency and helplessness may have difficulty making even a simple forced choice.

Isolation. Isolation is a common problem for many patients in hospice care. People may live alone at home or in long-term care facilities, or are in hospitals where it is more difficult for various people to visit. Many may be of an age where most of their friends and family have died. Others do not want people around to witness their decline. Some people avoid visiting friends at end-of-life, while other visitors do not know how to interact with someone who is withdrawn or may not communicate in a familiar way.

Socialization is an important component of quality of life (Hilliard, 2005). People have a need to feel as if they are accepted and belong. Integrating acceptance and belonging into musical interventions is typical and inherent in the musical process (see Chapter 3). When feasible and appropriate, group interactions take place within families, with friends, or with other residents of facilities. Making music together helps develop a sense of belonging, whether in a group situation or simply with the music therapist.

Family cohesion. When people gather at the end-of-life, there may be family members who have not seen each other since they were young. They may disagree on issues, and old patterns and resentments may reoccur. It can be a stressful time, with family members missing time from work and their own family responsibilities. Disagreement can be distressing for the patient as well as the family.

MUSIC THERAPY GOALS AND INTERVENTIONS COMMONLY USED IN HOSPICE AND PALLIATIVE CARE

The most widely used intervention, listening to live or recorded music, can reduce pain perception and anxiety; provide relaxation, comfort, and spiritual support;

and offer a means for life review and emotional expression. The music serves as a stimulus for active listening, which can offer a means for reminiscence, verbal discussions, and emotional expression. Music can also provide for a more passive means while creating a positive sensory environment, for enhancing relaxation, or for reducing anxiety and agitation (Krout, 2000).

According to Krout (2000), hospice and palliative care music therapists often use a combined treatment strategy to address multiple patients' needs and goals. Many interventions may be used in the treatment course or within a single session in order to provide individualized care; however, the techniques most often used are the following:

- Music listening
- Improvisation
- Singing
- Songwriting
- Music playing
- Song choice
- Music/imagery for relaxation—with progressive muscle relaxation and deep breathing
- Lyric analysis—music assisted cognitive reframing

(Hilliard, 2003; Krout, 2000; Mills-Groen, 2007)

Instrument playing, singing and *improvisation* are effective techniques for facilitating expression of emotions and improving communication with terminally ill patients (Krout, 2000). Many different kinds of instruments and styles of music can be utilized according to the preference of the patient. People of all ages and functioning levels are able to participate with adaptations prepared by the music therapist. Patients may play with great expression and musicality within a successful experience designed to foster creativity, enhance self-concept, and provide a means to the unconscious. Emotions not easily verbalized such as anger, fear, and existential concerns may be expressed unconsciously through improvisation (Krout, 2000).

The universal appeal and novelty of live music is an effective tool for distraction. *Listening to live or recorded music* may help patients focus their attention on something other than pain, **perseverative behavior**, painful procedures, daily cares, worry, or anxious thoughts. Distraction can be used with people of all ages and functioning levels; however, it works particularly well with infants and young children. Providing distraction with instruments of a **vibrotactile** nature may be effective for older patients with cognitive impairments. Utilizing a variety of easily adaptable and colorful vibrotactile instruments, which are both aurally and visually appealing, in combination with the skills of the music therapist allows for successful distraction.

Songwriting is a valuable technique for assisting patients with creative and emotional expression or self-awareness, enhancing self-esteem, providing validation, and creating a lasting gift for a loved one (Krout, 2000). A variety of songwriting techniques can be adapted for differences in functioning levels as well as age. Music therapists can design the music so that it is applicable to the situation and considers the musical preference of the patient as well.

Music-based cognitive reframing and *lyric analysis* use music to stimulate discussion about thoughts and feelings. Music listening, singing, songwriting, and song choice can all be used as a means for discussing the lyrics as they relate to a patient. Cognitive reframing refers to changing the way a person would view a situation by changing the way he or she would think about it.

Music can provide the structure for slow, deep breathing, and imagery may be added after *autogenic* or *progressive muscle relaxation* has occurred. Autogenic relaxation uses self-directed visual imagery like the repetition of a word, phrase, or feeling combined with body awareness. Progressive muscle relaxation involves slowly tensing and then relaxing different muscle groups within the body (Mayo Foundation for Medical Education and Research, 2008). The use of imagery in order to reduce anxiety or provide relaxation can be used with music assisted relaxation (MAR). However, in order to use the approaches of Guided Imagery and Music (GIM) or the Bonny Method of Guided Imagery and Music, one needs advanced training and certification. These methods also use music, imagery, and relaxation, but the goals of the practice are creativity, self-exploration, insight, and reorganization (Krout, 2000).

Music Therapy to Alleviate Physical Symptoms

Manage pain. Music therapy offers a comprehensive **nonpharmacological approach** for pain management, and there are many ways that music therapy interventions can be utilized to reduce pain perception. Because of the fragile interactive dimensions and complexity of total pain, music therapy as a multifaceted treatment is an effective modality for pain management. Standley (2000) compiled music research in medical treatment and generalized that music is most effective when:

- a patient experiences mild to moderate pain. As pain becomes severe, music is less effective.
- live music (as opposed to recorded music) is provided by a music therapist.
- it is patient preferred.

See Chapter 10 for descriptions of the following music therapy interventions associated with pain management:

- as a stimulus for **active focus** or **distraction**
- to facilitate a **relaxation response**
- as a **masking agent**
- as an **information agent**
- as a **positive environmental stimulus**

Jean was an elderly woman with dementia and severe arthritis who lived in a long-term care facility. Her days consisted of sitting in a reclining wheelchair with her eyes closed or lying in her bed. She sometimes would answer a closed question with "mm-huh" (yes) or a shake of her head meaning "no."

Because of her arthritis, Jean's hands had contracted so tightly that her fingernails were causing open sores in the palm of one of her hands. A hospice home health aide would soak and gently massage her hands over a period of time to help open them. The area could then be cleaned, medicated, and dressed. Even with pre-medication, this was a painful process; therefore, the music therapist would provide distraction, relaxation, deep breathing, and imagery to assist with pain control.

Jean would cry out and moan in pain during this process, so the music therapist provided live, slow, arpeggiated guitar accompaniment that matched the pitch of her moaning. The music therapist hummed the pitch of her moan and began gradually dropping the pitch as if in a sigh. Intermittent breathing in an audible manner by the music therapist (inhaling and exhaling slowly with music as the guide) as well as giving Jean cues to "keep breathing" gave her both a focal point and distraction from her pain. Jean began to follow the music therapist's drop in pitch with her moans as well as breathing more evenly and slowly. The music therapist continued to hum and sing, improvising and weaving images about Jean's farm into the music. Jean's grimace and furrowed brow disappeared and her face relaxed. Jean stopped moaning and listened as the music therapist sang about the sights, smells, sounds, and general feel of her farm on a warm, humid summer day. The nurse and the home health aide both reported that Jean had significantly less pain and discomfort when music therapy was provided during her dressing change. In addition, these caregivers also stated that they felt "much less stressed" during the procedure with support from music therapy.

This situation involved music therapy procedural support for acute pain. Music therapy provided the multifaceted approach that Jean needed to reduce her pain. The music therapist used the **iso-principle** (matching the patient's mood with the music) to provide sensory input, as well as cognitive strategies, breathing techniques, distraction, and a focal point in order to reduce Jean's pain perception.

Promote relaxation.

> *Bud's health had been declining rapidly for the last year; he lay in bed and was unable to move his arms. He was recently diagnosed with* **amyotrophic lateral sclerosis (ALS)**, *was becoming weaker, and had increasing pain and difficulty swallowing foods and liquids. His anxiety was increasing due to dyspnea. He had played guitar in the past and still enjoyed watching movies and listening to music. The music therapist provided live vocal and guitar music as requested by Bud.*

With the knowledge and skills of the therapist, the music was able to serve multiple purposes:

- As a focal point—Bud did not think about his pain or dyspnea as he concentrated on the lyrics and guitar.
- As a way of reducing anxiety through music assisted relaxation—As time progressed and Bud became more anxious, music was found to be the most comforting and effective means for relaxation. The music therapist was able to provide live sessions, recordings, and cognitive strategies with MAR to help Bud reduce his dyspnea and anxiety.
- As a stimulus for reminiscence—Bud was able to recall many happy times when he played the guitar. He was able to remember specific performances and how he felt at the time. This was a way of life review and validation of his life.
- As a means for spiritual support—Bud was unable to attend the services of his faith tradition, and he felt close to his Higher Power when his favorite spiritual music was provided.
- As a stimulus to improve social interaction—Bud's friends and family sometimes felt uncomfortable interacting with him. The music provided a vehicle for socialization. His grandchildren as well as his friends could all participate together and interact in a normalized way.
- As a means for control—Bud was able to make choices (e.g., fast or slow music, type of music, specific song, etc.) within an environment where he was slowly losing more and more control everyday.
- As a stimulus for finding meaning and purpose—Bud was able to teach the music therapist some advanced concepts for guitar. This helped give him purpose

and improved his self-concept as he was still able to help someone else despite his compromised health.

Bud's case illustrates the point that many patients in hospice care have more than one need. Bud had physical needs with his chronic pain and shortness of breath, as well as many psychosocial and spiritual needs. When a patient has more than one need, the music therapist must be able to assess quickly what need is most important to focus on at the time. Flexibility and the ability to change, modify, or create new plans at any time are vital when working in hospice care.

Using MAR at end-of-life can be an effective and powerful tool to relieve pain, reduce anxiety, and provide relaxation and a calm, soothing environment. However, level of functioning of the patient and disease progression need to be considered. Patients in the later stages of illness may not be able to participate in long relaxation and imagery sessions; therefore, shorter sessions may be advisable (O'Callaghan, 1996). Lower functioning patients may not be appropriate candidates for imagery but may be able to concentrate on breathing techniques paired with music. Patients with a history of emotional problems, abuse, low mental energy, or problems with concentration or reality may be better served by more passive music relaxation. MAR can be used with children when consideration is given to developmental level, goal of the approach, and type of intervention—sedative music listening, music facilitated deep breathing, music and imagery, or progressive muscle relaxation (Ghetti & Walker, in press).

Music can be tailored to calm, soothe, and orient people according to their specific requirements and musical preferences. Some lower functioning patients or those who have dementia may have increased agitation with daily cares such as bathing, dressing changes or other activities. Music therapists can co-treat and provide distraction and relaxation during procedures or daily cares to reduce agitative behaviors. A patient who is restless may be easily distracted or soothed by carefully administered musical stimuli. If a patient is observed to be restless, the music therapist can often reduce the likelihood of the patient becoming agitated. The music provides the same result as medication, but without the negative side effects that may accompany medications often administered to reduce agitation or restlessness.

Adjust sleep cycles. The music therapist can provide live or recorded music for people who have sleep problems. If patients sleep during the day, they are less likely to fall asleep easily at night, or remain asleep for a period of time. Therefore, stimulating music may be needed to keep the person awake during the day. Conversely, sedative music can be provided in order to help patients fall asleep. This can be a positive nonpharmacological strategy to assist patients who often do not want more medication. Taking less medication is less stressful for the patient and a cost saver for families and facilities. Music can also help mask unwanted noise from a hallway, a roommate, or medical equipment, while providing comfort.

Music Therapy for Psychosocial Support

Patients may be referred for music therapy services for an extensive range of psychological, emotional, and social issues including anxiety, depression, isolation, confusion, grief, impaired communication, ineffective coping, normalization, self-esteem, control, relationship/family problems, diversion, lack of insight, life review and reminiscence, disorientation, and motivation (Dileo & Dneaster, 2004; Krout, 2000; Maue-Johnson & Tanguay, 2006; Mills-Groen, 2007).

The music therapist enters the room of Dan, a 55-year-old nonresponsive male patient on the palliative care unit located within a hospital. Many family members are present; however, they are not interacting with each other. The television is on and they are sitting quietly around the perimeter of the room. The music therapist stands by the bed, talks directly to the patient and family, and gradually family members gather around the bed and begin interacting with each other and Dan. They respond to the statements by the music therapist, and a teenage son who was looking through a songbook states, "Dad always turned up the radio in the pickup when he heard this one." The music therapist suggests singing this song, and the family does so. The family begins telling stories about Dan, touching his arms and legs as they stand near the bed while others hold his hands. The music therapist encourages family to speak directly to Dan, as the sense of hearing is the last sense remaining before end-of-life. Dan may not be able to respond, but he possibly can hear what his family is saying to him. Family expresses a variety of emotions, sings, and talks to Dan, who responds by a slight raising of his eyebrows and barely noticeable nods of his head.

This situation is typical in hospice and palliative care when a patient is nearing end-of-life. Other patients in hospice care are active, fully functional, and continue to work, while most others fit somewhere between on the continuum of nonresponsive to fully functional. In the scenario above, the music therapist provided a focus for the family members to interact with each other, to express emotions, and to express themselves directly to their loved one. The variety of emotions expressed was directly related to the music and the skills of the therapist who helped normalize the environment. Family members were able to laugh and shed tears when telling stories. They were able to review life and help put things in perspective while working together in their grief. The music was a way for the family to feel as if they could do something for Dan; they at least had control within this one area. The music therapist helped create positive memories in a situation where the family felt helpless and distressed.

Music therapy can assist with providing the focal point for the family to work together, everyone at the same time, for the best quality of life for the patient. Family can be encouraged to sing or play tone chimes or other instruments, working together as a cohesive unit for the benefit of the patient and everyone involved.

Music therapy also provides psychosocial support through music assisted relaxation, through music-based discussions for expression of concerns and fears, and by offering a focus for living in the present moment while enjoying the simple pleasures in life. Patients often find that a familiar meaningful piece of music may offer a calming and soothing presence. Songwriting, lyric discussions, singing, and listening to music can all assist patients and families with identification and expression of concerns or fears. Live music facilitated by the therapist brings the focus on the here and now, enjoying the moment with loved ones instead of worrying about the uncertainty of the future.

Provide emotional support. The music therapist has the means to reach patients on an emotional level (see Chapter 3). Instead of talking on an intellectual level, patients may be able to express themselves on the feeling level with assistance from the musical stimulus. Salmon (1993) maintains that most people have experienced "being profoundly moved upon hearing a piece of music" (p. 49).

Low-functioning patients may be able to cry, smile, or respond motorically, or express other emotions that would be more difficult or impossible to do with only discussion involved. Patients can be reassured that is it socially acceptable to release feelings to music, which may help normalize the situation. Often patients will express a certain emotion in reaction to music and not realize that this is what they were feeling. The music therapist can help identify and encourage expression of this feeling through music listening, songwriting, singing, instrument playing, lyric discussion, song choice, relaxation and music imagery, or making a recording as a lasting gift.

Music may be used to help someone visualize different ways of thinking or become self-aware, either through lyrics, music-based counseling, or self-growth within musical experiences. Patients may not need or desire extensive reframing or interpretation by the music therapist. Offering support and comfort through music-assisted supportive counseling and active listening when applicable may be most effective in providing the best quality of life for each individual.

As a stimulus for reminiscence/life review. Looking back at one's life and putting things in perspective helps a person discover a sense of meaning (Salmon, 1993). Music can effectively stimulate the long-term memory of patients, making it possible to recall in great detail long-forgotten past events and emotions (Bonny, 2001). This is particularly effective with patients who have short-term memory problems but retain all or part of their long-term memory. Families are able to contribute to a life review, enjoy, express emotions, and reconnect with each other through shared memories and experiences. Varied musical interventions can help the life review process become more vivid, detailed, and effective (O'Callaghan, 1996).

A musical life review can contain a mixture of emotions with patients and families expressing sadness, joy, hope, meaning, and release through the verbal process as well as the music itself. The musical presence in a life review tends to bring the emotional content to the surface, possibly making it more meaningful to those involved. For patients who enjoy singing, the release of tension, emotion, and creativity can be cathartic.

Provide spiritual support and comfort. The music therapist may work with the patient and family to select religious music according to specific faith traditions or with other music that is deemed spiritual by the patient or family. Patients may be physically unable to attend their place of worship or enjoy nature in a direct manner, so the music therapist can create opportunities for spiritual expression. Although spiritual needs are considerable and diverse, music therapists often provide comfort, a stimulus for reminiscence/life review, and an outlet for creativity (Hilliard, 2005; Krout, 2003; Trauger-Querry & Haghighi, 1999).

Music may be most comforting for a patient at end-of-life, as the bond between music, emotions, and spirituality is strong (Walker, 1995). Music may bring a sense of familiarity, intimacy, connectedness, tenderness, and peace as it blocks or masks other undesirable noise in the environment. Listening to favorite music from the past may be soothing for the patient, caregivers, and families. One person may wish to listen to favorite hymns sung quietly at bedside, which also helps reduce agitation later in the day. Another person may choose to hear upbeat gospel music that lifts mood and provides structure for motor responses such as toe-tapping and clapping. Both interventions provide spiritual support and involve passive or active music listening.

Music also brings the added dimension of comfort for patients who are not affiliated with organized religious practices. Offering comfort through musical pieces that have specific function or ritual can be particularly meaningful for patients and families. Music provides a venue for worship (Bonny, 2001). It helps access the deeper inner nature of being, opens communication between people and the divine, and provides structure for comfort, peace, and release (Lipe, 2002). Music, prayer, and the beauty of nature are effective means to access the close connection to a Higher Power for some patients (Wein, 1987).

Opportunities for choice and decision making. Patients may have little independence or autonomy at end-of-life. Singing and song choice can add increased control and self-expression to music listening approaches. The familiarity of choosing and singing even parts of a song seems to help memories become more vivid. Music therapists can encourage autonomy with simple choice-making interventions. For example, the music therapist might ask, "Do you want to hear 'Home on the Range' or 'As Time Goes By'?" This begins the process of enhancing feelings of control in a small manner. Patients make a selection, and then the music therapist can continue to offer an additional choice, "Would you like a fast song or a slow song?" and so on. Some patients who feel helpless need to practice making small decisions, and as they become more comfortable, they can make choices more easily.

The music therapist might provide the patient with an age-appropriate instrument, adapted so it is easily played in a successful manner, to enhance self-esteem and feelings of accomplishment. Nonverbal patients can often express themselves through motoric responses on a drum or other instrument. Songwriting can be adapted to ensure that a positive experience occurs and that autonomy will be enhanced. For example, a patient may need to fill in only one word or part of a phrase in a song that the music therapist has created. Discussion of song lyrics can help people identify strategies to develop realistic ways of taking control of things that can be controlled. Conversely, serious discussions of what types of things are beyond control can help validate experience and motivate change. The music therapist can help patients adjust to limitations, gain a sense of control, and raise self-esteem through interventions including song choice, music listening, songwriting, playing instruments, singing, making a recording for others, or lyric discussion.

Lower functioning patients may also participate in song choice and singing approaches. Allowing extra time for response, providing a forced choice between two selections, or having a visual aid helps some patients with making choices. For example, a nonverbal patient may be able to make a selection by pointing or directing a gaze at a picture of a sun, choosing the song You Are My Sunshine. Lower functioning patients may frequently join singing when adaptations such as repetition, slower tempo, lower range, and close proximity are implemented. They may be able to mouth words to songs, hum, and sing parts or ends of phrases with pleasure and a feeling of achievement.

Emily was a 6-year-old female with an inoperable brain tumor, no longer active due to disease progression. Music therapy provided sessions for

Emily with her younger sibling and other family members. Emily preferred quiet voices and low stimulation due to her diagnosis, but wanted to sing and have everyone around her. She gained great comfort by singing her favorite song for others and from having her family repeatedly sing her favorite song to her. In addition to comfort, providing group sessions and a recording of Emily singing also helped create positive memories for Emily's younger sister and family.

Singing, music listening, and song choice are adaptable to all ages as well as levels of functioning. In addition to their illness, children in hospice care may have the stress of missing school, events, friends, and the normal situations of everyday life. Adolescents in particular may listen to music for peer acceptance, to tune out adults, and for an emotional outlet. Music helps provide a normalized environment for children, offers distraction and a means for emotional expression, as well as providing comfort.

Outlet for creativity. Using music and creativity as a means of living fully and finding inner peace brings comfort at end-of-life (Krout, 2001). People who have life-limiting or chronic conditions are still able to express themselves creatively through music-based interventions in a variety of ways (Hilliard, 2001; O'Callaghan, 1996). Patients can sing, play instruments, write songs or poems that can be set to music, make recordings for lasting gifts, and make creative suggestions while participating in music therapy sessions.

Support during bereavement. Music therapy services can also be tailored to effectively support individuals in their own grief process (Krout, 2000). Each person has his or her own time frame for healing because there is no typical way to grieve. **Bereavement** begins for families, friends, and others of significance after the death of a loved one (Krout, 2005). Some music therapists terminate services upon death, others provide music and support at funerals or memorial services, and others continue to see family members for grief support for a length of time. Music therapists may also provide music for memorial services offered through the hospice organization for all patients who have died within a certain time period. It is common practice to offer bereavement sessions through the hospice organization for specific groups based on age or type of loss. For example, there are music therapy sessions for children who are bereaved, and grief groups for teens, parents, or spouses who have lost a partner.

SUMMARY

Music therapy in hospice and palliative care is more about helping people live to the fullest in the moment than focusing on death and dying. Working with patients and families at end-of-life can be fulfilling and growth-producing for the therapist. Music therapists, along with the entire interdisciplinary hospice team, make a difference in the lives of others on a daily basis.

People in end-of-life care have needs related to physical symptoms such as pain and restlessness, emotional issues such as dealing with loss and self-expression, and family cohesion issues. Music therapists use interventions including music listening, singing, songwriting, song choice, instrument playing, lyric analysis, music-assisted cognitive reframing, improvisation, and music for imagery and relaxation to address the needs of the patient and families. Music therapy interventions are designed to help manage pain, increase relaxation, promote emotional expression, decrease isolation, improve family interactions, provide a spiritual outlet, and improve self-esteem. Music therapy interventions can be flexible and adapted to the functioning level and individual needs of each patient.

STUDY QUESTIONS

1. What are the primary goals of hospice and palliative care?

2. How does the music therapist contribute to the interdisciplinary team approach?

3. What are some of the primary physical needs of people who have terminal illness? What are the primary psychosocial needs of people who have terminal illness?

4. What are some of the ways that music can be used to manage pain?

5. How can music therapy be used to provide emotional comfort or emotional expression?

6. How can music therapy be used to engage family members and improve family cohesion?

7. What is bereavement and how can a music therapist contribute to this phase of the hospice program?

8. What are some challenges a music therapist might face when assessing a person who has a terminal illness?

REFERENCES

American Music Therapy Association. (2007). *AMTA member sourcebook*. Silver Spring, MD: Author.

Barrickman, J. (1989). A developmental music therapy approach for preschool hospitalized children. *Music Therapy Perspectives, 7*, 10–16.

Bonny, H. (2001). Music and spirituality. *Music Therapy Perspectives, 19*(1), 59–62.

Cohen-Mansfield, J., & Creedon, M. (2002). Nursing staff members' perceptions of pain indicators in persons with severe dementia. *Clinical Journal of Pain, 18*(1), 64–73.

Dileo, C., & Dneaster, D. (2005). Music therapy at the end of life: State of the art. In C. Dileo & J. L. Loewy (Eds.), *Music therapy at end of life* (pp. xix–xxvii). Cherry Hill, NJ: Jeffrey Books.

Ghetti, C., & Walker, J. (in press). Music therapy with pediatric units: Oncology, hematology, and bone marrow transplant. In D. Hanson-Abromeit & C. Colwell (Eds.), *Medical music therapy: Children to adults in the hospital setting.* Silver Spring, MD: American Music Therapy Association.

Hilliard, R. (2001). The use of music therapy in meeting the multidimensional needs of hospice patients and their families. *Journal of Palliative Care, 17*(3), 161–166.

Hilliard, R. E. (2003). The effects of music therapy on the quality and length of life of people diagnosed with terminal cancer. *Journal of Music Therapy, 40*(2), 117–137.

Hilliard, R. E. (2005). *Hospice and palliative care music therapy: A guide to program development and clinical care.* Cherry Hill, NJ: Jeffrey Books.

Hospice Patient Alliance. (2008). *Terminal agitation: A major distressful symptom in the dying.* Retrieved May 9, 2008, from http://hospicepatients.org

Kastenbaum, B. (2001). Pain and pain management. In G. Howarth & O. Leaman (Eds.), *Encyclopedia of death and dying.* Retrieved May 9, 2008, from http://deathreference.com

Krout, R. E. (2000). Hospice and palliative music therapy: A continuum of creative caring. In AMTA (Ed.), *Effectiveness of music therapy procedures: Documentation of research and clinical practice* (3rd ed.) (pp. 323–341). Silver Spring, MD: American Music Therapy Association.

Krout, R. E. (2001). The effects of single session music therapy interventions on the observed and self-reported levels of pain control, physical comfort, and relaxation of hospice patients. *American Journal of Hospice & Palliative Care, 18*(6), 383–390.

Krout, R. E. (2003). Music therapy with imminently dying hospice patients and their families: Facilitating release near time of death. *American Journal of Hospice & Palliative Care, 20*(2), 129–134.

Krout, R. E. (2005). Applications of music therapist-composed songs in creating participant connections and facilitating goals and rituals during on-time bereavement support groups and programs. *Music Therapy Perspectives, 23*(2), 118–128.

Lipe, A. (2002). Beyond therapy: Music, spirituality, and health in human experience: A review of literature. *Journal of Music Therapy, 39*(3), 209–240.

Mayo Foundation for Medical Education and Research. (2008). *Relaxation techniques: Learn ways to calm your stress.* Retrieved May 12, 2008, from http://mayoclinic.com

Maue-Johnson, E., & Tanguay, C. L. (2006). Assessing the unique needs of hospice patients: A tool for music therapists. *Music Therapy Perspectives, 24*(1), 13–21.

Mills-Groen, K. (2007). Pain assessment and management in end of life care: A survey of assessment and treatment practices of hospice music therapy and nursing professionals. *Journal of Music Therapy, 44*(2), 90–112.

National Foundation for the Treatment of Pain. (2008). *Perspectives in intractable pain management.* Retrieved May 10, 2008, from http://paincare.org

National Hospice & Palliative Care Organization. (2008). *The hospice team.* Retrieved May 9, 2008, from http://nhpco.org

O'Callaghan, C. C. (1996). Pain, music creativity and music therapy in palliative care. *The American Journal of Hospice and Palliative Care, 13*(2), 43–49.

Salmon, D. (1993). Music and emotion in palliative care. *Journal of Palliative Care, 9*(4), 48–52.

Standley, J. M. (2000). Music research in medical treatment. In AMTA (Ed.), *Effectiveness of music therapy procedures: Documentation of research and clinical practice* (3rd ed.) (pp. 1–64). Silver Spring, MD: American Music Therapy Association.

Trauger-Querry, B., & Haghighi, K. R. (1999). Balancing the focus: Art and music therapy for pain control and symptom management in hospice care. *The Hospice Journal, 14*(1), 25–38.

Walker, J. (1995). Music therapy, spirituality and chemically dependent clients. *Journal of Chemical Dependency Treatment, 5*(2), 145–166.

Warden, V., Hurley, A., & Volicer, L. (2003). Development and psychometric evaluation of the pain assessment in advanced dementia (PAINAD) scale. *American Medical Directors Association, 4*(1), 9–15.

Wein, B. (1987). Body and soul music. *American Health, 4*, 67–73.

CHAPTER 13

MUSIC THERAPY IN THE TREATMENT OF SENSORY DISORDERS

Kate E. Gfeller
Alice Ann Darrow

CHAPTER OUTLINE

PART I: HEARING
SOUND AND THE AUDITORY SYSTEM
Sound Energy
The Hearing Mechanism
PROFILES OF HEARING LOSS
Types of Hearing Loss
Degree of Hearing Losses
Configuration of Hearing Loss
Onset of Hearing Loss
Hearing Aids and Cochlear Implants
THE RELATIONSHIP BETWEEN HEARING LOSS AND MODE OF COMMUNICATION
OTHER TERMS AND SOCIOCULTURAL ISSUES RELATED TO HEARING LOSS
Deaf Culture
Music in Deaf Culture
PROBLEMS ASSOCIATED WITH HEARING LOSS
Problems Resulting from a Hearing Loss in Early Childhood
Problems Resulting from a Hearing Loss Acquired in Adulthood
MUSIC THERAPY WITH PERSONS WHO HAVE HEARING LOSSES
Music Perception and Enjoyment
Accommodations in Music Therapy and Music Education
TREATMENT GOALS FOR PERSONS WITH HEARING LOSSES
Music Therapy to Promote Auditory Training
Music Therapy for Speech Development
Music Therapy for Language Development

Music Therapy for Social Skills Development
PART II: VISION
VISUAL IMPAIRMENTS: DEFINITIONS AND ETIOLOGY
Definitions of Vision Loss
CHARACTERISTICS OF PERSONS WITH VISUAL IMPAIRMENTS
Cognition
Language
Academic Achievement
Social Development
Motor Development
MUSIC THERAPY OBJECTIVES
Listening Skills
Orientation and Mobility Skills
Daily Living Skills
Social and Interpersonal Communication Skills
Emotional Expression and Development
Academic Skills
Reducing Sensory Stimulation Behaviors That May Accompany Blindness

PART I: HEARING

Meganne is music therapist at a summer program intended to help children who have hearing losses to help develop speech, language, and reading skills. Meganne has been asked to develop music activities that will reinforce their communication goals, as well as expose them to music and other fine arts in an accessible format.

This morning, Meganne met the five children assigned to her music group for the first time. While they all share the common experience of having hearing loss, they are true individuals in many ways. Nathan, a 10-year-old who lives on a farm just outside of town, was born with a profound hearing loss. At age 3, he received a cochlear implant, a special bionic ear that helps him understand speech. Because he relied heavily on sign language prior to and while becoming accustomed to his implant, he is still comfortable with signing, though now he communicates primarily with speech. Nathan loves to play basketball, and last year he started playing the drums in band.

Enrique, who is 9 years old, is the son of Mexican migrant workers. Although he has only a moderate hearing loss, he did not receive any hearing aids or special services to develop language skills (including the use of sign language) until he was 8. Therefore, even though he is extremely bright, he is far behind his peers in the development of speech and language. Enrique has a close-knit family. He loves to play baseball and soccer with his brothers, and he especially enjoys social events such as Cinco de Mayo celebrations shared with other Mexican families in town. School, on the other hand, can be frustrating and lonely because he has difficulty with academics and communicating with the other kids.

Ten-year-old Kristin was born with a mild hearing loss, which is progressing in severity each year. At present, she has a moderate loss, but she still gets benefits from the use of hearing aids. Her speech sounds very much like that of any hearing person her age, though her language skills are a bit behind her classmates. Because of her progressive hearing loss, Kristin's parents have encouraged her to learn sign language as well as use spoken communication. She is quite comfortable communicating either way. Kristin loves country music and drawing; her dream is to have her own horse.

Yen-Ling is 10 years old. Her family moved to the States from Taiwan when she was 5. Her hearing loss is mild, and she hears pretty well as long as she uses her hearing aids. She is accustomed to communicating with speech (she knows only a few signs), but her speech and language development are a bit behind that of her peers—not only because of her hearing loss, but also because she started learning English at age 5. Yen-Ling's family has a strong commitment to education and also to the fine arts. She is enrolled in ballet and she started cello lessons last year. Yen-Ling is all excited about going to Disney World later this summer.

Shelley, an 11-year-old, was born deaf to deaf parents; Shelley's grandparents are deaf as well. Shelley's family members are leaders in their local Deaf Club, and Shelley's dad is a bit of a celebrity, since he was once a championship wrestler in the Deaf Olympics. Shelley has owned hearing aids for years, but she rarely uses them since she considers them of little assistance and "lame." Shelley communicates using American Sign Language, and her signing is simply beautiful—she is often chosen to do special signing "solos," such as signing the National Anthem at school assemblies. She has also performed several leads in a local drama company, Thespian Signs, that uses sign language rather than speech. This company, which was inspired by the National Theatre for the Deaf, is sponsored by the Deaf Club. Shelley hates using her voice, and she has already informed Meganne, the music therapist, that she doesn't see why she should waste her time coming to music—after all, music is for hearing people.

Meganne has an interesting challenge ahead of her: developing group activities that will meet the communicative and social needs as well as the personal interests of each group member. As she plans her sessions, she'll need to take into account the audiological profiles, modes of communication, functional strengths and needs, sociocultural values, and individual personalities in order to provide a meaningful and beneficial experience.

As the participants in Meganne's group illustrate, there is no single profile of hearing loss. People with hearing loss differ on a number of dimensions, including the characteristics of their hearing loss (how severe, what type, etc.), how they communicate, their cultural background, and their own unique interests and challenges. This chapter will (1) provide an overview of the audiological aspects of hearing loss, (2) introduce several prominent methods for communication, (3) present various cultural perspectives relevant to hearing loss, (4) identify problems of speech and language associated with hearing loss, and (5) describe different uses of music therapy and instructional accommodations that can be beneficial.

SOUND AND THE AUDITORY SYSTEM

Sound Energy

The sense of hearing is an important source of information and pleasure. The wail of a police siren signals possible danger, while the lilt of a mother's lullaby comforts her infant. The voice on the six o'clock news informs us of world events, and music from the car radio offers welcome distraction from the tedium of a long drive. Though we may not realize it, all of these sources of sound vibrate and create **sound waves** that travel through mediums such as air, water, or solids (e.g., metal) to reach your ear.

The term *frequency* is used to describe the number of cycles per second at which a sound source (voice, instrument, etc.) is vibrating. The unit of measurement of frequency is called Hertz (abbreviated as **Hz**, e.g., 440 Hz). If a sound source vibrates slowly, it produces a low-frequency sound (such as 20 Hz), and if it vibrates quickly, it produces a high-frequency sound (such as 4000 Hz). The term *pitch* is used to describe our *perception* of frequency—that is, how high or low it sounds to the listener. In music, we assign letter names of the musical scale to each pitch. For example, a sound wave of 440 Hz would be called A above middle C. Because hearing is the primary sense through which most people perceive music, and music is the primary medium in music therapy, this chapter includes information about the structure of the hearing mechanism as well as different types of hearing losses that alter enjoyment and perception of musical sounds.

The Hearing Mechanism

How do we perceive sound energy? The ear is made up of three major parts: the **outer ear**, the **middle ear**, and the **inner ear**. The **outer ear** includes the **pinna** (ear lobe), which is specially shaped to funnel sound waves into the ear canal. The **mechanical energy** of the sound wave is then transmitted to the portion of the hearing mechanism called the **middle ear**, which includes the **tympanic membrane** (eardrum), and **ossicles** (small middle ear bones). These ossicles act as levers to conduct the mechanical energy to the **inner ear**, which includes the **cochlea**.

The cochlea is made up of a narrow winding canal that houses a gelatinous type of fluid and a special lining called the **basilar membrane**. This membrane holds in place thousands of fine hair cells (a special kind of neuron, or nerve cell), known as **cilia**. The mechanical energy transmitted from the middle ear moves across the cilia. As these hair cells are stimulated, the mechanical energy is converted to electrochemical energy; this energy is sent via the **auditory nerve** to the brain, where the sound is processed and interpreted.

Disease, anatomical anomalies, or malfunction can impair hearing at any point along this auditory pathway, and thus affect the quality and loudness of sound that an individual hears. Different terms used to describe where the hearing loss originates are described below.

PROFILES OF HEARING LOSSES

Types of Hearing Loss

There are four primary types of hearing loss, each of which has a different origin in the hearing mechanism. A **conductive hearing loss** is caused by disease, malformation, or obstruction in the outer or middle ear. Conductive hearing losses often impede hearing acuity across a wide range of frequencies (i.e., low as well as high sounds). In some cases, the problem can be treated medically (i.e., reparative surgery). If the problem cannot be resolved medically, devices such as hearing aids (which will be described later in this chapter) that amplify sounds are often helpful.

Some hearing losses, known as **sensorineural hearing losses**, result from damage to, or absence of the delicate hair cells of the inner ear. This type of loss may be due to a variety of causes (etiology) such as infections, extended exposure to extremely loud sounds, or conditions present at birth. It is often the case that some frequencies are more easily heard than others. For example, many people with a sensorineural hearing loss will be able to hear low-pitched sounds (e.g., music from a cello) more easily than high-pitched sounds (e.g., music from a flute). In addition, some sounds may be distorted. Some persons with this type of loss often report that musical sounds are distorted or harsh in quality, as well as difficult to perceive.

With a sensorineural loss, there is a breakdown in the transmission of sound waves from mechanical to electrochemical energy. Providing more sound energy through amplification (as with a hearing aid) may or may not be of any benefit. Some persons with profound sensorineural loss who do not benefit from hearing aids may be candidates for an auditory prosthesis called a cochlear implant, which will be described later in this chapter.

A *mixed hearing loss* is a combination of conductive and sensorineural losses in one ear. If the hearing loss is due to damage or impairment to the brain or central nervous system, it is called a **central hearing loss.** In the case of a central hearing loss, although sound stimuli are transmitted to the inner ear at an adequate level of loudness, the listener, because of neurological deficits, has difficulty interpreting or understanding the sound signal. For example, the individual may acknowledge that he hears speech, but he may be unable to determine the meaning of the words. Rehabilitation of a central hearing loss is more closely related to interventions for brain injury than conductive or sensorineural losses, and therefore will not be covered in this chapter.

Degree of Hearing Losses

Hearing losses vary not only with regard to type (structural cause) but also with regard to **severity**. More specifically, the range of hearing losses is as follows (from least to most severe): slight, mild, moderate, severe, and profound. People with slight hearing losses may have difficulty hearing quiet or distant speech, but may be unaware that they have a problem. They may think that others are talking too softly or mumbling. At the other end of this continuum, people with profound losses can hear only very loud sounds and have considerable difficulty hearing normal conversational speech. Quiet sounds will most likely be completely undetected; loud sounds may be perceived, but are often experienced as a tactile (vibration) sensation rather than as a distinct sound with a specific pitch or timbre (tone quality). Profound or total deafness is rare. More often, people have some usable hearing, called **residual hearing.**

In general, the greater the severity of loss, the greater the impact the deficit has on communication, particularly among other hearing persons. Through training, people can learn to make maximum use of their residual hearing in order to better understand speech and environmental sounds.

Configuration of Hearing Loss

The configuration or shape of the hearing loss refers to the extent of hearing loss at each frequency and the overall profile of hearing that results (American Speech-Language-Hearing Association [ASHA], 2008). For example, some people have greater hearing loss in higher frequencies than in lower frequencies, while other people may have what is called a flat configuration—that is, a similar amount of hearing loss for low and high sounds. With regard to music, greater loss in higher frequencies can make it more difficult to hear instruments played in a higher frequency range (e.g., flute, triangle), as well as reduce the brilliance of tone quality. Other hearing problems related to configuration include (1) whether the loss is in one ear (**unilateral**) or in both ears (**bilateral**), or (2) the course of the loss over time (e.g., sudden onset, progressive, stable, fluctuating).

Onset of Hearing Loss

Another way in which hearing losses are categorized is by **age of onset**, or when the hearing loss first occurred. A **congenital** hearing loss is present *at birth*, while hearing losses that occur *after* birth are known as **acquired** or **adventitious** hearing losses.

Prelingual losses occur before the acquisition of spoken language (approximately 0–2 years of age), and **perilingual** losses occur as spoken language is developing (approximately 2–4 years). **Postlingual losses** are those that occur after the acquisition of language (approximately age 4 and up). The age of onset is particularly important with regard to speech and language development and music perception. Those losses that occur before the acquisition of language have a greater impact on speech and language development than postlingual losses.

In most cases, persons with postlingual losses will have developed a foundation for spoken language and mental concept of speech and musical sounds. However, children with postlingual losses often show a slower rate of more advanced language skills than do normally hearing children, and the quality of speech can deteriorate over time because the individual has difficulty monitoring his own speech sounds.

Keep in mind that the type, degree, configuration, and onset of hearing loss all interact with one another. Together, these factors influence the extent to which a hearing loss impacts everyday functioning. For example, a person with a slight postlingual hearing loss may require only minor adjustments (such as sitting closer to the person speaking, and watching their lips carefully) in order to function effectively in typical educational, vocational, or social settings. In contrast, when an individual has a severe or profound loss that occurs prelingually, acoustic prosthetics (e.g., hearing aids, cochlear implants) or alternative modes of communication may be necessary. For that reason, a therapist will want to learn as much as possible about a client's hearing profile in order to establish more suitable therapeutic objectives, to make suitable choices regarding accommodations, and to choose musical sounds compatible with the individual's auditory capabilities and acoustic prosthetics. The following section describes some of the most common types of acoustic prosthetics.

Hearing Aids and Cochlear Implants

Most people are familiar with **hearing aids**. Hearing aids, which are worn within the ear canal, essentially amplify sounds so they can be more easily detected. A personal hearing aid picks up the sound waves through a small ear-level microphone and converts it into electrical energy. After the electrical signal is amplified, it is converted back into sound waves, which are presented into the ear canal.

Hearing aids are dispensed by **audiologists**, professionals who test hearing and then make recommendations regarding the most appropriate type of amplification. Hearing aids do not cure hearing losses, but rather aid listeners in detecting sounds. They are most helpful for people who have slight to moderate conductive losses. Persons who have more severe damage to the inner ear may receive only partial or minimal benefit from personal hearing aids and are more likely to experience some distortion in sound quality, especially with louder sounds. The effectiveness of hearing aids with regard to music will be discussed later in this chapter.

Some persons who have severe to profound sensorineural hearing loss in both ears receive limited benefit from personal hearing aids. These individuals may be candidates for another type of device called the **cochlear implant (CI)**. This device, part of which is surgically implanted in the person's cochlea, does not amplify the sound. Rather, the CI provides direct electrical stimulation to the auditory nerve. The sound wave is picked up by a microphone worn at ear level and converted by a small externally-worn processor to an electrical signal. That signal is transmitted to a small electrode array implanted in the cochlea, which then stimulates the auditory nerve. The signal travels via the auditory neural pathway in the brain to the auditory cortex, or that part of the brain dedicated to perceiving and interpreting sounds. It is important to note that a cochlear implant does not cure deafness or transmit a replica of sound as heard through a healthy ear. Rather, the implant extracts specific parts of the signal that are considered especially helpful in understanding speech.

The extent to which CIs help speech perception varies from one person to the next depending upon the age at which the individual became deaf, the cause of hearing loss, and several other factors, including the structural features of the language being spoken. For example, some languages (such as Mandarin Chinese or Thai) are called tonal languages, because the tones (pitch contours) of the words convey meaning. Some tones are less effectively transmitted by cochlear implants than words used in non-tonal languages such as English (Hsiao, in press). However, most CI recipients find the CI quite helpful in understanding speech (Wilson, 2000).

On average, adults who grew up with normal hearing, but lost hearing well into adulthood, achieve approximately 80% accuracy on some speech perception tests with their implants. The extent to which CIs are effective in conveying musical sounds is described later in this chapter.

It is interesting to note that some individuals who affiliate primarily with Deaf culture (which is introduced later in this chapter) and communicate primarily with sign language, choose not to use cochlear implants, even if CIs might provide some benefit in spoken communication. Keep in mind that one of the primary reasons for using a CI is to aid spoken communication. If spoken communication is not a high priority, the CI may be considered irrelevant to one's daily life. Furthermore, for some, a cochlear implant is considered inconsistent with the cultural values of the Deaf community—even a threat to the future of American Sign Language.

As this section indicates, the profile of hearing loss has implications for prosthetic devices used, which, in turn, has implications for music enjoyment and candidacy for music therapy services. What's more, the hearing profile and hearing history also have an impact upon the type(s) of communication most often used. The next section describes different modes (types) of communication used by persons with hearing losses.

THE RELATIONSHIP BETWEEN HEARING LOSS AND MODE OF COMMUNICATION

The combination of type, severity, and onset of hearing loss is likely to influence the type of communication that is most effective for a given individual. For example, people with mild losses and greater residual hearing can generally communicate by speaking and speechreading (often referred to informally as lipreading) in conjunction with careful listening. This is known as an **oral communication system.**

The Oral Approach to developing communication is based upon the assumption that deaf and hard-of-hearing children can learn to talk; this approach encourages speech and speechreading as the primary means for the transmission of thoughts and ideas. Educators who believe in the Oral Approach philosophy rely exclusively on the use of residual hearing (with amplification) and speechreading in teaching speech. People with mild hearing losses who communicate orally may be virtually undistinguishable from normal-hearing people in superficial interactions, unless you happen to notice their hearing aids or very subtle differences in the sound of their speech.

Some people with more severe losses (especially those with early onset) may have great difficulty forming clear, intelligible speech sounds, or understanding other people's verbal communication. Persons with severe to profound hearing losses (especially those with congenital losses, or with deaf parents) often prefer to communicate manually. The **Manual Approach** includes the use of **signs** (symbolic representations of language made with the hands) and **fingerspelling** (hand shapes corresponding to the letters of the written alphabet). **Sign languages** are independent languages that have developed within communities of origin. There is no universal sign language. For example, **American Sign Language (ASL)** is different from British Sign Language, even though the oral language for both countries is English.

There are various forms of **Manual Communication**, which are described in Figure 1. These methods of communication include **English-based sign systems, fingerspelling**—also referred to as the **Rochester Method,** and **American Sign Language (ASL)**. Each form of manual communication employs different rules of syntax and semantics.

Some persons may use both oral and a form of manual communication, which is referred to as **Simultaneous Communication** or **SimmCom**. Though often used interchangeably with the term *Total Communication (TC)*, it is more appropriately a type of Total Communication.

Fingerspelling consists of specific hand shapes that correspond to the individual letters of the alphabet. These hand shapes are used to spell out words, much like writing in the air. When used exclusively, this mode of communication is referred to as the Rochester Method.

American Sign Language (ASL) is a true language in that it has its own syntactical structure, different from that of the English language. It is supplemented by fingerspelled words if no appropriate sign exists for a particular object or concept (e.g., proper names). The signs in ASL are word-like units, which have both concrete and abstract meanings.

Sign Systems differ from sign language in that they attempt to create visual equivalents of spoken words through manual symbols. Systems such as **Signed English** or **Signing Exact English** are forms of manually-coded English. While they may borrow signs from ASL, the signs are used in the syntactical structure of the English language and are used in one-to-one correspondence with words. Additional signs are used to indicate verb tense, prefixes, suffixes, and word endings.

Conceptually Accurate Signed English (CASE) is the use of ASL signs based on meaning, but in English word order. Users of CASE, like those who use American Sign Language, use ASL signs based on the meaning of the message and not on English words.

Simultaneous Communication (SimmCom) is used to denote the combined use of speech, signs, and fingerspelling. Receptively, an individual receives the message both by speechreading what is being said and by reading the signs and fingerspelling simultaneously. Spoken English rarely is used with ASL. The manual form of communication is most often one of the English sign systems or CASE.

Cued Speech is a form of simultaneous communication, but unlike SimmCom, the signs are specific hand shapes provided as cues to assist children in clarifying English speechreading. The hand shapes are used to help a child differentiate the various **phonemes** (sound segments of speech) of speech that look similar on the lips (such as map, pat, and bat).

Total Communication (TC) involves the use of any or all modes of communication—sign systems or sign language, spoken language, mime, facial expression, or gestures to facilitate children's language development and communication. The intention of this methodology is to provide a child with any modality, or combinations thereof, that might be successful in facilitating language development. Some educators believe that utilizing any or all forms of communication is unrealistic, and that one form of communication is emphasized at the expense of another (Schirmer, 1998).

Figure 1. Modes of Communication Used by People with Hearing Losses

Historically, there has been considerable dissention and debate among proponents of the various communication approaches. There is increasing consensus, however, that whatever system or method works most successfully for the child should be used to promote clear and understandable communication. The primary factors that influence choice of communication (oral or particular manual approach) include the degree of hearing loss, educational background, philosophy of communication, and the family's form of communication.

The majority of individuals with a hearing loss are able to use speech as their primary medium for language acquisition. However, children with severe to profound hearing losses who get little benefit from amplification have a much more difficult time learning to speak and in developing language skills. They will not be able to rely solely on their hearing for processing speech. In order to communicate orally, they will need to learn to speechread and/or rely on manual forms of communication. The type of manual communication used will ultimately depend upon the values and cultural background of their family—deaf or hearing, as well as the presence, background, and influence of early intervention educators.

Language development and competency. Language competency is influenced by a number of factors including onset of hearing loss, effectiveness of amplification, appropriate choice of communication mode, education, and also the availability of excellent language models in all aspects of the child's life (home, school, community). The extent to which a child's parents provide a rich language model that is accessible to the child is a particularly important factor (Marschark, 2007). Deaf children born into deaf families with parents who are excellent signers develop language at rates similar to hearing children born to hearing parents (Kuntze, 1998; Meier & Newport, 1990). Most deaf children, however, are born to hearing parents. It is important to provide competent language models to deaf children at as early an age as is possible. For children born into hearing families, special effort is required to provide a rich language environment to compensate for the child's auditory limitations.

One instructional approach related to language competence that is experiencing growing interest is the Bilingual-Bicultural Approach (Drasgow, 1998; Mahshie, 1995). Based upon the successful academic achievement of children born to deaf parents and other approaches used with second language learners, some educators are advocating a bilingual-bicultural approach to the education of deaf children. Advocates believe that American Sign Language as a first language can lead to linguistic competence, and that English is better learned as a second language and in the context of bilingual-bicultural instruction. The main obstacle to a bilingual-bicultural approach is finding teachers who are sufficiently fluent in American Sign

Language and educated enough about deaf culture such that instruction is truly bilingual and bicultural.

It is important to realize that language delays of deaf children do not indicate children who are "deficient," or slow learners (except in cases of hearing loss combined with intellectual deficits as described in Chapter 4), but rather reflect the absence of an appropriate model to emulate during their critical years of language development. In spite of frequent obstacles in learning language, many children with hearing losses— those who use signs or who learn to speak, do learn language and employ it freely and comfortably in their daily lives.

OTHER TERMS AND SOCIOCULTURAL ISSUES RELATED TO HEARING LOSS

This section introduces additional terms and concepts related to hearing loss and its conceptualization within society. Some terms are based in regulatory policy or cultural norms. For example, the term *hearing impairment* is a global term that describes all hearing losses, regardless of type, classification, or onset, and is often used in regulatory language related to the provision of special education services. It is also a term commonly used by hearing people in everyday conversations when they discuss hearing losses.

There are, however, individuals who find the term *hearing impaired* offensive— primarily persons who identify with Deaf culture. The word *impaired* is usually defined as "broken" or "defective." Persons who are deaf do not see themselves as defective, but rather as members of a linguistic minority within the hearing world (Padden, 1996). The Deaf community has made great strides in recent years to depathologize their disability.

Most professionals distinguish between individuals who are **hard-of-hearing** and those who are **deaf** (Hardman, Drew, & Egan, 2002; Heward, 2003, Turnbull, Turnbull, Shank, Smith, & Leal, 2001). Individuals who are described as hard-of-hearing generally respond to speech and other auditory sounds through the use of their residual hearing, hearing aids, or cochlear implants. Their primary and preferred mode of communication is speech. For individuals who are deaf, their residual hearing is not sufficient to process speech; therefore, the primary means of communication is through some form of manual communication.

Persons who identify with the Deaf culture further define the term *deaf* as either **Deaf (with a capital "D")** or **deaf (with lower case "d")**. Those who uphold the values of Deaf culture (described below) describe themselves as "Deaf." There are others, however, who do not share the language or social ties and thus function more in the hearing world. For example, people with serious hearing losses acquired well into adulthood may prefer to use speechreading and oral forms of communication rather than American Sign Language, since the majority of their friends and acquaintances are hearing people (Padden & Humphries, 1988). These individuals are more apt to describe themselves as *deaf* or with the term *hard-of-hearing* (Padden & Humphries, 1988). Given the considerable variation in hearing status and cultural values of those who have hearing losses, it is important to use these terms with sensitivity to the specific circumstance or individual preference.

Deaf Culture

Culture embodies the beliefs, experiences, and practices of an integrated group of people. These commonalities unify and strengthen the individual members who find understanding from others like themselves. Affiliation with Deaf culture is not simply a matter of degree of hearing loss. Those who uphold the values of **Deaf culture** and use ASL take pride in their cultural identity. Members of the Deaf community can also include hearing people (e.g., children or close friends of deaf individuals) who share the values of the culture (Padden & Humphries, 1988).[1]

Cultural subgroups develop distinct behaviors that are functional for survival within a larger sound-reliant community—such as the formation of Deaf clubs and organizations, schools, sporting events, and churches. The key feature that defines and maintains virtually all cultures is language. It is through language that people are able to socialize, and thereby they transmit group customs, mores, and expectations. Deaf people thus emerge as a unique group with strong solidarity and identity. American Sign Language (ASL) is the native language of people within the Deaf culture (Armstrong, 1999). It originated in the early 19th century through the efforts of Laurent Clerc, a Deaf French educator, and the Reverend Thomas Gallaudet, an American, who saw the need for Deaf education in the United States.

Increasingly, people who are Deaf are seen as a linguistic minority within the hearing world (Padden, 1996). They are not defective or impaired people who are intellectually or cognitively inferior to those who do hear. Misconceptions about sign language and competence have had an impact on the educational and political experiences of the Deaf. In recent years, the Deaf community has made great strides in exerting their issues by educating the public about their language, social and political organizations, and rich legacy of Deaf folklore, art, and literature.

Music in Deaf Culture

Music in Deaf culture has a long and varied history (Darrow & Heller, 1985; Sheldon, 1997). In respect for the Deaf community, it is important to discuss the role of music in a cultural context (Darrow & Loomis, 1999). This respect

---

[1]The second portion of this chapter is about visual impairments. It is important to note that an environment created solely by a sensory deprivation does not make a culture. While blind people bond as a result of similar circumstances associated with limited vision, this shared experience does not form a culture. Blind people are vision-impaired members of a variety of America's linguistic communities.

means expanding the conventional constructs through which music involvement is traditionally defined. First, keep in mind that the adaptability of music makes it accessible to people who are Deaf, especially given that most Deaf and hard-of-hearing people usually have some degree of residual hearing. Therefore, there are certain frequencies, timbres, and intensities of music that can be auditorily detected. Further, music can be processed visually and tactually.

Second, there are aspects of music participation that are particularly meaningful to some people who are Deaf, including vibrations, rhythm, movement, and expression. There are referential features of music, such as emotion and imagery, that even persons with little hearing are able to detect (Darrow, 2006; Darrow & Novak, 2007). There are instrumentalists, singers, rock band musicians, dancers, and concert fans who are Deaf.

Third, research indicates that not all people who are Deaf value music (Darrow, 1993) or feel any sense of loss at being unable to hear music. Some individuals reject music as a hearing value and find no use for it in their lives. These findings have implications for music therapy with individuals who are Deaf. Music therapists should be sensitive to their clients' place within or outside of Deaf culture. For example, Shelley, the child described at the beginning of this chapter who has strong affiliation with the Deaf community, may or may not be a suitable candidate for music therapy.

As this chapter has emphasized, there is no single profile of persons with hearing loss. Some will communicate primarily through speech and affiliate with hearing society. At the other end of the continuum are those who rely on manual communication and for whom sound is more or less irrelevant. That said, people who communicate through sign are a linguistic minority, and they must often function within a predominantly hearing society. The following section outlines some of the difficulties that a person with a hearing loss may have, particularly when functioning in the hearing world.

PROBLEMS ASSOCIATED WITH HEARING LOSS

Problems Resulting from a Hearing Loss in Early Childhood

The primary difficulty associated with hearing loss is in written and spoken forms of communication, particularly when the loss occurs early in life and is severe in nature. This difficulty is easier to understand when we consider how normally hearing children acquire language. Babies start to learn about their native language by listening to the speech of adults or children who demonstrate competent language models. In everyday life, children have many hours of exposure to **incidental language learning** (learning informally by engaging in or overhearing conversation).

Most children by ages 3 or 4 will have acquired most of the basic rules of grammar for their native culture simply by listening to language around them.

Contrast this usual scenario to that of a child (from a hearing family) with a serious hearing loss that is either undetected or little improved by hearing aids or CIs. This child will either miss or have poor examples of language in everyday life. Consequently, there are often delays in language development, including spoken language, internal language (the mental processes associated with language), and written forms.

Some typical problems associated with hearing loss include slower acquisition of vocabulary and proper syntax (rules of grammar), improperly formed speech sounds that make intelligibility problematic, and limited use of the voice. These difficulties in acquiring language and its spoken form (speech) have a negative impact on academic skills that are based in language (any academic subject that requires reading, writing, or verbal communication). Difficulties in understanding the speech of others or in producing intelligible speech also have a negative impact on everyday spoken communication and socialization. These problems in speech perception and/ or production may manifest themselves in difficulties following directions, poor discrimination of sounds, awkward social interactions, and social isolation (Davis & Hardick, 1981).

It is important to emphasize, however, that these difficulties are particular to acquisition of spoken language and the use of written language. Children with rich exposure to manual forms of communication in early life are likely to show similar progress in language development and social interaction in contexts where manual communication is used. However, special instructional methods are typically necessary in order for these same children to acquire competence in spoken and written language. It is toward that end that the music therapist may work in conjunction with other professionals (i.e., deaf education teachers, audiologists, speech-language pathologists) to maximize communication and academic development.

Problems Resulting from a Hearing Loss Acquired in Adulthood

Because adults who acquire hearing losses in adulthood have already mastered speech and language, the types of problems experienced by these individuals are somewhat different from those found in children. Although a few speech sounds may sound less clear or crisp, the speech and language of most adults with acquired hearing loss can still be understood. The problems that are more prevalent for adults with acquired loss include social isolation (i.e., difficulty understanding others in conversation, hearing the words on the radio, etc.), vocational disabilities (i.e., using a phone at work, understanding the instructions of supervisors, etc.), or changes in life style, including hobbies and cultural enrichment (i.e., reduced enjoyment of concerts, plays, religious services, holiday music, etc.). The problems associated with a hearing loss acquired well into adulthood are ameliorated primarily through hearing aids, cochlear implants, and assistive **hearing devices** (i.e., special electronic devices for replacing doorbells, alarm clocks, etc.).

MUSIC THERAPY WITH PERSONS WHO HAVE HEARING LOSSES

Because music is considered primarily an auditory art form, it is easy to assume that music is an inappropriate therapeutic medium for persons with hearing losses. However, music can be an enjoyable art form as well as an excellent tool for therapy, as long as the auditory and communicative characteristics of the individual are accommodated (Amir & Schuchman, 1985; Darrow & Gfeller, 1991, 1996; Edmonds, 1984; Fahey & Birkenshaw, 1972; Ford, 1985; Gfeller, 1986, 1987, 2000, 2007; Hummel, 1971; Riordian, 1971; Vettese, 1974). This section includes (1) a description of musical perception of persons with various types of hearing losses, (2) accommodations that can enhance music perception, and (3) some of the primary music therapy goals and methods for persons with significant hearing losses.

Music Perception and Enjoyment

When considering the musical perception and enjoyment of persons with hearing losses, it is essential to remember that most people have some residual hearing. However, the types of musical sounds most easily heard and the extent to which an individual actually enjoys music will depend upon (1) the hearing history and profile, (2) the particular structural features of the music itself, (3) the type of assistive device used, and (4) personal background and preferences of each individual.

The profile of hearing loss can make a difference with regard to which musical features are most easily perceived. For example, people with better hearing acuity in lower frequencies are more able to perceive the sounds of low-pitched musical instruments in the bass and baritone range than the relatively high frequency sounds that make up much of human speech. People who have mild to moderate hearing losses have more residual hearing through which they can perceive and enjoy music compared to those with severe or profound hearing losses, who may perceive little more than the rhythmic beat or the most low-frequency sounds. In such instances, music that has a strong rhythmic beat may be more readily perceived and enjoyed than music that emphasizes melody and harmony (Darrow, 1979, 1984, 1987; Korduba, 1975).

With regard to effective music participation, research studies indicate that children with hearing losses can perform at least as effectively or more so than normal-hearing children on some types of rhythmic tasks (such as imitating a beat) if tactile (the sense of touch) or visual cues are available (Darrow, 1979, 1984, 1987;

Korduba, 1975). For example, the child might keep a steady beat by watching a blinking light on a metronome, or by feeling the beat of a drum on the wooden frame of the instrument.

There may be greater limitation in the perception and production of melody or harmony, especially in the case of children with moderate to profound losses. For children with enough residual hearing to perceive some frequency information, pitch discrimination improves with increased intensity (loudness). Accuracy may also be greater for lower pitches (i.e., the lower half of the piano keyboard, trombone, or cello). Though large pitch changes are more easily perceived than small changes (i.e., stepwise changes such as C to D), children with severe hearing losses have been trained to recognize pitch changes as small as a minor third (i.e., C to E-flat) (Ford, 1985).

Music perception and enjoyment will also be affected by the type of technology used by the individual. Hearing aids function on a principle of amplifying (making louder) sounds, especially those considered most important in understanding speech. Consequently, musical sounds may not always sound as pleasant or natural through a hearing aid (Franks, 1982). Some people describe music as sounding somewhat unnatural in quality with some hearing aid settings. In addition, persons with more severe losses may have difficulty actually perceiving some of the key features of music (e.g., small pitch changes, the subtleties of the timbre) even in their best aided condition. The sound quality is also likely to be influenced by the acoustical characteristics of the listening environment (such as a noisy or reverberant environment).

Hearing aids, however, provide a much more natural signal with regard to music than do cochlear implants, which transmit to the individual only portions of the total sound wave. Most implant recipients are able to perceive the basic rhythmic features (beat, rhythmic patterns) of music with relative accuracy. Unfortunately, many implant recipients find it difficult to distinguish small changes in pitch and the contour of melody. Many CI recipients describe the timbre (tone quality) of music as mechanical or noisy (Gfeller et al., 2000; Gfeller, Knutson, Woodworth, Witt, & DeBus, 1998; Gfeller & Lansing, 1991, 1992; Gfeller, Olszewski, Turner, Gantz, & Oleson, 2006; Gfeller et al., 2007; Gfeller et al., 2002; Gfeller, Witt, Stordahl, Mehr, & Woodworth, 2001; Gfeller, Woodworth, Robin, Witt, & Knutson, 1997; Hsiao, in press). For example, a CI recipient might describe music as sounding like a cage full of squawking parrots, or like beeps and buzzes. The manufacturers of cochlear implants are making efforts to improve the technical features of the CI. Hopefully, future implants may provide a more satisfactory quality of sound for music listening (Gfeller, 2007).

CI recipients are clearly different from normal-hearing people when it comes to music perception and enjoyment. Interestingly, there is also considerable difference from one CI recipient to the next when it comes to music perception and enjoyment. Some implant recipients find music unpleasant to hear, while others enjoy listening to or making music. In addition, some CI recipients have improved their music perception and enjoyment as a result of focused music training (e.g., Driscoll et al., in press; Gfeller et al., 2000; Gfeller, Mehr, & Witt, 2001; Gfeller et al., 2007; Gfeller, Witt, et al., 2001; McDermott, 2004).

The technical limitations of the CI with regard to music perception and enjoyment have several implications for music therapists. On one hand, some CI recipients may find musical sounds unpleasant or less enjoyable than they did prior to acquiring a hearing loss. In such cases, these individuals may no longer find music a meaningful or motivating art form in everyday life or in music therapy for conditions not related to their hearing loss. For example, while music might typically be a motivating factor in physical therapy for a person who has had a stroke, a stroke victim who happens to use a CI may find the sound quality of music too aversive to use in rehabilitation. However, CI recipients who would like to regain musical enjoyment may be excellent candidates for music therapy, with a goal of aural rehabilitation and music training (Driscoll et al., in press; Gfeller, 2001; Gfeller, Mehr, & Witt, 2001).

The unique characteristics of the individual are also important with regard to music perception and enjoyment (Gfeller, 1997a). Just as is the case for normally hearing persons, people with hearing losses vary with regard to their musical background and preferences. For example, some adults who lost their hearing in adulthood may have had extensive musical experiences prior to hearing loss. Such people can draw on recollection of "normal" listening experiences, while those with early loss cannot. Thus conceptualization of music may be quite different depending upon the onset of loss. One advantage for those with limited listening experience prior to hearing loss is that they may have less demanding expectations regarding sound quality and what constitutes satisfactory musical sounds (Gfeller, 1997a; Gfeller et al., 2000).

For that segment of the population with hearing losses that does listen to and enjoy music, there are individual differences with regard to individual preference. For example, some people report particular enjoyment of popular music, while others indicate that classical music is especially meaningful. Like normally hearing people, people with hearing losses vary in their preference for different musical instruments or musical styles (Gfeller et al., 2000; Gfeller & Witt, 1997).

Accommodations in Music Therapy and Music Education

Many people with hearing losses can benefit from and enjoy participation in music therapy or music education experiences as long as the therapist or educator (1) sets up an optimal acoustical environment, (2) selects musical sounds and activities that are adequately accessible, and (3) communicates in a manner that facilitates clear and effective interaction.

Acoustical accommodations are important when working with persons who have significant hearing losses. Music therapists or educators should create an environment that supports optimal use of residual hearing and should also take into account the auditory profile of each individual. For example, a room with a lot of reverberation (echo) makes it much more difficult for anyone, but especially people with auditory prostheses, to hear spoken instructions or musical sounds. Therefore, it is best to work in a room with some carpeting, curtains, or other soft surfaces that can reduce reverberation. Good lighting without glare can support speechreading and the use of other visual cues that promote understanding. Some persons get particular benefit from an FM system or other sort of assistive listening device that provides more direct input of sound. A conversation with the client's audiologist or deaf education specialist can help you to better understand the sorts of modifications in the room or assistive listening devices that might be helpful (Darrow & Gfeller, 1991).

Selecting appropriate music and instruments can enhance music enjoyment. People with mild hearing losses may be able to enjoy most musical instruments as long as their hearing aid is properly adjusted. The characteristics of the person's loss may offer insights into which instruments are most accessible. For individuals with severe or profound losses, poor auditory acuity can be accommodated by selecting rhythmic musical instruments with large vibrating surfaces, such as drums, pianos, bass tone bars, and xylophones. The rhythmic pulses of these instruments can be felt as well as heard. Furthermore, some of these low frequency and percussive instruments are more easily heard than human speech (which is comprised of many high frequencies). Consequently, musical instruments can be a particularly valuable therapeutic tool in goals such as promoting use of residual hearing.

Persons who use cochlear implants and hearing aid users with severe losses will generally have greater perceptual acuity for rhythm instruments, but some have been successful at playing the piano or wind instruments that produce pitch changes by playing keys on the instrument. Instruments that require constant and fine tuning, such as violin or cello, are likely to be much more challenging. Keep in mind, however, that hearing aid and CI recipients vary considerably in how well they perceive and enjoy music. Therefore, it is a good idea to use some trial and error in conjunction with testing of pitch perception when selecting the most suitable musical instrument for these clients. In addition, it is also important to keep in mind individual preferences (Gfeller, 1997b; Gfeller et al., 2000).

Accommodations for communication are essential to effective music therapy sessions. The language deficiencies commonly experienced by children with serious hearing losses (Darrow & Gfeller, 1996; Ford, 1985) can also affect their ability to participate in music activities. In general, the music therapist needs to communicate with language that is within the present developmental level of the child (Gfeller & Baumann, 1988). For example, complex instructions and explanations may be beyond some children's language level. Words typically used to describe musical concepts may be difficult to conceptualize. Terms such as *minor key* or *harmony* are abstract descriptions of musical characteristics related to perceptual distinctions. In contrast, *fast* and *slow* are examples of more concrete terms that are easily demonstrated and more readily understood. Lyrics to songs should be examined for suitability and new vocabulary words carefully chosen and explained.

In addition to considering developmental issues of language acquisition, the music therapist should also be sensitive to the client's system of communication. If the child uses manual communication (i.e., ASL, Signed English, etc.), the therapist either should be able to engage in two-way communication through sign, or should ensure that a qualified interpreter is available for each session.

TREATMENT GOALS FOR PERSONS WITH HEARING LOSSES

A significant hearing loss that is congenital or acquired in early childhood is likely to have an impact on communication throughout life. If music therapy is considered a suitable option for a given individual, music therapy intervention in the areas of speech, language, or auditory perception is most likely to occur during the preschool, elementary, or middle school years.

As the child with a hearing loss enters adolescence and young adulthood, the music therapist may begin to emphasize the social and emotional aspects of music, such as participation in music ensembles as a leisure-time activity and art form. The music therapist's role may change from interventionist to consultant or resource person, thus encouraging greater self-determination and responsibility on the part of the adolescent or young adult. Given these patterns of rehabilitation, and more typical job placement of music therapists, this section will focus primarily on rehabilitation goals with children who are deaf or hard-of-hearing.

The music therapist contributes to the rehabilitation of children with significant hearing losses in four primary ways, by (1) supplementing auditory training, (2) improving speech production, (3) reinforcing language development, and (4) providing a structured activity for social skill attainment (Darrow & Gfeller, 1996). Each of these goals will be discussed below.

Music Therapy to Promote Auditory Training

Auditory training is an intervention that enables the individual to make maximum use of residual hearing, thus improving the ability to understand speech and environmental sounds. The ultimate goal of auditory training is typically to improve speech comprehension. Because music and speech share common structural characteristics (such as pitch and duration of sound), music can effectively contribute to an auditory training program by motivating the use of residual hearing (Amir & Schuchman, 1985; Bang, 1980; Darrow & Gfeller, 1996; Fisher & Parker, 1994; Gfeller, 2000).

For children with better low-frequency acuity and limited pitch perception, percussion instruments and low-pitched mallet instruments (such as xylophones or glockenspiels) can be used effectively to work on the following objectives: (1) **sound detection** (absence or presence of sound), (2) **sound discrimination** (same or different), (3) **sound identification** (recognizing the sound source), and (4) the **comprehension (understanding) of sound** (Darrow & Gfeller, 1996; Erber & Hirsh, 1978). The music therapist initially chooses sounds most accessible to the client and gradually increases the difficulty of the listening tasks.

> *Carol is a music therapist who works with a small group of preschool children (ages 3 and 4) with severe hearing losses who are enrolled in a special language rehabilitation program. One of the objectives in the children's Individualized Education Programs is to develop optimal use of their residual hearing. The first step toward this goal is detection of sound versus silence. For the session, Carol has decided to use a large tom-tom to introduce concepts of sound and silence. The head of the drum is large enough that young children with partially developed motor skills can successfully create a sound. In addition, the beat of the drum can be felt by touching the base of the instrument. As each child takes a turn striking the surface of the drum, the other children feel the vibrations on the wooden base of the drum. Carol and the other staff members speak and sign "I hear sound!" When the child stops playing, the adults all sign "Stop." As another way of reinforcing the concept of sound versus silence, Carol marches to the child's rhythmic pattern and then freezes in place when the beat stops. Little Alyssa loves to play this game, making people march and freeze by creating sound and silence.*

Although the treatment team will eventually establish goals more challenging than these basic listening tasks, musical sound sources offer positive benefits in the early stages of auditory training. First, because musical instruments are pitched in a wide range of frequencies (from low to high) and can be played relatively loudly, they may be heard more readily than speech sounds, which have a more limited frequency (pitch) and intensity (loudness) range. These musical sounds can provide successful experiences during the early stages of sound detection. Certain musical instruments with vibrating surfaces that are easily touched, such as the drum, piano, and xylophone, provide tactile as well as auditory sensations for the client experimenting with sound and silence. These tactile sensations (i.e., touching the drum while listening to the beat) can reinforce the distinction between sound and no sound (Fisher & Parker, 1994).

Playing rhythm instruments allows the individual to see a cause-effect relationship between an action (striking the instrument) and the subsequent sound. For many young children, playing rhythm instruments is also a positive, motivating experience, as they actively create and listen to sounds. A high level of motivation is helpful in keeping young children with short attention spans focused and involved during therapy. The music therapist assesses progress in auditory training both through informal testing and through the use of standardized assessment procedures (Darrow & Gfeller, 1996; Gfeller & Baumann, 1988). Formal tests of auditory comprehension are available and are outlined by Darrow, Gfeller, Gorsuch, and Thomas in the book *Effectiveness of Music Therapy Procedures: Documentation of Research and Clinical Practice* (American Music Therapy Association [AMTA], 2000). Some of these tests require the test administrator to have specialized training in speech-language pathology or audiology.

Music Therapy for Speech Development

Children with normal hearing learn to speak by imitating the sounds of others, hearing their own speech, and making necessary adjustments. Because children with significant hearing losses hear distorted or partial models of speech, some of their speech sounds may be formed improperly or omitted entirely (Davis & Hardick, 1981). It is also common for children with severe hearing losses to have speech with an improper pitch level (i.e., too high or low for age and gender) and unusual rhythm or inflection (i.e., sounding monotonous or mechanical). Individuals with profound hearing losses may use their voices very little, making only isolated sounds rather than forming clearly articulated words or phrases.

Although music therapists are not trained in specific methods to shape correct articulation (the correct production of speech sounds, such as forming a "sh" or "buh"), the music therapist can reinforce other aspects of speech production identified by the speech-language pathologist, which include (1) an increased use of the voice in free vocalization; and (2) an increased awareness of speech patterns and subsequent production of more natural speech rhythms, pitch, and inflections, factors that influence intelligibility (Bang, 1980; Darrow, 1990; Darrow & Cohen, 1991; Darrow & Gfeller, 1996; Darrow & Starmer, 1986; Gfeller, 1986).

Vocal imitation can be encouraged through singing activities, as in the following example:

> In Carol's preschool group, Alyssa, SooMie, and Kara are working on production of the sounds "mmmm" and "bah." In order to encourage use of these sounds, Carol has decided to introduce the song "Old MacDonald." As the verses about the cows and sheep are introduced, Carol models the sounds MOOO and BAAH (using methods of modeling recommended by the speech-language pathologist) and the children pretend that they are cows and sheep. Carol works cooperatively with Natalie, the speech-language pathologist, in helping each child to produce his or her best possible speech sounds. Although the initial utterances produced in rehabilitation are not always clear or correct, experimentation with and repeated practice using the voice is an important step toward improved speech production.

Progress in speech intelligibility is difficult to assess since it is subjective in nature. Over time, therapists will find the speech of persons with hearing losses easier to understand. Nevertheless, the music therapist can evaluate progress in speech intelligibility with a variety of tests, which are described by Darrow et al. in the book *Effectiveness of Music Therapy Procedures: Documentation of Research and Clinical Practice* (AMTA, 2000). Proper test administration, scoring, and requirements are described in that book.

Music Therapy for Language Development

A significant hearing loss affects not only the ability to hear and form intelligible speech sounds, but it also has a major impact on language development. Therefore, the development of language is dependent on early and comprehensive intervention. Common problems include reduced or improper use of vocabulary, errors in syntax, use of shorter and simpler sentences, and diminished spontaneous interactions (Davis & Hardick, 1981).

Because music is a nonverbal language, why is it used toward language development goals? First, music is often paired with words in songs. Furthermore, musical activities are often facilitated with verbal instructions or directives. Activities such as writing songs or pairing sign language with music provide motivating ways to introduce or practice new vocabulary words (Darrow & Gfeller, 1996; Galloway & Bean, 1974; Gfeller, 1987; Gfeller & Darrow, 1987; Gfeller & Schum, 1994). During the process of constructing a song, clients are encouraged to generate and express ideas using language skills. As group members discuss their ideas and formulate the lyrics and music, the music therapist encourages topic-related interaction among group members.

Carol provides music therapy for a group of lower elementary school-aged children who have moderate to profound hearing losses. Today in music therapy, the children are writing a song about favorite foods. This topic was chosen because Joey, the speech-language pathologist, shared with Carol that most of the children in the group are working on vocabulary regarding foods (i.e., spaghetti, pizza, French fries, broccoli, etc.). On a Velcro board, Carol has placed pictures of the foods in the vocabulary list and asks the children to guess which one each of their friends likes the best. Their responses are placed in a simple song entitled "My Favorite Food," which Carol composed for this particular activity. As each child shares his or her favorite food, Carol models the correct sign and speech sound for each food. Elizabeth signs and says that her favorite food is pizza, and Theresa signs enthusiastically, "Me, too!" Miki chimes in: "I like ice cream." Carol reinforces the written form of the vocabulary words by writing their ideas on a large chart. Then she praises how beautifully they took turns and used their best speech and sign, which promotes appropriate social use of communication.

Language development goals in music therapy typically focus on one of the following: (1) increased and appropriate use of vocabulary; (2) increased spontaneous or topic-related interaction; (3) increased complexity and completeness of sentences; and (4) **pragmatics**, which concerns the use of language its use in context (such as differences in communicating in a formal vs. informal social setting) (Darrow & Gfeller, 1996; Gfeller & Baumann, 1988). Interaction and sentence structure are complex and difficult to assess, and require that the therapist be fluent in the child's mode of communication. Furthermore, interpretation of the sample requires an understanding of normal, delayed, and deviant language patterns. Therefore, unless the music therapist has had extensive training in this area, he or she should collaborate with the speech therapist to monitor progress (Gfeller & Baumann, 1988).

Music Therapy for Social Skills Development

As a result of delayed language development and speech production problems, children with hearing losses miss out on many interactions with others. Furthermore, a child with limited language skills finds it difficult to understand instructions, ask questions, and express concerns or frustration. These limitations can contribute to problems in social adjustment (Meadow, 1980a; Schum & Gfeller, 1994).

Some children with significant hearing losses may demonstrate immature behaviors or revert to socially unacceptable ways of expressing themselves when communication breaks down. Because music tends to be a cooperative group event, a structured music activity offers a splendid opportunity to practice even the most basic social skills, such as taking turns, paying attention to others, following directions, sharing, working cooperatively toward a group goal, and expressing feelings appropriately (Bang, 1980; Darrow & Gfeller, 1996; Schum & Gfeller, 1994). For some individuals, music making (i.e., playing instruments, writing songs, etc.) can be a satisfying leisure-time activity and opportunity for personal achievement.

One of the most convenient ways to measure improvement in social skills is through changes over time in the occurrence of specific problem behaviors (e.g., interruptions, outbursts). The therapist can also use a specially designed scale, such as the Meadow/Kendall Social-Emotional Assessment Inventory for Deaf Students (Meadow, 1980b), to assess social/emotional competency.

SUMMARY

In summary, there is no single profile that characterizes all persons with hearing loss. A significant hearing loss can have a serious impact on a person's ability to understand speech and environmental sounds, speech production, language development, and social interaction. The extent to which speech and language development are affected depends on the type of loss, severity of loss, the onset of loss, the impact of any devices used to support hearing (e.g., hearing aids, cochlear implants), and the family and community environment in which the individual lives. For those individuals who have significant and early hearing losses, intervention is required to facilitate maximal speech and language development. The structural characteristics of music and the social nature of music activities can help to reduce the impact of these problems in the following ways:

1. Musical sounds, which encompass a wide range of frequencies, can be played at moderate to high intensity levels and produce tactile as well as auditory stimulation. These characteristics are useful in auditory training tasks, such as sound detection and discrimination.

2. Like speech, music is composed of patterns that differ in pitch, duration, and intensity. Musical patterns can therefore be used to demonstrate and reinforce similar characteristics of normal speech production.

3. Music is often paired with textual information, as in song lyrics. New vocabulary and correct language usage can be reinforced through activities such as songwriting and singing.

4. Musical ensembles require social skills: following instructions, taking turns, cooperating with others, and sharing ideas. These activities provide

a motivating and structured environment for learning and reinforcing appropriate social behaviors.

The decision to use music therapy should be made in the context of the individual's age, needs, and cultural affiliation. Music therapy may not be a suitable choice for persons who affiliate primarily with Deaf culture and who communicate primarily through American Sign Language.

PART II: VISION

With very little thought, the names of musicians who are blind comes to mind—Stevie Wonder, Ray Charles, Jose Feliciano, Andrea Bocelli, Ronnie Milsap, George Shearing, Marcus Roberts. Obviously, visual loss does not impair one's ability to become a good musician or even a famous musician. In fact, with the loss of sight, the subsequent development of aural skills is thought by many to enhance one's ability to develop musically, especially in cases of early-onset blindness. It is erroneous, however, to assume that when one sense is absent, other senses are naturally enhanced (Drake, 1939; Gougoux, Lepore, Voss, Zatorre, & Belin, 2004; Heim, 1963; Kwalwasser, 1955; Madsen & Darrow, 1989; Sakurabayashi, Satyo, & Uehara, 1956; Stankov & Spillsbury, 1978). Because blind persons rely more heavily on listening skills in order to function in everyday life, they are more likely to develop their hearing more fully. Since much of the information they receive about the world around them is through listening, young children require instruction and experiences in developing this skill to its fullest extent (Adamek & Darrow, 2005; Brown, 1990).

Vicarious learning is at risk for all students with vision loss. Much of what children learn is by observing and imitating what they see around them. The world meets the sighted child half way. Curious to explore what they see, children move toward objects and people, ever increasing their knowledge of the world around them. Children without sight are no less curious; however, they require an environment that is aurally and tactually inviting (Adamek & Darrow, 2005). A great deal of information is strictly visual and cannot be accessed in any other way. For example, consider the dilemma of explaining through an alternative sensory experience what a blue sky or sunset is like. In order to better understand the importance of augmenting the aural environment, encouraging the development of listening skills, as well as other related rehabilitative emphases, the following section provides an overview of various types of visual losses, terminology associated with those limitations, and the characteristics and needs of individuals with visual impairments.

VISUAL IMPAIRMENTS: DEFINITIONS AND ETIOLOGY

Very few individuals are completely without any sense of sight. Most individuals with visual impairments have sufficient **residual vision** to function in daily life, though they may require assistive devices such as glasses, contacts, or specialized technology when using computers, TVs, and phones. The general term *visual impairment* (see Figure 2) represents a range of visual acuity, as well as different amounts of functional vision. The degree and type of vision loss influence how individuals will be educated and how they will experience the environment (Individuals with Disabilities Educational Improvement Act of 2004 [IDEA], 2004).

Definitions of Vision Loss

Visual acuity is determined by measuring the distance at which an individual can clearly identify objects—usually letters, numbers, or symbols on the familiar Snellen chart. In general, people with visual impairments are classified into two major groups: those who are **blind**—without vision, and those with **low vision**—with partial sight (Adamek & Darrow, 2005). Beyond these two broad classifications, there are other terms listed in Figure 2 that describe specific types or aspects of vision loss.

Legally blind—20/200 vision; can see at 20 feet what a typical person can see at 200 feet

Levels of vision loss—
- Low vision (partial sight)—reads print; may depend on optical aids to enlarge the print
- Functionally blind—uses Braille for reading and writing; may use functional vision for mobility, cooking, dressing, etc.
- Blind—receives no useful input through their sense of vision; uses tactile and auditory senses for knowledge of environment

Restricted field of vision—
- Tunnel vision—able to see objects only within an area of 20 degrees or less from the normal 180-degree field
- Poor central vision—only good peripheral vision.

Visual efficiency—efficiency in using residual vision (e.g., adapting to varied visual stimuli, controlling eye movements, processing visual information)

Functional vision—residual vision sufficient for daily living tasks

Figure 2. Terms Related to Visual Impairments

Visual losses can be **congenital** or **acquired**. The **age of onset** has important implications for adjustment to vision loss. Those who have never experienced vision understandably have a different perception of the world around them than those who lost their vision gradually. Persons who were blind at birth have learned through hearing, touch, tastes, and smells, but without vision; those who gradually lost their sight generally have a memory bank of visual experiences to draw upon when compensating for vision impairments. However, individuals who have lost their vision adventitiously (acquired their vision loss) and who are therefore accustomed to relying on vision, must make major adjustments in their lifestyle. The etiology of blindness includes infections and diseases, accidents and injuries, and prenatal influences including heredity; these conditions can be stable or progressive in nature (Codding, 1982).

> *Julie is a music therapist at a state school for the deaf and blind. She works with children from preschool through high school who have either hearing losses or visual impairments. Today she is working with a group of upper elementary-aged students who have varying degrees of vision loss. Her goal for this class has been to work on self-help skills that will prepare them for middle school (changing classes, increasing independence on school work, grooming, etc.).*

> *Michelle has been totally blind since birth and has adjusted well to her disability. She reads Braille and uses a cane for mobility. She hopes to have a service dog when she is older. She has been learning to play the piano since 1st grade and recently began to learn Braille music.*

> *Achia and her brother Anthony both have Albinism—which results in low vision, nystagmus (rapid movement of the eye back and forth), and photophobia (hypersensitivity to light). They are able to read large print with indirect lighting. They enjoy singing in their church choir. Because they are African American and have pale skin and eyes, their greatest difficulty in school is not their visual impairment, but the taunts of partially sighted students who bully and ridicule them for "not being black or white."*

> *Jeremy has low vision, and his family has just found out that it is a progressive loss of vision that will ultimately lead to blindness. At first, he was able to read regular print with magnifying devices; he then progressed to large print, and now must learn to read Braille and use a cane. His adjustment to vision loss has not been easy, and he does not want to be at a school for "stupid blind kids." The only music he likes is hip hop.*

> *Julie has good ideas for music applications, but her challenges are preparing music and other visuals for the varying types and degrees of*

vision loss represented among her students, as well as for their different musical preferences and their unique social and emotional needs.

Some people who are have severe vision loss read Braille, a special form of print that was invented in 1842 by a Frenchman named Louis Braille. It is a tactile system of reading and writing that uses a configuration of dots to form letters of the alphabet as well as music. In recent years, modern technology has made large print materials more readily available to students with low vision. The American Printing House for the Blind produces books and music for students with low vision. When planning lessons or therapy sessions, it is important to remember that reading both large print and Braille generally takes more time to read than standard print.

CHARACTERISTICS OF PERSONS WITH VISUAL IMPAIRMENTS

As noted earlier, children typically learn much about the world around them by visual observation. For example, most children learn to use writing utensils by watching others use them. The child who cannot observe the use of such utensils must be taught, not only how to hold a crayon, a pencil, and a pen, but the function of each and the motions that facilitate their use. Most children with limited vision have learned to use other senses to acquire much of the information that is transmitted in their environment, and thus, the growth and development of children with visual disabilities is generally no different than that of their peers. There are, however, specific areas of learning and behavior that may be affected, depending upon on the age of onset, the severity of vision loss, family support, and the type and degree of educational intervention. These areas are described below.

Cognition

Many intellectual tasks, such as determining spatial relationships and science concepts, require or are more easily understood through visual illustrations, such as graphs and charts. A visual disability does not impair intellectual abilities, per se, but people with visual impairments have much less information upon which to rely. Thus, individuals with vision disabilities may score lower on tests of intellect. However, when individuals' intellectual abilities are measured on tasks that do not require vision, those with and without sight perform similarly (Stephens & Grub, 1982).

Language

Because vocabulary acquisition occurs to a great extent through the integration of visual experiences and words, children with severe vision loss are at a distinct disadvantage in language development. Children without sight who live in an environment rich in language may develop vocabulary as a sighted child would; however, they may have little understanding of many words used in everyday conversation. For example, imagine trying to understand the lyrics to "This Land Is Your Land" without the benefit of having had vision: "As I was walking a ribbon of highway, I saw above me an endless skyway, I saw below me a golden valley, this land was made for you and me."

Academic Achievement

Related to cognition and language is academic achievement. Several reports suggest that the academic achievement of many students with severe vision loss is delayed when compared to their sighted peers (Bishop, 1996; Rapp & Rapp, 1992). The general knowledge of students with vision loss may also be limited due to limited access to reading materials and experiences that bring meaning to reading materials (Adamek & Darrow, 2005). Test scores for academic achievement must be interpreted with caution, however, due to the different testing conditions required for students with vision problem, which includes extra time for reading large print and Braille.

Social Development

Crocker and Orr (1996) found that children with severe vision loss, who cannot see their peers, were less likely to initiate social interactions and had fewer opportunities to socialize. Children without sight must learn to listen for social opportunities, and, more importantly, learn to be appropriately assertive in initiating conversation. The inability to use and observe others' use of nonverbal communication can also impair interpersonal interactions, given that eye contact, facial expression, and gestures are all useful behaviors in relating to others. Children without vision can learn to use nonverbal communication, but it must be taught through senses other than vision— usually tactual.

Motor Development

One of the most noticeable delays in the development of visually impaired children is in motor areas, including gross motor skills and balance (Bouchard & Tetreault, 2000). Locomotion (e.g., creeping/crawling and/or walking) is delayed in young blind children because vision is the sense that motivates babies to venture out and explore their environment.

Persons with visual impairments have the potential for normal development in all of the areas cited above. However, the lack of typical experiences may result in developmental delays in some or all areas of physical, cognitive, and social development. For individuals whose only disability is vision loss, their rehabilitative goals should be directed toward strategies that will compensate for the effects of vision loss on everyday learning experiences.

MUSIC THERAPY OBJECTIVES

In contrast to the existing clinical and research literature on music therapy and hearing loss, there is a relatively small body of literature regarding music therapy and visual impairments. Because there is less current information to convey, this portion of the chapter is comparatively brief. Music therapists serving this population would benefit from a concerted effort by clinicians and researchers to increase available resources on this topic. From existing resources, however, it is clear that various rehabilitation objectives for persons with visual impairments can be addressed through music therapy. According to Codding (2000), music is used to achieve these objectives in several ways: (1) as a structured activity to facilitate learning of academic, motor, social, and verbal behavior; (2) as a stimulus cue or prompt for sound localization and other listening tasks; (3) as a contingent reward; and (4) as a part of music appreciation and enjoyment. Appropriate objectives for persons with vision loss are those that can negate or lessen the impact of vision loss on daily learning experiences. Such objectives include the development of skills in listening, **mobility** and **orientation**, socialization, interpersonal communication, and skills required in daily living (Davis, Gfeller, & Thaut, 1999; Hardman et al., 2002; Hunt & Marshall, 2005).

Listening Skills

The development of listening skills is perhaps the most important educational and rehabilitation objective for individuals with vision loss. Listening skills provide the foundation for learning and functioning in the environment. For example, improved discrimination of timbral differences may assist children in differentiating between male and female voices or an adult and a child's voice. Learning to detect minor changes in loudness may assist in detecting whether a sound source is approaching or retreating (Adamek & Darrow, 2005). Of particular importance are auditory training exercises related to sound localization and sustained attention to sound.

Orientation and Mobility Skills

Orientation is the ability to determine one's position in relation to the environment, while **mobility** is the ability to move safely and efficiently from one point to another (Heward, 2003). Orientation and mobility (O & M) instruction provides strategies for persons with visual impairments, which are mastered through ample practice. Typical O & M skills can be reinforced through music, such as using musical sounds to teach routes (Uslan, Malone, & De l'Aune, 1983), or the use of music with dance instruction to help develop balance, coordination, and gross motor skills (Duehl, 1979). Musical instruments can serve as aural stimuli—motivating the child to reach out (Gourgey, 1998).

Daily Living Skills

Skills such as cooking, dressing, housekeeping, and personal hygiene are essential to eventual independence in adulthood. These skills, which are taught to all students, must be taught to the student who is blind in alternative ways. Music has long been used to teach daily living skills to children with developmental disabilities. The same kind of musical interventions can be employed with children who are blind, with adaptations made for their lack of sight. Songs about hand washing or identifying body parts cannot be taught through visual imitation, but through hands-on experiences (Adamek & Darrow, 2005).

Social and Interpersonal Communication Skills

Students with severe vision loss are often delayed in the development of social skills. Music making and music listening with others is an effective strategy for bringing students with and without vision together. Such activities should be structured and monitored by therapists who understand how to facilitate positive social relationships and to teach social skills such as turn taking, greeting behaviors (shaking hands, introductions), the simulation of eye contact, and table etiquette (Adamek & Darrow, 2005; Gourgey, 1998; Kern & Wolery, 2001; Kersten, 1981).

Musical skills can also be useful in the development of leisure skills and community socialization. Much of the attraction to participating in music programs is the socialization that occurs at rehearsals and after performances. For adolescents and teens with impaired vision, the positive sense of self that comes from socializing with others, participating in communal music activities, and developing musical skills will do much to enhance their confidence and social well-being (Adamek & Darrow, 2005).

Jeff works as a public school music therapist in a large school district. For the past year, he has worked in the resource room with junior high students who are blind or functionally blind. The director of special education asked him to address goals directed toward "social and emotional development." Jeff was successful at planning music activities that addressed typical teen emotional issues (through lyric analysis), social etiquette (by taking them to musical events in the community), and social development (by organizing inclusive music performances with sighted students). At the end of the year, what he learned most about working with these students was not related to music. Through the course of the year, he came to realize how dependent he was on using various nonverbal means to communicate with others (pointing, head nodding, use of gestures, facial expression, visuals, etc.). On the last day of class, he thanked his blind students for teaching him "how to talk."

Emotional Expression and Development

Although visual impairment per se may not have a negative impact on personality development and self-concept, the attitudes of parents, siblings, and peers toward people who are blind can have a deleterious effect on self-esteem and emotional growth. Feelings of dependence, helplessness, and lack of acceptance may exist. Activities such as writing songs or listening to relevant lyrics in a discussion group can assist in appropriate expression of feelings. Successful involvement in musical activities can promote a sense of mastery, personal accomplishment, and healthy self-concept.

Academic Skills

As with daily living skills, songs have been used to teach academic skills. For example, the alphabet song has long been used to teach letters. This same song can be used with children who are blind, but with Braille letters or other tactile letters substituted for written letters. Songs can also be used to teach factual concepts that are generally acquired through vision.

Music instruction is also a valuable curricular component for students with visual impairments. Nearly all state and private schools for students with visual impairments still include music as an important part of the curriculum (Corn & Bailey, 1991).[2]

Reducing Sensory Stimulation Behaviors That May Accompany Blindness

Students with severe vision loss sometimes engage in stereotypic behaviors that can impair their social and interpersonal relationships. Behaviors such as body rocking, rubbing or poking the eyes, repetitive finger or hand movements, and head rolling are socially stigmatizing, and they often discourage classmates from approaching a student who engages in these behaviors (Hardman et al., 2002). Beyond the social implications, stereotypic behaviors can also interfere with learning.

Although the elimination of stereotypic behaviors is often difficult, contingent music has been shown to significantly reduce the number of stereotypic behaviors in children with stereotypic behaviors (Greene, Hoats, & Hornick, 1970; Greenwald, 1978; Kersten, 1981; Smeets, 1972). There are many musical behaviors that are incompatible with stereotypic behaviors. For example, students cannot play a

---

[2]A number of practical recommendations for modifying music instruction (such as the use of Braille music, large print, rote learning, and extra time for learning) are outlined in the textbook, *Music in Special Education* (Adamek & Darrow, 2005).

recorder (or at least not very easily) while moving their head in a figure eight, or play a drum while flailing their hands (Adamek & Darrow, 2005).

Regardless of the therapeutic objective being addressed, verbal explanations and physical assistance are necessary modes of instruction and feedback for students with vision loss. Pointing to a spot in the music, gestures, or visual demonstrations are lost to students who are blind, and generally to those with low vision as well. Head nodding has to be accompanied by phrases such as "you're getting it" or "that's right." In addition, many instructions such as "cross your arms" have no meaning for a student who has never seen arms crossed. In such cases, physical assistance is needed to place the student's arms in position.

Visual impairment sometimes accompanies other disabilities. In the case of multiple disabilities, the therapist must take into account all areas of need in addition to the impact of the visual impairment. Therapists working with people who are deaf-blind face particular challenges in establishing effective interpersonal communication, because the two sensory modes traditionally used in everyday interaction are limited. The therapist may use sign language formed in the client's hand in order to communicate. For this population, the vibrations made by musical instruments such as guitars, pianos, or drums can provide a valuable source of sensory stimulation.

A small proportion of music therapists serve individuals with vision loss (AMTA, 2004; Codding, 2000). Compared with other types of disabling conditions, visual impairment is a relatively low-incidence impairment among children and young adults. Furthermore, those individuals who have only a visual impairment (as opposed to multiple disabilities) make up an even smaller subgroup (Codding, 1988). Music therapy clientele with vision loss most often have accompanying disabilities such as cerebral palsy or other types of physical or developmental disabilities. Progressive loss of vision (along with hearing loss) is a common problem among the elderly, however. Consequently, this disability is characteristic of many music therapy clients in assisted living and nursing home settings.

SUMMARY

Persons with visual impairment make up a small segment of children and young adults with disabilities. Visual impairments are generally categorized as either blind or partially sighted, and may or may not be accompanied by other physical disabilities. Visual impairments may be stable or progressive in nature. People who are blind are not inherently gifted in auditory perception and musical skills, but extensive training and practice can result in optimal use of intact sensory modes.

Those persons with normal intelligence generally have normal development, except in specific skills where conceptual and language development is strongly correlated with visual experiences. Dependency and helplessness may result from over protectiveness or negative attitudes on the part of parents and peers toward the disability. One developmental area in which this population shows lower performance than sighted individuals is in motor coordination and mobility. The development of orientation and locomotor skills as well as the use of special technical supports (i.e., Braille, talking books, etc.) helps these individuals to function successfully.

The primary objective of music therapy is to reduce the impact of the visual impairment on social, emotional, and motor functioning. A number of general objectives is commonly found in music therapy with this population: development of skills in listening, orientation and mobility, academics, socialization, interpersonal communication, and emotional expression; development of daily living skills; and reduction of stigmatizing mannerisms. Music is used toward those objectives in a variety of ways: (1) as a structured activity to facilitate learning of academic, motor, social, and verbal behavior; (2) as a stimulus cue or prompt for sound localization and other listening tasks; (3) as a contingency, or reward for desired behavior; and (4) as part of musical appreciation and enjoyment (including lessons).

STUDY QUESTIONS

1. Which type of loss (conductive, sensorineural, or central hearing loss) is due to an obstruction or malformation in the outer or middle ear?

2. What is residual hearing?

3. Describe four modes of communication used by persons with hearing losses.

4. How does the melodic and rhythmic perception of children with hearing losses compare with that of normal-hearing children?

5. What types of instruments are best for use clients who have hearing losses?

6. What are four primary ways in which a music therapist can contribute to the rehabilitation of persons with hearing losses? Give an example of one therapeutic goal for each intervention focus.

7. What are the two broad terms used to describe individuals with vision loss?

8. Briefly define the following terms: *visual acuity, field of vision, visual efficiency,* and *functional vision.*

9. Briefly discuss the musical aptitude of individuals who are blind and how it relates to their lack of sight.

10. Identify four areas of human development that may be impacted by vision loss, and briefly discuss the potential effects of such a loss.

11. Identify at least five areas for therapeutic intervention that music therapists might address in their clinical work with clients who are blind.

REFERENCES

Adamek, M. S., & Darrow, A. A. (Eds.). (2005). *Music in special education.* Silver Spring, MD: American Music Therapy Association.

American Music Therapy Association (AMTA). (2000). *Effectiveness of music therapy procedures: Documentation of research and clinical practice* (3rd ed.). Silver Spring, MD: Author.

American Music Therapy Association (AMTA). (2004). AMTA *member sourcebook.* Silver Spring, MD: Author.

American Speech-Language-Hearing Association. (2008). *Type, degree, and configuration of hearing loss.* Retrieved May 12, 2008, from http://asha.org/public/hearing/disorders/types.htm

Amir, D., & Schuchman, G. (1985). Auditory training through music with hearing impaired preschool children. *Volta Review, 87,* 333–343.

Armstrong, D. F. (1999). *Original signs: Gesture, sign and the sources of language.* Washington, DC: Gallaudet University Press.

Bang, C. (1980). A work of sound and music. *Journal of the British Association for Teachers of the Deaf, 4,* 1–10.

Bishop, V. E. (1996). *Teaching visually impaired children* (2nd ed.). Springfield, IL: Charles C. Thomas.

Bouchard, D., & Tetreault, S. (2000). The motor development of sighted children and children with moderate low vision. *Journal of Visual Impairment and Blindness, 94,* 564–573.

Brown, K. R. (1990). Effects of a music-based memory training program on the auditory memory skills of visually impaired individuals (Doctoral dissertation, University of Houston, 1990). *Dissertation Abstracts International, 52* (03), 877A.

Codding, P. (1982). *Music therapy for handicapped children: Visually impaired.* Washington, DC: National Association for Music Therapy.

Codding, P. (1988). Music in the education/rehabilitation of visually disabled and multihandicapped persons: A review of literature from 1946–1987. In C. E. Furman (Ed.), *Effectiveness of music therapy procedures: Documentation of research and clinical practice.* Washington, DC: National Association for Music Therapy.

Codding, P. (2000). Music therapy literature and clinical applications for blind and severely visually impaired persons: 1940–2000. In AMTA (Ed.), *Effectiveness of music therapy procedures: Documentation of research and clinical practice* (pp. 159–198). Silver Spring, MD: American Music Therapy Association.

Corn, A. L., & Bailey, G. L. (1991). Profile of music programs at residential schools for blind and visually impaired students. *Journal of Visual Impairment and Blindness, 85,* 379–382.

Crocker, A. D., & Orr, R. R. (1996). Social behaviors of children with visual impairments enrolled in preschool programs. *Exceptional Children, 62,* 451–462.

Darrow, A. A. (1979). The beat reproduction response of subjects with normal and impaired hearing: An empirical comparison. *Journal of Music Therapy, 16,* 6–11.

Darrow, A. A. (1984). A comparison of the rhythmic responsiveness in normal hearing and hearing-impaired children and an investigation of the relationship of the rhythmic responsiveness to the suprasegmental aspects of speech perception. *Journal of Music Therapy, 21,* 48–66.

Darrow, A. A. (1987). An investigative study: The effect of hearing impairment on musical aptitude. *Journal of Music Therapy, 24*(2), 88–96.

Darrow, A. A. (1990). The effect of frequency adjustment on the vocal reproduction accuracy of hearing impaired children. *Journal of Music Therapy, 27*(1), 24–33.

Darrow, A. A. (1993). The role of music in deaf culture: Implications for music educators. *Journal of Research in Music Education, 43*(1), 2–15.

Darrow, A. A. (2006). The perception of emotion in music by deaf and hard-of-hearing children. *Journal of Music Therapy, 43*(1), 2–15.

Darrow, A. A., & Cohen, N. (1991). The effect of programmed pitch practice and private instruction on the vocal reproduction accuracy of hearing impaired children: Two case studies. *Music Therapy Perspectives, 9*, 61–65.

Darrow, A. A., & Gfeller, K. E. (1991). A study of public school music programs mainstreaming hearing impaired students. *Journal of Music Therapy, 28*(1), 23–39.

Darrow, A. A., & Gfeller, K. E. (1996). Music therapy with children who are deaf and hard of hearing. In C. E. Furman (Ed.), *Effectiveness of music therapy procedures: Documentation of research and clinical practice* (2nd ed., pp. 230–266). Washington, DC: National Association for Music Therapy.

Darrow, A. A., Gfeller, K. E., Gorsuch, A., & Thomas, K. (2000). Music therapy with children who are deaf and hard-of-hearing. In AMTA (Ed.), *Effectiveness of music therapy procedures: Documentation of research and clinical practice* (3rd ed., pp. 35–157). Silver Spring, MD: American Music Therapy Association.

Darrow, A. A., & Heller, G. N. (1985). William Wolcott Turner and David Ely Bartlett: Early advocates of music education for the hearing impaired. *Journal of Research in Music Education, 33*, 269–279.

Darrow, A. A., & Loomis, D. (1999). Music and deaf culture: Images from the media and their interpretation by deaf and hearing students. *Journal of Music Therapy, 36*(2), 88–109.

Darrow, A. A., & Novak, J. (2007). The effect of vision and hearing loss on listener's perception of referential meaning in music. *Journal of Music Therapy, 44*, 57–73.

Darrow, A. A., & Starmer, G. J. (1986). The effect of vocal training on the intonation and rate of hearing-impaired children's speech: A pilot study. *Journal of Music Therapy, 23*, 194–201.

Davis, J., & Hardick, E. J. (1981). *Rehabilitative audiology for children and adults.* New York: John Wiley and Sons.

Davis, W. B., Gfeller, K. E., & Thaut, M. H. (1999). *An introduction to music therapy: Theory and practice* (2nd ed.). Dubuque, IA: McGraw-Hill.

Drake, R. M. (1939). Factorial analysis of music tests by the Spearman tetrad difference technique. *Journal of Musicology, 1*, 6–10.

Drasgow, E. (1998). American Sign Language as a pathway to linguistic competence. *Exceptional Children, 64*, 329–342.

Driscoll, V., Oleson, J., Jiang, D., & Gfeller, K. (in press). The effects of training on recognition of musical instruments presented through cochlear implant simulations. *Journal of the American Academy of Audiology.*

Duehl, A. N. (1979). The effect of creative dance movement on large muscle control and balance in congenitally blind children. *Journal of Visual Impairment and Blindness, 73*, 127–133.

Edmonds, K. (1984). Is there a valid place for music in the education of deaf children? *ACEHI Journal, 10*, 164–169.

Erber, N. P., & Hirsh, I. J. (1978). Auditory training. In H. Davis & S. R. Silverman (Eds.), *Hearing and deafness.* Chicago: Holt, Rinehart and Winston.

Fahey, J. D., & Birkenshaw, L. (1972). Bypassing the ear: The perception of music by feeling and touch. *The Music Educators Journal, 58*, 44–49.

Fisher, K. V., & Parker, B. J. (1994). A multisensory system for the development of sound awareness and speech production. *Journal of the Academy of Rehabilitative Audiology, 25*, 13–24.

Ford, T. A. (1985). *The effect of musical experiences and age on the ability of deaf children to discriminate pitch of complex tones.* Unpublished doctoral dissertation, University of North Carolina, Chapel Hill.

Franks, J. R. (1982). Judgment of hearing aid processed music. *Ear and Hearing, 3*(1), 18–23.

Galloway, H. F., & Bean, M. F. (1974). The effects of action songs on the development of body-image and body-part identification in hearing-impaired preschool children. *Journal of Music Therapy, 11*, 125–134.

Gfeller, K. E. (1986). Music as a remedial tool for improving speech rhythm in the hearing-impaired: Clinical and research considerations. *MEH Bulletin, 2*, 3–19.

Gfeller, K. E. (1987). Songwriting as a tool for reading and language remediation. *Music Therapy, 6*, 28–38.

Gfeller, K. E. (1997a). *Music perception and aesthetic response of cochlear implant recipients.* Presented at the Multidisciplinary Perspectives on Musicality: The Seashore Symposium, Iowa City, IA.

Gfeller, K. E. (1997b). *Music therapy methods for children who are deaf or hard of hearing.* Presented at the Australian Music Therapy National Conference, Brisbane, Australia.

Gfeller, K. (2000). Accommodating children who use cochlear implants in the music therapy or educational setting. *Music Therapy Perspectives, 18*(2), 122–130.

Gfeller, K. (2001). Aural rehabilitation of music listening for adult cochlear implant recipients: Addressing learner characteristics. *Music Therapy Perspectives, 19*, 88–95.

Gfeller, K. E. (2007). Music therapy and hearing loss: A 30-year retrospective. *Music Therapy Perspectives, 20*(2), 100–107.

Gfeller, K. E., & Baumann, A. A. (1988). Assessment procedures for music therapy with hearing-impaired children: Language development. *Journal of Music Therapy, 25*, 192–205.

Gfeller, K., Christ, A., Knutson, J. F., Witt, S., Murray, K. T., & Tyler, R. S. (2000). Musical backgrounds, listening habits, and aesthetic enjoyment of adult cochlear implant recipients. *Journal of the American Academy of Audiology, 11*, 390–406.

Gfeller, K. E., & Darrow, A. A. (1987). Music as a remedial tool in the language education of hearing-impaired children. *The Arts in Psychotherapy, 14*, 229–235.

Gfeller, K., Knutson, J. F., Woodworth, G., Witt, S., & DeBus, B. (1998). Timbral recognition and appraisal by adult cochlear implant users and by normal-hearing adults. *Journal of the American Academy of Audiology, 9*(1), 1–19.

Gfeller, K., & Lansing, C. R. (1991). Melodic, rhythmic and timbral perception of adult cochlear implant users. *Journal of Speech and Hearing Research, 34*, 916–920.

Gfeller, K., & Lansing, C. (1992). Musical perception of cochlear implant users as measured by the Primary Measure of Music Audiation: An item analysis. *Journal of Music Therapy, 29*(1), 18–39.

Gfeller, K., Mehr, M., & Witt, S. (2001). Aural rehabilitation of music perception and enjoyment of adult cochlear implant users. *Journal of the Academy of Rehabilitative Audiology, 34*, 17–27.

Gfeller, K., Olszewski, C., Turner, C., Gantz, B., & Oleson, J. (2006). Music perception with cochlear implants and residual hearing. *Audiology & Neurotology, 11*(Suppl. 1), 12–15.

Gfeller, K. E., & Schum, R. (1994). Requisites for conversation: Engendering world knowledge. In N. Tye-Murray (Ed.), *Let's converse: A "how-to" guide to develop and expand conversational skills of children and teenagers who are hearing impaired* (pp. 177–214). Washington, DC: Alexander Graham Bell Association.

Gfeller, K., Turner, C., Oleson, J., Zhang, X., Gantz, B., Froman, R., et al. (2007). Accuracy of cochlear implant recipients on pitch perception, melody recognition and speech reception in noise. *Ear and Hearing, 28*(3), 412.

Gfeller, K. E., & Witt, S. (1997). *A qualitative assessment of music listening experiences by adult cochlear implant recipients.* Presented at the annual meeting of the National Association for Music Therapy National Conference, Los Angeles, CA.

Gfeller, K., Witt, S., Adamek, M., Mehr, M., Rogers, J., Stordahl, J., et al. (2002). Effects of training on timbre recognition and appraisal by postlingually deafened cochlear implant recipients. *Journal of the American Academy of Audiology, 13*, 132–145.

Gfeller, K., Witt, S., Stordahl, J., Mehr, M., & Woodworth, G. (2001). The effects of training on melody recognition and appraisal by adult cochlear implant recipients. *Journal of the Academy of Rehabilitative Audiology, 33*, 115–138.

Gfeller, K., Woodworth, G., Robin, D. A., Witt, S., & Knutson, J. F. (1997). Perception of rhythmic and sequential pitch patterns by normally hearing adults and adult cochlear implant users. *Ear and Hearing, 18*(3), 252–260.

Gougoux, F., Lepore, M., Voss, P., Zatorre, R. J., & Belin, R. (2004). Pitch discrimination in the early blind: People blinded in infancy have sharper listening skills than those who lost their sight later. *Nature, 430*, 309.

Gourgey, C. (1998). Music therapy in the treatment of social isolation in visually impaired children. *Review, 29*(4), 157–162.

Greene, R. J., Hoats, D. L., & Hornick, A. J. (1970). Music distortion: A new technique for behavior modification. *The Psychological Record, 20*, 107–109.

Greenwald, M. A. (1978). The effectiveness of distorted music versus interrupted music to decrease self stimulatory behavior in profoundly retarded adolescents. *Journal of Music Therapy, 15*, 58–66.

Hardman, M. L., Drew, C. J., & Egan, M. W. (2002). *Human exceptionality: Society, school and family* (7th ed.). Boston: Allyn and Bacon.

Heim, K. E. (1963). *Musical aptitude of seven high school students in residential schools for the blind as measured by the Wing Standardized Test of Musical Intelligence.* Unpublished master's thesis, University of Kansas, Lawrence, KS.

Heward, W. L. (2003). *Exceptional children: An introduction to special education* (7th ed.). Upper Saddle River, NJ: Merrill/Prentice Hall.

Hsiao, F.-L. (in press). Mandarin melody recognition by pediatric cochlear implant recipients. *Journal of Music Therapy.*

Hummel, C. J. (1971). The value of music in teaching deaf students. *Volta Review, 73*, 224–228.

Hunt, N., & Marshall, K. (2005). *Exceptional children and youth* (4th ed.). Boston: Houghton Mifflin.

Individuals with Disabilities Educational Improvement Act of 2004, 108th Cong. (2004).

Kern, P., & Wolery, M. (2001). Participation of a preschooler with visual impairments on the playground: Effects of musical adaptations and staff development. *Journal of Music Therapy, 38*, 149–164.

Kersten, F. (1981). Music as therapy for the visually impaired. *Music Educators Journal, 67*, 62–65.

Korduba, O. M. (1975). Duplicated rhythmic patterns between deaf and normal-hearing children. *Journal of Music Therapy, 12*, 136–146.

Kuntze, M. (1998). Literacy and deaf children: The language question. *Topics in Language Disorders, 18*(4), 1–15.

Kwalwasser, J. (1955). *Exploring the musical mind.* New York: Colman Ross.

Madsen, C. K., & Darrow, A. A. (1989). The relationship between music aptitude and sound conceptualization of the visually impaired. *Journal of Music Therapy, 26*, 71–78.

Mahshie, S. N. (1995). *Educating deaf children bilingually*. Washington, DC: Gallaudet University Press.

Marschark, M. (2007). Raising and educating a deaf child: A comprehensive guide to the choices, controversies and decisions faced by parents and educators. London: Oxford University Press.

McDermott, H. J. (2004). Music perception with cochlear implants: A review. *Trends in Amplification, 8*(2), 49–81.

Meadow, K. (1980a). *Deafness and child development*. Los Angeles: University of California Press.

Meadow, K. (1980b). *Meadow/Kendall Social-Emotional Assessment Inventory for deaf students*. Washington, DC: Gallaudet College.

Meier, R., & Newport, E. (1990). Out of the hands of babes: On a possible sign advantage in language acquisition. *Language, 66*, 1–23.

Padden, C. (1996). *From the cultural to the bicultural: The modern deaf community*. New York: Cambridge University Press.

Padden, C., & Humphries, T. (1988). *Deaf in America: Voices from a culture*. Cambridge, MA: Harvard University Press.

Rapp, D. W., & Rapp, A. J. (1992). A survey of the current status of visually impaired students in secondary mathematics. *Journal of Visual Impairment and Blindness, 86*, 115–117.

Riordan, J. T. (1971). *They can sing too: Rhythm for the deaf*. Springfield, VA: Jenrich Associates.

Sakurabayashi, H. Y., Satyo, Y., & Uehara, E. (1956). Auditory discrimination of the blind. *Japanese Journal of Psychology of the Blind, 1*, 3–10.

Schirmer, B. R. (1998). Hearing loss. In A. Turnbull, R. Turnbull, M. Shank & D. Leal (Eds.), *Exceptional lives: Special education in today's schools* (pp. 620–660). Upper Saddle River, NJ: Merrill/Prentice Hall.

Schum, R., & Gfeller, K. (1994). Engendering social skills. In N. Tye-Murray (Ed.), *Let's converse: A "how-to" guide to develop and expand conversational skills of children and teenagers who are hearing impaired* (pp. 147–176). Washington, DC: Alexander Graham Bell Association.

Sheldon, D. A. (1997). The Illinois School for the Deaf band: A historical perspective. *Journal of Research in Music Education, 45*, 580–600.

Smeets, P. M. (1972). The effects of various sounds and noise levels on stereotyped rocking behavior of blind retardates. *Training School Bulletin, 68*, 226.

Stankov, L., & Spillsbury, G. (1978). The measurement of auditory abilities of sighted, partially sighted, and blind children. *Applied Psychological Measurement, 2*, 491–503.

Stephens, W. B., & Grub, C. (1982). Development of Piagetian reasoning in congenitally blind children. *Journal of Visual Impairment and Blindness, 76*(4), 133–143.

Turnbull, R., Turnbull, A., Shank, M., Smith, S., & Leal, D. (2001). *Exceptional lives: Special education in today's schools* (3rd ed.). Upper Saddle River, NJ: Prentice Hall.

Uslan, M., Malone, S., & De l'Aune, W. (1983). Teaching route travel to multiply handicapped blind adults: An auditory approach. *Journal of Visual Impairment and Blindness, 77*, 18–20.

Vettese, J. (1974). Instrumental lessons for deaf children. *Volta Review, 76*(4), 19–22.

Wilson, B. (2000). Cochlear implant technology. In J. K. Niparko, K. I. Kirk, N. K. Mellon, A. M. Robbins, D. L. Tucci, & B. S. Wilson (Ed.), *Cochlear implants: Principles and practices* (pp. 109–118). New York: Lippincott, Williams & Wilkins.

CHAPTER 14

MUSIC THERAPY IN SPECIAL EDUCATION

Mary Adamek
Alice-Ann Darrow

CHAPTER OUTLINE

IMPORTANT EVENTS IN THE HISTORY OF SPECIAL EDUCATION
INDIVIDUALS WITH DISABILITIES EDUCATION ACT (IDEA)
    Disability Categories under IDEA
MAINSTREAMING AND INCLUSION
    Principles of Inclusion
    Models of Educational Services
CHANGING ROLES OF MUSIC THERAPISTS IN SCHOOLS
    Music Therapy as a Related Service
    Music Therapy in a District-wide Setting
ADAPTIVE STRATEGIES FOR INCLUDING STUDENTS WITH DISABILITIES IN MUSIC
THE IMPORTANCE AND ROLE OF COLLABORATION IN SCHOOLS
MANAGING THE THERAPEUTIC CLASSROOM
THE USE OF MUSIC AS A STRATEGY TO MANAGE BEHAVIOR
CONCLUSIONS

Public schools in the U.S. are mandated by Congress to provide a free and appropriate public education to all children, regardless of the child's abilities or disabilities. Currently there are over 6 million students with disabilities receiving special education services in schools. Music educators and music therapists are responsible for providing appropriate educational services to students with disabilities in all types of music settings, which may include performance groups, general music classes, adapted music classes, and music therapy sessions. All music professionals need to be prepared to work effectively with children across the continuum of abilities. Music therapists employed in schools typically work with students who have a wide range of disabilities, and who may be anywhere from preschool to high school age.

According to the *AMTA Member Sourcebook* (2007), one of the two largest client populations served by music therapists is public school children with disabilities, and schools K–12 have accounted for the largest number of new jobs in music therapy over the past five years (*AMTA Member Sourcebooks*, 2003–2008).

Music therapists typically work on improving students' social, communication, and academic skills through music-based interventions, while music educators focus almost exclusively on developing their musical skills. A music therapist might also collaborate with music educators to adapt the music education environment to better support students with disabilities, or the music therapist might work in small groups or one-to-one with students who have disabilities to enhance their acquisition of educational and social goals. Music therapists in schools today are generally itinerant, and thus attend to the needs of students and teachers at multiple sites. The role they play in the education of students with disabilities has changed over the years—primarily due to the concomitant changes that have occurred in special education practices.

IMPORTANT EVENTS IN THE HISTORY OF SPECIAL EDUCATION

Significant changes have occurred in the availability of educational services for students with disabilities over the past two centuries. The educational system in the U.S. has moved from no services for children with disabilities to opportunities for full inclusion in general education settings. In the early 1800s, students with disabilities were typically provided with public education. The public school system then moved to educating students with disabilities in segregated schools and separate classrooms, followed by mainstreaming practices and full inclusion with typically developing students. The current educational system in the U.S. mandates a free and appropriate public education (FAPE) for all children, no matter what their abilities or disabilities may be. Services are provided based on the requirements of federal legislation titled the Individuals with Disabilities Education Improvement Act 2004 (or IDEA 2004 or IDEA) (Adamek, 2002; Adamek & Darrow, 2005).

Table 1 demonstrates significant developments in the education of children with disabilities since the early 1900s. Factors such as changes in societal views, the Great Depression, civil rights cases, and legislative actions were catalysts for these important changes throughout history.

Table 1
Significant Issues and Developments in Special Education, Early 1900s–Present (Rothstein, 2000)

Date	Issues in Special Education
Early 1900s	• Students with disabilities educated in asylums or government institutions • Many had no educational opportunities • Primarily custodial care
Mid 1900s (1950–1970)	• Curriculum expanded, with emphasis on social participation and vocational skills • Basic rights being considered • *Brown v. Board of Education* (1954): landmark case that affected special education; civil rights case; separate education did not provide equal education
Late 1900s (1970–2000)	• Practice of mainstreaming began; moved to inclusion models • Early intervention services added • Individuals with Disabilities Education Act (IDEA)
Present	• Continued movement towards education of students with disabilities with same-aged peers without disabilities • More accountability for all children to learn (No Child Left Behind Education Act)

INDIVIDUALS WITH DISABILITIES EDUCATION ACT (IDEA)

The Individuals with Disabilities Education Act (IDEA) is a federal special education law that specifies who is eligible for services and the nature of those services. Mandates from IDEA are formulated on the basis of six principles that describe what parents and students can expect from their educational experience. The principles of IDEA are *zero reject, nondiscriminatory evaluation, appropriate education, least restrictive environment, procedural due process,* and *parent and student participation* (Table 2). These six principles guarantee educational access and govern the educational services for eligible students with disabilities (Turnbull, Turnbull, & Wehmeyer, 2007).

Table 2
Six Principles of IDEA

IDEA Principle	Definition
Zero reject	Students may not be excluded from educational services due to a disability, no matter how severe the disability.
Nondiscriminatory evaluation	Nonbiased and nondiscriminatory evaluation tools must be used to determine if a student has a disability that negatively affects the ability to benefit from his/her education.
Appropriate education	Educational plan must be individualized for the student, at no cost to the parent. The Individual Family Service Plan (IFSP) is developed for children ages birth–2, and the Individualized Education Program (IEP) is developed for students ages 3–21.
Least restrictive environment (LRE)	Students with disabilities must be educated with students who do not have disabilities, to the maximum extent possible for the student to benefit from the education experience. Students who cannot make educational progress in a general education setting may be educated in a more restrictive, less inclusive classroom.
Procedural due process	Process by which parents can challenge a decision made by the schools, consisting of procedural guidelines to protect students with disabilities from practices that deny their rights under IDEA.
Parent and student participation	Ensures parents' and students' rights to participate in the development, implementation, and decision-making process related to education services and placement.

According to data collected by the U.S. Department of Education (2007) over 6.6 million students ages 6 through 21 received special education services under the Individuals with Disabilities Education Act (IDEA). This number represents 9.1% of the total population of students ages 6 through 21 at that time. During this same year, close to 700,000 children ages 3–5 received special education services under IDEA, representing close to 6% of the total population of children in that age range. In addition, there were 270,000 children ages birth–2 who received services under IDEA, representing 2.2% of the population of that age range.

Disability Categories under IDEA

IDEA is based upon federal legislation, which specifies categories of disabilities or illnesses that are covered within this law, as well as guidelines for implementing educational services for students with disabilities. As this book goes into publication (August 2008), IDEA lists 13 categories under which students could be eligible for special education services. The specific categories currently listed under IDEA are specific learning disability, speech or language impairment, mental retardation, emotional disturbance, multiple disabilities, hearing impairment, orthopedic impairment, other health impairment, visual impairment, autism, deaf-blindness, traumatic brain injury, and developmental delay. The noncategorical developmental delay category may be used for students ages 3 through 9 for whom a diagnosis has not been determined or may not be appropriate due to delay rather than a specific disability.

You may be curious about the use of the terms *mental retardation, hearing impairment,* and *emotional disturbance* as categories within IDEA, rather than *intellectual disability* (as used in Chapter 4), *behavioral-emotional disorder* (as used in Chapter 8), or *deaf or hard-of-hearing* (as described in Chapter 13). As noted in previous chapters, specific terms used to describe illnesses or disabling conditions have changed over time. Furthermore, there can be differing opinions among professionals, organizations, or individuals regarding which terms are most accurate and/or socially acceptable for use. The category names used in this chapter are consistent with the current language found within federal legislation specific to educational policies and practices. These terms may be somewhat different from those terms used in other chapters in this book, as well as those recommended in other circumstances (such as medical settings or residential facilities). In addition, the terminology used in special education and health care will continue to evolve in response to societal and scientific changes. Consequently, music therapists need to stay abreast of changes in preferred terminology from one organization or circumstance to the next, as well as changes in language use over time.

IDEA focuses on the educational needs of students ages 3 through 21, with additional services for children birth through 2. Students who have a disability that adversely affects their ability to learn may be eligible for special education and **related services**. Related services are those additional services that are related to education but not typically an educational service that a student needs to make progress on educational goals. Examples of related services include occupational therapy, physical therapy, speech and language therapy, and music therapy. In order to receive related services, professionals certified in the particular discipline must complete an eligibility assessment to determine a student's needs. Related services are listed on the student's IEP as necessary services, and the school is mandated to provide services for which the student is eligible. IDEA uses a categorical approach to define eligibility for special education and related services. Specific disabilities will fall into one of three areas, including:

- Disabilities related to physical impairment/functioning
- Disabilities related to mental, emotional, or cognitive impairment/functioning
- Catch-all category for less specific disorders (developmental delay, multiple disabilities, other health impairments)

IDEA lists 13 specific disability categories under which students could be eligible for special education services. As shown in Table 3, nearly half of all students with disabilities served under IDEA have specific learning disabilities. The next largest categories are students with speech and language impairments (18%), students with mental retardation (10%), and student with emotional disturbance (8%). Of all students ages 6 through 21, 83% were classified under one of these four disability categories. Although autism is a relatively small category in terms of the entire population, the number of children with this diagnosis has increased dramatically over the past several years (U.S. Department of Education, 2007).

Table 3
Precentage of Students Receiving Services under IDEA, Ages 6-21, by Disability Category

Specific Disability Category	Percentage
Specific Learning Disability	47%
Speech or Language Impairment	18%
Mental Retardation	10%
Emotional Disturbance	8%
Other Health Impairments	7.5%
All remaining categories combined	8.8%
Multiple Disabilities	
Hearing Impairments	
Autism	
Orthopedic Impairments	
Developmental Delay	
Visual Impairments	
Traumatic Brain Injury	
Deaf-Blindness	

Source: *27rd Annual Report to Congress on the Implementation of the Individuals with Disabilities Education Act* (U.S. Department of Education, 2007)

MAINSTREAMING AND INCLUSION

Practices related to educating students with disabilities have had a great impact on the roles of music therapists and music educators over the past 35 years. Music in special education has changed from the early years of isolation and segregation, to the practice of mainstreaming in the mid 1970s, and continuing with IDEA's directives to educate students with disabilities in general education classes as much as possible. The term *mainstreaming* was originally used to describe the practice of including students with disabilities in general education classes for a portion of the day. Students with disabilities would join their peers without disabilities for part of the day, either in class for an academic subject or in a more social time, such as lunch or recess. In many instances, one of the student's first mainstreaming experiences included joining the music, art, and/or physical education class. This term came into use in the mid 1970s after the passage of PL 94-142, which was the precursor to IDEA in later years.

Principles of Inclusion

Currently, the practice of inclusion refers to educating all students in the same classroom, with additional supports provided for students with disabilities. In this model, students of all abilities may be educated in the regular education classroom for the entire day or part of the day. Appropriate educational interventions are provided to promote success of all students in the inclusive classroom (Adamek & Darrow, 2005). The practice of inclusion is based on some fundamental beliefs upon which educational practices for students with disabilities are developed, including:

- The *human potential movement*—The belief that everyone has the desire to develop in positive ways, and that basic rights and equal opportunities should be provided to ensure that positive development is based on the needs of the individual.
- The *general system theory*—The student must be seen as a whole person who is influenced by his or her interaction with the environment. Educational services should take all aspects of the student into consideration.
- The *principle of normalization*—Students with disabilities should have experiences as close as possible to those of typically developing peers.
- The *self-determination movement*—Students and families should be empowered through decision-making opportunities. Creativity, assertiveness, and problem solving are all part of the process to promote self-determination.

(Kochhar, West, & Taymans, 2000)

Models of Educational Services

IDEA mandates that students with disabilities be educated in the least restrictive environment but does not specify what that setting should be for students. The least restrictive environment may be different from one student to the next, based on student needs and abilities, family requests, and school district structures. A continuum of services exists to provide the best, most normalized educational environment for students to promote and support student success. Selected examples of this continuum of services are listed below, in order from the least restrictive or most normalized setting, to most restrictive settings. It is important to remember that for some students, the least restrictive environment, where they can be successful, will be a setting that is highly restricted and separated, and one with high levels of support (Mastropieri & Scruggs, 2000).

- **Full inclusion model**—Student with disabilities is educated in the regular education classroom 100% of the time, and special educators collaborate with classroom teachers to provide support and adaptations for student progress.
- **Mainstreaming or inclusion model**—Student attends selected general education classes with same-aged peers, but is also educated in a smaller classroom with more support for part of the day.
- **Social mainstreaming model**—Student with severe disabilities attends some classes with same-aged peers for the purpose of social interaction. Expectations for student participation and achievement are significantly adapted.
- **Self-contained classroom model**—Student is educated with a small number of students, all with disabilities, with a high teacher-to-student ratio.
- **Separate school or residential school model**—Student is educated in a separate school setting that serves students with severe disabilities who cannot be successfully educated in another, less restrictive, setting.

Music class is usually one of the first choices for including a student primarily educated in a self-contained classroom into a general education classroom (Jellison & Gainer, 1995). The music educator and music therapist can participate in the decision-making process to determine if the music class is an appropriate inclusive placement based on the educational benefits and/or the social benefits that a student is receiving in that setting (Patterson, 2003). The music educator and music therapist can suggest the most educationally beneficial placement for the child, considering the following issues. Placement suggestions can be made based on:

- the characteristics of the student, including the student's abilities
- the primary focus of the music class (a class that focuses on music making rather than music theory might be more appropriate for a student with severe mental retardation)
- the general education options that are available for that student in the school (is the student placed in the music class because it is the only option, or is there a more appropriate general education class for this student?)
- opportunities for partial participation (if the student is unable to successfully participate in the entire class every time, is there a possibility for the student to join the class for a portion of the class time and then move to another setting?)

(Adamek & Darrow, 2005, p. 105)

Music educators typically teach students with disabilities in a variety of inclusive or mainstreamed settings. Music educators may also teach music in self-contained classrooms with students who have disabilities so severe that they are not appropriate for the more normalized or inclusive classroom. This is sometimes termed *adapted music education* since the music educator teaches music skills; however, these skills may need to be adapted to meet the special needs of students with disabilities. Music therapists frequently collaborate with music educators to assist them in their work with students with disabilities.

CHANGING ROLES OF MUSIC THERAPISTS IN SCHOOLS

Throughout the U.S., music therapists work in school districts in a wide variety of roles. As mentioned previously, music therapists may collaborate with music educators to help provide appropriate adaptations to the music setting. In addition to functioning as a consultant to the music educator, the music therapist may also teach music in the self-contained classroom, provide music therapy as a related service to an individual student, and/or provide group music therapy to several children in a district-wide services model.

Music Therapy as a Related Service

Some students respond to music interventions in a way that they do not respond to other types of interventions. The student might be more engaged, focused, or verbal during a music activity than he or she is during other activities. Maybe the child sings but does not verbalize, or maybe the child will remain seated for a group activity if music is present but not if music is absent. If a parent or teacher believes that music therapy might be necessary for a student to make progress on his or her educational goals, someone from the team may request a music therapy eligibility assessment. This music therapy assessment, facilitated by a qualified board-certified music therapist, will help determine if a student functions at a significantly higher level with the assist of music interventions. If so, the team will discuss the possibility of adding music therapy as a "related service" on the student's Individualized Education Program (IEP). With music therapy as a related service, the student will be eligible for individual or small group music therapy sessions focusing on IEP goals and objectives. The Special Education Music Therapy Assessment Process (SEMTAP) is a music therapy assessment procedure used in many school districts. In this approach, the music therapist selects objectives from the student's IEP, develops music therapy interventions based on these objectives, facilitates one or two music therapy sessions with the student, and collects data on the student's responses in the music therapy setting with the aid of music, and in the classroom setting without the aid of music. If the student performs significantly better with the support of the music and music therapy interventions, music therapy as a related service may be recommended to the IEP team (Brunk & Coleman, 2002). See Table 4 for an overview of possible recommendations based on the music therapy assessment process.

Table 4
Potential Recommendations Following a Music Therapy Assessment

Recommendation for Services	Assessment Findings and Music Therapy Services
Direct music therapy service	*Assessment findings:* Music therapy provides a considerable assist for the student to make progress on IEP goals.
	Music therapist provides music therapy services directly with the student. Goals are taken directly from the IEP.
Consult to student service	*Assessment findings:* Music therapy assists student when involved in classroom activities (such as working with peers, sharing, completing tasks).
	Music therapist provides services to the student within the classroom or in other therapy settings (speech therapy, occupational therapy) and offers suggestions to teachers on how to implement music-based interventions throughout the school day. Goals are taken directly from the IEP.
Combination of direct service and consult to student service	*Assessment findings:* Music therapy assists the student on IEP goals individually and when involved in classroom activities.
	Music therapist provides individual 1-to-1 music therapy with the student and works with the student in the classroom, as well as with the teachers. Goals are taken directly from the IEP.
No music therapy services	*Assessment findings:* When comparing responses to music-based and non-music-based interventions, there was not a difference between the student's responses. Music therapy did not significantly assist the student to make progress on IEP objectives.

(Adamek & Darrow, 2005, p. 123)

Music Therapy in a District-wide Setting

Many school districts provide music therapy as one of many comprehensive special services available to students with disabilities. This model of music therapy service reaches many students who can benefit from music therapy services, but may or may not be eligible for music therapy as a related service. Music therapists work with students from early childhood special education through high school levels to enhance their social, academic, behavioral, communication, and leisure skill development. In this model, music therapy is not listed on a student's IEP as a related service, but could be listed as a service that is provided to the student as a complement to other special education services.

> *Emily is a music therapist in a Midwestern school district. Each week she serves students in six schools throughout the district, providing a variety of music therapy services to students with disabilities. Two days a week she provides music therapy in self-contained special education classrooms from early childhood special education through middle school special education classes. She works with these students on important educational skills such as improving attention to task and following directions, as well as working with other students. One day a week she works with students who are included in their grade level music class to remediate their behavior and music skills to promote success in their inclusive setting. The rest of the week she provides music therapy as a related service to individual students who have music therapy listed on their IEP; facilitates eligibility assessments on students who have been referred for a music therapy eligibility assessment; completes documentation and paperwork; and consults with music educators, special educators, and classroom teachers to help them either to adapt music education lessons or to support students in their classrooms using music.*

ADAPTIVE STRATEGIES FOR INCLUDING STUDENTS WITH DISABILITIES IN MUSIC

There are numerous **adaptive strategies** that can be utilized in music education classes and music therapy sessions to enhance the learning of students with disabilities. Strategies may involve adapting the way the teacher or therapist delivers instruction, offering alternative means for students to respond to instruction, modifying the curriculum to fit the student's needs, or adapting the environment (Ebeling, Deschenes, & Sprague, 1994; Kochhar & West, 1996). Table 5 includes a list of adaptive strategies that may be helpful in providing individualized, appropriate, and effective instruction to students. Some teachers and therapists may need to use very few of these adaptive strategies, while others may need to employ a number of them in order to meet the needs of their students.

Table 5
Adaptive Strategies Useful in Teaching Students with Disabilities

Strategy	Adaptation
Varying Student Participation	Vary the level of participation that is expected of the student—partial to full.
Varying Teacher Input	Adapt the way that instruction is delivered to the students by using a multimodal (visual, tactual, kinesthetic, etc.) approach to instruction.
Varying Student Output	Adapt how the students can respond to instruction. A student might be able to answer a question verbally or through an assistive communication device rather than speaking or in writing.
Varying Difficulty of Task	Adapt the skill level, the type of problem, or the rules on how a student may approach a task.
Varying Amount of Time	Adapt the amount of time allotted for completing a task, taking a test, or learning a new skill.
Varying the Number of Items	Adapt the number of items or amount of material that a student is expected to learn or complete.
Adapting Outcomes or Expectations	While using the same materials for all students, adapt the outcome expectations for some students.
Providing a Substitute Curriculum	Provide a different curriculum or instructional materials to meet the individual student's goals.
Adapting the Environment	Adapt the classroom to best suit the needs of the students. Adaptations can be wheelchair ramps, wide aisles, low shelving, visuals, sign language interpreter, adapted instruments, etc.
Providing Student Support	Additional support might be provided by a peer buddy, paraprofessional, or another adult.

Determining which adaptations are appropriate for students or the level of support they need to be successful in the classroom can be best established through consultation with classroom teachers or other school personnel. Collaborative decision making in planning for individual student needs allows music educators and music therapists the opportunity to consult with special education teachers, general education teachers, paraprofessionals, parents, and other health-related professionals such as speech-language pathologists, occupational therapists, and physical therapists.

THE IMPORTANCE AND ROLE OF COLLABORATION IN SCHOOLS

Collaboration is a mutually beneficial relationship entered into by individuals, groups, or organizations in order to achieve results they are more likely to achieve together than alone (Winer & Ray, 1994). In schools, it is an ongoing process among educational professionals and parents that is essential for the effective education of students. The collaborative process involves cooperation, meaningful communication, problem solving, idea sharing, information sharing, and planning and facilitating useful strategies for students. It can occur formally through the IEP process or other meetings, through co-teaching or directly serving a student with another professional, or informally through email and impromptu conversations.

Ongoing collaborative efforts can promote the strengths of all educational and therapeutic personnel and their programs. Collaboration means that therapists and teachers are working cooperatively with one another so that students receive the best possible education throughout their school day. While the general education teacher or special education teacher might have primary responsibility for a student, all professionals work together to assist the student in the accomplishment of his or her IEP goals.

One of the first steps in working effectively with students who have special needs in music classes or music therapy sessions is to gather information about the students. **Consultation** is an important part of collaborative efforts. In fact, according to some educators, consultation with school personnel is considered to be the most critical issue related to successfully including students with severe disabilities in music (Darrow, 1999). Music educators cited the need to obtain information about (1) students, their disabilities, and IEP goals; (2) adapting curriculum materials, instruments, and music; and (3) appropriate placement of students in music classrooms. Music educators often work in isolation, and thus they desire consultation with school personnel about the needs of students with disabilities. Music therapists in the schools, however, are frequently in contact with many of the classroom and special education teachers in their building—primarily because they often work exclusively with students who have disabilities, and because they generally move from room to room and are able to see others in passing, or in more formal ways such as IEP meetings. Important information for music therapists to gather includes (1) a student's strength or special skills; (2) a student's disability characteristics, limitations, or weaknesses; (3) IEP objectives that can be addressed through music; and (4) useful strategies for working with the student (Adamek, 2001; Ebeling et al., 1994). Simple forms asking for this information can be created and then distributed to classroom teachers, special education teachers, administrators, specialists, parents, and, in some cases, the student.

To achieve effective working relationships, it is imperative to have open and direct two-way communication between teachers and the music therapist. Barriers to effective communication include attitudes held by certain professionals, difficulties with interpersonal skills, or lack of time to share about the students. Some of the characteristics of successful collaborators are:

- A willingness to share information
- Good interpersonal skills
- The ability to be depersonalize and not become defensive
- A willingness to reserve judgment
- The ability to actively listen to others
- A genuine interest in others' opinions
- The ability to acknowledge the contributions of others

In a collaborative process, the goal is not only to achieve a desired outcome, but also to achieve that desired outcome in the most efficient and effective way possible for all parties involved (for more information on collaboration, see Chapter 15). The general process for school collaborations is:

- Gather the necessary parties for consultation
- Discuss and agree upon goals
- Define success or desired outcomes
- Determine how desired outcomes will be measured
- Discuss contributions of each member to meet goals
- Discuss possible barriers to collaboration and possible solutions
- Secure a commitment from each member to move forward under the agreed-upon collaborative guidelines
- Decide on method and frequency of future communication
- Set a timeline for future communications
- Prepare summary notes and distribute to team members

(Bauwens & Hourcade, 1995; Dieker & Barnett, 1996;
Walther-Thomas, Bryant, & Land, 1996)

Communicating openly and directly with others will help avert any misunderstandings in the collaborative process. Mutual respect and member parity is imperative to creating and maintaining a collaborative partnership. Successful collaboration can result in a win-win situation for all involved.

Jennifer is a music therapist in a large metropolitan school district. She services a number of students who have Asperger's Syndrome in their individual schools. She has determined that one of their greatest needs is social skills development. Jennifer wants to organize a community music group that specifically addresses these skills. She is going to need the cooperation of parents and the advice of the classroom and special education teachers who work with these students. She has called for a meeting of parents and related school personnel. Because the implementation of her community music group will require the input and time of all concerned, she will need to exercise her very best collaborative skills in order to realize the creative strategy she has designed for her students. Jennifer is more likely to be successful if she allows others to offer ideas and to be part of process, and if she is not defensive or hurt if others are not as enthusiastic as she is about the music group.

MANAGING THE THERAPEUTIC CLASSROOM

One area that music therapists may wish to consult with others about is effective **classroom management**. Music therapists often work with clients in one-to-one or small group settings, so when faced with large numbers of students, they are often at a loss as to how to shape and maintain appropriate behaviors. Music therapists are not alone—poor classroom management has been identified as the primary deterrent to effective instruction (Darrow, 1999). Classroom management should be considered not only as a way to deal with students' behavior problems, but also as a total process that affects all aspects of the classroom environment. Motivating students to want to learn and to make wise choices regarding their behaviors requires patience, knowledge about management strategies, and, most of all—practice. Many music therapists do their internships in well-established programs with procedures already in place that minimize behavior problems. In this type of situation, student teachers have few opportunities to practice the skills necessary for behavior management. When they begin working independently at their first jobs, they often realize how difficult it can be to motivate some students to learn and to follow directions (Adamek & Darrow, 2005). Sadly, many music teachers and therapists become discouraged and give up before they have been able to develop a repertoire of strategies that will allow them to be successful and to create a positive learning environment. The development of classroom management skills requires experience and practice.

Unfortunately, students who have behavioral challenges are often seen simply as troubled students vying for attention, and not as students with a disability who are deserving of the same educational provisions as students with physical, cognitive, or sensory disabilities. In addition to their challenging behaviors, such students are frequently diagnosed with accompanying disorders—such as learning disabilities, attention deficit and hyperactivity disorders, depression, and suicidal tendencies

(Stahl & Clarizio, 1999). These students usually have limited academic success. In addition, they can cause stress for the teacher or therapist as well as for other students in the classroom. Common student characteristics that contribute to behavioral and academic problems are:

- Overdependence on the teacher
- Difficulty concentrating and paying attention
- Becoming upset under pressure to achieve
- Sloppiness and impulsivity in responding
- Teasing, annoying, or interfering with other children
- Negativism about work, self, teacher, or peers
- Poor personal hygiene
- Extreme social withdrawal or refusal to respond
- Self-stimulation or self-injury
- Physical or verbal aggression toward teacher or peers

(Kauffman, Pullen, & Akers, 1986, p. 2)

These characteristics can cause negative reactions from teachers and therapists as well as from the students' peers, all of which can be detrimental to a positive learning environment. When students do not follow the classroom rules and exhibit problem behaviors in the music class, the teachers and therapists need an array of behavior management techniques to redirect or decrease negative behaviors. Preventing behavior problems is the best approach, but not all problem behaviors can be prevented. A clear and direct behavior management system with consistent follow-through and consequences is needed to ensure a classroom or therapy environment suitable for learning. The following list includes various strategies that can help to promote positive student behaviors:

- Having positive therapist attitude with high expectations for student learning
- Having clear expectations, known by all students
- Providing an appropriate and motivating curriculum
- Pacing the session such that student interest is maintained
- Giving clear directions
- Providing structure in the environment and routine in instruction
- Reinforcing appropriate behaviors rather than reprimanding inappropriate behaviors
- Following through with predetermined consequences
- Tolerating selected behaviors by remembering that positive behaviors need to be shaped and shaping requires time

- Using proximity control—sometimes just being near a student who is difficult can be effective in eliminating the problem, or placing them away from distractions or next to students who have no behavior problems

- Using planned ignoring— when a student engages in an inappropriate behavior, the teacher ignores that behavior and immediately reinforces the student when he or she exhibits the appropriate behavior

- Employing nonverbal signals to interrupt problem behaviors—nonverbal techniques such as eye contact, hand gestures, finger snapping, or clearing the throat can provide enough of a cue to alert a student to get back on task

- Prioritizing those behaviors that most interfere with learning

- Removing a student from the situation—asking a student to leave the session or the room for a brief time in order to gain self-control

- Having a sense of humor—well-placed humor can dissipate an anxiety-producing situation, and nearly all students will respond positively to someone who can make them laugh.

(Brophy, 1987; Kauffman et al., 1986;
Madsen & Madsen, 2000; Wood, 1998)

THE USE OF MUSIC AS A STRATEGY TO MANAGE BEHAVIOR

Music is a highly desirable activity for even the most challenging student. As a result of its desirability, the contingent use of music can be easily incorporated into a behavioral management program to reinforce appropriate behaviors. In addition, selected musical behaviors that are incompatible with inappropriate or negative behaviors can be taught. Music can also be used to induce mood change and relaxation in students who are anxious or stressed. Music therapists can serve as consultants to classroom teachers and music educators about these uses of music as strategies to manage behavior:

- There are many musical behaviors that are incompatible with undesirable behaviors. For example, a student cannot play a guitar while striking another student, or play the piano while walking around the room. A student cannot sing while swearing or yelling. Musical behaviors should be selected that compete with the problem behaviors a student exhibits.

- The use of contingent music has been used for many years by music therapists to effectively modify challenging behaviors. Music has been used effectively to reward appropriate behaviors and thus to encourage prosocial behaviors.

- The act of learning music, such as to play an instrument, requires many behavioral prerequisites—sitting still, holding an instrument, manipulating the instrument, and reading music. The process of music learning increases the likelihood that students with behavior disorders will engage in these adaptive behaviors, and that the musical product itself will motivate continued engagement.

- Music that induces positive changes in mood, or sedates hyperactive or inappropriate behavior, may be a quick, efficient, and noninvasive way to manage difficult behavior.

- Students with behavior disorders often choose inappropriate ways to express their emotions. Music therapy can provide these students with an alternative means of communication, and an opportunity to express their emotions through song writing or lyric analysis.

(Adamek & Darrow, 2005)

Brenda is a music therapist in a Southeastern school district. She has been asked to give an inservice to elementary teachers on effective uses of music to manage problem behaviors. She has asked teachers to submit, prior to the inservice workshop, a description of the behaviors they find to be most problematic. By doing so, she can target strategies for the specific problems teachers are experiencing with their students. Their problems included out-of-seat behaviors, lack of participation in class activities, use of inappropriate language, and physical abuse—hitting and kicking others. Brenda created three strategies to address each behavior. She also devised a data form for teachers to record these behaviors in order to determine the effectiveness of the strategies. She prioritized the three strategies according to which she thought would be most effective. Brenda designed a management program that employed student preferred music listening and drum lessons as reinforcers for appropriate behaviors, such as remaining in seat for increasing amounts of time or for participating in classroom activities. Brenda made CDs of music that she had heard students listening to during free time. She also made a list of music behaviors that are incompatible with inappropriate language (such as rapping, singing, vocal percussion) and behaviors that are incompatible with kicking and hitting (dancing and playing the drum machine). She encouraged teachers to dissipate tension in the classroom by quickly redirecting students to engage in these music behaviors. She also provided a list of songs that are appropriate for lyric analysis and classroom discussion regarding social situations.

The advantage of using music to manage classroom behavior is that music is an inherently nonthreatening and inviting medium. Music offers the reluctant student a safe environment in which to explore emotions. Musical preferences of the students must be considered as well as the sedative or stimulative characteristics of the music itself.

Music is adaptable in ways such as style, age appropriateness, and sophistication, and, as a result, is capable of targeting problem behaviors across a wide age range of students. Nearly all students respond to music. Their generally positive responses to music can serve as a strong foundation for therapeutic work.

CONCLUSIONS

Many students with disabilities in public schools today receive music therapy as a part of their educational experience. Developments in the field of special education have played an important role in the advancement of music therapy in schools. Music therapists work with students who have a wide range of ages and abilities. The knowledge base required to work effectively with such a diverse population increases with passage of each new amendment to the Individuals with Disabilities Education Act. The job description of music therapists in schools depends on the school district in which they work; however, some job responsibilities are common to most positions. The use of adaptive strategies to include students with disabilities, consulting with school personnel, and managing the music classroom are all important aspects of what music therapists do in schools.

The future of music therapists in schools is bright. Public schools presently account for the largest number of new jobs in music therapy, and school children constitute one of the largest music therapy client populations. Music therapists in schools carry greater accountability than ever before in the education of students with disabilities. Music therapy positions in schools are likely to remain secure due to the increasing number of students with disabilities identified each year.

SUMMARY

Music has long played a role in special education programs. Music was considered an essential part of the special class curricula—generally, for the purposes of achieving nonmusical goals. In these early accounts, music was used to diagnose and to treat various speech and hearing disorders, to facilitate the learning of students with cognitive disabilities, and to assist in the rehabilitation of students with physical disabilities. Such early recognition of music's therapeutic value paved the way for the later employment of music therapists in schools. With the passage of PL 94-142, increasing numbers of students with severe disabilities were mainstreamed into the music classroom. As a result, academic specialists, such as music therapists, became more involved in school programs for students with disabilities. The early role of music therapists was to provide services to students whose disabilities precluded their participation in the regular music classroom. Music therapists quickly became part of the treatment team, with their goals being primarily nonmusical. Under the current IDEA reauthorization, all students, regardless of their abilities, must have access to all subjects, including music. Therefore, music therapists' goals for students with disabilities have expanded to include both musical and nonmusical objectives. With present day inclusive practices where accommodations or modifications are to be made such that all children can participate in any area of academic study, music therapists are becoming increasingly valuable as team teachers with or as consultants to music educators.

The role of music therapists in schools today requires that they engage in collaborative and consultative efforts on behalf of students with disabilities. Music therapists work with a wide range of school personnel. They must develop interpersonal skills that will enable them to work effectively with parents, administrators, teachers, and other health-related school professionals. Effective communication is important when working with other professionals. Techniques such as active listening, depersonalizing situations, identifying and sharing goals and solutions, and monitoring students' progress are essential for effective communication and collaboration in schools.

Music therapists are encouraged to collaborate with classroom teachers, special educators, and paraprofessionals to develop and implement effective behavior management procedures in the music setting. The first step in the behavior management process is to create a positive environment for learning. Positive teacher attitude, clear expectations, and motivating classroom activities are a few elements that contribute to a positive classroom environment. There will be times when preventative measures are not enough and additional techniques need to be implemented to manage students' behaviors. Music can be a useful technique to manage the classroom. Because of music's pervasiveness, adaptability, and flexibility, music is seen as an effective strategy to manage classroom behavior.

The role of music therapists in schools appears to be secure, and the future of music therapy in schools is a viable option for employment. Fortunately for those interested in the education of children and youth and the use of music to meet their needs, schools will always be present in neighborhood communities and will continue to hold an important place in society.

STUDY QUESTIONS

1. What three decades included the move to inclusive schools and the passage of the Individuals with Disabilities Education Act?

2. What is meant by the term the *least restrictive environment*?

3. What is the age range of students with disabilities who can receive services in public schools? What disabilities are represented among these students?

4. How has the role of music therapists in schools changed over the years?

5. Identify at least five adaptive strategies that can be used to include students with disabilities in music.

6. What are some of the characteristics of successful collaborators?

7. Identify the major components of the collaborative process.

8. Identify at least five strategies that can help to promote positive classroom behaviors.

9. In what ways can music be used to manage problem classroom behaviors?

10. What music therapy setting has accounted for the greatest number of new jobs over the past five years?

REFERENCES

Adamek, M. (2001). Meeting special needs in music class. *Music Educators Journal, 87*(4), 23–26.

Adamek, M. (2002). In the beginning: A review of early special education services and legislative/regulatory activity affecting the teaching and placement of special learners. In B. Wilson (Ed.), *Models of music therapy interventions in school settings* (2nd ed., pp. 15–24). Silver Spring, MD: American Music Therapy Association.

Adamek, M., & Darrow, A. A. (2005). *Music in special education.* Silver Spring, MD: American Music Therapy Association.

American Music Therapy Association. (2003–2008). *AMTA member sourcebook.* Silver Spring, MD: Author.

Bauwens, J., & Hourcade, J. J. (1995). *Cooperative teaching: Rebuilding the schoolhouse for all students.* Austin, TX: Pro-Ed.

Brophy, J. (1987). Synthesis of research on strategies for motivating students to learn. *Educational Leadership, 45*(2), 40–48.

Brunk, B., & Coleman, K. (2002). A special education music therapy assessment process. In B. Wilson (Ed.), *Models of music therapy interventions in school settings* (2nd ed., pp. 69–82). Silver Spring, MD: American Music Therapy Association.

Darrow, A. A. (1999). Music educators' perceptions regarding the inclusion of students with severe disabilities in music classrooms. *Journal of Music Therapy, 36*, 254–273.

Dieker, L. A., & Barnett, C. A. (1996). Effective co-teaching. *TEACHING Exceptional Children, 29*(1), 5–7.

Ebeling, D., Deschenes, C., & Sprague, J. (1994). *Adapting curriculum and instruction in inclusive classrooms: A teacher's desk reference.* Bloomington, IN: Center for School and Community Integration–Institute for the Study of Developmental Disabilities.

Jellison, J., & Gainer, E. (1995). Into the mainstream: A case study of a child's participation in music education and music therapy. *Journal of Music Therapy, 32*, 228–247.

Kauffman, J. M., Pullen, P. L., & Akers, E. (1986). Classroom management: Teacher-child-peer relationships. *Focus on Exceptional Children, 19*(1), 1–10.

Kochhar, C. A., & West, L. L. (1996). *Handbook for successful inclusion.* Gaithersburg, MD: Aspen.

Kochhar, C., West, L., & Taymans, J. (2000). *Successful inclusion. Practical strategies for a shared responsibility*. Upper Saddle River, NJ: Prentice-Hall.

Madsen, C. H., & Madsen, C. K. (2000). *Teaching discipline: A positive approach for educational development* (4th ed.). Raleigh, NC: Contemporary.

Mastropieri, M., & Scruggs, T. (2000). *The inclusive classroom: Strategies for effective instruction*. Upper Saddle River, NJ: Prentice-Hall.

Patterson, A. (2003). Music teachers and music therapists: Helping children together. *Music Educators Journal, 89*(4), 35–38.

Rothstein, L. F. (2000). *Special education law* (3rd ed.). New York: Longman.

Stahl, N. D., & Clarizio, H. F. (1999). Conduct disorder and comorbidity. *Psychology in the Schools, 36*, 41–50.

Turnbull, A., Turnbull, H. R., & Wehmeyer, M. (2007). *Exceptional lives: Special education in today's schools* (5th ed.). Upper Saddle River, NJ: Prentice-Hall.

U.S. Department of Education. (2007). *Twenty-seventh annual report to Congress on the implementation of the Individuals with Disabilities Education Act*. Washington, DC: U.S. Government Printing Office.

Walther-Thomas, C. S., Bryant, M., & Land, S. (1996). Planning for effective co-teaching: The key to successful inclusion. *Remedial and Special Education, 17*(4), 255–264.

Winer, M. B., & Ray, K. L. (1994). *Collaboration handbook: Creating, sustaining, and enjoying the journey*. St. Paul, MN: Wilder.

Wood, J. W. (1998). *Adapting instruction to accommodate students in inclusive settings* (3rd ed.). Upper Saddle River, NJ: Prentice-Hall.

PART Three

Professional Issues in Music Therapy

CHAPTER 15

THE MUSIC THERAPY
TREATMENT PROCESS

Kate E. Gfeller
William B. Davis

CHAPTER OUTLINE

    PART I: THE CLINICAL PROCESS
        REFERRAL
        ASSESSMENT
            Why Is Assessment Important?
            Assessment Tools
        TREATMENT PLAN
            Therapeutic Goals and Objectives
        DOCUMENTATION OF PROGRESS
        EVALUATION AND TERMINATION OF TREATMENT
        PROFESSIONAL ETHICS AND PERSONAL QUALIFICATIONS
            Professional Ethics
            Cultural Competence
            Personal Qualifications

    PART II: MUSIC THERAPY APPROACHES
        DEFINITIONS
        HISTORICAL TRENDS THAT HAVE INFLUENCED MUSIC THERAPY APPROACHES
        RECENT TRENDS THAT HAVE INFLUENCED THE DEVELOPMENT OF MUSIC
            THERAPY APPROACHES
            Advances in Scientific Knowledge Regarding Health and Illness
            Societal Changes
            Research and Clinical Initiatives in the Music Therapy Field

FACTORS THAT INFLUENCE CLINICAL CHOICES
  Differences in Clientele Served
  Policies or Attitudes at the Work Place
  The Clinical and Educational Background of the Therapist
  The Personal Strengths, Limitations, and Beliefs of the Individual Therapist
PROMINENT APPROACHES TO MUSIC THERAPY
  Approaches Developed within Music Education and Pedagogy
  Approaches Developed within the Field of Music Therapy
  Music Therapy Approaches Reflecting or Based upon Psychological
    Philosophies, Theories, or Models
  Music Therapy Approaches Reflecting Biomedical Models
  Eclectic or Integrative Approach
CONCLUSIONS

PART I: THE CLINICAL PROCESS

According to Cohen and Gericke (1972), "The cornerstone upon which to develop a responsible and meaningful treatment-rehabilitation program is the accumulation and synthesis of accurate, significant patient data" (p. 161). After this information has been collected and analyzed, it is used to formulate treatment goals, objectives, and strategies. Assessment of client needs also assists the therapist in evaluating and documenting clinical change that occurs during treatment (Cohen & Gericke, 1972; Douglass, 2006; Hanser, 1987; Isenberg-Grezeda, 1988; Punwar, 1988). This chapter will discuss areas of professional accountability, including assessment of client needs, development of the treatment plan, evaluation of clinical change, and documentation of progress. In addition, several other key components to professional competence will be addressed: professional ethics, cultural competence, and personal qualifications.

> *Donna is a 68-year-old woman with chronic lower back pain. Even though the initial tissue damage from her back injury has healed, she still suffers from significant pain, and none of the interventions tried to date have resulted in sufficient relief. Pain has changed Donna's life. Prior to her back injury, she and her husband, Jim, were part of a ballroom dance club, and Donna was a faithful member of the local chapter of the Sweet Adelines Singers. She sang in the church choir, volunteered at the library, and was admired widely for her beautifully kept home and her fabulous dinner parties. Since her back injury, Donna has become somewhat of a recluse. Her pain has severely curtailed her daily activities around the house, her participation in community events, and her interest in hobbies*

that she used to enjoy. As the pain lingers on, she has become despondent and depressed, gradually giving up on ever having a normal life again. Her pain, and all that comes with it, is having a negative impact on her relationship with her husband as well. She has become what some specialists in pain management refer to as "a pain person." Her entire life revolves around her back pain. Donna's personal physician has referred her to the Backpain Clinic at Roseville Rehabilitation Center for a 4-week inpatient program intended to provide an intensive transdisciplinary approach to address Donna's physical, emotional, and social functioning.

In Part I of this chapter, we will follow Donna through her course of therapy, including referral, assessment, treatment, documentation, evaluation, and issues related to professional ethics.

REFERRAL

The first step in the treatment process is referral, which facilitates access to health care providers. Requests for services, including music therapy, may come from various sources, including physicians, psychologists, occupational therapists, physical therapists, speech and language pathologists, teachers, parents, social workers, and, occasionally, clients themselves. In a hospital setting, referral for music therapy services is generally initiated by a physician. In a public school setting, the referral may be generated by parents, the school psychologist, or the interdisciplinary team, as part of the student's Individualized Education Program. A request for music therapy in a nursing home may come from a staff member, physician, family member, or the activity director.

Upon admission to Roseville Rehabilitation Center, Donna goes through a battery of tests and interviews conducted by different members of the treatment team. Dr. Kim, the physician, administers a medical exam to determine if there is any remaining tissue damage or abnormality contributing to her back pain. Then, the psychologist conducts an evaluation to identify any psychological factors (such as depression or personality traits) associated with Donna's condition. Jon, the physical therapist, assesses Donna's functional movements (e.g., walking, sitting, turning her torso, etc.) to identify any maladaptive patterns of movement and to determine her level of fitness and activity prior to and after her injury. Brenda, the occupational therapist, is reviewing an assessment of everyday activities at home that Donna and her husband filled in prior to her admission at the center. Florencia, the social worker, interviews Donna to learn more about her lifestyle and interests prior to the onset of back pain, as well as the impact of pain on her life. The initial assessments identify that dance and music have had an important role in Donna's life, so music therapy is identified as another important treatment modality for Donna. Matt, the music therapist, will develop treatment goals and objectives for Donna's inpatient therapy and to facilitate her transition back into her community.

ASSESSMENT

An **initial assessment** is completed prior to the start of treatment. It provides an overall view of the client's history and present condition. According to the American Music Therapy Association's Standards of Clinical Practice (*AMTA Member Sourcebook*, 2007), assessment should be included as a general procedure prior to commencing services with a client. An assessment is an analysis of a person's abilities, needs, and problems (Cohen & Gericke, 1972; Lipe, 2001; Punwar, 1988). As the example above indicates, assessments often include nonmusical categories of psychological, cognitive, physiological functioning, communication, and social skills, as well as musical skills, music preferences, and response to music (Douglass, 2006). In addition to completing their own assessments, music therapists may refer to assessments conducted by other health professionals (physician, physical therapist, occupational therapist, social worker, etc.). Assessment information can be acquired by interviewing the client and/or family members; testing, observing, and documenting how well the client does in cognitive, physical, or other tasks; viewing the client's interactions with others; or reviewing the client's records. Ideally, assessment data are gathered in multiple ways (Douglass, 2006).

Assessment tools take a variety of forms, including tests, surveys, or measures of specific abilities most relevant to the therapeutic needs of the client (Bruscia, 1987; Douglass, 2006; Fraenkel & Wallen, 2000; Gantt, 2001; Hanser, 1987; Lowey, 2001; Standley, 1996a). The format and content of assessment tools vary considerably from one facility to the next, depending upon the age and type of population served, the policies of a given facility, state or federal requirements for documentation, length of treatment, and time available for assessment (Brunk, 2001; Brunk & Coleman, 2000; Cole, 2002; Douglass, 2006; Scalenghe & Murphy, 2000). The music therapist may evaluate musical interests and abilities as well as strengths and weaknesses in nonmusic domains that are amenable to assessment by musical stimuli (e.g., auditory perception, memory, auditory discrimination, gross and fine motor coordination, and social and emotional behaviors (Hanser, 1987).

There are three primary types of assessment currently used by music therapists: (1) an **initial assessment**, completed at the beginning of the therapeutic process to identify client strengths and weaknesses, and to help formulate treatment goals; (2) **comprehensive assessments**, completed when a client is referred for music therapy services only (as opposed to music therapy being one of many services provided by a treatment team); and (3) **ongoing assessment**, which tracks functional levels and progress through the treatment process (Douglass, 2006).

Why Is Assessment Important?

There are several reasons why music therapists need to know how to administer assessments. One of the most important reasons is that the information learned from an initial assessment helps to determine the nature and scope of treatment, including whether the client is suited for music therapy, and, if so, what treatment goals and techniques are appropriate.

A second reason for assessing client needs is to provide a reference against which progress during treatment can be measured (**ongoing assessment**). In other words, we can't tell how far we have gone if we don't know where we started. If ongoing progress is not satisfactory, the therapist may modify the treatment plan. At the end of treatment, a final evaluation helps to determine improvement since the initial evaluation.

Third, the continued growth and development of the music therapy profession is dependent upon the ability to accurately assess, monitor, and evaluate treatment (Douglass, 2006; Isenberg-Grezeda, 1988). According to Cohen, Averbach, and Katz (1978), no profession, whether it is music therapy or another discipline, can legitimately attain true professional stature without a viable assessment system, not merely the completion of an assessment form. Such an assessment system must underscore the uniqueness of music therapy and contribute to the fulfillment of an individualized client treatment, training, and habilitation plan.

Areas of assessment. In order to determine a treatment plan, the team will assess the strengths and needs of the client in the following areas: (1) **medical**, which includes past medical history and current health status; (2) **physical**, which includes range of motion, gross and fine motor coordination, strength, and endurance; (3) **cognitive**, which includes comprehension, concentration, attention span, memory, and problem-solving skills; (4) **emotional**, which includes appropriateness of affect and emotional responses to various situations; (5) **social**, which includes self-expression, self-control, and quality and quantity of interpersonal interaction; (6) **communication**, which includes expressive and receptive language skills; (7) **family**, which includes assessment of family relationships and needs; (8) **vocational/ education**, which includes adequacy of work skills and preparation for the workplace; and (9) **leisure skills**, which includes awareness of recreational needs, interests, and participation in meaningful leisure activities and knowledge of community resources. In addition, there may be specific music therapy assessments that address among other things musical background, interests, and skills.

Donna's interdisciplinary treatment team has completed an initial assessment during her first few days in the back pain program. The types of assessment conducted are outlined for each functional area.

Medical. *The doctor has conducted a lengthy interview with Donna and her husband to obtain a history of the pain problem, how it started and progressed, and interventions tried to manage it. This includes a record of dosage and frequency for pain and sleep medications used since the initial injury. A medical examination including x-rays and various tests has been completed to determine any physical conditions contributing to Donna's back pain. The doctor has identified no physiological abnormality that accounts for the extent of discomfort that Donna currently suffers, thus specific medical treatments to correct physical conditions are not indicated. Donna's exam indicates that she is slightly overweight (possibly due to her sedentary lifestyle), which adds to her back problems, and she has regular bouts of insomnia.*

Physical. *As a result of back pain, Donna's normal movement patterns (such as walking, sitting, standing, bending, and reaching) have been compromised. She has a self-protective walk (very slow and with a distinct limp), which has reduced the efficiency and speed of her movements, and she has lost muscle tone, flexibility, and endurance as a result of her sedentary life. In addition to analyzing the structural aspects of Donna's movements, Donna is asked to fill out several pain scales (such as those described in Chapter 11) to indicate the type and extent of pain that she experiences during different types of movements and tasks. She has also completed a shuttle walk test, which determines the rate at which she walks. These assessments provide a baseline for measuring progress in treatment.*

Cognitive. *Donna's psychological testing indicates intelligence within the normal range. She has difficulty concentrating (short attention span, poor memory, and poor problem-solving skills) that appears to be related to pain and depression.*

Emotional. *The psychologist has conducted an interview as well as administered several standardized assessments, including the Minnesota Multiphasic Personality Inventory (MMPI), the Beck Depression Inventory*

(BDI2), and a medical outcomes survey (SF-36). These assessments have been administered to better understand her current mood state as well as personality traits, which may suggest particular approaches for helping Donna control and manage her pain. These evaluations indicate a significant level of depression, resentment, and anger, and she has developed a sense of helplessness and dependency not atypical for patients with chronic pain (Sarafino, 2006). The evaluations also indicate that Donna would be a suitable candidate for specific types of intervention that are part of the treatment options at Roseville.

Social. *The social worker's interview reveals that Donna has withdrawn from most of her social activities (ballroom dancing, Sweet Adelines Singers, attending church, etc.) since her back injury. Donna reports feeling lonely, but she makes few attempts to leave the confines of her home or to invite friends to visit. The evaluation indicates that Donna would like to re-establish involvement in dancing and singing, and the one thing that brings her some consolation is listening to her favorite music, which she sometimes uses to help her sleep.*

Communication. *Donna has no medically-based difficulties with communication, though she finds it difficult to speak with others in a straightforward manner regarding personal matters. Her communication problems are more closely aligned with psychological and emotional functioning than any physical limitation.*

Family. *Both the social worker and psychologist have met with Donna and her husband, Jim, as well as with each individually. Jim has expressed considerable frustration that Donna's back problems have essentially "taken over" nearly every aspect of their life. Donna's pain is so prevalent that their life revolves around that, and he has become responsible for all household chores in addition to all of his usual responsibilities. He wants his "real wife" back.*

Vocational/Education. *Donna's career as a homemaker has been disrupted by her pain. She has difficulty with or delegates almost every task required to run a household (e.g., cleaning, laundry, shopping, cooking, etc.) and she has essentially given up any sense of pride in how her home is maintained or decorated. An occupational therapist has met with Donna to discuss her household duties with her and to discuss a plan of action for re-establishing her capabilities in this aspect of her life. In* *conjunction with the physical therapist, they have assessed the level of pain that Donna experiences in various functional tasks.*

Leisure skills. *Interviews with the social worker and the music therapist reveal that Donna and Jim used to be quite social. They enjoyed ballroom dancing nearly every week, and they often entertained guests in their home. Now, Jim occasionally meets with friends on his own, but then he feels guilty for leaving Donna home alone. Donna used to be a regular participant in the local chapter of Sweet Adelines, but she gave that up after her back injury made it difficult for her to stand or sit comfortably for any length of time during choral rehearsals and performances. Now, about all she does is watch TV, listen to music, and try to sleep. On a more positive note, Donna seems motivated to start dancing and singing again, and the team notes that Donna derives pleasure and comfort from listening to music.*

Music therapy assessment. *Matt, the music therapist, will refer to the assessments by the other team members as well as completing his own assessment in order to develop a treatment plan. Through his music therapy assessment, he determines prior musical background and interests as well as preferred musical styles and forms of participation that will be motivating and relevant to Donna's life. Because music will be used as part of Donna's exercise and relaxation programs, Matt has given Donna a questionnaire to determine her favorite musical styles, and to identify musical selections that might be suitable for relaxation sessions as well as to promote exercise. He has also interviewed Donna about her participation in the ballroom dance club, Sweet Adelines Singers, and her church choir in order to learn more about the practice schedule and required physical skills needed to participate successfully in each.*

Assessment Tools

Although the format and content of assessment tools will vary depending upon the type of disability and the focus of the person doing the assessment (e.g., physician vs. social worker), good assessments have in common the characteristics of being reliable and valid (Douglass, 2006; Fraenkel & Wallen, 2000). Reliability refers to the consistency with which a test measures a behavior or behaviors. To be reliable, a test must measure a behavior consistently. Validity, on the other hand, has to do with how well a test really measures what it is supposed to (Fraenkel & Wallen, 2000). For example, a bathroom scale is intended to measure one's weight, and therefore is valid if it measures how many pounds you weigh (as opposed to some other things such as your waistline circumference or your current mood). If a scale is reliable, you could step on the scale several times within a few minutes (without any major changes such as attire, food intake, or energy expenditure) and you should get a very similar reading of weight.

Music therapy assessments have been published for use with a variety of populations, including persons with developmental disabilities (intellectual disabilities and autism), children in special education, persons with behavioral-emotional disorders, children who have been hospitalized, hospice patients, and older adults (Adler, 2001; Bitcon, 1976; Boxill, 1985; Braswell et al., 1983, 1986; Bruscia, 1987; Cassity & Cassity, 2006; Cohen et al., 1978; Cohen & Gericke, 1972; Coleman & Brunk, 1999; Douglass, 2006; Groen, 2007; Hintz, 2001; Layman, Hussey, & Laing, 2002; Loewy, 2000; Maure-Johnson, 2006; Nordoff & Robbins, 1977; Wasserman, Plutchik, Deutsch, & Takemoto, 1973; Wells, 1988; Wigram, 2001; York, 1994). These tools vary in format and content in order to be useable and useful with the varied developmental levels, communication abilities, therapeutic needs, and treatment foci associated with the various populations and placements (e.g., educational, hospital, rehabilitation, etc.). The drawback for some of these tests is that reliability and validity have not yet been fully established. In such cases, caution must be used when interpreting the results.

As indicated previously, Donna's team is using a variety of assessment tools to evaluate her progress, including interviews, x-rays, charting of medication usage, psychological tests, pain scales, questionnaires, measures of Donna's walking and other functional movements (Sarafino, 2006), and observational tools. The treatment team now uses these initial assessments to develop a treatment plan that will address the various aspects of Donna's condition.

TREATMENT PLAN

Once the **initial assessment** data have been gathered and analyzed, the next step is to establish a treatment plan. In some treatment approaches, each specialist develops his or her own plan more or less independently. In care plans that are **multidisciplinary** in nature, each team member will focus on and report in team meetings on particular aspects of the client's needs that are considered closest to his or her disciplinary scope of practice (e.g., the physician focusing on medications, and the physical therapist focusing on functional movements such as standing and walking).

Some treatment teams have an **interdisciplinary** approach, in which each team member takes primary responsibility for particular treatment goals, but there is collaboration in the development of treatment goals and how those goals will be attained. This particular clinic uses a **transdisciplinary** approach, and therefore several specialists may collaborate on particular goals and objectives (Hobson, 2006). For example, the physical therapist and music therapist will collaborate on the exercise program, the psychologist and music therapist will collaborate on the relaxation program, and the music therapist and social worker will collaborate on the leisure skills program. Ongoing assessment will be gathered by each caregiver over the period of rehabilitation to evaluate Donna's response to treatment.

Therapeutic Goals and Objectives

The essence of a treatment plan lies in therapeutic goals and objectives, which are based on established treatment priorities. A goal may be defined as a broad statement of the desired outcome of treatment. Thus, the treatment team, in consultation with Donna, has developed the following treatment goals for Donna's four-week back pain rehabilitation (Sarafino, 2006):

Treatment goals for Donna:

1. *Reduce Donna's experience of pain, including psychological components (such as depression and helplessness)*
2. *Decrease or eliminate the use of medication for pain*
3. *Improve physical and lifestyle functioning (including her level of activity at home, physical exercise, and participation in the community)*
4. *Enhance her social support and restore her family life to pre-injury level of interaction and satisfaction*

Each team member will be contributing to one or more of these treatment goals.

Whereas goals are broad statements of desired changes in client behavior, objectives are more specific and short-term. A goal is broken down into a series of short-term objectives. Each objective describes an immediate goal, which is measurable, and may be viewed as a small step in the process of attaining a final goal. The extent of improvement anticipated within a specified time frame will vary depending upon the status of the client at the time of initial assessment. If clients show either slower or more rapid improvement than anticipated, the objectives may be changed to reflect more likely treatment outcomes. Various members of the treatment team will focus on particular objectives and maintain ongoing assessment of progress throughout her treatment program. Listed below are examples (not intended to be comprehensive) of (1) objectives that could reflect each of Donna's goals, and (2) assessment tools that could be used to measure ongoing progress:

Goal 1. Reduce Donna's experience of pain, including psychological components (such as depression and helplessness)

Objectives:

a. Reduce levels of pain experienced during walking, sitting, household chores, and at bedtime by 40%

b. Establish a regular program of exercises for strength, flexibility, and relaxation that will support the back in everyday activities

c. Achieve lessening of depression and perceived helplessness

Ongoing assessments:

a. Visual analog scale [see Chapter 11] for self-report of pain each day before and after walking, before and after relaxation exercises, before and after occupational therapy, and each evening at bedtime

b. Complete 20–30 minutes of strength, flexibility, and relaxation exercises 5 days per week

c. Pain diary

d. Beck Depression Inventory

Goal 2. Decrease or eliminate the use of medication for pain

Objectives:

a. Donna will demonstrate the use of 4 methods of cognitive pain strategies for reducing discomfort: progressive relaxation techniques, distraction, guided imagery, and pain redefinition, and be able to give examples of situations in which each can be applied in her everyday life.

b. Donna will learn healthy patterns of movements and accommodations to reduce discomfort during functional activities in the household and leisure activities

Ongoing assessments:

a. Therapist observation of Donna's use of each strategy, paired with measures from pain scales

b. Monitor dosage and frequency of pain medication

Goal 3. Improve physical and lifestyle functioning (including level of activity at home, physical exercises, and participation in the community)

Objectives:

a. Increase length of treadmill walking by 50% each of 4 weeks

    b. *Increase velocity of walking on shuttle walk test by 30% by end of 4 weeks*

    c. *Increase strength and endurance using weight-bearing exercises*

    d. *Complete 8 of 10 of the list of functional home activities by week 4*

    e. *Develop ergonomically suitable movements for completing two ballroom dances, and complete 10 minutes of ballroom dances with spouse (foxtrot and waltz) by week 4*

Ongoing assessments:

    a. *Chart duration of time spent on treadmill and weight-bearing exercises each week*

    b. *Measure distance walked in 1-minute increments*

    c. *Evaluate strength and range of motion in physical therapy clinic*

    d. *Structured observation of functional activities*

    e. *Chart length of time in ballroom dance practice*

Goal 4. *Enhance Donna's social support and restore her family life to pre-injury level of interaction and satisfaction*

Objectives:

    a. *Donna will accompany Jim to a ballroom dance club event for at least 15 minutes by week 3*

    b. *Develop strategies for sustained standing and sitting during choir rehearsals*

    c. *Donna will increase tolerance for standing during choir practice by week 4*

Ongoing assessments:

    a. *Checklist of attendance at sessions and social activities*

    b. *Pain scales and entry in pain diary to assess physical comfort during sitting, standing, and dancing*

Now that the treatment goals, objectives, and assessment tools have been established, Matt, the music therapist, has developed specific music therapy interventions that will be used to help Donna meet her objectives. As you have learned in previous chapters, music can be an effective therapeutic tool for the psychological, social, and physical challenges that Donna faces. Music is an excellent medium for exploring and expressing emotions. Music also has a strong social component, bringing people together in a variety of circumstances. From a physical standpoint, music can be an effective stimulus for use in cognitive pain management (as a distraction or to promote relaxation), and it can promote efficient movements and persistence in exercise. Consequently, there are many ways that music therapy can contribute to Donna's treatment goals and objectives. For some of the treatment objectives, Matt will work with Donna to select and create music recordings for use in her physical therapy and relaxation routines. For other treatment objectives, Matt will work with Donna to re-establish healthy behaviors that involve music participation. The list below summarizes the interventions that Matt will contribute to the treatment goals and objectives.

Music as a stimulus to reduce discomfort. (related to Goals 1 and 2)

Matt integrates information gathered from Donna's questionnaire to develop lists of music selections that Donna can use as part of relaxation and to promote sleep. Matt will confer with Donna about the final choice of songs, will prepare an easily-used CD, and will instruct Donna on how to use music for distraction and to promote a relaxation response. He will practice these skills with her during several sessions and provide written instructions that she can refer to after discharge.

Music to promote efficient movements and persistence. (related to Goals 1, 2, and 3)

Matt will develop an initial list of tunes that Donna enjoys (as indicated through her preference questionnaire) and that are appropriate in tempo and beat for the exercise program devised by the physical therapist. Donna can use her individualized exercise music during physical therapy as well as after discharge.

Music in group therapy. (related to Goals 1, 2, and 4)

Donna will participate in group music therapy during which lyric analysis, writing music, and group discussion will be used to help Donna with expression of feelings and modulation of her mood. This group will also provide an important form of social support as she practices new adaptive behaviors.

Music and leisure skills. (related to Goals 3 and 4)

Matt and the physical therapist will meet with Donna to analyze the kinds of movements required for successful participation in ballroom dancing and choirs. Matt provides input on the requirements of prolonged sitting and standing in choral rehearsals, use of breath support, etc., and he also outlines the primary movements required for the foxtrot and waltz, two of the dances most commonly played in the ballroom dance club. The physical therapist then suggests healthy movement patterns or accommodations that will allow Donna to persist in these social activities.

Matt will develop recording of ballroom music and choir selections that Donna can use in practicing these skills. Matt will also assist Donna in maintaining her participation checklist for ongoing assessment.

DOCUMENTATION OF PROGRESS

Monitoring progress throughout a client's therapeutic process is one of the most important aspects of a therapist's job (Ottenbacher, 1986). It allows the therapist to make adjustments in the treatment plan if progress is not occurring and it ultimately measures the success or failure of a treatment program.

As we have learned, objectives are carefully written to reflect precisely what the client needs to do to meet the treatment goal. Because the behavior can be observed by the therapist, it can also be accurately recorded and matched against a baseline, or level at which the behavior was occurring before treatment was begun (initial assessment). A baseline measure is important to obtain, because it indicates the severity of the problem and serves as a reference point for later evaluation of treatment effectiveness (Hall, 1974). Oftentimes a treatment team will meet to discuss a client's progress on each goal, and the various health professionals will report on progress or lack of progress in their areas. If the client is not making reasonable progress, then the team either will discuss possible modifications in the chosen interventions, or will modify the objectives based upon the present level of functioning.

Organizations must maintain accurate and complete records on the diagnosis, treatment, and care of all clients. This information provides a chronological account of the client's treatment and is considered a legal document (Miller, 1986). A client's record also contains information used to monitor quality (effectiveness of treatment), cost effectiveness, and efficiency. In some cases, music therapy progress reports are used to justify charges to school budgets, insurance companies, Medicare, and Medicaid (Lewis, 1989; Punwar, 1988). On a more immediate scale, the record establishes an important communication link among all caregivers involved with the client.

The submission of regular and accurate written reports is a fundamental responsibility of all music therapists. Although reporting requirements and formats vary greatly among organizations, most reports contain assessment data, goals and objectives, treatment plans, progress notes, and a final report at time of discharge or discontinuation of services. The information must be written in a clear, concise manner using nonjudgmental, objective terminology. In the case of private practice, the music therapist bears primary responsibility for documentation and determining appropriate dissemination of data to authorized agencies or individuals (Reuer, 2007; Wilhelm, 2004).

EVALUATION AND TERMINATION OF TREATMENT

When a client has met his or her treatment goals, or when the treatment team decides that the client has derived the greatest possible benefit from therapy, treatment is discontinued. In some circumstances, treatment centers or insurance coverage stipulates a typical length of treatment for a specific type of illness or condition. Thus, when setting objectives, there is an expectation that a particular level of improvement should be feasible within that predetermined length of treatment.

At the time of discharge or discontinuation of treatment, the music therapist writes an evaluation of the entire music therapy process, including the initial goals that were set and progress that was made. The therapist may include recommendations for further treatment or other services.

> *Donna has completed the 4-week back pain program and has met most of her goals. In Matt's summary, he recommends continued use of music to promote relaxation and exercise in her own home. He has also, with Donna's permission, contacted the choir director of Sweet Adelines to discuss some of the accommodations that were developed to help Donna with the physical requirements of choir rehearsal. Donna and her husband have attended two events of the ballroom dance club, the first time for 15 minutes, and the second time for 30 minutes. Although she is not without pain, she can now tolerate her discomfort and is more effective at maintaining a more normal level of social activity. Donna and Jim hope that, with persistence in her pain management and physical exercises, she will be able to eventually return to full participation.*

Donna's case study is just one example of the treatment process. Treatment protocols and assessment tools vary considerably depending upon the nature of the condition and the unique needs of each client. Hopefully, this case example helps you to see the general process that takes place in clinical practice.

The next section of this chapter focuses more on the therapist and the professional and personal qualifications that contribute to professional effectiveness.

PROFESSIONAL ETHICS AND PERSONAL QUALIFICATIONS

Professional Ethics

Most professional organizations, including Roseville Rehabilitation Center, are concerned not only with the knowledge of practitioners (as demonstrated through successful completion of required educational preparation and examinations) but also with their ethical behavior. The term *ethics* refers to the standards of conduct that guide professional practice. Ethical standards are sometimes related to legal statutes (i.e., through state or federal laws), but may sometimes be self-imposed by a professional organization.

Organizations such as the American Psychological Association, the National Association of Social Workers, the American Psychiatric Association, and the American Music Therapy Association, to name just a few, have formulated codes of ethics that outline appropriate behavior of the therapist in relation to the client and society in general (Corey, 2001; Corey, Corey, & Callanan, 1993). While the specific policies outlined within each code of ethics differ from organization to organization, there are several key issues that are considered of particular importance by most health care professions, including music therapy, and that will be covered in this chapter. These include confidentiality, appropriate therapist-client relationships, and professional competence.

Confidentiality. Confidentiality means that the therapist will not share or discuss matters (outside the group of professionals directly providing care) that arise in therapy. Confidentiality is specified in most codes of ethics and is also addressed in many state laws and institutional policies (Corey et al., 1993). Principles of confidentiality seek to protect the client's right to privacy within the boundaries of the law. They are applicable to all treatment settings, including public organizations, private organizations, and private practice. Confidentiality applies to students who are working with clients in fieldwork or internships.

Most health professions have addressed the issue of confidentiality in their professional standards of ethics. The Code of Ethics adopted by the American Music Therapy Association includes a section on confidentiality (AMTA, 2007). An important component is the expectation that the therapist keeps all client information confidential, whether that information is contained in a written record, a pictorial account, an audio recording, or an informal conversation. However, the release of confidential information to other health professionals involved with the client is acceptable, as is its release in other limited circumstances. For example, the words or actions of a client may be revealed: (1) when an individual poses imminent danger to himself or to others (i.e., if a client has informed a therapist that he intends to kill his former girlfriend, the therapist is legally obligated to inform the threatened individual and the proper authorities so protective action can be taken); (2) in the case of abuse of minors; (3) in cases in which the therapist determines that a client requires hospitalization; (4) when the information has become an issue in a court action; and (5) when the individual requests in writing that his or her records be released to the individual or to a third party (such as to another doctor or to a relative assisting with care) (Corey, 2001).

Confidentiality is a very important part of music therapy practice. Students need to understand and practice the principles of confidentiality prior to their first visit to a clinical site. Student and professional therapists also need to take precautions when sharing information about clients with other team members to ensure that written or verbal communication cannot be seen or heard by others who do not have reason for access to the information. For example, if discussing a client with another team member while in an open hallway or public place (e.g., a restaurant), comments can easily be overheard.

Avoiding dual relationships. Another important ethical guideline is to **avoid dual relationships** with clients. This means that the therapist avoids interacting with clients in situations outside of therapy that interfere with professional judgment or objectivity (i.e., a romantic relationship or personal friendship) (Corey, 2001). A dual (or multiple) relationship occurs when a therapist engages in two or more roles (such as friend, employer, relative, lover, borrowing money, business venture) simultaneously or sequentially with a client. Examples might include a therapist dating a client, or agreeing to serve as a therapist for one of his or her own office employees. Dual relationships are complex and multidimensional. For example, imagine if a therapist begins to date a client. Many couples eventually have spats or break up along the road of romance. These sorts of personal conflicts add an undesirable complexity to an already delicate relationship of therapist and client. Because there is often a power differential between a therapist and client (in other words, the therapist generally has greater authority in the therapy situation), there is also the risk of exploitation to the client in a dual relationship. Suggestions for minimizing the risk of dual relationships can be found in other more advanced resources on clinical practice (e.g., Corey, 2001, p. 56).

Professional competence. Professional competence, including working within one's **scope of practice**, is a complex issue, but several concerns are commonly found within the ethical codes of health care professions. One is an adequate preparation for the specific profession one intends to practice. In order to practice their profession, music therapists must have completed a music therapy program accredited by AMTA, have successfully completed an internship, and use methods that conform to standards of practice endorsed by their professional organization. The therapist should also be aware of personal and professional limitations that might interfere with appropriate provision of care. This is related to the term *scope of practice,* which refers to the range of skills or procedures for which a person within a given profession has been properly trained. For example, the music therapist is not qualified to administer or prescribe medication, whereas a physician is. If the music therapist suspects that the client's problem requires medication, that client should be referred to a physician for evaluation.

Most helping professions have established guidelines or policy statements regarding the scope of practice within their profession. For example, the American Speech-Language and Hearing Association defines those assessments and therapeutic interventions that speech-language pathologists are qualified to do following the required educational and clinical preparation and certification (Hobson, 2006). If a music therapist were collaborating with a speech-language pathologist in providing Melodic Intonation Therapy for a person with aphasia (see Chapter 10), then the music therapist should have a clear sense of the scope of practice for music therapy as well as that of their team member in order to select those treatment objectives most appropriately addressed through music therapy treatment.

The overriding concern in the therapist-client relationship should be the welfare of the client. This means that the client has the right to the most effective treatment in an environment that fosters safety, respect, and self-determination. In addition to providing good care, therapy should be terminated or referrals made when the client no longer benefits from therapy.

These are only a few of the many complex concerns that are addressed in ethical standards for music therapists and other health care professionals. Other ethical considerations include providing **informed consent** (i.e., providing clients with adequate information about their rights and responsibilities related to clinical or research practices), the use of **appropriate diagnostic and testing procedures**, and consideration of the **client's cultural context in therapeutic decisions and approaches** (cultural competency is discussed in the following section in this chapter) (Corey, 2001).   Not all ethical considerations are subject to formal legal action, but the individual who breeches ethical conduct may be subject to censure or sanctions by the professional organization. Over and above possible enforcement, each professional has an obligation to conform to these guidelines in order to protect the rights and dignity of each client as well as to uphold the standards of the profession.

Cultural Competence

Culture is difficult to define. According to one broad definition, culture encompasses many different identities, including but not limited to race, ethnicity, (dis)ability, sexual orientation, gender, socioeconomic status, religion, etc. Multicultural has been defined by some as the interactions and intermingling of people from different culture (Stowe, 2004). America is now a pluralistic society that includes persons from many diverse backgrounds (Darrow, 1998; Froman, 2006); consequently, therapists are likely to serve clients from many different cultural backgrounds.

In recent years, there has been increasing awareness of the importance of sensitivity to cultural differences by the helping professions. Though some individuals may be unaware that they have cultural biases (Stowe, 2004), therapists bring to their practice and everyday encounters their own cultural values and beliefs that impact therapeutic goals and approaches. Those values may differ in important ways from those of some of their clients (Corey, 2001; Shapiro, 2005; Stowe, 2004; Valentino, 2006). For example, a therapist working in a mental health facility may establish for a client the goal of making good eye contact when conversing as a part of good communication; direct eye contact is sometimes a problem for some individuals who suffer from depression or poor self-esteem. However, in some cultures, making direct eye contact (especially with elders) would be considered disrespectful. Consequently, a therapist who does not take into account the client's cultural values can inadvertently contribute to poor communication within the client's primary community and may also improperly judge this client as noncompliant or resistant to change.

The importance of cultural competence to the therapeutic process is reinforced by the fact that the American Counseling Association has implemented multicultural competencies. These competencies, developed by Sue, Arredondo, and McDavis (1992), fall into three broad competencies: counselor awareness of his or her own cultural values and biases, counselor awareness of the client's worldview, and culturally appropriate intervention strategies (Stowe, 2004).

In recent years, the issues of multiculturalism and cultural competence have gained greater recognition among music therapists as well. Studies by Toppozada (1995), Darrow and Malloy (1998), Chase (2003), Stowe (2004), and Froman (2006) all indicate the importance of sensitivity to multicultural issues and cultural competence in clinical practice. These studies have also pointed up shortcomings within the profession with regard to collegiate courses and continuing education. However, according to these studies, music therapists do seek training outside of collegiate requirements, such as in workshops or extra training sessions. Furthermore, the majority of music therapists surveyed uses multicultural music during music therapy sessions and sees its use as important.

The population in the United States is pluralistic, making it unrealistic for a music therapist to be an expert about all cultures, which may lead to occasional misunderstandings and problems (Froman, 2006). However, there are several common recommendations with regard to developing cultural competence. First, music therapists should be aware of their own cultural biases and perspectives, in addition to seeking new cultural experiences. One should be aware that differences can occur on many, sometimes subtle, dimensions (Stowe, 2004) and seek help in understanding cultural perspectives outside of one's own experiences (Chase, 2003). Music is an important part of all known cultures and is used to express cultural values and promote cultural affiliation (Froman, 2006; Gfeller, 2002); thus, it is important to be musically flexible and become familiar with music that is culturally significant to one's clients (Chase, 2003; Froman, 2006). Multicultural perspectives and sensitivity regarding different cultures, values, and perspectives should be integrated into music therapy practice (Froman, 2006).

Personal Qualifications

A student can achieve excellent grades on papers and exams in courses required for a therapy degree, yet lack the personal characteristics that are most essential to a helping professional. There are a number of personal characteristics that are associated with being an effective therapist: (1) a clear sense of one's own identity and healthy (though not inflated) self-esteem; (2) a willingness to admit mistakes; (3) a willingness to take responsibility for one's own actions; (4), a lifelong pattern of self reflection, learning, and change; (5) sincerity and honesty; (6) a sense of humor; (7) empathy for and an interest in others, paired with the ability to maintain healthy boundaries; and (8) the capacity to make realistic assessments (Corey, 2001; Fowler, 2006). Research indicates that those music therapists who have had a long-term and positive experience within the profession are those more likely to approach life challenges with a greater sense of personal control (internal locus of control), to perceive challenges as opportunities (as opposed to negative events), and to maintain their overall well-being through social connections and healthy lifestyle choices (Fowler, 2006).

Sometimes students consider majoring or taking classes in the helping professions (psychology, social work, music therapy, etc.) because they themselves are struggling with significant medical, emotional, or social challenges that either they have not faced directly, or which remain problematic, despite efforts to resolve the problem through treatment or other strategies. For example, there are people who have an unhealthy need to be in control and to dominate others in order to compensate for their own poor self-esteem. Persons who have an unhealthy need to control, and who choose to help persons that are medically or emotionally vulnerable primarily because of their own need to dominate others, would be considered self-serving and would be using an unethical way to meet their own needs. If you have read the book or seen the movie *One Flew Over the Cuckoo's Nest*, the character of "Big Nurse" presents an excellent example of this sort of ethical problem.

Therapists are not super human beings devoid of problems. Good therapists can, in fact, draw on their own personal challenges in order to understand and be empathic about the issues their clients face. However, when those same challenges overwhelm their capacity to function effectively and objectively (which can be hard for even healthy individuals to achieve in times of duress), professional competence can be compromised. For example, therapists who may be currently engaged in a difficult personal situation could unintentionally find themselves over relating to problems in relationships of their clients. Thus, while therapists will face their own everyday personal challenges, it is important that they have adequate stability in emotional and physical health to fulfill their professional obligations in a competent and ethical manner, or to seek professional help if necessary in order to regain healthy functioning.

> Maureen is a music therapist at a local mental health clinic. She is an excellent therapist, but lately she has found herself feeling easily irritated and critical of some clients. She realizes that her feelings toward her estranged husband, with whom divorce proceedings are pending, are spilling over into her interactions with some colleagues and clients who resemble her spouse—even in the most innocuous ways (similar hair color or build). Fortunately, Maureen is aware of her own feelings, and she is honest in her self-appraisal. She realizes that her personal concerns are interfering with her professional competence. Therefore, she meets with Kirsten, her supervisor, and has a confidential conversation regarding her situation. Together, they work out a plan for Maureen to take a temporary leave of absence while she resolves her personal issues.

As this example illustrates, it is not only important for therapists to have stable emotional and physical health, but it is also important that they take time for self-reflection, are open to feedback, and strive to keeping growing as a person and professional.

SUMMARY OF PART I

In Part I of this chapter, we have learned about the music therapy process, including referral, assessment, treatment, and documentation. Before treatment begins, an assessment is completed, generally by an interdisciplinary team made up of professionals from different specialties. This information helps to determine the proper approach to treatment.

Treatment begins with the development of goals and objectives. Goals are broad statements of intent, whereas objectives precisely describe what the client will accomplish. During the course of treatment, client progress is monitored by gathering objective and subjective data. This information helps to determine accountability, treatment effectiveness, and efficiency of the therapy. It allows the therapist to make changes in a program that is not working.

Progress is recorded in the client's record, generally after each session. There are a variety of formats for writing progress notes. Written reports, as well as other information pertaining to the client's treatment, are governed by principles of confidentiality.

The final step in the therapy process is the evaluation and termination of treatment. At that point, the therapist prepares a discharge summary of the treatment process and may make recommendations for follow-up.

Therapists should follow guidelines for ethical practice, including confidentiality, avoidance of dual relationships, and practicing within one's own scope of practice. Cultural competence and suitable personal characteristics are also important to professional success.

STUDY QUESTIONS FOR PART I

1. What is an assessment?
2. Why does an assessment need to be completed before treatment?
3. Name four types of treatment teams.
4. Define *reliability* and *validity*.
5. Discuss the personal qualifications that are associated with becoming a successful therapist.
6. Describe the elements of a treatment plan.
7. Define *goals* and *objectives* and discuss how they relate to the treatment plan.
8. What is the purpose of data collection?
9. Discuss the importance of documenting client progress.
10. Define *informed consent* and discuss why this is an important safeguard for the clients you work with.
11. When should a therapist terminate treatment?
12. When is it appropriate for a therapist to share confidential client information with persons not involved with the patient's treatment?

13. Define *scope of practice.*
14. Why is a code of ethics important to the profession of music therapy?

PART II: MUSIC THERAPY APPROACHES[1]

Emma is home after completing her freshman year in college. She's can't wait to see old friends at the beach, but she's not so excited about her bathing suit "situation."

Emma is a victim of the "Freshman 15"—15 pounds of extra weight that she gained during her freshman year as a result of snacking on junk food and endless hours of sitting at the computer. "Whale alert!" Emma moans, as she checks out her backside in the full-length mirror. She's got to get those pounds off, and in a hurry.

Emma goes to the Internet to find some helpful hints on taking off weight and is immediately overwhelmed: grapefruit diets, cabbage soup diets, low carbohydrate diets, no carbohydrate diets, low-fat diets, liquid diets, diet pills, fat-burning belts. Some diets claim that she'll take off 10 pounds in just 12 days, while other diets encourage slow but steady weight loss of around 2 pounds a week. What's right? Why is this so complicated? After all, doesn't everyone know that losing weight comes down to calories in, calories out?

Emma decides to call up her favorite Aunt Marcia, who is a nutritionist, to see if she can get the low-down on some of these diet claims. Aunt Marcia explains to Emma that a lot of people get caught in the trap of random quick-fix diets. Sure, people can lose weight quickly, but mostly from temporary loss of water weight; those pounds usually come right back. Fad diets tend to contribute to yo-yo dieting, actual weight gain in the long term, and even serious health problems. Marcia explains that the most successful programs are actually lifestyle changes based upon good scientific evidence regarding how the body metabolizes food paired with diet methods or approaches that address psychological (such as eating because of stress or boredom) and social factors (eating as a part of social events, holidays, etc.). These reliable approaches result in gradual but sustainable and healthy weight loss. Therefore, Marcia encourages

---

[1]We wish to acknowledge assistance from Michele Forinash and Cathy McKinney in reviewing and refining information regarding Nordoff-Robbins Music Therapy, The Bonny Method of Guided Imagery and Music, and the Psychodynamic Approach to Music Therapy.

Emma to try an approach that includes scientifically-based principles of nutrition and exercise, paired with methods or strategies that will help her to avoid junk food snacking and binge eating at social events. Emma wishes there were a quick fix, yet she knows that her Aunt Marcia is really smart, and Marcia looks amazing—even though she is over 50 years old! So maybe Marcia knows what she's talking about.

Most people in America are inundated with information about weight loss—it's a national pastime. Savvy consumers are aware that the most reliable and healthy weight loss approaches are based upon sound scientific principles of metabolic theories. They are also aware of various methods, such as keeping a food and exercise diary or finding social support, which can help people to succeed in weight management. Experts in the field will tell you there are a variety of sensible approaches and many methods that can work. Furthermore, one approach is not effective for *all* people.

This is also true when it comes to music therapy. Because music therapy is less widely known and understood (compared with diet plans), it is even easier for misconceptions to take hold—quick-fix uses of music that can "cure" everything from autism to cancer. The fact is that music therapy, like any other legitimate therapeutic specialty, has developed as a result of scientific and clinical studies and observations that have been tested and refined over many decades. As you learned in Chapter 2, humans have known for centuries that music could have a healing effect. It is during more recent history that we've understood more clearly the "how" and "why" of music's therapeutic benefit.

Part II of this chapter will introduce various approaches commonly used in the field of music therapy. Why have different approaches to music therapy been included in this orientation textbook? In reality, an in-depth understanding and appreciation of the various approaches typically develops as a result of (1) ample clinical experience, especially with different types of clients; (2) exposure to the clinical practice of other professionals through conference presentations and observation; (3) the study of more advanced books and articles regarding this topic; and (4) self-reflection regarding one's own attitudes and beliefs.

However, it is worthwhile at an early stage of exploration (1) to know that there are different approaches to music therapy, (2) to understand that different approaches may be more or less effective in different circumstances, and (3) to develop a basic familiarity with terms and categories that will be encountered in more advanced music therapy courses. This portion of the chapter will also explain how and why various approaches developed and will present some basic features that characterize some prominent approaches in contemporary music therapy. This portion of the book is not intended to provide in-depth or comprehensive coverage of this interesting topic, but rather to provide a foundation for more advanced studies.

Before introducing some common approaches in music therapy, let's consider some of the terms that are related to the topic of therapy approaches.

DEFINITIONS

Within the field of music therapy, there are terms that are commonly used to describe different aspects of music therapy principles and practice: approach, method, philosophy, theory, and model. These terms are sometimes used differently by different therapists, teachers, and scholars, but the definitions found in the fourth edition of *Webster's New World College Dictionary* (2005) provide a useful point of departure:

Approach—"A means of attaining a goal or purpose."

In music therapy, this term is often used to describe a way of teaching a musical skill (such as playing guitar or Orff instruments) or facilitating a session. **Please note that the term *approach* will sometimes be used in this chapter in a more general sense when discussing (in a collective fashion) approaches, methods, philosophies, theories, and models, for all of these terms could be considered a means or way of attaining a goal.**

Method—(a) "A way of doing anything; mode, procedure, process, esp. a regular, orderly, definite procedure or way of teaching, investigating, etc.; (b) Regularity and orderliness in action, thought, or expression; system in doing things or handling ideas; (c) Regular orderly arrangement."

In music therapy, this term is often used to describe organized and clearly prescribed ways of teaching a particular skill, or a system for conducting therapy.

Philosophy—"Theory or logical analysis of the principles underlying conduct, thought, knowledge, and the nature of the universe; the general principle or laws of a field of knowledge, activity, etc."

In music therapy, this term is sometimes used when linking music therapy with basic attitudes or beliefs about the nature of the human condition, or scientific laws of how the mind or human body works.

Theory—"A systematic statement of principles involved; a formulation of apparent relationships or underlying principles of certain observed phenomena which have been verified to some degree."

Within music therapy practice, this term is often used in conjunction with psychological or scientific explanations of behaviors, emotions, thoughts, or physical (biological) functioning that have been scrutinized through scientific methods of verification.

Model—"A generalized hypothetical description . . . used in analyzing or explaining something."

In music therapy, a model may be developed to illustrate the relationship of musical sounds and music engagement with behaviors, cognition, emotions, and physical functioning. Formal structural models are "built" when the various components within the model are subject to formal scientific testing and verification.

Before you read further, it is helpful to realize that different people may use particular terms in somewhat different ways. For example, one music therapist might refer to Orff-Schulwerk (which is discussed later) as an approach, while another might consider it more of a method. In any field, there is likely to be some healthy difference of opinion regarding terminology. Some of these differences will become easier to understand as you gain more experience in the field.

Just as people have strong personal opinions on cuisine, fashion, their favorite sports teams, politics, and religion, you will find that music therapists sometimes hold very strong opinions regarding music therapy approaches. At this point in your studies, it is premature to make hard and fast assumptions regarding the relative merits of different approaches, methods, or models. A genuine appreciation of various approaches will evolve with greater educational and clinical experience. Discussion and an open mind are important to the future development of any individual and the professional at large; therefore, we recommend that you use this chapter primarily as a starting point for familiarizing yourself with different music therapy methods, models, and approaches. These approaches will take on greater meaning as you gain depth of experience. The next section will help you to understand why different approaches to music therapy exist.

HISTORICAL TRENDS THAT HAVE INFLUENCED MUSIC THERAPY APPROACHES

As noted in Chapter 2, the field of music therapy was initially developed by persons from different disciplinary fields, including medicine, psychiatry, music, and education. Until 1900, music therapy practice in the United States was limited to a few isolated occurrences. The most significant came from medical doctors and psychiatrists who wrote about and occasionally practiced music therapy. During this time, there was no formal training available in music therapy, so much of what was written was based on intuition and personal philosophy.

This intuitive approach to therapy continued into the first decades of the 20th century, with musicians and educators joining those in the medical profession advocating for music therapy. The hallmark of early 20th-century practice was the development of interesting personal philosophies concerning the use of music in therapy, practicing what they advocated (as opposed to just writing about it), and, in some cases, establishing music therapy organizations that made use of volunteer musicians to visit the sick in hospitals and institutions.

About the time of World War II, an era of scientific interest was developing, beginning with the efforts to treat returning soldiers suffering from psychological and physical injuries. Spearheaded by some of the individuals that you met in Chapter 2, such as Harriet Ayer Seymour, Ira Altshuler, and E. Thayer Gaston, an emphasis on research began to develop that helped to refine music therapy practice. With this important step, the field of music therapy began to mature and develop into the profession of today.

One of the most remarkable trends taking place a few years after the founding of the National Association for Music Therapy in 1950 was the deinstitutionalization movement. This new approach to the care and treatment of adults and children with disabilities changed the scope of practice in music therapy. Instead of working almost exclusively in large institutions, mainly with individuals with behavioral and emotional disorders, music therapists found numerous employment opportunities in a variety of new community-based clinical settings. Some of these new facilities included schools, nursing homes, group homes, and hospice. This refreshing person-centered philosophy led to the development of many of the approaches to music therapy that you will become familiar with in following pages.

RECENT TRENDS THAT HAVE INFLUENCED THE DEVELOPMENT OF MUSIC THERAPY APPROACHES

As the previous paragraphs show, the current status of music therapy has been influenced by the attitudes of persons from the fields of music, psychiatry, and medicine. Music therapy practice continues to be influenced by a number of factors, including (1) advances in scientific knowledge regarding health and illness, (2) societal changes, and (3) clinical and research initiatives by leaders in the music therapy field.

Advances in Scientific Knowledge Regarding Health and Illness

In recent decades, medical science has evolved from a relatively singular focus on biological explanations of health and illness, to a realization that biology interacts with psychological and social factors. This is referred to as a biopsychosocial model of health and illness (Sarafino, 2006) (see Chapter 11). In a biopsychosocial model of health care, psychological and social factors are considered important aspects of a coordinated treatment plan. As noted in Chapter 3, music is associated with emotional expression and social integration. Therefore, music is a powerful tool for addressing psychological and social factors. An integrated model of health care has prompted new approaches as well as applications of music therapy.

Societal Changes

As previous chapters have reported, the manner in which health care is provided has changed dramatically since the initial founding of a professional music therapy association. Health care has evolved from long-term to short-term care, with outpatient and rehabilitation replacing long-term hospitalization and institutionalization (see Chapter 2). Educational practices have moved from institutionalization to a model of inclusion (see Chapter 14). While these changes reflect, in part, advances in medical care and societal attitudes, they also reflect economic pressures to provide affordable treatment and education. Practical considerations of reimbursement (insurance) and payment for special education have driven music therapy practice toward approaches that are consistent with short-term care or education that can be provided within the individual's home community.

Multiculturalism is another important societal change (Chase, 2003; Darrow & Malloy, 1998; Froman, 2006; Stowe, 2004; Sue, Arredondo, & McDavis, 1992; Toppozada, 1995). The U.S. is a pluralistic society, and music therapists serve persons from diverse backgrounds that have different attitudes and values regarding health and treatment. Multiculturalism is referred to by some as the "fourth force" in counseling (the first three being Freudian, behaviorism, and humanism) (Stowe, 2004). The importance of cultural competency and flexibility in providing treatment that is appropriate for persons from diverse cultures has influenced music therapy practice with regard to definitions of health and well-being, suitability of goals and objectives, the choice of music for use in therapy, and the use and facilitation of therapeutic approaches and methods.

Research and Clinical Initiatives in the Music Therapy Field

The field of music therapy will continue to change and develop as clinicians and researchers in the field and related fields chart new territory with regard to therapeutic approaches. These initiatives are disseminated in university courses, at professional conferences and workshops, and through books and articles. Later in this chapter, you will read about several approaches to music therapy that have been developed and that continue to be evaluated through ongoing clinical and research efforts.

FACTORS THAT INFLUENCE CLINICAL CHOICES

As noted earlier, experts will tell you there are a variety of sensible treatment or educational approaches and many methods that can work; one approach is not effective for all people. How do music therapists decide from many different approaches, methods, or models in their everyday work place and with individual clients?

There are a number of factors that influence the choice of approaches used: (1) the clientele served, (2) the policies or attitudes at the work place, (3) the clinical and educational background of the therapist, and (4) the personal strengths and beliefs of the individual therapist.

Differences in Clientele Served

One of the primary reasons that different approaches are needed is because music therapists serve clients who vary in (1) primary presenting problems, (2) age, (3) current developmental/functional level, (4) background and culture, and (5) personal attitudes (including motivation) and values. Compare, for example, the health care needs of a woman delivering a baby with those of a person who has just broken his leg. Imagine how odd it would seem if the woman's obstetrician set the expectant mother's ankle in a cast, rather than focusing on the delivery of a baby. In other words, the therapeutic approaches chosen need to match the primary needs of each client. With regard to music therapy approaches, low-stimulation rocking and lullabies might be a suitable approach for a premature baby in a NICU (neonatal intensive care unit), while a person recovering from a stroke might be a candidate for gait training with Rhythmic Auditory Stimulation. In short, the therapist needs to select music therapy approaches that are consistent with best practice for the presenting health or educational needs given the primary presenting condition.

The approach to therapy will be influenced not only by the particular condition or illness, but also by the prognosis or severity of that condition. For example, a person with a mild clinical depression will require very different treatment from that of a person with a chronic and severe depression. Or a person in remission from successful cancer treatment will have very different needs from a person whose cancer has not responded well to treatment and who likely faces imminent death.

The onset of an illness or condition can also influence the choice of music therapy approach. For example, as noted in Chapter 13, prelingual deafness results in very different therapeutic needs from those of persons who lost their hearing later in life. In the case of prelingual deafness, direct instruction of spoken language may be required, while spoken language will already be well established in persons who lost their hearing in later adulthood.

Chronological age. The chronological age of the client will also influence the choice of music therapy approaches. Singing nursery rhythms such as "The Wheels on the Bus" can be an excellent and age-appropriate method for developing vocabulary and language in preschoolers; these same wonderful songs would be anything but appropriate if working with a group of adolescents. Although some individuals with intellectual disabilities may function at a developmental age equivalent to preschoolers by young adulthood, the use of nursery songs would nevertheless be inappropriate. A music therapist working with young adults with intellectual deficits would search for materials and methods that are age appropriate while still within the developmental capabilities of his or her clients. Developmental age can influence functional capabilities in cognition, communication, social skills, and motor skills; thus, the approaches selected should account for the current functional level in these domain areas, no matter what the chronological age of the client. For example, some music therapy approaches are particularly effective for working with persons who have limited or no verbal communication. Other approaches require that the client have advanced cognitive skills and capacity for insight and verbalization.

Background and culture. The background and culture of individual clients should also influence music therapy materials and approaches (Chase, 2003; Darrow & Malloy, 1998; Froman, 2006; Stowe, 2004; Toppazada, 1995). Because music is such a powerful marker of culture, and because it can elicit powerful emotions, one type of music is not acceptable for all clients. For example, there are individuals who have lost family members or ancestors to the Nazi Holocaust. For persons with this particular life experience, there are musical selections (such as Wagner's "Ride of the Valkyries," which was once played in concentration camps) that could result in tremendous emotional turmoil (Froman, 2006). Or there are specific musical selections that may be associated with traumatic events for a person who suffers from post-traumatic stress disorder. On a more positive note, there are musical selections that represent cherished life events (weddings, graduations, etc.) or cultural heritage (e.g., songs associated with one's culture or holidays).

In addition to the music chosen, the cultural values of an individual can influence what therapeutic approaches are considered acceptable. For example, in some cultures, therapy approaches that emphasize **self-actualization** (according to Maslow, the basic human need of humans to strive to be the best they can be) to a greater extent than the good of the family and community would be inappropriate (Corey, 2001). Part of cultural competence as a therapist is learning the values held dear by various cultures, while also addressing the unique perspectives of each individual within the larger community (Gfeller, 2007).

This brings up the importance of individual differences among clients who may share similar conditions, age, and background. For example, two people may have grown up in similar families and have similar cultural backgrounds, yet one may really enjoy rap music, while the other may not. The fact remains that people who share many characteristics often differ with regard to personal musical preferences, motivation, and attitude toward treatment. In addition, one individual may differ in his or her capacity for insight or readiness for change at different points in the therapeutic process. Consequently, a music therapist may select different approaches because they are a better "fit" for particular individuals being served.

In addition, different therapy approaches are more or less suitable for the same client at different points in life, or at different stages in therapy. Think back to the story of Emma and the "Freshman 15." Many people have tried diets, and most know what it takes to lose weight. But many people fail to lose or maintain weight loss on the first try. They may not be "ready" to make the fundamental changes in lifestyle that are required for sustained weight management. Similarly, the music therapist is a partner with his or her client in therapeutic change. Some clients are ready for difficult challenges and sustained effort, while others are less so. The client's present situation, condition, and attitude should influence the choice of therapeutic approaches chosen for therapy.

Policies or Attitudes at the Work Place

The majority of music therapists work as part of a treatment team within a hospital, clinic, rehabilitation center, or educational setting. Most health care and educational facilities have established policies and treatment models that provide a foundation for setting priorities, establishing which clientele they will serve, and guiding the selection of treatment approaches. For example, many educational programs that serve children with autism now use an educational approach called ABA—Applied Behavior Analysis (see Chapter 5). When a music therapist is hired to fill a position in a school that adheres to this approach, the music therapist will generally be expected to choose music therapy approaches that are consistent with ABA.

Some facilities have a more eclectic approach to therapy; nevertheless, there are often approaches that are more consistent with typical care within the facility. For example, in short-term psychiatric care, approaches documented as providing quick and reliable change are more likely to be adopted than approaches that require possibly years of commitment to therapy.

Many times, the policies and approaches used within an agency are related to the primary types of clients served. For example, a hospice program will tend to emphasize therapeutic approaches that focus on pain management and overall quality of life (Groen, 2007), whereas a physical rehabilitation program may emphasize approaches known to yield clear and measurable physical improvement.

The Clinical and Educational Background of the Therapist

All of us are a product of our life experiences. For example, many people who grew up during the Great Depression of the 1930s are very parsimonious in their spending habits. The children of those Depression children may have adopted similar attitudes about spending, or they may have reacted against their parents' penny pinching and adopted lavish shopping habits. We are influenced by our families, our teachers, our friends, and social circumstances. Thus, many music therapists have developed opinions about particular therapeutic approaches that reflect (or reject) the attitudes of their instructors, internship supervisors, and colleagues. However, as clinicians obtain experience with different clientele, those initial influences may be modified or changed. For example, a person initially trained in a strict medical model of treatment may find his or her attitudes toward treatment change in response to working in end-of-life care, which tends to emphasize quality of life over specific recovery objectives.

The Personal Strengths, Limitations, and Beliefs of the Individual Therapist

Each therapist is, in the final analysis, an individual with personal strengths, limitations, and beliefs. As we mature and are influenced by experiences and influential persons in our life, we continue to grow and develop. Sometimes we find firmly held beliefs shaken by life-altering experiences, such as the 9/11 tragedy, a hurricane, or the loss of a loved one. Or we may be inspired by others in the field, who show us options we previously had not considered.

According to Baruth and Huber (1985), when selecting a therapeutic position or theory, it is important to consider how closely it matches your own personal philosophy of helping, which is influenced by your life experiences, your personality, your likes and dislikes, and your informal assumptions about what makes people tick. Many music therapists find that they are drawn to particular therapeutic approaches, and that will often influence their choice of clientele and facility that they approach for internship and in the job application process. Good therapists, however, will continue to evolve as human beings, and they will work to stay abreast of current knowledge and trends. Therefore, therapists may find that their own therapeutic position will evolve to some extent over the course of their professional career.

PROMINENT APPROACHES TO MUSIC THERAPY

The following section presents some of the prominent methods, approaches, and models frequently used today in music therapy practice. As indicated earlier, the field of music therapy has been influenced by professionals with expertise in music education and pedagogy, psychology, and medicine. Consequently, it is not surprising that the various approaches used in contemporary music therapy reflect or are consistent with approaches from each of those fields. Some approaches described below are essentially pedagogical methods used by music educators, which have been adapted for therapy. Some approaches might be considered unique to music therapy—approaches developed by music therapists that emphasize music as therapy (i.e., the process of music making and musical interaction as inherently therapeutic). Some music therapy approaches reflect or have been based upon philosophical or theoretical models from the fields of psychology or medicine.

Approaches Developed within Music Education and Pedagogy

Because music therapists often engage their clients in making or moving to music, it is important to have effective approaches that can facilitate successful participation by children and adults who have a wide range of functional levels in cognitive, motor, communicative, and social domains. Many music therapists in the early years of the field's professional development were initially educated within departments of music education and therefore drew upon that body of knowledge when developing music therapy approaches. Among those educational approaches that have been most readily adapted for music therapy (especially with children) have been those instructional methods made famous by Carl Orff, Emile-Henri Jaques-Dalcroze, and Zoltan Kodály. As you will learn, these music education approaches have been used successfully in music therapy clinical settings with a variety of children and adults with disabilities.

Orff-Schulwerk. Carl Orff (1895–1982) was born in Munich, Germany, into a family that valued training in music at an early age. Both a serious composer (probably best known for his composition *Carmina Burana*) and music educator, he championed his approach to music education by using the student's innate talent, energy, and curiosity to teach basic musical concepts through the elements of speech, rhythm, movement, dance, and song (Goodkin, 2002).

Orff-Schulwerk (or schoolwork) is a multisensory approach to music education that Orff called "**elemental music**." Developed by Orff during the 1920s in association with Gunild Keetman, the Orff method uses a holistic approach to learning music that emphasizes hearing music before learning to read and write musical notation. The use of the voice is stressed along with movement and performance on percussion and melody instruments, such as the recorder, xylophone, glockenspiel, and metallaphone (Colwell, Achey, Gillmeister, & Woolrich, 2004).

As his approach to teaching music to children became more and more popular, Orff began to publish his concepts in the early 1950s with a five-volume set titled *Music for Children*. Once *Music for Children* was translated into English, the movement to use Orff's methodology spread rapidly to the United States and Canada. Today, the American and Canadian Orff-Schulwerk Associations train music educators to use these specialized techniques in music education classes throughout North America (Colwell et al., 2004).

Orff readily acknowledged that his music education principles could be used in therapy and, as early as the 1960s, therapists were incorporating his techniques with special populations. During that time period, Wilhelm Keller successfully adapted Orff music education techniques for use with children who had a wide range of disabilities, including intellectual disability, emotional disturbances, and physical challenges (Voigt, 1999).

According to Colwell et al. (2004), in 1969, Judith Bevans incorporated modified Orff techniques with special populations. Bevans successfully used aspects of "elemental music" to assist children with visual impairments. In 1976, Carol Bitcon, a music therapist trained in Orff and practicing in the United States, authored *Alike and Different: The Clinical and Educational Uses of Orff-Schulwerk*, a text which included an extensive discussion about using elements of Orff with music therapy practice for a variety of clinical populations. The book, still available, is now in its second printing (Bitcon, 2000).

Today, we can apply many applications of the Orff methods to meet functional goals of our clients. For example, therapists can use chants and call-and-response songs to improve speech and language; body percussion is an excellent activity for developing motor skills, while ensemble playing can enhance socialization and communication. These are but a few examples of the way in which Orff-Schulwerk techniques are applicable to music therapy. Further information on the Orff method in general and how it can be used in therapy may be found in the following publications: *The Orff Music Therapy: Active Furthering of the Development of the Child* (Orff, 1974); *Key Concepts in the Orff Music Therapy* (Orff, 1989); *Alike and Different: The Clinical and Educational Uses of Orff-Schulwerk* (Bitcon, 2000); and "Orff Music Therapy with Multi-handicapped Children" (Voigt, 1999).

Dalcroze Eurhythmics. The Dalcroze approach (also known as **Eurhythmics**) was developed during the early years of the 20th century by Emile-Henri Jaques-Dalcroze (1865–1950). Born to Swiss parents, Dalcroze was part of a family that provided a rich musical environment at an early age. Dalcroze initially gained fame as a composer of art songs and works for orchestra and as a conductor. He developed his method of teaching music after observing that students learned rhythm more effectively when they were allowed to move freely, helping them to feel their innate sense of rhythm. After working with educators, physiologists, dancers, and musicians, he devised his now famous principles of music education (Frego, Liston, Hama, & Gillmeister, 2004). Dalcroze music education was introduced to the United States in 1968 at Carnegie Mellon University and has since expanded to nine additional training sites (Dalcroze Society of America, 2008).

The core of the Dalcroze approach is Eurhythmics. Eurhythmics uses movement extensively to teach musical concepts of rhythm, structure, and musical expression. The Dalcroze method teaches students to "feel" the elements of music, such as pulse, beat, meter, and rhythm, which are then connected to other arts and, more essentially, to human activities of language and emotion. In addition to movement as the foundation of his music education principles, Dalcroze also used singing, improvisation, reading and writing musical notation, and playing instruments that help to integrate music concepts (Dalcroze Society of America, 2008).

Dalcroze music education principles are applicable to music therapy. In fact, Dalcroze himself used his techniques to assist persons with visual impairments to become more confident in their ability to move. Movement, as you have learned in previous chapters, is an integral part of the music therapist's repertoire and can be applied to therapeutic goals set for adults and children functioning at different levels. For example, Eurhythmics has been used with persons who have AIDS, those with autism spectrum disorders, adults and children with intellectual disabilities, and many others. This approach combines physical, emotional, and intellectual properties of music to build self-confidence, mobility, social skills, self-awareness, and spatial relationships, and it provides a creative outlet. It was Dalcroze's belief that adults and children, no matter their level of ability, should engage in moving, improvising, singing, playing, and listening to music (Frego et al., 2004).

Additional resources that provide information about the Dalcroze approach used in music education and therapy are *Dalcroze Eurhythmics in Today's Music Classroom* (Mead, 1994); *Eurhythmics for Young Children: Six Lessons for Fall* (Dale, 2000); *Expressive Singing: Dalcroze Eurhythmics for Voice* (Caldwell, 1995); "Movement as Musical Expression in a Music Therapy Setting" (Hibben, 1984); and "Music Movement Therapy for People with AIDS" (Frego, 1995).

The Kodály Approach to Music Education. Zoltan Kodály (1882–1967) was a major Hungarian composer who, like Orff and Dalcroze, championed the belief that a holistic approach was most effective for developing musicality in children. His educational philosophy is founded on the idea that training in music must be centered on experiential learning beginning at an early age (Organization of American Kodály Educators, 2004).

Kodály, busy with his composing and teaching activities, did not become interested in music education until he was beyond age 40. When he heard school-age children singing poorly in concerts throughout Hungary, Kodály decided to change the system of music education by insisting on better teaching and music materials. Finally, in the mid 1940s, the Hungarian government took notice of his remarkable success at teaching music to children of all ages and abilities and implemented music education throughout the country. Beginning in 1958, other countries in Europe began to take notice of his successes. In 1973, the first Kodály conference was held in the United States, where the International Kodály Society was founded. Today his music education methods and training programs are popular throughout the world with music educators and music therapists (Brownell, Frego, Kwak, & Rayburn, 2004).

Kodály believed that musical literacy should be taught to all school children and that it was a right, not just a privilege for the gifted. He felt that music education should be part of a child's basic curriculum on equal footing with reading, math, and science. Musical training, according to Kodály, should begin at an early age and start with singing. He argued that singing was an important musical building block that should be taught before a child begins playing an instrument (Chosky, 1988).

Key elements of the Kodály approach include singing (and especially the use of folk songs native to the culture), solfege to develop listening skills, improvisation using the pentatonic scale, and (when developmentally appropriate) teaching the child to learn to read and write musical notation. According to this approach, the curriculum must be sequenced in a way appropriate for the age of the child to ensure successful experiences (Brownell et al., 2004).

According to Brownell et al. (2004), Kodály's music education approach is clearly appropriate for use in music therapy, in particular in special education settings. (For more information about music therapy in special education, see Chapter 14.) The strength with Kodály methodology, as well as the techniques used in Orff and Dalcroze education and therapy, is that it is developmental in approach. This means that music materials are not presented until a child is ready to master the new concepts. The beauty of these methods is that in inclusive public school settings, the music therapist can arrange therapeutic music experiences to the ability of each child, no matter the level of function. Appropriate functional goals may include communication, socialization, fine and gross motor development, and sense of accomplishment.

For further reading, please consult *The Kodály Method: Comprehensive Musical Education from Infant to Adult* (Chosky, 1988); *The Kodály Method I–III* (Chosky, 1999); "Application of Kodály Concepts in Music Therapy" (Lathom, 1974); and "The Kodály Method Applied to Special Education" (Strong, 1983).

Approaches Developed within the Field of Music Therapy

Two approaches that developed primarily within the field of music therapy are **Nordoff-Robbins Music Therapy** and the **Bonny Method of Guided Imagery and Music**. These psychotherapeutic forms of music therapy use a combination of the spoken word and music to elicit changes in client behavior. Depending upon the clientele and primary goals, as well as the therapist's own personal philosophy, some sessions use predominantly musical communication, and music is considered by some therapists to be inherently therapeutic—that is, no verbal processing is essential. These approaches to music therapy are intensely personal, frequently conducted on an individual basis, and used with a variety of clientele. Goals are usually broad and aimed at personal growth, self-actualization, and building self-worth in clients.

Nordoff-Robbins Music Therapy. Nordoff-Robbins Music Therapy developed from a unique partnership between Paul Nordoff, a composer, and Clive Robbins, a special education teacher. From 1959 until 1976, the year of Nordoff's death, the two collaborated on what they called "active" music therapy. Clive Robbins later worked for many years with his wife, Carol, to continue the team approach to therapy. Active music therapy primarily uses improvisation to attain therapeutic goals and is founded on the idea that all persons, no matter the level of (dis)ability, have inborn musical ability and creativity. The tapping into the client's innate musical ability leads to personal growth and development (Kim, 2004).

Internationally located facilities offer training programs and internships for music therapists interested in the Nordoff-Robbins approach. Students take classes in improvisation, musicianship, assessment, and theory of group music therapy. Each student must complete a prescribed set of clinical experiences under supervision, learn to document client progress, and complete an internship of 38 weeks. There are three levels of training available for those therapists who either have a master's degree or are enrolled in a graduate program in music therapy (Nordoff-Robbins Center for Music Therapy, 2008).

Nordoff and Robbins initially practiced music therapy as a team, one playing the piano while the other worked directly with the client. In current practice, therapists may work individually or, in the case of larger groups, work in pairs. Depending upon their needs, clients may be seen in individual sessions or a group setting, or may participate in both. The primary instrument used by the music therapist is either a piano or guitar. Participants engage in music making, playing high-quality instruments of various kinds, including pitched and percussion instruments. Singing and movement can be incorporated into the session to add variety and enhance communication between therapist and client. Nordoff-Robbins music therapists apply their techniques to a wide range of adults and children, including those with developmental disabilities or socioemotional problems, older adults, and clients in medical settings (Aigen et al., 2004).

Nordoff-Robbins music therapy emphasizes the concept of **self-actualization** and the meaningfulness of human destiny. Fundamental to this approach is the belief that within every human being is a musical self (sometimes referred to as the "music child"). The music serves as the primary clinical medium and agent of change. There is no specific format or procedure for a session; improvisation (and sometimes precomposed pieces) is used to begin a musical dialogue between participant and therapist. This form of communication is an important concept in active music therapy, with the therapist accepting whatever the client presents musically. This helps the adult or child to gain musical competence through using different rhythmic patterns, dynamics, and harmonies, and, ultimately, to improve expressive skills, self-confidence, and self-esteem. Nordoff-Robbins practitioners strive to build an effective relationship between themselves and their clients with the ultimate goal of helping the person to attain an improved quality of life (Aigen et al., 2004).

Clinical goals and objectives aim to develop the client's individual potential as opposed to working toward cultural expectations of "normality." Rather than establishing short-term behavioral objectives, clinicians generally focus on long-term therapeutic growth characterized by expressive freedom, creativity, self-confidence, and other human qualities associated with self-actualization (Aigen et al., 2004). Assessment does not typically focus on specific target behaviors; rather, sessions are recorded and then reviewed by clinicians, who study significant musical and nonmusical responses, changes, musical relationships, and teamwork. These observations are documented in a narrative style, which is referred to as "indexing the session" (Aigen et al., 2004).

For further information on the Nordoff-Robbins approach, the following are recommended sources: *Creative Music Therapy: A Guide to Fostering Clinical Musicianship* (Nordoff & Robbins, 2006); *Music Therapy for Handicapped Children* (Nordoff & Robbins, 1992); *Improvisational Models of Music Therapy* (Bruscia, 1987); *Paths of Development in Nordoff-Robbins Music Therapy* (Aigen, 1998); *Music Centered Music Therapy* (Aigen, 2004); *Healing Heritage: Paul Nordoff Exploring the Tonal Language of Music* (Robbins & Robbins, 1998); *Here We Are in Music: One Year with an Adolescent Creative Music Therapy Group* (Aigen, 1997); *Being in Music: Foundations of Nordoff-Robbins Music Therapy* (Aigen, 1996).

The Bonny Method of Guided Imagery and Music. Helen Bonny, the founder of Guided Imagery and Music (GIM), developed the idea of using classical music to stimulate and sustain a dynamic process through the imagination, which facilitates both self-exploration and what Abraham Maslow termed "peak experiences" in persons seeking self-awareness. Based on **humanistic** and **transpersonal** theories, GIM practitioners subscribe to the idea that the combination of music and **imagery** can help a client expand **self-awareness** that leads to a more healthy state of being (Bonny & Savary, 1990).

In an era where the drug LSD (lysergic acid diethylamide) was used in clinical research to enhance peak experiences for the purpose of self-actualization (with obvious drawbacks), Bonny proposed substituting music for the drug. Her subsequent research concluded that music, when properly applied, could intensify and safely contain imagery, thus aiding uncovering and working through detrimental thoughts, emotions, and feelings. By 1974, music and session protocols were in place leading to this form of music therapy practice (Burns & Woolrich, 2004).

GIM therapists use a combination of carefully selected and sequenced classical music to evoke and catalyze images, which may represent the participant's conscious and unconscious feelings from past and present events. As the music plays during individual sessions, the therapist facilitates an ongoing dialogue with the client as the imagery emerges, which fosters focus and engagement with the experience. Through the skillful use of music and imagery, the individual experiences a cathartic release of emotions, which leads to a transformation in the perception of the past events and the ability to view them from a new perspective. This cognitive reframing can then lead to positive behavior change and a renewed sense of self-worth (Burns & Woolrich, 2004). Therapeutic goals include creativity, self-exploration, spiritual insight, and cognitive reorganization (McKinney, 2007b).

The type of classical music used in GIM sessions is designed to challenge and expand the client's comfort level while providing sufficient structural support within which to explore images that arise during the GIM session. According to Goldberg (1992), music may evoke affective or feeling responses, which in turn evoke images. The music therapist chooses music that matches the client's affect, energy level, and issues. The arrangement of musical elements (dynamics, melody, harmony, rhythm, and orchestration) must suggest certain emotional qualities fitting client needs. The titles of many of the music programs for GIM suggest themes, such as Positive Affect, Relationships, Transitions, Affect Release, and Emotional Expression (Bonny, 2002). It is important to note that the music therapist's role in GIM is not to solve the client's problems but to guide, support, and serve as witness to the individual's process toward self-understanding and change. Persons who are most appropriate for GIM are those diagnosed with certain types of behavior or emotional disorders, those with chronic illness, or those seeking a better understanding of self. Individuals with psychosis are not appropriate candidates for GIM (Burns &

Woolrich, 2004). Facilitation of this approach requires advanced training in GIM as well as in counseling, psychotherapy, or music psychotherapy.

Desired clinical outcomes may include improved interpersonal relationships and lives that are more manageable and meaningful (Körelen & Wrangsjö, 2001). Research studies conducted with healthy adults as well as persons with depression or chronic illnesses (such as rheumatoid arthritis or cancer) have documented the following: significant decrease in emotional distress (including anxiety and depressed mood); significant improvement in relationships, and manageability and quality of life (Burns, 1999; Körelen & Wrangsjö, 2001; McKinney, Antoni, Kumar, Tims, & McCabe, 1997); reduced pain and improved physical functioning (Jacobi & Eisenberg, 2001–2002); and reduced blood pressure (McDonald, as cited in McKinney, Antoni, et al., 1997). Studies examining the potential use of GIM to reduce stress and enhance immune function (psychoneuroimmunology) have reported significant changes in neuro-endocrine responses associated with stress (McKinney, 2007a; McKinney, Antoni, et al., 1997; McKinney, Tims, Kumar, & Kumar, 1997).

For additional information, the following sources are recommended: *Music and Consciousness: The Evolution of Guided Imagery and Music* (Bonny, 2002); *Music and Your Mind: Listening with a New Consciousness* (Bonny & Savary, 1990).

Music Therapy Approaches Reflecting or Based upon Psychological Philosophies, Theories, or Models

Music therapists work with a variety of clientele, some who have as their primary diagnosis a behavioral-emotional disorder, and others who may have behavioral or emotional problems that accompany another primary diagnosis (e.g., learning disabilities, intellectual disabilities, some chronic illnesses, etc.). Consistent with a biopsychosocial model of health care, treatment should incorporate the psychological and social needs of the individual. Toward this end, music therapists often work collaboratively with other health care providers, including psychologists, social workers, and child life specialists, to address psychosocial issues.

While music therapists often feel more comfortable with particular approaches, they may need to select music therapy interventions that are congruent with philosophies, theories, or models of psychological functioning that have been adopted by their client's treatment team or the facility's overarching mission or philosophy. In this section, we have provided a summary of several prominent philosophies, theories, or models associated with the field of psychology, but which have informed and shaped music therapy practice as well. These include **behavioral therapy, cognitive behavioral therapy,** and **psychodynamic therapy.** In addition, an **eclectic** approach, which is the use of techniques from several different approaches, will be presented at the end of this chapter. You may recall reading about these terms in

Chapter 8. You may find it helpful to review that information in conjunction with reading this next section.

The Behavioral Approach to Music Therapy. The behavioral approach to music therapy is defined as the use of music in association with the therapist to change unhealthy patterns of socially important behavior (such as drug abuse) into more appropriate skills (abstaining from using drugs) (Standley, Johnson, Robb, Brownell, & Kim, 2004). Behavior is changed through a highly structured environment using **classical** or **operant** conditioning principles developed by psychologists, most notably B. F. Skinner and Albert Bandura. Behaviorism examines human behavior through **empirical methods** (quantifying observable and measurable behaviors) rather than focusing on thoughts and internal emotional conflicts. Behavioral psychology is the philosophical and theoretical basis for understanding human behavior. **Applied Behavior Analysis (ABA),** which is often used in educational and clinical settings, helps to link research with clinical practice. ABA consists of a variety of creative approaches and procedures that reflect behavioral theories to influence behavior change. These approaches and procedures have been validated through over 40 years of scientific research and are widely used in the United States (Standley et al., 2004; Sulzer-Azaroff & Mayer, 1991).

Procedures derived from behavioral therapy (including ABA) have been used to assess and treat a wide range of clinical entities, including persons with physically disabling conditions and behavioral-emotional disorders, and, in particular, adults and children with intellectual disabilities and autism spectrum disorders (Sturmey, 2002). Behavioral therapy can be used to modify a host of maladaptive behaviors, including self-injurious or self-stimulating behaviors, anxiety and phobias, depression, eating disorders, smoking, and antisocial behaviors (Corey, 2001).

Techniques common to behavioral therapy include **positive** and **negative reinforcement** of behavior, **punishment**, **extinction** of **undesirable** behaviors, **token economies** to strengthen socially desirable behaviors, and **shaping**. These are just of few of the terms that are commonly used in behavioral therapy and ABA. You can read definitions of these terms in the book's glossary and learn more about these techniques in other books and chapters that focus on behavioral therapy.

Techniques such as **reinforcement** and **shaping** can be easily integrated into music therapy sessions. In a general sense, music therapists often use these techniques to help clients participate successfully in the therapy session. Music therapists may use praise, award stickers (such as stars or happy faces), or other sorts of reward to reinforce appropriate behavior. But one of the special and powerful tools that music therapists have to offer is *music itself*. Most people find some sort of music beautiful and engaging. For example, adolescents often consider music central to their social and emotional life, and they will, on their own, spend hours a day listening to favorite music. Many research studies have shown that listening to or playing music can be a very powerful **reinforcement** that can be used to increase a target behavior. For example, a child with a behavioral disorder who is often verbally aggressive may "earn" the chance to take guitar lessons from the music therapist if he doesn't use offensive language throughout the day.

Music therapists also use techniques such as **shaping** in order to help clients develop new and challenging skills. For example, when first learning to play piano or guitar, most people sound pretty awkward and inept. Using principles of behavioral therapy, the music therapist can shape or gradually guide the client's skills toward a desirable level of competency, which in turn can support self-confidence.

Another therapeutic intervention that has emerged from the behavioral tradition is the pairing of relaxing music with special relaxations techniques (progressive relaxation or autogenic relaxation). The music eventually becomes **conditioned** with relaxation. These are only three of a panoply of ways in which behavioral principles integrate readily with music therapy interventions.

Since the formation of the National Association for Music Therapy in 1950, there has been a strong link between music therapy and behavioral therapy. The *Journal of Music Therapy* has published numerous research studies dating back to the 1960s and continuing today using behavioral strategies coupled with music therapy interventions (Gfeller, 1987). The field continues to grow through empirical research and development of new techniques that lead to more effective treatment.

The following resources provide more information on applied behavioral analysis and behavioral music therapy: *Principles of Behavior Modification* (Bandura, 1969); "Applied Behavior Analysis" (Hanser, 1995); "A Meta-analysis on the Effects of Music as a Reinforcement for Education/Therapy Objectives" (Standley, 1996b); "Four Decades of Music Therapy Behavioral Research Designs: A Content Analysis of *Journal of Music Therapy* Articles" (Gregory, 2002).

Cognitive-Behavioral Music Therapy. As noted in Chapter 8, cognitive therapies are based upon the premise that what we think about an event, object, or person has an enormous influence on what we feel and how we act (Corey, 2001). Cognitive approaches emphasize the importance of cognitive (mental) processes as determinants of behavior. The influence of behavioral therapy in this approach can be seen in the use of many techniques designed to alter maladaptive behaviors in conjunction with modifying irrational thoughts (Scoval & Gardstrom, 2002).

Cognitive-behavioral therapy is designed to help the clients replace undesirable, irrational thinking with healthier cognitive patterns. Cognitive-behavioral therapists do not delve into a person's past or probe internalized emotional conflicts; instead they focus on the client's current life situation and work toward a more satisfactory way of handling problems and seizing opportunities for positive growth. A music therapist may use this theoretical approach with persons having a variety of emotional and social problems, including anxiety disorders, substance abuse, eating disorders, and mood disorders. Cognitive-behavioral therapy has also proven useful to treat chronic pain and sleep disorders. Cognitive-behavioral therapy requires that the client be capable of insight and verbal communication; thus, this approach may not be suited for persons who are out of touch with reality (psychotic) or who have serious intellectual deficits (Corey, 2001). It is effective for use with groups or individuals.

The role of the music therapist who works within this therapeutic framework is almost like a coach or educator who encourages and supports the client in taking responsibility for his or her own changes, specifically to learn to adjust cognitive processes (thinking differently) and associated behaviors. Typically, a therapist will use a number of approaches to change feelings and behavior, such as role playing, rehearsal, and modeling. For example, within a structured music therapy intervention (such as playing instruments together), the music therapist may have members of the group rehearse or role play behaviors that are problematic in their everyday lives (Bryant, 1987). A very withdrawn person who is shy and reclusive may practice taking a leadership role in the musical ensemble. Or the music therapist might model (demonstrate) appropriate ways of communicating or behaving. The therapist may ask clients to complete assignments outside the session, and then keep a diary of specific thoughts and feelings that arise during situations. This provides practice and experimentation with new ways of responding to uncomfortable situations identified in therapy.

Cognitive-behavioral music therapy practice includes the components of music and verbal processing. Music therapists use guided listening strategies including lyric analysis, song writing, and relaxation experiences, which are described in Chapter 8. These experiences can help the client to identify issues in the song's content that have relevance to their personal situation (Bryant, 1987). Paring preferred relaxing music with an **autogenic** or **progressive relaxation** (a technique adopted from behavioral therapy) script can help clients with pain management and focus attention away from an unpleasant medical procedure (Standley et al., 2004). Music has also been effective in reducing stress in teachers as well as in adolescents who suffer from post-traumatic stress disorder, and in reducing cravings in persons suffering from alcohol abuse.

A recent study by Silverman (2007) indicates that music therapy practitioners use cognitive-behavioral strategies more frequently than other approaches with persons who have behavioral emotional disturbances. This is an important finding given that about 21% of music therapists work with this clinical population. According to Cassity (2007), the use of cognitive-behavioral therapy has grown over the past few decades and will continue to increase, as a philosophical orientation in psychiatric care and, consequently, also in music therapy.

References that provide more information about cognitive-behavior therapy and music therapy include: *Rational Emotive Behavioral Therapy: A Therapist's Guide* (Ellis & McLaren, 1998); "The Use of Rational Humorous Songs in Psychotherapy" (Ellis, 1987); "A Cognitive Approach to Therapy Through Music" (Bryant, 1987); and "The Use of Cognitive-Behavioral Music Therapy in the Treatment of Women with Eating Disorders" (Hilliard, 2001).

The Psychodynamic Approach to Music Therapy. This approach is related to psychodynamic theory of psychology, which had its origins in the theories of Sigmund Freud, as well as theories of later psychodynamic therapists (e.g., Jung, Adler, etc.) that extend or modify Freudian theory. These theories are described in detail in many psychology textbooks and courses. Briefly, the psychodynamic model is based upon the belief that human behavior is strongly influenced by unconscious psychological processes, such as internal conflicts, impulses, desires, and motives, of which we are largely unaware on a conscious level. Early childhood events are believed to have lifelong effects on our psychological states. A number of psychodynamic therapies have developed out of psychoanalytic principles, but all are concerned with explaining the motives behind why people think, feel, and behave as they do. Therapy is aimed at helping the individual gain insights or increased awareness of unconscious conflicts, in order to develop more adaptive and satisfying behaviors and relationships (Wilson, O'Leary, Nathan, & Clark, 1996).

Several models of psychodynamic music therapy are based upon psychodynamic theory. Among the pioneers of psychodynamic music therapy are Florence Tyson, an early American practitioner of this form of music therapy, Juliet Alvin (who used the term *psychodynamic music therapy*), and Mary Priestly (associated with a model of therapy known as Analytical Music Therapy); Alvin and Priestly were both British music therapists. As is true within the field of psychology, there are several approaches to psychodynamic music therapy. They differ on matters such as the role of music within therapy, the nature of the patient-client relationship, professional training methods, and therapy techniques. Some music therapy approaches used by psychodynamic music therapists include vocal and instrumental improvisation, song writing, patient-selected music, music imagery, and the Bonny Method of Guided Imagery and Music (described earlier in this chapter). It is important to note that some of these techniques are also used by music therapists who do not consider themselves to be psychodynamic therapists. These techniques are not inherently associated with psychodynamic principles, but they can be facilitated in such a manner that therapeutic goals associated with psychodynamic principles are addressed (Isenberg-Grezeda, Goldberg, & Dvorkin, 2004).

Psychodynamically-based music therapy is used to help patients develop insights into unconscious drives, motives, and conflicts that negatively impact present functioning. The relationship between the therapist and the client is fundamental to the treatment process and is used to help the patient gain insight into old relationships and patterns of behaviors, including defenses and resistance to change. Music and/or verbal interaction are the essential elements of change. According to Ruud (1980), music acts as a stimulus in which the abstract nature of music detours intellectual control and provides access to unconscious conflicts and emotions. These conflicts and emotions can then be expressed through music. In addition, musical activity can help clients to attain a stronger ego (sense of self) and improved self-esteem.

There has been debate regarding the role of music versus the role of the patient-therapist relationship in music psychotherapy. Bruscia (1998) has suggested four levels of engagement between the patient and therapist that fall on a continuum from exclusively musical interaction (in which therapeutic issues are accessed, worked through, and resolved through musical engagement), to predominantly verbal interactions in which the therapeutic issues are accessed, worked through, and resolved verbally, but music experiences are used to facilitate or enrich the discussion (Isenberg-Grezeda et al., 2004).

This type of music therapy practice requires extensive and advanced training in psychodynamic music psychotherapy therapy, exceptionally strong skills in musical improvisation on the part of the therapist, and a commitment to more extended therapy and capacity for insight on the part of the client.

For additional information, the following sources are recommended: *Music Therapy* (Alvin, 1975); *The Dynamics of Music Psychotherapy* (Bruscia, 1998); *Essays on Analytical Music Therapy* (Priestly, 1994).

Music Therapy Approaches Reflecting Biomedical Models

A large number of music therapists works with clientele whose primary diagnoses involves a disease or condition that requires medical treatment and/or specific forms of neurologic rehabilitation (e.g., strokes, Parkinson's disease, cancer, COPD, etc.). While music therapists often address the psychological and social needs of persons with medical problems (see Chapter 11), music therapists also collaborate with physicians, nurses, physical therapists, and other health-care providers to treat or ameliorate the physical, biological, or neurological aspects of the disease or condition. Those sorts of conditions and music therapy interventions are described in many chapters of this book, in particular Chapters 6, 7, 10, 11, and 12.

While music therapists may have personally preferred music therapy approaches, their choices of music therapy interventions should also be congruent with philosophies, theories, or models adopted by their client's treatment team or the mission or philosophy of the hospital, clinic, or rehabilitation center where they work. In some facilities, this may be a biomedical orientation to treatment. This section describes music therapy approaches that emphasize a biomedical approach, that is, from a brain and behavior perspective. Some core aspects of a biomedical perspective are (1) the focus on the neurobiological foundations of the human nervous system, (2) a strong emphasis on music perception and active music participation as a form of stimulation that activates physiological and neurophysiological processes in the body (which include affect and cognition as part of neural behavior), and (3) the belief that the unique structural and cultural properties of music can be harnessed to access brain and behavior functions to facilitate and to promote healing and rehabilitation.

Throughout this book are examples of music and biological functioning. In Chapter 2, the long history of music as an influence on human functioning and health is presented. Chapter 3 outlines many ways in which music influences physical functioning, including neurological processes. Chapters throughout the book illustrate the link between physical functioning and various aspects of music listening and involvement.

In recent years, there have been several notable connections between music and physical well-being that have been documented through clinical research. As Chapter 11 notes, preliminary studies consistent with **psychoneuroimmunology** (an interdisciplinary field that involves the bidirectional relationships between the mind, brain, and immune system) indicate that stress-related hormones and neurotransmitters can suppress immune functioning. Music in conjunction with stress reduction and relaxation can reduce levels of these hormones and neurotransmitters (McKinney, 2007a).

Therapeutic application of music (such as rhythm and melodic patterns) have been associated with improved neuromotor, speech/language, and cognitive functioning for persons suffering from neurologically-based conditions such as stroke, Parkinson's disease, multiple sclerosis, traumatic brain injury, or cerebral palsy. The following music therapy model, **Neurologic Music Therapy (NMT)**, developed by Michael Thaut, focuses on utilizing musical stimuli for a variety of neurological disorders. Michael Thaut has provided an overview of NMT in the following paragraphs.

Neurologic Music Therapy (**This section contributed by Michael H. Thaut**). The study of the neurobiological basis of music ability is inherently linked to the study of music's influence on brain function. In other words, when we study the biology of music in the brain, we inevitably recognize a reciprocal relationship in musical behavior: The brain that engages in music is changed by engaging in music. Although much has been learned since the early 1990s about the effect of music on brain structure and function, a transformational framework, a new theoretical model, explains how musical responses can be generalized and transferred into nonmusical therapeutic responses. This scientific model called the **Rational Scientific Mediating Model (R-SMM**—for more information refer to Chapter 10), searches for the therapeutic effect of music by studying if and how music stimulates and engages parallel or shared brain function in the following areas, based on the psychological and physiological processes in music perception: cognition, speech and language, motor control, and emotion. Therefore, one can also describe the paradigm shift in this model as a change from an interpretive "social science" model to a perceptual "neuroscience" model.

Since about 1990, there has been a large body of research conducted in the neurosciences of music. This research—by enabling a more complete understanding of the neurobiological basis of music—has led to the development of "clusters" of scientific evidence for the effectiveness of specific interventions of music within therapy, rehabilitation, and medicine. In a comprehensive effort by researchers and clinicians in music therapy, neurology, and the brain sciences, these "evidence clusters" have been codified into a system of therapeutic techniques subsequently termed *Neurologic Music Therapy* **(NMT)**. This codification—which began in the late 1990s—has resulted in the development of clinical techniques that are standardized in applications and terminology as well as supported by evidence through scientific research. Because the system of techniques is research-based, it is dynamically open-ended in terms of future development and knowledge.

Five basic definitions articulate the most important principles of neurologic music therapy:

- NMT is defined as the therapeutic application of music to cognitive, sensory, and motor dysfunctions due to neurologic disease of the human nervous system.

- NMT is based on a neuroscience model of music perception and production, and the influence of music on functional changes in nonmusical brain and behavior functions (R-SMM).

- Treatment techniques are evidence based; they are based on data from scientific and clinical research and are directed toward functional nonmusical therapeutic goals.

- Treatment techniques are standardized in terminology and application and are applied to therapy as therapeutic music interventions (TMI), which are adaptable to the patient's functional needs.

- In addition to training in music and NMT, practitioners are educated in the areas of neuroanatomy and physiology, brain pathologies, medical terminology, and rehabilitation of cognitive, motor, speech, and language functions.

Clinical applications of NMT are subdivided into three domains of rehabilitation: (1) sensorimotor rehabilitation, (2) speech and language rehabilitation, and (3) cognitive rehabilitation. In each domain, NMT can be applied to patient treatment within different clinical fields and disciplines, such as inpatient and outpatient neurologic rehabilitation, neurogeriatrics, neuropedioatrics, and neurodevelopmental therapies. Depending on the patients' needs, the therapeutic goals are directed toward functional rehabilitative, developmental, or adaptive goals. Within this framework, the primary major area of therapeutic rehabilitation not fully covered is psychiatric rehabilitation. However, as the understanding of the nature and the mechanisms of psychiatric disorders progresses, our understanding of effective rehabilitation strategies will improve. Within an emerging framework of neuropsychiatric models, it will be possible to design effective treatment techniques in NMT, most likely within the domain of cognitive rehabilitation (Unkefer & Thaut, 2002).

More detail about Neurologic Music Therapy is discussed in Chapter 10. Therefore, only two additional concepts will be specifically mentioned here due to their particular significance for music in rehabilitation.

1. *Technique standardization.* In current music therapy practice, there is considerable variety in how various therapy approaches are named, with some terms being essentially activity descriptions and some being borrowed from other fields. This lack of standardization can make communication among professionals difficult. Therefore, standardization can provide an important foundation for establishing treatment goals and intervention protocols that can be more consistently recognized by other health professionals and insurance companies.

In Neurologic Music Therapy, two parameters of technique definition are introduced to allow for the development of standardized descriptions and applications. The first parameter is based on the functional goals of the therapeutic music exercise—for example, to improve range of motion of arms, enhance declarative memory, train selective attention, or facilitate speech encoding in a patient with expressive aphasia. The second parameter is based on the mechanism in music that facilitates the therapeutic change, such as rhythm as a sensory timer for motor control, or musical pattern perception as a mnemonic device to enhance learning and recall through metrical organization of verbal materials; or singing to access alternative neural pathways to encode verbal output. Based on standardized descriptions, techniques can be uniquely and consistently defined in a way that separates them from each other. The actual design of the therapeutic exercise, on the other hand—within its standardized structure—draws on an unlimited number of musical resources and experiences to be translated in highly creative yet logical designs into a functional therapeutic experience for the client.

2. *Assessment.* Assessment is an essential component for implementing "best practice" standards embraced internationally by many rehabilitation professions to ensure quality care for patients. Assessment is a complex process that all professions wrestle with, and music therapy is no exception. Within NMT, assessment evolves out of a simple question: What do music therapists assess that is unique to their professional role in facilitating best treatment options for the patient? A second issue is that assessment plays the critical role in helping to select which treatment is the right one for the patient's diagnostic status and which treatment option has the greatest likelihood of success.

This process, however, can be effectively applied only when well-defined and standardized treatment techniques exist, and when something is known about treatment success rates. This knowledge can be obtained by clinical research investigating techniques and elements of their mechanisms. Without standardized treatment techniques and a comprehensive evidence basis that is grounded in scientific mechanism and outcome research, meaningful development of assessment procedures remains difficult. In NMT, assessment is aided by standardization of goals and interventions. Outcome data are available and will continue to shape the future of this model.

Additional information regarding NMT can be found in the following sources: "The Neurosciences and Music" (Avanzini, Faiena, Minciacchi, Lopez, & Majono, 2003); *Oxford Handbook of Music Psychology* (Hall, Cross, & Thaut, 2008); "Rationales for Improving Motor Function" (Hummelsheim, 1999); *Retraining Cognition: Techniques and Applications* (Parente & Herrmann, 1996); *Rhythm, Music, and the Brain* (Thaut, 2005); *Music Therapy in the Treatment of Adults with Mental Disorders: Theoretical Basis and Clinical Interventions* (Unkefer & Thaut, 2002).

Eclectic or Integrative Approach

An **eclectic** or **integrative** approach to therapy means that therapists draw freely on techniques from all types of therapy without necessarily accepting the theoretical frameworks behind them. This represents an overall trend away from exclusiveness or narrowness of adhering to a particular system or theory, with the goal of more efficient treatment (Baruth & Huber, 1985; Corey, 2001). According to Corey (2001), a trend toward eclecticism has been motivated by a proliferation of therapies throughout the 20th century, along with recognition that no single theory is comprehensive enough to account for the complexities of human behaviors, especially when taking into consideration the diverse characteristics and problems of client types. In addition, socioeconomic realities such as insurance reimbursement and short-term health care models are problematic with regard to some theoretical approaches that required long-term commitment, and result in gradual change or recovery. Furthermore, there has been limited evidence to differentiate among some therapy approaches with regard to effectiveness, paired with recognition among professionals regarding commonalities across different approaches. By accepting that each theory has its strengths and weaknesses, and by adopting an integrative perspective, therapists have the opportunity to more closely match therapeutic interventions with the needs and goals of individual clients (Baruth & Huber, 1985; Corey, 2001).

An integrative approach to therapy should not be a random selection of one's personally favorite techniques. It is important for the therapist to consider which theories provide the best basis for understanding cognitive, emotional, behavioral, and biophysical dimensions, and then reflect on therapeutic approaches that are the best fit for the client's presenting problems, cultural background, and individual personality. An integrated approach requires a solid understanding of different therapy approaches (obtained through formal study, continuing education, ongoing observation, review of research literature); the characteristics, needs, and strengths of different types of clients; self-reflection on one's own abilities; clarity regarding the mission of the agency in which one practices; and the knowledge, skill, art, and experience to determine what techniques are suitable for particular problems and circumstances (Corey, 2001).

In a survey of music therapists who work in psychiatric facilities, Silverman (2007) found that the largest proportion described themselves as having an eclectic philosophical orientation toward psychiatric treatment. Cassity and Cassity (2006) have advocated for a multimodal model of therapy for persons with behavioral and emotional disorders, which systematically addresses various domains of human functioning (e.g., behavior, affect, sensation, cognitions, etc.). Eclecticism or integrative therapy is commonly used within the field of music therapy, and its use is likely to increase.

This textbook has presented a wide range of approaches to therapy that reflect an extensive set of therapeutic techniques, some that are more or less suitable for a particular type clientele. Given the wide variety of clients served by music therapists, some level of eclectism is likely to remain an important part of music therapy practice.

CONCLUSIONS

Over an entire career, music therapists are likely to work within different clinical settings and with a variety of clientele who differ in age, clinical needs, background, and beliefs. Furthermore, a therapist who is aware of societal changes will seek input through professional collaborations, advanced studies, professional conferences, and information on scientific and clinical advances available through books and journals. As a result of life experiences, therapists also evolve in their understanding of themselves, the human condition, and their own personal responsibility to their clients and colleagues. All of these factors speak to the importance of being a lifelong learner who evolves personally as well as professionally with regard to music therapy approaches and the clinical contract with our clients.

SUMMARY OF PART II

In Part II of this chapter, you have learned about common music therapy approaches used to treat adults and children with disabilities. Also introduced were terms commonly used to describe music therapy approaches; terms such as *method, philosophy, theory,* and *model,* though having distinct meanings, are sometimes used interchangeably by music therapists. The field of music therapy was originally developed by musicians, educators, physicians, and psychiatrists who initially used an intuitive approach to music therapy practice that served the profession well for a time. But it was not until the mid 20th century that an emphasis was placed on the importance of research. As more research was carried out, the field of music therapy began to develop and mature at a rapid pace. In addition to better scientific knowledge about the way music influences cognitive, physiological, and socioemotional function, changes in society (including multiculturalism and the deinstitutionalization movement) have shaped today's practice in music therapy.

We also learned that not all approaches work equally well with all persons with disabilities, leaving it to the music therapist to select the most appropriate methods to meet client needs. Prominent approaches discussed in this chapter included educational models, approaches developed within the field of music therapy, and music therapy practice based on psychological philosophies. Finally, music therapy integrated with biomedical models and the increasingly popular eclectic approach to music therapy practice was discussed. Music therapists need to remain sensitive to the various factors that influence therapy effectiveness, and on-going developments in the field regarding best practice.

STUDY QUESTIONS FOR PART II

1. Distinguish between the terms *approach, method, theory,* and *philosophy.*

2. Describe the intuitive approach to music therapy and discuss the strengths and weakness of the intuitive approach.

3. What is the biopsychosocial model of health and illness?

4. Define *multiculturalism*.

5. There are four factors that influence the choice of approaches used by music therapists. List, and then describe, these four factors.

6. What difference does the background and culture of clients seen in music therapy matter when a music therapist develops a session plan?

7. Define *self-actualization*.

8. Why might a therapist's attitudes toward therapeutic approaches change over time?

9. Name and distinguish between the three music education approaches sometimes used by music therapists.

10. Compare and contrast the differences between the cognitive-behavioral approach and psychodynamic approach.

11. Define *Applied Behavioral Analysis*.

12. How is the Nordoff-Robbins approach to music therapy similar in philosophy to the Bonny Method of Guided Imagery in Music?

13. Define *psychoneuroimmunology*.

14. Describe the five basic principles of Neurologic Music Therapy.

15. Describe three reasons that an eclectic approach to music therapy has become more prevalent in recent years.

REFERENCES

Adler, R. S. (2001). *Musical assessment of gerontologic needs and treatment: The MAGNET survey*. St. Louis, MO: MMB Music.

Aigen, K. (1996). *Being in music: Foundations of Nordoff-Robbins music therapy*. The Nordoff-Robbins Music Therapy Monograph Series (Vol. 1). St. Louis, MO: MMB Music.

Aigen, K. (1997). *Here we are in music: One year with an adolescent creative music therapy group*. Gilsum, NH: Barcelona

Aigen, K. (1998). *Paths of development in Nordoff-Robbins music therapy*. Phoenixville, PA: Barcelona.

Aigen, K. (2004). *Music centered music therapy*. Gilsum, NH: Barcelona.

Aigen, K., Miller, C. K., Kim, Y. Pasiali, V., Kwak, E., & Tague, D. B. (2004). Nordoff-Robbins music therapy. In A. A. Darrow (Ed.), *Introduction to approaches in music therapy* (pp. 25–33). Silver Spring, MD: American Music Therapy Association.

Alvin, J. (1975). *Music therapy*. London: Hutchinson.

American Music Therapy Association. (2007). Code of ethics. *AMTA member sourcebook* (pp. 24–28). Silver Spring, MD: Author.

American Music Therapy Association. (2007). Standards of clinical practice. *AMTA member sourcebook* (pp. 24–28). Silver Spring, MD: Author.

Avanzini, G., Faiena, C., Minciacchi, D., Lopez, L., & Majono, M. (Eds.). (2003). The neurosciences and music. *Annals of the New York Academy of Sciences, 999.*

Bandura, A. (1969). *Principles of behavior modification.* San Francisco: Hole, Rinehart, & Winston.

Baruth, L.G., & Huber, C.H. (1985). *Counseling and psychotherapy: Theoretical analyses and skills applications.* Columbus, OH: Charles E. Merrill.

Bitcon, C. (1976). *Alike and different: The clinical and educational use of Orff-Schulwerk.* Anaheim, CA: Lincoln Music.

Bitcon, C. (2000). *Alike and different: The clinical and educational use of Orff-Schulwerk* (2nd ed.). Gilsum, NH: Barcelona.

Bonny, H. L. (2002). *Music and consciousness: The evolution of Guided Imagery and Music.* Gilsum, NH: Barcelona.

Bonny, H. L., & Savary, L. M. (1990). *Music and your mind: Listening with a new consciousness* (2nd ed.). New York: Station Hill Press.

Boxill, E. H. (1985). *Music therapy for the developmentally disabled.* Rockville, MD: Aspen Systems.

Braswell, C., Brooks, D. M., Decuir, A., Humphrey, T., Jacobs, K. W. & Sutton, K. (1983). Development and implementation of a music/activity therapy intake assessment for psychiatric patients. Part I: Initial standardization procedures on data from university students. *Journal of Music Therapy, 20*, 88–100.

Braswell, C., Brooks, D. M., Decuir, A., Humphrey, T., Jacobs, K. W. & Sutton, K. (1986). Development and implementation of a music/activity therapy intake assessment for psychiatric patients. Part II: Standardization procedures on data from psychiatric patients. *Journal of Music Therapy, 23*, 126–141.

Brownell, M. D., Frego, R. J. D., Kwak, E., & Rayburn, A. M. (2004). The Kodály approach to music therapy. In A. A. Darrow (Ed.), *Introduction to approaches in music therapy* (pp. 25–33). Silver Spring, MD: American Music Therapy Association.

Brunk, B. K., & Coleman, K. A. (2000). Development of a special education music therapy assessment process. *Music Therapy Perspectives, 18*(1), 59–68.

Bruscia, K. E. (1987). *Improvisational models of music therapy.* Springfield, IL: Charles C. Thomas.

Bruscia, K. E. (1998). *The dynamics of music psychotherapy.* Gilsum, NH: Barcelona.

Bryant, D. R. (1987). A cognitive approach to therapy through music. *Journal of Music Therapy, 24*, 27–34.

Burns, D., & Woolrich, J. (2004). The Bonny Method of Guided Imagery and Music. In A. A. Darrow (Ed.), *Introduction to approaches in music therapy* (pp. 53–62). Silver Spring, MD: American Music Therapy Association.

Burns, D. S. (1999). The effect of the Bonny Method of Guided Imagery and Music on mood and life quality of cancer patients. *Journal of Music Therapy, 38*, 51–65.

Caldwell, J. T. (1995). *Expressive singing: Dalcroze Eurhythmics for voice.* Englewood Cliffs, NJ: Prentice Hall.

Cassity, M., & Cassity, J. (2006). *Multimodal psychiatric music therapy for adults, adolescents, and children: A clinical manual* (3rd ed.). Philadelphia: Jessica Kingsley.

Cassity, M. D. (2007). Psychiatric music therapy in 2016: A Delphi poll of the future. *Music Therapy Perspectives, 25*(2), 86–93.

Chase, K. M. (2003). Multicultural music therapy: A review of literature. *Music Therapy Perspectives, 21*(2), 84–88.

Chosky, L. (1988). *The Kodály Method: Comprehensive musical education from infant to adult* (2nd ed.). Englewood Cliffs, NJ: Prentice Hall.

Chosky, L. (1999). *The Kodály Method I–III*. Englewood Cliffs, NJ: Prentice Hall.

Cohen, G., Averbach, J., & Katz, E. (1978). Music therapy assessment of the client. *Journal of Music Therapy, 15*, 88–99.

Cohen, G., & Gericke, O. L. (1972). Music therapy assessment: Prime requisite for determining patient objectives. *Journal of Music Therapy, 9*, 161–189.

Cole, K. M. (2002). *The music therapy assessment handbook*. Columbus, MS: SouthernPen.

Coleman, K. A., & Brunk, B. K. (1999). *SEMTAP: Special education music therapy assessment process handbook*. Grapevine, TX: Prelude Music Therapy.

Colwell, C. M., Achey, C., Gillmeister, G., & Woolrich, J. (2004). The Orff approach to music therapy. In A. A. Darrow (Ed.), *Introduction to approaches in music therapy* (pp. 3–13). Silver Spring, MD: American Music Therapy Association.

Corey, G. (2001). *Theory and practice of counseling and psychotherapy* (6th ed.). Pacific Grove, CA: Cole.

Corey, G., Corey, M., & Callanan, P. (1993). *Issues and ethics in the helping professions* (4th ed.). Monterey, CA: Brooks/Cole.

Dalcroze Society of America. (2008). *Introduction to Dalcroze*. Retrieved May 31, 2008, from http://www.dalcrozeusa.org/about.html

Dale, M. (2000). *Eurhythmics for young children: Six lessons for fall*. Ellicott City, MD: MusiKinesis.

Darrow, A., & Malloy, D. (1998). Multicultural perspectives in music therapy: An examination of the literature, educational curricula, and clinical practices in culturally diverse cities of the United States. *Music Therapy Perspectives, 16*(1), 27–32.

Douglass, E. T. (2006). The development of a music therapy assessment tool for hospitalized children. *Music Therapy Perspectives, 24*(2), 73–79.

Ellis, A. (1987). The use of rational humorous songs in psychotherapy. In W. F. Fry, Jr. & W. A. Salameh (Eds.), *Handbook of humor and psychotherapy* (pp. 265–285). Sarasota, FL: Professional Resource Exchange.

Ellis, A., & MacLaren, C. (1998). *Rational emotive behavioral therapy: A therapist's guide*. Atascadero, CA: Impact.

Fowler, K. L. (2006). The relations between personality characteristics, work environment, and the professional well-being of music therapists. *Journal of Music Therapy, 43*(3), 174–197.

Fraenkel, J. R., & Wallen, N. E. (2000). *How to design and evaluate research in education* (4th ed.). Dubuque, IA: McGraw-Hill Higher Education.

Frego, R. J. D. (1995). Music movement therapy for people with AIDS. *International Journal of Arts Medicine, 4*(2), 21–25.

Frego, R. J. D., Liston, R. E., Hama, M., & Gillmeister, G. (2004). The Dalcroze approach to music therapy. In A. A. Darrow (Ed.), *Introduction to approaches in music therapy* (pp. 15–24). Silver Spring, MD: American Music Therapy Association.

Froman, R. (2006, November). *Music therapy with Jewish clients in the United States of America*. Paper presented at the 8th annual national conference of the American Music Therapy Association, Kansas City, MO.

Gantt, L. (2001). Music psychotherapy assessment. *Music Therapy Perspectives, 18*(1), 47–58.

Gfeller, K. E. (1987). Music therapy theory and practice as reflected in research literature. *Journal of Music Therapy, 24*, 178–194.

Gfeller, K. E. (2002). Music as a therapeutic agent: Historical and sociocultural perspectives. In R. F. Unkefer & M. H. Thaut (Eds.), *Music therapy in the treatment of adults with mental disorders* (pp. 60–67). St. Louis, MO: MMB.

Gfeller, K. E. (2007). Music therapy and hearing loss: A 30 year retrospective. *Music Therapy Perspectives, 25*(2), 100–107.

Goldberg, F. S. (1992). Images of emotions: The role of emotion in Guided Imagery and Music. *Journal of the Association for Music and Imagery, 1*, 5–17.

Goodkin, D. (2002). *Play sing and dance: An introduction to Orff-Schulwerk.* New York: Schott-EAMC.

Gregory, D. (2002). Four decades of music therapy behavioral research designs: A content analysis of *Journal of Music Therapy* articles. *Journal of Music Therapy, 39*, 56–71.

Groen, K. M. (2007). Pain assessment and management in end of life care: A survey of assessment and treatment practices of hospice music therapy and nursing professionals. *Journal of Music Therapy, 44*(2), 90–112.

Hall, R. V. (1974). *Managing behavior: 1.* Lawrence, KS: H & H Enterprises.

Hall, S., Cross, I., & Thaut, M. H. (Eds.). (2008). *Oxford handbook of music psychology.* Oxford, UK: Oxford University Press.

Hanser, S. B. (1987). *Music therapist's handbook.* St. Louis, MO: Warren H. Green.

Hanser, S. B. (1995). Applied behavior analysis. In B. L. Wheeler (Ed.), *Music therapy research: Quantitative and qualitative perspectives* (pp. 149–164). Phoenixville, PA: Barcelona.

Hibben, J. K. (1984). Movement as a musical expression in a music therapy setting. *Music Therapy, 4*, 91–97.

Hilliard, R. E. (2001). The use of cognitive-behavioral music therapy in the treatment of women with eating disorders. *Music Therapy Perspectives, 19*, 109–113.

Hintz, M. R. (2001). Geriatric music therapy clinical assessment—Assessment of music skills and related behaviors. *Music Therapy Perspectives, 18*(1), 31–40.

Hobson, M. R. (2006). The collaboration of music therapy and speech-language pathology in the treatment of neurogenic communication disorders: Part II–Collaborative strategies and scope of practice. *Music Therapy Perspectives, 24*(2), 66–72.

Hummelsheim, H. (1999). Rationales for improving motor function. *Current Opinion in Neurology, 12*, 697–701.

Isenberg-Grezeda, C. (1988). Music therapy assessment: A reflection of professional identity. *Journal of Music Therapy, 25*, 156–169.

Isenberg-Grezeda, C., Goldberg, F., & Dvorkin, J. (2004). Psychodynamic approach to music therapy. In A. A. Darrow (Ed.), *Introduction to approaches in music therapy* (pp. 15–24). Silver Spring, MD: American Music Therapy Association.

Jacobi, E. M., & Eisenberg, G. M. (2001–2002). The efficacy of Guided Imagery and Music (GIM) in the treatment of rheumatoid arthritis. *Journal of the Association for Music and Imagery, 8*, 57–74.

Kim, Y. (2004). The early beginnings of Nordoff-Robbins music therapy. *Journal of Music Therapy, 41*(4), 321–339.

Körelen, D., & Wrangsjö, B. (2001). Treatment effects of GIM therapy. *Nordic Journal of Music Therapy, 11*, 3–15.

Lathom, W. (1974). Application of Kodály concepts in music therapy. *Journal of Music Therapy, 11*, 13–20.

Layman, D. L., Hussey, D. L., & Laing, S. J. (2002). Music therapy assessment for severely emotionally disturbed children: A pilot study. *Journal of Music Therapy, 39*(3), 164–187.

Lewis, S. C. (1989). *Elder care in occupational therapy.* Thorofare, NJ: SLACK.

Lipe, A. (2001). Guest editorial. Special issue on assessment in music therapy. *Music Therapy Perspectives, 18*(1), 11–12.

Lowey, J. (2000). Music psychotherapy assessment. *Music Therapy Perspectives, 18*(1), 47–58.

Maure-Johnson, E. L. (2006). Assessing the unique needs of hospice patients: A tool for music therapists. *Music Therapy Perspectives, 24*(1), 13–20.

McDonald, R. (1990). *The efficacy of Guided Imagery and Music: A strategy of self concept and blood pressure change among adults with essential hypertension.* Unpublished doctoral dissertation, Walden University, Minneapolis, MN.

McKinney, C. (2007a, October). *Music therapy and psychoneuroimmunology.* Presentation for Music, Medicine, and Wellbeing Series. The University of Iowa, Iowa City.

McKinney, C. (2007b, October). *The psychobiology of the Bonny Method of Guided Imagery and Music.* Presentation for Music, Medicine, and Wellbeing Series. The University of Iowa, Iowa City.

McKinney, C. H., Antoni, M. H., Kumar, M., Tims, F. C., & McCabe, P. M. (1997). Effects of Guided Imagery and Music (GIM) therapy on mood and cortisol in healthy adults. *Health Psychology, 16*, 1–12.

McKinney, C. H., Tims, F. C., Kumar, A., & Kumar, M. (1997). The effect of selected classical music and spontaneous imagery on plasma beta-endorphin. *Journal of Behavior Medicine, 20*, 85–99.

Mead, V. H. (1994). *Dalcroze Eurhythmics in today's music.* Upper Saddle River, NJ: Prentice Hall.

Miller, R. D. (1986). *Problems in hospital law* (5th ed.). Rockville, MD: Aspen.

Nordoff, P., & Robbins, C. (1977). *Creative music therapy.* New York: John Day.

Nordoff, P., & Robbins, C. (1992). *Music therapy for handicapped* children. Bury St. Edmonds, Great Britain: St. Edmundsbury Press.

Nordoff, P., & Robbins, C. (2006). *Creative music therapy: A guide to fostering clinical musicianship.* Gilsum, NH: Barcelona.

Nordoff-Robbins Center for Music Therapy. (2008). *About the practice.* Retrieved May 31, 2008, from http://steinhardt.nyu.edu/music/nordoff/training/

Orff, G. (1974). *The Orff music therapy: Active furthering of the development of the child.* London: Schott.

Orff, G. (1989). *Key concepts in the Orff music therapy.* London: Schott.

Organization of American Kodály Educators. (2004). *Kodály Methods.* Retrieved May 30, 2008, from http://oake.org/php/kodalyphilosophy.php

Ottenbacher, K. J. (1986). *Evaluating clinical change.* Baltimore: Williams and Wilkins.

Parente, R., & Herrmann, D. (1996). *Retraining cognition: Techniques and applications.* Gaithersburg MD: Aspen.

Priestly, M. (1994). *Essays on analytical music therapy.* Phoenixville, PA: Barcelona.

Punwar, A. J. (1988). *Occupational therapy: Principles and practice.* Baltimore: Williams and Wilkins.

Reuer, B. (2007). An entrepreneurial journey: A music therapist's story-personal reflections. *Music Therapy Perspectives, 25*(2), 108–114.

Robbins, C., & Robbins, C. (1998). *Healing heritage: Paul Nordoff exploring the tonal language of music.* Gilsum, NH: Barcelona.

Ruud, E. (1980). *Music therapy and its relationship to current treatment theories.* St. Louis, MO: Magnamusic-Baton.

Sarafino, E. P. (2006). *Health psychology: Biopsychosocial interactions* (5th ed.). Hoboken, NJ: John Wiley & Sons.

Scalenghe, R., & Murphy, K.A. (2000). Music therapy assessment in the managed care environment. *Music Therapy Perspectives, 18*(1), 23–30.

Scovel, M. A., & Gardstrom, S. C. (2002). Music therapy within the context of psychotherapeutic models. In R. F. Unkefer & M. H. Thaut (Eds.), *Music therapy in the treatment of adults with mental disorders* (pp. 117–132). St. Louis, MO: MMB.

Shapiro, N. (2005). Sounds in the world: Multicultural influences in music therapy in clinical practice and training. *Music Therapy Perspectives, 23*(1), 29–35.

Silverman, M. J. (2007). Evaluating current trends in psychiatric music therapy: A descriptive analysis. *Journal of Music Therapy, 44*(4), 388–414.

Standley, J., Johnson, C. M., Robb, S. L., Brownell, M. D., & Kim, S. (2004). Behavioral approach to music therapy. In A. A. Darrow (Ed.), *Introduction to approaches in music therapy* (pp. 15–24). Silver Spring, MD: American Music Therapy Association.

Standley, J. M. (1996a). Documenting developmentally appropriate objectives and benefits of a music therapy program for early intervention: A behavioral analysis. *Music Therapy Perspectives, 14*(2), 87–94.

Standley, J. M. (1996b). A meta-analysis on the effects of music as a reinforcement for education/therapy objectives. *Journal of Research in Music Education, 44*, 105–133.

Stowe, A. (2004). *The application of multicultural principles to music therapy practice: A survey of experts.* Unpublished master's thesis, The University of Iowa, Iowa City.

Strong, A. D. (1983). The Kodály Method applied to special education. *Kodály Envoy, 9*, 3–8.

Sturmey, P. (2002). Mental retardation and concurrent psychiatric disorder: Assessment and treatment. *Current Opinion in Psychiatry, 15*(5), 489–495.

Sue, D. W., Arredondo, P., & McDavis, R. J. (1992). Multicultural counseling competencies and standards: A call to the profession. *Journal of Multicultural Counseling and Development, 20*, 64–88.

Sulzer-Azaroff, B., & Mayer, R. (1991). *Behavior analysis for lasting change.* Fort Worth, TX: Holt, Reinhart & Winston.

Thaut, M. H. (2005). *Rhythm, music, and the brain.* New York: Taylor & Francis.

Toppozada, M. R. (1995). Multicultural training for music therapists: An examination of current issues based on a national survey of professional music therapists. *Journal of Music Therapy, 32*(2), 65–90.

Unkefer, R. F., & Thaut, M. H. (2002). *Music therapy in the treatment of adults with mental disorders: Theoretical basis and clinical interventions.* St. Louis, MO: MMB Music.

Valentino, R. E. (2006). Attitudes toward cross-cultural empathy in music therapy. *Music Therapy Perspectives, 24*(2), 108–114.

Voigt, M. (1999). Orff music therapy with multi-handicapped children. In T. Wigram & J. De Backer (Eds.), *Clinical applications of music therapy: Developmental disability, paediatrics and neurology.* London: Jessica Kingsley.

Wasserman, N., Plutchik, R., Deutsch, R., & Takemoto, Y. (1973). A music therapy evaluation scale and its clinical applications to mentally retarded adult patients. *Journal of Music Therapy, 10*, 64–77.

Webster's New World College Dictionary (4th ed.) (2005).Cleveland, OH: Wiley.

Wells, N. F. (1988). An individual music therapy assessment procedure for emotionally disturbed young adolescents. *Arts in Psychotherapy, 15*, 47–54.

Wigram, T. (2001) A method of music therapy assessment for the diagnosis of autism and communication disorders in children. *Music Therapy Perspectives, 18*(1), 13–22.

Wilhelm, K. (2004). Music therapy and private practice: Recommendations on financial viability and marketing. *Music Therapy Perspectives, 22*(2), 68–83.

Wilson, G. T., O'Leary, K. D., Nathan, P. E., & Clark, L. A. (1996). *Abnormal psychology: Integrating Perspectives Test Bank.* Columbus, OH: Allyn and Bacon.

York, E. (1994). The development of a quantitative music skills test for patients with Alzheimer's disease. *Journal of Music Therapy, 31,* 280–296.

CHAPTER 16

THE ROLE OF RESEARCH IN MUSIC THERAPY

Kate E. Gfeller
William B. Davis
Michael H. Thaut
Michele Forinash

CHAPTER OUTLINE

INTRODUCTION TO RESEARCH IN MUSIC THERAPY
THE VALUE OF RESEARCH
DEFINITION OF RESEARCH
HOW RESEARCH CAN INFLUENCE MUSIC THERAPY PRACTICE
TYPES OF RESEARCH
    Descriptive Research
    Experimental Research
    Historical Research
    Qualitative Research
CURRENT STATUS OF RESEARCH IN THE PROFESSION

INTRODUCTION TO RESEARCH IN MUSIC THERAPY

The word *research* may bring to mind mysterious scientists in remote, sterile laboratories filled with test tubes and cages of white rats. As the white-coated researchers peer through microscopes, they mumble polysyllabic formulas for obscure chemical reactions. This image shrouds research in a "white coat" of isolation and obscurity. But in reality, research is often related to basic events of everyday life. Why do leaves turn different colors in the fall? What causes heart attacks? How do birds find their winter homes during migration? More relevant to the field of music therapy, we ask questions about how music affects moods, attitudes, or behaviors. For example, you might wonder why music at a horror movie makes us feel anxious, or why some people get teary-eyed when they listen to a special song.

The effect of music on mood and behavior has long been a subject of curiosity. In ancient times, people believed that music was a magical force that could affect how we think, feel, and act. Modern scientists still believe that music influences human behavior; however, we no longer credit its effects to supernatural powers. Rather, as a result of scientific inquiries, we have identified many characteristics of music that influence social, physiological, and psychological response (Juslin & Sloboda, 2001).

Intellectual curiosity alone has motivated extensive inquiry into musical response. This is the basis for the field known as Psychology of Music. Music therapists are interested not only in basic musical response, but also in applied research regarding therapeutic uses of music. As health care providers, music therapists serve individuals with specific physical, psychological, and social needs. It is the ethical responsibility of the therapist to provide the most effective and efficient care possible. To do so, the therapist compares possible interventions and evaluates each one for its relative merit. Systematic research plays an important role in this process. This chapter will introduce you to some important research concepts and types of research commonly used in music therapy.

THE VALUE OF RESEARCH

Music therapists have formally acknowledged the value of research for many years. In 1964, the National Association for Music Therapy (NAMT) established the *Journal of Music Therapy*, a publication dedicated to the dissemination of current research and clinical practice (Solomon, 1984). In 1969, the Constitutional Bylaws of NAMT were expanded to state that the basic purpose of NAMT was the advancement of training and research in the music therapy profession (National Association for Music Therapy, Article II, *Constitution and Bylaws,* 1969). For over five decades, research studies have been reported regularly at professional meetings and in journals of music therapy organizations (NAMT, AAMT, AMTA; see Chapter 2). According to Duerksen (1968), the "advancement of knowledge and practice in music therapy depends on the quality of the research performed and used by its practitioners." That statement is as true today as it was in 1968.

DEFINITION OF RESEARCH

Research may be defined as a goal-directed process of seeking specific answers to specific questions in an organized and reliable way (Payton, 1994). Research produces new knowledge and involves the collection, analysis, and interpretation of data. When done properly, research helps to explain and predict behavior. The ultimate benefit within our field is to assist the music therapist in selecting the most useful treatment for his or her clients.

HOW RESEARCH CAN INFLUENCE MUSIC THERAPY PRACTICE

There are three ways in which research can influence music therapy practice. First, because music is the therapeutic medium through which music therapists work, the clinician needs to understand normal reactions to musical stimuli. The therapist's use of music should take into account the many cultural, physiological, and psychological aspects of musical response. An understanding of normal musical response assists the therapist in selecting appropriate music for a given situation.

Second, music therapists need to evaluate the effectiveness of specific interventions with different types of disorders. Just as doctors prescribe medicine based on knowledge about how certain diseases react to different chemicals, the music therapist should select an intervention based on reliable information regarding how people with a particular disorder typically respond to specific applications of music and music activity.

Finally, research findings help to refine theories about music therapy practice. According to Webster's Dictionary, a theory is a systematic statement of principles that guides and acts as a rationale for any given discipline. These principles are the basis for practical actions (Feder & Feder, 1998). Music therapists base their clinical practice on theories, or beliefs, about how music influences behavior. Over the years, research findings have differentially supported, refuted, and refined various commonly held views about music therapy practice.

For example, one theory states that music is a unique stimulus that is intrinsically (for its own sake) enjoyable, which can therefore serve as an effective reinforcement or reward to modify behavior. This theory likely arose from clinical observations of many therapists who noted that clients often became more alert or cooperative when allowed to hear or play music. A number of research studies have since supported the theory that music can be an effective reinforcement. One such study by Hanser (1974) showed that children with behavioral disorders, who showed a high incidence of disruptive behavior in a classroom, reduced their interruptions when rewarded with the opportunity to listen to their favorite musical selections.

Subsequent studies, however, have helped music therapists to refine this theory. In a study of music therapy for persons with multiple disabilities, Wolfe (1980) investigated the use of music as a reward to encourage control of neck muscles. The participants in this study, due to their physical disability (cerebral palsy), had difficulty holding their heads erect, which interfered with eye contact, attending skills, and interpersonal interaction. Wolfe wanted to find out if music would serve as a reinforcement to control neck muscles. Participants wore a special head device (somewhat like a helmet with earphones) that allowed them to listen to music as long as the head was held erect. If the chin dropped, the music was stopped. As predicted, some individuals did indeed strive to maintain head and neck control; we would surmise that they made this effort because they enjoyed hearing the music. Interestingly, other participants in the study made little or no effort to hold their heads erect, so there was silence rather than music. These individuals did not respond in the predicted manner, that is, controlling their neck muscles in order to receive the reinforcement of listening to music. Why might this outcome have occurred?

The author noted that several of the participants who failed to establish erect head posture lived in a care facility that was often noisy and filled with unpleasant sounds. Wolfe hypothesized that some individuals may have found silence a novel relief and preferred quiet more than hearing music. It is also possible that the particular musical selection used in the study was not enjoyable to some of the participants. Wolfe's objective inquiry pointed out that music may not be intrinsically rewarding in every instance. Music may be more or less effective as a reinforcement in different situations and under different conditions. This is just one example of how music therapists, through research, continue to challenge their methods of practice, refining and improving interventions.

In summary, demonstrating the effectiveness of music therapy techniques is essential. It is accomplished by carefully accumulating data that support a theory or show its limitations. As therapists, we must be able to show that our interventions for specific populations and clinical environments produce beneficial results. Lacking such documentation, the music therapy profession risks skepticism from our clients and other health care professionals (Ottenbacher, 1986).

Research is the most important tool that we have to validate the music therapy profession. Fortunately, there are many types of research available. Let us consider a hypothetical clinical situation in which research can influence music therapy practice.

> Jamal is a music therapist working in a rehabilitation center. At a team meeting, the physical therapist has expressed concern about a group of elderly patients who have gait irregularity (uneven walking patterns) as a result of strokes. The physical therapist would like to use gait training to improve gait irregularities. Unfortunately, the group as a whole has poor tolerance for physical discomfort and lacks motivation to maintain regular exercise. Jamal knows that some of these patients will endure a long, difficult walk down the corridor in order to attend music therapy sessions in the day room. He wonders whether music might be incorporated into rehabilitation plans to improve motivation. As he ponders this problem, a number of questions come to mind. Has music ever proven effective for rehabilitation of gait disorders? If so, what kind of music would be best? Are there particular techniques that can improve therapy efficiency or effectiveness?

Jamal could answer some of these questions through a long process of trial and error. However, he can make more intelligent choices if he considers the research findings reported by others who have asked similar questions. Where can he find this information?

A common practice among researchers is to report the results of their experiments in professional publications, such as the *Journal of Music Therapy* (JMT). Jamal could visit the library or use the Internet to determine if there are published studies in JMT related to his area of interest. A second approach is to attend professional meetings, such as the American Music Therapy Association's annual national conference, where research papers are presented that detail the latest findings. Jamal may find one or more presentations that will be helpful in designing his treatment plan. He might also find articles using music as therapy that are sometimes published in journals of other health professions (such as the second research study presented later in this chapter, which is reported in the journal *Neurorehabilitation and Neural Repair*). Through these methods of distributing research results, music therapists can benefit from the work of others.

TYPES OF RESEARCH

There are many types of research, and no single approach is inherently superior. You might compare the use of different research methods to the use of various tools in household repair. To hang a picture, you are most likely to use a hammer, nails, and a level. If you are trying to shut off a leaky valve, however, then a wrench, not a hammer, is likely to be the tool of choice. Similarly, different types of research methods are used in order to answer different types of questions.

In this portion of the chapter, we present just a few of the many types of research that provide valuable information for music therapists. We will describe the sorts of questions addressed by each type of research, as well as associated methods. In order to illustrate some of the characteristics of several commonly used categories of research, we will present and describe existing published articles from the music therapy literature.

Because this is an introductory text book, this chapter will include only four types of research commonly found within music therapy journals: descriptive research, experimental research, historical research, and qualitative research. Additional types of research and in-depth analysis of research methods can be found in textbooks and courses about research methods.

Descriptive Research

Descriptive research, as its name implies, *describes* "what currently exists." Most likely, you have come across findings from this kind of research in everyday life. For example, when a Web site (Duke University Medical Center, 2006) reports that frequent bouts of depression, anxiety, hostility, and anger are found among persons with heart disease, they are reporting descriptive research. An article in *USA Today* (Findlay, 2003), reporting that 65% of U.S. adults are now overweight or obese, is based upon descriptive research.

Descriptive research normally uses **quantitative** data—that is, numerical information. The results in descriptive research might be reported as percent, **rank**, or amounts. Descriptive research usually focuses on typical results for relatively large groups of people, as opposed to describing the experiences of individuals. Gathering data from as many people as possible improves the generalizability of the results. **Generalizability** refers to the extent to which the results of a study will be applicable to other similar types of people not directly tested in the study. For example, a study of the musical preferences of 100,000 senior citizens in the United States would be more generalizable to (likely to reflect the preferences of) other older adults in the U.S. than a study based upon the responses of only 15 older adults (who may have unique tastes specific to one region or cultural subgroup).

In music therapy, descriptive research is used to answer questions such as where music therapists work, what methods they use most frequently, or what kinds of music are preferred by different types of clients. Descriptive research studies usually have a similar organizational structure with specific components, and they contain similar types of information. Just as shelves or bins that organize space can help you to find food quickly in your refrigerator or articles of clothing in your closet, the organizational structure of a descriptive research article helps you to dig out specific kinds of information quickly.

In order for you to better understand the typical structure and methods used in descriptive research, we have obtained permission to reprint an article that was published in the *Journal of Music Therapy* in 1991. The authors (Darrow and Gfeller, whom you may recognize as the authors of Chapter 13) conducted this descriptive research in order to learn about how extensively and how effectively students who are deaf or hard-of-hearing (d/hh) are included in regular music classes. You may find it helpful to refer back to Chapter 13 (which covers hearing losses) or Chapter 14 (which covers special education) if you run across technical terms or concepts about which you are unsure.

As you read this article, look for (1) the specific research questions asked by the authors, (2) what methods they used to answer these questions, and (3) what they discovered. In addition, it is important to learn some of the common components (e.g., title, abstract, methods, results, etc.) of research articles. We have highlighted and will later describe some of the important parts of the following article that are commonly found in descriptive and experimental research studies. Some of these components appear in other types of research as well.

Journal of Music Therapy, XXVIII (1), 1991, 23-29
© 1991 by the National Association for Music Therapy, Inc.

PUBLICATION INFORMATION
TITLE OF ARTICLE

A Study of Public School Music Programs Mainstreaming Hearing Impaired Students

AUTHOR(S) AND AFFILIATION

Alice-Ann Darrow
Kate Gfeller

The University of Kansas
The University of Iowa

ABSTRACT

The purposes of this study were to (a) examine the status of public school music instruction for hearing impaired students, and (b) examine the factors that contribute to the successful mainstreaming of hearing impaired students in the regular music classroom. A questionnaire was developed with items concerning demographic information, educational preparation, extent of instructional and administrative support, the extent to which musical and nonmusical goals are set by music educators, factors related to the successful mainstreaming of hearing impaired students, obstructions to mainstreaming, and activities and curricula successfully implemented in mainstreaming programs. Results of the study revealed the following: (a) more than half of all hearing impaired students attend regular music classes; (b) of those students not mainstreamed, less than half receive no music education in the self-contained classroom or otherwise; (c) many music educators are lacking in the educational preparation necessary for teaching hearing impaired students; (d) important instructional or administrative support is often not available; (e) several factors, such as lack of appropriate curricula or poor communication with other professionals, and identified as obstructions to the successful mainstreaming of hearing impaired students; (f) only 35% of the respondents reported that they have the same objectives for hearing impaired students as for normal hearing students; and (g) methodologies, materials, and activities were identified that were helpful in integrating hearing impaired students into the regular music classroom. Implications for public school music educators are cited.

INTRODUCTION AND REVIEW OF LITERATURE

Educational opportunities for hearing impaired children in regular public schools have become widespread only in recent years. Today, more than 60% of hearing impaired children in the United States attend local public schools; nearly 45% of these students are mainstreamed into the regular classroom to some degree (Moores, 1987; Quigley & Paul, 1986). Many of these students attend special classes such as music with their normal hearing peers. Music education has long been advocated for hearing impaired students as a means of self-expression and cultural awareness as well as for rehabilitative purposes. The history of music education for the hearing impaired extends nearly 150 years (Darrow & Heller, 1985; Solomon, 1980). Until recently, however, music programs were in self-contained classrooms in residential schools for the deaf, where the problems of mainstreaming did not exist.

A study by Gfeller, Darrow, and Hedden (1990) found that hearing impaired students, along with behaviorally or emotionally handicapped students, were perceived by music educators to be the most difficult exceptional student populations to mainstream into the music classroom. This is not surprising, considering the ear is the sensory channel through which music is most often perceived. Music educators' wariness in mainstreaming hearing impaired students is due not only to the nature of the impairment, but also to the lack of specialized information required to adapt procedures which accommodate the learning needs of the hearing impaired child.

A report to the President and Congress of the United States by The National Commission on Education of the Deaf (1988) stated:

> Although a growing percentage of deaf students are being educated in regular classroom settings to some extent, teachers often have no prior experience in teaching them. (p. 102)

This lack of preparation is unfortunate since research by Stephens and Braun (1980) indicates that teachers who had taken courses in special education were more willing to accept handicapped children into their classes than were teachers who had not taken such studies. Information regarding the disability was found to be positively related to their willingness to integrate handicapped children into their classroom.

In particular, the learning characteristics and communication style of hearing impaired children require specialized skills and preparation (Heward & Orlansky, 1988), such as speech and hearing science, audiology, aural habilitation, manual and oral communication methods, and the impact of hearing loss on speech and language development. Without this teacher preparation, the music educator is often at a loss concerning appropriate instructional methods. While formal instruction in the aforementioned areas is not always practical for music educators, knowledge of mainstreaming practices found to be useful by other music educators could be of considerable value.

A number of studies have examined mainstreaming practices for children with varying exceptionalities in the music classroom, or of hearing impaired children in the regular classroom. No studies could be found that specifically address the mainstreaming practices of hearing impaired students into the public school music classroom. Several related studies, however, examined the scope and sequence of music programs in residential and day school educational programs for hearing impaired students. These studies (Ford & Shroyer, 1987; Shroyer & Ford, 1986; Spitzer, 1984) investigated the extent to which day and residential programs for the hearing impaired offer music programs and the methods and objectives most commonly employed in these programs. Results of these studies revealed that only a little over half of these residential and day school programs offered music. The most commonly cited reason was lack of a qualified teacher. Other findings included a lack of participation by many students in schools where music was offered, and program objectives that were commonly concerned with speech improvement as well as the development of music concepts; in addition, music teachers often had degrees in academic areas other than music and often had additional teaching responsibilities other than music. While a review of these studies is helpful, residential and day school music programs commonly have self-contained classrooms for hearing impaired students, and are therefore rarely concerned with the mainstreaming accommodations that must be made in the regular music classroom.

Several research studies (Craig, Salem, & Craig, 1976; Karchmer & Trybus, 1977; Rawlings & Trybus, 1978) have examined the extent to which hearing impaired students are mainstreamed into the regular classroom and the distribution of hearing impaired students in different types of educational programs. Partial integration was found to be the most common type of mainstreaming program, with very few hearing impaired students mainstreamed on a full-time basis. Mainstreamed programs enroll two to five times as many postlingually hearing impaired students as other educational programs. Academics are most often taught in the self-contained classroom; consequently, hearing impaired students are usually mainstreamed into special or elective classes such as music, art, and physical education.

Unfortunately for music educators and others, very few studies have examined the effects of mainstreaming on the education of hearing impaired students. Salem and Herward (1978) found that residential school enrollments have greatly decreased, presumably because of recent mainstreaming trends. Pflaster (1980) examined factors that contribute to the placement decisions and academic success of hearing impaired students; important factors identified included: (a) highly developed oral skills; (b) high levels of motivation; (c) a high degree of ability to use spoken and written language, including paraphrasing, idiomatic expressions, and the use of varying sentence structure; (d) artistic and synthetic abilities; and (e) involved family members.

The severe communication problems of many hearing impaired students continue to make mainstreaming decisions difficult for all educators. Past studies (Atterbury, 1986; Gfeller, Darrow, & Hedden, 1990; Gilbert & Asmus, 1981) which examined the mainstreaming practices of children with varying handicaps into music found that important factors included grade level taught, area of music instruction (choral, instrumental, or general), availability of instructional support, educational preparation of the music educator, and involvement of music educators in mainstreaming decisions.

Because hearing impairments pose unique educational problems in music, the present study focused on those students within the mainstreamed music class. The purposes of this study were to (a) examine the status of public school music instruction for mainstreamed hearing impaired students, and (b) examine factors which contribute to the successful mainstreaming of hearing impaired students in the regular music classroom. The following research questions were formulated:

1.   To what extent are hearing impaired public school students mainstreamed into music classes with their normal hearing peers?
2.   If hearing impaired students are not mainstreamed into regular programs, are self-contained programs provided as an alternative?
3.   To what extent are music educators prepared to work with hearing impaired students in the mainstreamed music classroom?
4.   To what extent is support available from deaf education or special education staff?
5.   Which factors most frequently obstruct effective music education for hearing impaired students?
6.   What are the primary objectives of the music program? Are they the same for both hearing and hearing impaired students?
7.   Which teaching materials and/or methodologies have been most helpful in integrating hearing impaired students into the music classroom?

Method

A questionnaire was developed for distribution to music educators who have hearing impaired students mainstreamed in their regular music classes. Because the intent of the study was to focus on the quality, extent, and nature of student participation in the mainstream, teachers were asked to exclude any comments on music education practices used specifically in self-contained classes comprised of only hearing impaired students.

Development of the Questionnaire

Questionnaire items were designed to address the research questions. These items were developed by: (a) adapting questions used in a previous study by the authors concerned with the mainstreaming practices of exceptional children; (b) examining the suitability of items from other extant questionnaires on music education for hearing impaired students in the self-contained classroom; (c) reviewing methodological and experimental articles concerned with the music capabilities of hearing impaired children and the educational methods commonly used with them; (d) noting curricular objectives listed in the MENC document, *The School Music Program: Description and Standards;* and (e) drawing on the professional experiences of the authors and their colleagues in public schools and rehabilitation settings.

Questionnaire items fell into the following categories: demographic information on age group and area of music instruction; enrollment figures of hearing impaired students, both in the school and in the music program; information concerning placement practices; music teacher preparation for working with hearing impaired students; sources of support; types and success of various activities used in the music classroom; obstacles which obstruct the musical participation of hearing impaired students; instructional objectives; and particular techniques and methods that facilitate music education for hearing impaired students.

The questionnaire was refined using nine judges who were professionals in music education, deaf education/ speech pathology, and music therapy. The panel of judges all had extensive training and field experience with hearing impaired students. Judges were asked to critique items for clarity, format, and relevance to the research questions. Adjustments were made and a final form was sent to music educators via the directors of deaf education in school districts representing all 50 states.

Procedure

Three hundred surveys were sent to a stratified random sample of directors of deaf education programs included in a national list published annually in the April issue of the *American Annals of the Deaf.* Because the names of specific music educators were unavailable, directors of deaf education programs were asked to send the surveys to the attention of the music teacher at schools where hearing impaired students were enrolled. Each director was contacted by phone prior to receiving the surveys. A second survey was sent to nonrespondents within 2 weeks of the return date of the initial survey. Directors of the deaf education programs were again contacted by phone prior to the mailing of follow-up surveys to nonrespondents. Because of the inability to contact the individual teachers and the need to process the survey through an intermediary source, a modest 32% return rate was achieved. Nevertheless, valuable information was secured concerning the characteristics of various public school music education programs mainstreaming hearing impaired students.

Results

Eighty-six percent of the surveys returned were sent by music educators. Table 1 provided a breakdown of specialty areas and age groups taught by the music educators. The remaining surveys were completed by deaf education staff who reported that their students do not attend music, or that music programs are not available in their schools or to their students.

Respondents indicated the number of hearing impaired students in their school systems with totals ranging from 1 to 91. Those enrolled in music per school system ranged in "umber from none to as many as 91.

The following data are related to the research questions postulated for this study:

1. To what extent are hearing impaired students in public schools mainstreamed into music classes with their normal hearing peers?

Fifty-two percent of the hearing impaired students in responding school systems attend regular music classes, leading to the next research question which addressed the music education of those not attending music with their normal hearing peers.

2. If hearing impaired students are not mainstreamed into regular programs, are self-contained programs provided as an alternative?

Nearly half of the schools (47%) offer no self-contained music classes for hearing impaired students. Another 26% responded that self-contained classes are offered for all hearing impaired students, and 8% responded that some of the students have self-contained classes in music. A small percentage of music educators (8%) indicated that self-contained programs were not considered an option, since mainstreaming was expected for all students.

TABLE 1
Demographic Information on Respondents

Area of Instruction	Percentage*	Grade Groups	Percentage
General music	60%	K-6	52.5%
Vocal music	25%	7-12	7.5%
Instrumental music	9%	6-8	10%
Other (deaf education staff)	14%	9-12	7.5%
		K-5	7.5%
		K-12	2.5%
		4-6	2.5%
		10-12	2.5%
		K-4	2.5%
		1-6	2.5%
		K-8	1%
		4-5	1%
		7-8	1%
		1-5	1%

*Exceeds 100% because several music educators indicated more than one primary area of instruction.

Twenty-three percent of the students with hearing impairments receive no music education. The open-ended responses explaining their exclusion from music were analyzed and grouped into the following types of responses: no music is available in the district; no music programs appropriate for hearing impaired students are available; music is an elective (in secondary education programs) and not of interest to the students; there is lack of time for music; and hearing impaired students are preschool age and too young for elementary school music programs.

The placement of hearing impaired students in the mainstream as opposed to the self-contained classroom or exclusion from music is seldom within the control of the music educator. Only 31% of the music specialists indicated that they are consulted regarding placement in music. Twenty-one percent are consulted regarding the Individualized Education Program (IEP), and only 15% actually participate in team meetings.

3. To what extent are music educators prepared to work with hearing impaired students in the mainstreamed music class- room?

TABLE 2
Teacher Preparation for Working with Hearing Impaired Students

Type of Preparation	Percentage
Know basic sign language	19%
Know a few signs	31%
Rely on an interpreter	42%
Read articles, books on adapting music	43.5%
Attend workshop, clinics	21%
University instruction	16%
Solicit suggestions from teachers of the hearing impaired	68%
Rely on trial and error	58%

Table 2 summarizes the types of preparation music educators have for working with hearing impaired students. Only 19% know basic sign language, while 68% of the hearing impaired students use sign as well as speech for communication purposes. This implies that most music educators must rely heavily on the services of an interpreter for music instruction.

4. To what extent is support available from deaf education or special education staff?

The greater majority of music educators report the deaf education teacher as their primary source of consultation (85%). Speech pathologists (74%), audiologists (35%), interpreters (52%), itinerant teachers of the deaf (21%). and supervisors of deaf education (29%) also provide consultation services. In only a few schools (6%) are music therapists available for consultation. Respondents reported little support on the part of administrators in assuring effective mainstreaming accommodations in the music classroom. Teachers report the provision of a sign language interpreter (47%) as the most common source of support. A much smaller percentage have been provided with inservice about hearing impairments (26%) or on adapting music for hearing impaired students (8%). Only one of the teachers reported any provision of extra planning time, and only three reported support for continuing education to help them better serve these special needs students.

5. Which factors most frequently obstruct effective music education for hearing impaired students?

TABLE 3

Rank Order of Factors which Obstruct Effective Music Education for Students with Hearing Impairments

Factors	Rank Order
Lack of appropriate materials, equipment, and/or specialized curriculum for hearing-impaired students in music	1
Lack of knowledge specific to the disability of hearing impairment	2
Lack of or poor communication with teachers of the hearing impaired	3
Limited musical abilities that hearing impaired students demonstrate in class	4
Lack of additional planning time to prepare for students with special needs	5
Poor or limited communication between the normal hearing and hearing impaired students in the classroom	6
Lack of support staff (teacher's aide or interpreter)	7
Lack of cooperation from other professionals	8

Table 3 indicates the rank order (from most to least) of those factors perceived as obstructing effective music education for hearing impaired students. Factors ranked first, second, and third in order were, "lack of appropriate materials, equipment, and/or specialized curriculum for hearing impaired students in music," "lack of knowledge specific to the disability of hearing impairment," and "lack of or poor communication with teachers of the hearing impaired."

6. What are the primary objectives of the music program? Are they the same for both hearing and hearing impaired students?

Only 81% of the music educators responded to the items concerning classroom objectives. Of those respondents, 32% reported that they have the same objectives for hearing impaired students as for normal hearing students, while 12% adapt their objectives for hearing impaired students. Fifty percent reported that they adapt some objectives and maintain other objectives as they are for normal hearing students.

All respondents indicated that musical skills and knowledge are important objectives, and at least 54% indicated that they do include nonmusical secondary objectives for their hearing impaired students. Table 4 indicates a breakdown of objectives by program emphasis.

TABLE 4
Music Education Objectives for Hearing Impaired Students

Objectives	Percentage*r
Same as those for normal hearing students	32%
Adapted for hearing impaired students	12%
Combination of similar and adapted objectives	50%
Strictly musical	12%
Strictly nonmusical	0%
Primarily musical, with some nonmusical	54%
Primarily nonmusical, with some musical	6%
Evenly distributed between music and nonmusical	22%

*Response represents 81% of the music educators in the sample.

Table 5 indicates that hearing impaired students participate in a wide variety of musical activities: singing, playing instruments, movement activities, music listening, and learning music facts being the most common. However, these activities are not equally successful for hearing impaired students, as responses to research Question 7 indicate.

7. Which teaching materials and/or methodologies have been most helpful in integrating hearing impaired students into the music classroom?

Table 6 indicates the ranking of music activities perceived as most successful to least successful. Twenty-seven percent of the music educators indicated that, of traditional music education methodology, Orff techniques were the most successful with hearing impaired students. Other cited methodologies were Kodaly and Dalcroze; no existing curriculum seems to be widely accepted.

TABLE 5
Categories of Activities in which Hearing Impaired Students Participate

Categories	Percentage*
Singing	95.5%
Playing instruments	91%
Listening to music	87%
Reading musical notation	67%
Composition and improvisation	29%
Movement	87%
Learning music facts	84%

* Item responses given by 72.5% of the music educators.

Table 6

Rank Order of Activities Perceived by Music Educators as Successful for Hearing Impaired Students

Activities	Rank Order (Most Successful to Least Successful)
Movement	1
Playing instruments	2
Singing	3
Learning musical facts	4
Reading music	5
Listening to music	6
Composition and improvisation	7

In addition to traditional methodology, teachers indicated the following adaptations as beneficial: careful selection of instruments (i.e., low-frequency instruments, instruments with vibrotactile surfaces, percussive instruments), sign singing, careful physical placement of the student (to facilitate speech reading and imitation), rhythm and movement activities, extensive use of visual aids, peer assistance, and use of special auditory trainers or amplification systems, interpreters, and Kodaly hand signs.

Discussion

In February 1988, the National Commission on the Education of the Deaf reported to the President and Congress of the United States that:

> Of the children thus "mainstreamed," only about half actually experience any true integration, even on a part-time basis. Due to a lack of understanding of the nature and diversity of hearing impairment, the unique communicative, linguistic and social needs of the deaf child have seldom been met appropriately, particularly in the mainstream setting. (p. 9)

This report on the status of the education of the deaf holds true not only in academics, but in arts education as well. The purposes of this study were to: (a) examine the status of music instruction for mainstreamed hearing impaired students, and (b) examine the factors that contribute to the successful mainstreaming of hearing impaired students in public school music programs.

Several of the recommendations from the National Commission were related to the need for teacher training. Results from the present study indicate a lack of appropriate skills and training by music educators of hearing impaired students. The primary source of preparation reported was the solicitation of suggestions from classroom teachers of the deaf (Table 2); yet, "lack of or poor communication with teachers of the hearing impaired" was ranked third among factors which obstruct effective music education (Table 3). The question then obviously arises as to the quality and quantity of assistance provided by classroom teachers of the deaf. Lack of communication is often due to the fact that many deaf educators are itinerant, visiting some schools only once a week, which allows little time for consultation with the music educator. In addition, normal school scheduling unfortunately allows little time for communication among professionals working with exceptional children.

Over 50% of the respondents rely on trial and error, which corroborates the lack of procedures and structured curriculum appropriate for hearing impaired students reported in Table 3. Flexibility and trial and error will undoubtedly continue to be important coping mechanisms for music educators; however, it would seem that respondents are eager and motivated to learn more since 43% of the respondents indicated that they had read articles or other material on adapting music. Related reading was probably independent of course assignments, since only 16% of the respondents reported any university instruction in deaf education.

Given the data that 68% of students use bath sign or sign and speech, it is unfortunate that so few music educators have a working knowledge of sign language. Certainly the interpreter provides a useful service here;

however, instruction must go through the usual channels of translation, which has two major disadvantages: (a) additional class time must be spent duplicating the message; and (b) the interpreter, for a variety of reasons, may unwittingly misconstrue the true intent of the message. Several important advantages of speaking the language of the child are: (a) acknowledged acceptance of the child and his/her language, (b) greater facility in developing rapport, and (c) increased opportunity for personal communication. Manual communication courses are a part of all education programs for deaf educators except for the very few programs which strictly emphasize oral methods. Prior research has indicated that teacher preparation, not merely exposure to exceptional students, results in satisfactory mainstreaming practices (Gfeller, Darrow, & Hedden, 1990; Stephens & Braun, 1980).

The factor ranked fourth among those obstructing effective music education for students with hearing impairments was "limited musical abilities which hearing impaired students demonstrate in class." Much of the research in the perception and performance of music, however, indicates that the skills of hearing impaired students are not significantly different from their hearing peers if appropriate and/or supplementary procedures are utilized (Darrow, 1987, 1989a, 1989b; Darrow & Goll, 1989).

Another issue which appears to influence the effectiveness of mainstreaming is the extent of administrative support for instructional purposes. Data in Tables 2 and 3 indicate limited resources in terms of extra time for planning and consultation, provision of teacher's aides, interpreters, and inservice. According to PL 94-142, a student should be mainstreamed only if the regular classroom setting provides adequate educational support.

Table 4 indicates a lack of consensus in determining appropriate educational objectives for hearing impaired students in the music classroom. The lower response rate on questions concerning instructional objectives may also reflect possible lack of direction or uncertainty concerning these special needs students. To what extent should musical as opposed to nonmusical objectives be emphasized when working with hearing impaired students? Unfortunately, if this question has not been addressed, it is difficult not only to plan instructional units, but also to evaluate achievement or the extent to which mainstreaming has been successful. Thirty-two percent of the respondents indicated that music education objectives for hearing impaired students were the same as those for normal hearing students. For these teachers, instruction closely befits the true spirit of mainstreaming. Most likely, it is their classroom procedures, rather than their instructional objectives, that require adapting. While most educators do not object to adapting music objectives for special students when necessary, the question raised by many music educators is whether they should be expected to adapt objectives in the regular music classroom.

Considering the unique vocal quality of most hearing impaired singers and the extant research on the musical aptitude of hearing impaired children that indicates stronger rhythmic skills than tonal skills (Darrow, 1987), it is interesting to note that the type of activity most often reported was singing. This may reflect the typical activity of group singing common in general music classes and the fact that sign singing has received increased attention in the last several years. Frequent references to other general music activities and Orff methodology raise the question of whether hearing impaired students can find a meaningful place in middle or secondary music programs that rely heavily on music performance. Several secondary teachers indicated that no music curricula are available for hearing impaired students. Other deaf education teachers indicated that music was an elective at the secondary level and was not chosen by their students.

Reference to Orff methodology is not particularly surprising given its inherent visual, imitative, and rhythmic aspects. More consistent exploitation of these methodological strengths could easily transfer to other activities, thus reinforcing the learning styles and participation of hearing impaired students.

This study points to several key areas that influence the success of mainstreaming hearing impaired students in the music classroom: (a) the need for clearly identified educational objectives, (b) the need for adequate educational preparation of teachers, and (c) the need for instructional support in the classroom and in curriculum planning. It is important that teachers responsible for the music education of hearing impaired students take the initiative in supplementing their education by attending workshops or perhaps enrolling in additional college courses related to the field of deaf education. Hearing impairment is a low incidence handicap; therefore, for some music educators with few hearing impaired students, additional training may not be considered to be cost effective or time efficient. These educators could possibly consolidate the hearing impaired student populations from several schools and entrust their music instruction to a music educator or music therapist with a special interest in deaf education.

It is also important that music educators in turn educate their administrators regarding the unique educational needs of hearing impaired students as well as request inservice and instructional support. This can best be accomplished by communicating to administrators clearly defined music objectives for hearing impaired students and the necessary assistance required to meet these objectives. Such initiatives will not only improve and further the music education of hearing impaired students, but can also alleviate many of the problems faced by music educators mainstreaming hearing impaired students.

References

Atterbury, B. (1986). A survey of present mainstreaming practices in the Southern United States. *Journal of Music Therapy, 23*, 202-207.

Craig, W., Salem, J., & Craig, H. (1976). Mainstreaming and partial integration of deaf with hearing students. *American Annals of the Deaf, 121*, 63-68.

Darrow, A. A. (1987). An investigative study: The effect of hearing impairment on the music aptitude of young children. *Journal of Music Therapy, 24*, 88-96

Darrow, A. A. (1989a) *Comparison of rhythmic performances by normal hearing children and mainstreamed hearing-impaired children.* Unpublished paper, The University of Kansas.

Darrow, A. A. (1989b). The effect of adjusted frequency response on hearing impaired children's vocal reproduction accuracy *Journal of Music Therapy, 27*, 24-33.

Darrow, A. A.. & Goll. H. (1989). The effect of vibrotactile stimuli on the recognition of rhythmic change by hearing impaired children. *Journal of Music Therapy, 26*, 115-124.

Darrow, A. A., & Heller, G N. (1985). Early advocates of music education for the hearing impaired: William Wolcott Turner and David Ely Bartlett. *Journal of Research in Music Education, 33*, 269-279.

Ford, T. A., & Shroyer, E. H. (1987). Survey of music teachers in residential and day programs for hearing-impaired students. *Journal of the International Association of Music for the Handicapped, 3*. 16-25.

Gfeller, K., Darrow, A. A., & Hedden, S. K. (1990). On the ten-year anniversary of P.L. 94-142: The perceived status of mainstreaming among music educators in the states of Iowa and Kansas. *Journal of Research in Music Educatkm, 38,* 90-101.

Gilbert. J. P., & Asmus, E. P. (1981). Mainstreaming: Music educators' participation and professional needs. *Journal of Research in Music Education, 25*, 283-289.

Heward, W. L., & Orlansky, M. D. (1988). *Exceptional children.* Columbus, OH: Merrill Publishing Company.

Karchmer, M., & Trybus, R. (1977). *Who are the deaf children in the "mainstream" program?* Series R, No. 4. Office of Demographic Studies, Gallaudet University, Washington, DC,

Moores, D. F. (1987). *Educating the deaf: Psychology, principles and practices* (3rd ed.). Boston: Houghton Mifflin.

National Commission on Education of the Deaf. (1988). *Toward equality: Education of the deaf.* Report to the President and the Congress of the United States.

Pflaster, G. (1980). A factor analysis of variables related to academic performance of hearing-impaired children in regular classes. *Volta Review, 82*, 71-84.

Quigley, S. P., & Paul, P. V. (1986). A perspective on academic achievement. In D. M. Luterman (Ed.), *Deafness in perspective* (pp. 55-86). San Diego: College-Hill.

Rawlings, B., & Trybus, R. (1978). Personnel, facilities and services available in schools and classes for hearing impaired children in the United States. *American Annals of the Deaf Directory of Program and Service, 123*, 99-114.

Salem, J., & Herward, P. (1978). A survey to determine the impact of P.L. 94-142 on residential schools for the deaf. *American Annals of the Deaf, 123*, 524-527.

Shroyer, E. H., & Ford, T.A (1986). Survey of music instruction and activities in residential and day schools for hearing-impaired students. *Music Education for the Handicapped Bulletin, 2,* 28-45.

Solomon, A. L. (1980). Music in special education before 1930: Hearing and speech development. *Journal of Research in Music Education, 28,* 236-242.

Spitzer, M. (1984). A survey of the use of music in schools for the hearing impaired. *The Volta Review, 86,* 362-363.

Stephens, T. M., & Braun, B. L. (1980). Measures of regular classroom teachers' attitudes toward handicapped children. *Exceptional Children, 46,* 292-294.

Reprinted with permission of the *Journal of Music Therapy*

Now that you've read the article by Darrow and Gfeller, let's examine the specific organizational components of this article. Each of these components provides the reader with specific kinds of information.

Publication information. Publication information, which is found in nearly all types of research articles, helps you to locate an article in the library or online. Usually, this information includes the name of the journal (in this case, the *Journal of Music Therapy*) and the year in which the journal was published (for this article, 1991). Similar to magazines, research journals often have several volumes that come out each year (e.g., monthly, quarterly, biannually). The listing of the volume (28th year that this journal was published), issue number (1, meaning the first issue for that year), and page numbers (pages 23–39) helps you to find the article or chapter.

Title of article. The title of a research article is often lengthy and therefore may seem cumbersome. However, the author wants the title to include as much information as possible about what is being studied and with whom, so that readers can decide whether the article is relevant to their current interests. A clear and informative research title is an important component for all types of research articles. The title of this article, "A Study of Public School Music Programs in Mainstreaming Hearing Impaired Students," tells the reader that the article is about students with hearing losses and their participation in music programs in public schools. If you were a music therapist working in a school system who has just been assigned to work with a deaf student, then you might find this article especially useful.

Author and affiliation. Most all research studies list the name(s) of the author(s), as well as the institution(s) where the research was carried out. In this example, Alice Ann Darrow was affiliated with the University of Kansas and Kate Gfeller with the University of Iowa when this research was completed. This information helps the reader to contact the author if they would like to find out more about this study.

Abstract. Not all research studies include an abstract, though many do. The abstract provides a brief summary of the information found in the article. It usually includes the purpose of the study, who participated in the study (referred to as "subjects" or "participants"), behaviors or events that were observed and analyzed, and the main results of the study. The abstract is a valuable tool for the reader, because it helps to determine whether the research paper contains information relevant to the reader's current interests, without having to read the entire article. From reading this abstract, the reader will determine that the authors used a questionnaire to examine the participation (or lack thereof) of students with hearing losses in public school music, and those factors that contribute to successful instruction. The results of the study regarding extent of participation, teacher preparation, instructional support and instructional methods, and objectives are summarized in points (a) through (g).

Introduction and Related Literature. The Introduction of an article provides the reader with some background about the topic being studied and why it is of interest. The Review of Literature expands on the topic, summarizing information from previous articles or books, and explaining (1) what is already known about this topic, and (2) what questions remain unanswered. The authors also explain what they plan to study, based on questions unanswered in previous research. In some articles, such as this one, the review of literature will close with a series of research questions that will be addressed and described in the following section, which is called the Method section.

Method. The Method section describes how the author(s) conducted the study, including a description of people who participated in the study (referred to in most articles as either participants or subjects), where the study took place, and specific measures and procedures used to collect information. The author(s) should provide enough detail so that another researcher could replicate (repeat) the study, and so that the reader gets a clear sense of how the research was carried out.

In this particular study, Darrow and Gfeller developed a questionnaire (survey) designed specifically to answer the research questions listed at the end of the review of literature. They describe how the questionnaire was developed, the nature of the questions asked, and who received the survey. An important part of descriptive research is describing who you studied, and how they were chosen and invited to participate. Because descriptive research generally tries to determine responses or behaviors that are common or typical for the specific population being studied (in this case, public school music teachers), it is preferable to study as large a group as possible. In addition, special effort is made to avoid biased or preconceived responses by participants. For example, rather than simply contacting a few of their own personal friends who are music teachers, Darrow and Gfeller sought the opinions and experiences of teachers all over the United States. Therefore, the questionnaires were sent to schools listed in a national directory.

Results. The Results section describes what the authors discovered. In both descriptive and experimental research (which will be described next), there is usually a statistical analysis of the quantitative data (percentages, **rankings**, **mean** or average scores, etc.) collected by the researcher that summarizes the overall trends for the entire group. In descriptive research, the author often describes the results using both a narrative form (a written description of what they found) as well as numerical summaries in a table or figure (see next section). For example, Darrow and Gfeller explain that nearly half of the schools surveyed (47%) had no self-contained (special) music classes specifically for students with hearing losses. What's more, of the schools included in this study, nearly a fourth (23%) of the students with hearing losses received no music education. The narrative (written description) in this article brings the reader's attention to some of the key findings in six tables, which summarize the primary research findings.

Tables. Because descriptive research usually involves numerical information, an efficient way to present the results is through tables that present a summary of the data. In this example, the author reports the results using either a percentage (Tables 1, 2, 4, and 5) or **rank order** (Tables 3 and 6). In many descriptive and experimental studies, there are also special statistical tests used to determine if there are significant differences among different groups or treatment approaches.

Figures. Many descriptive studies also use figures (graphs, charts, photographs, etc.) as a helpful visual representation of the results. This particular study does not include figures, but you will see an example in an experimental study that appears later in this chapter.

Discussion or summary. Many articles have a separate Discussion section. In the Discussion, the author interprets the findings of the study. In other words, what do the results mean? Are there any implications for clinical practice? Are there any interesting differences between the findings of this study and previous studies that were described in the review of literature? Are there special considerations that the reader should take into account when interpreting the outcome? This section may also suggest areas that merit future study.

References. The Reference section includes a list of all previous research studies to which the author referred when writing the current article. Each entry is comprised of the title of the article, the name of the author, and information about the publication in which it appeared. References appear at the end of nearly all types of research studies. The Reference section provides a valuable source for finding additional information on topics related to the study.

This descriptive research study by Darrow and Gfeller describes what **already exists**, but there was no attempt to change the instructional conditions. In educational and health-related research, it is common to find research studies in which specific interventions are tested in order to determine benefit. Experimental research is commonly used to test the effectiveness of specific interventions with particular types of clients.

Experimental Research

Experimental research is similar to descriptive research in a number of ways. Both types of research have similar sections: publication information, title, author affiliation, abstract, Introduction and Review of Literature, Methods, Results, tables, figures, Discussion, and References. Both types of research answer questions using quantitative (numerical) data, and they usually report the results for groups of people rather than for individuals. As is the case for descriptive research, using a larger numbers of participants makes a study more generalizable. As in descriptive studies, researchers use specific methods designed to reduce bias and increase objectivity; those methods are usually described in considerable detail. While descriptive and experimental research share many common features, there are important differences in the kind of information we can learn. Descriptive research describes "what exists," whereas experimental research suggests what "**would happen under particular circumstances**."

In an experimental study, the researcher uses a controlled environment to determine whether a particular **variable** (such as a particular type of medicine, method of teaching, or brand of toothpaste) has an important effect on a specific outcome (such as recovery from an illness, rate of learning, number of cavities). For example, a researcher in dentistry may have some patients use Brand X toothpaste, while others are given Brand Y. At the end of six months, the researcher may find that the patients using Brand X had fewer cavities than those using Brand Y.

Can the researcher assume that Brand X is more effective? Only if he or she has eliminated all other possible explanations for the difference between the two groups. Perhaps many more of the patients using Brand X lived in a neighborhood with fluoridated water, or perhaps the Brand X patients were simply more conscientious about brushing their teeth. In order for the researcher to feel confident that the difference in number of cavities was because Brand X worked more effectively, she must have controlled for other factors (such as fluoridation, or tooth brushing and flossing habits) that could have influenced the outcome.

Experimental research begins by asking a specific question, which researchers call a **hypothesis**. In the hypothesis, researchers predict how they think the results will turn out. For example, the dental researcher described above might hypothesize that Brand X toothpaste, which contains a new and more powerful type of fluoride, will result in fewer cavities than the older commercially available toothpaste (Brand Y). After the prediction has been made, tests are carried out and statistical analyses (special mathematical calculations) are used to determine whether there was an important difference (called **statistically significant difference**) as a result of the particular treatment or intervention. Experimental research methods are powerful tools commonly used for evaluating the effectiveness of specific medications and treatment procedures. Many music therapy programs (especially graduate programs) include courses on statistical and research methods that explain how hypotheses are developed and tested, and some of the basic principles behind statistical methods.

Just as a dentist might compare two toothpaste brands in order to help patients have fewer cavities, a music therapist might compare different treatment interventions to determine if one is more effective. The next article is an example of an experimental study that examines the effectiveness of **Rhythmic Auditory Stimulation (RAS)**, an intervention that you read about in Chapter 10. Because therapists should provide their clients with the most effective and efficient interventions possible, the researchers of this study wanted to determine in a systematic and objective way whether RAS is as effective, or possibly more effective, than another type of neurological intervention often used with persons who have suffered from strokes. As you read this article, you will find a similar organizational structure to that of the descriptive article by Darrow and Gfeller. Look for the parts of the article (title, abstract, results, etc.) that you learned about previously.

In this article, Thaut and his colleagues carry out statistical analyses to determine if one treatment intervention is more effective than the other. For example, in the results of this study, you will read that "**Significant differences** were found in favor of RAS training in all 4 gait parameters: **velocity** ($df = 76$, $t = 2.83$, $P = .006$), **cadence** ($df = 76$, $t = 5.13$, $P = .0001$), **stride length** ($df = 76$, $t = 4.6$, $P = .0001$), and **symmetry** ($df = 76$, $t = 2.13$, $P = .049$)." What do initials like df, t, and P mean? What are those numbers all about? If you have not yet had a statistics class and don't understand those symbols or numerical values, the written explanation of these results will give you a basic idea of what the researchers found out. The visual representation in Figure 1 can also help to clarify the results.

If you have some difficulty with some of the terms related to strokes or RAS used in this article, you may find it helpful to review parts of Chapter 10 to reacquaint yourself with this population and type of intervention.

Neurorehabilitation and Neural Repair 20(10), 1-5; 2007
© 2007 by the American Society of Neurorehabilitation

Rhythmic Auditory Stimulation Improves Gait More Than NDT/Bobath Training in Near-Ambulatory Patients Early Poststroke: A Single-Blind, Randomized Trial

M. H. Thaut, PhD, A. K. Leins, PhD, R. R. Rice, MS, H. Argstatter, MA, G. P. Kenyon, MS, G. C. McIntosh, MD, H. V. Bolay, PhD, and M. Fetter, MD

Objectives. The effectiveness of 2 different types of gait training in stroke rehabilitation, rhythmic auditory stimulation (RAS) versus neurodevelopmental therapy (NDT)/Bobath-based training, was compared in 2 groups of hemiparetic stroke patients over a 3-week period of daily training (RAS group, n =43; NDT/Bobath group =35). *Methods.* Mean entry date into the study was 21.3 days poststroke for the RAS group and 22.3 days for the control group. Patients entered the study as soon as they were able to complete 5 stride cycles with handheld assistance. Patients were closely equated by age, gender, and lesion site. Motor function in both groups was preassessed by the Barthel Index and the Fugl-Meyer Scales. *Results.* Pre- to posttest measures showed a significant improvement in the RAS group for velocity (P =.006), stride length (P =.0001), cadence (P =.0001) and symmetry (P = .0049) over the NDT/Bobath group. Effect sizes for RAS over NDT/Bobath training were 13.1 m/min for velocity, 0.18 m for stride length, and 19 steps/min for cadence. *Conclusions.* The data show that after 3 weeks of gait training, RAS is an effective therapeutic method to enhance gait training in hemiparetic stroke rehabilitation. Gains were significantly higher for RAS compared to NDT/Bobath training.

Restoration of mobility is critical to successful rehabilitation after stroke, which makes recovery of functional gait a high priority. Each year, 750,000 individuals have a stroke in the United States, a prevalence of 200 to 300 per 100,000 inhabitants.[1,2] The vast majority of individuals in whom at least partial recovery is observed experience persistent problems especially in the area of neurological motor deficits. For example, epidemiological studies have shown that 20% of stroke survivors remain wheelchair bound and 60% show gait deficits of varying degrees.[3] However, intensive rehabilitation programs have shown to improve gait function[4] and continued research into the efficacy of various treatment approaches continues to hold great benefit.

A number of intervention techniques are in current use, based on different models of motor physiology and disease recovery. Traditional but still widely used techniques include neurodevelopmental therapy (NDT), in Europe known as Bobath-therapy, the Brunnstrom method, proprioceptive neuromuscular facilitation (PNF), and the Rood method.[4,5] However, the research evidence base for the effectiveness of one approach over another has not been demonstrated.

One recent form of gait therapy, rhythmic auditory stimulation (RAS), involves the use of rhythmic sensory cuing of the motor system. RAS is based on entrainment models in which rhythmic auditory cues synchronize motor responses into stable time relationships, similar to oscillator coupling models. Rhythm serves as an anticipatory and continuous time reference on which movements are mapped within a stable temporal template. The fast-acting physiological entrainment mechanisms between auditory rhythm and motor response serve as coupling mechanisms to stabilize and regulate gait patterns. In several clinical research studies, RAS significantly improved gait and other movement parameters (eg, upper extremity function) during rehabilitation for hemiparesis.[6-13] RAS can be used as a self-contained training protocol, but its principles of rhythmic cuing and temporal regulation can also be integrated into other interventions.

The purpose of this study was to examine the clinical efficacy of RAS, based on the experimental design of the study by Thaut et al,[7] by comparing 3 weeks of RAS against the NDT/Bobath method. which is one of the most widely used gait therapies.

METHODS

Subject Selection

From an eligible catchment pool of 155 patients, 78 patients from 2 research centers in Germany and the United States were selected by a random number table. Patients were randomly assigned to either the experimental (RAS; n = 43; male = 22, female = 21) or control (neurodevelopmental technique/Bobath; n = 35; male = 19, female = 16) training group (see Table 1). Treatment allocation was accomplished by computerized random number generators in both centers. Random numbers for the allocation-to-treatment sequence were concealed from the recruiter and the therapists carrying out the training. Patients were informed of the 2 possible treatment allocations but blinded to the aims of an experimental versus control condition. Ethical review board clearance was obtained for all patients.

Subject Characteristics

Table 1 describes the patients. Mean age for the RAS group was 69.2 ±11.5 and for the NDT/Bobath group 69.7 ±11.2 years. Lesion site was closely matched in both groups. Mild to moderate sensory dysfunction was present in all middle cerebral artery distribution strokes. Both groups had lower limb spasticity, most pronounced in knee flexors/extensors, plantar flexion, and hip flexors/extensors, as typical for a stage 4 or early stage 3 on the Brunnstrom hemiplegia recovery scale.[14]

Subject Assessment and Training

Both groups were assessed by blinded physical therapists who performed the Barthel Index[15] and the Fugl-Meyer Scale.[16] The Fugl-Meyer score was 31.4 for the control group and 33.3 for the RAS group (balance and lower extremity function combined). The Barthel Index score was 45.5 for the control group and 47.5 for the RAS group. Patients entered the study within 4 weeks of onset, as soon as they could complete 5 stride cycles with handheld assistance by the therapist, that is, with no more than support of the forearm, wrist, and elbow at approximately 90 degrees of elbow flexion on the nonparetic side. Handheld assistance was available to all patients throughout training when needed.

TABLE 1. Subject Characteristics

	RAS	NDT/ Bobath*
N	43	35
Age	69.2 ±11	69.7 ±11
Gender M/F	22/21	19/16
Side of hemiplegia (R:L)	20:23	16:19
Time between (days) stroke and admission to study	21.3 ±11	22.2 ±12
Location of stroke		
Middle cerebral artery	35	30
Internal capsule	4	4
Basal ganglia/thalamus	3	1
Subdural hematoma	1	

RAS = rhythmic auditory stimulation; NDT = neurodevelopmental therapy.

Mean entry date poststroke was 21.3 ±10.8 days for the RAS group and 22.3 ±14.7 for the NDT/Bobath group. The study duration was 3 weeks, with gait training daily for 30 minutes, 5 times per week. Four gait therapists for each group conducted the training to ensure consistency in training protocols and procedures. Each center had its own independently trained pool of therapists. Therapists were not blinded to the treatment conditions of the study. However, because both conditions are considered full treatment conditions, no performance bias was expected. Total walking time was tracked in both groups to ensure consistent exercise duration. Pre-gait exercises were not included in the actual training period of the experimental trials and were carried out in similar fashion in both groups if therapeutically indicated.

RAS training followed established protocols[7,17] using a metronome and specifically prepared music tapes in digital MIDI format to ensure temporal precision and tempo stability as well as full capacity for frequency modulation of the stimulus based on patient needs. After an initial cadence assessment, cuing frequencies were matched to the gait cadence for the first quarter of the session. During the second quarter, cue frequencies were increased in 5% increments as kinematically indicated without compromising postural and dynamic stability. During the third quarter, adaptive gait patterns, for example, ramp or step walking, were practiced. The last quarter was spent fading the cues intermittently to train for independent carryover. The control group trained the same amount of time and distance, following NDT and Bobath principles as well as using similar instructions about gait parameters to practice, but without rhythmic auditory cuing.

TABLE 2. Pretest and Posttest Means and Standard Deviations, Mean Differences Within and Between Groups, and 95% Confidence Intervals Around Mean Differences Between Groups

	Pretest Week 0		Posttest Week 3		Differences Within Groups Week 3 - Week 0		Differences Between Groups* Week 6 - Week 0-
	Exp	Ctrl	Exp	Ctrl	Exp	Ctrl	
Velocity (m/min)	14.1 (6.3)	13.0 (5.9)	34.5 (9.1)	20.3 (6.5)	20.4	7.3	13.1 (6.9, 19.3)
Stride length (m)	0.53 (0.12)	0.50 (0.12)	0.88 (0.21)	0.67 (0.24)	0.35	0.17	0.18 (0.13, 0.23)
Cadence (steps/min)	53 (10.8)	50 (9.9)	82 (12.9)	60 (9.9)	29 10	19	(10.4, 27.6)
Symmetry (swing ratios)	0.42 (0.12)	0.40 (0.12)	0.58 (0.05)	0.46 (0.07)	0.16	0.06	0.10 (−0.04, 0.24)

*CI boundaries in parentheses.

Testing

All patients were tested 1 day before the training sessions started and 1 day after the last training session. All available participant data after removing dropout participants were analyzed in an intention-to-treat analysis. Testing was carried out without RAS present. For testing, patients walked along a 10 m flat walkway. Two meters on either side were available for acceleration and deceleration without data recording. Gait parameters were recorded at a sampling rate of 500/sec with a computerized foot sensor system consisting of 4 foot contact sensors (heel, first metatarsal, fifth metatarsal, big toe) embedded into shoe inserts. Sensor data were stored online in a portable microprocessor and downloaded after the test walk into a PC with interface hardware and analysis software.

RESULTS

The dropout rate in one center was 23% of initially included patients. There was a 10% dropout rate in the other center. Dropout reasons were due to hospital transfer, early discharge, medical complication, or unspecified personal reasons.

Four major gait parameters critical for improved functional gait were measured and statistically analyzed: velocity, stride length, cadence, swing symmetry (calculated as the ratio between the swing times of 2 consecutive steps using the longer step—ie, paretic vs nonparetic leg—as the denominator). After statistical checks for equivalence of variance (Levene's F test) in each parameter, 2-tailed t test comparisons for independent samples were carried out for pretest differences between the RAS group and the NDT/Bobath group. Pre- and posttest means as well as effect size differences and confidence intervals are given in Table 2. At pretest, there were no significant differences between the 2 groups in each parameter: velocity (df=76, t =1.01, P =.347), stride length (df=76, t =1.75, P =.111), cadence (df=76, t =1.49, P =.141), and swing symmetry (df=76, t =1.13, P =.285).

After 3 weeks of gait training, t test comparisons for posttest differences between groups were carried out. Significant differences were found in favor of RAS training in all 4 gait parameters: velocity (df=76, t =2.83, P =.006), cadence (df=76, t =5.13, P =.0001), stride length (df=76, t =4.6, P =.0001), and symmetry (df=76, t =2.13, P =.049). Effect size analysis showed improvements for RAS over NDT/Bobath training of 13.1 m/min for velocity, 0.18 m in stride length, 19 steps/min in cadence, and 0.10 in gait symmetry (swing ratio) (Table 2).

Data of patient satisfaction showed a significant main effect in favor of the RAS group (df=1,24, F =6.35, P =.019). However, both groups showed continued increases in satisfaction ratings across therapy (RAS: 77%-84%-87%; NDT/Bobath: 64%-70%-75%).

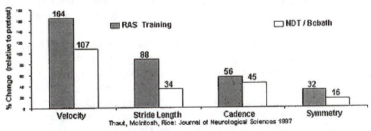

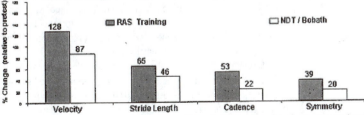

Figure 1. Comparison data for treatment duration.

DISCUSSION

Statistical analysis of 4 gait parameters after a 3-week gait training period in subacute hemiparetic stroke rehabilitation showed significantly greater improvements for training with rhythmic auditory stimulation relative to training within a standard NDT/Bobath protocol. Differences between pre- and posttest as expressed in percent change showed substantial differences between the 2 groups in favor of RAS: velocity 128.8% (RAS) versus 87.6% (NDT/Bobath); stride length 65.9% versus 46.1%; cadence 53.8% versus 22.2%; symmetry 39.1% versus 20.2% (Figure 1). Noteworthy is that RAS training produced mean effects substantially higher in improvement over NDT/Bobath training: 13.1 m/min for velocity, 0.18 m for stride length, 19 steps/min for cadence, and 0.10 in symmetry (swing ratio) over NDT/Bobath training (Table 2).

In the RAS group, significant increases in gait velocity were driven by somewhat larger increases in stride length than cadence. In the control group, a similar pattern of contribution was observed; however, with a much larger differential in magnitude for stride length relative to cadence, which only improved by 22% on average. Because changes in stride length and cadence are kinematically linked in healthy gait, increases in those parameters that are coupled more closely may suggest a more functional recovery of gait mechanics. Improvements in velocity that are mostly driven by stride length and a disproportionally smaller cadence change may indicate uncoupling of kinematic linkages due to compromised asymmetric step patterns.[4]

Although substantial increases in swing symmetry were seen for RAS relative to NDT/Bobath, the smaller improvement compared to the other parameters shows the higher resistance of this parameter to rehabilitation efforts.[1] However, the isochronous nature of the rhythmic timing cue still showed higher efficacy in symmetry restoration than NDT/Bobath alone. Similarly, moderate results in regard to swing symmetry were obtained by our group in a previous study,[7] but improvements in this parameter did not reach statistical significance.

Improvements in velocity, stride length, and cadence were statistically similar to previous data,[7] but with smaller percentage increase rates in this study compared to previous data. Velocity improved 128% versus 164% in previous research (control group improvement 87.6% vs 107%). The main difference in treatment dosage between the 2 studies was the duration (3 vs 6 weeks). Therefore, the difference in percent improvement suggests that the additional 3 weeks of training had a substantial effect on speed of walking, which is a critical parameter in functional gait recovery. Although the current study was not designed to statistically compare different treatment durations, the similarity in treatment design and diagnostic patient selection criteria allows for a descriptive comparison between the current data and the previous study data,[7] showing the dosage benefit of 6 weeks of therapy over 3 weeks (Figure 1).

When referenced to percent of healthy normative data,[18] results showed substantial differences in favor of RAS. RAS-training patients reached 43.6% of healthy control velocity but only 26.3% in NDT/Bobath, in cadence 66.4% versus 48%, and in stride length 60.5 versus 51.8%.

Considering that predictive states in motor planning, as well as attentional and executive brain networks, reduce performance variability, the intrinsic time structure of rhythmic cues and their almost instantaneous synchronization effect on motor responses can play a critical role in performance regulation by enhancing temporal predictability via interval scaling. It has been shown in optimization models that a rhythmic cue as a predictive time constraint can result in the complete specification of the dynamics of the movement over the entire movement cycle, reducing variability, enhancing temporal precision, and facilitating the selection of optimal movement trajectories, velocity, and acceleration parameters. Thus, temporal-rhythmic motor cues do not only cue speed and timing of movement but also regulate comprehensive spatiotemporal and force parameters[19,20] in restoring motor function in brain rehabilitation.[5,21,22]

In summary, RAS significantly improved gait performance in subacute hemiparetic stroke rehabilitation over NDT/Bobath-based training. The 3-week training period showed smaller overall improvements when compared to a 6-week study with an identical therapy protocol, suggesting the functional importance of additional training for the patient's functional locomotor recovery. Future studies may follow 4 directions to further establish the role of RAS in gait rehabilitation: (a) test other treatment dosages for RAS, (b) compare RAS against other current gait-training methods besides NDT/Bobath, (c) investigate the potential to enhance RAS by adding other current gait therapy techniques, (d) study the effect of RAS in long-term outpatient or community-based settings.

REFERENCES

1. Resse S, Werner C. Post-stroke motor dysfunction and spasticity: novel pharmacological and physical treatment strategies. *CNS Drugs.* 2003;17:1070-1093.
2. Williams GR, Jiang JG, Matchar DB, Samsa GP. Incidence and occurrence of total (first-ever and recurrent) stroke. *Stroke.* 1999;30:2523-2528.
3. Jorgensen HS, Nakayama H, Pedersen PM, Kammersgaard L, Raaschou HO, Olsen TS. Epidemiology of stroke-related disability. *Clin Geriatr Med.* 1999;15:785-799.
4. Mauritz KH. Gait training in hemiplegia. *Eur J Neurol.* 2002;9:23-29.
5. Hummelsheim H. Rationales for improving motor function. *Curr Opin Neurol.* 1999;12:697-701.
6. Thaut MH, McIntosh GC, Prassas SG, Rice RR. The effect of auditory rhythmic cuing on stride and EMG patterns in hemiparetic gait of stroke patients. *J Neurol Rehabil.* 1993;7:9-16.
7. Thaut MH, McIntosh GC, Rice RR. Rhythmic facilitation of gait training in hemiparetic stroke rehabilitation. *J Neurol Sci.* 1997;151:207-212.
8. Thaut MH, Kenyon GP, Hurt CP, McIntosh GC, Hoemberg V. Kinematic optimization of spatiotemporal patterns in paretic arm training with stroke patients. *Neuropsychol.* 2002;40:1073-1081.
9. Whitall J, McCombe Waller S, Silver KH, Macko RF. Repetitive bilateral arm training with rhythmic auditory cueing improves motor function in chronic hemiparetic stroke. *Stroke.* 2000;31: 2390-2395.
10. Luft AR, McCombe Waller S, Whitall J, et al. Repetitive bilateral arm training and motor cortex activation in chronic stroke: a randomized controlled trial. *JAMA.* 2004;292:1853-1861.
11. Mandel AR, Nymark JR, Balmer SJ, Grinnell DM, O'Riain MD. Electromyographic feedback versus rhythmic positional biofeedback in computerized gait retraining with stroke patients. *Arch Phys Med Rehabil.* 1990;71:649-654.
12. McCombe WS, Whitall J. Hand dominance and side of stroke affect rehabilitation in chronic stroke. *Clin Rehabil.* 2005;19:544-551.
13. Schauer M, Mauritz KH. Musical motor feedback (MMF) in walking hemiparetic stroke patients: randomized trials of gait improvement. *Clin Rehabil.* 2003;17:713-722.
14. Brunnstrom S. *Movement Therapy in Hemiplegia: A Neurophysiological Approach.* Philadelphia, PA: Harper & Row; 1970.
15. Mahoney FI, Barthel DW. Rehabilitation of the hemiplegic patient: a clinical evaluation. *Arch Phys Med Rehabil.* 1954; 35:359-362.
16. Fugl-Meyer AR, Jääskö L, Leyman I, Olsson S, Steglind S. The post-stroke hemiplegic patient: a method for evaluation of physical performance. *Scand J Rehabil Med.* 1975;7:13-31.
17. Thaut MH. *Rhythm, Music, and the Brain: Scientific Foundations and Clinical Applications.* New York: Taylor & Francis; 2005.
18. Oeberg T, Karsznia A, Oeberg K. Basic gait parameters; reference data for normal subjects, 10-79 years of age. *J Rehabil Res Dev.* 1993;30:210-223.
19. Kenyon GP, Thaut MH. Rhythmic-driven optimization of motor control. *Recent Res Dev Biomech.* 2003;1:29-47.
20. Harris CM, Wolpert DM. Signal-dependent noise determines motor planning. Nature. 1998;194:780-784.
21. Hoemberg V. Evidence-based medicine in neurological rehabilitation—a critical review. *Acta Neurochir.* 2005;93: 3-14.
22. Molinari M, Leggio MG, De Martin M, Cerasa A, Thaut M. Neurobiology of rhythmic motor entrainment. *Ann N Y Acad Sci.* 2003;999:313-321.

From Molecular, Cellular, and Integrative Neuroscience Programs, Colorado State University, Fort Collins (MHT); University of Applied Sciences Heidelberg, Heidelberg, Germany (AKL, HA, HVB); Poudre Valley Hospital, Fort Collins, CO (RRR, GCM); Colorado State University, Fort Collins (GPK); SRH-Hospitals Karlsbad-Langensteinbach, Karlsbad, Germany (MF).

Address correspondence to Michael H. Thaut, PhD, Molecular, Cellular, and Integrative Neuroscience Programs, Center for Biomedical Research in Music, 102 Music Building, Colorado State University, Fort Collins, CO 80523. E-mail: michael.thaut@colostate.edu.

Thaut MH, Nickel AK, Rice RR, Argstatter H, Kenyon GP, McIntosh GC, Bolay HV, Fetter M. Rhythmic auditory stimulation improves gait more than NDT/Bobath training in near-ambulatory patients early post stroke: a single-blind, randomized trial. Neurorehabil Neural Repair 2007;20(10), 1-5.

DOI: 10.1177/1545968307300523

Key Words: Gait rehabilitation—Stroke—Rhythmic auditory stimulation.

Introduction and Review of Literature. In this study, the authors compared the effectiveness of two different types of gait training designed to improve the gait (walking) of persons recovering from strokes: (1) rhythmic auditory stimulation (RAS) (which is described in greater detail in Chapter 10), and (2) neurodevelopmental therapy (NDT)/Bobath-based training. As the Review of Literature indicates, NDT has been used widely for a number of years, while RAS has been developed more recently. By determining if one method is more effective than another, a therapist can make more judicious choices about which methods promote faster recovery in rehabilitation and are therefore less costly in terms of **cost-benefit ratios.**

Methods. This study includes a large number of patients (78 people) so that the researchers can determine with greater confidence whether these results can be generalized to other people who have similar problems or characteristics. In order to compare the two treatment methods (RAS and NDT), the participants were **randomly assigned** to one of the two conditions. The article tells us that the participants had **hemiplegia** as a result of the stroke. From reviewing the information in Chapter 10, you should already know something about gait problems associated with strokes.

Specific details about the participants in each group (RAS and NDT) for this study can be found in Table 1. For example, in Table 1, the letter *N* (initial for the word *number*) stands for the number of participants. There are 43 in the RAS treatment group, and 35 in the NDT treatment. You can also determine that the **mean** (average) age of those in the RAS group was 69.2 years of age (with a **range** of 11 years more or less than 69.2 years), and that the participants in the NDT group were of a similar age (**mean** age of 69.7 years). The table also outlines (1) how many men and women were in each group, (2) the side of the hemiplegia, (3) the average number of days between the event of the stroke and participation in the study, and (4) the location of the stroke in the brain. By knowing more about the people who were involved in this study, the reader gets a better idea whether the results of this study might apply to patients in his or her own music therapy practice.

While the article by Darrow and Gfeller used a questionnaire to gather information, this study uses several assessment tools commonly used in motor therapy and physical rehabilitation: Barthel Index and Fugl-Meyer Scales, which are measures that assess walking performance (velocity = speed of walking; stride length; cadence = step frequency; symmetry between left and right leg stride times). These tools were used to measure any change that occurred as a result of training. As the Methods section indicates, the participants in the two groups trained for the same amount and distance, but only participants in the RAS group walked to rhythmic auditory cueing. The Methods section also describes when and how testing was done before (**pretest**) and after (**posttest**) training.

Methods sections of experimental research often include technical terms that have specific meaning. For example, the authors write that "Both groups were assessed by *blinded* physical therapists that performed the Barthel Index and the Fugl-Meyer Scale." This does not mean that the research was carried out by physical therapists who could not see. Rather, ***blind*** in the context of research is a term that means that the physical therapists were not informed about the specific research questions or interventions being studied. This is one method used in experimental research to reduce the chance of biased results. Another method that is used to reduce potential bias is ***random assignment*** of participants. This term indicates that people are assigned by chance to different groups in order to keep the two groups as similar as possible on factors such as age, gender, and other characteristics that might influence the results. These are just two of many technical terms that are used in research. These terms can seem a little confusing at times, but these terms are often learned in books or classes about research methods, or in more advanced music therapy classes.

Results. The results of this study are described in a narrative, but also in Table 2. Table 2 summarizes the **mean** (average) scores for all the patients before training (**Pretest** Week 10), after training (**Posttest** Week 3) and the change from pre- to posttest on four different measures: velocity, stride length, cadence, and symmetry. Each of these measures (which are described in Chapter 10) gives us some idea of how well these stroke patients can walk before and after gait training.

In addition to examining the effectiveness of this 3-week training program, the researchers wondered how 3 weeks of rehabilitation would compare with a 6-week training program examined in a prior study (Thaut, McIntosh, & Rice, 1997). The results of the 3-week program studied in the present study and the 6-week program reported in an earlier study (Thaut et al., 1997) are compared in **Figure 1**. The percent of change (improvement) for those in the RAS group appears in the gray bars, and the change for those in the NDT group appears in the white bars. As the graph shows, the stroke patients randomly assigned to the RAS group showed greater improvement than the NDT group after both 3 and 6 weeks on all four measures. However, the figure indicates that greater gains were achieved as a result of 6 weeks of training.

Discussion. In the Discussion section, the authors interpret the results (that is, give an educated guess about why the results turned out as they did), linking the superior benefit of RAS to specific theories of neuromotor functioning. They also note that 6 weeks of training results in greater recovery than 3 weeks of training on functional **locomotor** recovery. This suggests that music therapists may want to provide at least 6 weeks of treatment in order to optimize treatment benefit for this type of intervention. Like the descriptive study presented previously, the experimental article concludes with **References**, a list of articles or books that acted as a foundation for this study.

As you can see, these descriptive and experimental research studies are similar in the use of quantitative data, the study of groups, specific components (e.g., abstract, Results, etc.) and methodological efforts to avoid bias. However, these two types of research contrast in the sorts of questions they ask, with descriptive research describing what already exists, while experimental research examines what would happen under certain prescribed conditions.

The following two research examples, **historical** and **qualitative** research, differ from the previous types of research in organizational structure, types of questions asked, and the type of information presented.

Historical Research

Whereas descriptive and experimental researchers seek to discover what is and what will be under particular circumstances, historical researchers attempt to learn, in a precise and systematic manner, what has happened in the past. Of interest to music therapists are the people, places, events, and past practices that have helped shape the profession.

According to Phelps, Sadoff, Warburton, and Ferrara (2004), there are a number of reasons for pursuing historical research. First, the past may be helpful in understanding present conditions that influence music therapy practice. For example, in a historical study, Solomon (1980) found evidence that special education classrooms in the 19th and early 20th centuries used music as an important tool to diagnose and treat speech and hearing defects. Solomon concluded that the use of music in special education classrooms is not a new idea, but one with a lengthy history that can be traced to the early 19th century. Thus, today's practice of using music to help diagnose and treat children with hearing impairments comes from a precedent set 100 years ago.

A second reason for undertaking historical research is to understand more about past practices in our profession. We can identify the institutions, hospitals, and schools where music therapy has been practiced. We know, for example, that music therapy was used on Blackwell's Island (now known as Roosevelt's Island) in New York City during the latter part of the 19th century. However, we lack specific information about the daily routine of the hospital and the music therapy techniques used with the many hundreds of clients suffering from behavioral-emotional disorders. A more complete account of music therapy practiced on Blackwell's Island would help us better understand the techniques and status of the profession during the last few decades of the 19th century.

Third, biographical data concerning early, prominent music therapists are important but also scarce. For example, Ray Green was an important music therapist and one of the founders of the National Association for Music Therapy. He lived during the early and mid 20th century, yet we know very little about his life or music therapy activities beyond his role during the early days of NAMT. Without a record of the contributions of music therapy pioneers, we are missing worthwhile information that could provide encouragement for today's music therapists (Solomon & Heller, 1982). This kind of information, to which you have been introduced in Chapter 2 of this book, is discovered through historical research methods.

The following article is an example of historical research written by William Davis. The article describes the efforts of three women who were pioneers in promoting music therapy during the first half of the 20th century. Each of the three women independently established an organization of volunteer musicians to provide music therapy services to people with physical and mental disorders. Davis indicates that due to the work of these women, music therapy played an important role in physical and psychological rehabilitation in clinics, hospitals, and other medical settings in New York City many years before the establishment of the National Association for Music Therapy in 1950. This article is important because it compiles information from a variety of sources, which demonstrates an ongoing interest in music therapy training and practice during the first decades of the 20th century and helps us to better understand some early initiatives that enabled the profession to take hold in the United States.

Journal of Music Therapy, XXX (1), 1993, 34-45
© 1993 by the National Association for Music Therapy, Inc.

Keeping the Dream Alive: Profiles of Three Early Twentieth Century Music Therapists

William B. Davis

Colorado State University

Until 1900, music therapy clinical practice in the United States was limited to a few isolated occurrences. The most significant of these events happened during the last 25 years of the nineteenth century, and, although important historically, did little to promote the growth and development of music therapy as the United States entered the twentieth century. Owing the first years of the twentieth century, music therapy clinical practice was more vigorously promoted than ever before, due mostly to the efforts of three women music educators/ therapists who flourished during this time. Eva Agusta Vescelius, Isa Maud Ilsen, and Harriet Ayer Seymour were strong-willed individuals who developed interesting personal philosophies concerning the use of music in therapy, practiced what they advocated (unlike many of the people writing about music therapy at the time), and each, in her career, established music therapy organizations devoted to treating the physically and mentally ill with music. Although none left a lasting legacy, all should be recognized as twentieth century pioneers in music therapy.

Until 1900, music therapy clinical practice in the United States was limited to a few isolated occurrences. The most significant, including the establishment of programs at Blackwell's Island and Utica State Hospital in New York, happened during the last 25 years of the nineteenth century and, although important historically, did little to promote the growth and development of music therapy (Davis, 1989).

During the first years of the twentieth century, music therapy clinical practice was promoted more vigorously than ever before, due to the efforts of three women. Eva Augusta Vescelius, Isa Maud Ilsen, and Harriet Ayer Seymour were all strong-willed individuals who developed interesting personal philosophies concerning the use of music in therapy, practiced what they advocated, and late in their careers, established music therapy organizations devoted to treating physically and mentally ill patients with live music. Although they ultimately failed to develop music therapy programs that lasted more than a few years, their work established music therapy as a viable therapeutic modality that was recognized by such organizations as the Red Cross and United States Army (Davis & Gfeller, 1992).

Eva Augusta Vescelius (Activity Span: 1900-1917)

Eva Augusta Vescelius was the first of the three to practice music therapy. She and her two sisters were brought up in an environment that nurtured their musical talents. As a young woman, Vescelius was privileged to study voice with excellent teachers in the United States and Europe. Later, she and her sisters sang professionally around the world, sometimes performing in hospitals and asylums. After 10 years of constant touring, she tired of this endeavor and returned home to study "mental therapy" and applications of music in healing. She perfected her theories at home before venturing out to apply her ideas to patients in hospitals and institutions (Vescelius-Sheldon, 1919).

The first documented evidence of Vescelius' interest in music therapy was in 1900, when she presented a lecture at the second annual meeting of the International Metaphysical League, held at Madison Square Garden in New York City ("Effect of Music," 1900). Her lecture, entitled "Musical Vibration in the Healing of the Sick," was well-received despite skepticism among some of the conference organizers—they granted Vescelius only 12 minutes to present her paper (Vescelius, 1913). The success of this presentation and numerous other lectures and demonstrations led Vescelius to establish the National Society for Musical Therapeutics in 1903. The purpose of the organization was "to be the study and advancement of music in its relation to life and health and to promote the intelligent employment of music in homes of the sick, in hospitals, and in asylums" ("Home of the New Thought," 1906). Vescelius remained the organization's president until her death in 1917.

At the time the National Society for Musical Therapeutics was founded, Vescelius rented a studio in Carnegie Hall, where she taught applied voice and piano lessons as well as classes about music therapy. She was also in demand as a speaker. In the summer of 1907, she was scheduled to present a series of lectures at the Upland Farmers Alliance meeting near Peekskill, New York. Members of this group gathered each summer under the leadership of Charles Brodie Patterson, an influential proponent of New Thought, to share ideas, make music, and relax in the idyllic, rural setting ("Home of the New Thought," 1906).

New Thought was an important, though controversial mental and therapeutics movement that flourished during the late nineteenth and early twentieth centuries. Following the principles espoused by Phineas Parkhust Quimby and Ralph Waldo Emerson, New Thought advocates believed in a personal, nonliturgical religion that stressed the importance of the power of the mind to heal physical and mental illness ("New Thought," 1982). The philosophical precepts that comprised New Thought clearly influenced the music therapy practice of Vescelius, who believed that a combination of music and mental healing was best for treating mental and physical illness (Vescelius, 1913).

The philosophy and music therapy techniques espoused by Vescelius were developed over the years during her numerous visits to hospitals and asylums. She had very definite ideas about the way music should be used with the sick. Specifically, she believed that the selection of key, rhythm, and composition was very important in helping people change unhealthy physical, mental, and spiritual conditions. She considered rhythm the most important factor in a cure, although she did not elaborate. Also sketchy were claims that her experiments using voice, piano, harp, and other stringed instruments proved the efficacy of using live music to treat illness (Vescelius, 1918).

Vescelius sometimes grouped together diverse medical conditions she believed could be treated by a particular style of music (selected compositions by Beethoven were favorites). For example, soft, rhythmical music could be used to break a fever, reduce pulse and respiration, and calm the patient.

Interestingly, Vescelius believed that the therapist's personality should not intrude on the musical treatment; musical healing should be impersonal, with the individuality of the artist reflected in the music. Because of this factor, music therapists who worked for Vescelius had to be exceptional musicians. Consequently, when members of the NSMT visited hospitals, they nearly always played while outside the patient's room (Vescelius, 1918).

Perhaps Eva Augusta Vescelius' greatest contribution to music therapy was the establishment in 1913 of the first American music therapy periodical, Music and Health. Although this publication was short-lived (lasting only three issues), it was a fitting testimony to her long-standing commitment to music therapy. One reason for the journal's early demise may have been its questionable quality; it contained poems, anecdotes culled from music and medical periodicals (many of which were old), and a few testimonials about the benefits of music therapy from musicians and physicians, but very few substantial articles. One of the more substantive articles authored by Vescelius in the first issue later formed the basis of her last known writing, "Music and Health," which appeared posthumously in an issue of The Musical Quarterly (1918).

After Vescelius sudden death from heart failure in 1917, her sister, Louise Vescelius-Sheldon (also a professional musician and writer) carried on her work for a short period of time. As a final tribute to her sister, Vescelius-Sheldon wrote an article in 1919 that summarized her work as a music therapist, noting that Vescelius "started the ball rolling; the world gave it a kick, and it rolled away and is still going" (Vescelius-Sheldon, 1919, P. 3).

Isa Maud Ilsen (Activity Span: 1905-1930)

Unfortunately, very little information exists about the early experiences that shaped Isa Maud Ilsen's desire to become a music therapist. However, it is known that in 1905 as an undergraduate in nursing school, she became interested in using music to treat physical and mental disorders and, like Vescelius spent several years testing her theories on clinical populations, including the mentally ill, terminally ill, and mentally retarded. She was also active in promoting music in factories and other businesses to humanize often difficult working conditions ("Musical Prescriptions," 1919).

Before the United States entered World War I in 1917, Ilsen moved to Canada to offer music therapy services to injured Canadian veterans returning from the European Theater. It was during this time that she claimed to have established a practical and scientific method for treating physical and mental disease "almost as precise as any existing medicine or surgery" ("Musical Prescriptions," 1919).

In 1918, Ilsen returned to the United States to work for the Commission on Training Camp Activities of the War Department as a music therapist. A short time later, she became Director of Hospital Music in Reconstruction Hospitals for the Red Cross, where she vigorously promoted the use of music therapy for injured American soldiers with surgical, medical, corrective, and reconstruction needs. After the War, Ilsen briefly changed the focus of her music therapy activity from that of clinician to teacher. In 1919, she accepted the position of lecturer in "Musico-therapy" at Columbia University in New York City. This was the first time that music therapy was taught on a regular basis at a college or university in the United States. She noted that 12 graduates from her first class used her system of music therapy in area hospitals and institutions ("Musical Prescriptions for the Ailing," 1919). Apparently, it took but a short period of time to learn the principles of Ilsen's methods, because her students worked as clinicians after only one semester of study!

In 1925, she was employed as Associate Secretary, Department of Hospital Services, New York Tuberculosis and Health Association. For a year or two, she worked as an administrator and clinician to bring music therapy services to children and adults suffering from tuberculosis. At that time, the treatment for tuberculosis consisted of rest, proper diet, and fresh air—there were no effective drugs for this dreaded condition (Bell & Ilsen, 1925). As a consequence, persons afflicted with tuberculosis spent months and sometimes years in hospitals and sanitariums while the disease ran its course. Music was used in conjunction with other treatment modalities, such as occupational therapy, to enrich the dreadfully monotonous lifestyle imposed on tuberculosis patients.

Ilsen's crowning achievement occurred in New York City during 1926, with the founding of the National Association for Music in Hospitals. The purpose of the group was to bring properly prepared music programs into hospitals to be used as an adjunct to medical treatment. She firmly believed that the success of her program depended on trained staff and the cooperation of medical staff. As early as 1919, she developed the following specific rules of conduct for performing in hospitals:

- obtaining the permission of the physician in charge
- establishing rapport with the chief nurse and assistants
- wearing clothing that was bright and cheerful
- avoiding somber music
- avoiding the use of trumpet, cello, or portable organ
- using tact and common sense

These and other results provided valuable guidelines for the volunteer musicians entering a hospital for the first time. Ilsen recognized early on that cooperation with the medical staff was imperative for the success of her program. She did not want to jeopardize hospital privileges by allowing well-meaning musicians to participate without adequate preparation ("Music Therapy," 1919). Some of her rules are as relevant today as they were in 1919, while others, such as the ban on the use of trumpet, cello, and portable organ from hospital wards, would be less acceptable.

In September 1926, a short announcement appeared in the New York Times offering free scholarships to musicians willing to be trained as music therapists. Because of the demand, classes were to begin immediately after the screening and admittance of approved candidates. Perhaps most importantly, funds had been raised by a group of philanthropic women to train and transport the music therapists to local hospitals and institutions. Ilsen remarked that, even though the Association had only recently been established, she had received requests for music therapy services from as far away as New Mexico and Tennessee ("A Society," 1926).

Isa Maud Ilsen carefully cultivated her ideas and theories concerning the uses of music in hospitals. Based on her many years as a clinician, educator, and administrator, she offered strong opinions as to the proper manner in which music therapy should be used with clients. In addition to insisting on the use of trained professionals, she firmly believed in using a variety of music along with other creative arts therapies, including dancers, magicians, and elocutionists (trained public speakers). She favored the violin and voice but also endorsed other instruments, including the harp. Unlike Vescelius, Ilsen believed that a therapist's personality played an important role in the therapeutic process. Because the music was performed live and often at the patient's bedside, it was important to hire musicians who were not only well-trained but also able to relate to clients and staff effectively (Ilsen, 1927).

Ilsen, like Vescelius, had definite ideas about the stylistic qualities of the music to be used. Songs should not be pitched in a minor key or contain sad lyrics; they should be bright and cheerful, while instrumental music should be short, tuneful, familiar, and "not too classical," and jazz should be used sparingly if at all. Ilsen believed that music aroused vital functions (undefined) of the body—a state of perfect health indicated that all vital functions were rhythmic, whereas illness indicated just the opposite. Ilsen envisioned music therapy as a permanent part of hospital service in the near future, because "I have yet to find a single case where the right kind of music, rendered by the right kind of instrument, in the right way by the right people has anything but a remedial agent for the sick" (Ilsen, 1926, p. 15).

Despite the substantial attention given to Ilsen and the National Association for Music in Hospitals by the media, there is no evidence that her dream survived for long. The last reference to her work occurred in a 1930 article (Ilsen, 1930) which reiterated her ideas concerning the use of music therapy in hospitals.

Harriet Ayer Seymour (Activity Span: 1915-1944)

Harriet Ayer Seymour was born on August 27, 1867 in Chicago to a wealthy family that was willing and able to provide her with the best musical training available. She studied in New York City and later at the Royal Conservatory of Music in Stuttgart, Germany, where she graduated in 1886. She gave up her musical career for marriage but resumed it a short time later as a teacher when her husband, a stockbroker, suffered financial reversals. She was a skilled pianist and teacher who taught for a number of years at the Institute of Musical Art, later renamed the Julliard School of Music ("Harriet Ayer Seymour," 1947).

She supported her four children with a number of interesting teaching and administrative positions, including 11 years as head of the music department of the Third Street Musical Settlement (settlement schools provided educational and social pro- grams to poor families) in New York City. In 1924, she founded the Seymour School of Musical Reeducation where, in addition to her teaching duties, she published one issue of an ill-fated journal promoting her ideas about music education and therapy. During the time that she headed the music school bearing her name, she also lectured on music topics for the New York Public Schools and served as Chairwoman of the Music Committee of the New York State Charities Aid Association, an organization that brought musical entertainment to the New York hospitals that cared for indigent patients. From 1930-1935, Harriet Ayer Seymour regularly hosted a music appreciation program for NBC radio ("Harriet Ayer Seymour," 1947).

Like Eva Augusta Vescelius Seymour began her music therapy training by informally conducting experiments with friends in her home. A short time later, she tried out her ideas in hospitals and institutions with a wide range of clientele. During World War I, Seymour provided music therapy services to "shell shocked" American soldiers returning to hospitals from Europe ("Music for Shellshock," 1944). It is interesting to note that even though Seymour and Isa Maud Ilsen both worked with returning soldiers who had mental and physical injuries sustained in the war, there is no evidence that the two ever crossed paths during this or any other time.

Harriet Ayer Seymour was also an accomplished author, publishing a number of books on music education and, later in life, devoting much time to writing about music therapy. In 1920, she penned a book entitled, *What Music Can Do For You*. One chapter, "Music and Health," elucidated her thoughts about music therapy for the first time.

At about the same time that *What Music Can Do For You* was published, Seymour's spiritual preferences became apparent through other writings. This was important because her adherence to the teachings of the Unity Church and New Thought Movement shaped her philosophy of music education and therapy for life. As an example, she often used "musical meditation" to reach the emotions of both her private piano students and music therapy clients. She would improvise at the piano on a phrase, such as "infinite goodness," while her students/clients repeated the expression to themselves, either audibly or silently (Seymour, 1920).

As evidence of her leadership in this type of "mental healing," Seymour participated in a music therapy demonstration for 200 delegates attending a New Thought Alliance meeting in New York City during the spring of 1933. As referenced in the discussion of Vescelius, adherents of New Thought philosophy believed in the power to heal through thought. She played the piano while another participant asked the members to close their eyes and concentrate on the phrase "power and plenty." At the conclusion of the demonstration, several members of the audience claimed that their headaches had been cured. One audience member even remarked that her heart condition was improved ("200 Test Music Cure," 1933).

Seymour's career as a teacher, therapist, and writer culminated with the 1941 founding of the third music therapy organization during the twentieth century—the National Foundation of Musical Therapy (Stewart, 1941). During the short existence of her organization, Seymour claimed to have trained more than 500 "musical doctors" to work in New York City hospitals, primarily with sick or injured World War II veterans. Shortly before her death in July, 1944, Seymour published what may have been the first music therapy text devoted to clinical practice. *An Instruction Course in the Use and Practice of Musical Therapy* contained information about appropriate applications of music with a variety of clinical populations. For example, she devoted chapters to "Musical Therapy for Children, " "Instructions for Visiting Mental and Tubercular Hospitals," and "Instruction Programs for Hospital Wards." In addition, she provided useful guidelines for prospective music therapists. Unlike Ilsen and Vescelius, Seymour did not believe that a music therapist must be an extraordinarily gifted musician. Instead, she looked for individuals who possessed a basic knowledge of music, with the ability to play simple tunes with good tone and rhythm and, if possible, without using music. She sought people who were sensitive to clients' reactions and had a desire to become a "channel" for the healing properties of the music (Seymour, 1944).

The cornerstone of Seymour's treatment philosophy was music used in conjunction with "constructive thought." As Seymour matured, she developed specific ideas concerning the use of particular styles of music for a variety of disorders. According to Seymour, patients suffering from heart ailments should be treated with music having a predictable, even rhythm in order to correct an irregular heartbeat. For patients with paralysis, the use of mental imagery coupled with rhythmic music (especially marches) improved the function of the affected limbs. Depressed individuals benefitted from folk tunes of their culture ("Music for Shellshock," 1944). Most of the time, Seymour did not explain why a specific combination of music and constructive thought worked better with some disorders than with others. Presumably her many years of work as a music therapist led her to develop distinctive treatment strategies for a particular illness.

Like Vescelius and Ilsen, Seymour was skeptical of the value of jazz. Having perhaps the greatest bias against the musical style of the three women, Seymour remarked that "The irregular pulse and lack of form are more disturbing than healing. Jazz stimulates, but on a low level, and a little goes a long way. You play boogie woogie in a psychiatric ward and the patients get frightfully agitated" ("Music for Shellshock," 1944). Seymour died in New York City on July 31, 1944 at age 77.

Conclusion

For many reasons, Eva Augusta Vescelius, Isa Maud Ilsen, and Harriet Ayer Seymour were three of the most important figures in early twentieth century music therapy. They were the first Americans to practice clinical music therapy for an extended length of time. All had impressive careers that touched many lives, including the clients who received music therapy and the volunteer musicians who provided the service. Through adherence to high standards of conduct, empirical research over many years, and the establishment of organizations to carry out their work, these three women provided the impetus for the continued growth and development of music therapy during the second half of the twentieth century.

The three were also educators dedicated to training musicians in the proper methods of using music in hospitals, asylums, and schools, and as a preventive measure against stress and disease. There is ample evidence to conclude that all three women lectured and taught on a regular basis throughout their careers, training many volunteers (very few music therapists were paid) to provide music therapy services to adults and children in charity hospitals, asylums, prisons, and schools.

Why then, despite good intentions, hard work, and media attention, did none of the three music therapy pioneers leave a lasting legacy? One probable reason was the lack of a formal structure in their organizations. There is no evidence that any of the three music therapy societies had anything more than a rudimentary administrative organization; therefore, it would have been difficult for another individual to assume a leadership role once the founder died or stepped down. Perhaps the women did not perceive a need to formalize their operations, relying instead on personal charisma to maintain a viable organization. Another possible reason for the demise of the organizations was the general reluctance of many to accept the idea of music therapy. Louise Vescelius-Sheldon remarked that "reporters [who attended Eva Augusta Vescelius' lecturers on music therapy] insisted on data which they used for the most part in editorial ridicule" (Vescelius-Sheldon, 1919, p. 3). Even today, music therapy organizations as well as individual music therapists spend much time educating the public about music therapy. In 1900, the job would have perhaps been overwhelming, even to dedicated people like Vescelius, Ilsen, and Seymour, who had the courage, conviction, and skill to promote this unusual therapy (Davis & Gfeller, 1992).

Despite the ultimate failure of each woman to leave a lasting reputation, all should be recognized as twentieth century pioneers in the field of music therapy. As Harriet Ayer Seymour noted in 1944 just months before her death, "Fortunate indeed is the therapist of today who walks straightway into pioneered territory, where he may begin work at once without being questioned by skeptics" (Seymour, 1944, p. 1). These words are perhaps even more applicable today than they were almost 50 years ago.

References

A society for hospital music. (1926, May 8). The Literary Digest, 24. Bell, F. D., & Ilsen, I. M. (1925). The psycho-physiological effect of music on tuberculosis patients. Modern Hospital, 25, 227-229.

Davis, W. B. (1989). Music therapy in nineteenth century America. Journal of Music Therapy, 24, 76-87.

Davis, W. B., & Gfeller, K. (1992) (1992). Music therapy: An historical perspective. In W. B. Davis, K. E. Gfeller, and H. H. Thaut (Eds.), An introduction to music therapy: Theory and practice (pp. 16-37). Dubuque, IA: Brown and Benchmark.

Effect of music on the sick. (1900, October 24). New York Times, 14.

Harriet Ayer Seymour. (1947). National Cyclopedia of American Biography, 33, 294.

Home of the new thought. (1906, September 1). Highland Democrat, 7.

Ilsen, I. M. (1926). How music is used in hospitals. Musician, 31, 15, 30.

Ilsen, I. M. (1927). The value of music in hospitals. Clinical Medicine, 34, 765-768.

Ilsen, I. M. (1930). Music as a medicine and a tonic in restoring health. The Modern Hospital, 34, 81-84.

Musical prescriptions. (1919, August 23). Literary Digest, 26.

Musical prescriptions for the ailing. (1919, July 13). New York Times Magazine, 5.

Musical therapy--an opportunity. (August, 1919). Musician, 24, 9, 37.

Music for shellshock. (1944, January 24). Newsweek, 66.

New thought. (1982). Encyclopedia Americana. Danbury, CT: Grolier.

Seymour. H. A. (1920). Music and health. In H. A. Seymour (Ed.), *What music can do for you* (pp. 146163). New York: Harper & Brothers.

Seymour, H. A. (1944). *An instruction course in the use and practice of musical therapy.* New York: National Foundation of Musical Therapy, Inc.

Stewart, 0. (1941). Music that cures. *Scribner's Commentary, 10,* 83-87.

200 test music cure. (1933, May 29). *New York Times,* 22.

Vescelius, E. A. (1913). Music in its relation to life. *Music and Health, 1,* 5-10.

Vescelius, E. A. (1918). Music and health. *Musical Quarterly, 4,* 377-401.

Vescelius-Sheldon, L. (1919, May 10). Music attuned to the patient's pulse beat a life renewer. *Musical America, 30,* 3-4.

Reprinted with permission of the *Journal of Music Therapy*

From reading Davis's article, music therapists can determine that music therapy was used in many clinical environments years before the formation of NAMT in 1950. This article provides a strong historical precedent for the use of therapeutic music in treating persons with disabilities. Now let's consider the structure and content of historical research.

Examination of Davis's article reveals that the structure of the study differs considerably from that used in descriptive and experimental research. It does not contain Methods, Results, or Discussion sections, and it does not include statistical analyses of numerical data. The form of historical research emerges from the data by using logical and critical thinking and varies from problem to problem. The structure of the narrative is not evident from the beginning of the project but takes shape as it is being written (Solomon & Heller, 1982). Rather than having distinct sections (such as Methods, Results, etc.), a historical study often reads more like a story and may include reproductions of pictures, objects, or documents that add richness and depth as well as illustrate some of the key findings.

Historians use different types of data (information) than we find in descriptive or experimental research. Rather than using quantitative (numerical) data, questions are often answered by examining artifacts such as old photographs, objects (such as old equipment or personal possessions), personal letters, diaries, articles in newspapers, official documents or policy statements, and other materials that provide insights into the past. These materials may be found in places such as libraries, museums, archives, governmental records, newspaper files, special collections, and in the possession of individual citizens. One of the tasks of the historian is to verify that the materials used in his or her study are **authentic** (that is, genuine, and not falsified information). In addition, the historian must endeavor to uncover as much relevant information as possible in order to present as comprehensive and balanced perspective of the question at hand as is possible.

Sometimes historians ask questions about events more recent than those found in Davis's article. For example, a historian may wish to learn more about the merger of the National Association for Music Therapy and the American Association for Music Therapy in 1998. Many people, such as the presidents of those two organizations, who observed those events firsthand, are still alive. In such instances, the historian may want to interview people to gather their recollections and to determine if those individuals have possession of letters, pictures, or documents that might be relevant to the research study.

The final type of research that we will cover in this chapter is called **qualitative research.** Like historical research, qualitative research uses written narratives rather than statistical analyses of quantitative (numerical) data to answer questions. The term *qualitative research* refers to a category of many different research methods (outlined below), which share common principles.

Qualitative Research

Qualitative research answers questions using rich and detailed narratives or written or poetic accounts of specific situations. Qualitative research in music therapy has a rich and diverse history both nationally and internationally. Beginning with a seminal work in 1983 by music therapist Carolyn Kenny, the qualitative tradition continues to flourish (Abrams, 2005; Aigen, 1993; Aldridge, 1989; Amir, 1993; Ansdell, 2003, Assgaard, 2005; Bruscia, 1995; Forinash & Gonzalez, 1989; Kenny, 1987; Ruud, 2005; Smeijsters, 1997; Stige, 2005; Wheeler, 1999, 2005).

All research emanates from an **ontology** or world view that defines what is considered "reality." **Quantitative** research (such as descriptive and experimental research) comes from a perspective in which "reality" is seen as something that can be uncovered and known, or at least approximated (Edwards, 1999). Quantitative researchers go to great lengths to use methods that will result in objective and unbiased answers to questions such as "Is music therapy an effective treatment strategy for children with autism?" or "Was music therapy effective this group of adults with behavioral-emotional disorders?"

Qualitative research comes from a different perspective on what constitutes "reality." In **qualitative** research, "reality" is seen as something that is negotiated or constructed by those who are experiencing the event. In other words, rather than trying to set up an objective and unbiased experiment, the qualitative researcher will embrace the unique life experiences and beliefs of those involved in the study; their perspectives influence how the study unfolds and how the results are interpreted. The sorts of questions that emanate from a qualitative perspective might include:

"What did this group of adolescent girls with eating disorders experience in music therapy?" or "What meaning do cancer patients find in group music therapy?" So rather than looking for an objective or single "truth," in qualitative research one seeks to examine and understand human experience.

The qualitative mind set. Within qualitative research are many different research methods, each with various research **protocols** (steps or approaches). Examples include ethnographic, arts-based, naturalistic, participatory action, morphological, first-person, heuristic, narrative, qualitative case study, hermeneutic, grounded theory, and phenomenology[1]. At this point in your studies, it is not important to understand completely each of these aforementioned methods. But it is important to realize that there is no single research protocol for any of these methods. Consequently, you may come across qualitative case studies or phenomenological studies that use very different research protocols. You can learn much more about these different qualitative methods in more advanced courses that focus specifically on research methods.

Qualitative research is more of a mind set or a philosophy than an actual series of research protocols or methodological rules. Several authors have described general characteristics of qualitative research in an attempt to provide guidelines for the qualitative research mind set (Aigen, 1993; Bogdan & Biklen, 1982; Creswell, 2007, Forinash & Lee, 1998; Lincoln & Guba, 1985; Wheeler & Kenny, 2005). Thus, while the reader may not encounter each of the following concepts or principles in all qualitative research, it is likely that you will encounter some or many of the following concepts or principles when reading qualitative research:

1. **Qualitative research happens in the natural setting.** You will find qualitative researchers out in the field, interviewing or observing research participants in their school, group, or internship site, doing what they would be doing naturally. This is why you will also hear qualitative research referred to as **naturalistic research.** Qualitative research is descriptive rather than numeric, with **thick** (lengthy and detailed) descriptions of experience, pictures, images, poems, or metaphors used to depict experiences. Arts-based research (Austin & Forinash, 2005) in particular, uses an artistic process for each step of the research endeavor (generating the question, collecting data, data analysis, and presentation of results).

2. **Research participants are indeed participants and not "subjects"** as they truly take part in the research endeavor and have an impact on the findings. They are chosen on purpose, rather than randomly, for their particular life experience or

---

[1]See B. W. Wheeler (2005) for a thorough discussion of qualitative research approaches.

perspective. For example, if one wants to understand the experience of a therapist practicing from a particular music therapy model (as shown in the article that follows), one would seek out clinicians practicing in that model who were articulate and thoughtful, as they would be able to accurately describe their experiences and help the researcher gain a new understanding of their experience.

3. An emergent research design is common in qualitative research. Emergent means that not all the research steps need to be spelled out before the research begins. One may start out with a basic question about understanding the meaning of a music therapy experience and begin the research process by observing clients in music therapy. However, after observing, the researcher might decide that to better understand the phenomenon, he or she needed to take additional steps, such as interviewing the music therapist, interviewing the clients' families, or observing the clients in a setting outside of music therapy. Much like the process of practicing as a music therapist in a **client-centered** way, while there is an end goal in mind, the process of getting to that goal is negotiated along the way. While this may sound "simple," it actually requires great focus and concentration to stay attuned to the research process as it unfolds and not go off course. To maintain focus, researchers keep a journal in which they record all decisions made relating to the research process and a discussion of why choices are made.

4. Research outcomes are negotiated, meaning that once the researcher has formed conclusions, he or she would share these conclusions with the research participants (where appropriate) or with peers to help ensure that he or she had indeed captured the participants' experience. Oftentimes, as in the example below, research participants have additional insights that are included in the outcomes.

Because the qualitative researcher selects participants with specific characteristics and often studies individuals or small groups, the findings of the article are not easily generalized (i.e., applied) to many other people or circumstances. The researcher is describing what the experience was only for this particular group of participants; he or she is not implying that other clients would have the same experience. However, research consumers can evaluate the findings and decide whether their clients are similar enough to those in the study and if the findings might apply to them as well.

Often the researchers will share their thoughts and beliefs about the study as well as how the study impacted them. This allows the reader to understand the perspective the researcher brings to the study. Acknowledging one's own biases also enables the researcher some ability to suspend his or her beliefs and attend to the phenomenon under investigation.

So we see that qualitative research is not one "thing." It is more of a perspective or a philosophy of knowing. The focus of research is to construct meaning based on input from those who have experienced the phenomenon.

In qualitative research, there is no magic or "sufficient" number of participants that indicates a good study. Studies may have 1 participant, or 4, or 7, or 15. Because qualitative researchers do not emphasize generalizability, there is no need for a large number of participants. In fact, it would be nearly impossible to do a good qualitative study with 50 participants! The guidance here is that you keep collecting data until you are satiated, that is, until you feel you have captured the experience you are studying in both breadth and depth.

Evaluating qualitative research. Evaluating qualitative research is complex, as there are no agreed-upon set of standards that one must follow to ensure quality work. Several authors (Bruscia, 1998; Creswell, 2007; Lincoln & Guba, 1985; Stige, 2002) have grappled with providing standards, though it is important to acknowledge that there simply is no checklist to follow and no minimum number of standards that guarantee a robust (strong and well executed) study. The burden is on the consumer of research to be familiar with various standards, and thus be able to evaluate the study.

Ken Bruscia (1998), a music therapist well known for his qualitative research studies, does a masterful job of discussing standards of integrity in qualitative research and likens it to the process of learning and performing a Chopin nocturne. He created four broad categories of integrity: **Methodological, Personal, Interpersonal,** and **Aesthetic**. Evaluating a research study's methodological integrity (Bruscia, 1998, pp. 182–184) means determining that the research method is appropriate to the question being asked and making sure that the research method chosen allows us to learn something new about the topic being studied.

Evaluating **personal integrity** (Bruscia, 1998, pp. 189–191) has to do with evidence that the researcher was fully present and honest, both professionally and personally, while doing the study. Readers will want to know that the researcher took the work seriously, stayed focused on the study, and took responsibility for all decisions made in the research process. Readers would also want to evaluate that the researcher sought and offered new insights and discoveries about the topic being studied.

Assessing **interpersonal integrity** (Bruscia, 1998, pp. 185–189) means evaluating the researcher's commitment to understanding the world of the research participant, being clear about how his or her beliefs impact the study. It also means being clear about the distinction between the words and ideas of the participant and the words and ideas of the researcher. While we don't often talk about the beauty of research, evaluating **aesthetic integrity** (pp. 192–196) means looking for creativity in the research, meaningful outcomes for those involved in the study as well as for readers of the study. The study should give us new knowledge about the topic being studied.

Now that you've learned about some basic characteristics of qualitative research, here is an article that illustrates those characteristics.

Music Therapy, 11 (1), 120-141, 1992

A Phenomenological Analysis of Nordoff-Robbins Model of Music Therapy: The Lived Experience of Clinical Improvisation[2]

Introduction

The purpose of this study was to examine the experience of therapists who use clinical improvisation as practiced by Nordoff-Robbins trained clinicians. Clinical improvisation is the basis of the Nordoff-Robbins model of music therapy and rests on the assumption that in every child, regardless of ability or disability, lives an inborn musicality and musical sensitivity. This inherent musicality is referred to as the "music child."

> *...the term has reference to the universality of musical sensitivity – the heritage of complex sensitivity to the ordering and relationship of tonal and rhythmic movement; it also points to the distinctly personal significance of each child's musical responsiveness. (1977, p. 1).*

Clinical improvisation is the technique of engaging a child through the therapist's creation of a musical-emotional environment, thus accessing the "music child." In this environment the child's responses and expressions are accepted as meaningful and used to facilitate further contact and communication. The therapist's role in this process is to improvise clinical significant music, music that will reach the child and provide the possibility for a relationship in which the child can grow and develop.

Method

All of the 10 music therapists on staff at the Nordoff–Robbins Center for Music Therapy accepted the invitation to be research participants. The research protocol included individual face to face interviews with participants while watching video segments video of them improvising in a session. Interviews took the form of open ended questions regarding the improvisation. Each interview was audio recorded, transcribed, and analyzed as follows (Giorgi, 1984).

Step 1. Each transcript was reviewed to get an overall sense of the experience.
Step 2. Each transcript was reviewed multiple times and phrases that seemed important were highlighted.

---

[2]Adapted from Forinash, M. (1992) A phenomenological analysis of Nordoff-Robbins model of music therapy: The lived experience of clinical improvisation. *Music Therapy, 11*(1), 120–141. Reprinted with permission.

Step 3 Highlighted phrases that seemed similar from various transcripts were grouped together.

Step 4 Grouped phrases were placed in categories and were given short titles such as "Vulnerability" etc. which described the experience

Step 5 Emerging categories and phrases were continually reviewed until the categories and supporting quotes from the transcripts made sense.

Step 6. Descriptions of the categories were created and quotes were included as examples of the types of statements which led to the creation of the category.

Step 7. Transcripts of the interviews along with the descriptions of the categories were submitted to the participants.

Step 8. Responses from the participants were integrated into the conclusion section and a general description of clinical improvisation was offered.

Results

The following categories emerged from the data analysis: Natural Ability; Musical Biography; The Unknown; Vulnerability; Pressure; Hard to Define; Spontaneity, Creativity, and Intuition; Interplay of Intuition and Rationality; Rational Conscious Choice; Self; Music; and The Child. These categories are discussed below and supported by quotes from the research interviews. In keeping with the phenomenological ideal to study experience in its lived form, the interview material is included as it transpired. The therapists were responding spontaneously as the research process unfolded. Therefore, some of the quotations have a rough, process oriented quality to them rather than the more finished phrasing usually given to one's thoughts when they are allowed to develop over an extended period of time. (For the purposes of this chapter only 3 of the 11 categories are discussed.) It is important to note that there was not a focus on finding agreement between participants about what they had experienced. Categories that appeared for only one or two participants were considered important as they address the breadth of the experience.

Musical Biography

Participants spoke of the significance of their own unique musical background, their "musical biography": their history as a musician which encompasses their musical preferences, training, and personality. This can be summarized as an awareness of one's musical background and an ability to use one's natural resources to build from these assets.

> Participant 9: Musical biography is not only your gifts but what you have been exposed to, what you have acquired, your tastes and prejudices.

The participants represented a diversity of musical biographies. Some learned to play music by ear and grew up playing primarily popular music. One participant related an early musical memory of hearing and imitating music, and of the subsequent connections made between emotions and music and how this affected current improvisations.

> Participant 2: I remember watching TV as a child and connecting certain scenes to emotions. Like on "Star Trek" when Kirk saw his love. [Therapist moves to the piano and plays music from that scene.] Those things stick with me. It becomes part of my history.

Other participants grew up with classical training and technique. In describing an improvisation, one spoke of the influence of her classical training.

> Participant 1: I didn't grow up with improvisation. I tend to play in a more classical style. Even this theme [referring to video tape] is more "Bachian" because I have been listening to that music all my life.

Although the participants stated that musical history as essential, they assumed that no one particular musical biography was correct or the best. They indicated that musical biography was an important part of the preparation for improvisation. It was not seen as a limitation to overcome, but as a building block from which to grow.

The Unknown

When asked to describe the experience of improvising the participants spoke of improvisation as facing the unknown, which they recognized as a very powerful force.

> Participant 1: It is like a mystery story where the end is unknown. It has yet to happen. The only way to find out is to do it.

> Participant 5: There is a lot of living in the moment to see what will happen and not even knowing what I will be playing.

> Participant 2: I have a sense of preparation and direction, but I do not know what will happen. I must be open to that.

> Participant 9: It is a stepping into the unknown. It is a mysterious thing about the creative process.

These statements indicate that clinical improvisation involves a necessary willingness on the part of the therapist to step into the unknown, to enter into a relationship

Vulnerability

The participants spoke of the feeling of vulnerability that accompanies stepping into the unknown:

> Participant 5: It is a vulnerable situation because defenses are stripped away. It is really letting yourself go and it is a vulnerable place to be in.

> Participant 8: You are vulnerable in that …even if you have a plan it might be totally not what is needed at the moment. You have to be vulnerable. If you were controlling and rigid, I don't think you could do this kind of work.

Perhaps this participant sums it up most clearly:

> Participant 3: You can't hide. It comes out in the music.

While participants felt this sense of vulnerability was uncomfortable to some degree, they saw their discomfort as unavoidable and something to be accepted as part of the improvisation experience. Permitting and accepting the feelings of vulnerability seemed critical to these participants.

Interplay of Intuition and Rationality

At times both intuition and rationality are working together in a balance. The participants spoke of the constant interaction between their spontaneous, intuitive choices and their rational choices. One might intuitively begin the music in a session but once started the music can become more clinically directed

> Participant 4: The music comes out, you are hearing it, then you catch up to your fingers. It is a split. After you start improvising, then your mind is listening and develops it. You have to become conscious of what you are playing. It may come from an unknown place, but you have to know it and be aware of it to bring it back to the child, even as it is happening.

The transformation was from the spontaneous, creative impulse to deliberate, clinical significant intentionality. The reverse may also happen. One may decide to play a certain musical style but, once begun, the development may occur spontaneously.

Participant 7: For this improvisation I had picked a mode based on the instrument the child was playing. When he changed to a different instrument I stayed with the music I had started because, I don't know, it just felt right to stay with it. I don't know why I did that.

For these participants there is a flow that occurs during the sessions from intuition to rational choices and from rational choices to intuitive choices.

Discussion

The results indicate that, for these participants, the experience of improvisation encompasses more than the interaction between therapist and child in the session. The experience also extends back in time to the participants individual and complex music histories, and reaches forward to encompass their learning as they analyze their improvisations after the sessions.

The participants also conveyed that there is a profound sense of facing the unknown and the accompanying vulnerability that comes with improvising. Another insight into the experience of improvisation came in the participants' discussions about the interplay of intuition and rationality.[3] There is a place and necessity for all positions along the rational to intuitive continuum. While it is probably easier to teach the rational and logical aspects of clinical improvisation, the experience of these participants suggests that the creative and intuitive aspects were vital to their process of improvisation.

For these participants clinical improvisation is bringing personal, unique musical ability and history to life in the present moment. It requires one to step into the unknown moment of clinical interaction and to meet that moment with musical and therapeutic creativity and intuition as well as rational intention. Clinical improvisation requires a sense of trust and the ability to "let go" into the process. It requires a willingness to be open and vulnerable to the experience.

Conclusion

In qualitative research trustworthiness is often established in terms of what meaning the results have for the research participants. For that reason the results were submitted to the participants and their responses to the portrait of clinical improvisation are offered here.

Comments from the participants indicated that they were pleased and surprised that their experiences were paralleled by other participants. While an individual participant may not have been able to verbalize an aspect of the experience clearly, they gained a deeper understanding by reading someone else's attempt to describe the experience.

Participant 1: I found the comments from my colleagues to be insightful and interesting. Especially one in particular who said "You can't hide. It comes out in the music."

Participant 4: While I couldn't verbalize it myself, the words "Facing the Unknown" with their accompanying feelings of vulnerability rang true for me. These elements make the work so challenging and a bit scary at times.

Clinical improvisation remains a complex process. This study began to uncover aspects of what these participants experienced and might be of use for those teaching in the Nordoff-Robbins model.

In terms of further research, each of the categories of experience could be looked at in more depth and additional Nordoff-Robbins therapists could be interviewed to provide more breadth to what is experienced in improvisation.

---

[3]And other themes which are discussed more fully in the original article.

References

Bruscia, K.E. (2001). A qualitative approach to analyzing client improvisations. *Music Therapy Perspectives, 19,* 7-21.

Forinash, M. & Grocke, D. (2005). Phenomenological inquiry. In B.W. Wheeler (Ed.). *Music therapy research,* 2nd ed. Gilsum, NH: Barcelona Publishers.

Giorgi, A. (1984). A phenomenological psychological analysis of the artistic process. In J.G. Gilbert (Ed.), *Qualitative Evaluation in the Arts.* New York: NYU Publishing.

Kenny, C.B. (1983, May). *Phenomenological research: A promise for the healing arts.* Paper presented at the meeting of the Canadian Association for Music Therapy, Toronto, Ontario, Canada.

Nordoff, P & Robbins, C. (1977) *Creative music therapy.* New York: John Day. (this edition is out of print – see below for second edition).

Nordoff, P. & Robbins, C. (2006). *Creative music therapy: A guide to fostering clinical musicianship.* Gilsum, NH: Barcelona Publishers.

As one can see from this qualitative study, a relatively small number (10 people) participated in this study. The format and content of the study are much less prescribed and predictable than descriptive or experimental research, and you do not find tables of numerical data or statistical analyses. The primary technique used in this study is an open-ended interview (gathered using videotapes), in which some basic questions are asked, but the researcher leaves the door open for each participant to share his or her own perspectives (rather than asking prescribed and uniform questions). One of the striking features of this article is the presence of detailed narratives describing individual participants' responses (as opposed to tables with average results for groups).

Perhaps you might be asking yourself which of these four research methods is the best. No single research method is sufficient or appropriate for answering all types of questions. Particular types of research are more effective for answering specific types of questions. For example, if you are interested in the use of music therapy in pain control, you might use descriptive research to determine what types of pain management methods or types of music are most commonly used by music therapists in hospitals or hospice settings. Through experimental research, you could determine whether one type of pain management approach is more effective than another. A historical researcher could provide information on uses of music to reduce pain in military hospitals during World War II. A qualitative researcher might interview patients in an oncology unit to gather their individual opinions on how music therapy has affected their management of pain.

You can learn more about the strengths and limitations of each type of research, along with its best use, in books and courses about research methodology. You can also gain insights into these methods as you read more research studies as part of your ongoing professional development.

If you found the articles in this chapter somewhat challenging to read and understand, keep in mind that music therapy students often take courses in basic statistics or research methods as part of undergraduate or graduate studies. These courses help them understand and interpret these studies more effectively. Furthermore, as is the case with learning any new skill, reading research studies such as these becomes easier as a result of practice and experience. The more research you read, the easier and more interesting it becomes.

CURRENT STATUS OF RESEARCH IN THE PROFESSION

The advancement of research has been a primary purpose of the National Association for Music Therapy (NAMT) since it was founded in 1950 (National Association for Music Therapy, 1950). In comparison to some professions established hundreds of years ago, however, this is a short history of research involvement. Therefore, a comparatively small quantity of research knowledge has been gathered by music therapists.

The first coordinated effort to share research findings came in 1951, when NAMT published research papers in its *Book of Proceedings*. This annual compendium primarily consisted of professional papers and presentations given at the organization's annual conferences.

In 1964, NAMT began publishing the *Journal of Music Therapy*, a periodical that disseminated original music therapy research. By 1973, music therapists had access to an additional forum for clinical and research papers in a journal entitled *Arts Psychotherapy: An International Journal*, now published under the title *Arts in Psychotherapy*. This journal includes papers from a variety of allied health professionals, such as psychologists, art therapists, and counselors, as well as music therapists. Still another journal, *Music Therapy*, was established by the American Association for Music Therapy (AAMT) in 1981. (This journal ceased publication in 1997, when NAMT and AAMT unified.) One year later, in 1982, NAMT approved and commenced publication of *Music Therapy Perspectives*, a journal that addresses primarily clinical matters but that also includes data-based research. With the merger of NAMT and AAMT into AMTA, the *Journal of Music Therapy* and *Music Therapy Perspectives* were adopted as the two journals sponsored by this organization. These periodicals are by no means the only ones of professional interest to music therapists in the United States (professional music therapy associations from many other countries also publish research journals). Many music therapists often read and write for journals in related fields, such as counseling, special education, neurology, and psychology. However, the aforementioned journals do represent the primary collection of research information dedicated to the use of music in therapy.

SUMMARY

Descriptive, experimental, historical, and qualitative research are all valuable forms of inquiry, and each type has its particular strengths and limitations. Descriptive and qualitative research are used to determine current conditions (e.g., how a client feels about a particular type of music), while experimental research methods explore what will be (e.g., whether music will have a significant effect on increasing verbal responses in a child with intellectual disabilities). Historical research is less commonly conducted in the field of music therapy than descriptive and experimental research, though it is no less important. Historical research is concerned with the people, places, and events that have shaped the music therapy profession. In qualitative research, "reality" is seen as something that is negotiated or constructed by those who are experiencing the event. The qualitative researcher embraces the unique life experiences and beliefs of those involved in the study and reports on those experiences using thick narratives.

As noted earlier, one type of research is not inherently better than another. Rather, it is important for the researcher to select the method best suited to answer a particular question. In addition, one type of research can have an important effect on another. For example, the information gathered in a descriptive, qualitative, or historical study may highlight problems that require special intervention, which can be tested through experimental research methods. Or a historical study might help to clarify some of the environmental circumstances or key personnel that lead to what is found in a descriptive study. Finally, it is important to understand that research findings are always in flux. As a result of new and more sophisticated research methods, past studies may be refuted or findings clarified or expanded. And with each research finding, new questions emerge. Theories and methods will be continually tested and refined as a result of the cumulative efforts of researchers of the past, present, and future.

STUDY QUESTIONS

1. What are the three ways that research can influence music therapy practice?
2. Define *descriptive research* and provide one example of a research study that would use this technique.
3. Why is the related literature section of a research project important?
4. What function does the research abstract serve in research articles?
5. How are descriptive and qualitative research different?
6. How do the *Journal of Music Therapy* and *Music Therapy Perspectives* differ in their focus?

7. What was the purpose of NAMT's publication, *Book of Proceedings?*

8. What are at least two differences between qualitative research and experimental research?

REFERENCES

Abrams, B. (2005). Evaluating qualitative music therapy research. In B. W. Wheeler (Ed.), *Music therapy research* (2nd ed.). Gilsum, NH: Barcelona.

Aigen, K. (1993). The music therapist as qualitative researcher. *Music Therapy, 12,* 16–19.

Aldridge, D. (1989). A phenomenological comparison of the organization of music and the self. *The Arts in Psychotherapy, 16,* 91–97.

Amir, D. (1993). Moments of insight in the music therapy experience. *Music Therapy, 12,* 85–100.

Ansdell, G. (2003) The stories we tell: Some meta-theoretical reflections on music therapy. *Nordic Journal of Music Therapy, 12,* 152–159.

Assgaard. T. (2005). Song creations by children with cancer—Process and meaning. In D. Aldridge (Ed.), *Case study designs in music therapy.* London: Jessica Kingsley.

Austin, D., & Forinash, M. (2005). Arts-based research. In B. W. Wheeler (Ed.), *Music therapy research* (2nd ed.). Gilsum, NH: Barcelona.

Bogdan, R., & Biklen, S. (1982). *Qualitative research for education.* Boston: Allyn & Bacon.

Bruscia, K. E. (1998). Standards of integrity for qualitative music therapy research. *Journal of Music Therapy, 35*(3), 176–200.

Bruscia, K. E. (1995). Modes of consciousness in Guided Imagery and Music: A therapist's experience of the guiding process. In C. Kenny (Ed.), *Listening, playing, creating: Essays on the power of sound* (pp. 165–197). Albany: State University of New York Press.

Creswell, J. W. (2007). *Qualitative inquiry and research design: Choosing among five approaches* (2nd ed.). Thousand Oaks, CA: Sage.

Darrow, A. A., & Gfeller, K. E. (1991). A study of public school music programs in mainstreaming hearing impaired students. *Journal of Music Therapy, 28*(1), 23–39.

Davis, W. B. (1993). Keeping the dream alive: Profiles of three early twentieth century music therapists. *Journal of Music Therapy, 30,* 34–45.

Duerksen, G. (1968). The research process. In E. T. Gaston (Ed.), *Music in therapy* (pp. 409-419). New York: Macmillan.

Duke University Medical Center. (2006, November 16). Combination of personality traits increases risk for heart disease. *Science Daily.* Retrieved May 26, 2008, from http://www.sciencedaily.com /releases/2006/11/061116122150.htm

Edwards, J. (1999). Considering the paradigmatic frame: Social science research approaches relevant to research in music therapy. *The Arts in Psychotherapy, 26*(2), 73–80.

Feder, E., & Feder, B. (1998). *The art and science evaluation in the arts therapies: How do you know what's working?* Springfield, IL: Charles C. Thomas.

Findlay, S. (2003, December 15). Designate obesity as disease. *USA Today.* Retrieved May 26, 2008, from http://www.usatoday.com/news/opinion/editorials/2003-12-15-obesity-edit_x.htm

Forinash, M. (1992). A phenomenological analysis of Nordoff-Robbins model of music therapy: The lived experience of clinical improvisation. *Music Therapy, 11*(1), 120–141.

Forinash, M., & Gonzalez, D. (1989). A phenomenological perspective of music therapy. *Music Therapy, 8,* 35–46.

Forinash, M., & Lee, C. (1998). Guest editorial. *Journal of Music Therapy, 33*(3), 142–149.

Hanser, S. B. (1974). Group contingent music listening with emotionally disturbed boys. *Journal of Music Therapy, 11*, 220–225.

Juslin, P. N., & Sloboda, J. A. (2001). Music and emotion: Introduction. In P. Juslin, & J. Sloboda (Eds.), *Music and emotion: Theory and research* (pp. 3–20). New York: Oxford University Press.

Kenny, C. B. (1987). The field of play: A theoretical study of music therapy process. *Dissertation Abstracts International, 48*(2), 3067A. (UMI No. DEV88-02367)

Lincoln, Y. S., & Guba, E. G. (1985). *Naturalistic inquiry.* London: Sage.

National Association for Music Therapy. (1950). *Constitution and bylaws of the National Association for Music Therapy.* Lawrence, KS: Author.

National Association for Music Therapy. (1969). Constitution and bylaws of the National Association for Music Therapy. *Journal of Music Therapy, 8*, 59–67.

Ottenbacher, K. J. (1986). *Evaluating clinical change: Strategies for occupational and physical therapists.* Baltimore: Williams and Wilkins.

Payton, O. D. (1994). *Research: The validation of clinical practice* (3rd ed.). Philadelphia: F.A. Davis.

Phelps, R., Sadoff, R. H., Warburton, E. C., & Ferrara, L. (2004). *A guide to research in music education* (5th ed.). Lanham, MD: Scarecrow Press.

Rainbow, E. L., & Froehlich, H. C. (1987). *Research in music education: An introduction to systematic inquiry.* New York: Schirmer Books.

Ruud, E. (2005). Philosophy and theory of science. In B. W. Wheeler (Ed.), *Music therapy research* (2nd ed.). Gilsum, NH: Barcelona.

Smeijsters, H. (1997). *Multiple perspectives: A guide to qualitative research in music therapy.* Gilsum, NH: Barcelona.

Solomon, A. I. (1980). Music for the feeble-minded in nineteenth century America. *Journal of Music Therapy, 11*, 119–122.

Solomon, A. I. (1984). *A historical study of the National Association for Music Therapy, 1960–1980.* Unpublished doctoral dissertation, University of Kansas, Lawrence.

Solomon, A. I., & Heller, G. N. (1982). Historical research in music therapy: An important avenue for studying the profession. *Journal of Music Therapy, 19*, 236–242.

Stige, B. (2002). Do we need general criteria for the evaluation of qualitative research? *Nordic Journal of Music Therapy 11*(1), 65–71.

Stige, B. (2005). Ethnography and ethnographically informed research. In B. W. Wheeler (Ed.), *Music therapy research* (2nd ed.). Gilsum, NH: Barcelona.

Thaut, M. H., Leins, A. K., Rice, R. R., Argstatter, H., Kenyon, G. P., McIntosh, G. C., et al. (2007). Rhythmic auditory stimulation improves gait more than NDT/Bobath training in near-ambulatory patients early poststroke: A single-blind randomized trial. *Neurorehabilitation and Neural Repair, 20*(10), 1–5.

Thaut, M. H., McIntosh, G. C., & Rice, R. R. (1997). Rhythmic facilitation of gait training in hemiparetic stroke rehabilitation. *Journal of Neurological Sciences, 151*, 207–212.

Wheeler, B. L. (1999). Experiencing pleasure in working with severely disabled children. *Journal of Music Therapy, 36*, 56–80.

Wheeler, B. L. (Ed.). (2005). *Music therapy research* (2nd ed.). Gilsum, NH: Barcelona.

Wheeler, B. L., & Kenny, C. (2005). Principles of qualitative research. In B. W. Wheeler (Ed.), *Music therapy research* (2nd ed.). Gilsum, NH: Barcelona.

Wolfe, D. (1980). The effect of automated interrupted music on head posturing of cerebral palsied individuals. *Journal of Music Therapy, 17*, 184–206.

Additional Resources

GLOSSARY OF TERMS

Acquired hearing loss: A hearing loss acquired after birth.

Adaptive behavior: Behavior that changes to fit the demands of a situation.

Adventitious: Not present at birth.

Aesthetic enjoyment: Appreciating the intrinsic beauty or importance in a work (of art, of music, etc.) without necessarily gaining any entertainment value from the work.

Aesthetic integrity: Working to introduce creative and enjoyable aspects into research so as to provide meaningful outcomes for those involved in the study as well as for readers of the study.

Affect: The observable aspects of behavior that tell others how one feels; for example, facial expression, tone of voice, and posture.

Age of onset: The person's age during which the symptoms of a particular condition first appeared.

Alternative and Augmentative Communication system (AAC): Products or methods used to aid communication for persons with disorders of speech, language, or writing. AACs can range from pointing at pictures to using sophisticated electronic equipment.

Alzheimer's/dementia: Refers to a group of diseases that cause a gradual, steady decline in various areas of cognitive function due to structural changes in the brain.

American Association for Music Therapy: A music therapy organization that existed from 1971 until 1998, when it merged with the National Association for Music Therapy.

American Association on Intellectual and Developmental Disabilities (AAIDD): A professional organization that comprises professionals who work with and/or support people with intellectual and developmental disabilities. Formerly the American Association on Mental Retardation (AAMR).

American Music Therapy Association: The principal music therapy organization of the United States, which serves (among other things) to promote awareness of the profession, to advance clinical and scientific knowledge in the field, and to set and maintain standards of music therapy practice. This organization was formed in 1998 with the unification of the American Association for Music Therapy and the National Association for Music Therapy.

American Sign Language (ASL): A true language that has its own structure that differs from that of the English language. Finger spelling is used only when there is no appropriate ASL sign for a given word or concept.

Amyotrophic lateral sclerosis (ALS): A terminal, progressive disease of the motor neurons in the brain stem and spinal chord that eventually leads to muscular paralysis.

Aphasia: Impaired ability to use or understand oral language.

Arthritis: An affliction in which joints become inflamed or begin to deteriorate.

Asperger's Syndrome: A condition on the autism spectrum that is characterized by repetitive or stereotyped behavior and deficits in social interaction, but in which language and intellectual development progress more or less normally.

Assessment tools: Tools that are used to provide a view of a person's abilities, needs, and problems. These tools can vary widely depending on what a person is being treated for and the focus of the person doing the assessment.

Assistive hearing device: An apparatus that is designed to improve an individual's perception of sound.

Association through contiguity: The association of two separate events due to temporal proximity.

Atherosclerosis: A disease affecting the arterial blood vessels. It is the name of a process in which fatty substances are deposited on the inner lining of the arteries and over time build up, causing a stroke or heart attack.

Atlantoaxial instability: A type of misalignment of the upper spinal column that is often found in people with Down syndrome.

Attention: The process of seeking out stimuli that are of interest.

Audiologist: A health care professional who deals with the science of hearing. An audiologist often tests hearing, fits hearing aids, and directs the rehabilitation of individuals with significant hearing losses

Auditory awareness: The perception of sounds in the environment.

Auditory discrimination: The ability to differentiate between two (or more) sounds in the acoustic environment.

Auditory nerve: The nerve fibers that carry sound information, in the form of electrochemical energy, from the inner ear (cochlea) to the brain, where the information is processed.

Authentic: Refers to historical research that is supported by an abundance of solid evidence rather than speculation.

Autism: A developmental disorder that is manifested through deficits in speech and language capacity, responses to sensory stimuli, social interaction, and developmental rate or sequence.

Autism spectrum disorders: A group of disorders that are characterized by difficulties in communication, social interaction, and/or cognitive functioning as a result of uneven or delayed development, while sensory abilities remain intact.

Basilar membrane: A lining inside the cochlea that holds in place thousands of cilia.

Beat competency: The ability to follow and maintain a simple beat.

Bereavement: The process of grieving over the death of a loved one.

Bilateral: Referring to two sides; for example, a bilateral hearing loss indicates a loss in both ears.

Bilingual-Bicultural approach to language learning: A method in which a child learns American Sign Language as his/her primary language, but is taught English as a second language so that the child can ultimately use both languages and socialize in both Deaf and hearing cultures.

Blindness: Visual acuity of no less than 20/200 in the better eye after best possible correction; or, a visual field of 20 degrees or less in the better eye.

Board Certification exam: A test that measures a prospective music therapist's knowledge about music therapy principles and foundations, clinical theories and techniques, general knowledge about music, and professional roles and responsibilities. Passing this test is one requirement to become certified as a music therapist.

Cadence: In gait training, the degree to which a person's steps stay in rhythm.

Catatonic behavior: Marked abnormal in motor behavior, such as long periods of remaining in the same position without moving.

Central hearing loss: Hearing loss due to damage to or impairment of the brain or central nervous system.

Cerebrovascular Accident (CVA): Occurs when blood flow to the brain is restricted, sometimes due to a ruptured cerebral blood vessel. The resulting lack of oxygen to brain cells can cause permanent damage or death. CVA is also known as stroke.

Chronic obstructive pulmonary disorder (COPD): A disease in which air sacs of the lungs lose their elasticity and become overly porous, which can result in dyspnea, fatigue, and eventually lead to death.

Cilia: Tiny hair cells that lie on the basilar membrane. They act as transducers, converting sound from mechanical energy into electrochemical energy.

Client-centered: An approach to therapy in which the client has significant input into the way in which progress is made toward the end therapeutic goal.

Cochlea: A small snail-shaped structure of the inner ear that contains sensory receptors important in the transmission of sound to the auditory nerve.

Cochlear implant: An assistive hearing device designed for individuals with severe to profound sensorineural loss.

Cognitive behavior modification: A behavior modification technique that includes self-reinforcement and self-evaluation.

Cognitive-behavior therapy: A form of therapy that emphasizes the two-way interaction between faulty thoughts and beliefs and maladaptive behavior in treating mental illness.

Compression: An increase in density of air molecules.

Compulsions: Repetitive behaviors that a person feels they must carry out in response to their obsessions, despite the fact that these responses are not realistically connected to such obsessions.

Concrete operations: Third stage of Piaget's theory of development (approximately ages 7–11) during which children develop the ability to think logically and solve problems mentally as long as the situation is related to their own experience. They have also developed the ability for community involvement and to execute refined motor movements.

Conditioning: Learning by associating one stimulus with another, or by associating one's behavior with a particular consequence.

Conductive hearing loss: Hearing loss caused by disease or obstruction in the outer or middle ear.

Configuration of hearing loss: Refers to the extent of hearing loss at each frequency and the overall prospect of hearing that is created. For example, some people experience hearing loss at only low frequencies and may have different needs than someone who has hearing loss across the entire hearing spectrum.

Congenital: Present at birth.

Cost benefit ratio: An assessment of a treatment modality that weighs its perceived effectiveness against how much the treatment is expected to cost.

Cultural convention: A set of agreed upon or generally accepted social norms or standards of a given group of people.

Degree of hearing loss: Refers to the severity of hearing loss, which can range from mild, moderate, severe, to profound levels.

Delusions: Invalid beliefs that lack evidence in reality.

Descriptive research: A type of research that describes "what is" under current conditions. Surveys are a common tool used to gather data for this mode of inquiry.

Developmental disability: A condition, such as mental retardation or cerebral palsy, that begins before age 18 and continues indefinitely, causing substantial limitations.

Direct instruction: Explicit teaching of a lesson or set of skills using lecture or demonstration, as opposed to, for example, "hands-on" learning or group discussion.

Disorganized speech: Refers to switching topics with no natural transition, or answering questions in a tangential way, which often renders speech incoherent or illogical.

Divided attention: Focusing one's spotlight of awareness on more than one task at a time.

Down syndrome: A specific form of mental retardation resulting from a chromosomal abnormality.

DSM-IV-TR: An abbreviation for the 2000 text revision of the fourth edition of the *Diagnostic and Statistical Manual of Mental Disorders*, a publication of the American Psychiatric Association that systematically organizes and categorizes the many forms of mental illness into a uniform system.

Dysarthria: Imperfect articulation of speech because of loss of muscle control as a result of damage to the central or peripheral nervous system.

Dyspnea: Shortness of breath.

Dyspraxia: Disturbance in the sequence of spoken language resulting from decreased ability to plan and position the muscles involved in word articulation.

Ear canal: Part of the ear that forms a tunnel in which sounds funneled by the pinna travel from the exterior environment to the tympanic membrane (eardrum).

Early intervention program: A special education program implemented under IDEA for children under the age of 3 who have been diagnosed with some sort of disability or developmental delay.

Echolalic: Describes speech in which previously heard words or phrases are repeated without intent to convey meaning.

Eclectic: An approach to therapy that draws from a variety of different models to serve an individual client based on his/her particular needs.

Education for All Handicapped Children Act of 1975: Also known as PL-142. A landmark law that declares that all handicapped children are entitled to "free and appropriate" public education.

Electrochemical energy: Energy controlled by chemical changes resulting from electric current, such the energy transmitted by neurons in the nervous system.

Electroconvulsive therapy: A treatment involving the discharge of electricity into the brain, which can be used for severe depression that is unresponsive to other forms of therapy.

Emergent: A research design common in qualitative research in which it is not necessary for all the research steps to be spelled out before the research begins.

Encephalitis: Swelling or infection of the brain.

Encoding: The act of processing information from our senses into memory, either by automatic processes or intentional effort.

End-of-life care: Treatment provided to persons with a terminal illness who are usually projected to live six months or less.

English-based sign systems: Refers to sign systems that use many of the same signs as does ASL, but they are used within the syntactical structure of English language, and additional signs must be used to indicate parts of speech such as word endings, verb tenses, and prefixes/suffixes.

Entertainment: Characterized by amusement or diversion. Entertaining things are not necessarily appreciated as art objects, but they help people enjoy themselves and forget the cares of everyday life.

Episodes: Discrete periods of time during which a person has a number of specific symptoms that reflect a marked change from previous functioning.

Etiology: Cause or origin of a condition.

Executive function: The ability of a person's brain to effectively carry out commands or plans that the person intends to complete.

Experimental blindness: Refers to a characteristic of research in which the persons carrying out the actual treatment are not informed about the specific research questions or interventions being studied.

Expressionism: As related to the philosophy of the arts, the belief that music's ability to evoke emotions and take on meaning results from the structural characteristics of the music itself.

Extramusical associations: Instances in which music produces thoughts, feelings, and sensations about things other than the music itself; for example, when a trumpet call is recognized as a symbol for victory in battle.

Fetal alcohol syndrome: A disorder caused by alcohol ingestion during pregnancy, which can result in a variety of problems in the child, including intellectual disabilities, attention problems, growth deficiencies, and facial deformities.

Fingerspelling: A method that uses hand shapes and positions that correspond to the letters of the alphabet to spell out words.

Formal operations: Fourth stage of Piaget's theory of development (approximately ages 12 and beyond). Formal operations is characterized by development of the ability to think abstractly, that is, to conceive of a concept, such as global warming, merely by looking at a chart of climate-related numbers and figures.

Fragile X syndrome: A genetic disorder that causes mental retardation.

Frequency: The number of sound waves per second generated by a sound-producing source (measured in Hertz [Hz]). The greater the number of waves per second, the higher the sound.

Functions of music: The various ways that music is used in society, including the purposes of communicating, producing a physical response, symbolizing a nonmusical concept, promoting social integration, expressing and/or affecting emotions, and providing aesthetic enjoyment or entertainment.

Generalizability: The ability to apply knowledge gained from research to situations beyond the specific conditions contained in the research.

Genetic abnormalities: Changes in normal human development that result from broken, damaged, or missing genetic material.

Glasgow Coma Scale (GCS): A tool for assessment of comatose states that measures three features—eye movement, motor response to stimuli, and verbal response—according to severity.

Good Gestalts: Refers to a principle of Gestalt psychology that states that figures and patterns tend be perceived in the most stable (or "best") form as sensory input will allow.

Grossly disorganized behavior: Refers to the inability to manage one's own behavior enough to complete basic activities of everyday life.

Hallucinations: Perceptions of sensory input, often sounds or tactile sensations, which are not occurring in reality.

Harmonics: Overtones that occur in periodic patterns.

Hearing aids: Assistive hearing devices that work primarily by amplifying and/or modifying the incoming acoustic signal.

Hemiplegia: Paralysis on either the left or the right side of the body.

Hertz (Hz): Unit of measure of frequency. As a point of reference, 440 Hz is the value assigned to the musical note A above middle C on the piano.

Hospice: In relation to terminal illness, the reduction and abatement of pain and other troubling symptoms in the absence of any measures to cure the illness.

Huntington's disease: A relatively rare, inherited neurological disorder affecting motor control, which tends to appear in middle age.

Hydrocephaly: A medical condition resulting from an excess of cerebrospinal fluid in and around the brain.

Hypothesis: In research, a proposition (or set of propositions) given to explain the expected outcome of the study. A hypothesis can be a provisional prediction used to guide research, or it can be accepted as highly probable given a bulk of already existing evidence.

Hypotonia: A lack of muscle tone.

Iconicity: The imitation of a feeling, object, or event through the structural properties of an art form.

Incidental language learning: The process of "picking up" language skills by being in an environment in which the language is used. This ability is especially sharp in infants and young children.

Incus: One of three small bones (ossicles) in the middle ear that act as levers to transmit mechanical energy to the cochlea.

Individual Education Program (IEP): An individualized plan for children with disabilities who qualify for special education services, required through IDEA. This document is written by a team of special education professionals in consultation with the child's parents or guardian and acts as a blueprint for determining the best possible educational program for each child.

Individual Family Service Program (IFSP): An individualized treatment program designed for children under age 3 who qualify for services under the Early Intervention provision of the Individual with Disabilities Education Act (IDEA).

Individuals with Disabilities Education Act (IDEA): A federal law passed in 1990, based on PL 94-142, mandating nondiscriminatory assessment of educational needs, free and appropriate public education, individualized education programs, least restrictive environment, parental involvement, and due process.

Infant-directed speech: An innate speech tendency of mothers in the presence of their babies characterized by elevated vocal pitch, exaggerated affect and speech contour, and stretched-out vowel sounds.

Inner ear: The part of the hearing mechanism that houses the cochlea, in which sound is changed from mechanical energy into electrochemical information that can be interpreted by the brain. Also includes the vestibular canals, which are involved in balance.

Intellectual disability: A term that refers to significantly subaverage general intellectual functioning existing concurrently with deficits in adaptive behavior, and manifested during the developmental period before age 18. Causes of intellectual disabilities may occur before birth (prenatal), during birth (perinatal), or after birth (postnatal).

Interpersonal integrity: Making a commitment to understand the world of each research participant, being clear about how his or her beliefs may impact the study.

Irrational thoughts: Patterns of thinking that cause stress and/or feelings of inadequacy that do not aid in adapting to one's environment.

Iso principle: A technique by which music is matched with the mood of a client, then gradually altered to affect the desired mood state. This technique can also be used to affect physiological responses such as heart rate and blood pressure.

Isomorphism: In Gestalt psychology, the principle that there is a parallel between Gestalt perception of a pattern and the actual "experience" of the pattern structure in the brain. This term is sometimes used to refer to structural characteristics of music that "mimic" human emotions or behaviors.

Kanner, Leo: A psychiatrist who in the early 1940s first identified autism as a distinct developmental disorder, labeling it "infantile autism."

Least restrictive environment (LRE): A component of IDEA that states that students with disabilities must be educated with students who do not have disabilities to the greatest extent possible. Additional supports and services should be provided to help the student achieve educational goals.

Locomotion: The act of moving from place to place.

Long-term memory: Information that has been rehearsed and stored in the brain and is retrievable over a long period of time, sometimes over the span of a lifetime.

Low vision: Visual acuity greater than 20/200 but no greater than 20/70 in the better eye after correction.

Malleus: One of three small bones (ossicles) in the middle ear that act as levers to transmit mechanical energy to the cochlea.

Manual approach to communication: Any system that uses hand shapes to represent letters or words.

Mean: The average of a set of values, obtained by adding all values together and dividing by the total number of values.

Mechanical energy: Energy controlled by physical forces.

Medical model: An approach that considers emotional and behavioral disturbances as originating from biological factors such as chemical imbalances, genetic problems, or physical illness.

Medicare-certified: A medical product or treatment that has been approved by Medicare and is thus covered to the extent that the plan allows.

Memory: The means by which we draw on past knowledge that has been retained to use that knowledge in the present (retrieval).

Meningitis: A disease that arises from infection of the spinal fluid and can cause hearing loss and other serious complications, including death.

Mental retardation: A phrase that is a precursor to the term intellectual disability.

Metabolic errors: Conditions in which the body cannot properly break down (metabolize) a substance.

Methodological integrity: Determining that the research method is appropriate to the question being asked and ensuring that this chosen method allows us to learn something new about the topic being studied.

Middle ear: The part of the hearing mechanism that dampens sound from the ear canal and passes it on to the inner ear; includes the tympanic membrane (eardrum) and the ossicles.

Mixed loss: A term that describes hearing difficulties due to structural deficiencies in both the outer or middle and the inner ear.

Mnemonic device: A technique or system used to assist the memory.

Mobility: Movement from present position to a desired location in space.

Multidisciplinary assessment: An evaluation of an individual's needs by a variety of individuals and along a range of different dimensions, as opposed to a single, "expert" opinion. In the special education setting, multidisciplinary assessment may include input from doctors, teachers, parents, aides, speech therapists, music therapists, and others.

Multiple sclerosis (MS): A chronic, degenerative disease of the central nervous system in which the myelin sheaths surrounding nerve fibers degrade, resulting in neuromuscular symptoms such as weakness in the limbs and sensory impairment.

Music as a masking agent: Refers to the use of music to cover or mask undesirable sounds in order to reduce patients' anxiety.

Music as an agent for active focus/distraction: Refers to the using preferred selections of music as a positive and competing stimulus to reduce attention to the negative aspects of pain or an uncomfortable medical procedure.

Music as an agent for relaxation response: Refers to the therapeutic use of music in conjunction with structured techniques that promote mental and physical relaxation.

Music as an information agent: Refers to the use of music to convey information important to a particular treatment goal, such as a children's song whose lyrics introduce the various individuals encountered during the surgical process.

Music therapy as a related service: A way of directly providing special education music therapy services to children as part of their individual education programs, as provisions of the Individuals with Disabilities Education Act specify that music therapy can be included on such programs as a "related service" if considered essential to the child's success.

National Association for Music Therapy: A music therapy organization that existed from 1950 until 1998, when it merged with the American Association for Music Therapy.

Naturalistic research: Research that involves observing people in their natural setting, doing what they would normally be doing, with a minimum amount of interference by the researchers.

Negative symptoms: Symptoms of schizophrenia that are characterized by the lack of something; for example, avolition is a negative symptom which refers to a lack of will to accomplish basic tasks.

Neurologic music therapy (NMT): The research-based, therapeutic application of music to deficits in cognitive, sensory, and motor function due to diseases of the nervous system.

Neuromuscular disease: A broad term for diseases that affect muscular movement due to damage to the central or peripheral nervous system.

Neuropsychologist: A healthcare professional whose approach to understanding and treating psychological conditions focuses on the structures and functions of the brain and nervous system.

Nonpharmacological approach: A method of treatment that excludes or minimizes pharmacological intervention (drug treatment).

Numeric Rating Scale (NRS): An assessment method in which a client provides a number to "rate" some aspect of his or her being. For example, a patient using a NRS for pain may indicate a "5" on a scale of 1–10 to indicate moderate pain.

Observational learning: Learning by watching others.

Obsessions: Persistent thoughts that are intrusive and inappropriate and that a person realizes are a product of his or her own mind.

Onset of hearing loss: A way of categorizing hearing loss according to when the loss first occurred.

Ontology: A world view that defines what is considered "reality" for a given line of research.

Optimal complexity theory: Theory associated with Daniel Berlyne that specifies that we feel the most pleasurable feelings if music has an ideal level of complexity and/or familiarity. This ideal level can change depending on situational circumstances.

Oral communication system: Communicating by speaking, speech reading, and careful listening. Individuals with less severe hearing losses can often manage to communicate in this manner.

Orientation: Utilization of sensory processes to establish one's position in relation to significant objects in the environment.

Ossicles: The three small bones (malleus, incus, and stapes) found in the middle ear that move in response to acoustical energy transmitted by the tympanic membrane.

Outer ear: The part of the hearing mechanism which includes the pinna (fleshy outer part of the ear) and the ear canal. Its main function is to funnel sound toward the middle ear.

Overtones: Any frequencies that sound above the fundamental (lowest frequency) of a pitch.

Palliative care: A term for care that is focused on the relief of pain or suffering. In end-of-life circumstances, palliative care may be given in conjunction with curative measures.

Parallel play: Characterizes a stage of development in which very young children will play beside each other but not engage in social interaction.

Parkinson's disease: A neurological disorder that affects movement.

Perceptual processing: Organizing or interpreting information taken in through the senses.

Perilingual: Occurring during the acquisition of the principal structures of adult speech and language.

Periodic: A quality that describes the regular repetition of compression and rarefaction.

Personal integrity: Ensuring that, during the course of the study, the researcher was fully present and honest both professionally and personally.

Pervasive Developmental Disorders (PDDs): A group of disorders that are characterized by delays in multiple areas of development, including communication and social functioning.

Phenomenological research: The examination of human experience by studying extensively a small number of people to develop patterns of meaning.

Phenylketonuria (PKU): A genetic metabolic disorder that causes severe brain damage due to the body's inability to break down the chemical phenylalanine.

Picture Exchange Communication System (PECS): A form of augmentative and alternative communication (AAC) that is typically used as an aid for children with autism.

Pinna: The outer portion of the ear that funnels sound into the ear canal.

Pitch: Term used to denote how high or low a musical note sounds.

Postlingual: Occurring after the acquisition of the principal structures of adult speech and language.

Posttest: In experimental research, the assessment of a particular variable or variables after the experimental intervention has taken place.

Prelingual: Occurring in the period before acquisition of the principal structures of adult speech and language (approximately the first three years of life).

Preoperational: Second stage of Piaget's theory of development (approximately ages 2–7) during which children experience rapid growth in language skills, conceptual understanding, and social awareness.

Pretest: In experimental research, the assessment of a particular variable or variables prior to the experimental intervention.

Protocols: The particular steps or approaches of a research methodology.

Psychodynamic: An approach to therapy rooted in the work of Sigmund Freud that attributes emotional problems to internal conflicts that have resulted from negative events of the past.

Psychosocial: Referring to interrelated aspects of emotional and social functioning.

Psychotherapy: A way of addressing mental disorders or maladjustments that involves consulting with a professional to confront issues ranging from problems of everyday life to deep-seated psychological conflicts.

Public Law 94-142 (PL 94-142): Also known as the Education for All Handicapped Children Act of 1975. A landmark law that declares that all children with disabilities are entitled to "free and appropriate" public education.

Qualitative research: A research style that is descriptive and focuses on people's perceptions and feelings. Qualitative research is conducted with individuals or small groups in the client's social environment over extended periods of time.

Quantitative research: A research style that is often experimental and focuses on seeing "what might be" under certain controlled circumstances. In quantitative research, phenomena are examined through the numerical representation of observations and statistical analysis.

Random assignment: The process of assigning research participants to groups by chance instead of by some other method that might make the groups inequivalent.

Range: The highest and lowest values in a set of data.

Rank order: An organization of pieces of information hierarchically from top to bottom, without indicating the exact numerical differences between each.

Rarefaction: A decrease in density of air molecules.

Rational Scientific Mediating Model: A systematic approach to studying the interactions of music and the brain whose groundwork lies in the scientific foundation of music perception and production.

Reality orientation: A technique used with the elderly that emphasizes the repetition of information to reeducate clients who may be disoriented and confused. Accurate perception of person, place, date, time, and other environmental objects or events.

Reconstructive music therapy: Music therapy activities that are used to uncover or resolve subconscious conflicts that continue to hamper personal development.

Re-educative music therapy: Music therapy activities that emphasize verbal reflection and processing about interpersonal relationships and emotions, while still highlighting active participation of group members.

Referentialist philosophy: The philosophical belief that the meaning in music arises from connections the listener makes between music and a nonmusical object or event.

Residual hearing: Usable hearing (associated with people with hearing losses who can hear some sounds but not others).

Residual vision: Remaining visual ability in a person with vision loss; varies widely among individuals.

Retrieval: Calling up information stored in long-term memory so it may be used in the present.

Rett's Syndrome: A disorder in females which, following an apparently normal development of up to two and a half years, a child shows decelerated head growth, diminishing physical coordination, and impaired social and language development.

Rhythmic Auditory Stimulation: A technique used to facilitate rhythmic movement, especially gait.

Rochester Method: An English-based sign system that focuses on fingerspelling and speech sounds.

Safety valve function: Using music to "let off steam," that is, to express deep-felt emotions or to speak out about societal concerns.

Self-injurious behavior: Actions that physically and directly harm one's self.

Sensorimotor: First stage of Piaget's theory of development (approximately ages 0–2 years) during which children learn about their environment through their senses and motor activity.

Sensorineural hearing loss: Loss in hearing usually due to defects in the sensory or neural mechanisms of the ear (cochlea and auditory nerve).

Sensory processing: Refers to ability to make sense of information incoming from the senses.

Severity (of hearing loss): A term that refers to the continuum of how much actual hearing is lost and what communication difficulties occur as a result.

Shifting attention: Continually changing one's focus of attention from one aspect of the environment to another.

Significant difference: In quantitative research, the difference between two results is said to be significant if the difference would not have been expected to happen by chance. In statistical terms, significance is usually defined as something that would have been likely to happen by chance at most 5% of the time.

Simultaneous Communication (SimCom): A communication technique in which both a spoken language and a manual version of that language (such as English and Signed Exact English) are used simultaneously.

Social Communication Training: Refers to activities and exercises aimed at maximizing individuals' ability to function in social situations.

Social stories: Narrative tools that can be used to teach children with autism appropriate social responses in situations they may find challenging or confusing.

Sound comprehension: Understanding a sound, that is, being able to discuss aspects of it that distinguish it from others, such as its timbre, its pitch, and so on.

Sound detection: The ability to distinguish the presence or absence of sound.

Sound discrimination: The ability to tell that two sounds are the same or different.

Sound identification: Being able to identify the source of a particular sound.

Spina bifida: An open defect in the spinal column caused by failure of the back arches of the vertebra to close before birth.

Stapes: One of three small bones (ossicles) in the middle ear that act as levers to transmit mechanical energy to the cochlea.

Stereotypical behaviors: Repetitive behaviors, such as arm flapping, rocking, and vocalizing vowel sounds that appear to serve only to create sensory stimulation.

Storage: The act of retaining information in short-term or long-term memory following adequate rehearsal.

Stride length: The distance a person travels with each step.

Stroke: Occurs when blood flow to the brain is restricted, sometimes due to a ruptured cerebral blood vessel. The resulting lack of oxygen to brain cells can cause permanent damage or death. Stroke is also known by the term cerebrovascular accident (CVA).

Supportive music therapy: Music therapy activities that are designed to promote adaptive behavior and are oriented toward participants' active involvement and awareness of the present.

Sustained attention: The act of maintaining one's spotlight of attention on a particular task for an extended period.

Symmetry: In gait training, the degree to which a person's right and left steps are similar with respect to their location from the center of the body.

Tactile: Related to the sense of touch.

Tactile defensiveness: Being overly responsive to the sense of touch, especially in the case of another person's touch.

Team-oriented approach: End-of-life care in which a variety of professionals collaborate to meet a client's needs, sometimes crossing or transcending disciplinary lines. Such approaches may include services of nurses, counselors, music therapists, clergy, and trained volunteers, depending on the particular needs of a given client.

Terminal illness: A medical condition that is incurable and progressively worsening.

Theory of expectations: Theory associated with Leonard Meyer that specifies that emotions are aroused when a tendency to respond a certain way is inhibited; for example, the last few notes being left out of a familiar melody.

Therapeutic music interventions: Activities in which music is a primary focal point but which are designed mainly to address nonmusical treatment goals.

Total Communication (TC): Refers to the simultaneous use of one of more manual communication systems and spoken language, in which the recipients of the messages select those aspects of the communication to which they will attend.

Total pain: Pain or suffering resulting from the combined effect of physical, emotional, social, and spiritual pain.

Transformational Design Model (TDM): A specific framework for music therapy treatment. Five stages include assessment of the patient, development of goals and objectives, designing functional nonmusic activities, converting nonmusical activities to musical experiences, and generalization of training to real-life situations.

Traumatic brain injury (TBI): A head injury that causes significant damage to the brain. TBI can result in a variety of combinations of cognitive, physical, emotional, and behavioral deficits, depending on the particular nature of the injury.

Tympanic membrane: A flexible, elastic structure in the middle ear that vibrates at the frequency of incoming sound waves to transmit mechanical energy to the ossicles.

Unilateral: Referring to one side only; for example, a unilateral hearing loss indicates a loss in one ear.

Variable: In research, any aspect that is purposely measured.

Velocity: In gait training, number of steps taken in a given period of time.

Vibrotactile aid: A mechanism that aids individuals who are deaf or hard of hearing to detect and interpret the vibration of sounds through the sense of touch.

INDEX

A

Abel, H. H. 314
Abraham, I. L. 201
Abrams, B. 525
Achey, C. 461
acquired amputations 150
acquired hearing loss 379
Adamek, M. S. 50, 117, 125, 130, 131, 132, 133, 137, 310, 311, 343, 390, 391, 394, 395, 396, 397, 398, 405, 406, 411, 412, 414, 417, 419, 422
Adams, H. 271
adaptive behavior 82, 83, 85, 235, 422, 441
Adler, R. S. 437
adventitious 371, 392
aesthetic enjoyment 53
affect 174, 195, 212, 213, 224, 243, 292, 433, 467, 474, 478
ageism 186
age of onset 83, 371, 391, 393
Aigen, K. 466, 525, 526
Akers, E. 420
Alaimo, D. F. 122
Albert, M. L. 162
Aldridge, D. 196, 201, 298, 525
Aldridge, G. 196, 201
Alexander, T. 200
Allen, K. 320, 324, 332
Alternative and Augmentative Communication System (AAC) 122, 129
Alvin, J. 472, 473
Alzheimer's disease 9, 50, 183, 187, 188, 198, 200, 203, 291, 309, 311, 344

Alzheimer, Alois 188
American Association for Music Therapy (AAMT) 34, 36, 488, 525, 534
American Association on Intellectual and Developmental Disabilities (AAIDD) 82, 84, 85, 87
American Association on Mental Retardation (AAMR) 82
American Music Therapy Association (AMTA) 7, 8, 9, 12, 13, 14, 15, 34, 36, 97, 202, 241, 312, 332, 345, 386, 387, 398, 432, 444, 445, 488, 491, 534
American Psychiatric Association (APA) 85, 86, 87, 88, 118, 138, 211, 213, 215, 216, 219, 220, 444
American Sign Language (ASL) 367, 373, 374, 375, 376, 377, 384, 390
American Speech-Language-Hearing Association (ASHA) 371
Amir, D. 380, 385, 525
Amyotrophic Lateral Sclerosis (ALS) 354
Anastasiow, N. J. 92
Anderson, A. K. 169, 267
Anderson, K. O. 316, 317, 320, 322
Anderson, M. A. 186, 187, 189
Anderson, V. 127
Andreason, N. 214, 222, 223, 229
aneurism 190
Ansdell, G. 525
Antoni, M. H. 56, 309, 311, 330, 468
anxiety 30, 31, 67, 100, 130, 168, 174, 188, 214, 217, 218, 220, 222, 227, 228, 230, 248, 249, 252, 266, 276, 280, 282, 289, 292, 293, 298, 309, 310, 311, 314, 316, 318, 320, 321, 322, 323, 325, 326, 327, 329, 330, 331, 332, 333, 346, 347, 348, 349, 350, 351, 352, 354, 355, 356, 421, 468, 469, 471, 492
anxiety disorders 120, 187, 217, 218, 222, 471

aphasia 161, 162, 165, 264, 268, 274, 284, 285, 446, 476

Applebaum, E. 124

apraxia 161, 268, 269, 275

Armstrong, D. F. 377

Arredondo, P. 447, 456

arteriosclerosis 190

arthritis 144, 148, 175, 182, 186, 189, 353, 468

arthrogryposis 148

Asenbauer, B. 174

Ashcraft, M. H. 170

Ashley, M. J. 279

Ashton, V. J. 155

Asmus, E. 62, 495

Asperger's Syndrome 118, 119, 131, 138, 418

assessment 13, 84, 95, 99, 195, 196, 237, 273, 278, 284, 291, 296, 331, 332, 333, 345, 346, 347, 386, 389, 409, 413, 415, 430, 431, 432, 433, 434, 435, 436, 437

assessment tools 292, 296, 331, 333, 347, 432, 436, 437, 438, 440, 443, 515

Assgaard, T. 525

assistive hearing devices 380

association through contiguity 64

Associative Mood and Memory Training (AAMT) 171, 175, 267

Associative Mood and Memory Training (AMMT) 267

ataxia 146

atherosclerosis 190

athetosis 146

atlantoaxial instability 94

Atlee, E. A. 23, 24

atonia 146

attention 31, 45, 52, 57, 58, 59, 60, 65, 82, 91, 94, 98, 104, 105, 106, 107, 122, 124, 125, 126, 128, 130, 135, 136, 146, 152, 164, 168, 169, 170, 174, 195, 225, 226, 232, 264, 267, 273, 279, 282, 283, 292, 293, 297, 298, 316, 317, 319, 351, 386, 389, 395, 415, 433, 434, 476

Atterbury, B. W. 97, 98, 104, 106, 495

audiologist 372, 379, 383, 498

auditory awareness 104, 128

auditory discrimination 128, 169, 432

auditory nerve 54, 287, 369, 372

Auditory Perception Training (APT) 169, 267

Austin, D. 526

authentic 524

autism 82, 117, 118, 119, 120, 121, 122, 123, 124, 125, 127, 128, 130, 131, 132, 133, 135, 136, 137, 138, 409, 410, 437, 452, 459, 525

Autism Society of America 117, 118, 120, 121

Autism Speaks 121

Autism Spectrum Disorder (ASD) 117, 118, 119, 120, 122, 123, 131, 133, 134, 138, 463, 469

Avanzini, G. 477

Averbach, J. 433

Axen, K. 165, 269

Ayoub, C. M. 320, 332

Babai, E. M. 166

Bach-y-Rita, P. 281

Bailey, G. L. 397

Bailey, L. 330

Balch, W. 61

Balkwill, L. 66

Balmer, S. J. 155

Bandura, A. 469, 470

Bang, C. 385, 386, 389

Barnett, C. A. 418

Baroff, G. S. 93, 94

Barrickman, J. 47, 323, 327, 328, 329, 346

Bartlett, D. E. 24

Baruth, L. G. 460, 477, 478

Baryza, M. J. 320

basilar membrane 369

Basmajian, J. V. 265

Basso, A. 166, 268, 284

Baumann, A. A. 384, 386, 388

Bauwens, J. 418

Bayless, K. M. 45, 47

Beal, M. 50

Bean, M. F. 387

beat competency 47

Bedard, P. J. 294

Bednarz, C. F. 222

Beer, A. S. 11, 98

behavioral disorder 210

behavioral-emotional disorder 210

Behrens, G. A. 313

Belin, P. 284

Belin, R. 390

Belleville, S. 125
bereavement 12, 266, 310, 344, 345, 360
Berlyne, D. E. 60, 64, 65
Bernatzky, G. 155
Bernatzky, P. 155
Bernstein, B. 198, 200, 201
Bettison, S. 127, 135, 267
Biklen, D. 11
Biklen, S. 526
bilateral 276, 283, 371
Bilbrey, M. 200
bilingual-bicultural Approach to language learning 375
Bindman, A. B. 199
Birkenshaw, L. 380
Bishop, B. L. 321
Bishop, S. 225, 234
Bishop, V. E. 394
Bitcon, C. 437, 462
Blackstock, E. G. 124
Blake 234
Blake, R. 225
Bleck, E. 145
blindness 10, 86, 144, 190, 390, 391, 392, 394, 396,
       397, 398, 409
Bloom, L. J. 257
Blumer, G. A. 26
Board Certification exam 34
Bogdan, R. 526
Boldt, S. 330
Bolger, E. P. 313
Bolton, C. 310
Bondy, A. 122
Bonk, V. A. 320
Bonny, H. L. 225, 236, 240, 241, 321, 324, 352, 358,
       465, 466, 467, 468, 472
Bouchard, D. 394
Boucher, J. 164, 269
Boucher, V. 162
Bower, G. H. 168, 171, 268
Bowman, K. 61
Boxberger, R. 19, 20, 21, 29, 31, 32, 33
Boxhill, E. H. 101, 104
Boxill, E. H. 437
Boyle, J. D. 42, 62, 64, 68, 69
Brady, M. 118
bradykinesia 290
Brantley, D. 86
Braswell, C. 437

Breniere, Y. 145
Brewer, J. E. 97
Bright, R. 51, 200
Bril, B. 145
bronchitis 191
Brooks, B. H. 132
Brooks, D. M. 49, 233
Brookshire, R. H. 272
Brophy, J. 421
Brotons, M. 200, 201
Brown, I. 94
Brown, K. R. 390
Brown, L. 132
Brown, S. H. 57, 88, 155, 294
Brown, S. W. 317
Brownell, M. D. 464, 469
Browning, C. A. 318, 320, 321, 322
Bruer, A. B. 200
Brunk, B. K. 414, 432, 437
Brunnstrom, S. 265, 276, 508, 509
Bruscia, K. E. 432, 437, 466, 473, 525, 528
Bryant, D. R. 219, 228, 234, 239, 471, 472
Bryant, M. 418
Bryen, D. N. 104
Bullock, C. 109
Bumanis, A. 200
Burdick, W. P. 30
Burney, C. 23, 25
Burns, D. S. 330, 467, 468
Burt, R. K. 320
Burton, R. 21
Bushong, D. J. 257
Byrne, L. A. 200
Byrnes, S. R. 230

Cacioppo, J. T. 174
cadence 57, 156, 270, 288, 294
Cahill, L. 268
Caine, J. 314
Caird, F. I. 290
Caldwell, J. T. 463
Callanan, P. 444
Calne, D. B. 292
Camp, C. J. 183

Campbell, P. S. 45, 46, 47, 48
Capatini, E. 268
Carapetyan, A. 21
Carder, M. P. H. 24
Carey, A. 104
Carlson, E. T. 24
Carter, S. A. 98
Casby, J. A. 201
Casey, L. 330
Cassidy, J. W. 314
Cassileth, B. R. 330
Cassity, J. 66, 214, 217, 219, 221, 222, 225, 226, 227, 228, 230, 231, 233, 234, 235, 236, 237, 239, 242, 437, 478
Cassity, M. 66, 214, 217, 219, 221, 222, 224, 225, 226, 227, 228, 229, 230, 231, 233, 234, 235, 236, 237, 239, 241, 242, 437, 472, 478
cataracts 190
catatonic behavior 213
Centers for Disease Control and Prevention 119, 121
central hearing loss 370
Central Wisconsin Center for People with Developmental Disabilities 95
cerebral aneurysm 272
Cerebrovascular Accident (CVA) 190, 271, 272, 276, 299
Cevasco, A. M. 200, 222, 235, 236
Chadwick, D. 160, 173, 270
Chadwick, P. 127
Chase, K. M. 447, 448, 456, 458
Chen, C. 154
Chetta, H. 323, 332
Chosky, L. 464
Christenberry, E. 324, 325
Christenson, P. G. 49
Chronic Obstructive Pulmonary Disorder (COPD) 191, 312, 331, 348, 473
Cicerone, K. D. 169
cilia 369
Cioni, M. 294
Clair, A. A. 42, 50, 51, 52, 53, 61, 63, 66, 67, 68, 70, 181, 195, 196, 198, 200, 201, 310, 311
Clarizio, H. F. 420
Clark, C. 118, 160, 173, 270
Clark, F. 127, 131
Clark, L. A. 212, 472
Clark, M. 323, 329
Clark, M. E. 200, 316, 318, 319, 320, 321, 322
Claussen, D. 267, 283

client-centered 527
Cloninger, C. R. 200
clubfoot 148
Coates, P. 97, 98, 110
cochlea 54, 369, 372
cochlear implant 366, 370, 371, 372, 373, 376, 380, 381, 383, 389
Codding, P. A. 248, 332, 392, 395, 398
Cody, F. W. 155
Coffman, D. D. 50, 62, 310, 311
cognitive-behavior therapy 472
Cohen, G. 430, 432, 433, 437
Cohen, H. 273
Cohen, N. 386
Cohen-Mansfield, J. 347
Cohn, C. 310
Cole, K. M. 432
Coleman, J. M. 314
Coleman, K. A. 414, 432, 437
Coleman, M. R. 92
Collins, S. K. 314
Columbia University 28, 31, 520
Colwell, C. M. 318, 320, 321, 325, 331, 461, 462
coma 299
compression 54
compulsions 217
concentration 170
concrete operations 44, 48, 49
conditioning 225
conductive hearing loss 369
congenital 88, 144, 145, 148, 149, 150, 175, 272, 371, 373, 384, 391
congenital hearing loss 371
congenital vision loss 391
Corain, B. 187
Corey, G. 218, 220, 225, 226, 227, 228, 232, 233, 240, 241, 444, 445, 446, 447, 448, 458, 469, 470, 471, 477, 478
Corey, M. 233, 444
Corn, A. L. 397
Corning, J. L. 26
coronary heart disease 190
Cotter, V. W. 200
Cotton, E. 154
coup-contrecoup injury 277
Cratty, B. J. 101, 152
Crawford, M. J. 174
Creedon, M. 347

Creswell, J. W. 526, 528
Crocker, A. D. 394
Cross, I. 477
Crozier, W. R. 67, 68
Cudeiro, J. 155
cultural convention 63, 66
Cutler, N. R. 188, 189

Dainow, E. 55
Dalcroze, E. J. 461, 462, 463
Dalcroze Eurhythmics Approach to Music Education 462, 463, 464
Dalcroze Society of America 463
Dale, M. 463
Daly, J. 199
Darrow, A. A. 11, 24, 125, 130, 131, 132, 133, 137, 365, 377, 378, 380, 383, 384, 385, 386, 387, 388, 389, 390, 391, 394, 395, 396, 398, 405, 406, 411, 412, 414, 417, 419, 422, 447, 456, 458, 492, 493, 495, 501, 503, 504, 505, 506, 507, 515
Dassa, A. 200
Daveson, B. A. 320, 321, 322, 324, 327
David, A. S. 230
David, R. M. 265
Davids, J. R. 145
Davidson, L. 46
Davis, B. A. 313
Davis, J. 386, 387
Davis, R. 379
Davis, R. K. 127
Davis, W. B. 3, 17, 21, 27, 28, 29, 30, 32, 56, 67, 79, 181, 395, 429, 487, 517, 518, 523, 524, 525
DeBout, J. K. 98, 104
DeBus, B. 381
DeGagne, R. 320
degree of hearing loss 370, 375, 377
delusions 212, 213, 214
Del Olmo, M. F. 155
dementia 50, 183, 187, 188, 193, 196, 198, 292, 311, 344, 347, 353, 355
Denny, A. 201
DeNora, T. 173
Depperschmidt, K. A. 201
depression 187

depressive episode 215
Deschenes, C. 415
descriptive research 491, 492, 504, 505, 506, 516, 533
Deutsch, D. 267
Deutsch, G. 274
Deutsch, R. 437
developmental disability 117, 137
Developmental Speech and Language Training Through Music (DSLM) 166
De l'Aune, W. 395
De L'Etoile, S. K. 45, 173, 174
diabetes 191
Dieker, L. A. 418
Dileo, C. 356
Dileo Maranto, C. 228
diplegia 146
direct instruction 123, 457
disorganized speech 213
Distenfeld, S. 165, 269
divided attention 59, 170
Dneaster, D. 356
Doherty, C. P. 174
Dolan, R. J. 171, 172, 268
Douglass, E. T. 331, 332, 430, 432, 433, 436, 437
Down syndrome 88, 90, 93, 94, 102
Dragon, D. 155
Drake, R. M. 390
Drasgow, E. 375
Drew, C. J. 80, 82, 83, 84, 87, 89, 90, 91, 94, 376
Driscoll, V. 382
Drolet, P. 320
DSM-IV-TR 85, 86, 87, 88, 211, 212, 213, 215, 216, 219, 220, 221, 222, 237
Dubner, R. 316
Duehl, A. N. 395
Duerksen, G. 488
Duffy, J. R. 294
Duke University Medical Center 492
Dunn, J. 94
Dura, J. R. 309
Durham, P. 278
Dvorkin, J. 473
dwarfism 149
dysarthria 162, 165, 265, 268, 269, 274, 285, 292, 293, 294, 297
dyspnea 348, 349, 354
dyspraxia 265, 285

$\mathscr{E}$

Eagle, C. 173, 226
early intervention 90, 375
ear canal 54, 369, 372
Ebberts, G. 200
Ebeling, D. 415, 417
echolalic 120, 121
Eckert, E. 62
Eckert, M. 62
eclectic 224, 232, 243, 459, 468, 477, 478, 479
Edgerton, C. 127, 128
Edmonds, K. 380
Education for All Handicapped Children Act of 1975 11, 95, 97
Edwards, J. 127, 131, 321, 322, 324, 327, 525
Edwards, L. B. 25
Egan, M. W. 376
Egel, A. L. 124
Eich, E. 61
Eisenberg, G. M. 468
El'ner, A. M. 56
electrochemical energy 369, 370
Electroconvulsive Therapy (ECT) 216, 230
Elliot, B. 160, 173, 270
Ellis, A. 472
emergent 527
encephalitis 89, 291
encoding 171, 267, 476
end-of-life care 344, 361, 460
Engen, R. L. 313, 326, 329, 331, 332
English-based sign systems 374
entertainment 31, 53, 521
entrainment 286
episodes 148, 211, 215, 216, 218, 223, 292
Erber, J. T. 182, 183, 184, 185, 187, 188, 189, 190, 191, 192
Erber, N. P. 385
Erdman, A. F. 31
etiology 87, 88, 111, 120, 230, 271, 277, 291, 295, 369, 391, 392
Etten, M. J. 189
Evans, A. 154
executive function 91, 92, 135, 168, 172, 267, 268, 292, 293, 297
expressionism 62
extramusical associations 62

$\mathscr{F}$

Fahey, J. D. 380
Fahn, S. 292
Faiena, C. 477
Fait, H. 94
Farnan, L. A. 46, 55, 57, 79, 80, 82, 97, 98, 99, 102, 104
Farthing, G. W. 317
Faunce, G. 330
Feder, B. 19, 20, 489
Feder, E. 19, 20, 489
Feil, N. 198
Feldman, R. D. 183
Ferrara, L. 516
Ferraro, K. F. 183
Ferrer, A. J. 323, 329, 332
fetal alcohol syndrome 88
Ficken, T. 235, 239
Findlay, S. 492
fingerspelling 374
Fisher, J. 297
Fisher, K. V. 385, 386
Fitzgerald-Cloutier, M. L. 201
Fitzsimons, M. 174
Fleurant, J. 162
Flodmark, A. 158
Flowers, P. 127
Floyd, J. 324
Ford, T. A. 380, 381, 384, 494
Forinash, M. 487, 525, 526
formal operations 44, 49
Foster, N. A. 201
Fowler, K. L. 448
Fox, L. 91
Foxton, J. M. 125
Fraenkel, J. R. 432, 436
Fragile X syndrome 88, 90, 106
France, C. R. 320
Franks, J. R. 381
Frasinetti, F. 267
Fratianne, R. 320, 321, 322, 324, 325, 331, 332
Freed, B. S. 221, 222, 235, 239
Freeland, R. L. 155
Frego, R. J. D. 463, 464
frequency
    in research 86, 165, 192, 210, 214, 216, 220, 286, 297, 332, 418, 434, 439, 515

in sound 55, 368, 371, 380, 381, 383, 385, 386, 500, 510

Friedman, M. 104

Frith, U. 119, 121, 124

Froelich, M. A. 327, 328

Froman, R. 68, 69, 447, 448, 456, 458

Frost, L. 122

Fulford, M. 251

functions of music 8, 53, 70

G

Gaab, N. 160

Gaal, D. 320

Gage, J. R. 145

Gagnon, L. 166

Gainer, E. 412

Galizio, M. 62

Gallagher, J. J. 92

Gallagher, L. M. 249

Gallahue, D. 286

Gallaudet, T. 377

Galloway, H. F. 387

Gantt, L. 432

Gantz, B. 381

Garand, J. 123

Garand, L. 198

Garcia, L. J. 162

Gardener, E. 320

Gardiner, J. C. 217, 225, 227, 229, 230, 232, 234, 293

Gardner, H. 46

Gardner, J. E. 200

Gardstrom, S. C. 49, 470

Garrett, E. E. 29

Gaston, E. T. 33, 34, 42, 61, 62, 67, 455

gastritis 191

generalizability 492, 528

Generally, N. 222

genetic abnormalities 90

Gerdner, L. A. 201

Gericke, O. L. 430, 432, 437

Gerstmann, D. R. 314

Gfeller, K. E. 3, 17, 41, 48, 50, 51, 52, 55, 57, 59, 60, 61, 62, 64, 66, 70, 108, 198, 209, 267, 283, 305, 310, 317, 318, 319, 320, 322, 323, 328, 331, 365, 380, 381, 382, 383, 384, 385, 386, 387, 388, 389, 395, 429, 448, 458, 470, 487, 492, 493, 495, 501, 503, 504, 505, 506, 507, 515, 518, 523

Ghetti, C. M. 310, 347, 355

Gibbons, A. C. 50, 198, 200

Gilbert, J. P. 24, 50, 495

Gillmeister, G. 461, 463

Girard, M. 320

Glaser, R. 309

Glasgow Coma Scale (GCS) 278

glaucoma 190

Glover, G. H. 164

Glover, H. 269

Glynn, N. J. 196

Goatcher, S. 109

Goddaer, J. 201

Godley, C. A. 318, 319, 320, 321, 325

Gold, C. 174

Goldberg, F. S. 225, 241, 467, 473

Goldstein, A. 324

Goldstein, C. 127, 131, 136

Goldstein, M. 292

Gonzales, A. 127

Gonzalez, D. 525

Good, D. C. 57

Good, M. 309, 317, 318, 320, 321, 332

Goodkin, D. 461

Goodwin, D. 217

good Gestalts 59

Gorsuch, A. 386

Gorsuch, R. L. 332

Gottselig, J. M. 61, 64

Gougoux, F. 390

Gourgey, C. 395, 396

Gowensmith, W. N. 257

Gracely, R. H. 316

Graham, R. M. 11, 98

Granot, A. 200

Grant, R. E. 104, 200

Gray, C. 123

Greenberg, L. 66

Greenberg, M. 46

Greene, R. J. 397

Greenwald, M. A. 397

Greenwald Furman, A. 117

Gregory, D. 200, 470
Grenier, Y. 320
Grinnell, D. M. 155
Groen, K. M. 333, 437, 460
Groene, R. W. 200, 201
grossly disorganized behavior 213
Grub, C. 393
Guba, E. G. 526, 528
Guthrie, P. T. 313, 323, 325, 327, 328, 329
Guyn, L. H. 298
Guze, S. 217
Gwede, C. 330

H

Haaland, K. Y. 154
Haas, E. 269
Haas, F. 165
Hachinski, V. 271
Hagen, C. 278, 279
Haghighi, K. R. 346, 349, 358
Hai, S. 200
Haimov, I. 200
Hairston, M. 127
Hakvoort, L. 251
Hall, R. V. 442
Hall, S. 477
Hall, V. 225, 226
Halligan, P. W. 230
hallucinations 212, 213, 214, 222, 231, 324
Hama, M. 310, 463
Hamburg, J. 200
Haneishi, E. 294
Hanser, S. B. 230, 236, 313, 318, 320, 322, 430, 432, 470, 489
Hanson, N. 52, 198
Hanson-Abromeit, D. 45, 46, 313, 314, 315
Hardick, E. J. 379, 386, 387
Hardman, M. L. 80, 82, 83, 84, 87, 89, 90, 91, 94, 376, 395, 397
Hargreaves, D. J. 49
Harrington, D. L. 154
Harris, D. K. 183, 184, 185, 187, 188
Harris, J. C. 86, 87, 89, 105, 106, 109
Harris, M. R. 322
Hart, T. 274

Hatfield, E. 174
Havlicek, L. 50
Hayden, M. 274
Heaney, C. J. 222, 232
hearing aids 367, 369, 370, 371, 372, 373, 376, 379, 380, 381, 389
Heaton, P. 125, 267
Hébert, S. 166, 170
Heflin, L. J. 122
Heim, K. E. 390
Heitman, R. 200
Heller, G. N. 11, 22, 23, 24, 25, 377, 493, 517, 524
Helm, N. A. 162, 268
hemiplegia 146, 275, 509, 514
Hendrick, C. 62
Hermelin, B. 125, 127, 135, 267
Herrmann, D. 477
hertz (Hz) 368
Hesse, H. P. 155
Heward, W. L. 376, 395, 494
Hibben, J. K. 463
Hilliard, R. E. 219, 227, 228, 234, 239, 345, 348, 349, 350, 351, 358, 360, 472
Hintz, M. R. 437
Hirsh, I. J. 385
Hoats, D. L. 397
Hobson, M. R. 61, 438, 446
Hodges, D. A. 17, 55
Hoehn, M. M. 292
Hoemberg, V. 155, 162, 294, 295
Holbrook, M. 266
Hollander, F. M. 127, 131
Holme, M. B. 201
Hommel, M. 169, 267
Hornick, A. J. 397
hospice care 8, 10, 12, 318, 333, 343, 344, 345, 346, 347, 348, 349, 350, 351, 353, 355, 356, 360, 361, 437, 455, 459
Hospice Patient Alliance 348
Houghton, B. A. 214
Hourcade, J. J. 418
Howe, J. W. 24
Howe, S. G. 24
Howe, T. E. 155
Howery, B. I. 97, 110
Hoyer, W. J. 50, 184
Hsiao, F. L. 372, 381
Huber, C. H. 460, 477, 478

Huck, A. M. 132
Hullmann, K. 293
Hummel, C. J. 380
Hummelsheim, H. 477
Humpal, M. E. 47, 127
Humphries, T. 377
Hunt, N. 395
Hunter, B. C. 321
Huntington's disease (HD) 188, 266, 290, 291, 292, 293, 294, 295, 299, 300
Hurley, A. 347
Huron, D. 42, 50, 53
Hurt, C. P. 155, 295
Hussey, D. L. 437
hydrocephaly 90
hypertension 190, 272
hypokenetic dysarthria 293
hypokinesia 290
hypothesis 507
hypotonia 94

iconicity 63, 64
Ilsen, I. M. 28, 29, 30, 31, 32, 36, 518, 520, 521, 522, 523
Imhoff, B. 124
incidental language learning 378
Individualized Education Program (IEP) 11, 95, 385, 409, 413, 414, 415, 417, 431, 497
Individuals with Disabilities Education Act (IDEA) 95, 118, 391, 406, 407, 408, 409, 410, 411, 423, 424
infant-directed speech 45
inner ear 54, 369, 370, 372
Intellectual Disability (ID) 80, 81, 82, 83, 85, 86, 87, 91, 92, 94, 97, 106, 108, 111, 409, 462
International Kodály Society 464
interpersonal integrity 528
intracranial hemorrhage 271, 272, 299
irrational thoughts 218, 228, 229, 470
ischemia 271, 299
Isenberg-Grezeda, C. 430, 433, 473
Isern, B. 97
isomorphism 64
iso principle 23, 30

Jackson, S. A. 164, 269
Jacobi, E. M. 468
Jacobson, E. 252
Jacox, A. D. 316, 317, 318, 320, 321, 322
James, M. R. 221, 222
Jeffery, D. R. 57
Jellison, J. A. 132, 151, 282, 412
Johns, D. F. 272
Johnson, C. M. 469
Johnson, C. P. 119
Johnson, D. 330
Johnson, G. 201
Johnson, R. E. 34
Johnson, S. 200
Jones, C. J. 87, 94
Jones, G. 56
Joyce, C. A. 311
Juhrs, P. D. 127, 131
Junkala, J. 158
Juslin, P. N. 64, 173, 488
juvenile rheumatoid arthritis 148

Kain, Z. N. 320
Kalinowski, J. 164, 269
Kamps, D. M. 122
Kandel, E. 284
Kane, E. O. 30
Kanner, L. 118
Kaps, M. 293
Kastenbaum, B. 345
Katz, E. 433
Kauffman, J. M. 420, 421
Keller, W. 462
Kemmerer, K. 122
Kennelly, J. 327
Kenny, C. B. 525, 526
Kenyon, G. P. 155, 270
Kern, P. 396
Kerr, T. 311
Kersten, F. 396, 397
Kiecolt-Glaser, J. K. 309

Kim, Y. 465, 469
Kirk, S. A. 92, 93, 94, 96
Kirkpatrick, J. 324
Knoll, C. D. 10
Knutson, J. F. 267, 381
Kochhar, C. A. 411, 415
Kodály, Z. 461, 463, 464
Kodály Approach to Music Education 463, 464
Koegel, R. L. 124, 136
Korduba, O. M. 380, 381
Körelen, D. 468
Korn, G. W. 320
Kostka, M. 127
Kraft, I. 81, 96
Kravits, T. R. 122
Kreitler, H. 60, 64
Kreitler, S. 60, 64
Krevsky, B. 317, 318, 320, 332
Kroger, S. 200
Krout, R. E. 345, 348, 351, 352, 356, 358, 360
Kruse, J. 321, 323, 329, 330
Krych, D. K. 279
Kuck, K. 314
Kumar, A. 56, 309, 468
Kumar, M. 56, 309, 468
Kuntze, M. 375
Kurz, C. E. 200
Kwak, E. E. 156, 464
Kwalwasser, J. 390
Kwoun, S. 61, 62, 64, 66, 310

Ladavos, E. 267
Ladurner, G. 155
LaGasse, B. 261
Laing, S. J. 437
Lancaster, L. C. 192
Land, S. 418
Lange, H. W. 295
Langer, E. 323
Langer, S. 61, 310
Langton-Hewer, R. 265
Lansing, C. R. 381
Larsen, J. D. 171
Larson, P. S. 50

Larson, S. C. 318
Laskerk, R. D. 199
Lathom, W. 50, 97, 98, 99, 101, 102, 104, 106, 173, 226, 464
Layman, D. L. 437
Leal, D. 376
Least Restrictive Environment (LRE) 95, 407, 411
Lee, C. 526
Lee, M. 127
Lee, P. R. 199
Lee, S. 125, 127
Lefcourt, H. 323
Lehr, S. 11
Leins, A. K. 143, 174
Leitner, M. J. 186
Lepage, C. 320, 332
Lepore, M. 390
Leuchter, A. F. 247
Levenson, R. W. 62
Levine, C. B. 290
Lewis, S. C. 187, 442
Lezak, M. D. 280
Licklider, J. C. 320
Liesveld, J. L. 321
Lim, H. A. 127
Lim, I. 155
Lincoln, Y. S. 526, 528
Lipe, A. W. 196, 200, 201, 359, 432
Liston, R. E. 463
Litchman, M. D. 127, 128
locomotion 101, 136, 155, 394
Locsin, R. 320, 324
Logan, D. R. 90
Logan, E. H. 317
long-term memory 59, 60, 200, 358
Longino, C. F. 184, 186
Loomis, D. 377
Lopez, L. 477
Lord, T. R. 200
Lou, M. F. 201
Loven, M. F. 97
Lovgreen, B. 155
Lowey, J. 432
low vision 391, 392, 393, 398
Luce, D. 217, 219, 227, 228, 234, 239
Lucia, C. M. 313
Luft, A. R. 155
Luschene, R. 332

Lussier, I. 166
Lynch, W. J. 280

manic episode 215, 216
Ma, Y. 127, 135
Macaulay, D. 61
MacDonald, R. A. R. 319
Macko, R. F. 155
Madsen, C. H. 421
Madsen, C. K. 390, 421
Madsen, C. M. 45
Maeller, D. H. 267
Magill, L. A. 330
magnetic resonance imaging (MRI) 296
Mahlberg, M. 127, 128, 136
Mahon, M. 109
Mahshie, S. N. 375
Majono, M. 477
Malherbe, V. 145
Malkmus, D. 278
Malloy, D. 447, 456, 458
Malone, A. 320
Malone, S. 395
Malouin, F. 294
Mandel, A. R. 155
Mandel, S. E. 313, 326, 329, 330, 331
manic episodes 216
Manton, K. G. 184
manual approach to communication 373, 375
Maratos, A. S. 174
Marcionetti, M. J. 214, 217, 219, 223, 231, 232, 235, 236, 242
Markson, E. W. 185
Marley, L. S. 323, 328
Marschark, M. 375
Marsden, C. D. 292
Marshall, A. 311
Marshall, K. 395
Marteniuk, R. G. 57
Martin, A. 268
Masataka, N. 173
Mastropieri, M. 119, 412
Masur, F. T. 316, 317, 320, 322
Mathenius, L. 102

Mathews, R. M. 200
Mathews, S. J. 23, 24
Maue-Johnson 347
Maultsby, M. 228
Maure-Johnson, E. L. 437
Mauritz, K. H. 155
Maus, N. K. 280
Mayer, A. R. 154
Mayer, R. 469
Mayo Foundation for Medical Education and Research 352
McCabe, P. M. 56, 309, 468
McCaffery, M. 323
McClosky, L. J. 200
McCombe, W. S. 155
McCombe-Waller, S. 155
McDavis, R. J. 447, 456
McDermott, F. 330
McDermott, H. J. 382
McDonald, D. T. 45, 46, 47, 48, 328
McDonald, R. 468
McDonald, W. I. 296
McFarland, R. A. 62
McGlinn, J. A. 30, 31
McGrath, P. 316
McIntosh, G. C. 57, 154, 155, 162, 270, 294, 298, 515
McIntosh, K. W. 162, 285, 294
McKernon, P. 46
McKinney, C. H. 56, 309, 311, 330, 467, 468, 474
McNeil, C. 188
Mead, V. H. 463
Meadow, K. 388, 389
mean 149, 505, 508, 509, 510, 514, 515
mechanical energy 54, 369
Medicaid 442
medical model 97, 460
Medical Powers of Music 24
Medicare 442
Medicare-certified 350
Mehr, M. 381, 382
Meier, R. 375
Meinhart, N. T. 323
Melodic Intonation Therapy (MIT) 162, 268, 284, 285
Melvill Jones, G. 287
Melzack, R. 316, 317, 331
Memmot, J. 195, 196

memory 8, 48, 51, 58, 59, 60, 97, 108, 124, 128, 135, 136, 157, 161, 166, 168, 169, 170, 171, 175, 181, 185, 188, 190, 195, 200, 232, 264, 267, 268, 272, 273, 274, 276, 279, 283, 284, 288, 292, 297, 298, 358, 392, 432, 433, 434, 476, 530

Menard, E. 125

meningitis 89

mental retardation 81, 82, 85, 147, 408, 409, 410, 412

Merriam, A. P. 18, 20, 53, 62, 63, 68, 70, 310

Mertel, K. 143

metabolic errors 90

methodological integrity 528

Metzger, L. K. 313, 326

Meyer, L. B. 63, 65

Michel, D. E. 98

middle ear 54, 369

Miles, B. S. 125

Millard, K. O. 200

Miller, A. 295, 296, 297

Miller, R. A. 56, 57, 155, 270, 294

Miller, R. D. 442

Mills-Groen, K. 347, 351, 356

Miltner, R. 295

Minciacchi, D. 477

Minimal Record of Disability (MRD) 296

Mitchell, L. A. 319

mixed hearing loss 370

mnemonic devices 59, 60, 170, 171, 267, 283, 288, 476

mobility 6, 83, 102, 148, 149, 151, 154, 172, 193, 200, 269, 328, 333, 392, 395, 399, 463, 508

Mohler, L. 61

Molinari, M. 154

monoplegia 146

Monsey, H. L. 320

mood disorders 215

Moog, H. 46

Moore, R. S. 102, 200, 201

Morris, G. S. 155

motor coordination 276

motor memory 288

Mottron, L. 125

Mountain, G. 189

multidisciplinary assessment 95

Multiple sclerosis (MS) 266, 295, 297, 298, 299, 300, 474

Mundy, P. 122

Munro, S. 51, 318, 325, 329

Murphy, K. A. 432

Murphy, M. 222

muscular dystrophy 146

music
  as an information agent 319, 322, 333, 353
  as a masking agent 319, 322, 333, 353
  as a positive environmental stimulus 319, 323, 353
  as a stimulus for active focus or distraction 319, 353
  to facilitate a relaxation response 319, 353

Musical Attention Control Training (MACT) 169, 267, 282

Musical Executive Function Training (MEFT) 171, 175, 268, 293

musical memory 157, 530

Musical Mnemonics Training (MMT) 171, 175, 232, 267, 298

Musical Mnemonic Training (MMT) 283

Musical Neglect Training (MNT) 169, 267, 283

Musical Prescriptions 520

Musical Prescriptions for the Ailing 520

Musical Sensory Orientation Training (MSOT) 168, 169, 175, 267, 282

Musical Speech Stimulation (MUSTIM) 268, 284, 285

Music Attention Control Training (MACT) 293

Music Physically Considered 22

music therapy assessment 195, 243, 413, 414, 415, 432, 433, 434, 436, 437

music therapy as a related service 413, 414, 415

Myocardial infarction (MI) 190

Nagel, D. 145

Nagler, J. 127

Nakata, T. 174

Namazi, K. 200

Nash, S. 127

Nathan, P. E. 212, 472

National Association for Music Therapy (NAMT) 7, 32, 33, 34, 36, 173, 455, 470, 488, 517, 524, 525, 534

National Foundation for the Treatment of Pain 346

National Head Injury Foundation 277

National Hospice & Palliative Care Organization 345

National Institutes of Mental Health 213, 217, 218, 224

National Research Council 122, 125

naturalistic research 526

negative symptoms 213, 223, 320

Nelson, D. 127

Nettelbeck, T. 125
Nettl, B. 18, 42, 53, 63, 68
Neurologic Music Therapy (NMT) 155, 157, 175, 232, 265, 266, 267, 268, 269, 281, 282, 284, 285, 286, 293, 294, 295, 298, 299, 474, 475, 476, 477
neuromuscular disease 344
neuropsychologist 273
Newport, E. 375
Nichols, R. J. 321
Nieto del Rincon, P. L. 125
Nieuwboer, A. 294
Nikkel, B. 222
Noel, P. S. 24
Noguchi, L. K. 319
Nolan, P. 225, 240, 241
nonpharmacological approach 352
Nordoff, P. 437, 465, 466
Nordoff-Robbins Center for Music Therapy 465
Nordoff-Robbins Model of Music Therapy 465, 466, 529, 532
Norris, J. W. 271
North, A. C. 49
Northern Wisconsin Center 96
Novak, J. 378
Numeric Rating Scale (NRS) 347
Nymark, J. R. 155

Oleson, J. 381
Olson, B. K. 200
Olszewski, C. 381
oncology 533
onset of hearing loss 371, 373, 375
ontology 525
optimal complexity theory 64
oral communication system 373
Oral Motor and Respiratory Exercises (OMREX) 164, 269, 285, 286, 294
Orff, C. 461, 462, 463
Orff-Schulwerk Method 453, 454, 461, 462, 464, 501
Organization of American Kodály Educators 463
orientation
  in awareness 168, 169, 196, 200, 232, 237, 238, 241, 267
  in mobility 395, 399
  in philosophy of treatment 194, 223, 224, 225, 227, 228, 232, 233, 243, 472, 474, 478
Orr, R. R. 394
ossicles 54, 369
osteoarthritis 189
osteogenesis imperfecta 149
osteoporosis 189
Ostermann, T. 298
Ottenbacher, K. J. 442, 490
Otto, D. 201
outer ear 369
Oyama, T. 324

O'Briant, M. P. 62
O'Callaghan, C. C. 330, 355, 358, 360
O'Connell, A. S. 318
O'Connell, T. 124
O'Connor, N. 127
O'Leary, K. D. 212, 472
O'Neill, S. A. 49, 61, 310
O'Riain, M. D. 155
O'Shanick, G. J. 278
observational learning 225
obsessions 217, 218, 238
obsessive-compulsive disorder (OCD) 217
Ogata, D. 169
Ogata, S. 267
Okun, M. 310
Oldham, J. A. 155
Olding 310

Pacchetti, C. 155
Padden, C. 376, 377
Paivio, S. C. 66
Pal'tsev, Y. I. 56
palliative care 10, 318, 343, 344, 347, 350, 351, 356, 361
Palmer, M. D. 51
panic disorder 217, 218
Papalia, D. E. 183, 184, 187, 188, 189, 191
Paradis, J. 162
parallel play 47
paraplegia 146
Parente, R. 477
Parker, B. J. 385, 386

Parker, J. C. 321
Parkinson's disease (PD) 155, 187, 188, 266, 290, 291, 292, 293, 294, 299, 300, 473, 474
Patterned Sensory Enhancement (PSE) 155, 156, 270, 289, 294
Patterson, A. 412
Patterson, C. B. 519
Paul, D. 226
Paul, P. V. 493
Pavani, F. 267
Payton, O. D. 488
Pedretti, L. W. 272, 279
Pelletier, C. I. 310, 318, 321, 322, 324
Penhune, V. B. 154
perceptual processing 58, 60
Percy, M. 88, 94
Peretz, I. 58, 61, 64, 125, 166, 170, 172
perilingual 371
Perilli, G. G. 254
periodic 7
personality disorders 219, 220
personal integrity 528
Pervasive Developmental Disorder (PDD) 118, 138
Peterson, D. A. 298
Peterson, E. D. 97
Peterson, M. 50
Phelps, E. A. 169, 267
Phelps, R. 516
phenomenonological research 526, 527, 528, 529, 530
Phenylketonuria (PKU) 88
Pickett-Cooper, P. 200, 201
Picture Exchange Communication System (PECS) 122
Pilon, M. A. 162, 285
pinna 369
pitch 52, 54, 58, 128, 368, 386
Plach, T. 234, 236
Platel, H. 154
Plutchik, R. 437
poliomyelitis 151
Pollock, N. 200
Polman, C. H. 296
Posner, R. A. 182
post-traumatic stress disorder (PTSD) 217
postlingual 371, 494
posttest 515
Potucek, J. 122
Prassas, S. G. 57, 154
Pratt, R. R. 314

prelingual 371, 457
preoperational 44, 47, 48
presbycusis 190
pretest 515
Prickett, C. A. 200, 201
Priestly, M. 472, 473
Pring, L. 125, 267
Pronovost, W. 124
protocols 52, 242, 268, 270, 443, 467, 476, 508, 510, 512, 526, 529
psychodynamic 224, 241, 468, 472, 473
psychosocial 182, 183, 184, 185, 186, 192, 193, 195, 203, 214, 217, 222, 233, 241, 243, 248, 249, 266, 299, 309, 313, 316, 327, 329, 330, 332, 344, 345, 346, 348, 355, 356, 357, 468
psychotherapy 8, 66, 187, 216, 217, 221, 224, 230, 235, 242, 247, 248, 251, 252, 253, 468, 473
Public Law 94-142 (PL 94-142) 11, 95, 97, 151, 411, 423, 501
Pullen, P. L. 420
Punwar, A. J. 430, 432, 442

quadriplegia 146
qualitative research 491, 516, 525, 526, 527, 528, 529, 532, 535
quantitative research 525

Radocy, R. E. 42, 62, 64, 68, 69
Raffman, D. 253
Rainey, D. W. 171
Rajput, A. 290
Rajput, A. H. 290
Rajput, M. 290
Ramsey, M. E. 45, 47
random assignment 515
range
  in music 55, 70, 104, 164, 269, 294, 313, 359, 369, 371, 380, 385, 389
  of motion 150, 152, 154, 155, 158, 160, 200, 265,

269, 270, 275, 280, 289, 433, 440, 476
Rankin, J. A. 322
rank order 498, 505
Rao, S. M. 154
Rapp, A. J. 394
Rapp, D. W. 394
Rapson, R. L. 174
rarefaction 54
Rastatter, M. 164, 269
RAS frequency 270
Rational Scientific Mediating Model (R-SMM) 266, 475
Rauscher, F. H. 167
Ray, K. L. 417
Rayburn, A. M. 464
reality orientation 196, 200, 232, 237, 238, 241
reconstructive music therapy 238, 240, 241, 242, 243
Redinbaugh, E. M. 200
Reed, K. J. 251
reeducative music therapy 238, 239, 242, 243
referentialist philosophy 63
Reigler, J. 200
Reimer, M. A. 298
Reitman, M. R. 127, 135
Remarkable Cure of a Fever by Music 22
residual hearing 370, 373, 376, 378, 380, 381, 383, 385
residual vision 391
retrieval 58, 59, 170, 171
Rett's syndrome 118, 138
Reuer, B. L. 310, 443
Reuter, I. 293
Reynolds, B. J. 97
Rhythmic Auditory Stimulation (RAS) 155, 156, 175, 270, 288, 294, 507, 508, 509, 510, 511, 512, 513, 514, 516
Rhythmic Speech Cuing (RSC) 162, 269, 285
Rice, C. 117
Rice, R. R. 57, 154, 155, 294, 515
Richards, C. L. 294
Rider, M. 324
Riggin, O. Z. 330
rigidity 146
Rimland, B. 124
Ringgenberg, S. 47
Rio, R. E. 249
Riordian, J. T. 380
Rizk, L. B. 320
Robb, S. L. 33, 174, 321, 322, 323, 325, 326, 327, 328, 329, 331, 469

Robbins, Carol 466
Robbins, Clive 437, 465, 466
Roberts, D. F. 49
Robin, D. A. 267, 381
Rochester 155
Rochester Method 374
Roederer, J. G. 167
Roodin, P. A. 50, 184
Rorke, M. A. 32
Roskam, K. S. 200
Rossignol, S. 56, 287
Rothstein, L. F. 407
Rouleau, N. 125
Royka, A. M. 313, 325
Rudenberg, M. T. 10, 313, 323, 325
Rutan, R. L. 321
Ruud, E. 225, 240, 473, 525
Ryan, L. 61
Rybash, J. M. 184

Sachs, C. 18
Sadoff, R. H. 516
safety valve function 62
Safran, J. 66
Sahler 321, 330
Sakurabayashi, H. Y. 390
Salmon, D. 357, 358
Sambandham, M. 201
Sammer, G. 293
Santeramo, B. 196
Saperston, B. 127, 128, 136
Sarafino, E. P. 242, 308, 309, 312, 315, 316, 317, 318, 320, 321, 322, 323, 324, 325, 326, 329, 331, 332, 435, 437, 438, 455
Satyo, Y. 390
Savary, L. M. 467, 468
Saxon, S. V. 189
Scalenghe, R. 432
Scartelli, J. P. 174, 231, 236, 319, 321, 322, 324
Schauer, M. L. 56, 155, 270
Scheerenberger, R. C. 81, 82
Scheinberg, L. 296
Schirm, V. 201
schizophrenia 212, 213, 214

Schlaug, G. 154
Schmid, W. 298
Schmidt, D. 127, 131
Schuchman, G. 380, 385
Schulenburg, D. 253
Schum, R. 387, 388, 389
Schwankovsky, L. M. 313, 323, 325, 327, 328, 329
Schwarz, J. 284
Scott, J. 118, 119, 122, 123, 124, 130
Scott-Kassner, C. 45, 46, 47, 48
Scruggs, T. 119, 412
Scully, J. H. 213, 218, 220
Searl, S. 11
Sears. W. 33, 69
Secic, M. 313
self-injurious behavior 94, 101, 124, 125
Sena, K. M. 298
sensorimotor 44, 45, 46, 47, 70, 136, 153, 154, 155, 157, 169, 266, 269, 279, 280, 294, 299, 476
sensorineural hearing loss 369, 370, 372
sensory processing 55, 124
severity (of hearing loss) 370, 373, 389
Seymour, H. A. 29, 30, 31, 32, 36, 455, 518, 521, 522, 523
Shank, M. 376
Shapiro, D. W. 199
Shapiro, N. 447
Sheldon, D. A. 377
Shenfield, T. 174
Sheridan, R. L. 320
Sherrill, C. 144, 147, 148, 149
Sherwin, A. 124
shifting attention 59, 170
Shore, K. 11
short-term memory 108, 200, 358
Shumway-Cook, A. 262
Siegel, S. L. 322
Sigerist, H. E. 18, 19, 20
significant difference 505, 507, 511
Silver, K. H. 155
Silverman, M. J. 214, 217, 219, 221, 222, 223, 224, 230, 231, 232, 235, 236, 242, 471, 478
Simons, G. A. 45, 46, 47, 48, 328
Simpson, R. L. 125
Simultaneous Communication (SimmCom) 374
Skilbeck, C. E. 265
Skinner, B. F. 225, 469
Skole, K. S. 317, 318, 320, 332

Sloboda, J. A. 61, 64, 173, 255, 310, 488
Smeets, P. M. 397
Smeijsters, H. 525
Smeltekop, R. A. 214
Smith, C. 296
Smith, G. H. 201
Smith, J. C. 311
Smith, J. M. 200
Smith, M. 330
Smith, S. 376
Smith-Marchese, K. 200
social communication training 123
social phobia 217, 218
social stories 123
Soldo, B. J. 184
Solomon, A. L. 488, 493, 516, 517, 524
somatosensory symptoms 297
Soshensky, R. 222
sound comprehension 385
sound detection 385, 386, 389
sound discrimination 385
sound identification 128, 385
Sparks, R. W. 162, 268, 284
spasticity 145
Special Education Music Therapy Assessment Process (SEMTAP) 413
Speech Stimulation (STIM) 165
Speicher, C. E. 309
Spiegler, D. 45
Spielberger, D. D. 332
Spillsbury, G. 390
spinal cord injuries 150
spina bifida 90, 93, 144, 147, 148, 175
Spitznagel, E. 200
Sprague, J. 415
Springer, S. P. 274
Sramek, J. J. 188, 189
Staffen, W. 155
Stahl, N. D. 420
Standley, J. M. 45, 46, 174, 311, 312, 313, 314, 315, 317, 318, 319, 320, 321, 322, 324, 329, 331, 332, 352, 432, 469, 470, 471
Stankov, L. 390
Starmer, G. J. 386
Starr, P. 27
State of Wisconsin Department of Health and Family Services 98
statistically significant difference 507

Staum, M. 57, 127, 313
Staunton, H. 174
Steele, A. L. 249
Steele, M. 298
Stella, J. 122
Stephens, W. B. 393
stereotypical behaviors 124, 138
Stevens, E. 127
Stevenson, B. 17
Stewart, M. L. 332
Stewart, O. 522
Stige, B. 525, 528
Stillman, D. 192
Stoddard, R. A. 314
storage 58, 59, 167, 283, 284
Stordahl, J. 381
Stowe, A. 447, 448, 456, 458
Strick, E. 201
stride length 156, 294, 511, 512, 515
stroke 4, 57, 155, 190, 266, 271, 272, 273, 274, 275,
    276, 277, 280, 281, 283, 288, 292, 299, 300, 313,
    382, 457, 473, 474, 490, 507, 508, 509, 512, 514,
    515, 516
Strong, A. D. 464
Strunk, D. 21
Stuart, A. 164, 269
Sturmey, P. 469
substance-related disorders 221, 222
Sue, D. W. 447, 456
Sullivan, J. M. 33
Sulzer-Azaroff, B. 469
Super 320
supportive music therapy 237, 238, 242, 243, 251, 258
sustained attention 59, 106, 107, 170, 174, 395
Sutherland, D. H. 145
Swanson, E. A. 198, 201
Swenson, J. R. 272
Symbolic Communication Training Through Music (SY-
    COM) 167, 269
symmetry 74, 288, 511, 512, 515

tactile 54, 55, 57, 70, 105, 136, 153, 169, 264, 267,
    274, 314, 315, 370, 380, 386, 389, 393, 397
tactile defensiveness 126

Takemoto, Y. 437
Talbot, M. L. 158
Tan, X. 320, 321, 322, 324, 325, 331, 332
Tanguay, C. L. 347, 356
Tanioka, F. 324
tardive dyskinesia 189
Taub, E. 281
Taylor, B. K. 320
Taylor, D. B. 27, 28, 30, 31
Taylor, S. 11
Taymans, J. 411
team-oriented approach 344
Tebb, A. 198
Tenney, K. S. 249
terminal illness 29, 34, 344
Tetreault, S. 394
Thaut, C. 261
Thaut, M. H. 55, 56, 57, 58, 59, 60, 61, 67, 104, 117,
    124, 127, 131, 135, 136, 143, 154, 155, 162, 175,
    196, 209, 214, 217, 219, 221, 223, 225, 227, 228,
    229, 230, 231, 233, 234, 235, 236, 237, 238, 239,
    240, 241, 242, 247, 248, 249, 251, 252, 255, 257,
    261, 267, 270, 283, 285, 286, 287, 294, 298, 313,
    395, 474, 476, 477, 487, 507, 509, 515, 516
Thayer, J. F. 62
theory of expectations 65
Therapeutic Instrumental Music Performance (TIMP)
    155, 270, 289
Therapeutic Instrumental Music Playing (TIMP) 157,
    159, 294
Therapeutic Music Experience (TME) 288
Therapeutic Music Interventions (TMI) 4, 98, 102, 182,
    266, 475
Therapeutic Singing (TS) 164, 269, 286, 294, 298
thermal injuries 149
Thomas, D. 200
Thomas, G. E. 84, 92, 95
Thomas, K. 386
Thompson, W. F. 66
Tims, F. C. 56, 309, 311, 330, 468
Toombs-Rudenberg, M. 151
Toppozada, M. R. 447, 456
Total Communication (TC) 374
total pain 345, 352
Trainor, L. J. 174
Transformational Design Model (TDM) 196
transient ischemic attack (TIA) 271
Trask, O. J. 309

Trauger-Querry, B. 346, 349, 358

Traumatic Brain Injury (TBI) 266, 277, 281, 289, 292, 300, 409, 474

treatment plan 224, 333, 430, 433, 436, 437, 438, 442, 455, 491

Treharne, D. A. 164, 269

Trehub, S. E. 45, 174

tremor 146

tremor frequency 291

Trent, J. W. 10, 27

triplegia 146

Turnbull, A. 376, 407

Turnbull, H. R. 407

Turnbull, R. 376

Turner, C. 381

Turner, W. W. 24

tympanic membrane 54, 369

U. S. Department of Education 11, 117, 408, 410

Uehara, E. 390

ulcers 191

Umbarger, G. 127

unilateral 276, 297, 371

Unkefer, R. F. 214, 217, 219, 221, 223, 225, 227, 228, 229, 230, 231, 233, 234, 235, 236, 237, 238, 239, 240, 241, 242, 252, 257, 476, 477

Uslan, M. 395

Vaitl, D. 293

Valdiserri, E. V. 247

Valentine, E. R. 201

Valentino, R. E. 447

Van de Wall, W. 31, 32, 36

variable 506

velocity 156, 288, 440, 511, 512, 515

Venturino, M. 317

Verghese, J. 50

Verghese, M. 311

Vescelius, E. A. 27, 28, 29, 30, 32, 36, 518, 519, 520, 521, 522, 523

Vescelius-Sheldon, L. 519, 523

Vettese, J. 380

vibrotactile 55, 351, 500

Vickers, A. J. 330

Vigndo, L. S. 166

Vignolo, L. A. 268

visual evoked potentials (VEP) 296

Vladimir, H. 271

Vocal Intonation Therapy (VIT) 163, 269, 286, 294, 298

Voigt, M. 462

Volicer, L. 347

Voracek, M. 174

Voss, P. 390

Wade, D. T. 265, 271, 272, 273, 274, 275, 281

Wade, L. M. 313, 332

Wagner, M. J. 54

Waldon, E. G. 330

Walker, F. 290

Walker, J. 222, 317, 343, 347, 355, 358

Wall, P. D. 316, 317

Wallace, W. T. 125, 166, 170, 267, 283

Wallen, N. E. 432, 436

Walsh, J. 311

Walters, C. 320

Walther-Thomas, C. S. 418

Walworth, D. D. 127, 214, 218

Wang, X. 174

Warburton, E. C. 516

Warden, V. 347

Warja, M. 225, 240

Warwick, A. 127, 131

Wasserman, N. 437

Waters, D. J. 183, 185

Watson, D. M. 252

Watson, J. B. 225

Webster's New World College Dictionary 453, 489

Wehmeyer, M. 407

Weideman, D. A. 200

Wein, B. 359

Weis, R. 85, 86

Wells, N. F. 437

Wendelin, A. 97
West, L. L. 411, 415
Westling, D. L. 91
Wheeler, B. L. 225, 237, 238, 239, 240, 241, 525, 526
Whipple, J. 127, 313, 314, 315, 319, 320, 323, 326, 327, 328, 331, 332
Whitall, J. 155
Whitbourne, S. K. 185
Whitehead-Pleaux, A. M. 320, 323, 331
Whittaker, J. T. 25
Wiens, M. E. 298
Wigram, T. 174, 437
Wilhelm, K. 225, 443
Willbanks, W. A. 62
Willems, A. M. 294
Williams, S. B. 316
Wilmoth, J. M. 184, 186
Wilson, B. 372
Wilson, G. T. 212, 213, 215, 216, 219, 220, 221, 222, 223, 225, 229, 230, 239, 241
Wimpory, D. 127, 135
Winer, M. B. 417
Winner, E. 17, 60, 61
Winokur, M. A. 332
Wintle, R. R. 62
Witt, S. 267, 381, 382
Wolery, M. 396
Wolfe, D. 322, 326, 489, 490
Wolfe, J. R. 200
Wollock, J. L. 24
Wood, J. W. 421
Woodworth, G. 198, 267, 381
Woollacott, M. H. 262
Woolrich, J. 310, 461, 467, 468
Woolsey, W. 322, 326
Worden, M. C. 98, 104
World Health Organization (WHO) 90, 193, 194
Wrangsjö, B. 468
Wundt, W. 225
Wyatt, J. G. 249
Wylie, M. E. 200

Yalom, I. 257
Yoder, J. W. 200
York, E. 437
Young, R. L. 125
Yowler, C. J. 320

Zatorre, R. 58, 61, 154, 310, 390
Zebrowski, N. 320
Zillman, D. 49
Zimmerman, M. P. 46
Ziv, N. 200

Yaacoub, C. I. 320
Yahr, M. D. 292